An Expanding World
Volume 2

The European Opportunity

AN EXPANDING WORLD
The European Impact On World History 1450–1800

General Editor: A.J.R. Russell-Wood
with the assistance of Mark Steele

An Expanding World
The European Impact on World History 1450–1800

Volume 2

The European Opportunity

edited by
Felipe Fernández-Armesto

VARIORUM
1995

Published by VARIORUM
      Ashgate Publishing Limited
      Gower House, Croft Road
      Aldershot, Hampshire GU11 3HR
      Great Britain

      Ashgate Publishing Company
      Old Post Road
      Brookfield, Vermont 05036
      USA

ISBN 0-86078-501-7

British Library CIP data
      European Opportunity, — (Expanding World Series; vol. 2)
      I. Fernández-Armesto, Felipe   II. Series
      940.1

US Library of Congress CIP data
      The European Opportunity / [edited by] Felipe Fernández-Armesto.
      p. cm. — (An Expanding World: vol. 2)
      Includes three articles in French. Collection of previously
      published material, 1960–92. Includes bibliographical references.
      ISBN 0-86078-501-7
      1. Discoveries in geography—Asian. I. Fernández-Armesto, Felipe
      II. Series.
      G400.E97   1995   95-3136
      941.085'092—dc20 [B]   CIP

Printed in Great Britain at the University Press, Cambridge

AN EXPANDING WORLD 2

Contents

MOMENTUM

Acknowledgements

The chapters in this volume are taken from the sources listed below. The editor and publishers wish to thank their authors, original publishers or other copyright holders for permission to use their material, as follows:

Chapter 1: Thomas Goldstein, 'Geography in Fifteenth-Century Florence', *Merchants and Scholars*, ed. J. Parker (Minneapolis, 1965), pp. 11–32. Copyright © 1965 by the University of Minnesota.

Chapter 2: Paul Adam, 'Navigation primitive et navigation astronomique', *Les aspects internationaux de la découverte océanique au quinzième et seizième siècles: Actes du cinquième Colloque international d'histoire maritime*, ed. M. Mollat and P. Adam (Paris, 1960), pp. 61–85. © 1960 SEVPEN, Paris.

Chapter 3: Richard W. Unger, 'Portuguese Shipbuilding and the Early Voyages to the Guinea Coast', *Vice-Almirante A. Teixeira Da Mota In Memoriam* I (Lisbon: Academia da Marinha e Instituto de Investigação Científico Tropical, 1987), pp. 229–49.

Chapter 4: J. Heers, 'La rôle des capitaux internationaux dans les voyages de découvertes au quinzième et seizième siècles', *Les aspects internationaux de la découverte océanique au quinzième et seizième siècles: Actes du cinquième Colloque international d'histoire maritime*, ed. M. Mollatt and P. Adam (Paris, 1960), pp. 273–93. © 1960 SEVPEN, Paris.

Chapter 5: Charles Verlinden, 'Italian Influences in Iberian Colonization', *Hispanic American Historical Review* XXXIII (New York, 1953), pp. 199–211. By Permission of Duke University.

Chapter 6: P.E. Russell, 'Prince Henry the Navigator', *Diamante* XI (London: The Hispanic and Luso-Brazilian Council, 1960), pp. 3–30.

Chapter 7: Guy Beaujouan, 'Fernand Colomb et le traité d'astrologie d'Henri le Navigateur', *Romania* LXXXII (Paris: Cassirer, 1961), pp. 96–105.

Chapter 8: Andrew M. Watson, 'Back to Gold - and Silver', *Economic History Review* XX (Oxford: Blackwell, 1967), pp. 1–34.

Chapter 9: C.F. Beckingham, 'The Quest for Prester John', *Bulletin of the John Rylands University Library of Manchester* LXII (Manchester, 1980), pp. 291–310. Reproduced by courtesy of the Director and University Librarian, the John Rylands University Library of Manchester.

Chapter 10: Pauline Moffitt Watts, 'Prophecy and Discovery: On the Spiritual Origins of Christopher Columbus's Enterprise in the Indies', *American Historical Review* XC (Washington, D.C., 1985), pp. 73–102.

Chapter 11: Charles Verlinden, 'The Transfer of Colonial Techniques from the Mediterranean to the Atlantic', *The Beginnings of Modern Colonisation: Eleven Essays with an Introduction*, ed. C. Verlinden, tr. Yvonne Freccero (Ithaca and London, 1970), pp. 3–32. Copyright © 1970 by Cornell University. Used by permission of the publisher, Cornell University Press.

Chapter 12: C.J. Bishko, 'The Castilian as Plainsman: The Medieval Ranching Frontier in La Mancha and Extremadura', reprinted from *The New World Looks at its History*, edited by Archibald R. Lewis and Thomas F. McGann, pp. 47–69. Copyright © 1963. By permission of the University of Texas Press.

Chapter 13: Felipe Fernández-Armesto, 'Atlantic Exploration Before Columbus: the Evidence of Maps', *Renaissance and Modern Studies* XXX (University of Nottingham, 1986), pp. 12–34. By permission of the editors of *Renaissance and Modern Studies*.

Chapter 14: R.S. Lopez, 'European Merchants in the Medieval Indies: the Evidence of Commercial Documents', *Journal of Economic History* (Cambridge, 1943), pp. 164–84. © 1943 Economic History Association, Cambridge University Press.

Chapter 15: Rees Davies, 'Frontier Arrangements in Fragmented Societies: Ireland and Wales', *Medieval Frontier Societies*, ed. R. Bartlett and A. MacKay (Oxford, 1992), pp. 77–100. © 1992 Oxford University Press.

Every effort has been made to trace all the copyright holders, but if any have been inadvertently overlooked the publishers will be pleased to make the necessary arrangement at the first opportunity.

General Editor's Preface

A.J.R. Russell-Wood

An Expanding World: The European Impact on World History, 1450–1800 is designed to meet two objectives: first, each volume covers a specific aspect of the European initiative and reaction across time and space; second, the series represents a superb overview and compendium of knowledge and is an invaluable reference source on the European presence beyond Europe in the early modern period, interaction with non-Europeans, and experiences of peoples of other continents, religions, and races in relation to Europe and Europeans. The series reflects revisionist interpretations and new approaches to what has been called 'the expansion of Europe' and whose historiography traditionally bore the hallmarks of a narrowly Eurocentric perspective, focus on the achievements of individual nations, and characterization of the European presence as one of dominance, conquest, and control. Fragmentation characterized much of this literature: fragmentation by national groups, by geography, and by chronology.

The volumes of *An Expanding World* seek to transcend nationalist histories and to examine on the global stage rather than in discrete regions important selected facets of the European presence overseas. One result has been to bring to the fore the multicontinental, multi-oceanic and multinational dimension of the European activities. A further outcome is compensatory in the emphasis placed on the cross-cultural context of European activities and on how collaboration and cooperation between peoples transcended real or perceived boundaries of religion, nationality, race, and language and were no less important aspects of the European experience in Africa, Asia, the Americas, and Australia than the highly publicized confrontational, bellicose, and exploitative dimensions. Recent scholarship has not only led to greater understanding of peoples, cultures, and institutions of Africa, Asia, the Americas, and Australasia with whom Europeans interacted and the complexity of such interactions and transactions, but also of relations between Europeans of different nationalities and religious persuasions.

The initial five volumes reflect the changing historiography and set the stage for volumes encompassing the broad themes of technology and science, trade and commerce, exploitation as reflected in agriculture and the extractive industries and through systems of forced and coerced labour, government of empire, and society and culture in European colonies and settlements overseas. Final volumes examine the image of Europe and Europeans as 'the other' and the impact of the wider world on European *mentalités* and mores.

An international team of editors was selected to reflect a diversity of educational backgrounds, nationalities, and scholars at different stages of their professional careers. Few would claim to be 'world historians', but each is a recognized authority in his or her field and has the demonstrated capacity to ask the significant questions and provide a conceptual framework for the selection of articles which combine analysis with interpretation. Editors were exhorted to place their specific subjects within a global context and over the *longue durée*. I have been delighted by the enthusiasm with which they took up this intellectual challenge, their courage in venturing beyond their immediate research fields to look over the fences into the gardens of their academic neighbours, and the collegiality which has led to a generous informal exchange of information. Editors were posed the daunting task of surveying a rich historical literature and selecting those essays which they regarded as significant contributions to an understanding of the specific field or representative of the historiography. They were asked to give priority to articles in scholarly journals; essays from conference volumes and *Festschriften* were acceptable; excluded (with some few exceptions) were excerpts from recent monographs or paperback volumes. After much discussion and agonizing, the decision was taken to incorporate essays only in English, French, and Spanish. This has led to the exclusion of the extensive scholarly literature in Danish, Dutch, German and Portuguese. The ramifications of these decisions and how these have had an impact on the representative quality of selections of articles have varied, depending on the theme, and have been addressed by editors in their introductions.

The introduction to each volume enables readers to assess the importance of the topic *per se* and place this in the broader context of European activities overseas. It acquaints readers with broad trends in the historiography and alerts them to controversies and conflicting interpretations. Editors clarify the conceptual framework for each volume and explain the rationale for the selection of articles and how they relate to each other. Introductions permit volume editors to assess the impact on their treatments of discrete topics of constraints of language, format, and chronology, assess the completeness of the journal literature, and address *lacunae*. A further charge to editors was to describe and evaluate the importance of change over time, explain differences attributable to differing geographical, cultural, institutional, and economic circumstances and suggest the potential for cross-cultural, comparative, and interdisciplinary approaches. The addition of notes and bibliographies enhances the scholarly value of the introductions and suggests avenues for further enquiry.

I should like to express my thanks to the volume editors for their willing participation, enthusiasm, sage counsel, invaluable suggestions, and good judgment. Evidence of the timeliness and importance of the series was illustrated by the decision, based on extensive consultation with the scholarly community, to expand a series, which had originally been projected not to exceed eight volumes, to more than thirty volumes. As General Editor, my task has been facilitated by the tireless assistance of Dr Mark Steele who was responsible for the 'operations' component of the series, and of John Smedley whose initiative gave rise to discussion as to the viability and need for such a series and who has overseen the publishing, publicity, and marketing of *An Expanding World.*

The Department of History,
The Johns Hopkins University

Introduction

Felipe Fernández-Armesto

An observer at large in the world of the fifteenth century would have noticed a number of cultures and civilizations separated by great distances, poor communications and, in some cases, mutual ignorance or lack of interest. He might, however, have detected – in places, for the most part, outside Latin Christendom – some stirrings at the edges: the dilation of political frontiers or the beginnings of movements of expansion, of settlement, trade, conquest and proselytization, which would make the world of the next few centuries an arena of imperial competition, where expanding civilizations collided and where virtually all human communities were joined in conflict, commerce and contagion.

The accomplishment of this enormous and conspicuous change depended on the creation and exploitation of practical routes of access between previously isolated or barely-communicating groups of people. The process came to be dominated from Latin Christendom: western European preponderance in exploration and colonization was built up gradually, but a critical decade was that of the 1490s, when navigators from starting-points on the Atlantic seaboard of the Iberian peninsula, making voyages of unprecedented audacity, opened new and reliable routes to and from the New World and the Indian Ocean. Yet our hypothetical observer would probably not have been able to predict such an outcome until the century was well advanced. There was nothing inevitable about this episode in the 'European miracle'. Such sources of motivation as material exigency, scientific curiosity, missionary zeal, commercial spirit or wanton aggression were not peculiar to any one part of the world, and, compared with China and Islam, Latin Christendom was under-equipped in the technical resources with which to undertake long journeys, to sustain life during them, to find directions in unfamiliar places, to record and communicate the information gathered.[1]

Some otherwise promising cultures were subject to even graver technical limitations which perhaps inhibited or disqualified them from further big achievements in exploration. In Mesoamerica, for instance, as among the indigenous peoples of sub-Saharan Africa, there was no means of long-range navigation by sea; in Peru, no maps. The Polynesians, surrounded by the vast Pacific, may have attained the limits of the world accessible to them with the

---

[1] J. Needham, *Science and Civilisation in China* (Cambridge, 1954 – in progress), IV, part III (1971), pp. 379–699. G.R. Tibbetts, *Arab Navigation in the Indian Ocean before the Coming of the Portuguese* (London, 1980); generally, see vol. I in An Expanding World series, *The Global Opportunity*.

technology at their disposal. Yet the record of these societies, from which routes were explored and recorded over vast distances – extending in the Peruvian case across thirty degrees of latitude and in the Polynesian case over thousands of miles of sea – shows how much can be achieved in defiance of technical insufficiency.[2]

The best equipped people, indeed, failed to fulfil their promise as explorers. Java, for instance, probably had by the late fourteenth century cartographical traditions and shipbuilding techniques at least as good as those of anywhere else; but all her shipping was absorbed by the demands of trade within a fairly restricted zone between south Asia and the far east. By the mid-fourteenth century, Arabic travel literature and pilgrims' guides covered the whole Islamic world and extended selectively beyond it, for instance, into Sardinia and China; and Arabic sailing directions of the second half of the fifteenth century covered the Indian Ocean from southern Africa to the South China Sea. Yet after the Arab commercial world had attained its desired limits in the Mediterranean and the Far East, Islamic exploration further afield became fitful and slight. In particular, little attempt was made to imitate the achievements of Indian Ocean navigators in Atlantic waters, and mariners satiated with the profits of well-known routes showed no inclination to venture beyond the stormy latitudes which screen the Indian Ocean to the south. When the New World became an extension of Christendom and the Portuguese discovered an Atlantic highway to the east, the Ottoman sultans came, too late, to regret their failings.[3]

Meanwhile, development of the exploring traditions of China was similarly arrested. The range of travel had long been limited to the reach of trade and diplomacy; but in China that meant including a huge swathe of the world, exceeding the length of the silk roads and the breadth of the Indian Ocean. Geographical scholars collated and mapped the information collected. In about 1220, for instance, a detailed account of the South China Sea and of countries of south-east Asia and India was produced, partly from personal observation, by a scholar and diplomat. A century later, passable maps of the Indian Ocean were made, perhaps including the coast of Africa to beyond the Cape of Good Hope.[4] Between 1405 and 1433, a series of tribute-gathering missions under the eunuch-admiral, Cheng Ho [Pinyin: Zheng He], consolidated knowledge of commercial routes and reported, from direct experience, on places as distant as Jiddah and Malindi. Yet for a combination of imperfectly understood reasons – which

---

[2] F. Fernández-Armesto, (ed.), *The Times Atlas of World Exploration* (London and New York, 1991), pp. 15–39.

[3] A.C. Hess, 'Piri Reis and the Ottoman Response to the Voyages of Discovery', *Terrae Incognitae* VI (1974), pp. 19–38.

[4] Kuei-Sheng Chang, 'The Ming Maritime Enterprise and China's Knowledge of Africa prior to the Age of Great Discoveries', *Terrae Incognitae* III (1971), pp. 33–44.

included the effects of the ebb and flow of factional conflicts, the hostility of the mandarin élite to eunuchs and traders and the prohibitive cost of the ventures – this potentially imperial initiative was aborted. Naval shipbuilding was discontinued and many official records of Cheng Ho's achievements were destroyed.[5]

Thus while more prosperous and proficient civilizations rested content with the exploitation of their traditional contacts, it was left to explorers from Latin Christendom to search for new resources, extend their reach and ultimately enmesh most of the world in their routes.

Their biggest source of advantage was probably their starting-place on the edge of the Atlantic. In the age of sail, maritime route-finding depended on access to favourable winds and currents. Navigators from the Indian Ocean and western Pacific would not have found conditions particularly favourable for long-range navigation outside the zone of monsoons, even had they wished to do so. The only navigable route eastwards across the Pacific was an effective dead end until trading-places developed on the west coast of America in colonial times. The ways out of the Indian Ocean to the south were laborious and dangerous and led, as far as was known, only to unrewarding destinations. The Atlantic, by contrast, was a highway to the rest of the world. Its wind systems provided potential links with the Pacific and Indian Oceans as well as routes between the Old and New Worlds. The location and exploitation of these routes was a labour, accomplished in the fifteenth and sixteenth centuries, which deserves its reputation as a revolutionary achievement in world history.

The background of that achievement – the prerequisites and preconditions supplied in parts of western Europe – forms the subject of the essays which follow.

In part one, the means are explored: science, technology and material resources. Though historians' search for connexions between 'the Renaissance' and 'the Age of Discovery' has sometimes been conducted with an air of desperation,[6] re-discoveries from classical antiquity, along with texts which formed a continuous part of the erudite tradition in the medieval west, did contribute to the atmosphere of speculation in which explorers' expeditions were launched. Thomas Goldstein's essay focusses on one of the most influential centres,

---

[5] E.L. Dreyer, *Early Ming China: a Political History, 1355–1435* (Stanford, Mass., 1982), pp. 220–33.

[6] The subject is admirably treated, however, in J.H. Elliott, 'The Discovery of America and the Discovery of Man', *Proceedings of the British Academy* LVIII (1972), pp. 101–25, and, on a broader front but still with particular reference to America, by C.H.C. Clough, 'The New World and the Italian Renaissance', in ed. C.H.C. Clough and P.E.H. Hair, *The European Outthrust and Encounter – the First Phase, c. 1400–c. 1700: Essays Presented to David Beers Quinn on His 85th Birthday* (Liverpool, 1994), pp. 291–328. See also Goldstein, 'The role of the Italian Merchant Class', cited n. 17 below.

Florence, and some of the most important texts, though this should be seen as a representative case:[7] it would have been just as appropriate to illustrate the point with work on fourteenth-century Majorca, say, or fifteenth-century Nuremberg or Salamanca.[8] Moreover, the limitations of scientific cosmography and long-range exploration grew more intimate as time went on;[9] in the late middle ages, however, travellers' tales, mirabilia, chivalric romance and hagiography all probably contributed more to the inspiration of overseas ventures.[10]

In the early stages, European expansion depended less on technological progress than might be supposed. Although an enormous amount of literature has been devoted to the problem of how and when navigation by means of astronomical instruments developed,[11] primitive celestial navigation, as explained

[7] See also G. Beaujouan, 'Science livresque et art nautique au XVe siècle', in ed. M. Mollat and P. Adam, *Les aspects internationaux de la découverte océanique au XVe et XVIe siècles: Actes du cinquième Colloque international d'histoire maritime* (Paris, 1960), pp. 61–85; W.G.L. Randles, *De la Terre plate au globe terrestre* (Paris, 1980) and 'The Evaluation of Columbus's 'India Project' in the Light of the Geographical Science of the Period', *Imago Mundi* XLII (1990), pp. 50–65.

[8] On Majorca, see Y.K. Fall, *L'Afrique à la naissance de la cartographie moderne. Les cartes majorquines, XIVe au XVe siècles* (Paris, 1985) and F. Yates, 'Ramon Llull and John Scotus Erigena', *Journal of the Warburg and Courtauld Institutes* XVII (1954), pp. 1–44; on the Majorcan background generally, D.S. Abulafia, *A Mediterranean Emporium: the Catalan Kingdom of Mallorca* (Cambridge, 1994); on Nuremberg, see ed. J.K.W. Willers, *Focus Behaim Globus*, 2 vols (exhibition catalogue, Germanisches Nationalmuseum, Nuremberg, 1992), I, pp. 143–66, 217–22, 239–72 and E.P. Goldschmidt, *Hieronymus Münzer und seiner Bibliothek* (London, 1938); on Salamanca, see J.L. Espinel Marcos, 'Cristal Colón y Salamanca', in ed. J.L. Espinel Marcos and R. Hernández Martín, *Colón en Salamanca: los Dominicos* (Salamanca, 1988), pp. 18–49; E. Jos, *El plan y la genesis del descubrimiento colombino* (Valladolid, 1980) and A.M. Carabias, 'Pasos, leguas, millas, miriadas: la contribución salmantina al conocimiento del espacio', *Jornadas rotarias histórico-jurídicas en el quinto centenario de las paces de Tordesillas* (forthcoming).

[9] See U. Lamb, 'La nueva ciencia geográfica', *Revista de Occidente*, 2nd s., XXXVII (April–June, 1972), pp. 162–83.

[10] J.K. Hyde, 'Real and Imaginary Journeys in the Later Middle Ages', *Bulletin of the John Rylands University Library of Manchester*, LXV (1982), pp. 125–47; V.I.J. Flint, *The Imaginative Landscape of Christopher Columbus* (Princeton, 1992); J. Le Goff, 'The Medieval West and the Indian Ocean', in *Time, Work and Culture in the Middle Ages* (Chicago, 1980), pp. 189–200 and 341–7; F. Fernández-Armesto, 'Sea and Chivalry in Late Medieval Spain', in ed. J.B. Hattendorff, *Maritime History in the Age of Discovery* (provisional title) (New York, forthcoming).

[11] See D.W. Waters, 'Science and the Techniques of Navigation in the Renaissance', in ed. C.S. Singleton, *Art, Science and History in the Renaissance* (Baltimore, 1967); A. Teixeira da Mota, 'L'Art de naviguer en Méditerrannée du XIIIe au XVIIe siècle et la création de la navigation astronomique dans les océans', in ed. M. Mollat and P. Adam, *Le navire et l'économie maritime du Moyen-age au XVIIe siècle, principalement en Méditerrannée: Travaux du IIe Colloque international d'histoire maritime*, (Paris, 1958), pp. 127–54; G. Beaujouan and E. Poulle, 'Les Origines de la navigation astronomique aux XIVe et XVe siècles', ibid., pp. 103–16; on navigation generally, see E.G.R. Taylor, *The Haven-Finding Art* (London, 1956).

below by P. Adam, sufficed to launch ocean-going exploration.[12] It was important not only to find routes but also to record them so that they could be lastingly exploited and the successes of explorers were matched by developments in cartography:[13] for practical purposes, however, Chinese, south-east Asian and Arab cartography remained equal or superior to that of Europe until well into the sixteenth century, at least.[14] Most of the long-range voyages of the era could be accomplished with traditional ship types, though the kind of developments dealt with in Richard Unger's contribution below were vital for particular tasks and routes.[15] The problems of keeping food and water for long journeys were probably of at least equal importance but, until recently, have been little studied. Portuguese and, to a lesser extent, Spanish seafarers in the Atlantic in the late fourteenth and fifteenth centuries made expeditions of unprecedented length, in terms of numbers of days out of sight of land; by the end of the fifteenth century, journeys of ninety days on the open sea were possible. These achievements demanded casks of the highest quality and of improved design.[16]

The early stages of European expansion were accomplished despite severe material constraints in a part of the world which, by comparison with some potential rivals, was under-productive, under-populated and under-equipped. It was a drive from behind to supplement the resources of an inadequate home-base. Unlike the Chinese naval expeditions in the Indian Ocean, European ventures in this period were small-scale affairs, demanding little by way of ships and men. On the other hand, exploration was an activity generally slow to yield returns on investment and the final studies in part one below by Jacques Heers and Charles Verlinden illustrate the vital role of independent merchant-capitalists in promoting voyages.[17] While royal and princely patronage was important to the

---

[12] See also C. Verlinden, 'La découverte des archipels de la 'Méditerrannée Atlantique' (Canaries, Madères, Açores) et la navigation astronomique primitive', *Revista portuguesa de história* XVI (1978), pp. 105–31.

[13] T. Campbell, 'Portolan Charts from the late Thirteenth Century to 1500', in ed. J.B. Harley and D. Woodward, *The History of Cartography, I: Cartography in Prehistoric, Ancient and Medieval Europe and the Mediterranean* (Chicago, 1987), pp. 371–93; M. Mollat du Jourdain and M. de La Roncière, *Sea Charts of the Early Explorers* (London and New York, 1984).

[14] Needham, *Science and Civilisation*, op. cit. (n. 1), III (1959), pp. 497–590.

[15] See additionally on Spanish shipbuilding, C. Rahn Phillips, 'Sizes and Configurations of Spanish Ships in the Age of Discovery', in ed. D.T. Gerace, *Columbus and His World: Proceedings of the First San Salvador Conference* (Fort Lauderdale, 1987), pp. 69–98.

[16] R. Barker 'Shipshape for Discoveries, and Return', *The Mariner's Mirror* LXXVIII (1992), pp. 433–47, pp. 444–6.

[17] See also T. Goldstein, 'The Role of the Italian Merchant Class in Renaissance and Discoveries', *Terrae Incognitae* VIII (1976), pp. 19–28; C. Varela, *Colón y los florentinos* (Madrid, 1988); L.A. Vigneras, *The Discovery of South America and the Andalusian Voyages* (Chicago and London, 1976); F. Fernández-Armesto, 'La financiación de la conquista de las Islas Canarias en el tiempo de los Reyes Católicos', *Anuario de estudios atlánticos* XXVIII (1982), pp. 342–77.

legitimation, protection and prestige of overseas ventures, only in Portugal can public sources of finance be said to have contributed much directly by way of investment. Though western European peoples had the advantage of a culture propitious to the generation of venture-capital, they were short of surplus resources by comparison with some of the expanding societies of Asia: European success – it may be fair to say – was only possible on the cheap.

While other societies were better equipped, those of western Europe had the advantage of some highly motivated manpower. In part two below, a range of motives of explorers, traders, settlers and promoters is covered. While similar motives existed in other parts of the world, they amounted in Latin Christendom to what might be called a culture of expansion which was, perhaps, stronger than in other civilizations at the time. A vital part of it was the great aristocratic ethos of the late middle ages in the west, the 'code' of chivalry. Its role-models were the footloose princes who won themselves kingdoms by deeds of derring-do in popular romance, often in a maritime setting:[18] their spirit of seaborne knight-errantry contrasted with the landlubbers' complacency that dominated prevailing values in China and parts of Islam. A further contribution to the culture of expansion was made by militant, evangelizing Christianity. A framework of classification of mankind was to hand, which, while remaining a subject of vigorous debate among scholars, made pagans, 'primitives' and 'barbarians' potentially proper objects of imperial victimization. Popes and, to some extent, secular rulers, could also apply a universalist imperial tradition inherited from Europe's Roman past and supplemented and modified by Christian influences.[19]

It is important to realise that motivation is one of the hardest elements to generalize about and in the essays below by Pauline Moffitt Watts, Peter Russell and Guy Beaujouan the focus is on two particular cases: those of Columbus and the Infante Dom Henrique of Portugal. The influence of milleniarianism and astrology revealed in those cases is typical, however, of the period. Expansion was not necessarily born of self-confidence: at one level, it was a response to the consciousness of inferiority induced by the threat from an expanding Islamic world. C.F. Beckingham's lecture on the quest for Prester John is a reminder that European exploration was motivated, in part, by a search for allies in an unequal conflict.[20]

---

[18] A. Navarro González, *El mar en la literatura medieval castellana* (La Laguna, 1962); Fernández-Armesto, 'Sea and Chivalry', loc. cit., n.10 above.

[19] J. Muldoon, *Popes, Lawyers and Infidels* (Liverpool, 1979). See also on the problem of classification of 'barbarians' M. Hodgen, *Early Anthropology in the Sixteenth and Seventeenth Centuries* (Philadelphia, 1971) and A.R.D. Pagden, *The Fall of Natural Man* (Cambridge, 1982), and on the influence of millenarianism, A. Milhou, *Colón y su mentalidad mesiánica en el ambiente franciscanista español* (Valladolid, 1983).

[20] See also F.M. Rogers, *The Quest for Eastern Christians: Travels and Rumour in the Age of Discovery* (Minneapolis, 1962).

Latin Christendom had other features suited to an imperial civilization: a social structure prolific in ambitious outcasts who were prepared to take risks; an emulous state-system which encouraged a long-range search for resources; and an economy neither too poor to generate venture-capital nor too rich to relax in complacency. Whereas demand in the Islamic world, China, Japan, India and south-east Asia could be met by autarchic methods or from the gleanings of long-established trade-routes, Europeans had to look far afield for the products and outlets they wanted or needed.

Among the economic objectives of their early explorations by land and sea – which included food, slaves, dyestuffs, exotic textiles, markets for their own wares and, increasingly, spices – precious metals stand out as of overwhelming importance. A.H. Watson's article reproduced below depicts the economic background to western Europeans' late-medieval search for new sources of gold.[21] Some of the most important new routes of the fifteenth century – across and around the Sahara, across the west African bulge and across the central Atlantic to the discoveries of Columbus – were opened, largely or entirely, in pursuit of rumoured gold. To be appreciated in the terms of the time, gold should be seen as more than an economic commodity: it had a mystical, numinous and in some respects a religious significance and explorers' searches for the 'river' or 'mine' of gold had something of the fantastic flavour of the alchemists' hunt for the philosopher's stone.

In the last fifty years, in the context of a wide-ranging historical project to establish elements of continuity between the 'middle ages' and 'modern times', it has become increasingly evident that European civilization was carried to other regions of the world in part by the momentum of a long, slow and fitful history of medieval expansion. The search for origins can be rewarded only by taking a very long-term view and acknowledging that the process grew, cumulatively but unevenly, from modest beginnings. It can be traced, in a sense, to Latin Christendom's era of self-discovery in the late eleventh and twelfth centuries, when the riverbankers conquered the wild wood, in a vast project of domestication of little-explored and under-exploited environments, while observers and travellers turned inward to find and describe Europe's inner barbarians: the remote peoples of forest, bog and mountains, the imperfectly-assimilated marchland-dwellers, whose evangelization was sketchy and whose habitats were often blanks on the map.[22] At about the same time, knowledge of the world beyond these recesses and thresholds was increased by the colonists and crusaders who extended the

---

[21] See also F. Braudel, 'Monnaies et civilisations: de l'or du Soudan à l'argent d'Amérique', *Annales, Économies, Sociétés, Civilisations* II (1947), pp. 9–22; V. Magalhães Godinho, *O 'Mediterraneo' saariano e as caravanas do ouro* (São Paulo, 1956).

[22] R. Bartlett, *The Making of Europe* (London, 1993); E. Christiansen, *The Northern Crusades* (London, 1980); see also R. Bechmann, *Les racines des cathédrales* (Paris, 1981).

frontiers of Latin Christendom. Scholars in western Europe were acquainted with the vastness of the world by the experience of the crusades – reinforced, in the thirteenth and early fourteenth centuries, by the reports of merchants and missionaries who travelled the Mongol road as far as China or sailed, with indigenous shipping, on the Indian Ocean.

The northern and eastern frontiers of Latin Christendom remained important schools of colonialism in the late middle ages; however, the momentum which led towards the oceans of the world was built up in the five areas represented by the essays in part three below. The seepage of Mediterranean techniques and personnel from the Mediterranean to the Atlantic is the essential starting-point: Atlantic exploration, though it became a speciality of ringside communities of Europe's Atlantic shores, began from havens deep in the western Mediterranean, in Genoa and Mallorca.[23] When Portugal and Castile took on the initiative, they still relied heavily on Italian finance and savoir-faire: Charles Verlinden, who is the doyen of study of this subject, is responsible for presenting it here.[24] The Iberian peninsula, a theatre of 'a vast and uninterrupted project of colonization'[25] which prepared Spain and Portugal to be world powers, is represented by C.J. Bishko's essay on the Iberian background of the ranching economy and culture of parts of the New World.[26] The African Atlantic – the necessary springboard for expansion further into the ocean – is dealt with in a piece by me which also provides some light on the nautical cartography of the period.[27] An essay by Rees Davies profiles English imperialism in Wales and Ireland,[28] which, with the long English and Scandinavian experience of Atlantic navigation, contributed to the creation and development of north Atlantic routes of trade and colonization in

---

[23] On Majorca, A. Rumeu de Armas, *El obispado de Telde* (Madrid and Telde, 1986) and Abulafia, op. cit., n. 8 above; on Genoa, F.M. Rogers, 'The Vivaldi Expedition', *Annual Report of the Dante Society* LXXIII (1955), pp. 31–45; L. de la Rosa Oliveira, 'Francisco de Riberol y la colonia genovesa en Canarias', *Anuario de estudios atlánticos* XVIII (1972), pp. 61–198.

[24] See also the same author's, *Précédents médiévaux de la colonie en Amérique* (Mexico, 1954); 'The Rise of Spanish Trade in the Middle Ages', *Economic History Review* X (1960), pp. 44–59; and M.A. Ladero Quesada, 'Los genoveses en Sevilla y su región (siglos XII–XVI): elementos de permanencia y arraigo', in *Los mudéjares de Castilla y otros estudios de historia medieval andaluz* (Granada, 1989), pp. 283–312.

[25] C. Sánchez-Albornoz, *España: un enigma histórico*, 2 vols (Buenos Aires, 1956–57), II, p. 156. See also the same author's 'The Frontier and Castilian Liberties', in ed. A.R. Lewis and T.F. McGann, *The New World Looks at its History* (Austin, Texas, 1963), pp. 25–46.

[26] See A. de la Torre, J.M. Lacarra et al., *La reconquista española y la repoblación del país* (Madrid, 1951); A. McKay, *Spain from Frontier to Empire, 1000–1500* (London, 1977).

[27] Also A. Rumeu de Armas, *España en el Africa Atlántica*, 2 vols (Madrid, 1955); R. Mauny, *Les navigations médiévales aux côtes sahariennes* (Lisbon, 1960); P.E. Russell, *O infante Dom Henrique e as Ilhas Canárias* (Lisbon, 1979); F. Fernández-Armesto, 'Spanish Atlantic Voyages before Columbus', in ed. Hattendorf, op. cit. (n. 10 above) (forthcoming).

[28] See J.F. Lydon, ed., *The English in Medieval Ireland* (Dublin, 1984); R.R. Davies, (ed.), *The British Isles, 1100–1500: Comparisons, Contrasts and Connexions* (Edinburgh, 1988).

early modern times.[29] As a result of the confluence of means, motives and momentum, the preponderance of European peoples in the expanding world was, if not assured, at least prefigured by the sixteenth century.

Select Additional Bibliography

C. Allmand, ed., *New Cambridge Medieval History* VII (Cambridge, forthcoming).

C.R. Beazely, *The Dawn of Modern Geography*, 3 vols (Oxford, 1897–1906).

P. Chaunu, *European Overseas Expansion in the Later Middle Ages* (Amsterdam, 1979).

F. Fernández-Armesto, *Before Columbus: Exploration and Colonisation from the Mediterranean to the Atlantic* (London and Philadelphia, 1987).

V. Magalhães Godinho, *Os decobrimentos e a economia mundial*, 3 vols (Lisbon, 1981–82).

J. Heers, *L'Occident aux XIVe et XVe siècles: aspects économiques et sociales* (Paris, 1970).

H.A. Miskimin, *The Economy of Early Renaissance Europe* (Englewood Cliffs, N.J., 1969).

J.H. Parry, *The Age of Reconnaissance* (London, 1965).

J.R.S. Phillips, *The Medieval Expansion of Europe* (Oxford, 1988).

C. de la Roncière, *La découverte de la Terre* (Paris, 1934).

G.V. Scammell, *The World Encompassed: the First European Maritime Empires* (London and New York, 1981).

— *The First Imperial Age: European Overseas Expansion, c. 1400–1715* (London, 1989).

C. Verlinden, *Les Origines de la civilisation atlantique* (Paris, 1966).

---

[29] D.B. Quinn, 'England and the Atlantic', in *England and the Discovery of America, 1481–1620* (New York, 1974), pp. 47–84.

1
Geography in Fifteenth-Century Florence

Thomas Goldstein

FLORENCE in the quattrocento calls forth associations that have little enough to do with a fairly specialized branch in the history of science. The memories it evokes are of the unfolding of early Renaissance art; the flourishing of humanist studies; the cult of Plato; a setting of lovely churches and palazzi capped by Brunelleschi's cupola — one of the rare moments in history, in short, when a city rose to the heights of the enjoyment of living, amidst the loveliness of the Tuscan hills.

We are not used to thinking of this setting as sheltering scientific studies of major import, least of all a development in geographic theory that paved the way for the age of the great explorations. Nor do our notions of the age of discoveries include a phase of theoretical preparation in which Florence, about two generations before Columbus — at the very height of the early Renaissance — played a significant role. Standard ideas, in fact, have it the other way around: as though the explorers, thrusting into the unknown without benefit of any theoretical insights to speak of, were the cause of a geographic science that was a mere afterthought, crystallizing not before the sixteenth century, at any rate.

The lone exception these notions admit of is the famous "Toscanelli letter" containing the equally famous theory of the "westward route" from Portugal or Spain to the Indies. History presents this often-cited document essentially as a confirmation — one of many — of Columbus's own presumably highly fantastic scheme, in this instance by one of the most eminent and most highly respected scientists of his day. The modern reader is left with the inference that Toscanelli's theory must have been equally fantastic — and that geographic theory before Columbus was of no serious consequence.

Of late years, this image of a naive age — innocent of important scientific thought, steeped in a rarefied atmosphere of pure aesthetics, barren of any major theoretical contribution to the geographic discoveries — has been marred by a number of disturbing findings. To name just a few:

Our growing appreciation of the stature of medieval science makes it increasingly

NOTES for *Geography in Fifteenth-Century Florence* are to be found on pages 26 to 32.

MERCHANTS AND SCHOLARS

difficult to overlook the sturdy role of geography, roughly since the twelfth century. Geography was by no means a neglected field either among the Arabs — from whom the West inherited an almost complete body of scientific practice and thought — nor among the thirteenth- and fourteenth-century scientific thinkers of the Latin West.[1] Why should this long-standing concern with geographic problems have failed to supply a consistent theoretical basis for the age of discoveries?

The Portuguese expeditions into the eastern Atlantic and down the west coast of Africa since early in the fifteenth century proceeded with such evident circumspection that a thorough grounding in geographic theory — assimilated at Prince Henry the Navigator's home base at Sagres — has by now been universally accepted.[2] Could the Sagres academy have worked in a vacuum, outside any significant context of contemporary European thought?

In 1410 — five years before the first of the Portuguese expeditions — a Florentine humanist, Jacopo Angelo de' Scarperia, completed his Latin translation of the most important compendium of ancient geographical knowledge and theory, Claudius Ptolemaeus's *Geography*. Modern Renaissance specialists have wondered whether the recovery of this vital classical work could really have had no effect upon the thinking of the explorers.[3]

The whole idea that the fifteenth-century Renaissance evolved in a climate of pure aesthetic delight, inhospitable to the rise of science,[4] has come in for serious challenge. Not only was the art of the early Renaissance grounded in solid mathematics, optics, perspective, and anatomy,[5] which had been thriving in Florence since the early quattrocento. Not only did the philological and historical studies of the humanists contribute important elements to the evolution of the modern scientific method.[6] Even the very roots of Renaissance art and architecture have been traced to a body of concepts with far-reaching implications for science — above all a philosophy of space based on a consistent mathematical world view.[7]

The beginnings of modern science, we see with increasing clarity, lie back in the later Middle Ages. The subject of geography — above all intense speculation about the shape of the earth — formed part of this evolution. Nor did the evolution cease during the fifteenth century. The idea of the discoverers groping about in the dark, with no more theoretical backing than a few rather absurd hunches, would seem increasingly to conflict with the perspectives of historical scholarship.

These considerations might be reason enough for a critical return to the available evidence. In point of fact, a close reading of the Toscanelli correspondence itself reveals a far more substantial body of underlying geographic knowledge than the offhand, theoretically worthless suggestion of a westward route would seem to imply. When examined against the background of the history of geographic thought, the purely practical suggestion that the "Indies" could be reached by sailing west proves to be underlain by a major theoretical premise. With one, or perhaps two lone exceptions, unknown to the West until the middle of the fifteenth century, this premise had

THOMAS GOLDSTEIN

never been stated before.[8] What it involved was nothing less than a complete revision of the basic concept of the earth: the theory, that is, that the ocean could be used as an intercontinental waterway. Added to this was a second equally revolutionary premise — equally subversive of the entire medieval tradition of geography: that the navigable Ocean Sea included the Southern Hemisphere. Taken together these premises meant the decisive abandonment of the traditional (ancient as well as medieval) concept of the *orbis terrarum* — the idea that a severely foreshortened three-continental land mass (Europe, Asia, and Africa) was forever confined within its own limits by an all-encircling Ocean Sea, conceived of very much as we today look upon outer space, as another orbit,[9] believed to be by its very nature inaccessible to the efforts of man. And it meant, by the same token, the abandonment of the idea that man's habitat was limited to the Northern Hemisphere. It meant the substitution of the modern concept of the earth for the one that — those one or two lone exceptions notwithstanding — had dominated geographic thinking ever since ancient times.

It seems axiomatic that the new concept, with all its psychological and practical implications, could hardly have occurred to Toscanelli out of the blue Florentine sky, while he was writing his letter. Behind it lay in fact an arduous intellectual development. Toscanelli's letter of 1474 represented no more than an exceedingly brief summary of a long and vigorous evolution of geographic thought, whose body had taken shape in Florence more than a generation before, during the earlier part of the fifteenth century, and which had culminated at the time of the Council of Florence.

It was this evolution during the early fifteenth century that formed the historical bridge between the medieval tradition of science and the age of the discoveries. The principal strength and primary inspiration of this process of thought lay in the revival of the best fruits of ancient geography — not the bare philological recovery and translation of the texts, but the active reintegration of the leading classical theories, in particular those of Strabo and Ptolemy. The intellectual conquest of the earth thus preceded Columbus's first voyage by more than half a century — a conquest based on classical sources, the legacy of medieval geographic theory and lore, and the systematic use of contemporary maritime experience and travelers' reports. It had been accomplished in the same place and at the same time that the Renaissance was directing man's senses toward other aspects of his earthly habitat, as an integral part of the process which Jacob Burckhardt has called the "discovery of the world." [10]

Paolo dal Pozzo Toscanelli's famous letter to Columbus is obviously the work of a tired and celebrated old man writing to a young unknown. In a few short lines, with somewhat perfunctory courtesy, "Paul, the Physician" advises young Columbus that some time before — on June 24, 1474, to be exact — he had written about the subject of Columbus's inquiry (that is, the theory of a new route to the spice areas) to an old acquaintance, the canon of the Lisbon cathedral, Fernão Martins. For the young man's benefit he enclosed a copy of that earlier letter as well as a copy of the sailing chart he had sent Martins to illustrate his theory.[11]

MERCHANTS AND SCHOLARS

Yet even the letter to Martins, written in Toscanelli's seventy-fifth or seventy-sixth year, is clearly a tight-lipped summary of a highly complex theory, although designed expressly for the benefit of a layman. Reading it with this background in mind, one cannot help feeling that, because of his age and in view of this inexpert (though otherwise distinguished) audience — perhaps also because his own more intense concern with these problems lay by now more than thirty years back — the old scholar did not care to bother with a longer, more detailed explanation: The king of Portugal, he writes, Afonso V, through the services of the good canon, "now seeks from me some statement, or rather a demonstration to the eye, *by which the slightly learned may take in and understand*" [12] his suggestion of a sea route to the spice areas, shorter than the circumnavigation of Africa toward which the Portuguese were then bending their efforts. "I have already spoken with you respecting a shorter way to the places of spices than that which you take by Guinea, *by means of maritime navigation.*" [13]

The marked brevity of his style in dealing with a complicated subject may help to explain the astounding fact that historians have consistently tended to overlook the theoretical premise upon which his proposal was based. Besides, the originality of his thought is further obscured by the presence of two major "errors" in the westward-route proposal: Toscanelli's underestimation of the circumference of the globe,[14] and his obvious ignorance of the existence of the American continent — both common, if not inevitable errors in 1474 — combining, by understandable logic, into a vision of "the Indies" at the western end of the ocean, within a relatively short distance from Europe.

In point of fact, however, the understanding of his proposal required first and foremost an accurate conception of global geography (not just the knowledge that the earth was round, which had been familiar to geographers since antiquity. "Of all the vulgar errors connected with Columbus, the most persistent and the most absurd is that he had to convince people 'the earth was round,'" Samuel Eliot Morison said.) [15] Which was why Toscanelli seems at first to have thought of achieving the requested "demonstration to the eye" by sending a globe along with his letter ("I know this can be shown from the spherical shape of the earth," he writes), but had at last settled for a sailing chart, presumably because the old gentleman found the constructing of a globe a bit too cumbersome.[16]

Actually, despite the reluctant brevity of his style, he tries, as clearly as he can, to evoke a global concept in his reader's mind which is, at least in principle, altogether identical with that of modern geography. Instead of the traditional three-continental land mass of the *orbis terrarum,* surrounded by an impenetrable Ocean Sea, he clearly presupposes an ocean which had become an integral part of the earth, open to navigation, interspersed with habitable land formations. For Toscanelli's mind the entire earth had become accessible to man.

"You must not be surprised," he writes, trying to adjust his reader's vision to this

THOMAS GOLDSTEIN

new global view, "if I call the parts where the spices are west, when they usually call them east, because to those sailing west, those parts are found by navigation on the under side of the earth. But if by land and on the upper side, they will always be found to the east." Crucial, succinct, full of new meaning, the sentences look at first glance a little obscure. But for Fernão Martins, for King Afonso V, for Columbus, or for any other contemporary reader, they meant that he had to discard all at once the time-honored notion that the "habitable earth" was wrapped around with a kind of watery orbit. In his mind's eye, he had to link the two ends of the known earth by an enormous navigable waterway, thus in effect constructing a mental image of the modern globe (although still with a much smaller circumference, and as yet limited to three continents — plus whatever land formations the unknown ocean might still contain).[17]

But why "on the under side"? Toscanelli was evidently aware that the bulk of the Sunda archipelago — where most of the spice islands were — is in the Southern Hemisphere, to be reached at least partly "by navigation on the under side of the earth." His implicit premise is that the Southern Hemisphere was navigable, rather than covered by an unnavigable "torrid zone." Offhand one might assume that Portuguese navigation down the African coast had already demonstrated this fact beyond dispute. But in reality the Portuguese had crossed the equator for the first time only the year before, in 1473, under Lopo Gonçalves.[18] (The year is open to question; it may have been 1474.[19] Rui de Sequeira's expedition to Cape Catarina reached there on St. Catherine's Day, November 25, 1474 — possibly 1475,[20] but in any case later than the date of the Toscanelli letter.) What was more, the area covered by these pioneer expeditions extended over no more than one or two degrees S. Strictly speaking then, sufficient evidence did not exist by June 1474 to disprove the age-old belief in a "torrid zone" covering the entire Southern Hemisphere. Nor had the problem, patently of the highest importance for the Portuguese, been completely solved by Ptolemy, whose *Geography* contains some statements implying, mostly by inference and indirection, a rejection of the "torrid zone." [21] Since neither Portuguese maritime experience nor Ptolemy's inferences had firmly established the navigability of the Southern Hemisphere as a whole, Toscanelli's assumption that the spice islands of the Far East could be reached "by navigation on the under side of the earth" is remarkable in putting forth the idea of a navigable lower half of the globe.

Like the concept of a navigable Ocean Sea linking the continents, this assumption reflected a vigorous, original process of thought, synthesizing and transcending fragments of empirical evidence and hypothetical theory to reach definite and independent conclusions. It was the collective process of thought of a group of early fifteenth-century geographers which lay behind Toscanelli's brief but very bold statements.

Though a re-examination of his letter helps to clarify these implications and thereby to establish Toscanelli's precise contribution to the history of geographic

MERCHANTS AND SCHOLARS

thought, he may in one sense have received too much credit.[22] As long as his letter to Martins is considered the only important document of fifteenth-century geographic science, he necessarily appears to be the only outstanding scientist of his time to delve into geographic problems. This view not only overlooks the role of the large — albeit amorphous — group which had been carrying on geographic discussions (in which Toscanelli may well have been a guiding spirit, due both to his early training at the famous School of Padua and to his high achievement in other scientific fields).[23] It also fails to give proper credit to the often highly informal (by rigid modern standards we might say "dilettante") ways in which early modern science sometimes reached important results.

Without denying Toscanelli's role as the only known fully qualified scientist among this motley group — or his apparently magnetic and inspiring personality — one has to acknowledge that his fame in history rests on his having communicated the "global" theory to the Portuguese, rather than on any substantial evidence that he was its exclusive author. Though he was undoubtedly considered an authoritative spokesman for the new theory, he makes no claim in either of the documents of having originated the new concepts all by himself.

The revision of geographic thought — from the traditional *orbis terrarum* cum Ocean Sea to global — was unquestionably not the work of only one man. It was evolved by an apparently sizable group of scholars and dilettantes, mostly with characteristic humanist leanings, between 1410 or shortly thereafter and 1439–1440, the time of the Council of Florence (and possibly for a few years after that), in a long series of discussions — informal "symposia" probably similar in setting and atmosphere to those held on loftier subjects at the Platonic Academy, almost half a century afterward. We do not have a complete list of the participants, nor anything like a consistent record of the proceedings.[24] In time more light may be thrown on these discussions by new, more sharply focused research. Some aspects shall probably remain forever lost to us — not only because of the notorious capriciousness of archivistic history, but because there may have been reasons for conducting these meetings under cover of relative secrecy.[25] Besides, the very informality of a lively intellectual exchange — the kind of milieu in which the new concepts were undoubtedly worked out — may be sufficient reason for the absence of any major geographical studies reflecting the thought processes of this group.[26] But the evidence suffices to show that a number of well-known humanists took part in these talks;[27] that Florence soon became a center of geographic studies so that interested people from abroad, including Portugal, would consult with the Florentines; that such eminent scholars as the Byzantine Gemistos Plethon took part in some of these symposia; and above all that the discussions, however informal, followed a remarkably systematic approach to the knowledge of the earth and showed vigorous conceptual progress.

The appearance in 1410 of the Latin version of Ptolemy's *Geography* (in itself an indication in Florence of substantial interest in geography even before 1406, when

THOMAS GOLDSTEIN

Scarperia began his translation) [28] had first loosed a spate of discussions leading to major revisions of the medieval picture of the earth.[29] The identity of the participants in these early discussions is lit up by little more than occasional glimpses — somewhat like faces carved out of the dark by the flicker of a candle. Poggio gives us such a glimpse when he sketches a picture of Niccolò Niccoli, Aeneas Sylvius, and Cosimo Medici bending their heads over a copy of the *Geography* ("Hos ego [i.e., Poggio] Ptolemei Geographiam inspicientes cum imprimis, ut mos est, salutassem").[30] Humanists vied to possess a copy of the Ptolemaic manuscript.[31] The study of the *Geography* stimulated a new interest in cartography which in time resulted in decisive cartographic reforms.[32]

The *Geography* was also studied at Henry the Navigator's Sagres academy. (Diogo Gomes, whose narrative of Henry's activities was later written down by Martin Behaim, reported that one of the Navigator's explicit aims was the exploration of the ocean beyond Ptolemy's scope.)[33] In mid-1428 Henry's older brother, Prince Pedro, came to Florence during a trip devoted to the collecting of maps and general pointers for his brother's enterprise.[34] By that time, the geographic symposia held at various places around Florence and attended by a number of the well-known humanists of the time were undoubtedly well enough advanced for Prince Pedro to find a group of deeply interested men, steeped in the essentials of Ptolemaic geography, enabling him to discuss his brother's enterprise in an unusually qualified group.

How decisively the Florentine group may have influenced Portuguese thinking during these meetings cannot be precisely established until the theoretical evolution of the Sagres school — and Prince Pedro's contribution to it — has been more fully reconstructed.[35] But the possibility might have to be considered in future Portuguese research that that influence may indeed have been marked. The Florentines were at any rate qualified to discuss the two Ptolemaic theories most relevant to the Portuguese project — the extension of the African continent beyond the equator, and the possibility that the Southern Hemisphere might be navigable.[36] Besides, the intense cartographic activities stimulated in Florence by the *Geography*[37] should have confronted Prince Pedro with a highly expert group of mapmakers, well versed in the mathematical implications of cartography, from whom he could get valuable advice on a subject of crucial importance for the Portuguese enterprise. Broadly speaking, what the Florentines had to offer Prince Pedro (and to Portuguese leaders on later occasions) was more than a mere familiarity with the Ptolemaic text. As the study of the evolution of Florentine geographic thought shows, the Florentines were intent upon collecting additional evidence for Ptolemy's theories, in order to have a complete picture of the earth. For example, Ptolemy's inference about the navigability of the Southern Hemisphere could be corroborated by a number of considerations about the navigability of the ocean in general — especially certain conclusions resulting from the geographic position of the spice islands, a problem uppermost in Florentine thought.[38] And the Florentines, out of the same preoccupation with the evolving of a

[17]

MERCHANTS AND SCHOLARS

new "global" geography, had reason to be especially interested in the Portuguese explorations of the eastern Atlantic island world (already well advanced by 1428).[39]
The exchange of information and ideas on these subjects should have lent the talks
with Prince Pedro a global dimension.

In fact, discussion between Florence and Portugal of problems of geography did
not end with the Prince's visit. Throughout the fifteenth century Italian merchants in
the Iberian peninsula were to act as middlemen in a lively two-way exchange of geographic information and theory.[40] When the Portuguese turned to Toscanelli in the
time of Afonso V, through the good offices of Fernão Martins (and, later, when one
of his younger associates, Piero Vaglienti, credited him with the original idea for the
rounding of the Cape of Good Hope), Florence had been a kind of theoretical store-
house for the Portuguese expeditions, at least on crucial occasions, for quite some
time.

In 1439 another distinguished visitor from abroad found himself drawn into the
geographic symposia. Gemistos Plethon had come to Florence to attend the sessions
of the Ecumenical Council in the entourage of the Byzantine emperor, John VII Pa-
laeologus. During his many fruitful meetings with Florentine humanists he found their
geographic interests so one-sidedly Ptolemaic that he decided to round out their view
of classical geography with a forceful exposition of the theories of Strabo.[41] Even Plethon, however, succumbed to the Ptolemaic orientation of his Florentine friends with
respect to a number of important concepts, so that the result was a lively give and
take in which both sides ultimately managed to reconstruct and exchange the essential theories of the two leading geographers of the ancient world, creating an integrated picture of classical geography.[42]

Strabo's influence upon the course of Florentine thought — stemming from Plethon's vigorous advocacy — can clearly be traced, and was in fact highly important.[43]
We find the Ptolemaic influence upon Plethon in his *Diórthosis* — or "Correction"; the
full title is: "A Correction of Certain Errors Made by Strabo"[44] — written either
while he was in Florence or immediately afterward, i.e., under the direct impact of
his discussions with the Florentines.[45] One of the Ptolemaic theories he absorbed in
this way was the principle of presenting the earth or its segments through spherical
projection (which Ptolemy expounds in Book I, ch. XXIV, of the *Geography*).[46]

The critical sifting of Ptolemaic theories was to prove especially fruitful in the
field of accurate projection of the earth's surface. Two Florentines, Leon Battista
Alberti and Filippo Brunelleschi, pioneers both of Renaissance architecture and of
the mathematical principle of perspective, were intrigued by the problem of applying
the latter to cartography.[47] Alberti (who developed the final solution of perspective)
introduced the principle of polar (or conic) projection in his *Descriptio Urbis Ro-
mae*.[48] A simplification of the spherical projection method, it had been suggested by
Ptolemy as an alternative. Toward the end of the century both the spherical projec-

THOMAS GOLDSTEIN

tion method and the text of the *Geography* itself (in which the method was set forth) combined to bring about the beginning of full-fledged modern cartography. A series of editions of the *Geography,* first in manuscript form, then printed, came to include maps drawn on the Ptolemaic principle; thus Ptolemy's text became, from the sixteenth century on,[49] the prototype of the modern atlas. Florence continued to play a leading part in this development: the terza rima version of the *Geography,* completed in Florence in 1482 by Francesco Berlinghieri,[50] contained a reproduction of the projection employed by Ptolemy himself,[51] and helped to establish the use of the Ptolemaic method in modern cartography.

Several elements predestined the Council of Florence to become the natural setting for a final synthesis of Florentine geographic thought. The council itself had been moved from Ferrara to Florence at Cosimo Medici's invitation, mainly for the purpose of raising the international prestige of Florence.[52] The pageant of delegates from Byzantium, Russia, and the Near and even Far East (as well as from all of Roman Catholic Europe) made Florence for one brief moment the capital of the Christian world. The council's efforts to effect a reconciliation between Western Catholicism and the Eastern church — culminating in a formal agreement to re-establish Christian unity [53] — clearly enhanced its ecumenical importance. By the same token the citizens of Florence were exposed to the dazzle of foreign civilizations. (Some of that exotic glamor has been captured in Benozzo Gozzoli's "Visit of the Magi.") Byzantine scholars such as Plethon made deliberate efforts to help the Florentines get the fullest benefit from this unique cultural opportunity. His geographic expositions were only a minor part of his effort to round out Western knowledge of the ancient legacy — to complement the West's knowledge of Aristotelian philosophy by expounding Plato, and to complement its one-sided Ptolemaic picture of the earth by expounding Strabo.

Geography-minded Florentines found themselves suddenly facing a microcosmic mirror of the known world, aided by an expert interpretation of a body of ancient geographic knowledge and theory that had until then been unknown to them. Toscanelli and his friends seized the opportunity to talk with foreign delegates to the council about remote parts of the earth, filling in details missing from their mental map of the world. In the symposia with Plethon on Strabo's and Ptolemy's major theories — one might imagine the talks with the delegates as taking place mostly in the daytime, during the proceedings of the council; the symposia in the quiet of the Tuscan night — they made spectacular progress in filling the larger gaps in the *terra incognita.*

One of the subjects in the foreground of both the discussions and the talks with the council delegates was the geography of the Far East. The entire land mass to the east of India had been hazy ever since antiquity. Strabo had thought of all Asia as an indistinct land complex, calling it "India" (the term "Indies" in the Toscanelli correspondence still reflects this traditional haziness; in fact, despite the clarifying efforts at the time of the council, maps into the sixteenth century still tend to fade out in the

MERCHANTS AND SCHOLARS

Far East [54] — an indication of how very gradual was the focusing on that part of the world). Of the Southeast Asian island world Strabo merely mentions one major formation, "Taprobane," presumably a legendary elaboration upon reports about Ceylon.[55] Ptolemy — who wrote some hundred and fifty years later — was a great deal more specific in visualizing a distinct land mass to the east of India which he calls Sinae. He also saw a multitudinous island world.[56]

The Middle Ages had turned the whole world east and southeast of India into a vast, glittering stage for their exotic legends, though the more practical influence of travelers like Marco Polo can occasionally be traced on medieval maps. The Florentines had a particular reason for trying to clarify their picture of this remote part of the earth: their keen interest in the location of the spice islands.[57] Toscanelli appears to have taken copious notes from his talks with the council delegates, among whom was an emissary from "the country of the Great Khan," with whom he had a "long conversation . . . on many subjects, about the magnitude of their rivers in length and breadth, and on the multitude of cities on the banks of the rivers," as he was much later to recall in his letter to Martins.[58] Toscanelli amassed a great many notes about geographic subjects during his life (when the news of Columbus's discovery began to stir up the old interests, Ercole d'Este instructed his Florentine ambassador to recover Toscanelli's notes from his nephew).[59] The fate of his notes is unknown, but we may safely assume that his collection included those he took during the council.

Plethon too was keenly interested in the Far East. His "Correction" of Strabo shows that he absorbed important new information about the area while in Florence.[60] His sources may have been three: conversations with delegates, similar to Toscanelli's fact-gathering talks; the store of medieval travelers' reports (like Marco Polo's), available in the West; and Ptolemy's superior picture of Far Eastern geography.[61] The Florentines would have introduced him to the last two of these sources. Even if he was familiar with Ptolemy, as has been assumed,[62] before coming to Florence, the Ptolemaic imprint on his revisions of Strabo is so unmistakable that they clearly reflect the persuasive arguments of the Florentine followers of Ptolemy. But the whole Far Eastern problem was no doubt bandied about during their meetings. Part of his "Correction," incidentally, shows clearly that he too talked with delegates about various other parts of the world — with, for example, Isidore of Kiev and his fellow delegates about details of the geography of Russia.[63] Fact-gathering as well as the exchange of ideas was obviously intense on both sides.

Approximately at that time — probably during the council and while Plethon was there — the Florentines heard a report by a Venetian traveler, Niccolò de' Conti, who had been some twenty-five years in the East.[64] His detailed picture of the Southeast Asian island world [65] gave the Florentines important knowledge about an area they were particularly interested in.[66] When Toscanelli in the letter to Martins refers to an unspecified source of information about the Far East and its islands (in phrases like

THOMAS GOLDSTEIN

"it is asserted that . . . ," "they affirm that . . ."), the source was presumably Conti.

One listener was so fascinated by what Conti had to tell that he took detailed notes and later incorporated a transcription of them in his own works. As a reminder that these painstaking efforts to piece together a consistent picture of the earth were considered an exciting subject by eminent humanists we should note that the listener was Poggio Bracciolini.[67]

While the substance of these discussions (and their precise step-by-step evolution) remains somewhat shadowy in the absence of direct documentary evidence, we are aided by at least four major elements in reconstructing the essentials of Florentine geographic theory. They are (a) our knowledge of the discussions' point of departure; (b) our equally firm knowledge of the final result; (c) our knowledge of the major sources from which they drew their inspiration in piecing together a new concept of the globe; and (d) the inner logic of a thought process which, through several decades and many sessions of informal give and take (including, no doubt, countless trips over detours and up blind alleys), could essentially have followed only one course to arrive where it did.

The point of departure — to look ahead before tracing that thought process in more detail — was the Florentines' paramount interest in finding a new route to the spice islands. The final result, we know, was the premise of the Toscanelli letter: the theory of the navigability of the Ocean Sea, its place as an intercontinental waterway within a new, global concept of the earth. Their major sources, as we have seen, were first Ptolemy, then Strabo, and later the integration of these geographies, achieved during the exchanges between the Toscanelli group and Gemistos Plethon. Even without any more solid evidence on this point than the lively geographic communications between Florence and Portugal after Prince Pedro's visit, it is evident that the news of the progress of the Portuguese discoveries roughly till 1440 (i.e., up to the passing of Cape Bojador and a little further down the coast; and the exploration of the Madeira group, the Canary Islands, and the Azores) presented an additional vital source for the Florentines. We may assume with equal certainty that the Florentines studied the classical geographers principally for what they had to add to traditional medieval knowledge. Pierre d'Ailly's famous *Imago Mundi* (completed about 1410 and not yet influenced by Ptolemy's *Geography*)[68] can be considered a representative, up-to-date version of that tradition.

Lastly, while we are trying to retrace the thought process by which the Florentines arrived at a totally new concept of the earth, the other three elements will always have to be kept in mind.

Although the humanists were naturally attracted to the geographic symposia by the opportunity to delve into highly detailed aspects of ancient thought — and by a characteristic Renaissance pleasure in exploring foreign civilizations and countries,

MERCHANTS AND SCHOLARS

or in other words "the earth" [69] — the primary motive of the discussions was a great deal more pragmatic, if not downright commercial.

In both the letters Toscanelli stated the object of his proposal in unambiguously commercial terms — as a new "way to where the spices grow." Moreover, when writing to Columbus ("I perceive your magnificent and great desire to find a way to where the spices grow"), he implied that this desire had also been the object of Columbus's original inquiry. Both men had been active in the spice trade — Toscanelli as a member of his family's firm,[70] Columbus as an associate of several Genoese business groups.[71] And if it is not altogether certain whether Columbus, in his activities as an independent merchant on Porto Santo (where he established himself about 1480), continued to deal in spices,[72] he was definitely engaged in trade at the time he wrote to Toscanelli.

Most of the Italian businessmen in Portugal and Spain who transmitted geographic information between Italy and the Iberian Peninsula for the better part of the fifteenth century were also engaged in the spice business.[73] One of this group, Piero Vaglienti of Pisa (who collected reports on the voyages of discovery), commented upon Bartholomeu Dias's rounding of the Cape of Good Hope by neatly summing up the commercial result: "And thus an enterprise has been carried out that arouses the admiration of the whole world. The spices that should, or used to, go to Cairo by way of the Red Sea are now carried to Lisbon by this other route, and with this the Sultan has lost some five or six thousand ducats a year, and the Venetians the same." [74]

What Vaglienti was referring to was the historic reason behind the search for a new route, from the Florentines to the Portuguese and, finally, Columbus. By the fifteenth century the Turkish advances and other upheavals in the Near East had seriously dislocated traditional trade patterns, with the Turks imposing heavy tolls upon the European traders. Though a few privileged commercial groups faced with this problem succeeded either in offsetting their losses by virtually monopolizing the remaining import routes (like the Venetians),[75] or in avoiding the high tolls to the sultan through a kind of "most-favored-nation" agreement (like Lorenzo Medici's firm) — though a few solved the problem in these ways, less-favored business groups, in Italy and outside, were casting about for a more profitable business based on a direct access to the spice-producing areas.[76] It was this situation which led not only to a substantial transfer of Italian capital to Portugal and Spain,[77] but also to the intense intellectual efforts to find an alternative route, an effort that eventually required nothing less than a radical revision of the concept of the globe.

We shall have to envisage this background in order to appreciate why the recovery of first Ptolemy and then Strabo held such exciting new implications for the Florentines.

The first thing Ptolemy did for his fifteenth-century readers was to put the Far East, including its spice-producing island world, in sharper focus.[78] His notion of a

THOMAS GOLDSTEIN

great multitude of Southeast Asian islands agreed with Marco Polo's (and, later, Conti's) reports. But how could one reach these islands if not over the age-old spice routes across Asia, now the scene of intensified rivalry among the chief European economic powers? Traditional medieval notions offered no conceivable alternative. To the new approaches the fifteenth century was finally to work out, Pierre d'Ailly's *Imago Mundi* opposed three distinct traditional barriers.

Toward the east, Asia (including its island world) was blocked by the surrounding, proverbially impenetrable Ocean Sea. (D'Ailly restated this Homeric conception in authoritative terms in his chapter "De Mari" — although mentioning, with somewhat chilly sarcasm, that "quidam moderni philosophi" had begun to question this time-honored belief.) [79] The Far East, then, could certainly not be reached "by sailing west."

If the spice islands, on the other hand, were in the Indian Ocean (as d'Ailly — and with him, of course, the Florentine geographers — knew), [80] here was a second, additional barrier: for d'Ailly — in fact for virtually the entire geographic tradition from antiquity through the Middle Ages — the Indian Ocean appeared landlocked, blocked by a major land mass, toward the east. The only way to reach it was by an eastward voyage which d'Ailly thought would take about a year. [81]

As for reaching the spice islands by sailing around Africa, the very idea of the impenetrable Ocean Sea surrounding all three continents, obviously precluded that.

Ptolemy's *Geography* destroyed at least two of these traditional barriers. By introducing the concept of an African continent extending considerably south of the equator (i.e., to 16°25′S) (Book VII, ch. V), he not only replaced the highly contracted northern sliver of the ancient — and later, again, medieval — maps by a far more accurate image, but, what was more decisive, he suggested that the Southern Hemisphere was at least partly inhabitable (Book IV, ch. VIII). To the early fifteenth century this meant the exciting possibility that the traditional "torrid zone" (in which ships would burn to a crisp and white men turn black) did not in fact cover the southern half of the globe. It gave impressive encouragement to Henry the Navigator's efforts to reach "the Indies" by sailing around the African continent. [82] And the Florentines might have detected at least an encouraging general implication: that an Ocean Sea without a torrid zone might perhaps be accessible to ships. The idea was startling enough to cause Plethon to correct Strabo on this point. [83]

Ptolemy is not, however, explicit in suggesting that the ocean could be used as a waterway (some modern scholarly assumptions notwithstanding). [84] Nor — again contrary to a modern assumption — did he doubt that the Indian Ocean was "landlocked." [85] It was Strabo through Plethon's advocacy, who on both these points supplied the missing pieces. Though Strabo had no clear idea of the Indian Ocean as such (the term does not even occur in his voluminous work), [86] nor of the Southeast Asian island world, [87] the startling idea fifteenth-century geographers did find in him was that the Asiatic land mass as a whole, south as well as east, was washed by the Ocean

MERCHANTS AND SCHOLARS

Sea. ("But the Southern and Eastern sides [of 'India'] which are much greater than the other two, extend out into the Atlantic sea," he had said.) [88]

What this meant was neither more nor less than that Southeast Asia, including its island world (which the Florentines had come to see with growing clarity),[89] was accessible from the east — or, as Toscanelli was to put it in his letter, by "always sailing west." Provided, of course, that the ocean was indeed navigable in all directions.

The final, and all-important, conclusion that the Ocean Sea was open to navigation was prepared for by several cumulative pieces of evidence, and should therefore have been reached in a series of corresponding steps.

1. Portuguese navigation since 1415 demonstrated progressively that the eastern Atlantic, at least as far out as the Azores, as well as southward down the African coast, was indeed navigable, at least for a relatively short distance offshore.

2. Portuguese exploration of Atlantic island groups inevitably suggested the likelihood of additional land formations farther out. Since the discovered islands turned out to be habitable (permitting an island-hopping kind of sailing between them), the Ocean Sea was evidently not an alien element, destructive of human life (an assumption which a host of medieval legends had perpetuated).[90]

3. Strabo's over-all conception of Asia implied that its island world — instead of being situated in a landlocked Indian Ocean — jutted out into the surrounding Ocean Sea. Strabo actually said as much, at least regarding the one major island formation of which he was aware: "We have strong assurance that Taprobane is a large island *in the open sea, which lies off India to the South* . . ."[91] The open sea, south of "India," was for Strabo the surrounding ocean, as we have seen. The same assumptions (1 and 2 above) would have to hold true when the Ocean Sea was regarded from its Asiatic end, as from the eastern or "Atlantic." Before the discovery of the New World, the Atlantic and Pacific were of course thought of as one sea; in other words, the ocean must be navigable and its land formations accessible from both ends. Incidentally, the reasonable assumption of possible further, as yet unknown land formations was also true of the ocean when viewed from the Asiatic shore.

Speculation that the Ocean Sea might contain land formations, possibly entire continents — and thus be able to accommodate human life — was by no means altogether new. A thin thread of this kind of speculation had run from Plato's *Timaeus* through the late Graeco-Roman and medieval world all the way into the fifteenth century.[92]

The Middle Ages had made their own contribution to this age-old tradition by peopling the Ocean Sea with legendary islands. Our modern concept of "legendary" should not preclude our realization that the Middle Ages thought these islands were real.[93] Moreover, the *Timaeus*, with its assumption of a mid-oceanic continent, Atlantis, was well known during the Middle Ages.[94] During the fifteenth century all this long-standing speculation about oceanic land formations (including the idea that the

THOMAS GOLDSTEIN

ocean was accessible to man and hospitable to human life) generated a new spate of similar prognostications, culminating in Lorenzo Buonincontri's emphatic statement in 1476 that the existence of a "fourth continent" had become a foregone conclusion.[95]

If all these elements were by their very nature at best inferential and speculative (although undoubtedly influential for a systematic approach to the problem of the ocean's navigability), in Strabo the Florentines found at last the definite suggestion that the ocean could be crossed from east to west.[96] More importantly, Strabo's hypothetical statement to this effect (based on Eratosthenes) emerges from a distinctly global conception of the habitable earth, with the ocean forming an integral part of the habitable globe — and the further idea that it might contain habitable land formations, possibly entire continents. "The inhabited world," he wrote, "forms a complete circle, itself meeting itself; so that if the immensity of the Atlantic Sea did not prevent, we could sail from Iberia to India along one and the same parallel over the remainder of the circle." [97] Strabo explicitly points out in this context that the concept of the "habitable earth" (or oikoumène) should not be limited to the traditional three-continental land mass. "It is possible," he wrote, "that in the same temperate zone [i.e., that inhabited by us] there are actually two inhabited worlds, or even more, and particularly in the proximity of the parallel through Athens that is drawn across the Atlantic Sea." [98]

Strabo (basing his theories on a long tradition of Greek geographic thought which had assumed the sphericity of the earth since the time of Pythagoras in the sixth century B.C.) [99] conveyed to the Florentines his original — though inspired by Eratosthenes — concept of a navigable Ocean Sea embedded in a global concept of the habitable earth. The mere mathematical assumption that the earth was a sphere had of course not in itself affected the belief that the human habitat was limited to a small portion of the globe, a portion hedged in by a hostile and impenetrable element. Like Toscanelli's letter, Strabo's practical suggestion (tossed off as a mere hypothesis) formed part of a comprehensive theory of the globe. Just as for Toscanelli the novelty of his conception was in his emphasis upon the ocean as a potential intercontinental waterway, containing habitable land formations as well as being navigable — the navigability qualified only by a mention of the ocean's "immensity," and not specifying any inherently hostile properties.

For the process of global reconstruction in which the Florentines were engaged Strabo supplied a classical conceptual framework. But then the fifteenth century was ahead of Strabo's time in a crucial, practical way: Portuguese maritime experience had added an empirical element to classical theory.

Florentine thought in the fifteenth century had progressed by stages to a conception of the modern globe. The Far East and its spice islands had moved into sharper focus. The site of these islands — the Indian Ocean — had been mentally unlocked toward the east, made accessible across the Ocean Sea. Old Oceanus itself had been

[25]

MERCHANTS AND SCHOLARS

moved from its orbital status, integrated with the habitable world, tamed for the existence of human life, opened up for navigation. The Southern Hemisphere had been wrested from its "torrid" state — always by a mental combination of actual maritime or travelers' experience and classical theory — opened up for human life and navigation as well. The modern globe was ready, mentally and in outline at any rate. The spice islands could be approached "by navigation," sailing from east to west, even "on the under side of the earth."

All that was missing was an explorer's boldness to demonstrate the validity of the new theories, and, of course, such further details or refinements as an accurate measuring of the circumference of the earth (for which Magellan's voyage supplied the empirical basis); the discovery of the New World and its identification as a separate continent (for which Amerigo Vespucci supplied the data); the recognition of the separate identities of the Atlantic and Pacific oceans (based on Nuñez de Balboa's original observations); and the discovery and exploration in detail of the remaining continents — until the modern globe would at last be complete. Yet the fundamental principle of modern geography, even including a basically accurate cartographic method, had been developed in full, through a forceful adaptation of classical theory to fifteenth-century practical experience, by an impressive thought process, in the shadow of the quattrocento Renaissance.

NOTES

page 12

[1] See Boies Penrose, *Travel and Discovery in the Renaissance*, New York, 1962, pp. 11ff., for a brief, up-to-date survey. Pliny's *Natural History*, including its four books on geography, was used as a textbook throughout the Middle Ages (see A. C. Crombie, *Medieval and Early Modern Science*, New York, 1959, vol. 1, p. 11). Ptolemaic concepts had been reaching the West through the Arabs (through Edrisi's influence and through the *Almagest*, as well as through John of Holywood's abstract of the latter, the *Sphaera Mundi*) since the twelfth century. See Penrose, *op. cit.*, pp. 11f.; Philip K. Hitti, *The Arabs: A Short History*, Chicago, 1956, p. 149. For Albertus Magnus's, Roger Bacon's, and other thirteenth- and fourteenth-century scholars' mostly Aristotelian speculations on geographic subjects, see also R. Beazley, *The Dawn of Modern Geography*, Oxford, 1897–1906, vol. 3, p. 502 (and *passim*).

[2] See Penrose, *op. cit.*, pp. 45f. Carlos Coimbra, "O Infante e o objectivo geografico dos descobrimentos," in *Actas do Congresso Internacional de Historia dos Descobrimentos*, Lisbon, 1961, vol. 4, pp. 77ff., gives an idea of the extremely inferential nature of our information on this subject so far.

[3] Thus B. L. Ullman, *Studies in the Renaissance*, Rome, 1955, pp. 22f.: "Perhaps we should start anew to test, cautiously and scientifically, the impact of the Renaissance on the various aspects of civilization . . . Did the enormous influence of the translation of Ptolemy's Geography, finished in 1410 by Iacopo Angeli da Scarperia . . . have a bearing on the voyages of discovery?" See also *ibid.*, p. 23, n. 25.

[4] See, e.g., John H. Randall, Jr., *The Making of the Modern Mind*, Cambridge, Mass., 1940 (rev. ed. 1954), pp. 212f.

[5] See Rudolph Wittkower, *Architectural Principles in the Age of Humanism*, 2nd ed., London, 1952; Erwin Panofsky, "The History of the Theory of Human Proportions as a Re-

THOMAS GOLDSTEIN

flection of the History of Styles," in *Meaning in the Visual Arts*, New York, 1955, pp. 55–107; Erwin Panofsky, "Das perspektivische Verfahren Leone Battista Albertis," in *Kunstchronik*, vol. 25, August 1915, pp. 504–516.

[6] See the valid survey in Myron P. Gilmore, *The World of Humanism*, New York, 1952, pp. 254ff.

[7] See Joan Gadol, "Leon Battista Alberti: The Renaissance of Geometric Space in Art and Science," Columbia University dissertation, 1963.

page 13

[8] I.e., Strabo (see below, p. 25), who, in his crucial passage, explicitly refers to Eratosthenes as the original author of the concept. Sporadic speculation about habitable parts of the globe, outside of the *oikouméne*, occurs in Greek thought since Plato; see also note 92 below. Some of this is echoed during the Middle Ages; see Penrose, *op. cit.*, pp. 12f. However, for the evolution of geographic theory one will have to keep in mind that all this speculation lacked Strabo's solid conceptual context. The same is true for Pierre d'Ailly's extremely casual remark about the navigability of the Ocean "if the wind be fair," in his *Cosmologiae Tractatus Duo*, c.1414. The fact that Columbus was excited about d'Ailly's remark — see Samuel Eliot Morison, *Admiral of the Ocean Sea: A Life of Christopher Columbus*, Boston, 1942, p. 93 — speaks for Columbus's fairly crude theoretical understanding, not for the importance of d'Ailly's revised theories for the evolution of a systematic concept of the earth.

[9] See below, p. 23, for Pierre d'Ailly's restatement of this classical concept in his *Imago Mundi*, c.1410. Lloyd A. Brown, *The Story of Maps*, Boston, 1950, mentions a Sumerian (or Akkadian) clay tablet, c.2300 or 2100, depicting the Oceanus river (p. 33) and discusses the Homeric concept (pp. 22f.). The idea of the surrounding Ocean river is entirely endemic to ancient and medieval cartography — the latter from Cosmas in the sixth century through the fifteenth century, up to Toscanelli's and Behaim's times — with a highly qualified implication in Ptolemy's *Geography* the only major exception (see below, p. 23), and, of course, Strabo's totally different concept (see note 8 above).

[10] For an argument in support of the continued validity of the Burckhardtian view of the Renaissance, see Thomas Goldstein, "Medieval Civilization from the World-Historical View," in *Journal of World History*, UNESCO, vol. 6, 1960, no. 3, pp. 503ff. (especially p. 505, n. 7).

[11] For a critical evaluation of the Toscanelli correspondence see Norbert Sumien, *La Correspondence du savant florentin Paolo del Pozzo Toscanelli avec Christophe Colomb*, Paris, 1927.

page 14

[12] The version used here is C. R. Markham's translation from the Latin in *The Journal of Christopher Columbus*, London, 1893, *Works Issued by the Hakluyt Society*, vol. 86 (italics mine).

[13] Toscanelli and Martins may have discussed the subject at length (and Toscanelli may thus have felt that he could rely on Martins's more elaborate explanations to the king) at the house of Nicholas Cusanus in San Pietro in Vincoli in Rome, where the three men met frequently during Cusanus's last years (Cusanus died in 1464). See Gustavo Uzielli, *La Vita ed i tempi di Paolo del Pozzo Toscanelli; ricerche e studi*, part V, vol. 1 of *Raccolta di documenti e studi pubblicati dalla R. Commissione Colombiana pel quarto centenario della scoperta dell'America* (from here on cited as Uzielli, *vita*), Rome, 1894, pp. 261ff. See also Paolo Rotta, *Nicolò Cusano*, Milan, 1942, pp. 111, 297. Martins together with Toscanelli witnessed Cusanus's testament.

[14] See the discussion of the circumference problem in Morison, *op. cit.*, pp. 64ff. Eratosthenes's near-accurate calculation had been lost in the tradition.

[15] Morison, *op. cit.*, p. 33. For the history and implications of the spheric concept since antiquity see W. G. L. Randles, *Quelques modifications apportées par les grandes découvertes à la conception mediévale du monde*, Lisbon, 1959, p. 5; Lloyd A. Brown, *op. cit.*, pp. 25ff.

[16] Toscanelli suggests two reasons why he preferred to send a portolano instead of a globe ("yet, to make the comprehension of it easier, *and to facilitate the work*, I have determined to show that way by means of a sailing chart"). One tends to suspect that the first reason is somewhat spurious — his global theory should

MERCHANTS AND SCHOLARS

have been easier to demonstrate with the help of a globe than a portolano — so that the real reason should have been that the producing of a chart involved less effort.

page 15

[17] "Et non miremini, si voco occidentales partes ubi sunt aromata, cum communiter dicantur orientales, quia navigantibus per subterraneas navigationes ad occidentem semper illae partes inveniuntur; si, enim, per terram et per superiora itinera, ad orientem semper reperientur."

The scope of his theory becomes more evident if one compares Toscanelli's sailing chart with the earth as presented on earlier maps, still dominated by the notion of the surrounding Ocean Sea. Since both copies of his chart are lost, one might consult the reconstruction in Uzielli, *vita*. Both of Toscanelli's letters contain sufficiently specific references, including distances, to permit an essentially accurate reconstruction. See also the discussion in Sumien, *op. cit.*, p. 3; also H. Wagner, "Die Rekonstruktion der Toscanelli-Karte vom Jahre 1474 und die Pseudo-Faksimilia des Behaim-Globus vom Jahre 1492," *Goettinger Gelehrte Nachrichten*, Philosophisch-Historische Klasse (1894), pp. 208ff. (The Latin text of the letter to Martins can be found, e.g., in Sumien, *op. cit.*, pp. 9ff.) On the assumption of land formations inside the Ocean, see n. 92 and n. 95 below.

[18] See Penrose, *op. cit.*, p. 55; Damião Peres, *A History of the Portuguese Discoveries*, Lisbon, 1960, p. 48.

[19] Peres, *op. cit.*, places Gonçalves's and de Sequeira's discoveries between 1474 and 1475.

[20] *Ibid.*

[21] See below, p. 23.

page 16

[22] The principal studies about Toscanelli are by Gustavo Uzielli (see n. 13 for his monumental *vita*). Through a lifetime of enthusiastic devotion Uzielli managed to collect many essential documents and to establish Toscanelli's important contribution to the age of discoveries. Although subsequent historians have largely relied on Uzielli's work (see, e.g., Germán Arciniegas, *Amerigo and the New World: The Life and Times of Amerigo Vespucci*, New York, 1955), a critical re-examination of his conclusions and evidence would seem indicated

in view of his heavily apologetic bias, aiming at establishing Toscanelli's fame. Uzielli fully recognizes the role of the informal discussions of geographic subjects (in which Toscanelli participated) on which this essay is focused, and in fact has assembled most of the available evidence (Arciniegas's *Amerigo* contains additional significant material). He fails, however, to give a consistent reconstruction of the evolution of geographic theory in these debates, for which Professor Anastos's study has supplied a crucial element (see below, n. 42ff.).

[23] For Toscanelli's studies at the School of Padua, see Uzielli, *vita*, pp. 13ff. (See Uzielli, *vita*, pp. 22ff. for a detailed survey of his education.) The influence of the Padua tradition should be viewed in the light of John H. Randall, Jr.'s *The School of Padua and the Emergence of Modern Science* (especially ch. I, "The Development of the Scientific Method in the School of Padua"), Padua, 1961. For Toscanelli's only surviving manuscript, concerning problems of astronomy, geodesy, and geography (including the location of the manuscript in the Florentine Biblioteca Nazionale Centrale, which should be verified or relocated), see Uzielli, *vita*, p. 452.

[24] A detailed survey can be found in G. Uzielli, *Paolo dal Pozzo Toscanelli iniziatore della scoperta d'America*, Florence, 1892 (with appendix of documentary sources, "Osservazioni e documenti"), pp. 76, 208n, 209n. Also his *vita*, pp. 54ff., 72ff. Uzielli places these meetings in the Convento degli Angeli at Camaldoli in the years between 1420 and 1440. He lists Toscanelli, Leonardo Bruni, Palla Strozzi, Antonio Corbinelli, Filippo Pieruzzi, and Niccolò Niccoli among the participants. Arciniegas, *op. cit.*, pp. 45ff., discusses a continuation of these meetings at the Badia a Settimo. Unfortunately, his inspiring study works without consistent source references.

[25] Uzielli, *vita*, pp. 475ff. and *passim* assumes Toscanelli and his friends were conducting these discussions, at any rate after Cosimo's return in 1434, in the shadow of potential persecution by the Medici and those who shared the effective power over Florence with them. Uzielli's thesis seems to have been implicitly accepted by Arciniegas, *op. cit.*, pp. 85ff. Though Uzielli presents some telling evidence on the connection of the geographers with the anti-Medici opposition, the political undercur-

THOMAS GOLDSTEIN

rents of fifteenth-century Florence may have to be clarified more thoroughly before the underground character of these meetings could be considered as established. However, economic motives for escaping the prohibitive Medici taxation through outside investments may have been strong (see below, n. 77); and it is noteworthy that the discussions seem to have been held consistently at some distance from the city. On the tendency of the contemporary governments to keep matters of geographic discovery a secret, see Jaime Cortesão, *The National Secret of the Portuguese Discoveries of the 15th Century*, London, n.d.; Morison, *op. cit.*, p. 344.

[26] See Pearl Kibre, "Intellectual Interests as Reflected in 14th and 15th Century Libraries," *Journal of the History of Ideas*, vol. 7, 1946, pp. 257ff., on the fact that fifteenth-century libraries contain little else on the subject of geography than maps or the texts of classical geographers. A careful study of the correspondence and other writings of the contemporary humanists (even on subjects not overtly related to geography) may yet produce a tenuous accumulation of supporting evidence through which the evolution of certain concepts — and, above all, the scope of humanist interest in these matters — might be more palpably traced.

[27] See n. 24 above. Specialized studies of the geographic interests of the fifteenth-century humanists, made on the basis of the available evidence, include Siegmund Günther, "Der Humanismus in seinem Einfluss auf die Entwicklung der Erdkunde," *Heffners Geographische Zeitschrift*, vol. 6, 1900, pp. 65ff.; Waldemar Sensburg, "Poggio Bracciolini und Nicolo de' Conti in ihrer Bedeutung für die Geographie des Rennaisse-Zeitalters," *Mitteilungen der K. K. Geographischen Gesellschaft in Wien*, vol. 48, 1905, pp. 257ff.; Alfred Berg, *Enea Silvio de' Piccolomini in seiner Bedeutung als Geograph* (Ein Beitrag zur Geschichte der Erdkunde im Quattrocento), Halle a.S., 1901. Besides these, G. Voigt, *Enea Piccolomini und sein Zeitalter*, Berlin, 1862, 2 vols., contains interesting material on Aeneas Sylvius's geographic interests. Arciniegas's cited study of Vespucci offers a wealth of material embedding Amerigo's education in the background of geographic studies in Florence since early in the fifteenth century. There seems little doubt that

humanist concern for geographic questions was first stimulated by the Florentine discussions; see below, pp. 17 and 20, for Aeneas Sylvius's and Conti's connections with this group.

page 17

[28] The possibility that the translation may have been begun by Chrysoloras has been suggested by Brown, *op. cit.*, p. 145. Scarperia may at any rate have been urged to undertake the translation by the man who introduced the study of Greek at the "Studio fiorentino."

[29] See below, pp. 18, 22, 23.

[30] Poggio Bracciolini, *De Infelicitate princip.*, op. 392 (cited in Sensburg, *op. cit.*, p. 342, n. 1).

[31] See, e.g., Sensburg, *op. cit.*, p. 342, about Poggio writing to Niccolò Niccoli concerning his desire to own a copy of the *Geography*.

[32] See below, p. 19.

[33] See D. Peres, *op. cit.*, pp. 24f.

[34] Prince Pedro, sometime around June, "tornò in casa di Matteo Scolari dall'albergo della Corona" (Uzielli, *Toscanelli iniziatore*, p. 73). See *ibid.*, pp. 73ff. and 208n for a discussion of Dom Pedro's probable moves in Florence.

[35] See n. 2 above. Also R. Beazley, *Prince Henry the Navigator*, London, n.d. The plain fact is that the reconstruction of Portuguese geographic theory, despite the intense interest of Portuguese historians, has made little headway so far. This is partly due to the scarcity of direct evidence, and partly, perhaps, to a general omission of attempts to reconstruct fifteenth-century geographic thought as a serious phase in the history of science.

[36] See also below, p. 20.

[37] See below, p. 17.

[38] See below, p. 21.

page 18

[39] By that time, the Portuguese had explored the Madeira group, the Canary Islands, and, in all probability, the Azores; see Penrose, *op. cit.*, pp. 46f.; D. Peres, *op. cit.*, pp. 30ff.

[40] See Charles Verlinden, "Les Découvertes portugaises et la collaboration italienne d'Alphonse IV à Alphonse V," *Actas do Congresso Internacional de Historia dos Descobrimentos*, Lisbon, 1961, vol. 3, pp. 593ff. (who discusses several instances of Italian contributions to fifteenth-century Portuguese discoveries). Actually, examples where Italian businessmen in

MERCHANTS AND SCHOLARS

the Iberian Peninsula have played a crucial role in the transmission of geographic information are strikingly frequent and would deserve a special study: e.g., Columbus's contact with Toscanelli was arranged by Lorenzo Berardi (Morison, *op. cit.*, pp. 83f.), who belonged to a Florentine business firm with branch offices in Lisbon and Seville (cf. Uzielli, *vita*, p. 498). Giovanni (Gianetto) Berardi (friend of Amerigo Vespucci's first employer, Lorenzo di Pier Francesco de' Medici, and himself Vespucci's employer after 1492) brought about Vespucci's meeting with Columbus and may have helped finance Columbus's second voyage. The story, somewhat spread out through Arciniegas's volume, can be pieced together with the help of his index, by looking under "Berardi, Gianetto." Bartolomeo Marchionni, member of a Florentine house in Lisbon, was credited by Piero Vaglienti with having conveyed Toscanelli's support for Bartholomeu Dias's rounding of the Cape of Good Hope to the Portuguese court (Arciniegas, *op. cit.*, pp. 111f., 198). Piero Vaglienti, a Florentine with a small business firm in Pisa who collected reports on the Portuguese (and, later, Spanish) voyages, had grown up in the firm of Benedetto Dei, a Florentine businessman who was an authority on foreign travel, especially the geography of the interior of Africa (a subject evidently of primary importance for the Portuguese) (Arciniegas, *op. cit.*, pp. 111f., 125).

[41] See M. V. Anastos, "Pletho, Strabo and Columbus," *Annuaire de l'Institut de Philologie et d'Histoire Orientales et Slaves*, vol. 12, 1952, Brussels, *Mélanges Henri Grégoire, IV*, pp. 6f.

[42] Professor Anastos's highly stimulating study clearly establishes that Plethon, during his stay in Florence, met Toscanelli (and apparently others associated with the geographic symposia), and that, when confronted with the one-sided cult of Ptolemy among the Florentines, he countered by expounding Strabo's theories (especially where these conflicted with Ptolemy), thus bringing knowledge of Strabo to the West quite some time before Guarino da Verona's translation, completed in 1458, or that by Gregory Tiphernias (who finished his translation of books 11–17 of the *Geographikà* in 1456). (See Anastos, *op. cit.*, pp. 10, 11.) What Anastos fails to recognize is that the rather substantial corrections in Plethon's own

geographic concepts, as evident from his explicit corrections of Strabo's geography, clearly reflect Ptolemaic influence (except for some detail which he had obviously gathered from individual Council delegates) (see Anastos, *op. cit.*, p. 3). Therefore, the analysis of the substance of the theories which were assimilated by both sides on this occasion can leave no doubt that an extensive exchange of Strabonic and Ptolemaic views took place during the Council of Florence, and that the discussions between Plethon and the Florentines must have been thorough enough to allow what amounted to an essential integration of classical geographic thought.

[43] See Anastos, *op. cit.*, pp. 7, 13ff. for further discussion.

[44] See Anastos, *op. cit.*, pp. 1f.

[45] *Ibid.*

[46] See Anastos, *op. cit.*, p. 3, on Plethon criticizing Strabo for his un-Ptolemaic view that meridians may be represented by straight lines. Several of the other criticisms clearly reflect Ptolemaic concepts (see below). (Joseph Fischer, *C. Ptolemaes Geographiae Codex Urbinas Graecus 82 Phototypice Depictus*, Leyden-Leipzig, 1932.)

[47] See Günther, *op. cit.*, p. 86.

[48] See Gadol, *op. cit.*; Brown, *op. cit.*, pp. 69f.

page 19

[49] Brown, *op. cit.*, pp. 152ff.

[50] See Arciniegas, *op. cit.*, p. 94.

[51] Brown, *op. cit.*, p. 155.

[52] The role of the intangibles of prestige in Cosimo Medici's policy (and of Eugene the Fourth's and the Council of Florence's place within his scheme) is well presented in Ferdinand Schevill, *The Medici*, New York, 1949, pp. 70ff.

[53] Schevill, *op. cit.*, p. 74.

page 20

[54] Cf., e.g., the Mercator map of the world of 1538 (see A. E. Nordenskjöld, *Facsimile-atlas to the Early History of Cartography*, Stockholm, 1889, pl. XLIII).

[55] *The Geography of Strabo*; translated by H. L. Jones, Loeb Classical Library, London–New York, 1917, 8 vols., 2.1.14; vol. 1, p. 271.

[56] Book VII, ch. 3 ("Sinae"). "There are many islands around Taprobane," Ptolemy says

THOMAS GOLDSTEIN

(Book VII, ch. 4), "which are said to number more than one thousand three hundred and seventy-eight."

[57] See below, pp. 22f.

[58] The reference in the letter to Martins is, somewhat vaguely (presumably in keeping with the whole tenor of the letter), to "the time of Eugenius," rather than to the Council. Eugenius the Fourth, 1431–1447, presided over the Council of Ferrara-Florence. See Uzielli, *vita*, p. 163, for Toscanelli's reference to the notes he took during the Council.

[59] Cf. Sumien, *op. cit.*, p. 7.

[60] Anastos, *op. cit.*, pp. 3, 5. '

[61] See earlier discussion.

[62] Anastos, *op. cit.*, p. 6.

[63] *Ibid.*, p. 5.

[64] See Sensburg, *op. cit.* (n. 27 above). The date of Conti's return to Italy (and his stay in Florence) has been placed by Sensburg between 1439 and 1442, but with a good likelihood that he may have been there during the Council.

[65] Sensburg, *op. cit.*, pp. 257, 319ff., presents an extensive catalogue of the Southeast Asian islands identified by Conti. For a comparison, one might consult the thorough list of Far Eastern islands as identified by Marco Polo; see Leonardo Olschki, *L'Asia di Marco Polo*, Venice-Rome, 1957. Olschki's "island catalogue" has to be compiled with the help of the indexes — "Indice geografico ed etnografico" and "Indice delle cose notabili," *ibid.* See also, in English, *Marco Polo's Asia*, translated by John Scott, Berkeley, 1960.

[66] See below, p. 22.

page 21

[67] Sensburg's assumption that Poggio's relation was based on notes taken during Conti's talk seems more plausible than his alternative suggestion that it was based on dictation (*op. cit.*, p. 328). The oldest known manuscript of Poggio's relation dates from 1447–1448, but an older manuscript may have existed (*ibid.*, pp. 261f.). The report was finally incorporated into Book IV of Poggio's *Historiae de varietate fortunae libri IV* (see *ibid.*, p. 328).

[68] Latin and French text, ed. E. Guron, Paris, 1930, 3 vols. George H. T. Kimble, *Geography in the Middle Ages*, London, 1938, p. 211, has suggested that in his subsequent treatise, *Cosmographiae Tractatus Duo*, written c.1414,

d'Ailly made some major revisions in his geographic picture under the influence of Ptolemy's *Geography*, following the latter's Latin translation. Although Kimble's suggestion appears to have been rather generally accepted — see, e.g., Penrose, *op. cit.*, p. 13; Morison, *op. cit.*, p. 93 — some of d'Ailly's revised concepts are clearly Ptolemaic (such as the southward extension of Africa), but others are definitely not (such as the concept of an "open" Indian Ocean) (see below, p. 24). There is the possibility that stray concepts of Strabo were known during the Middle Ages and therefore may have influenced d'Ailly (d'Ailly's *Imago* in fact contains a doubtful reference to him; see Anastos, *op. cit.*, pp. 8ff., 10). On the whole, d'Ailly represents such a jumble of conventional medieval notions and surprisingly fresh concepts that a new critical study would seem indicated.

page 22

[69] See T. Goldstein, "Florentine Humanism and the Vision of the New World," *Actas do Congresso Internacional da Historia dos Descobrimentos*, Lisbon, 1961, vol. 4, pp. 195ff. (especially p. 203).

[70] See Uzielli, *vita*, pp. 504–511 (especially p. 506).

[71] See Morison, *op. cit.*, p. 22.

[72] *Ibid.*, pp. 39f.

[73] See above n. 40.

[74] See Arciniegas, *op. cit.*, pp. 111f.

[75] See Wallace K. Ferguson, *Europe in Transition; 1300–1520*, Boston, 1962, p. 425; Frederick C. Lane, "Venetian Shipping During the Commercial Revolution," *American Historical Review*, vol. 38, 1933.

[76] See R. Lopez and H. A. Miskimin, "The Economic Depression of the Renaissance," *The Economic History Review*, vol. 14, 1962, pp. 408ff.; R. de Roover, *The Medici Bank*, New York, 1948 (rev. ed. 1963); also see C. Barbagallo, "La crisi economico-sociale dell'Italia della Rinascenza," *Nuova Rivista Storica*, vol. 25, 1950.

[77] See n. 76, also Arciniegas, *op. cit.*, pp. 96f.

[78] See above, p. 20.

page 23

[79] *Imago Mundi*, vol. 2, pp. 542f.

[80] *Ibid.*, p. 140.

[81] *Ibid.*

MERCHANTS AND SCHOLARS

[52] See above, p. 17.

[83] Anastos, *op. cit.*, p. 3.

[84] Ptolemy (generally far less boldly speculative than Strabo) makes no explicit statement about the navigability of the Ocean Sea. Kimble's assumption that d'Ailly's revised concept of an "open" Indian Ocean reflected Ptolemy's influence (see n. 68 above) implies that the spice islands could be reached both from the West and the East, the latter obviously by crossing the Ocean Sea. The crucial deduction would thereby have been made by d'Ailly, on the basis of a Ptolemaic theory — an assumption that seems generally to have been perpetuated in the literature (*ibid.*). Both theories are in fact alien to Ptolemy's mind, which is conservative rather than speculative on all major global concepts, original mostly in his cartographic — i.e., basically mathematical — ideas.

[85] In Book VII, ch. 5, Ptolemy says: "The Hyrcanium sea, called also the Caspian, is surrounded on all sides by land and has the shape of an island . . . *and we may say the same of the Indian sea, for with its gulfs . . . it is entirely shut in, like the Caspian, on all sides.*"

[80] See the index in vol. 8 of the Loeb ed., or the map reconstructed from the text, "The Inhabited World According to Strabo," by L. A. Lawrence, adapted from C. Müller's "Orbis Terrarum Secundum Strabonem" on the inside cover of vol. 1.

[87] See above, p. 20.

page 24

[88] Strabo, *op. cit.*, 15.1.11, Loeb ed., vol. 7, p. 15.

[89] See above, p. 20.

[90] See the fascinating collection of ocean and mariners' legends in W. Frahm, *Das Meer und die Seefahrt in der altfranzösischen Literatur*, Göttingen, 1914, especially pp. 21ff.

[91] Strabo, *op. cit.*, 2.1.14, Loeb ed., vol. 1, p. 271.

[92] See Goldstein, *Florentine Humanism*, pp. 199ff.

[93] See the perceptive discussion of "mythological" versus "empirical" geography in Leonardo Olschki, *Storia letteraria delle scoperte geografiche*, Florence, 1937.

[94] See P. O. Kristeller, *The Classics and Renaissance Thought*, Cambridge, Mass., 1956, p. 56; R. Klibansky, "The School of Chartres," in *Twelfth-Century Europe and the Foundations of Modern Society*, Madison, Wisc., 1961, pp. 6f.

page 25

[95] See Uzielli, *Toscanelli iniziatore*, p. 79. It is intriguing to note, in this context, that Toscanelli's chart — according to Uzielli's reconstruction (see n. 17 above) — contains a number of legendary oceanic land formations which in fact overlap with actual parts of the American continent. See Goldstein, *Florentine Humanism*, p. 206, n. 31.

[96] See Anastos, *op. cit.*, pp. 14ff. about the impact of Strabo's theory, according to Ferdinand Columbus, upon Columbus's cosmography. Professor Anastos's study demonstrates throughout that this — along with other major Strabonic theories — was conveyed to the Florentines by Plethon at the time of the Council.

[97] Strabo, *op. cit.*, 1.4.6, Loeb ed., vol. 1, p. 241.

[98] *Ibid.*, p. 243; the conceptual context, as well as the speculation about other "inhabited worlds," are presented as Strabo's own speculations.

[90] See above, n. 15.

2
Navigation primitive et navigation astronomique

Paul Adam

Pour toutes les périodes d'avant les grandes découvertes, il est de coutume d'expliquer l'habileté des navigateurs capables de trouver leur chemin en mer par une série, non limitative, de moyens variés : repérage à vue possible à cause des courtes distances ; connaissance des étoiles ; sens marin d'hommes en contact direct avec la nature ; observation des oiseaux migrateurs ou autres ; particularités remarquables des vagues, nuages, etc. ; observation des poissons ou animaux marins... On aboutit ainsi à des formules, reprises et accrues par tous ceux qui écrivent sur la question, dont les éléments restent vagues et sont employés, un peu au hasard, pour justifier n'importe quelle navigation [1].

Il m'a paru intéressant de chercher plus de précision et de déterminer les composantes exactes de ce « sens marin primitif » ou « naturel » en choisissant des cas où il fut porté à sa quasi-perfection. En effet, en dehors de l'intérêt qu'il y a à expliquer les conditions exactes de certaines navigations dites primitives, incontestables mais mal connues, on rencontre là une question de principe dont certaines conséquences pourraient être généralisées afin d'expliquer un aspect capital des grandes découvertes : la naissance de la naviga-

---

(1) Voici un exemple tiré de J.E. WECKLER Jr., *Polynesian Explorer of the Pacific*, Smithsonian Institute, Washington, tome 13, 1943 :

« ... The Polynesians knew many constellations of stars and their positions in the sky at different seasons. This knowledge was used to maintain the ship's course as was also their extensive knowledge of the significance of different kinds of ocean swells and their directions... » (p. 17). En dehors de quelques commentaires sur les îles qui se reflètent sur les nuages et qu'on peut ainsi apercevoir de loin, ce sera tout sur les procédés de navigation des Polynésiens ; il est évident qu'après une pareille justification, il est possible de tracer sur une carte n'importe quelle navigation et de prétendre que les Polynésiens l'ont faite.

tion astronomique qui a soulevé et soulève encore tant de discussions.

Le problème précis auquel je me bornerai est le suivant : des marins primitifs ont-ils pu s'orienter et se sont-ils orientés en pleine mer sans le secours d'instruments d'observation ou avec des instruments très rudimentaires ? En d'autres termes, une navigation astronomique a-t-elle existé avant que sa naissance ne soit effectivement prouvée par des traités de navigation ou par des tables utilisables pour traduire géographiquement le résultat des observations astronomiques ?

Je ne parlerai pas de l'orientation en direction, connue depuis trop longtemps pour qu'il soit utile d'insister à son sujet [1]. Elle est d'ailleurs trop aléatoire dès que la distance à parcourir prend des dimensions que l'on pourrait appeler océaniques par opposition aux dimensions méditerranéennes.

La véritable navigation astronomique, selon le sens que l'on peut lui donner à l'époque des grandes découvertes, est celle du repérage en latitude puisque le repérage en longitude, lié à l'existence de montres précises, est beaucoup plus tardif. Ce repérage en latitude, même très sommaire, est capital pour l'objet qui nous occupe. Si, du point de vue astronomique et géographique, ce n'est plus aujourd'hui que quelque chose d'élémentaire, il ne faut pas oublier que sa connaissance ou son ignorance pouvaient permettre ou empêcher de traverser un océan, c'est-à-dire permettre ou empêcher les grandes découvertes. Longtemps encore après Christophe Colomb on a traversé l'Atlantique sur un simple repérage en latitude ne se différenciant qu'à peine de ceux qui vont être étudiés dans la présente communication ; les marins se sont beaucoup servis et certains se servent encore de la navigation astronomique comme s'il s'agissait de recettes utilisables pour aller d'un endroit précis à un autre endroit précis, sans la moindre généralisation traduisible sur un carroyage cartographique exact.

Les exemples choisis sont deux navigations au long cours, antérieures aux grandes découvertes, qui ont eu lieu de manière certaine et qui ont dû, semble-t-il, faire appel à des observations astronomiques donnant la latitude. Il s'agit, en premier lieu, de la navigation, découverte par Hippalus, qui, à l'époque de l'Empire romain, relia directement le détroit de Bab el Mandeb à la côte sud de l'Inde. En second lieu, la navigation des Polynésiens qui, en partant des îles de l'hémisphère sud, purent assurer des liaisons aller et retour avec les îles Hawaii. L'examen détaillé de ces navigations peut donner

---

(1) Parmi les orientations possibles en direction, il en est une qui s'apparente au repérage en latitude : viser une étoile au moment où elle apparaît ou au moment où elle disparaît à l'horizon.

des enseignements, ou du moins des présomptions solides, permettant de combler certaines lacunes de nos connaissances sur la naissance de la navigation astronomique scientifique.

I. — LA ROUTE D'HIPPALUS ET LA NAVIGATION VERS LES ILES HAWAII

Hippalus, romain d'origine grecque du premier siècle de notre ère, est connu comme ayant le premier relié la sortie de la mer Rouge aux Indes par une route directe faite hors de la vue des côtes ; soit vers les abords du port actuel de Bombay, soit sur le sud de la côte occidentale des Indes, où l'on a trouvé plus de traces romaines qu'ailleurs, vraisemblablement à cause de cette liaison maritime qui eut la forme d'un véritable commerce régulier [1]... Preuves écrites s'ajoutant à ces preuves archéologiques, cette navigation nous est indiquée comme ayant été régulièrement faite pour les besoins du commerce par le *Périple de la Mer Érythrée* [2] et par le *Livre VI de l'Histoire Naturelle* de Pline le Jeune. Il suffit de regarder la carte pour constater que la route était approximativement ouest-est ou est-ouest, c'est-à-dire qu'elle s'effectuait par latitude presque constante, et se prolongeait, sans la moindre escale possible sur une longue distance (près de 2 000 milles marins).

Le peuplement des îles Hawaii par les Polynésiens est le second exemple retenu. D'après l'étude des légendes et quelques fouilles archéologiques [3], on peut affirmer que les Polynésiens se trouvaient aux îles Hawaii bien avant que les Européens n'y arrivent, mais néanmoins à une époque relativement récente correspondant à notre ère. Ils n'ont pu faire cette route que par mer et ils la connaissaient suffisamment bien pour l'avoir faite et refaite pendant un certain temps et ensuite pour en avoir gardé un souvenir qui nous permet aujourd'hui d'en retrouver la trace. La distance de Tahiti aux Hawaii est d'un peu plus de 2 000 milles marins et celle des Marquises aux Hawaii approximativement équivalente : il semble en effet que ce soit au départ des Marquises que la route ait été faite,

---

(1) Cf. Jacques Schwartz, « L'Empire Romain, l'Égypte et le commerce oriental », dans *Annales*, Paris, janvier-février 1960, pp. 18-44, qui donne le dernier état de la question.

(2) Cf. W.H. Schoff, *The Periplus of the Erythrean Sea*, 1912. Il s'agit d'une édition critique comportant en plus du texte latin et de sa traduction en anglais un très important appareil de notes et commentaires.

(3) Cf. les recherches archéologiques et les datations au carbone 14 effectuées dans l'archipel des Hawaii par le Professeur Emory, dans le cadre du Bishop Museum d'Honolulu. En ce qui concerne les légendes, cf. P.H. Buck, *Les migrations des polynésiens*, Paris, 1952 (le titre anglais, plus évocateur, est : *Vikings of the Sunrise*).

ce qui serait parfaitement logique étant donné les vents dominants. Entre Tahiti et les Hawaii, il existe quelques îlots de corail, mais les viser et les atteindre avec certitude devait être difficile ; en tout cas, entre les Marquises et les Hawaii, il n'y a rien que de l'eau. Ajoutons à cela que cette traversée, plus longue un peu que celle d'Hippalus, était au moins aussi difficile, sinon davantage, à cause de la traversée déprimante de la zone équatoriale, le fameux « pot au noir ».

Ces deux routes d'Hippalus et des Polynésiens se caractérisent toutes deux par une longueur très anormale pour des navigations dites primitives, ainsi que par les parages fréquentés : les tropiques.

Voyons d'abord la question de la distance. On peut imaginer qu'en se repérant la nuit aux étoiles et le jour au soleil on puisse conserver une direction constante pendant une certaine distance. Mais après 2 000 milles marins la précision de l'atterrissage deviendrait totalement illusoire. Une erreur de direction, très possible, de 10° donnerait une erreur d'atterrissage de 353 milles marins, soit près de 20% de la route à parcourir, chiffres à multiplier par deux, car, *a priori* on ne peut savoir si l'erreur a été faite dans un sens ou dans l'autre [1]. Etant donné les difficultés propres à la navigation à voile (obligation d'utiliser les vents favorables) et les dangers non négligeables de piraterie quand on fréquentait des parages mal connus (dangers qui étaient réels sur la côte des Indes), le risque n'aurait pas été payant et une navigation réussie dans des circonstances exceptionnelles n'aurait pas donné naissance à une série de liaisons régulières. Plutôt que de manquer le port qui était visé, les successeurs d'Hippalus auraient eu intérêt à se contenter des anciennes relations commerciales par relais successifs. Quant aux Polynésiens, s'ils avaient manqué les Hawaii, ils se seraient irrémédiablement perdus dans l'immensité de l'Océan Pacifique.

Il est un moyen facile, et souvent suggéré, d'éluder cette difficulté. Ces navigations primitives n'auraient été possibles qu'avec des pertes nombreuses... comme si les marins avaient été des êtres à part, candidats conscients ou inconscients au suicide. Même si cette explication pouvait être invoquée dans le cas des Polynésiens primitifs, dont on ne sait rien, ce qui permet de tout imaginer, elle serait totalement invraisemblable dans le cas des commerçants de l'Empire romain qui, comme tous les commerçants de tous les pays et de

---

(1) Le calcul de l'erreur en distance pour une erreur d'angle déterminé est donné par formule : distance parcourue multipliée par la tangente de l'angle en question. Soit :
pour 5° : 175 milles pour une route directe idéale de 2 000 milles,
pour 10° : 353 milles pour une route directe idéale de 2 000 milles,
pour 15° : 434 milles pour une route directe idéale de 2 000 milles.

tous les temps, étaient désireux de conserver leur vie comme leurs propriétés.

Il semble donc vraisemblable que ces traversées, qui ont été effectuées, on en est certain, de manière régulière, n'ont pu l'être que par un repérage quelconque permettant de réussir des atterrissages précis. Comme, dans les deux cas, il n'y avait rien que de l'eau, ce repérage ne pouvait être qu'astronomique et devait donner, d'une manière ou d'une autre, la latitude. C'est là qu'intervient la seconde des caractéristiques de ces deux navigations. Sous les tropiques, dans les deux navigations considérées, soufflent la mousson ou les alizés. S'il arrive qu'il y ait pluies, tempêtes, ciels couverts, les mauvaises conditions atmosphériques ne se prolongent jamais très longtemps et les pilotes avaient un ciel clair et un horizon net assez souvent pour que des observations puissent être faites à intervalles suffisamment rapprochés. D'ailleurs, là comme ailleurs, on ne se lançait pas à l'aventure sur les océans à n'importe quelle époque de l'année. Les traversées se faisaient, selon les conditions atmosphériques bien connues, aux périodes les plus favorables.

II. — LE REPÉRAGE EN LATITUDE
SANS L'AIDE D'INSTRUMENTS D'OBSERVATION

Le problème étant exposé par les descriptions qui précèdent, comment peut-on imaginer ce repérage en latitude ? Pour l'hémisphère nord, ce qui est le cas aussi bien dans l'atterrissage sur les Hawaii que dans la route d'Hippalus, on pense immédiatement à utiliser la hauteur de la polaire qui, actuellement, donne à peu de choses près la latitude exacte.

A ce sujet, deux problèmes se posent :

1º Peut-on évaluer, sans instrument, la hauteur de la polaire avec une précision suffisante ?

2º Peut-on créditer les marins de ces époques de connaissances leur permettant de déduire le pôle géographique vrai de la position changeante de la polaire ?

A la première question répond de manière satisfaisante l'expérience des marins d'aujourd'hui. Les habitués de la navigation dans les eaux tropicales savent que quand l'horizon est clair (ce qui arrive souvent là où souffle la mousson ou l'alizé), si la nuit tombe vite, on a néanmoins le temps de prendre une hauteur d'étoile très correcte au moment où les étoiles sont déjà visibles et où l'horizon est encore parfaitement net. D'autre part, pendant la nuit, il arrive souvent que l'on ait un horizon, moins précis qu'en plein jour bien sûr, mais à peu près suffisant à environ 1° près [1].

Or, s'il est de fait qu'à nos latitudes on ne saurait, sans un instrument, observer la hauteur de la polaire (39° à Lisbonne, 49° à Paris, 59° à Stockholm), l'appréciation d'une différence d'un degré peut se faire à l'œil quand la distance angulaire, à partir de l'horizon, ne dépasse pas une quinzaine de degrés. Il y faut un œil bien exercé, certes, mais c'est très possible et on peut toujours y ajouter des trucs dont le plus simple est la main tendue à bout de bras qui peut donner des résultats d'une précision s'approchant de celle obtenue avec le « kamal » utilisé dans l'Océan Indien par les Arabes au moment de la découverte de Vasco de Gama [2].

Reste la difficulté de la seconde question. La polaire n'indique pas le pôle géographique réel. Aujourd'hui elle en est éloignée d'un peu moins d'un degré, c'est-à-dire qu'elle décrit autour de ce pôle réel un cercle dont le rayon est inférieur à un degré. Aussi, une observation exacte de la hauteur de la polaire, sans faire intervenir de rectification, donnerait une erreur maximum inférieure au degré. Mais la position de la polaire varie au cours des siècles et nous sommes actuellement à une période très favorable puisque nous sommes à quelque 100 ans de la position de la polaire la plus proche du pôle réel avec lequel elle ne se confondra jamais exactement. Au fur et à mesure que l'on remonte dans le temps, le cercle décrit par la polaire était plus grand. En 4 300 avant notre ère, le rayon du cercle atteignait 23° et il en sera de même si l'on en croit les astronomes, en l'an 8 500 de notre ère. En l'an 0, c'est-à-dire, peu avant la découverte d'Hippalus, cet angle était proche de 4° ; à l'époque d'Hippalus, entre 3 et 4° [3]. En conséquence, si on visait la polaire au moment où elle était à la même hauteur que le pôle réel (cela arrive deux fois en une révolution, aux deux points d'intersection du cercle et de son diamètre horizontal), on avait la latitude exacte ; dans tous les autres cas, on faisait une erreur qui pouvait aller jusqu'à environ

---

(1) Les marins modernes n'ont plus tellement l'habitude de regarder le ciel, du moins en observateurs attentifs. Pour trouver des exemples de ce genre il faut interroger de « ces aventuriers » modernes du genre d'Éric de Bisschop, de Michel Brun qui l'accompagna dans sa première traversée du Pacifique en radeau ; ce sont eux qui conservent les dernières traditions de la navigation à voiles. A ce sujet, plutôt qu'un livre d'astronomie, il vaut mieux consulter : Pierre Sizaire et Marin Marie, *Le ciel et la mer*, Paris, 1958, ou P. Sizaire, *Petit guide des étoiles*. Cf. d'autre part E.H. Bryan Jr., *Stars over Hawaii*, Honolulu, 1955 et surtout Maud W. Makenson, *The Morning Star rises, an Account of Polynesian Astronomy*, New Haven, Yale University Press, 1941.

(2) Cf. E.G.R. Taylor, *The Haven-finding Art*, Londres, 1958, pp. 128 et ss.

(3) Cf. Dr Paul V. Neugebauer, *Tafeln zur astronomischen Chronologie*, Leipzig, 1912-14, qui donne les positions des astres de 4000 avant notre ère jusqu'à 4000 après en divisant de 100 ans en 100 ans.

4°, ce qui est énorme puisqu'il faut compter 60 milles marins par degré de latitude, soit 240 milles marins.

La question se résume donc à savoir si les marins, à l'époque d'Hippalus ou à l'époque des Polynésiens primitifs, pouvaient repérer cette différence et la corriger. La repérer ? c'est évident ; ils s'en étaient certainement rendu compte. La corriger ? c'est une autre affaire et nous n'avons aucune trace que ce soit fait de manière courante. Mais nous n'avons pas les traités de navigation que manipulaient les pilotes du temps d'Auguste puisqu'alors l'enseignement nautique se faisait exclusivement par tradition orale. Taylor, dans son *Haven Finding Art*, pose la question et incline à penser qu'ils en étaient capables. Il faut en effet que toute navigation astronomique en direction, que ce soit par la polaire ou à plus forte raison par quelque autre moyen, exigeait des rectifications de ce genre auxquelles les marins devaient avoir eu l'occasion de s'entraîner. J'y ajouterai un autre argument. Nous avons tendance à regarder le ciel dans les livres d'astronomie plus que dans sa réalité en plein air. Nous désirons comprendre et placer nos connaissances dans des ensembles de lois générales qui nous dispensent d'observer. Nous raisonnons comme des exposés d'astronomie car c'est de ces exposés que nous tenons nos connaissances. Or, en l'occurrence, il faut oublier notre science et nous mettre à la place du paysan ou du pêcheur qui ne porte jamais de montre mais sait toujours l'heure à un quart d'heure près ; il ne saurait exposer les lois des mouvements célestes, mais il a, si l'on peut dire, le corps et le soleil qui marchent selon le même rythme, car, même sans s'en rendre compte, il observe continuellement le soleil et les ombres. Série de trucs, souvent devenus automatiques, qui n'est pas due à l'existence d'un sens que notre civilisation scientifique nous aurait fait perdre, mais qui est la somme de multiples expériences pratiques. De même, on peut dire que les trucs pratiques permettant de savoir où se trouve la polaire par rapport au pôle réel sont assez simples. Taylor en donne un [1]. Blondel, dans un recueil de calculs nautiques simples [2], en donne un autre qui y ressemble. Et puis, on sait qu'en prolongeant les deux roues arrière du chariot de la Grande Ourse on tombe sur la polaire : l'inclinaison de cette droite permet de savoir la position de la polaire par rapport au pôle réel. D'autres astuces peuvent être imaginées... et ont dû être utilisées.

Pour nous, le ciel est trop souvent quelque chose de fixe et de cartographié que l'on regarde, une fois par hasard, en vacances, un soir

---

(1) Cf. Taylor, *op. cit.*, note 7, pp. 145 et ss.

(2) Cf. Blondel, *Notes pratiques pour les calculs nautiques à l'usage des plaisanciers*, Lib. Maritime, Le Yacht, Paris.

d'été. Pour des marins qui ne savaient pas lire et n'avaient pas idée de ce que serait un jour une carte, le ciel ne devait exister que bougeant continuellement selon un rythme connu et observé à longueur d'années pendant les heures interminables des quarts de nuit.

III. — LES MÉTHODES DE NAVIGATION D'HIPPALUS ET DES POLYNÉSIENS

On ne sait rien des méthodes de navigation d'Hippalus, du moins directement, et son nom donné au vent que nous connaissons comme la mousson a conduit beaucoup d'historiens à simplifier les choses en disant qu'Hippalus avait découvert la mousson et, par le fait même, la route directe vers les Indes [1]. Or, si l'on se reporte au texte du *Périple*, cette conclusion hâtive semble erronée.

Alors que le voyage se faisait auparavant par un grand détour, en longeant les côtes, « Hippalus fut le navigateur qui, en observant la position des ports et les conditions à la mer, découvrit le premier comment tracer sa course directement à travers l'Océan ». Il n'est pas question là d'une découverte de la mousson ; au contraire, le *Périple* poursuit en indiquant que le vent utilisé pour cette navigation fut appelé Hippalus « du nom de celui qui le premier découvrit la voie qui l'utilisait » [2].

Ces citations ne donnent pas les précisions définitives que l'on pourrait souhaiter ; mais il ne faut pas oublier que l'auteur du *Périple* devait être un marchand qui s'adressait à des marchands et non à des marins ; toutefois, à défaut de certitudes, on peut en tirer des présomptions solides en faveur d'un repérage en latitude par des observations astronomiques :

1° la mousson était déjà connue ; ce qui manquait, c'était le moyen de s'en servir [3];

2° un des deux moyens indiqué pour utiliser la mousson était... « de repérer la position des ports », ce qui semble bien être la technique de la navigation par la latitude, résumée par un non technicien ; sachant la position du port que l'on veut atteindre, on se place le plus vite possible sur la latitude dudit port, puis on fait selon le

---

(1) Cf. notamment l'article de SCHWARTZ cité p. 93, n. 1, qui parle à plusieurs reprises de la « découverte de la mousson » comme étant également la découverte de la route directe des Indes.

(2) Cf. SCHOFF, cité p. 93, n. 3, ainsi que les notes correspondantes.

(3) Sur la mousson, cf. P. PÉDELABORDE, *Les moussons*, Paris, 1958. Il est à souhaiter que les alizés donnent lieu prochainement à un travail de même nature.

NAVIGATION PRIMITIVE ET NAVIGATION ASTRONOMIQUE   99

cas de l'ouest-est ou de l'est-ouest ; je ne vois aucune autre manière raisonnable d'interpréter l'expression « position des ports » ;

3° le second moyen indiqué par le *Périple* est « la connaissance de la mer »... ce qui est l'habituelle explication des terriens qui, voyant un marin diriger son navire hors de la vue des côtes, ont tendance à y voir une sorte de communion intime entre le navigateur et les flots : on connaîtrait la mer comme on connaît les rues de la ville où on habite depuis des années ; sorte d'instinct, plus ou moins créé par l'expérience, qui, si on ne le précise pas davantage, ne veut pas dire grand-chose.

Pour les Polynésiens allant aux Hawaii, la discussion est plus simple puisque des légendes nous ont gardé la trace irréfutable d'un repérage en latitude. Je ne fais évidemment là aucune allusion à la fameuse calebasse sacrée, amusant « canular » qui, quoique basé sur une idée de départ très juste, a fait long feu depuis longtemps [1].

Eric de Bisschop a, dans une étude encore inédite, donné l'explication de façon telle qu'il n'y a pratiquement rien à ajouter à son commentaire :

« Les légendes des Hawaii, nous parlant de la découverte de cet archipel, nous apprennent que Hawaiiloa fit voile en direction des Pléiades : nous aurions tort de les croire à la lettre comme le firent de nombreux ethnologues. On ne peut évidemment faire route sur un point déterminé de l'océan... en gouvernant sur une étoile laquelle change continuellement de position sur son cercle de déclinaison entre son lever et son coucher : D'autres légendes, concernant le même archipel nous parlent d'Aldébaran, étoile sur laquelle « gouvernaient » les découvreurs. Cela s'explique intelligemment si nous regardons les déclinaisons des Pléiades et d'Aldébaran. Le premier groupe est environ par 24° nord et l'étoile par 16° 1/2. Or, l'archipel des Hawaii est compris entre 18° 1/2 et 22° 1/2 de latitude nord...

...Le marin gagnait une position géographique correspondant à la culmination d'Aldébaran (c'est-à-dire vers 16 ou 17° de latitude nord ; il savait alors qu'il approchait et continuait sa route vers le nord, avec les

---

(1) La calebasse sacrée prend son origine dans une étude faite par Hugh Rodman, alors Lieutenant de Vaisseau, qui, paraît-il, trouva là un moyen de s'amuser tout en insistant sur une évidence : la nécessité d'avoir un moyen quelconque pour se repérer quand on est en pleine mer. L'histoire devient moins amusante quand le même Rodman, devenu Amiral, se mit à prendre au sérieux son travail de jeunesse (innombrables sont les gens qui ont cité ses conclusions, vraisemblablement sans se référer aux textes de l'auteur : Journal of the Polynesian Society, et le directeur du Bishop Museum fut obligé de remiser à la cave la calebasse en question qui était à peu près certainement un étui destiné à recueillir des restes vénérables d'ancêtres : le couvercle en était lacé sur le corps de la calebasse, ce qui explique les nombreux trous, par lesquels on peut repérer la polaire, si on le désire, comme de multiples autres étoiles. Mais BRYAN (cf. p. 96, n. 1) détruit cette baudruche de telle manière qu'il est inutile de s'appesantir sur cette question.

alizés, de manière à se mettre entre les deux culminations . des Pléiades et d'Aldébaran. » [1]

Ensuite de quoi il n'y avait plus qu'à conserver la même latitude en allant vers l'Ouest. C'est pour cette raison qu'il valait mieux partir des Marquises puisque les alizés soufflent vers l'Est ; de cette manière on ne risquait pas d'être dérouté par le vent dominant et de manquer les Hawaii en étant poussé vers l'Est tout en faisant route Nord.

Avec quelle précision pouvait se faire cette appréciation de la culmination ? Un œil bien exercé devait y parvenir à un ou deux degrés près, sans compter que les « astronomes » qui se trouvaient toujours sur les pirogues océaniques des Polynésiens devaient avoir d'autres points de repère, du même genre, permettant des vérifications [2]. D'autre part les Hawaii s'étendent sur plus de 3° et ont des sommets importants qui peuvent se repérer de loin. Des volcans en éruption ont peut-être été à l'origine de la première découverte ?...

IV. — TENTATIVE DE GÉNÉRALISATION

Les deux navigations qui précèdent sont, à ma connaissance, les seules navigations primitives océaniques permettant une étude, qui n'est peut-être pas définitive, mais qui apporte des présomptions solides. On peut mentionner d'autres navigations de ce type, qui ont

---

(1) Ce texte est extrait d'inédits laissés par Eric de Bisschop et mis en ordre par le Commandant Argod. Buck (*op. cit.*, p. 93, n. 3) parle des Pléiades (p. 230), mais aussi du Baudrier d'Orion (p. 222 et 234, et même de la Polaire, p. 335). Ceci indique bien la multiplicité des combinaisons possibles suggérée par Maud Makenson (*op. cit.*, p. 96, n. 1, chapitre sur la navigation qui est évidemment à lire entièrement). En ce qui concerne le Baudrier d'Orion, à noter que sa culmination correspond à peu près à l'équateur et se trouve à mi-chemin entre Tahiti et les Hawaii. Il n'est donc pas impossible de s'en servir pour se repérer d'une manière comparable à celle avec laquelle peuvent servir les Pléiades et Aldébaran.

(2) Il est curieux de voir, en lisant le livre de Maud Makenson, à quel point les Polynésiens étaient d'excellents astronomes pratiques, mais aussi à quel point nous savons mal quelle était exactement l'étendue précise de leurs connaissances. Pour le vocabulaire, par exemple, les dictionnaires de polynésien sont en fait très pauvres, vraisemblablement parce que les premiers enquêteurs, ignorants en astronomie, ne pouvaient ni traduire ce qu'ils apprenaient, ni vérifier ce qui leur était dit (cf. à ce sujet, Bryan, *op. cit.*, p. 93, n. 3). Si une étude approfondie pouvait être faite, peut-être arriverait-on à des conclusions aussi étonnantes que celles des fouilles de Novgorod sur l'écriture : cf. M.N. Tikhomirov, « L'Écriture urbaine dans l'ancienne Russie des XIe-XIIIe siècles », dans *Cahiers d'Histoire Mondiale*, V, 3, 1960, p. 661 et ss.

NAVIGATION PRIMITIVE ET NAVIGATION ASTRONOMIQUE 101

vraisemblablement eu lieu, mais sur lesquelles, malheureusement, les renseignements sont aujourd'hui encore insuffisants : par exemple les Phéniciens et Carthaginois allant sur les côtes d'Afrique ou jusqu'en Angleterre [1], ou le peuplement de Madagascar par des éléments d'origine non-africaine [2]... Mais, je voudrais ne retenir ces derniers cas que dans la mesure où leur existence montre qu'il y a des trous importants dans nos connaissances sur l'histoire de la navigation ; ainsi, l'étude de deux navigations d'Hippalus et des Polynésiens allant aux Hawaii en prend une valeur accrue car elle donne une base solide indispensable en montrant comment les choses ont pu se passer dans un cas déterminé.

En fait, si l'on ne peut pas nier qu'il y ait eu des navigations primitives véritablement océaniques, on doit tout de suite ajouter que ce furent toujours des cas particuliers à étudier en tenant chaque fois compte des conditions de parages et d'époques. Les extrapolations générales sont à proscrire car il ne s'est jamais agi de méthodes prenant une forme systématique ou générale et susceptibles d'être appliquées en d'autres circonstances.

La caractéristique des deux navigations en question, en dehors de leur caractère astronomique, est d'avoir été des « astuces » de marins pour aller d'un point déterminé à un autre point déterminé sans aucun lien avec des considérations scientifiques quelconques. Cette constatation suggère l'existence d'un type de navigation, dont les historiens ne parlent pas, mais qui aurait eu, notamment dans le domaine des travaux de notre Colloque, une importance capitale.

Si, en effet, on peut justifier cette incursion dans des siècles très éloignés des xve et xvie, ce sera, me semble-t-il, par une conclusion de prudence scientifique, ou, en termes plus précis, par l'addition d'une catégorie supplémentaire à la classification la plus habituellement retenue par les historiens de la navigation. Il faudrait faire la place, entre les navigations dites primitives et les navigations dites scientifiques, à un échelon intermédiaire, débordant sur l'une et sur l'autre ; la navigation que l'on pourrait appeler *astronomique primitive*.

La navigation astronomique date-t-elle de 1450, de 1480 ou de 1496 ? On discute encore et on discutera encore longtemps sur cette

---

(1) Cf. J. CARCOPINO, *Le Maroc Antique*, ou autre version du même problème, les études de Raymond MAUNY citées dans sa thèse complémentaire, *Les navigations médiévales sur les côtes sahariennes antérieures à la découverte portugaise (1434)*, Centro de Estudos Históricos Ultramarinos, Lisbonne, 1960.

(2) A. LEROI-GOURHAN et J. POIRIER, *Ethnologie de l'Union Française*, chapitre sur Madagascar.

question parce qu'elle est mal posée. En fait, la première trace que l'on ait de navigation astronomique date d'Hippalus, premier siècle de notre ère, et on ne peut même pas dire si Hippalus l'a découverte tout seul ou l'a apprise d'autres marins [1]. D'un autre côté, même après Cook et pratiquement jusqu'au xxᵉ siècle, il y a eu des navigations au long cours faites par des procédés astronomiques primitifs semblables à ceux d'Hippalus ou des Polynésiens [2].

Evidemment, si l'on se borne, de manière restrictive, à l'histoire des sciences, on peut arriver, avec des raisonnements rigoureux effectués sur les documents connus, à fixer une date relativement précise. Mais, comme l'ajoute immédiatement Beaujouan ce point d'arrivée n'est pas le résultat d'une illumination soudaine, bien plutôt celui d'une recherche aussi patiente que systématique dans laquelle Henri le Navigateur, son école et ses continuateurs, ont eu le rôle déterminant « par un remarquable effort d'organisation et de coordination ». Ce commentaire, indispensable à la sécheresse de sa conclusion chronologique, incline à faire une incursion dans un domaine où Beaujouan refuse de se lancer. Il existe dans notre documentation écrite des trous immenses parce que nous n'avons pas ou pratiquement pas de renseignements sur le navigateur moyen, celui dont l'histoire ne saura jamais le nom mais sans qui l'« organisation » portugaise n'aurait pas donné le moindre résultat et sans qui, ensuite, les grandes découvertes n'auraient pas été utilisées.

Pour essayer de fixer les idées en un schéma clair, j'aimerais suggérer la division suivante, en trois parties, dont les limites chronologiques se chevauchent largement et sans discontinuer depuis l'an 0 de notre ère jusqu'à nos jours :

Primo : Des navigations astronomiques primitives et empiriques, limitées à quelques cas précis (Hippalus, les Polynésiens vers les Hawaii...), sans liens les unes avec les autres et avec des prolongements jusqu'à nos jours ou presque.

Secundo : Une période européenne, avec prépondérance ibérique, de navigation vers les côtes d'Afrique pendant laquelle a été faite une navigation astronomique primitive du même type qu'au primo,

---

(1) Il existe un texte de Pline, très curieux, qui se recoupe exactement, sans aucun autre intermédiaire, avec les observations modernes de HADDON et HORNELL, *Canoes of Oceania*. On pourrait peut-être en déduire une présomption selon laquelle les populations indonésiennes découvrirent l'Inde avant que les populations hindoues ne découvrent l'Indonésie.

(2) Jusqu'à tout récemment, des habitants des Canaries émigraient au Vénézuela en utilisant des barques de pêche et en se repérant par la polaire à l'aide de la main tendue à bout de bras. Cela leur permettait, à l'atterrissage, de savoir à laquelle des îles des Antilles ils avaient affaire.

mais en même temps, une recherche systématique tendant à ration-
naliser et à généraliser les résultats obtenus afin de bâtir une méthode
de navigation et une cartographie dignes de ce nom (d'abord les
navigations des Gênois jusqu'aux Canaries... ; les voyages vers le
Sud, notamment au départ de Séville... ; le « Canarien » de Béthencourt [1]... ; enfin les expéditions d'Henri le Navigateur qui inaugu-
rent vraiment cette période nouvelle).

Tertio : Le résultat a été la mise au point des bases de la navigation
scientifique moderne aux dates fixées de manière précise, notamment
par Beaujouan, étant entendu que ce tournant capital a tout natu-
rellement accompagné les grandes découvertes auxquelles sont liés
les trois noms de Vasco de Gama, Christophe Colomb et Magellan,
mais étant entendu aussi que ce tournant n'a pas tellement été perçu
comme tel par les marins dont les méthodes pratiques de navigation
n'ont évolué que de manière très progressive. Cette troisième période,
en apportant des possibilités immenses, a aussi demandé un travail
immense dont le moindre n'a pas été celui de l'établissement de
cartes à la fois précises et utilisables par les marins.

Je m'explique sur ce dernier point par un exemple imaginaire.
Je suis persuadé (de nombreux documents le prouvent de façon
implicite) qu'un marin portugais de 1470-80 savait aller aux Canaries ou à Madère sans instrument ou avec des instruments très primitifs en ne faisant que des erreurs qui ne devaient pas dépasser le
degré. Or, quelque 10-20 ans plus tard, ce même marin, ne sachant
qu'à peine lire mais ayant entendu parler de Ptolémée, de la découverte des Indes et d'un certain nombre d'autres choses dont il devait
mélanger les éléments divers, si on l'avait brusquement lancé au
milieu de la mer des Caraïbes, aurait très bien pu placer les Bahamas
à la longitude des îles de la Société et à la latitude des Grenadines...
Cet exemple n'est qu'imaginaire, je le répète, mais ne se présente-t-il
pas comme une simple exagération des erreurs que l'on prête si
volontiers à Christophe Colomb ?

D'ailleurs, à propos de Christophe Colomb, sait-on vraiment ce
qu'il a appris des Portugais pendant son séjour de quelques années
à Lisbonne ? Certainement par les projets et programmes précis
qui ont préparé des expéditions comme celles de Vasco de Gama.
Par contre, et où en trouver la trace ?, il a certainement fréquenté
des pilotes de qui il a dû tirer des renseignements de seconde main,

---

(1) Cf. par exemple, les nombreuses références données par MAUNY (p. 101, n. 1), ainsi
que P. MARGRY, *La conquête et les conquérants des Iles Canaries, le vrai manuscrit du Canarien*,
Paris, 1896.

plus ou moins sûrs, et des trucs pratiques sans lesquels il est vraisemblable qu'il ne se serait jamais lancé dans l'inconnu. Pour ces pilotes, pour ces praticiens, les systématisations générales (comme la connaissance de la longueur exacte du degré) devaient être des choses dont on entendait parler mais que personne encore ne maîtrisait de manière certaine autrement que dans des études que beaucoup devaient considérer comme des spéculations abstraites. La science et l'intuition du savant qui préparait les techniques futures, aujourd'hui considérées comme élémentaires, étaient une chose. L'habileté des navigateurs, faite en partie d'astuces qui se passaient de bouche à oreille [1], en était une autre.

C'est en utilisant cette notion de navigation astronomique primitive que l'on pourrait peut-être formuler une suggestion au sujet de la fameuse politique du *secret* à laquelle Jaime Cortesão a apporté la puissance de sa conviction et de sa science. Le secret aurait véritablement existé ; mais aurait-il été le résultat d'un plan, d'une politique parfaitement consciente ? C'est là, me semble-t-il, que l'on peut faire des réserves. On cherchait, on était à une période de gestation. Il n'était pas encore question de fixer les règles définitives qui sont la routine des marins d'aujourd'hui. On essayait bien sûr de garder pour soi les progrès que l'on avait faits et on ne négligeait aucun effort dans ce sens. Mais on ne peut pas tout cacher d'abord parce que les voyages finissent par se savoir, ensuite parce qu'il faut bien éduquer les marins qui naviguent. Même en forçant ces derniers au secret, on ne pouvait empêcher quelques fuites ; la compensation est que ces fuites ne pouvaient être que partielles étant donné une double raison : les organisateurs de l'époque n'étaient pas aussi sûrs d'eux que beaucoup d'historiens d'aujourd'hui, et les marins praticiens, s'ils se croyaient vraiment sûrs d'eux-mêmes (la conviction d'un Christophe Colomb fait parfois peur, rétrospectivement, quand on songe aux arguments avec lesquels il la défendait), n'étaient en fait sur un terrain solide que quand il s'agissait de ce qu'ils avaient effectivement réalisé et savaient refaire... N'oublions pas que c'est seulement avec Cook que nous aurons le premier voyage satisfaisant sur le plan scientifique [2].

---

(1) Les nombreuses histoires qui se racontent à propos de Christophe Colomb (comme celle du pilote, mort chez lui, qui lui aurait confié des secrets sur les routes inconnues) sont inacceptables en elles-mêmes, mais indiquent une atmosphère dont il serait absurde de ne pas tenir compte. Comment imaginer, par exemple, que Colomb, connaissant, en partie par ouï-dire, les mers du Nord (cf. *Studi Colombiani*, tome 3, pp. 249-256, Gaston E. Broche, *Christophe Colomb a-t-il atteint l'Irlande* ?) n'ait pas entendu parler, même de manière indirecte, des voyages des Vikings vers l'Ouest ?

(2) ... et que la première édition scientifique des journaux de Cook vient seulement d'être entreprise car il n'avait jamais paru, jusqu'à présent, que des « rewriting » plus ou moins erronés.

NAVIGATION PRIMITIVE ET NAVIGATION ASTRONOMIQUE 105

Il y a certes un tournant très net vers 1480 ; mais il y a aussi, avec ses temps d'arrêt, ses retours en arrière et ses accélérations, une évolution très longue dont on trouve les premières traces avec Hippalus et qui se prolonge pratiquement jusqu'à l'époque contemporaine [1].

---

(1) Depuis la présentation de cette communication, le regretté L. Massignon a fait paraître une étude sur *Les nuages de Magellan et leur découverte par les arabes* (Lib. Orientaliste, Paul Geuthner, Paris, 1962). On y trouve des indications précieuses sur l'utilisation de ces nuages comme point de repère astronomique dans l'hémisphère sud. C'est là, par un autre exemple pris dans l'hémisphère sud, une intéressante confirmation de la thèse ici défendue.

Discussion de la communication
de M. Adam

M. WATERS. — Toutes ces communications posent des questions fondamentales pour la compréhension des grandes découvertes des xve et xvie siècles. Je suis tout à fait d'accord avec M. Cortesão lorsqu'il dit qu'il faut tenter des extrapolations sérieuses et mesurées là où l'on manque de connaissances et de sources certaines.

Je pense que les marins font un voyage parce que c'est leur unique moyen de subsister et qu'ils ne se mettent pas en route sinon dans ce but.

On se demande pourquoi au xve siècle les Portugais allèrent sur des mers inconnues et entreprirent des voyages plus longs ?

Mais j'aimerais poser des questions qui, je l'espère, ne paraîtront pas trop élémentaires : comment va-t-on sur mer à de longues distances lorsqu'on ne sait pas où l'on va, comment s'assure-t-on les moyens d'un long voyage ?

Mais si l'on fait abstraction de ma première affirmation — qu'aucun voyage sur mer n'est entrepris sans nécessité — il faut immédiatement poser l'hypothèse qu'il existe quelqu'un voulant que l'on parte, qui est muni du nécessaire pour un tel voyage et — chose plus importante dans cette perspective — qui attend le retour, pour apprendre ce qui a été vu et fait.

Au xve siècle, cette nécessité, à mon avis, suscita une organisation nautique aussi poussée qu'actuellement pour une fusée ou un spoutnik. Elle ne pouvait être mise sur pied par les petites communautés de villages isolées qui groupaient à cette époque la plus grande partie de la population de l'Europe. Il n'y avait que peu de villes, et elles étaient petites : Lisbonne était, je suppose, la plus grande ville du Portugal, mais ses ressources étaient très limitées.

Il y a eu voilà deux mois, au British Museum, une exposition intitulée : *Prince Henry the Navigator and Portuguese maritime Enterprise*. Les notices du catalogue sont extrêmement bien faites et l'introduction contient des passages qui éclairent certaines des questions que j'ai posées. Ils expliquent pourquoi l'Infant Henri voulait reconnaître l'Afrique et la contourner ; ils décrivent la colonisation des îles de l'Atlantique et la circumnavigation de l'Inde. Je ne résumerai pas davantage le contenu de ce catalogue. Je ne suis pas spécialiste du xve siècle, je m'occupe des explorations et de la navigation anglaises aux xvie et xviie siècles. Mais cela m'a été utile, car lorsque, pour des raisons de nécessités économiques, les Anglais décidèrent d'entreprendre des explorations, ils allèrent à la *Casa de la Contratación* de Séville pour y apprendre comment on organise des voyages de longue durée. Ils engagèrent le maître pilote Sébastien Cabot et entreprirent leur première expédition en 1553. Ils avaient fait appel aux meilleurs techniciens étrangers : un Espagnol, un hydrographe portugais, et des Français.

Par comparaison, il me semble que les Portugais durent faire au xve siècle le même genre d'efforts : mobilisation et organisation sur le plan national de tous les savants et de toutes les connaissances scientifiques.

Il y a 14 ans, j'ai été invité à écrire une histoire de la bataille de l'Atlantique. Cela m'a amené à étudier évidemment la précédente guerre de 1914-18. J'ai été impressionné par le fait suivant qui doit être une loi générale des guerres maritimes. Aucune arme n'a été inventée par des marins, mais par des terriens, des savants. Ceux parmi vous qui sont quelque peu familiarisés avec l'histoire de la dernière guerre se rappelleront que les Anglais firent appel aux savants pour préparer les opérations de la Marine et des armées de Terre et de l'Air. Tous les progrès stratégiques et tactiques fondamentaux de la dernière guerre sont dus à des savants civils.

De façon analogue, à mon avis, les Portugais du xve siècle s'adressèrent aux hommes de sciences : astronomes, astrologues, mathématiciens et leur dirent : « Nous voulons envoyer des bateaux au loin ; nous voulons qu'ils reviennent et qu'ils nous indiquent où ils ont été afin que d'autres puissent refaire leur parcours ». Je suis certain que, pour en apprendre davantage sur cette découverte fondamentale de l'application de l'astronomie à la science nautique, il faut remonter à l'histoire de l'astronomie portugaise et espagnole. On y trouvera, je pense, la réponse à la question de l'évolution maritime des Portugais.

Toutes ces expéditions, il ne faut pas l'oublier, exigèrent une organisation parfaite : et les Portugais ont le mérite d'avoir été les premiers à la mettre en œuvre et à faire collaborer leurs marins et leurs savants à l'élaboration et à l'exécution de leurs projets.

Commandant TEIXEIRA DA MOTA. — Quelques mots seulement au sujet de ce qu'a dit le Commandant Waters : il a touché le point essentiel de l'histoire de la navigation astronomique. Jusqu'il y a peu d'années les historiens ne l'avaient pas vu ; on confondait constamment les connaissances astronomiques avec la navigation astronomique. Le grand mérite des efforts des Portugais au xve siècle est d'avoir pour la première fois fait, à une grande échelle, la liaison entre l'astronome et le pilote. Je crois que c'est la base de tout le problème, et c'est fondamental. Je regrette que M. Luis de Albuquerque, Professeur à Coïmbre, ne soit pas ici ; il a publié des travaux remarquables sur la navigation astronomique et il avait écrit il y a cinq ans : « Il ne faut pas oublier ce fait fondamental : la barrière qui, dans les dernières années du Moyen Age encore, séparait les lettres des hommes qui exerçaient des professions pratiques, dont fait partie le pilotage. A cause de cela, si nous ne voulons expliquer que par la science livresque l'époque des premières conquêtes cartographiques des pilotes, nous posons la question sur une base erronée ». C'est exactement ce que vient de souligner le Commandant Waters et c'est très important. Le grand mérite des hommes du xvᵉ siècle est d'avoir uni pour toujours le savant, le théoricien, et l'homme de la mer, le praticien.

M. A. Cortesão. — Je félicite M. Adam de sa communication ainsi que les Commandants Waters et Teixeira da Mota. Je voudrais ajouter quelque chose au sujet de la navigation ancienne, découverte par les Phéniciens 3000 ans avant notre ère. On sait que par la suite, et avant l'expansion grecque, ces Phéniciens allèrent aux îles Cassitérides qui devaient se trouver quelque part au Sud de l'Angleterre et nous savons, par les auteurs classiques, qu'ils allèrent le long de la côte occidentale de l'Afrique.

Un historien, Diodore de Sicile, décrit les aventures d'un bateau phénicien qui avait dépassé le détroit de Gibraltar. Il fut surpris par une tempête et poussé pendant 40 jours sur la mer avant d'arriver à une grande île, d'où il revint.

Nous savons que les Phéniciens n'avaient que des bateaux à voiles carrées et qu'un bateau surpris par une tempête au-delà du détroit de Gibraltar ne pouvait qu'être poussé au Nord ou au Sud de l'Amérique. Nous n'avons pas de raison de douter de l'information de Diodore de Sicile, mais nous en avons de supposer que les Phéniciens avaient des notions de navigation astronomique et ce que nous en savons tend à le confirmer.

Les Phéniciens ont certainement été en Amérique quelques siècles avant J.-C. Ils devaient pratiquer une sorte de navigation astronomique que nous ignorons, mais dont on trouve des indications chez les auteurs classiques. Elles sont souvent peu connues. Hérodote dit qu'Homère apprit tout ce qu'il savait en fait de navigation des Phéniciens. Il dit aussi que les Phéniciens naviguaient d'après la Petite Ourse et que les Grecs reprirent d'eux cette méthode. Il est possible que les Phéniciens se soient orientés à l'aide de la Petite Ourse pour trouver le Nord. Lorsque les Romains occupèrent la Phénicie, ses habitants avaient 3000 ans d'expérience de navigation sur diverses mers ; ils étaient versés dans les mathématiques. Ils avaient recueilli les connaissances des Babyloniens, des Égyptiens : on a des indications, mais non des faits positifs de leurs connaissances astronomiques.

Ce que je voudrais souligner, c'est que les Phéniciens furent à leur époque dans la même situation que les Portugais au xvᵉ siècle et au début du xviᵉ siècle : peuple commerçant qui devait naviguer en haute mer, qui avait des connaissances mathématiques. Les Portugais en avaient, puisqu'au début du xivᵉ siècle fut écrit à Coïmbre un almanach nautique conservé à la Bibliothèque Nationale de Madrid et qui contient des tables astronomiques de déclinaison solaire et de planètes, des indications cosmographiques. Je suis convaincu que certains traités astronomiques furent envoyés par Alphonse le Sage au roi Denis du Portugal. Certes, ces connaissances n'étaient ni portugaises, ni espagnoles mais d'origine arabe ; elles passaient de génération en génération, et de pays en pays.

Les Phéniciens et les Portugais étaient donc dans la même situation. Ce qui se passa pour les Portugais qui étaient dans la nécessité de créer un processus d'utilisation des connaissances astronomiques, est semblable à ce que connurent les Phéniciens. Les quelques indications des auteurs classiques nous apprennent autre chose encore. Nous savons que des peuples très primitifs ont utilisé une sorte de navigation astronomique. Les Polynésiens naviguaient sur 3000 milles et réussissaient à retrouver la latitude d'Hawaï. Ils connaissaient certains phénomènes astronomiques et savaient les utiliser. Si donc un peuple, au stade de l'âge de la pierre, avait trouvé des moyens semblables, à plus forte raison, un peuple évolué comme les Phéniciens, devait-il connaître certaines méthodes d'orientation que nous ne connaissons malheureusement pas.

Amiral GUILLÉN. — Je voudrais parler du facteur humain. Je suis passionné par les origines des choses ; je m'occupe des origines de la cartographie et je pourrais ne jamais en finir. Quant à l'origine de la navigation, je suis tout à fait d'accord avec M. Cortesão. Il faut se rendre compte que l'homme ancien savait davantage de choses que nous ne le croyons. A mesure que la technique avance, l'intuition tombe. Quand je commandais la caravelle, nous avions 79 hommes et nous ne pouvions presque pas lever l'ancre. Est-ce qu'avec 3-400 matelots, on pourrait lever aujourd'hui l'ancre d'un bateau de trois ou quatre ponts ? Je vous assure que non. Et pourtant, jadis, un bateau de trois ponts levait l'ancre. Nous avons perdu l'intuition et la technique de la force.

L'homme des cavernes savait sans boussole plus que les explorateurs actuels. Un explorateur peut se perdre. L'homme de l'âge de la pierre se perdait certainement quelquefois; mais, le plus souvent, il devait savoir retrouver son chemin alors qu'aujourd'hui, avec les moyens dont il disposait, nous nous perdrions. Il faut comprendre que le pilote savait lui aussi plus que nous ne le croyons. Pour trouver l'origine de l'art nautique, il faut se mettre dans la peau de l'homme primitif. On ne peut pas raisonner avec notre ignorance de l'époque ancienne et avec nos connaissances actuelles.

Le Commandant Teixeira da Mota a très bien vu le pilote qui navigue avec intuition, sans instrument, puis avec un instrument. Moi, je vois deux navigations astronomiques, l'une d'instinct, l'autre technique.

Commandant WATERS. — Ce que l'Amiral Guillén vient de dire est très intéressant. Je pense avec lui que certains peuples ont navigué « de tête ». Il y en a un bon exemple dans les papiers du *piloto mayor* Rubiosa. Un marin désirait passer l'examen de pilote de la *Casa de Contratación* pour faire le voyage des Indes. Il ne savait ni lire, ni écrire, et avait déjà fait plusieurs voyages aux Indes, bien qu'il ignorât tout de l'art nautique. C'est une preuve à l'appui de la thèse de l'Amiral Guillén.

Je voudrais relever deux autres points : le premier est celui du secret dont il a été question. On peut le comprendre si l'on songe que toutes ces expéditions étaient payées. Lorsque les Anglais songèrent à organiser des voyages vers l'Extrême-Orient en contournant le cap de Bonne-Espérance, comme ils le firent en 1599, ils durent fonder une compagnie des Indes Orientales pour financer l'entreprise. Or, il fut absolument interdit à tout autre Anglais d'aller aux Indes Orientales, parce que la compagnie aurait perdu de l'argent en perdant son monopole et elle n'aurait plus eu les moyens de financer les expéditions prévues. Nécessairement, il y avait donc une sorte de secret autour des voyages aux Indes Orientales, mais c'était un secret commercial, tel qu'il en existe actuellement encore pour les méthodes de production. Cela explique un des aspects du « secret » des Portugais, de cette conspiration du silence du xve siècle. Nous nous souvenons également qu'au début du xvie siècle, toutes les expéditions espagnoles étaient confirmées à Séville. Dans toutes ces expéditions on payait au service hydrographique de la *Casa de Contratación*.

Fait intéressant : au xvie siècle, les Anglais, à l'exception de l'Extrême-Orient, n'avaient pas de monopole et ne purent jamais s'offrir un service hydrographique. Celui-ci date de l'extrême fin du xviiie siècle.

Second point : le développement de la navigation. Je pense avec l'Amiral Guillén qu'il y eut une navigation d'instinct qui précéda la navigation à l'aide d'instruments. A vrai dire, on ne naviguait pas très bien « de tête ». Lorsque Sir Walter Raleigh voulut coloniser la Virginie, ce qu'il fit en 1585, quatre ans auparavant environ il fit venir un mathématicien anglais nommé Hariot auprès de lui et lui demanda d'établir un programme en vue de la navigation, car le but de la colonisation de la Virginie était d'en recevoir régulièrement les produits. Hariot trouva quatre points à perfectionner :

1°) Les cartes étaient inutilisables car elles ne donnaient pas une représentation sphérique de la terre.

2°) Les tables de navigation de l'étoile polaire n'étaient pas utilisables car elles ne tenaient pas compte de la latitude.

3°) Les variations de l'aiguille du compas n'étaient pas assez précises.

4°) Les tables de déclinaison solaire n'étaient pas exactes.

Durant les quatre années qui précédèrent l'expédition de 1585, Hariot observa le soleil et fit de nouvelles tables de déclinaison solaire ; il prépara une correction de la position de l'étoile polaire en tenant compte de la latitude ; il prépara des tables d'amplitude pour trouver la variation et il résolut mathématiquement la projection de Mercator. Il est intéressant de savoir que les résultats de Hariot demeurèrent secrets, limités à quelques rares capitaines, et écrits en manuscrit. Le manuscrit a été étudié pour la première fois il y a six ans seulement à Oxford. Ses découvertes qui étaient presque ignorées, sont ainsi connues.

Or, il serait très possible que l'on trouve un manuscrit espagnol ou portugais expliquant comment étaient résolus les problèmes astronomiques au xve siècle, tout comme on a découvert tout à fait par hasard ce manuscrit en Angleterre.

3

Portuguese Shipbuilding and the Early Voyages to the Guinea Coast

Richard W. Unger

Early in his life Avelino Teixeira da Mota spent four years in what was then Portuguese Guinea. In that time he gained a lasting interest in the region and the role of Portugal in the history of that part of Africa (Teixeira da Mota, 1969: 4). It was only natural given his major contribution — work on Portuguese cartography in the age of discovery — that the centre of his study of west Africa should be the early voyages of Portuguese explorers and traders along that coast.

The history of those early years of Portuguese expansion is only a part of the complex and varied history of the growth of Europe which began in the High Middle Ages and continued to this century. Portugal's role was important and so has been subjected to extensive scrutiny over the last one hundred years. Portuguese historians have done much of the work and men such as Teixeira da Mota have brought the results of those labours to the attention of scholars outside Portugal. It might be helpful to review what can be learned about one aspect of Portugal's part in early expansion from available material in English, in a place far from the centre of studies on that history. Readers limited to libraries and repositories with a small range of works on Portuguese history and limited largely to works in English can and do find it difficult to discover the facts about the ships, the design and building methods used that made possible those early voyages to the Guinea coast. It is even more difficult to uncover the explanations for the behaviour of Portuguese shipowners and builders during those years. This review then can not be definitive nor can it be complete. Perhaps though it can show the effects of Portuguese scholarship and point to those problems where historians of shipping and shipbuilding outside Portugal need some help in their understanding of the achievements of early exploration.

The study of Portuguese shipbuilding and exploration invariably and immediately becomes involved in the general discussion of early Portuguese expansion, why it was done, what effects it had. The discussion of ship types has become deeply imbeded in the controversey over the role of Prince

Henry (1394-1460), called the Navigator, in carrying out the voyages of discovery. If he was the driving force behind exploration then it is possible, so it has been argued, that it was he who had a new type of vessel, the caravelle, designed and built specifically for the voyages. The importance of the caravelle and the association with the role of Prince Henry explains the attention given to the vessel type. The works of the specialists Quirino da Fonseca and Gago Coutinho offer the most exhaustive studies of the characteristics of caravelles (Teixeira da Mota, 1960a: 179). They followed Henrique Lopes de Mendonça who, writing in 1892, claimed the caravelle was a Portuguese invention created especially to explore the African coast (J. Cortesão, 1950: I, 327, 348, 498; Leite, 1958: 182). Writers in English always discuss the caravelle and even attribute development of the type to Prince Henry. Obviously they have been deeply influenced by the work of Mendonça especially as presented by Fonseca. Fortunately now work is underway on a new edition of his standard book and the process of bringing the results of some forty years of Portuguese scholarship to the attention of scholars outside of Portugal is underway. Unfortunately little of the Portuguese literature is known outside of Portugal (Boxer, 1969: 27; Bell, 1974: 77; Penrose, 1952: 35, 269-270; Barata, 1975: 404).

The most important date in the study of fifteenth century Portuguese shipbuilding seems to be from the eighteenth century. The Lisbon earthquake of 1755 destroyed masses of documents and especially documents related to the government. Since the royal family took an active part in shipping the loss of that material leaves the study of shipbuilding with a weak base. Two chronicles form the most commonly used source of information. For some years and voyages Gomes Eannes de Azurara (1404?--1474), usually just called Zurara, and Alvise de Cadamosto (1434-1488) give the only material available. The former was apparently biased while the latter covered only a short period and was interested in a wide variety of subjects, seafaring being only one among many (Beazley and Prestage, 1896 and 1897; Crone, 1937; Diffie and Winius, 1977: 48, n 4, 96). An early sixteenth century chronicler, Resende, is at times cited as well. A few documents from outside of Portugal, for exemple papal bulls, give a rare passing reference to Portuguese ships. The normal principal source of design detail for medieval ships, illustrations, is sorely lacking. Most pictures come from manuscripts and few Portuguese manuscripts have survived. It is that gap which makes it so difficult to describe with any accuracy the development of ships used in early voyages to the Guinea coast. Maps did often have pictures of ships and the early sixteenth century Portuguese cartographic masterpieces offer illustrations of many different types of vessels (for example A. Cortesão and Teixeira da Mota, 1960: 37-38, 55-61). But for the fifteenth century and especially for the early voyages maps do not yield information about the ships.

While chroniclers say little about the ships they do report the step-by--step progress of exploration down the coast. Voyages to the Canary Islands were already made in the fourteenth century. Starting in the early fifteenth sailors set off from Portugal to push their way down the coast of Morocco. The area was known to fishermen and so there was no dramatic change in knowledge until Gil Eannes doubled Cape Bojador in 1434. Nuno Tristão rounded Cape Branco and explored the region of Arguim in 1443. Dinis Dias doubled Cape Verde in 1444. Pedro de Sintra visited Sierra Leone in 1460. Portuguese sailors were travelling along the coast of Ghana by 1471. They crossed the equator by about 1475 and in 1483 Diogo Cão reached the mouth of the Congo River. In the 1430's they were visiting the Azores. About 1460 they visited the Cape Verde Islands for the first time and explored the islands of the Gulf of Guinea between 1471 and 1475 (Teixeira da Mota, 1969: 3; Morison, 1940: 11-14). It was an impressive record of accomplishment.

The chroniclers say the sailors used four different types of vessels for their explorations: barque, barinel, fusta and caravelle. Of these the caravelle was the most important. For the other three there is only scanty information. Barques were commonly mentioned in the fourteenth and fifteenth centuries and not just in Portugal. Because the word was used so frequently it is very difficult to say exactly what a barque was. It was in a *barcha* that Eannes doubled Cape Bojador (Beazley and Prestage, 1896: 33). The term, used at times interchangeably with barge, applied to many different types of vessel from ship's boats to seagoing commercial and military craft. Barques could range in size from 25 to 240 tons. It may be what distinguished barques was that they carried both oars and sails. In the fourteenth century there seems to have been one mast with a single sail but the number of masts appears to have risen to three by the end of the fifteenth century (Burwash, 1947: 108-117). Barques were known in the Mediterranean as well. At Ragusa for example the word was used for a small boat. In Sicily the *barche* was a small ship used on rivers, for fishing and for carrying goods. The size of such vessels varied a great deal (Gatti, 1975a: 37; Gatti, 1975b: 73; Bresc, 1975: 12-14). At Genoa they were small boats which were no more than coasters. But at Barcelona where the word *barca* was in use by 1415, it was a vessel of reasonable size and capable of making voyages throughout the Mediterranean (Heers, 1958: 107-108; Capmany, 1779-1792: III, 90; Dufourcq, 1966: 38).

The barque of Portuguese exploration may well have been a descendant of the Scandinavian sailing ship developed in the eighth century. Vessels like those earlier Viking ships were built in western Europe throughout the Middle Ages. Called keels, they even survived in one form or another into the twentieth century. It is doubtful that the *barca* was descended from Celtic boats or that it was flatbottomed as has been suggested. But it certainly was true that by the thirteenth century *barcas* carried heavy cargoes such as wine and coal along the Atlantic shores of western Europe (Lewis, 1975: 23-24). Bordeaux barques of the early sixteenth century had a keel about 10 metres long and were rated at 35 tons. Such vessels had a full deck with a cabin at the stern and a forecastle. But such barques already had three masts (Bernard, 1968: 356-358). Barques were known along the Biscayan coast of Iberia and Portuguese vessels for exploration were probably most like those. The barque was a common visitor to Basque ports, usually carrying about, 40 tons but ranging up to 120 and even 150 tons (Childs, 1977: 158). The seals of the towns of Santander (first half of the thirteenth century) and from San Sebastian (thirteenth century) show vessels very similar to the keels on contemporary seals of southern English ports (Ewe, 1972: 187). The dimensions of the Basque vessels may have been about 15 metres long, 4 metres wide and $2^1/_2$ metres deep (Soto, 1975).

The *barca* of the earlier explorers was probably a boat of about 25 tons but as large as 50 tons. They had partial decks and perhaps a crew of 15. There was certainly a single mast with a square sail and perhaps at times even a second small mast at the stern also carrying a square sail. Length would have been between 21 and 27 metres, the width about 8 metres giving it a length to breadth ratio of around 3.5, similar to that for Scandinavian cargo ships of the High Middle Ages (Penrose, 1952: 269; Fonseca, 1934: 619; David, 1966: 153). The vessel used was a well-known and common type, not particularly different in any way from fishing boats which worked along the coast of Morocco or made voyages to the Canary Islands.

The second type of ship mentioned by Zurara was the barinel. Barinels are presumably related to what northern European sailors called balingers. They were originally propelled with both oars and sails but by the fifteenth century as the type got bigger the oars were abandoned. Balingers could get very large, even up to 600 tons with a crew of 109. The barinel probably originated in the Bay of Biscay since it was most common there. It was usually a vessel of moderate size used for both fishing and carrying cargo, sometimes over long distances as far as from England to Spain (Burwash, 1947: 106-108). The balinger was also known in the Mediterranean where it seems to have been more closely related to the galley, a relatively long oared vessel which was descended from a classical ship type. Four *balenieri* showed up in Sicilian registers of 1460 (Bresc, 1975: 15; Dufourcq, 1966: 40). The barinel of the voyages of the 1430's probably still had oars. It was typically larger than the *barca* that travelled with it but had the same or similar rig. There were two masts with two square sails (Penrose, 1952: 269; David, 1966: 154). The barinel is very problematical since mention of it is extremely rare, even by the chroniclers. Explorers used the barinel for over a century but it was never the most popular vessel for voyages to Africa.

Zurara also mentions the fusta or pinnance and three vessels of unspecified type. The fusta is even more of a mystery. It too is mentioned as a small ship in the Mediterranean (Heers, 1958: 107). It turned up in a number of fleets for exploration but seeminly only as an auxiliary, as one ship among many.

The caravelle is most closely associated with Portuguese voyages of exploration. It is first mentioned as part of a voyage of 1440 past Cape

Bojador to Rio d'Oro. After that caravelles dominated the fleets sent out from Portugal, to Africa. From 1448 to 1460 no other type is mentioned (Diffie and Winius, 1977: 118). Certainly Prince Henry did not invent the caravelle. A careful critical examination of the evidence shows that there is no substantial base for the grandiose claims for Henry's contribution to advances in seafaring (Diffie and Winius, 1977: 113-119). It seems he financed no more than one-fourth of all the Portuguese voyages to the African coast before his death (Scammell, 1981: 228). His famous centre at Sagres may not even have existed. As for the caravelle, the type was known long before Henry was born.

The caravelle appears in mid-thirteenth century documents as a coastal fishing boat (Fonseca, 1934: 597; Landström, 1961: 100; Godinho, 1962: 33). By the late fifteenth or early sixteenth century the term was so widely used for smaller vessels it may even have become a generic term, not describing any specific type. It is possible that chroniclers were guilty of identifying any ship sent out on a voyage of exploration as a caravelle (Haring, 1918: 263; Beazley and Prestage, 1899: 150-153; Gille, 1966: 175). The confusion about the essential features of the caravelle is increased by the use in northern Europe of the term *carvel* or *karveel* or other variations to describe a ship of framefirst construction and with the exterior hull planks fitted edge--to-edge. That form of building had been developed in the Early Middle Ages in the Mediterranean. Shipbuilders in northern Europe began to use the method in the fifteenth century. Breton shipcarpenters seem to have been the first in the North to perfect using the new approach so many ships along the Biscay coast got called carvels. In a port like Bordeaux term could refer to the type of construction or to the design of the ship. Size did not matter (Hagedorn, 1914: 56-59; Anderson, 1932: 189; Bernard, 1968: 359-365). *Karveel* continued in use down into the seventeenth century to describe inland vessels of frame-first construction (van Beylen, 1970: 166).

The Portuguese caravelle apparently always had frame first construction. The design came originally from the Mediterranean, related to the Arab *carib* or *caravo* which carried two or three lateen or triangular sails on two or three masts. The lateen sail had been known in Antiquity. Romans used it on smaller vessels (Casson, 1959: 219). It gave the sailor the ability to sail closer to the wind. Lateen-rigged Arab ships could get to within 60-65° of the wind and Portuguese caravelles probably approached that (Parry, 1975: 13-14, 24-26). What seems to have distinguished the Portuguese caravelle was the design of the hull. It was long, narrow, light and had little freeboard and little draft. In those features it revealed its connection with the whaling, fishing and river boats of the Biscay coast of Iberia. The ratio of length to breadth was at least 3:1 and often higher, even reaching 4:1. At most there was a single deck. Smaller caravelles had only a half deck or were completely open. There was no forecastle which gave it a rakish look. The lack of upperworks also decreased resistance in a cross wind. The deck at the stern was very short to make handling the yards easier. There was a tall stempost and a straight keel. The stern like the bow was rounded, the latter looking in some cases almost bluff (J. Cortesão, 1961: between 80 and 81; Diffie and Winius, 1977: 118-119; Bernard, 1966: 203; David, 1966: 154-155). Caravelles on exploration voyages were relatively small, at most 60-70 tons and about 20-35 metres long with a breadth amidships of 6-9 metres. Such ships would have crews of more than 20 men. The lateen sails were more difficult and dangerous to handle than square ones. They were better on long runs with favourable winds than on short stretches where the sail often had to be changed from one side to the other. Portuguese builders improved the handling of the lateen by making the yards shorter, fitting them closer to the mast and setting them more upright. The sail combined with the hull form made the type highly maneouvrable, especially along coasts with changeable winds and unknown hazards. In fact caravelles had an excellent record, very few being lost (Parry, 1961: 23-24; Marques, 1976: I, 134).

Though the caravelle evolved over time the essential features always remained. In the fifteenth century it got larger with more decking and perhaps even a third mast with a third lateen sail. The rig limited the size of the ship since the yards could carry only one sail and the yards could not get too long. Otherwise they would have become too difficult to handle. The type was called a *latine de Portogau* or *caravella latina* as well as simply a caravelle (Bernard, 1968: 367). It proved to be a very fast ship making speeds on long reaches out in the Atlantic matched only in the nineteenth century by clipper ships (Penrose, 1952: 270; Chaunu, 1969: 287). Pope Nicolas V praised the caravelle in a bull of 1454 and Cadamosto in his chronicle wrote that the caravelle was the best ship on the seas (David, 1966: 155-156; Leite, 1958: 182). While Cadamosto may have exaggerated, for his voyages going down the coast of Africa and to the Atlantic islands it was far better than any contemporary ocean going ship.

There was a number of reasons for the extensive development and effective evolution of the Portuguese caravelle during the fourteenth and fifteenth centuries. Certainly one reason for the success of Portuguese shipbuilding was the wide variety of influences that met along the Atlantic coast of Iberia (Marques, 1976: I, 134; Chaunu, 1969: 284; Parry, 1975: 24). During the Middle Ages European shipbuilding was divided into two distinct and separate technical traditions. Mediterraean shipwrights built their vessels differently from workers in western and northern Europe. Portugal, because of its location and because of changes in ship design in the thirteenth and fourteenth centuries, became the place in Europe where the two traditions met and merged.

Sailing ships from northern Europe visited the Iberian coast in the Roman period and before. In the Early Middle Ages Vikings in their longships raided the coast and even travelled into the Mediterranean. During the Crusades northern Europeans travelled to the Holy Land via Portugal in in their new deep sea cogs. There were vessels from the Low Countries in the Holy Land in the First Crusade in 1097, vessels which must have made their way south along the Atlantic coast of Europe. A fleet of more than 160 ships on their way to the Second Crusade in 1147 from England and Germany stopped in Portugal long enough to help the king take Lisbon from the Muslims. The pattern was similar in the Third Crusade in 1189 and again in a new crusade in 1217. Those trips were the precursors of regular commercial contact between Portugal and the shores of the North Sea and the English Channel. For example there were Portuguese merchants at Bruges by 1200. In the fourteenth century trading relations and contacts between Portugal and northwest Europe improved markedly. Regular trading connections had been firmly established with vessels from the Low Countries going to Lisbon and then travelling directly to the Baltic before returning home (Vogel, 1915: I, 125-129, 295; Engelbrecht, 1940: 1-9; Diffie, 1960: 55-56, 75-76). Large hulks from towns in the Baltic made their way to Lisbon in the fifteenth century, that is if English pirates did not stop them. These were hulks or *urcas* of up to 300 tons, closely related to cogs and among the largest of northern European ships. They were certainly much larger than contemporary Portuguese ships (Marques, 1959: 479-480; Marques, 1960: 329-332; Diffie, 1960: 12, 17-18, 26; Lewis, 1976: 144, 148-158).

In the High Middle Ages Portugal was also exposed to direct influence from the Mediterranean. The crown imported Italian, especially Genoese, sailors to improve naval forces for use against the Muslims. Above all those Mediterranean experts brought knowledge of how to build and use galleys. By the late of the twelfth century Mediterranean galleys could make their way out through the Straits of Gibraltar against the prevailing winds and current as well as back. By the late thirteenth century galleys were making regular trips to England and the Low Countries passing by and even stopping along the coast of Portugal on the way. Certainly galleys were an integral part of Portuguese naval forces in the fourteenth and fifteenth centuries (David, 1966: 157; Diffie, 1960: 48-55, 64; Prestage, 1933: 10; Lewis, 1976; 139-140). The regular commercial contacts between Genoa and Portugal led to the involvement of Italians in trading voyages and voyages of discovery to the Canaries and even down the coast of Africa (Verlinden, 1980: 5; Lewis, 1976: 158-160). Some features of Mediterranean shipbuilding, only known in specific places, still turn up in traditional Portuguese boatbuilding (Johnstone and Tilley, 1976: 20). But the Italian technicians who came to Portugal came to serve in the galley fleets with a view to coastal and naval operations and so they did not intervene in the development of the Portuguese sailing fleet (Teixeira da Mota, 1957: 128).

Taking advantage of knowledge of both northern and Mediterranean practices Portuguese shipbuilders produced vessels with a great deal of versatility. In fact it may have been Portuguese or at least Iberian shipwrights who first hit upon the combination of square sails and lateen sails on a large cargo carrier to create the full-rigged ship. The earliest illustration of the new highly practical ocean sailing ship comes from a Spanish-Moorish plate dated to about 1400. The ship depicted is Portuguese (Landström, 1961: 96; David, 1966: 167-168). The new type was a product of modifications made in the cog which had been brought from northern Europe. The resulting carrack or *nau* as it was called in Portugal had the advantages of manouevrability from the lateen sail and easy expansion or contraction of the driving power from square sails. The full-rigged ship dominated ocean sailing until the advent of steam. In building *naus* Portuguese shipwrights proved themselves capable of creating a whole new type of ship which could perform tasks more effectively than its predecessors. The development of the new type was based on past experience but more important on very different traditional patterns of technology. Obviously Portuguese shipbuilding was vibrant, active and in a condition to receive knowledge from elsewhere and turn it to advantage.

The choice to develop the caravelle and the *nau* however was the result of the perceived needs of shipowners and buyers. In that Prince Henry may have had some role to play. In the fourteenth century the rising income of artisans, the general growth in trade and navigation in the face of falling noble incomes made investment in commerce more attractive. For Henry, a relatively poor member of the royal family, trade and the fishery looked rather attractive (Marques, 1976: 108-109, 144; Godinho, 1969: 40-41). Henry may simply represent a general trend among the nobility in the years around 1400 toward investment in commerce, colonization and expansion.

In the fourteenth and fifteenth centuries the Portuguese economy was based on the export of wine, fish and especially salt. Cork, olive oil and subtropical fruits were of lesser importance. Imports included precious metals, especially gold, other metals, cloth, wood and spices like pepper from the Mediterranean. But increasingly and especially after 1400 in terms of volume the major import was grain. The increasing bulk of Portuguese exports led to a growth in the average size of ships built (J. Cortesao, 1950: 192-193; Godinho, 1969: 37-38; Marques, 1976: I, 92-94; Marques, 1959: 482-484). The two industries of primary importance to exports were salt--making and fishing. Both typically were carried on by small units in the many little towns and villages along the coast. Production was traded through the major ports. Imports came through those same ports. The dominance of Oporto and Lisbon may have been because of the size of the ships involved in long distance trade. The development of the *nau* may have been a response to the need for a bulk carrier.

The one exception to the need for large ships was in the fishery. Fishing boats could not be made too large since they had to make their way into small harbours and often had to be beached at night. Fishing boats had to be highly maneouvrable since they often worked very close to shore. The fishery relied on a number of different types of ships but among them were all the types used in the early voyages of exploration; *barcas, barinéis, caravelas* (Godinho, 1962: 187). It was exactly those types that made trips to the northwest coast of Africa for fishing long before Prince Henry or any Portuguese nobleman thought of exploring further to the south. The typical pattern throughout Europe for all the voyages of discovery was to use ordinary vessels, the type of ship that was familiar and easily at hand. Explorers preferred if anything vessels designed for the coastal trade. The caravelle fit all the criteria (Parry, 1963: 67-68, 130).

Up through the 1440's and the voyages down to Senegambia sailors used the caravelle for the traditional tasks of the type. When it came time to extend the voyages further difficulties arose. Regular voyages to the Canaries had been going on since the mid-fourteenth century and in caravelles. In the fifteenth century not only the Canaries but Madeira, the Azores and the Cape Verde were colonized and so became regular goals of trading ships (Verlinden, 1980: 11; Mauny, 1970: 219-220). As distances travelled increased so too did the demands made on carrying capacity. Caravelles as a result became bigger. Crews were always relatively large on voyages of exploration. The men had to be fed so much of the hold was taken up with their food and especially water, a serious consideration along the Saharan coast. On typical voyages caravelles would carry four months worth of food and one month worth of water per man or about one-half ton. But for voyages of exploration that would more than double to over one ton per man. Given the size of the first caravelles and the size of the crews almost the entire carrying capacity would have been taken up with supplies (Denoix, 1966: 142-143; Chaunu, 1969: 287). That must have limitated reconnaissance along the northwest coast of Africa. By giving up oared vessels, barques and barinels, shippers decreased crew size. Improvements in the latten rig meant the caravelle could be built bigger without increasing the number of sailors. In the fifteenth century the caravelle also served effectively for many types of coastal navigation which explains its appearance in Bordeaux and in England. The growth in the size of the caravelle could have come from its role as a coastal trader along the Atlantic front as much as from the needs of explorers. Whatever the case by the mid-fifteenth century caravelles made trading voyages to Senegambia and to England, in both cases profitably.

There were two major changes in the equipment of Portuguese exploration. The first came about 1440, the second about 1460. In 1439-1440 the Portuguese first used caravelles and in 1441 they first traded in slaves along African coast (Chaunu, 1969: 141). The change in ship type was certainly related to the move south of Cape Bojador but it was also seeminly related to the need for greater carrying capacity and smaller crew to carry economically the new slave cargoes. While the caravelle dominated from 1440 to 1460 after that increasingly *naus* appeared in the fleets going to Africa. It is possible that *naus* were just as effective as caravelles on the west Africa route (Leite, 1958: 138-139). In 1452 an *urca* traded to Arguim (J. de Cortesão, 1950: I, 326). In the fleet that was sent out to set up the fortress at Mina there were 90 caravelles but 2 *urcas* of 400 tons each which carried much of the artillery and stone (Martinez-Hidalgo, 1966: 23; Haring, 1918: 264). By the late 1450's Portuguese traders were active in Senegambia which was perhaps the most highly developed part of black Africa. It was more urbanized and had better access to gold as well as other trade goods. Prince Henry not long before his death in 1460 called for a change in the character of African exploration. Rather than fighting the natives he urged seeking alliances with them, trying to trade with them and trying to convert them to Christianity (Scammell, 1981: 253; Mauny, 1970: 227). By the last quarter of the fifteenth century the *nau* was the type preferred for voyages to west Africa (Leite, 1958: 181, 183). In both instances as the Portuguese moved down the coast it was necessary to change ship type in response to the needs of expanding commercial opportunities.

When it came time for the voyages to India the ship, the *nau,* unequivocally replaced the caravelle. Once across the equator Portuguese navigators thought it might be possible to find a way to India. Bartholomeu Dias left Lisbon in 1487 on a voyage of exploration with three caravelles, doubled the Cape of Good Hope and showed the way to India. When Vasco da Gama set out for the Orient in 1498 principally to trade he took one caravelle and three *naus* for their greater durability and cargo capacity. The latter was certainly the most important consideration (Penrose, 1952: 270; Parry, 1975: 165-167, 171; Godinho, 1969: 550-551). The ships carrying trade goods out to India and spices back in the early sixteenth century were typically full-rigged with capacities of 500 tons but to get the spices from Lisbon to their principal market in the North, Antwerp, Portuguese shippers used caravelles (Godinho, 1969: 673, 727).

As the fifteenth century progressed Portuguese shipbuilders developed more specialized types of caravelles. A 1478 document for example mentions a *caravela de descobrir,* (J. Cortesão, 1950: I, 490). By 1500 a kind of caravelle was built especially for trading voyages along the Atlantic front. Called the *caravela redonda* to distinguish it from the older and now traditional *caravelas latinas,* it showed connections with the fifteenth century caravelles of the Andalusian style (Martinez-Hidalgo, 1966: 25; Parry, 1975: 170; Fonseca, 1934: 608-609). The *Nina* and *Pinta* of Columbus's first expedition in 1492 were good examples of that Andalusian variation. Hull design was typical of caravelles with shallow draft and little upperworks. Sometimes the vessels were rigged with just lateen sails but captains, like Columbus at Las Palmas, would and did rerig them with square sails on the fore and mainmasts and a lateen mizzen when they thought it appropriate. Columbus' caravelles performed well especially in sailing close to the wind (Martinez-Hidalgo, 1966: 8-9, 25, 87-100; Haring, 1918: 261, 263; Gille, 1966: 175). The sixteenth century version had three or four masts. The foremast carried two or even three square sails while the other masts rigged lateens. The stern was square. The hull form was the same as that of earlier caravelles but with a lower ratio of length to breadth. It was the round caravelle that appeared in northern Europe in the sixteenth century bringing cargoes from Iberia (Unger, 1975: 110-112; David, 1966: 155). The type also served to carry sugar from the Atlantic islands and black slaves from the Guinea coast. For the slave trade speed was important since delays at sea would increase the mortality of the valuable cargo. As the volume of Portuguese trade increased so too did the size of ships, the averaging doubling from the mid-fifteenth to the mid-sixteenth century. The round caravelle was part of that general growth. The *redondas* got to be as big as 200 tons with lengths of over 18 metres (Barata, 1965: 405; Denoix, 1966: 145; Godinho, 1969: 28; Prestage, 1933: 332). As time went on the greater carrying capacity of the round caravelle probably made it possible for it to dominate its ancestor.

Caravelles found a use by being smaller and therefore more versatile than the contemporary *nau*. Writing in the early sixteenth century a Venetian spy noted that for voyages to Brazil and the Guinea coast the Portuguese used small ships (Teixeira da Mota, 1966: 179). Shippers bringing sugar from Brazil to Lisbon preferred caravelles. Because of their size their holds could be filled more quickly so they had a chance of making two round trip voyages a year. Ships could not sit too long with the sugar since the cargo would deteriorate. The caravelle travelling alone was more vulnerable to pirates than the *nau* but despite that shippers still used round caravelles (Boxer, 1969: 220-221). The type also made its way into the Mediterranean. The first caravelles appeared there in the 1460's bringing sugar from the Atlantic islands. By the end of the century they were making long distance voyages all the way to the eastern shores of the Mediterranean. Trade goods in the Levant were increasingly luxuries, lighter goods and caravelles had no disadvantage in competing with large ships for the carriage of such goods (Heers, 1958: 116-118). Trade to the Antilles gave employment to both lateen and round caravelles, at least in the early decades of the sixteenth century. From 1506 to 1550 of the 285 ships which went from Spain to the New World and were identified by type 163 or over half were called caravelles. The 285 made up only a small proportion of the total of 4,385 ships making such voyages. In the seconde half of the sixteenth century, 1551--1600, the proportion of caravelles among the identified ships fell to just 63 out of 1,086 which in turn was a larger proportion of the 7,110 ships which made the voyages. Throughout the greatest use of the caravelle was for carrying slaves from the Guinea coast to the newly colonized islands in the Caribbean (J. Cortesão, 1950: I, 328-329; H. and P. Chaunu, 1955: VI, table 12E; Teixeira da Mota, 1969: 15).

What started as voyages to catch fish became in the fifteenth century voyages of exploration. Starting in the 1450's the trips became trading ventures. As exploration continued so the volume and scope of trade expanded. In each case the changes led to different transportation needs and shipbuilders adjusted to try to meet those needs. Often they did. In some cases other technological developments let them avoid confronting the problem. Improvements in navigational techniques saved shipbuilders from dealing with even greater problems. The prevailing winds and currents on the northwest coast of Africa are northerly. It is very easy to get down the coast but extremely difficult to return. It was possible to claw back up the coast using the variation of shore and sea breezes. But it was a great deal of work and sailing like that could never prove economical. The solution was to stand out to sea away from the coast on the return journey and describe a great arc in the Atlantic going north to about the position of the Azores and then turn east to use the prevailing westerly wind to bring the ship back to Portugal. In other words it was necessary to practice oceanic navigation. Certainly by the 1440's Portuguese sailors were able to do that (Boxer, 1961: 9-10; Teixeira da Mota, 1958: 130-132). In fact it is likely that they knew how to use the stars to guide them at sea for a long time before the voyages of discovery. Portuguese sailors made it to the Canary Islands and back in the fourteenth century so presumably they had developed some method of celestial observation which could allow long trips out of sight of land (Verlinden, 1980: 9; Chaunu, 1969: 289-293). There is a long-standing controversey over the exact date for the start of celestial navigation but it seems clear that Iberian sailors had developed many of the necessary skills long before there is any written indication of their accomplishments. Maps made in Portugal show that certainly by the 1470's pilots were using latitude observations to mark their position so they must have already been using celestial observations before that time. The transfer of the traditional practice to paper led to a revolution in mapmaking (Teixeira da Mota, 1958: 140; Teixeira da Mota, 1966b: 229-232).

The caravelle was the ship capable of making both the coastal voyage down to west Africa and the long run on the high seas to the Azores and then back to Portugal. Their speed on those long reaches at sea combined with their maneouvrability along the coast made them ideal for work to Guinea. The caravelles could follow the prevailing current south to Cape Verde. They stopped to take on fresh water at Beziguiche and then picked up the Guinea current which runs steadily eastward. Once along the coast they had to be careful of the many shoals and hidden rocks. For the return voyage the caravelles sailed south until they picked up the equatorial current. That ran parallel to the Guinea current but in the opposite direction. Making a wide sweep they got back to the Cape Verde Islands and from there they made that wide arc which took them to the Azores and then home (Blake, 1977: 13-14; Mauny, 1970: 229-230). One chronicler claimed that the reason for using caravelles as opposed to round ships, *naus,* was the currents (J. Cortesão, 1950: I, 490). The caravelles carried relatively high value cargoes. They competed with the caravans which carried goods across the desert between west and north Africa. Ibn Khaldun of Tunis writing about 1370 mentions slaves shipped from the Canaries to Moroccan markets. Portuguese ships brought pepper and gold north too in exchange for cloth and copper goods (Verlinden, 1980: 8; Teixeira da Mota, 1969: 6, 9-15). By the 1530's century Portuguese shipping had come to completely dominate the Muslim caravan routes across the desert (Godinho, 1969: 217).

The Portuguese government maintained the myth that only caravelles could make a round trip to the Guinea coast. The king ordered the two *urcas* sent to carry supplies for setting up the fortress at Mina destroyed rather than allow them to return to Portugal. There is a story that one day over lunch a famous pilot told the king of Portugal that he was sure he could make a round voyage to west Africa with any good ship. The king said he was exaggerating but took him aside later telling him that though he was right he should keep it to himself for the good of the king's service (Martinez-Hidalgo, 1966: 23-24). Even if the government insisted that only caravelles could make it back that would not have prevented sailors from other countries from making voyages to west Africa. Caravelles could be and were built in a number of places outside of Portugal. In Bordeaux in 1493 a builder contracted to supply a *caravela redonda* of 80 tons (Bernard, 1966: 217). Andalusia certainly produced caravelles in the last decade of the fifteenth century and probably for many years before that. Portugal forbade the export of caravelles. The date of the law is not certain. It could be from the first quarter of the sixteenth century but in 1454 a man was executed for having sold a caravelle to an English buyer. Even if the legislation is from the early fifteenth century and the time of Prince Henry it was not only caravelles that worried the lawmakers. The law forbade the export not only of carvelles but also of *naus*. It also prohibited Portuguese pilots and masters from serving on foreign ships (J. Cortesão, 1950: I, 328-300; Teixeira da Mota, 1966a: 181). The lawmakers were trying to keep all Portuguese maritime skills at home, not just the design of the caravelle. The type may have had unique characteristics but those characteristics were widely known certainly by the late fifteenth century if not well before. Since the caravelle found use in a variety of different trades travelling to many different parts of Europe it is doubtful that the Portuguese government could have kept others from building them.

The Portuguese protected their African trading monopoly not so much by denying technical information about shipbuilding to potential competitors as by the use of force. The caravelle proved itself capable of performing that task as well. The Portuguese navy used caravelles as warships against Castile in 1476. It was a year later that the Castilians sent their own caravelles against the Portuguese in Africa (J. Cortesão, 1950: I, 471-473). The ability to deploy armed caravelles, that is armed with artillery, was a critical factor in the voyages of discovery (Teixeira da Mota, 1966a: 180). It was also a critical factor in maintaining the Portuguese hold on African trade. In 1557 3 Portuguese caravelles sailing with 2 *naus* off the Guinea coast defeated a combined French and English force of sailing ships. The nameless battle set the pattern for naval warfare for the next two and one--half centuries. The Portuguese demonstrated the defensive advantages of lining ships up one behind the other, of firing broadside at the enemy

and of getting to windward of the enemy.   The fire from the caravelles proved
devastating.   Since the Portuguese were only interested in driving off their
enemies they did not have to bother with trying to board the English and
French ships.   They took advantage of the essentially defensive nature of
their armed sailing ships (Guilmartin, 1974: 84, 91-93).   In actions like
that against Europeans and non-Europeans alike Portugal asserted her dominance of navigation and trade in the south Atlantic and Indian Ocean.

It is abundantly clear that the small Portuguese shipbuilding industry
of the late Middle Ages was a vibrant and active one.   It was capable of
meeting the needs of local shippers and fishermen while at the same time
supplying or evolving new forms of vessels.   By the early fifteenth century
Portugal already had the capacity in its shipbuilding industry to deal with
any of the desires or ambitions of her rulers.   Shipbuilding benefitted from
the exposure over the centuries to different techniques from all over Europe.
Shipbuilding and shipping too for that matter benefitted from the active
support of the government.   Kings like Diniz (1279-1325) and Ferdinand I
(1367-1383) gave a great impetus to naval shipbuilding.   Dinis planted the
royal pine forest at Leiria which later furnished large quantities of wood for
building ships.   He also in 1293 set up a unique insurance system for all
ships leaving Portugal (David, 1966: 156-157; Duffy, 1955: 3; Diffie, 1960:
39, 44-45).   A more extensive insurance plan was instituted by Ferdinand.
A charge of 2% was made on the value of all cargoes of ships over 50 tons
leaving Portugal.   The funds so collected were used to pay for any loss at
sea of goods or, if the loss was total, of the ship as well.   It may well be
that the insurance scheme was never fully implemented but other legislation
of Ferdinand to aid shipping proclaimed in 1377 and 1380 does seem to
have been effective.   He authorised purchase of wood from the royal forests
by native shipbuilders without paying tax.   If they built a ship of 100 tons
or more then they paid nothing for the right to cut and carry the wood.   He
gave those same men the rights to all duties on imported shipbuilding supplies
like hemp, pitch and sails.   Shipowners were exempted from military service
on land or sea.   They got freedom from any duties on the first cargo a new
ship brought into the country (Boiteux, 1968: 40-41; Engelbrecht, 1940:
5-6; Prestage, 1933, 10-12; Diffie, 1960: 68-69).   The king of Portugal was
involved in trading and trading ventures (Diffie, 1960: 30).   Both the royal
example and extensive legislation served to promote the Portuguese merchant marine and in its train shipbuilding.   It is not suprising that kings
took a hand in the voyages to new lands in search of potential trade.

The caravelle was not just a small vessel with some features which made
it well-suited to exploration.   Sailors and landsmen used the term to describe a range of vessels built and used in Portugal from the thirteenth century
through the seventeenth.   In the fifteenth and sixteenth centuries Portuguese shipwrights produced a number of variations on the essential caravelle
design.   To concentrate on a single type, on a single precise set of attributes
would be incorrect.   It is excuseable given the limited nature of the sources

but none the less wrong. The caravelle had a number of uses. The range of uses increased through the fifteenth century as explorers found their way to the Guinea coast and back. First used as a fishing vessel the caravelle became important and then critical to the altogether new and suddenly thriving trade between Portugal and western of Africa. On the first voyage to some new region the problem was to get down the coast and back but on the second and all subsequent voyages the ships had to get back with a cargo which would pay for the cost of the trip as well as have something left over for the investors. The caravelle in its different forms solved a number of economic problems for shippers.

It may never be exactly clear what the products of Portuguese shipbuilding yards looked like in the fifteenth century. Discussion will always be made up of some guesswork because of the shortage of accurate information from the period. It is somewhat presumptuous to suggest where, some answers might be found since Portuguese scholars have long been devoted to the quest to find out more about caravelles, how they were built and how they were sailed. Still experience with the study of shipbuilding elsewhere in Europe may offer some guide. At least it is possible to suggest what might be of interest to those outside of Portugal where little is known of contemporary Portuguese research. The search can and will go on for now unknown illustrations of late medieval Portuguese ships. After so much research has already been done though it is not likely that that avenue will be very fruitful.

It is always hard to work backward, that is to interpolate the design of ships from vessels built later, but Scandinavian scholars have had some success in learning about Viking shipbuilding techniques from traditional boatbuilding practice still in use in small yards in Norway and Sweden. There were without doubt descendants of the caravelle and barque in Portugal into the twentieth century. *Barco* means simply boat now and boatbuilders often do not bother to distinguish one type from another. Yet it may well be that in one of the older types still being constructed along the north coast of Portugal hints can be found for the basic design of the barques of the fifteenth century voyages (Johnstone and Tilley, 1976: 15-17). The caravelle seems to have spawned a number of different types, some where the connection with the original became in time unrecognizeable. The frigate was probably a descendant of the caravelle, at least in its early seventeenth century form when it was brought to northern Europe (Mauro, 1966: 192-193; van Beylen, 1970: 67). The xebec or chebec, a popular two-masted lateen rig coaster of the Mediterranean through to the early twentieth century, showed many similarities with the caravelle in both rig and in hull design. A mass of information has survived about that type (Martinez-Hidalgo, 1966: 96-97). Along the Tagus River before Lisbon a number of small sailing vessels still remain in use. Some of them are probably related to the caravelle. The *fragata* bears many similarities to the caravelle but then so do almost all round-bottomed boats on the Tagus. The most likely candidate for direct descent is the now extinct *falua*. This may have been a smaller version of the *felucca,* a lateen rigged coastal trader which frequented many Portuguese ports. The *falua* carried two lateen sails on two masts and also had 4 oars. It had finer lines than the *fragata* (Landström, 1961: 210; Kochiss, 1978: 169-171, 175-177). Information about the construction and sailing qualities of these later types may help to fill gaps in knowledge about the fifteenth century caravelle.

Archaeology for the last three decades has provided a wealth of new information by turning up the ships themselves from the past. While archaeological finds have meant a great deal to the study of Roman, medieval Mediterranean and Viking ships it is doubtful that archaeology will be able to produce much about ships used to trade to Africa. Not many caravelles were lost and the waters along the African coast are not the type to aid in the preservation of a sunken ship. The high temperatures and salinity of the water make ideal conditions for shipworms which devour wood. Certainly it would be worth looking for wrecks underwater but the chances of such a search producing a major source of new information is small.

While Portuguese observers knew about the variety of types produced in domestic shipyards in the fourteenth and fifteenth centuries modern readers, especially outside of Portugal hardly know about them. Knowledge of those other designs would show why certain types were chosen for voyages of discovery over others. Also knowledge of the variety of products which came from Portuguese yards would reinforce the idea of the vibrancy and versatility of the Portuguese industry in the period. It would show that it was not just one man, by his own will, but rather a society with a wide range of seafaring skills, an expanding commercial and shipping sector and a strong interest in trade and navigation which produced travel and trade to Africa. After all in 1439, when the Duke of Burgundy wanted to build ships of the latest design using the most modern methods he sent for Portuguese shipwrights to come to Brussels to build such ships (van Beylen, 1970: 7; J. Cortesão, 1950: I, 193). Contemporaries thought highly of the skills and resources of Portuguese shipbuilding. It would be wrong for historians in the twentieth century to have a lesser view. While only a small proportion of the Portuguese population in the fourteenth and fifteenth centuries was involved in seafaring still there were skilled sailors and shipwrights capable of making the voyage of exploration and of building ships suited for such voyages. It was from the vigourous and innovative shipbuilding industry that the caravelle and many other types came.

The organization of shipbuilding yards is another part of the history of Portuguese industry which seems absent and which might add something to the study of ships and the early voyages to the Guinea coast. It was common in the High Middle Ages for governments in the Mediterraean to set up their own shipyards, arsenals like those in Venice and Barcelona. Castilians followed a similar practice when they conquered Seville in 1246. There shipbuilding, naval and commercial, was restricted to one part of the city (Godinho, 1969: 35; Dufourcq, 1966: 88; Galdacano, 1920: 18). Portugal followed suit with royal shipyards in existence in Lisbon by at least 1237. There were royal officials responsible for the proper operation of those yards (Diffie, 1960: 33-34; Godinho, 1962: 33). The centralization of naval construction must have helped to direct production of ships, at least of naval vessels (David, 1966: 165). The number of people involved in shipbuilding in Lisbon and other major centres was small in 1400 but over time it grew dramatically. In the mid-fifteenth century Lisbon boasted some 50-60 caulkers. In 1551 there were 100 caulkers along with 227, shipcarpenters and 18 riggers in the Lisbon yards alone. By the seventeenth century the royal dockyards in Lisbon employed 1500 men (Boxer, 1969: 11, 210; Duffy, 1955: 50-51). The problem of lack of sources is perhaps most critical in the case of study of the shipbuilding yards. Yet the organization of the yards in Portugal and in different parts of the Portuguese empire should reveal something about how the ships were built, about how the men who built them acted and were rewarded and most important about the ability of the Portuguese shipbuilding industry to adjust designs to perceived needs. Portuguese shipbuilding apparently bears important similarities to industries in other parts of Europe. Comparison with organization elsewhere might prove productive.

It is no longer necessary it seems for scholars either in or outside Portugal to worry about the invention of the caravelle. It is clear that a traditional type, a fishing boat with a long and probably Mediterranean ancestry became the subject of modification for Portuguese shipwrights. The builders took that ship type through at least four stages from fishing boat through exploration vessel to cargo ship and finally to the large round cargo ship. The first of those adjustments seems to have come around 1440 while the second came in the late 1450's. The final one appears to have been made at the close of the fifteenth century. Of course, shipbuilders while they might develop modified versions never gave up the established designs. Nor did they ever stop modifying the new variation on the traditional type. So many forms of caravelles always existed side by side. The same was true of all ship types. In general it is no longer necessary to unearth specific great Portuguese inventions to explain the successful voyages of exploration in the fifteenth century. This is true as much of the history of navigation as in other fields of the history of technology. As Teixeira da Mota and many other scholars have shown over the last generation there was a wide variety of scientific and technological activity in fifteenth century Portugal which laid the basis for expansion. The voyages of discovery had many different sources, political, economic, religious and they did not grow out of a single invention nor did any one single development make them possible. It was the choice of the right ship types combined with courage, obstinance and advanced cartographic and astronomical knowledge which assured Portuguese success (Gille, 1966: 176). Portugal was already a maritime nation in the fourteenth century well before embarking on the adventure of expansion.

It is not novel to suggest that the internal history of Portuguese shipbuilding, its organization, the variety of its products and the vestiges of those
products in the nineteenth and twentieth century is worthy of investigation.
However, it is audacious for an observer far away, limited in the works available and in the ability to use many of them, to explain what is needed to scholars
already very familiar with such study. The caravelle finally virtually
disappeared in the seventeenth century. The last mention of it was in Portugal in 1738 where it stayed in use longer than anywhere else in Europe
(Martinez-Hidalgo, 1966: 27). The modification of the caravelle and its
evolution was and is important as part of the general technical advance made
in Europe in closing years of the Middle Ages. The results of those advances
were massive and still too great for historians to properly describe or even
comprehend. In the case of Portuguese shipbuilding, technical advance
meant the creation of vessels capable of handling high value cargoes and
thus of making economically profitable voyages to the Guinea coast. It
was the caravelle in the fifteenth century which served to integrate Guinea
geographically and commercially with Europe. So the products of Portuguese shipbuilding yards an immediate impact on interregional trade. The
discovery of the sea route to India and the New World by Europeans meant
the ultimate integration of the regional economy of west Africa with the
economies and societies of other continents (Teixeira da Mota, 1969: 4, 16-18).
The value and importance to the economic and cultural history of west Africa
of that integration makes the study of Portuguese shipbuilding both more
interesting and more important. But ultimately it is from the study of the
internal history of the industry that the most valuable results for all historical
study will come.

SOURCES

ANDERSON, R. C. (1932) — «'Carvel' and 'caravel',» *The Mariner's Mirror*, 28: 189.

BARATA, João da Gama Pimentel (1975) — «Note: Four Dordrecht Ships of the Sixteenth Century», *The Mariner's Mirror*, 61: 404-405.

BEAZLEY, Charles R. and Edgar Prestage, trans. and eds. (1896 and 1899) — *Gomes Eannes de Azurara The Chronicle of the Discovery and Conquest of Guinea*, 2 volumes, London.

BELL, Christopher (1974) — *Portugal and the Quest for the Indies*, London.

BERNARD, Jacques (1968) — *Navires et Gens de Mer à Bordeaux (vers 1400-vers 1550)*, 3 volumes, Paris.

——, (1965) — «Les Types de Navires Ibériques et Leur Influence sur la Construction Navale dans les Ports du Sud-Ouest de la France (XVᵉ-XVIᵉ Siècles),» *Actes du Cinquième Colloque International D'Histoire Maritime*, Michel Mollat, ed., Paris: 195-217.

VAN BEYLEN, Jan (1970) — *Schepen van de Nederlanden*, Amsterdam.

BLAKE, John W., trans and ed. (1942) — *Europeans in West Africa, 1450-1560*, 2 volumes, London.

—— (1977) — *West Africa Quest for God and Gold 1454-1578*, London.

BOITEUX, L. A. (1968) — *La Fortune de Mer, le Besoin de Securité et les Débuts de l'Assurance Maritime*, Paris.

BOXER, Charles R. (1961) — *Four Centuries of Portuguese Expansion, 1415-1825: A Succinct Survey*, Johannesburg.

—— (1969) — *The Portuguese Seaborne Empire*, London.

BRESC, Henri (1975) — «Una flotta mercantile periferica: la marina siciliana medievale,» Henri Bresc *et al.*, *Studi di storia navale*, 4: 7-24.

BURWASH, Dorothy (1947) — *English Merchant Shipping, 1460-1540*, Toronto.

DE CAPMANY, Antonio (1779-1792) — *Memorias Historicas sobre la marina commercio y artes de la antigua ciudad de Barcelona*, 5 volumes, Madrid.

CASSON, Lionel (1959) — *The Ancient Mariners Seafarers and Sea Fighters of the Mediterranean in Ancient Times*, London.

CHAUNU, Pierre (1969) — *L'Expansion Européenne du XIIIᵉ au XVᵉ Siècle*, Paris.

—— and Huguette (1955) — *Séville et l'Atlantique 1540-1650*, 8 volumes, Paris.

CHILDS, Wendy R. (1977) — *Anglo-Castilian Trade in the Later Middle Ages*, Manchester.

CORTESÃO, Armando and Avelino Teixeira da Mota (1960) — *Portugaliae Monumenta Carthographica*, Lisbon.

CORTESÃO, Jaime [1950] — *Os Descobrimentos Portugueses*, 2 volumes, Lisbon.

—— (1961) — *Os Descobrimentos Pré-Colombinos Dos Portugueses*, Lisbon.

CRONE, G. R., trans. and ed. (1937) — *The Voyages of Cadamosto*, London.

DAVID, J. Ferreira (1966) — «Aperçu Historique des Types des Navires à Travers les Siècles et Influence des Navires Ibériques sur la Construction Navale Européenne,» *Actes du Cinquième Colloque International D'Histoire Maritime*, Michel Mollat, ed., Paris: 149-169.

DENOIX, L. (1966) — «Charactéristiques des Navires de l'Epoque des Grandes Découvertes,» *Actes du Cinquième Colloque International D'Histoire Maritime*, Michel Mollat, ed., Paris: 137-147.

DIFFIE, Bailey W. (1960) — *Prelude to Empire Portugal Overseas before Henry the Navigator*, Lincoln.

—— (1977) — *Foundations of the Portuguese Empire 1415-1580*, Minneapolis.

DUFFY, James (1955) — *Shipwreck and Empire*, Cambridge, Mass.

248   RICHARD W. UNGER

DUFOURCQ, Charles-Emmanuel (1966) — *L'Espagne Catalane et Le Maghrib aux XIIIe et XIVe Siècles*, Paris.

ENGELBRECHT, W. A. (1940) — *Schets der Historische Betrekkingen Portugal-Nederland*, The Hague.

EWE, Herbert (1972) — *Schiffe Auf Siegeln*, Rostock.

DA FONSECA, Quirino (1934) — *A Caravela Portuguesa e a prioridade téchnica das Navegações Henriquinas*, Coimbra.

GALDÁCANO, Gervasio de Artiñano y (1920) — *Arquitectura Naval Española (en Madera)*, Madrid.

GATTI, Luciana (1975a) — «Construzioni Navali in Liguria Fra XV e XVI Secolo,» Henri Bresc *et al.*, *Studi di storia navale*, 4: 25-72.

—— (1975b) — «Imbarcazioni Ragusee Nel Secolo XVI,» Henri Bresc *et al.*, *Studi di storia navale*, 4: 73-96.

GILLE, Paul (1966) — «Navires Lourds et Navires Rapides avant et après les Caravelles», *Actes du Cinquième Colloque International D'Histoire Maritime*, Michel Mollat, ed., Paris: 171-178.

GODINHO, Vitorino Magalhães (1969) — *L'Economie de L'Empire Portugais aux XVe et XVIe Siècles*, Paris.

—— (1962) — *A Economia Os Descobrimentos Henriquinos*, Lisbon.

GUILMARTIN, John F. (1974) — *Gunpowder and Galleys*, Cambridge, Mass.

HAGERDON, Bernhard (1914) — *Die Entwicklung der wichtigsten Schiffstypen bis ins 19. Jahrhundert*, Berlin.

HARING, Charles H. (1918) — *Trade and Navigation between Spain and the Indies in the Times of the Hapsburgs*, Cambridge, Mass.

HEERS, Jacques (1958) — «Type de Navires et Spécialization des Trafics en Méditerranée à la Fin du Moyen Age,» *Actes du Deuxième Colloque International d'Histoire Maritime*, Michel Mollat, ed., Paris: 107-117.

JOHNSTONE, Paul and A. F. TILLEY (1976) — «An Unusual Portuguese Fishing Boat», *The Mariner's Mirror*, 62: 15-21.

KOCHISS, John M. (1978) — «Tagus River Barges and Passenger Carriers», *The Mariner's Mirror*, 64: 169-185.

LANDSTRÖM, Bjorn (1961) — *The Ship*, London.

LEITE, Duarte (1958) — *Historia dos Descobrimentos Colectânea de esparsos*, Lisbon.

LEWIS, Archibald R. (1975) — «The Medieval Background of American Atlantic Development,» *The Atlantic World of Robert G. Albion*, Benjamin W. Labaree, ed., Middletown, Conn.: 18-39.

—— (1976) — «Northern European Sea Power and the Straits of Gibralter, 1031-1350 A. D.,» *Order and Innovation in the Middle Ages: Essays in Honor of Joseph R. Strayer*, Wiliam C. Jordan *et al.*, eds., Princeton: 139-164.

MARQUES, A. H. de Oliveira (1976) — *History of Portugal*, 2 volumes, New York.

—— (1960) — «Navegação Prussiana Para Portugal Nos Principios Do Século XV,» *Revista da Universidade de Coimbra*: 19, 329-349.

—— (1959) — «Navigation entre la Prusse et le Portugal au début du XVe Siècle,» *Vierteljahrschrift für Sozial -und Wirtschaftsgeschichte*, 46: 477-490.

MARTINEZ-HIDALGO, José M. (1966) — *Columbus' Ships*, Barre, Mass.

MAUNY, Raymond (1970) — *Les Siècles Obscurs de l'Afrique Noire Histoire et Archéologie*, Paris.

MAURO, Frédéric (1966) — «Navires et Constructions Navales en Europe Occidentale aux XVIe et XVIIe Siècles Points de Départ pour une Etude Comparée», *Actes du Cinquième Colloque International D'Histoire Maritime*, Michel Mollat, ed., Paris: 183-193.

MORISON, Samuel E. (1940) — *Portuguese Voyages to America in the Fifteenth Century*, Cambridge, Mass.

PARRY, John H. (1963) — *The Age of Reconnaisance*, New York.

"IN MEMORIAM" DO VICE-ALMIRANTE AVELINO TEIXEIRA DA MOTA   249

—— (1975) — *Discovery of the Sea*, London.
—— (1961) — *The Establishment of the European Hegemony, 1415-1715*, New York.
PENROSE, Boies (1952) — *Travel and Discovery in the Renaissance, 1420-1620*, Cambridge, Mass.
PRESTAGE, Edgar (1933) — *The Portuguese Pioneers*, London.
SCAMMELL, Geoffrey V. (1981) — *The World Encompassed The First European Maritime Empire c. 800-1650*, London.
SOTO, José L. Casado (1975) — «Arquitectura naval en el Cantabrico durante el siglo XIII», *Altamira* (Santander), 23-56.
TEIXEIRA DA MOTA, Avelino (1958) — «L'Art de Naviguer en Méditerranée du XIIIe au XVIIe Siècle et la Création de la Navigation Astronomique dans les Océans», *Actes du Deuxième Colloque International d'Histoire Maritime*, Michel Mollat, ed., Paris: 127-148.
—— (1966a) — «Discussion des communications de MM. Denoix, Ferreira David et Gille», *Actes du Cinquième Colloque International D'Histoire Maritime*, Michel Mollat, ed., Paris: 179-181.
—— (1966b) — «Influence de la Cartographie Portugaise sur la Cartographie Européenne à l'Epoque des Découvertes,» *Actes du Cinquième Colloque International D'Histoire Maritime*, Michel Mollat, ed., Paris: 223-248.
—— (1969) — *Der Portugiesische Seehandel in Westafrika im 15. und 16. Jahrhundert und seine Bedeutung für die Entwicklung überregionalen Handelsverkehrs*, Köln.
UNGER, Richard W. (1975) — «Four Dordrecht Ships of the Sixteenth Century,» *The Mariner's Mirror*, 61: 109-116.
VERLINDEN, VERLINDEN, Charles (1980) — «Perspectief-Verschuivingen in de Vroege Geschiedenis der Europese Expansie», *Mededelingen van de Koninklijkke Academie voor Wetenschappen, Letteren en Schone Kunsten van België, Klasse der Letteren*, 42: 3-22.
VOGEL, Walther (1915) — *Geschichte der deutschen Seeschiffahrt*, Volume I, Berlin.

4

Le rôle des capitaux internationaux dans les voyages de découvertes aux XVe et XVIe siècles

Jacques Heers

Les récits des contemporains, chroniqueurs, capitaines et marins mettent surtout l'accent sur le caractère aventureux ou dramatique des grands voyages de découverte ; nouvelles épopées dont les épisodes provoquaient angoisse ou émerveillement, mais où manquent le plus souvent les détails précis sur l'organisation des expéditions.

De ces entreprises, les historiens modernes ont voulu donner une image plus complexe, une analyse plus scientifique. Leurs efforts ont surtout porté sur l'aspect technique du problème : types de navires, évolution des instruments et des techniques de la navigation. Ces études ont fait, depuis peu d'années, des progrès considérables[1]. Beaucoup plus rares sont, au contraire, les travaux qui s'intéressent aux côtés économiques et financiers de l'affaire. On peut se demander, en effet, comment ont été rassemblés les capitaux nécessaires à l'armement des navires, l'entretien des équipages, l'achat des produits offerts en échange aux indigènes des terres lointaines. Dans quelle mesure cet armement, pour des voyages tout de même très risqués où les profits ne paraissaient pas assurés, est-il différent de celui des bâtiments qui naviguent sur les itinéraires du grand trafic maritime, reconnus depuis des siècles ? Les

---

(1) Cf. en particulier les récents travaux des historiens portugais et plus particulièrement ceux du Cdt. Teixeira da Mota ; voir aussi les études rassemblées dans les Actes des précédents Colloques d'Histoire Maritime, surtout : 1957, communication de G. Beaujouau et E. Poulle ; 1957, communication du Cdt. A. Teixeira da Mota.

Cf. d'autre part : J. BENSAUDE, *Histoire de la science nautique portugaise* (résumé), Genève, 1957 ; A. FONTOURA DA COSTA, *A Marinharia dos descobrimentos*, Lisbonne, 1933. ; Cdt. G. LA ROËRIE, *Navires et marins de la rame à l'hélice*, t. I, Paris, 1956. ; sur l'ensemble du sujet : Jaime CORTESÃO, *Os descobrimentos portugueses*, Lisbonne, 1960, t. I et II.

274   *PROBLÈMES ÉCONOMIQUES DE LA DÉCOUVERTE*

hommes d'affaires européens, ceux dont l'audience dépassait le cadre étroit de leur ville, ont-ils pensé aux profits à venir, ont-ils accepté de courir le risque ? Quel rôle revient ainsi aux capitaux internationaux dans la préparation des grands voyages de découverte aux xve et xvie siècles ?

Ce rapport est rédigé par le Professeur J. Heers, de l'Université de Caen, et soumis au Professeur Ch. Verlinden, de l'Université de Gand, qui a fait une série d'observations dont M. Heers a tenu compte.

Mais les réponses varient forcément selon la façon dont on définit le voyage de découverte. On sait, quelques rares et spectaculaires exceptions mises à part, les difficultés pour déterminer avec certitude le « Premier voyage ». Pour tant d'expéditions inventées longtemps après, par intérêt ou chauvinisme des écrivains pressés de vanter l'esprit d'entreprise de leurs pays, combien de voyages inconnus, passés sous silence par souci de discrétion, par désir de se réserver les profits éventuels, un nouveau banc de pêche, un marché plus aisé, à une époque où l'appât du gain l'emportait presque toujours sur le goût de la publicité tapageuse. De toutes façons, avant le premier voyage, officiel, homologué, et qui s'accompagne d'une sorte de prise de possession de la route maritime et des terres découvertes, il faudrait parler de tous ceux, imparfaits, qui l'ont précédé, ont ouvert la voie, perfectionné les techniques et entraîné les équipages ; de toutes ces approches laborieuses, plus obscures, dues au hasard ou à l'obstination des pêcheurs en quête de bancs plus éloignés mais moins fréquents [1].

A l'opposé, faut-il s'en tenir au moment où la route nouvelle est reconnue pour la première fois ? Pendant longtemps elle l'est

---

(1) Cf. l'ouvrage de S.E. MORISON, *Portuguese Voyages to America in the XVth. Century*, Cambridge, Mass., Harvard U.P., 1940, qui après Fr. MACHADO, (*Historia da expansão, portuguesa no mundo*, Lisbonne, 1937, p. 272-273), rappelle que le terme de « découvrir *o* n'était pas toujours utilisé lors d'un premier voyage accidentel et hasardeux ; « découvrir », c'était parfois chercher une terre dont on avait déjà une idée, même imparfaite ou erronée ; sur l'emploi du mot « découvrir » au Portugal, voir aussi J. CORTESÃO dans *Os descobrimentos...*, chapitre intitulé « Que è o Descobrimento ? » (t. II, p. 9 et *sq.*) et encore t. I p. 364 : « Os descobrimentos fez-se certamente por saltos... ou por fases sucessivas e sobre postas em que a um primeiro descobrimento global se seguia o reconhecimento metodico dos acidentes e os contactos comerciais com os indigenas, no interior dos estuarios » (sur les côtes d'Afrique). Cependant, M. Verlinden fait précisément remarquer que, bien souvent, la distinction entre voyage de « découverte » et voyage commercial n'est pas très aisée à définir.

D'autre part, S.E. MORISON étudie le problème des « premiers voyages » portugais en Amérique, eeux qui auraient précédé Colomb ou Pedro Alvares Cabral. Ses conclusions nient l'existence de ces voyages. Pour la thèse contraire, voir en particulier : M. HELENO, *O descobrimento da America*, Lisbonne, 1933. J. CORTESÃO, « Pre-Columbian Discovery of America », dans *Geographical Journal*, C 1937. E. PRESTAGE, *The Portuguese Pioneers*, Londres, 1933. S. LARSEN, *La découverte de l'Amérique septentrionale en 1472-1473 par les Danois et les Portugais*, Coïmbre, 1926. Voir aussi : CH. VERLINDEN, « Un précurseur de Colomb : Le Flamand Ferdinand van Olmen (1487) », *Revista Portuguesa de História*, X, Coïmbre, 1963.

encore très mal et il faudra parfois plusieurs voyages avant que l'on puisse s'y risquer sans crainte, assuré des escales, du régime des vents, des mauvais passages à éviter. La « découverte » ne cesse que lorsque le voyage d'exploration cède le pas au véritable trafic, à la routine marchande qui, à l'avance, peut calculer ses profits. Moment crucial, mais bien difficile à préciser car il varie considérablement selon les difficultés du trajet, les moyens mis en œuvre, l'importance des bénéfices escomptés, la concurrence des nations rivales. Une étude des assurances maritimes permettrait sans doute de situer avec précision ce passage ; il faudrait déterminer à partir de quel voyage les risques ont été volontiers couverts par les assureurs ou, s'ils l'ont été dès le début, à quelle date la prime se stabilise et le taux de l'assurance se rapproche de celui demandé sur les itinéraires du trafic traditionnel. Mais cette étude de l'assurance des grands voyages de découvertes et du premier trafic commercial reste, semble-t-il, à faire.

De toutes façons, les hommes d'affaires qui savent calculer les risques, qui ne cherchent pas l'acte gratuit, ont su voir ce moment. Faut-il penser qu'ils l'aient attendu pour investir leurs capitaux ? Avant d'étudier les faits, on conçoit aisément qu'une connaissance de la mentalité du capitaliste, et de son attitude : goût du risque, esprit d'entreprise ou timidité et recherche des seuls profits certains, apporte déjà des éléments de réponse ; attitude à vrai dire fortement influencée par les difficultés économiques, la conjoncture de l'époque. Les « temps difficiles », là où ils sévissent, sont-ils favorables à de tels investissements ?

Cependant cette participation du grand capitalisme de l'époque semblait-elle nécessaire, indispensable, à l'armement des navires ? Les voyages de découvertes ont-ils été, du point de vue financier, une affaire importante ?

A première vue on est frappé par la modestie, la médiocrité des moyens mis en œuvre tout au long du xve siècle et encore très tard au xvie siècle. Les navires sont peu nombreux, deux ou trois dans la plupart des cas ; parfois un seul : pour Jean Cabot au printemps de 1497, ou pour Paulmier de Bonneville en 1503 [1]. Mais surtout ce sont des bâtiments de faible importance. Navires atlantiques presque toujours dont, dès le début du xve siècle, le tonnage est exprimé en tonneaux ; navires aptes à la navigation en estuaire ou sur les côtes difficiles ; en somme navires d'exploration capables

---

(1) Pour le nombre de caravelles employées lors des voyages de découverte, entre le cap Bojador et le cap Vert, cf. la carte établie par J. CORTESÃO (*Os descobrimentos...*, t. I, p. 283) : à chaque fois un seul bâtiment ; sauf cependant en 1444 où on note six caravelles avec Lançarote, mais ce n'est pas là un véritable voyage de première exploration ; la même année, Dias va beaucoup plus au Sud, jusqu'au cap Vert, mais avec un seul navire.

d'être conduits dans les passes les plus dangereuses, maniables, de faible tirant d'eau. C'est sans aucun doute le gros avantage du vaisseau atlantique, et en particulier de la caravelle, sur son rival méditerranéen, beaucoup plus lourd, construit pour des trafics assurés et sans surprise. Les Castillans et les Portugais ont ainsi choisi très régulièrement, au début du moins, pour leurs voyages d'exploration les unités les plus légères, bien plus faibles que celles dont ils se servaient pour leurs commerces réguliers à la même époque ou peu de temps auparavant. Face aux quelque 300 tonneaux des navires basques qui, très nombreux, sillonnent depuis le début du xve siècle toutes les routes de la Méditerranée, les caravelles de Colomb ne jaugent que 120, et 60 tonneaux ; les cinq navires de Magellan lancés pourtant dans une entreprise que l'on sait dangereuse mais peut-être aussi très profitable, n'ont que 130, 130, 90, 60 et 60 tonneaux. En Angleterre, le 15 juillet 1840, c'est avec un bâtiment de 80 tonneaux que Thomas Lloyd, « le meilleur marin d'Angleterre » prend la mer pour atteindre de nouvelles terres loin à l'Ouest de l'Irlande [1].

Et cette prédilection pour le petit navire se maintient fort longtemps. Celui de Jean Cabot, lors du premier voyage en 1497, n'a que 18 hommes d'équipage [2]; l' « Espoir » de Gonneville qui en a pourtant 60 ne fait que 120 tonneaux [3], la « Pensée » et le « Sacre » de Jean et Raoul Parmentier en 1529, 200 et 120 tonneaux [4]; et ce ne sont pas non plus ses plus gros navires qu'à Dieppe Jean Ango arme pour les expéditions lointaines [5]. Pour le second voyage de Jean Cabot, les marchands de Bristol n'ont donné que quatre « petits navires » [6], alors que dès 1480 ils en construisaient qui atteignaient 500 tonneaux [7]; mais ces derniers étaient pour le commerce. Un peu plus tard, le « Paul » de Plymouth en route vers le Brésil (mais est-ce encore une découverte ?) fait tout au plus 250 tonneaux [8]; et en 1552-1553 à la flotte de Thomas Windham qui lève l'ancre pour la deuxième fois vers la Guinée avec le « Lyon » de 150 tonneaux, le « Buttolfe » de 150 tonneaux et une caravelle portugaise

---

(1) S.E. Morison, *op. cit.*, p. 51 ; à leur tour les Castillans achètent, au début du xvie siècle, des caravelles aux Portugais pour leur trafic de semi-cabotage dans la Mer des Antilles, (J. Cortesão, *Os descobrimentos...*, p. 328-329).

(2) J.A. Williamson, *A Short History of British Expansion*, t. I, *The Old Colonial Empire*, Londres, 1941, p. 68-69.

(3) M. Mollat, *Le commerce maritime normand à la fin du Moyen Age*, Paris, 1952, p. 250.

(4) Ch.-A. Julien, *Les débuts de l'expansion et de la colonisation françaises*, Paris, 1947, p. 100.

(5) *Ibidem*, p. 98 et M. Mollat, *op. cit.*, pp. 342, 501 *sqq.*

(6) J.A. Williamson, *op. cit.*, p. 70.

(7) Cf. Miss Carus-Wilson, *The Overseas Trade of Bristol*, Londres 1954 ; navires armés par W. Canynges (la *Mary Caninges* de 400 t., la *Mary Redcliffe* de 500 t.).

(8) J.W. Blake, *Europeans in West Africa*, 1450-1560, Londres, 1942, 2 vol., p. 249.

de 60 tonneaux [1], répond celle des Merchants Adventurers en quête du passage du Cathay par le Nord-Est, dont les trois navires jaugent respectivement 160, 120 et 90 tonneaux [2]. Et pourtant à cette époque on savait armer en Angleterre des bâtiments beaucoup plus puissants : le « Great Harry » de 1 500 tonneaux en 1514, le « New Great Harry » de 1 000 tonneaux en 1539 et ces six navires de plus de 500 tonneaux que comptait, parmi ses 53 vaisseaux, la marine anglaise à la fin du règne de Henry VIII [3].

Même politique dans les ports normands où l'on note aussi une nette opposition entre le petit navire des premiers voyages lointains, et ceux plus puissants armés pour le commerce. Lors de son second voyage, en 1535, J. Cartier ne commande que trois faibles bâtiments : l' « Ermillon » de 40 tonneaux, la « Petite Hermine » de 60 tonneaux, et la « Grande Hermine » de 110 tonneaux.

Dans ces conditions, la mise sur pied d'un navire ou d'une flotte de découverte ne demande que des investissements très limités. Investissements qui, semble-t-il, peuvent être dans la plupart des cas aisément réunis sur place. Comment comparer le prix de revient de ces navires, de ces esquifs, à celui des vaisseaux de commerce de l'époque : galées ou énormes nefs de Florence, Venise et Gênes qui jaugent de 400 à 1 500 tonnes métriques, kogge de la Hanse, nefs et barques de Marseille ou de Catalogne, de Séville, ou encore ces basques et portugais de Méditerranée dont on parlait tout à l'heure ?

Les deux navires que Louis XI envoie au Cap Vert en 1483, avec 300 soldats pourtant, ne lui ont coûté que 1 000 écus [4]. Les Sociétés, fondées à l'occasion des grands voyages du début du XVIe siècle n'engagent encore que des capitaux assez modestes ; pour Verrazzano, en 1523, certains actionnaires n'ont donné que 100, 200 ou 300 écus [5]; en 1526, l'association Jean Ango-amiral Chabot a dépensé environ 4 000 livres pour les deux galéasses de l'amiral, et 2 000 pour la nef du vicomte de Dieppe [6]. Certes les dépenses engagées en Castille, lors des expéditions de Colomb et Magellan paraissent plus importantes ; on a estimé celles de la flotte de Palos à 2 millions de maravedis, et l'on sait que celle du tour du monde

---

(1) *Ibidem*, p. 305.

(2) J.A. WILLIAMSON, *op. cit.*, p. 87.

(3) *Ibidem*, p. 78-80.

(4) Ch. de LA RONCIÈRE, *Histoire de la marine française*, t. II, p. 391 (en 1483) ; cf. aussi R. GANDILHON, *La politique économique de Louis XI*, Paris, 1941.

(5) LA RONCIÈRE, *op. cit.*, t. III, p. 258.

(6) La Société formée à cette occasion rassemblait au total un capital de 20 000 livres (cf. LA RONCIÈRE, *op. cit.*, t. III, p. 265).

a mobilisé au départ 9 millions de maravedis [1]; soit respectivement environ 5 000 et 24 000 doubles de Castille. Mais ces chiffres sont sans doute bien supérieurs à la propre valeur des navires; pour les cinq bâtiments de Magellan il n'a fallu que 4 millions de maravedis [2].

Or dès le milieu du xve siècle, il fallait dépenser à Gênes environ la valeur de *600* à *800* doubles castillanes rien que pour acheter le bois brut nécessaire à la construction d'une nef ; le mât principal coûtait facilement *1 000* doubles et il fallait encore, pour ne citer que le principal, *1 400* à *1 500* doubles pour les voiles et les cordages. Complètement terminée et armée, une nef de Gênes valait facilement *8 000* à *10 000* doubles [3].

Chez les Italiens donc, et pour le commerce, l'apport de grand capital était indispensable, ou du moins la participation d'hommes d'affaires puissants, disposant de moyens considérables. Tout au contraire la caravelle, ou tout navire utilisé lors des premières découvertes, est une *production artisanale ;* elle demande assez peu de matériel, peu d'argent aussi ; seulement une grande habileté et une belle expérience technique. Ceci explique sans doute que ces navires, les plus glorieux de l'époque, aient été construits et armés non pas dans les grands ports qui disposaient des capitaux et s'adonnaient avant tout au grand trafic et à la banque, mais dans ceux où la vie maritime était restée plus simple, limitée à l'armement et aux transports, souvent pour le compte des étrangers, vers les grands marchés étrangers. Il existe, à la fin du Moyen Age, *une sorte de divorce* entre les très grands ports de commerce, et ceux beaucoup plus nombreux où la vie maritime est encore en plein essor ; entre, d'une part l'activité des Italiens qui connaît une assez étroite spécialisation au service de quelques rares itinéraires et trafics, et d'autre part celle des Ibériques beaucoup plus variée et entreprenante.

Les voyages de découverte furent ainsi non pas l'œuvre des grands capitalistes italiens qui, maîtres de gros profits, négligent quantités de secteurs et paient les gens d'Espagne et de Lisbonne pour assurer leur propre ravitaillement [4], mais des Atlantiques qui sont encore plus marins que négociants. Ils furent l'œuvre davantage des petits ports, basques ou portugais, et de Palos, que de Séville ou Cadix; en Angleterre aussi, les marins de Bristol ont joué un rôle beaucoup plus important que les gros marchands ou financiers

---

(1) St. Zweig, *Magellan*, Paris, 1953, p. 321 et *sq.*

(2) *Ibidem.*

(3) Cf. J. Heers, *Gênes au xve siècle*, Paris, 1961.

(4) Cf. J. Heers, « Navires et marchands basques en Méditerranée », dans *Bulletin Hispanique*, 1955.

italiens de Londres. Question de tradition, d'expérience et de savoir faire, plus que d'argent.

C'est souvent quant à l'armement du moins, une entreprise modeste, parfois obscure. Une des caravelles de Colomb, la « Pinta », était la propriété des membres de l'équipage.

En outre, les cargaisons emportées ne représentent la plupart du temps que de faibles sommes. Ce sont de pauvres marchandises destinées aux opérations de troc avec les indigènes, de la pacotille, objet de la petite industrie locale : clous, quincaillerie, peignes, miroirs et bimbeloterie, chandeliers, montres et horloges tout au plus. Peu d'étoffes et toujours des toiles, non des draps. Ajoutons les perles dont Venise avait pu se réserver une sorte de monopole et dont les Français qui les appellent les « rassades de voires » chargent six quintaux sur l' « Espoir », en 1503. Au total, tout de même, choses sans grande valeur, « besognes de petit prix » [1]. Magellan qui pourtant va chercher des épices dans l'Océan Indien, là où les marchands sont difficiles, ne prend à bord que pour 1 700 000 maravédis de marchandises pour commencer [2], soit à peine 4 500 doubles ; somme suffisante certes pour que l'on fasse appel à un vrai marchand, Cristobla de Haro, mais qui reste cependant plusieurs fois (20 ou 30 fois souvent) inférieure à la valeur des marchandises chargées par les Italiens sur un seul de leurs navires au départ de Levant ou d'Angleterre.

Bâtiments peu nombreux et modestes, investissements en marchandises bien plus médiocres encore, le voyage de découverte reste, du point de vue financier, une petite affaire comparée à l'entreprise commerciale classique, qui emprunte les itinéraires reconnus et qui, elle, ne peut se passer des capitaux internationaux.

Aussi faut-il constater que nombre d'expéditions maritimes lancées à l'aventure vers des terres inconnues ont été préparées par des gens qui ne disposaient parfois que de très faibles moyens. Souvent ce sont de simples entreprises individuelles ou familiales. Lorsqu'en 1402, Jean de Béthencourt quitte la Normandie, il doit, pour acheter un navire, hypothéquer une bonne part de ses biens [3]; ainsi fut montée, avec des ressources très limitées, la grande expédition normande. Autres aventuriers conquérants : les Gascons de Peyrot de Monluc qui, en 1566, vendent ou engagent leurs terres pour, avec 800 hommes, aller découvrir et conquérir une base afri-

(1) Ch.-A. JULIEN, *Les Français en Amérique pendant la première moitié du* XVIe *siècle*, Paris, 1946, p. 29.

(2) St. ZWEIG, *op. cit.*, tables en appendice.

(3) M. MOLLAT, « La place de la conquête normande dans l'histoire coloniale française », *Anuario de Estudios Atlanticos*, Madrid, 1958.

caine d'où ils auraient pu intercepter le trafic des épices; ils réussissent ainsi à armer deux navires guidés par deux pilotes portugais, et deux « roberges » pour porter les hommes [1]; expédition malheureuse dont le seul résultat fut, désastreux à tous points de vue, le sac de Funchal, mais qui prouve que, sans appui des marchands hommes ou d'affaires, on pouvait ainsi se lancer sur les mers, à l'aventure.

Il faudrait aussi réserver une large place aux découvertes, mal connues, des pêcheurs qui, par leurs approches laborieuses, souvent secrètes, ont permis ensuite de lancer sur les mêmes routes devenues plus familières des navires de « découvreurs », puis de marchands. Sans les renseignements, incomplets sans doute et difficiles à obtenir et à interpréter, des patrons pêcheurs on expliquerait mal les succès des découvertes dans l'Atlantique Nord. Très tôt, au xv⁰ siècle, les pêcheurs de Hull et de Bristol ont trouvé la route directe vers l'Islande sans passer par Bergen, sur de très petits bâtiments, ouvrant la voie aux marchands de Bristol qui ne sont venus que plusieurs années après, sur de plus gros navires ; plus tard encore, ces pêcheurs anglais, délaissant l'Islande où leurs campagnes étaient toujours plus difficiles, se sont lancés vers le Nord-Ouest jusqu'aux bancs lointains de Terre-Neuve. De même pour les patrons bretons et normands qui, eux aussi, ont fréquenté ces passages ; de là sans doute l'expérience des ports français de la Manche pour ces lointains voyages et l'habileté des pilotes de Dieppe et de Saint-Malo. De même enfin pour les Basques, ou pour les Portugais de Lisbonne et des Açores (ces derniers également pilotes réputés et fort recherchés au xvi⁰ siècle) qui entreprenaient de grandes expéditions pour la pêche à la baleine dans les mers nordiques et ont alors exploré toute la Baie d'Hudson [2].

Sans aucun doute, toutes ces activités des pêcheurs d'Occident étaient à l'époque purement artisanales ; les hommes d'affaires du port ne s'y intéressaient pas toujours, et jamais en tout cas les financiers internationaux. La pêche est affaire de petites gens ; sauf parfois en Andalousie, ou en Méditerranée où l'exploitation des madragues [3] et des pêcheries de corail [4] attire les grandes

---

(1) Ch.-A. Julien, *Les débuts...*, p. 263-266.

(2) Sur le rôle des pêcheurs espagnols et portugais dans le mouvement d'expansion vers les terres lointaines, Cf. H.P. Biggar, *Precursors of Cartier*, et aussi S.E. Morison, *op. cit.*, qui rappelle que Terre-Neuve fut d'abord appelée par les Espagnols « Tierra de los Bacallãos » et que les gens des Açores cherchaient constamment de nouvelles terres pour leur propre compte, et ceci bien après la découverte de l'Amérique, jusqu'en 1770.

(3) Celles d'Andalousie affermées par le duc de Medina Sidonia et exploitées par des Génois ; celles de Sousse, également exploitées par une Compagnie Génoise (cf. R. Brunschvig, *Deux récits de voyages en Afrique du Nord au xv⁰ siècle*, Paris, 1936).

(4) Celles de la Calle surtout, près de Bône ; cf. O. Pastine, *L'arte dei corallieri...*, Gênes, 1933 ; cf. ensuite les études sur le « Bastion de France ».

maisons de commerce de Venise et Gênes ; mais ce sont là des entre-prises assurées d'importants profits, de véritables routines, une industrie en somme qui n'a rien à voir avec la découverte.

En dehors même des chevaliers aventuriers, découvreurs ou conquérants, et des obscurs et anonymes patrons pêcheurs, les arma-teurs ou marchands ont été souvent à l'origine des grands voyages de découvertes sans recevoir, pour cela, l'aide des hommes d'affaires maîtres du trafic international ; ils se contentent aisément de leurs propres capitaux ou de ceux qu'ils ont pu recueillir sur place parmi les gens de leur milieu. Au début du xviᵉ siècle, lorsque Paulmier de Gonneville revient de son séjour à Lisbonne, il forme une société de 9 armateurs ou marchands tous bourgeois de Honfleur pour armer un seul navire [1]; malgré l'importance des relations écono-miques entre Honfleur et Lisbonne, ou Séville [2], on ne peut parler ici de capitaux internationaux. De même d'ailleurs pour les mar-chands de Bristol, qui eux aussi fréquentent très volontiers Lisbonne et Séville, y font de longs séjours [3], mais restent cependant des hommes d'affaires dont l'audience ne dépasse pas un cadre assez étroit. Et lorsqu'en 1501 le roi Henry VII avait accordé à Sébastien Cabot licence de monter une expédition pour découvrir « toute terre non encore occupée par des Chrétiens », le marin avait trouvé l'argent chez ces hommes de Bristol, aidés par trois Portugais, pilotes sans doute, nés aux Açores [4]. C'est avec son propre navire que W. Hawkins entreprit le voyage au Brésil en 1530.

Les Pinzon qui ont permis, assure-t-on, le voyage de Colomb en s'engageant, soit directement, soit sous forme de prêts, pour environ un million de maravédis, ne sont que des armateurs de Palos, port actif sans doute et en plein essor, mais où les compagnies étrangères ne semblent avoir qu'un rôle bien médiocre, inférieur en tout cas à celui qu'elles tiennent à Séville, Cadix ou San Lucar. A Bristol, Dieppe, Honfleur ou Palos non plus, n'intervien-nent alors les grands hommes d'affaires, capitalistes interna-tionaux.

Au total on doit ainsi considérer que très nombreux sont les voyages de découverte entrepris sans aide immédiate des grands financiers.

---

(1) Ch.-A. JULIEN, *Les Français...*, p. 30.

(2) Ch. VERLINDEN, « The rise of Spanish trade in the middle ages », dans *The Economic History Review*, 1940.

(3) Miss CARUS-WILSON, *The Overseas Trade...*, et B. PENROSE, *Travel and Discovery in the Renaissance, 1420-1620*, Cambridge, Mass., 1955, p. 170.

(4) *Ibidem*, p. 143-144, et J.A. WILLIAMSON, *op. cit.*, p. 75 et *sq.*

Pourtant, ils interviennent parfois, dans des conditions qu'il n'est pas toujours facile de préciser. Tel est le cas d'abord des *entreprises officielles*, conçues et réalisées sous l'autorité du souverain. Ici l'origine des capitaux est souvent incertaine : le roi lui-même, quelque grand personnage, le trésor de l'État, avec bien souvent une participation du capital privé ; mais celle-ci n'est pas forcément importante. On sait que la Couronne aurait fourni à elle seule un million de maravédis sur les deux millions qu'aurait coûté le premier voyage de Colomb [1]. Sur les 9 millions de maravédis rassemblés pour le départ de Magellan, Cristobal de Haro, riche marchand d'Anvers qui a séjourné à Lisbonne, entretient d'étroites relations avec les banquiers allemands, et que l'on présente volontiers comme le capitaliste, le financier de l'expédition, a donné moins de deux millions ; expédition d'ailleurs malheureuse du point de vue commercial et financier car elle ne permit de distribuer au retour, après plus de 1 000 jours de navigation et la vente des 533 quintaux de poivre, qu'un profit de 4 %.

Mais comment apprécier et définir la part des capitaux et des marchands dans les explorations organisées par les souverains portugais le long des côtes d'Afrique et vers les îles, à la recherche du marché de l'or et plus tard de la route de l'Océan Indien ? Les premiers voyages préparés par Henri le Navigateur semblent vraiment des voyages de découvertes, des entreprises scientifiques; or ces aventures n'engagent qu'une ou deux caravelles, conduites par des gentilshommes, chevaliers et en somme serviteurs du Roi : un Gil Eanes par exemple, ou l'échanson Alfonso Baldaya, ou encore le plus entreprenant, Pedro de Sintra ; tous des hommes d'action et capitaines, plus qu'hommes d'argent. Lorsque le Roi fait appel à des étrangers, génois ou vénitiens, Antonio da Noli, Antonio Usodimare, Ca di Mosto, ce sont encore des capitaines, pilotes, personnages plus ou moins isolés, en quête d'aventures et de profits exceptionnels, animés par le goût du risque, et non des hommes d'affaires disposant de moyens considérables [2].

---

(1) S. de Madariaga, *C. Colomb*, Paris, 1951.

(2) Ainsi Ferdinand van Olm (Fernão Dulmo), flamand établi aux Açores mais aussi gentilhomme de la maison royale; en 1486, lettres patentes qui lui réservent toute terre à découvrir vers l'Ouest ; il s'associe ensuite avec Alfonso do Estreito de Funchal qui lui fournit deux caravelles ; ils ont avec eux un « chevalier allemand » (Cf. S.E. Morison, p. 45-46).

Pourtant J. Cortesão (*Os descobrimentos...*, t. I, p. 352) reprenant les indications de R. Caddeo, présente A. Usodimare comme un homme « de grandes possibilités financières »; mais ce que l'on peut savoir de l'activité économique génoise à l'époque, permet d'avancer que les affirmations de Caddeo semblentbien trop optimistes. Le fait qu'il possède des titres de la *Casa di San Giorgio* ne prouve pas que l'homme appartienne au milieu des hommes d'affaires de la cité ; plus de 10 000 personnes sont alors inscrites sur les registres de la *Casa*, très souvent pour des sommes dérisoires.

Pour la politique d'Henri le Navigateur, voir enfin : Duarte Leite, *Historia dos descobrimentos — Colectanea e espansão*, publiée par V. Magalhães Godinho, Lisbonne, 1958.

On ne peut considérer leur participation à la découverte des îles de l'Atlantique et des côtes d'Afrique, comme une intervention du capitalisme international.

Après la mort d'Henri le Navigateur les circonstances ne sont plus les mêmes. Certaines entreprises sont directement organisées par les grands marchands, isolés ou groupés en sociétés disposant d'importants capitaux, rassemblés dans les centres bancaires de l'époque. Dès 1496, Alfonso V afferme pour cinq années le droit de commercer en Guinée à un marchand de Lisbonne nommé Fernão Gomes ; celui-ci s'engageait non seulement à payer chaque année 60 000 cruzados d'or et à réserver au Roi tout l'ivoire récolté, mais à découvrir, au moins tous les ans, 100 lieues de côtes vers le Sud [1]. C'était laisser l'exploration aux mains d'un particulier, qui n'était certes pas une des grandes puissances du moment mais qui, financier de Lisbonne, disposait cependant d'importants moyens et pouvait compter sur les maisons italiennes établies dans la capitale. Pendant quelques années le fermier du Roi ne s'occupa que du commerce des esclaves ; mais les explorations reprennent ensuite : 1470 la Côte d'Ivoire, 1741 arrivée de ses pilotes, João de Santarem et Pedro de Escobar à la Mina de la Côte de l'Or, 1474 atteinte du Cap Sainte-Catherine au-delà de l'équateur. A vrai dire cet intermède privé et capitaliste dans l'histoire des découvertes portugaises en Afrique ne s'impose pas d'une façon définitive. Avec João II les voyages sont de nouveau organisés par le Roi, les navires commandés par des familiers du souverain [2].

En d'autres pays, et sur d'autres routes, les exemples de grands voyages financés directement par le grand capital ne manquent pas. Le cas le plus net est peut-être, en France, celui des 4 voyages de Verrazano au départ des ports normands. Ceux de 1520 et 1528 ont été mis sur pied grâce au capitalisme international : banque florentine de Rouen et surtout de Lyon avec les Guadagni, Albizzi, Buonaccorsi, Nasi ; Lombards de Paris avec leur « principal », Cipriano Relia ; gros marchands de Rouen [3]. Navigateur d'origine florentine, Verrazano était apparenté aux Ruccellai [4]. Pierre Rousselay, marchand de Rouen, allié à ceux de Lyon, l'a puissamment soutenu ; comme un peu plus tard Mario et Allessandro Rousselay pouvaient

---

(1) J.W. BLAKE, *op. cit.*, p. 67 et *sq.*

(2) En 1473, le roi cède à l'avance à Gonçalves de Camara, pour les services rendus en Afrique, « une île à découvrir par lui-même ou les navires envoyés en son nom » ; de même en 1474 pour Fernão Teles. (Cf. S.E. MORISON, p. 32) ; aventuriers en somme tous ces seigneurs qui reçoivent du Roi, avant de partir, une « promesa da capytanya de qualquer ilha que descubryr ».

(3) M. MOLLAT, *op. cit.*, p. 250 à 253.

(4) LA RONCIÈRE, *op. cit.*, t. III, p. 245-247, 258-260.

cautionner un autre grand voyageur, Girolamo Fer, descendant d'une vieille famille de patrons de Savone. L'expédition de 1526 fut, elle, surtout patronnée par des Français, mais toujours de puissants personnages : Ango l'armateur de Dieppe, l'amiral Chabot qui fournit deux galions, un bourgeois de Lyon, Adam Godefroy, Prud-homme qui était général des finances de Normandie, et aussi Pietro de Spinola, manifestement un marchand génois installé depuis peu en France [1]. Ainsi ces voyages de Verrazano, dont les fortunes furent assez diverses, semblent bien l'œuvre des grands bourgeois et finan-ciers des ports normands, ou des banques italiennes de Lyon.

Les grandes maisons allemandes ne sont pas restées inactives. On sait le rôle des Welser dans les années 1531-1534 et de leurs facteurs Ehringer et Federmann au Venezuela pour reconnaître les côtes du lac Maracaïbo ou les régions de l'intérieur [2]; type même des expéditions privées et capitalistes organisées par des fermiers qui disposent de grands moyens. En Angleterre, les voyages de découvertes furent plus volontiers subventionnés par des associa-tions particulières, formées tout exprès à cette occasion. Ainsi la « fellowship and company » qui groupe cinq ou six marchands de Londres pour préparer, en 1540, le second voyage de Thomas Windham [3]. Ainsi celle fondée en 1555 pour l'armement de la « Grace of God » que J. Hopkins veut conduire en Guinée ; mais on trouve, parmi les actionnaires, à côté de gros marchands de la Cité de Londres (dont le futur Lord Maire, sir Th. White, un des promoteurs un peu plus tard de la Moscovy Company), des gens dont la situation semble bien plus modeste : des tailleurs et des peaussiers [4].

Beaucoup plus significatives sont les véritables compagnies de découvertes, fondées pour plusieurs années et poursuivant un but précis. C'est en 1552 que Sébastien Cabot qui avait déjà obtenu pour son premier voyage d'importants capitaux de plusieurs grands armateurs de Séville, réussit à mettre sur pied une Compagnie pour l'aider à trouver le passages vers le Cathy par le Nord-Ouest. La Société compte plusieurs grands nobles anglais (le duc d'Arundel, de Bedford), des personnalités très en vue (Th. Gresham, sir G. Bar-nes) et de nombreux marchands de Londres ; le capital est au total

---

(1) *Ibidem*, III, p. 265.
(2) R. EHRENBERG, *Le temps des Függer*, trad. française, Paris, 1957, p. 91. M.T. SCHÖRER, « Notas para o estudo das relaçoes dos banqueiros alemâes con o empreemdimento colonial dos paises ibéricos na América no seculo XVI », dans *Revista de Historia*, São Paulo, 1957, p. 275-355. Cf. aussi : J. HUMBERT, *L'occupation allemande du Venezuela au XVIe siècle, période dite des Welser*, 1528-1558, Paris, 1905. G. ARCINIEGES, *Germans in the Conquest of America. A 16 th Century Venture*, New York, 1943.
(3) J.W. BLAKE, *op. cit.*, p. 305.
(4) *Ibidem*, p. 347.

de 6 000 livres sterlings, réparties en parts de 25 livres ; cette Compagnie des « Merchants Adventurers of England for the Discovery of lands, isles, dominions and seignories unknown », devait prendre plus tard le nom de « Muscovy Company »[1]. En 1586, autre grosse affaire : celle de sir Th. Cavendish qui obtient de la Couronne une charte de 15 ans et dispose d'un capital initial de plus de 30 000 Lb. st., ensuite porté à 70 000 Lb. st.[2]; ce sont là des moyens considérables qui témoignent de l'entrée en jeu du grand capitalisme.

Mais toutes ces expéditions montées par des compagnies privées, peuvent-elles être réellement qualifiées de « voyages de découverte » ? Dans la plupart des cas, il ne semble pas. Leur caractère a été nettement souligné par M. M. Mollat lorsqu'il étudie les voyages au départ des ports normands[3]. Dès 1503 l'itinéraire de l' « Espoir » était précisé à l'avance et son capitaine se comporte au Brésil surtout comme un marchand. De même les Parmentier cherchaient avant tout à réaliser des opérations commerciales sur des itinéraires et des marchés bien reconnus. Quant aux voyages de Verrazano, dès 1527 la recherche des terres inconnues est définitivement reléguée au second plan et M. Mollat conclut à leur sujet :

« Trois d'entre eux furent des entreprises purement commerciales. Les projets d'exploration n'avaient pas trouvé beaucoup d'écho auprès des marchands ».

Il est très net que les Florentins de Lyon, empressés à financer l'expédition de 1523, aient laissé aux Normands le soin de prendre à leur charge celle de 1526 et ne sont revenus, après le succès de celle-ci, à coup sûr, qu'en 1528. De même les grands marchands de Londres qui avaient fourni de l'argent à Jean Cabot en 1498, déçus par l'échec commercial et financier de l'expédition, se tiennent désormais à l'écart pendant une quinzaine d'années et laissent aux gens de Bristol, plus actifs, plus tentés par le risque, le soin d'intervenir ; ce sont eux qui, en 1501, s'associent aux pilotes portugais. La première expédition de Sébastien Cabot financée par la Compagnie de Londres, qui aboutit à la découverte d'une nouvelle route maritime jusqu'à Arkangelsk, s'est soldée par un tel succès commercial que les armateurs ne se sont plus préoccupés que de commerce

---

(1) J.A. WILLIAMSON, *op. cit.*, p. 87, et B. PENROSE, *op. cit.*, p. 170, 175-6.
(2) *Ibidem*, p. 189-190.
(3) M. MOLLAT, *op. cit.*, p. 256.

et que la découverte du Passage par le Nord-Est ne fut plus qu'un objectif très lointain et secondaire ; les explorations ne reprennent qu'en 1580 avec le voyage d'Arthur Pet et Charles Jakman [1].

Ainsi est-il difficile de ranger toutes ces dernières entreprises, mises sur pied par les grands financiers, parmi les voyages de découverte proprement dits.

Au total, à ne considérer que l'action directe et immédiate, matérielle en somme, de l'organisation des expéditions et l'armement des navires, il semble donc que le rôle des capitaux internationaux ait été, dans ces grands voyages lointains, généralement assez limité. La véritable exploration est plutôt l'œuvre de marins, d'armateurs ou marchands modestes mais entreprenants, d'artisans, d'aventuriers ou de pêcheurs, ou bien encore des souverains servis par leur propre trésorerie et leurs capitaines. Quelques exceptions mises à part, ce n'est qu'assez tard que la grande finance s'est intéressée à l'affaire, lorsque les routes étaient déjà reconnues et les profits déjà assurés. Commerce et non plus aventure.

Cependant, s'en tenir aux armements et à l'intervention directe, c'est forcément conclure trop vite. Le rôle du capital s'est exercé d'une façon moins facile à définir, assez indirecte, mais en commerce coup plus profonde et solide. Si les grandes maisons de fait beau-et de banque n'ont pas payé, ou rarement, les coques des navires et les équipages, ce sont elles qui presque toujours ont suscité les voyages ; elles qui par leur action diffuse les ont rendu nécessaires. C'est l'essor du capitalisme qui dans une large mesure explique l'expansion maritime et coloniale ; et, pour reprendre la belle formule de F. Braudel :

« Derrière la fortune ibérique, il y a cet élan des XIVe et XVe siècles, cette complicité du capitalisme international [2] ».

C'est en fait dès le Moyen Age qu'il faut rechercher l'action des grands marchands et banquiers dans les futures métropoles commerciales de l'Occident [3].

---

(1) J.A. WILLIAMSON, *op. cit.*, p. 89 et *sq.*

(2) F. BRAUDEL, « La double faillite coloniale de la France », dans *Annales E.S.C.*, 1949.

(3) P. PERAGALLO, *Cenni intorno alla colonia italiana in Portogallo nei secoli* XIV, XV, XVI, Gênes, 1907. H. Sancho de SOPRANIS, « Los Genoveses en la region gaditano-xericiense », dans *Hispania*, Madrid, 1948. Cf. aussi les études récentes de Ch. VERLINDEN, « Navigateurs, marchands et colons italiens au service de la découverte et de la colonisation portugaise sous Henri le Navigateur », dans *Moyen Age*, 1958 et *Rev. belge de Philologie et d'Histoire*, 1958.

Il faut, à vrai dire, remonter jusqu'à l'extrême fin du XIIIe siècle, au moment où s'établissent, par voie de mer, des relations régulières entre les marchés méditerranéens (Levant et Italie) et ceux du Nord, de l'Angleterre et de Flandre. Ces relations sont assurées, pour l'essentiel et pour les grands itinéraires, par les flottes italiennes de Venise, Gênes puis Florence. C'est l'escale italienne qui fit alors la fortune des ports d'Andalousie et de Lisbonne, après avoir fait celles de Tunis et de Palma. Ainsi s'établit et s'affirme sur la carte marchande du monde occidental une sorte de hiérarchie, de rupture même. D'une part les ports visités par le trafic international, actifs et pleins d'allant, d'autre part ceux restés en marge de la route, voués au commerce régional : les ports français de la Méditerranée, de l'Atlantique et même ceux de la Manche. D'où la « première faillite coloniale » de la France. Alors qu'à Séville, Cadix, Lisbonne, les marchands, puis les grands banquiers, suivent les marins et suscitent dans la ville un vaste mouvement d'affaires : développement du trafic, essor de l'armement et des constructions navales, demande considérablement accrue des produits du sol, entrepôt et commissions ; au total, enrichissement et formation d'une riche classe bourgeoise orientée vers le commerce.

On ne saurait trop insister sur l'importance de cette pénétration des pays ibériques par les hommes d'affaires italiens (et plus tard allemands, puisque dès le milieu du XVe siècle les négociants de Ravensburg avaient une grande plantation de canne à sucre près de Valence) [1]. Et cette pénétration est liée, avant tout, à l'escale maritime du grand trafic. A tel point que lorsque Henri le Navigateur s'intéresse aux ports de l'Algarve, aménage Lagos et fonde Sagres tout à l'extrémité du Cap, c'est, dit-on, « afin de créer un marché spécial pour le commerce et pour que les bâtiments passant *de l'Est vers l'Ouest* puissent y faire le point et prendre pilotes et provisions ».

Il ne faut pas d'ailleurs négliger l'autre courant, celui qui a mis les marins ibériques en contact direct avec le domaine méditerranéen, dès la fin du XIIIe siècle ; c'est en Méditerranée sur les itinéraires du ravitaillement italien ou catalan que les patrons des navires basques ou portugais sont allés s'initier aux techniques capitalistes plus évoluées, sont allés surtout faire de l'argent [2]. On

---

(1) Ch. VERLINDEN et M. MOLLAT, « Économie européenne à la fin du Moyen Age », dans *Rapport du Congrès International d'Histoire*, Rome, 1955, p. 899-902 et : C. VINAS Y MEY, « La Economia maritima de Castilla en el Atlantico durante la Baja Edad Media » (communication au même Congrès, résumée dans le vol. VII, p. 230-235).

(2) J. HEERS, « Navires et marchands ... » » et « L'expansion portugaise à la fin du Moyen Age : la Méditerranée », *Bul. Fac. de Letras*, Univ. de Lisbonne, 1956.

s'expliquerait plus difficilement l'essor considérable des marines marchandes ibériques au xvᵉ siècle s'il n'y avait pas eu ce trafic intense du blé de Sicile, ou du sel d'Iviça, toujours au service des grandes maisons de commerce de Gênes, Florence ou Barcelone ; et d'autre part le commerce des laines, du fer et des vins vers l'Angleterre ou la Flandre, cette fois pour les maisons italiennes, espagnoles ou allemandes de Bruges. D'où le développement de ces puissantes institutions maritimes et plus tard marchandes, en Castille : d'abord cette Hermandad de las Marismas, forte association de marins, sorte de Hanse castillane ; puis, à la fin du siècle, le Consulado de Burgos (1494), celui de Bilbao (1511) et l'Universidad de Mareantes de Séville [1]. A l'essor commercial et financier de Séville, grand centre des banques italiennes dans la péninsule, répond celui des villes du Nord de l'Espagne, dont les marchands très tôt vont partout vendre leurs laines mérinos améliorées grâce à l'intervention du capitalisme florentin et génois ; dès la fin du xvᵉ siècle, Burgos centre bancaire de l'intérieur connaît une prospérité remarquable et voit s'affirmer une riche bourgeoisie ; en 1510, les Pardo de Burgos dirigeaient une factorie dans le Sud marocain de Gué portugais et avaient obtenu le monopole de l'exportation du sucre [2]. En 1514, d'autres grands marchands de Burgos, Cristoforo de Haro et son frère Diégo, fondent une importante compagnie pour affermer le commerce avec la Sierra Leone ; un peu plus tard, ils signent avec le Roi Manuel un contrat qui leur donne le droit de « commercer pendant quelques années sur certaines rivières de Guinée » [3]; d'où la fortune du futur commanditaire de Magellan et son goût pour les expéditions lointaines.

Au total il est certain que l'action du capitalisme international fut ici prédominante, surtout, semble-t-il, en Castille où les ports étaient davantage pénétrés par l'influence étrangère, et qui offrait un marché intérieur infiniment plus vaste et plus riche. Ce sont ces capitaux qui ont donné aux États ibériques *les moyens* de préparer le grand mouvement d'expansion maritime et coloniale. Et finalement, en analysant les conséquences de cette pénétration du capitalisme international en Castille, on peut affirmer avec M. Viñas y Mey :

« La considérable exportation des laines, l'abondance des flottes dues au commerce de transit et au développement de l'affrètement et de la vente des navires, en provoquant une large augmentation du numéraire,

---

(1) C. Viñas y Mey, *op. cit.*
(2) M. Mollat, *Commerce maritime...*, p. 246.
(3) J.W. Blake, *op. cit.*, p. 38.

détermina une forte vitalité économique en Castille, et le début du capitalisme, en relation étroite avec celui de Flandre, de Bourgogne et du Portugal dont l'évolution est similaire et parallèle. »

Dans les autres pays d'Occident, l'action fut sans aucun doute plus tardive et limitée. En France ce sont pourtant les Italiens de Lyon et de Rouen qui ont souvent provoqué l'essor financier des deux villes. Situation beaucoup plus nette enfin en Flandre où Anvers doit sa fortune aux grandes maisons étrangères.

Mais les capitaux internationaux n'ont pas seulement donné aux grands ports d'Occident, aux ports ibériques surtout, les moyens techniques, maritimes et financiers d'entreprendre les grandes expéditions d'outre-mer ; ils ont aussi été indirectement *les promoteurs* en suscitant une véritable course aux nouveaux marchés. Ce sont les banques et les maisons de commerce qui ont aussi lancé les hommes et les navires d'Espagne à la recherche de nouvelles terres.

Avant tout, ce dynamisme vise *l'or* : d'abord celui du Soudan que l'on voulait atteindre le plus rapidement possible et que les Portugais, ce fut leur grande fortune, enlevèrent au marché italien et méditerranéen ; puis l'or, beaucoup plus incertain, du Cathay qui suscita pourtant nombre d'entreprises hardies. Ce trafic de l'or à la fin du Moyen Age, n'est pas affaire d'artisans ou d'aventuriers ; il a ses routes régulières, ses grands centres de distribution, il est surtout contrôlé par les grandes banques d'Italie souvent concurrentes. Ces rivalités incitent certes à rechercher les voies les plus directes et le voyage d'Antonio Malfante, en 1447 vers le Touat et l'intérieur du Sahara, sur la route de Tombouctou, voyage commandité par la banque génoise des Centurioni [1] est un parfait exemple d'entreprise, terrestre certes, mais lointaine et risquée, due à l'influence du capitalisme international [2].

L'image des premiers explorateurs lancés à la recherche d'une nouvelle route *des épices*, capable de concurrencer le monopole d'Alexandrie et de Venise, est tellement classique, qu'il semble à peine utile de montrer que ce fut là une des formes d'action du capitalisme international sur les voyages de découverte. Mais encore faut-il préciser les caractères de ce capitalisme nouveau susceptible de s'opposer à celui des Vénitiens. Ainsi s'expliquent, bien sûr, les efforts des Portugais sur la route maritime de l'Inde, ceux de

---

(1) Ch. de La Roncière, *La découverte de l'Afrique au Moyen Age*, 3 vol., Le Caire, 1925-1927, et bibliographie dans A. Sapori, *Le marchand italien au Moyen Age*, Paris, 1951, p. 73.

(2) Même si l'on n'adopte pas complètement la thèse de La Roncière qui fait sans doute la part trop belle à l'influence des grands banquiers dans cette affaire.

Paolo Centurione qui rêve d'une route terrestre directe par la Russie, et plus tard ceux constamment renouvelés des navigateurs en quête du fameux passage du Nord-Ouest.

Mais l'exemple si parfait des épices n'est pas le seul, loin de là. Ce serait une grave erreur d'y voir l'unique moteur de l'expansion maritime. Il faudrait pour cela que le poivre et les drogues, aient été à la fin du Moyen Age, les produits les plus importants du grand trafic international ; ce qui n'est pas du tout exact. Le commerce d'Orient était infiniment plus varié et ne comprenait pas uniquement les produits de l'Inde et des Moluques, mais aussi ceux des terres du Levant méditerranéen, terres souvent exploitées par les Latins au profit des grandes maisons de commerce. Lorsque la conquête turque a interdit l'exploitation des pays d'Orient et ruiné les marchés traditionnels, il a fallu se tourner vers l'Occident. Alors les capitaux internationaux ont provoqué un transfert des colonies de l'Est vers l'Ouest. Transfert qui en bien des cas s'est limité aux rivages de la Tyrrhénienne (alun de Tolfa puis Marañon, soie de Grenade et de Calabre, sucre de l'Algarve et de Malaga), mais qui parfois a suscité un mouvement beaucoup plus ambitieux : la recherche de terres inconnues.

Ainsi le mouvement d'expansion coloniale procède de l'Orient médiéval et latin ; ce qui a amené M. Verlinden à rechercher les « précédents médiévaux » de la colonisation espagnole en Amérique et à en préciser les caractères [1]. M. Magalhães Godinho a bien montré, pour sa part, comment la première phase des grands voyages de découvertes a été provoquée par le « dynamisme » des intérêts capitalistes et en particulier des intérêts sucriers [2]. Recherche des colorants (cochenille, cremex, sang de dragon, pastel), recherche des terres où faire des vins liquoreux qui se vendent au loin, mais surtout, en effet, recherche des terres à sucre. Les plantations de canne jalonnent la prise de possession de l'Occident par les maîtres du commerce international : de Syrie à Chypre, en Crète, Sicile, Andalousie et Algarve, région de Ceuta-Tanger, Sous, Canaries São Tomé ensuite, avant les Antilles et enfin la Nouvelle-Espagne. N'est-ce pas, bien souvent, la recherche de nouvelles terres où développer les plantations qui a ouvert la voie ? Le sucre, culture essentiellement « coloniale », spéculative, de caractère nette-

---

(1) Ch. VERLINDEN, « Les influences médiévales dans la colonisation de l'Amérique », dans *Revista de Historia de America*, Mexico, 1950.

(2) V. MAGALHÃES GODINHO, *A expansão quatrocentista portuguesa*, Lisbonne, 1947. « Les grandes découvertes », dans *Bul. Études Portugaises*, 1952. — *Historia da expansão no mundo*, Lisbonne, 1938.

ment capitaliste, réclame de vastes domaines et surtout une très nombreuse main-d'œuvre.

Le trafic du sucre, et donc l'action des grandes sociétés marchandes qui le contrôlent, explique ainsi celui des *esclaves*. A la recherche des marchés d'esclaves on trouve très vite les grands financiers : génois, florentins, portugais ; en 1486-1488, le trafic du Rio dos Escravos fut affermé par Bartolomeo Marchione, banquier florentin, que l'on retrouve au début du XVIe siècle à la tête d'une société d'hommes d'affaires italiens engagés dans le commerce direct avec l'Inde (en 1504 dit-on, sur les 15 navires de Francisco de Almeira, 3 appartiennent à une société de marchands allemands (Függer, Welser, Hochstetter) et italiens). Car cette intervention du capitalisme international ne se limite pas à reconnaître et à exploiter les parties du littoral déjà découvertes, mais à lancer les navires plus loin, vers d'autres escales. Les colons de l'île de Santiago dans l'archipel du Cap Vert, Portugais certes, mais aussi Génois et Castillans, qui dirigent une bonne part du commerce entre la Guinée et le Portugal, ont aussi lancé leurs navires sur toutes les côtes d'Afrique, du Sénégal à la Sierra Leone ; véritables voyages d'exploration et de découverte qui recherchaient les endroits encore restés à l'écart, remontaient les cours des fleuves prenaient partout contact avec des rives inconnues [1].

De toutes façons, les financiers, en organisant des expéditions sur les côtes de Guinée, même lorsque celles-ci avaient un caractère surtout commercial, ont puissamment aidé les autres grands voyages vers l'Ouest, ceux-ci plus lointains et désintéressés. Ce sont les profits de la traite des Noirs qui ont fourni au Roi les capitaux pour les voyages d'exploration. D'autres voyages ont eu pour résultats de former les équipages, année par année, à la navigation lointaine. Il faut ici insister sur le rôle important des financiers génois de Séville, sans aucun doute avec les Centurioni et Grimaldi les représentants les plus authentiques du grand capitalisme génois. Non contents d'exploiter le domaine castillan : Andalousie et îles des Canaries où ils ont introduit canne à sucre et malvoisie, ils s'en prennent, de Séville, aux marchés portugais d'Afrique. D'où ce trafic interlope des navires de Séville, Palos, San Lucar et Cadix sur les côtes de Guinée ; trafic considérable, capable de concurrencer celui officiel et régulier des Portugais, mais dirigé par les Génois ; dès 1453 une caravelle aventurée dans ces parages portait un marchand génois de Séville [2]. D'où la grande expérience acquise par

---

(1) J.W. BLAKE, *op. cit.*, p. 27 et *sq.*

(2) V. RAU et B.W. DIFFIÉ, « Alleged xv c. portuguese joint-stock companies and the articles of Dr. Fitzler », dans *Bull. of Institute of Historical Research*, 1953, p. 181-199.

les pilotes castillans qui préparent ainsi l'expédition de Colomb ; la plupart des marins de Colomb, et peut-être Martin Pinzon lui-même, ont été entraînés lors de ces voyages de contrebande en Guinée.

Ainsi, par l'essor économique et financier qu'ils ont donné aux pays où se sont installées les maisons de commerce ou banques italiennes puis allemandes et même ibériques, par la compétition qu'ils ont suscitée pour la recherche en Occident de nouveaux marchés capables de prendre le relais de ceux d'Orient, les capitaux internationaux ont joué sans aucun doute un rôle considérable dans le mouvement d'expansion maritime et coloniale aux xvᵉ et xvıᵉ siècles.

Certes, il faut laisser à cette influence du capitalisme et ses limites, et ses caractères particuliers. Mlle Rau a nettement insisté sur ce fait, qu'en ce qui concerne du moins la colonisation, les Portugais ont accompli une œuvre originale et que, se trouvant face à des circonstances très différentes, ils ne pouvaient toujours faire tout le profit des expériences italiennes en Orient [1].

D'autre part, la présence au Portugal ou en Espagne de riches et puissantes familles italiennes n'implique pas forcément l'intervention du grand capitalisme de leur ville d'origine, du moins pas de tous les capitaux. J'ai essayé de le montrer dans une communication ici même au Congrès de 1957, à propos du capitalisme génois à Lisbonne [2]. Les Génois du Portugal même les Lomellini beaucoup plus influents que tous les autres [3] — n'ont plus que des liens très lâches avec les marchands de leur ville. Leurs domaines sont très différents ; ils ne participent pas au trafic Méditerranée-Flandre, mais seulement au grand cabotage atlantique de Lisbonne à Bruges par tous les ports français de l'Atlantique et de la Manche [4]. D'où leur hostilité aux monopoles méditerranéens-vénitiens, florentins, et même génois, et leur empressement à chercher vers l'Ouest d'autres routes et d'autres marchés. Ce sont eux, et non les Génois de Gênes, qui pourront approuver et aider le mouvement d'expansion portugais. Ainsi, à l'origine du moins, l'influence qui l'a

---

(1) *Ibidem*, p. 198.

(2) J. Heers, « Portugais et Génois au xvᵉ siècle : la rivalité Atlantique-Méditerranée », dans *III Colòquio Internacional de Estudos Luso-Brasileiros; Actas*, Vol. II, p. 138-147, Lisbonne, 1960.

(3) V. Rau, « Uma famiglia de mercadores italianos em Portugal no século XV : os Lomellini », dans *Bul. Fac. Letras. Lisboa*, 1956.

(4) Notons que c'est en Irlande, à Galway, qu'Henri le Navigateur a établi un de ses serviteurs, sans doute pour acheter les toiles irlandaises nécessaires au commerce de Guinée (cf. J. Cortesão, *Os descobrimentos...*, I, p. 39, d'après *Cronica dos Feitos de Guinéo*, cap. XCIII).

LE ROLE DES CAPITAUX INTERNATIONAUX 293

emporté fut celle des financiers du lieu, plus prompts à servir les intérêts du pays, plus novateurs aussi. Un capitalisme certes, mais à vocation plus occidentale que celui des villes méditerranéennes encore attachées à leurs traditions. Remarques qui valent peut-être pour d'autres villes et d'autres ports.

Au total, influence certaine du grand capitalisme international sur les voyages de découvertes. Mais sans doute, influence diffuse, profonde, plutôt que rôle de promoteur et d'organisateur.

5
Italian Influences in Iberian Colonization

Charles Verlinden

When studying the beginnings of modern colonization, one must always remember that the Spaniards and Portuguese, who occupied the stage almost alone for more than a century, had the opportunity to make use of the experience gathered by the Italians and above all by the Genoese in the technique of commerce in general, as well as especially in the field of colonial economy, as this economy had gradually developed in their possessions in the Levant and on the shores of the Black Sea. Many features, characteristic of the economic and colonial activity of the Iberian nations, can only be understood when their connection and resemblance with Italian precedents is kept in mind.

Italy was the only really colonizing nation during the middle ages. From the beginning of the crusades onwards, Venice, Pisa, Genoa, later Florence, and southern Italy under the Angevins as well as under the Aragonese, were interested in the Levant and in the economic and colonial possibilities offered there by the gradual waning of the Byzantine empire.[1] It is also at about the same time that Italian merchants appear in the Iberian peninsula, and obtain an influence that will persist until far into the modern period, both in European and colonial economy.[2]

Some facts, for instance the presence of a large number of Italians in Seville and Lisbon in the times of Henry the Navi-

---

[1] A. Schaube, *Handelsgeschichte der Romanischen Völker des Mittelmeergebietes* (Munich-Berlin, 1906); W. Miller, *The Latins in the Levant* (London, 1908), and *idem, Essays on the Latin Orient* (Cambridge, 1921); R. Lopez, *Storia delle colonie genovesi nel Mediterraneo* (Bologna, 1938); R. Dudan, *Il dominio veneziano di Levante* (Bologna, 1938); G. M. Monti, *La espansione mediterranea del Mezzogiorno d'Italia e della Sicilia* (Bologna, 1942); J. Müller, *Documenti sulle relazioni delle città toscane coll' Oriente* (Florence, 1879).

[2] C. Verlinden, "The Rise of Spanish Trade in the Middle Ages," *The Economic History Review*, X (1940) 44 ff., and *idem*, "Le problème de l'expansion commerciale portugaise au moyen age," *Biblos* (Coimbra), XXIII (1948) 453 ff.

gator, Columbus and Vasco da Gama, are well known.[3] But how and when did those Italians arrive there? What kind of influence did they exert? These problems have not yet been sufficiently examined. Nevertheless, many questions arise about them and are crying for a solution. To bring this solution in sight by offering an outline—even though a tentative one—of the evolution from the twelfth century onward is the scope of this paper.

Pisans and Genoese appear in Catalonia at the beginning of the twelfth century. They draw Spain and Portugal into the sphere of the "international" trade of the time. Everywhere along the shores of the Iberian peninsula they create centers for an activity marked by long-distance maritime trade. They seem the torch-bearers of economic progress and surround the peninsula as a wood-shed to which they set fire from every side. But destruction is not brought by them; new life awakes which they help to keep active together with Iberian merchants and seamen.

Everywhere, thus, along the eastern and western coasts of the Iberian peninsula Italians animate during the twelfth century the economic revival and the long-distance sea trade. Genoese and Pisans play the leading part. During the thirteenth century the influence of the Genoese increases, that of the Pisans falls behind.[4]

Italian archives, and in the first place those of the notaries, should be investigated more thoroughly than has been done until now. But for the late twelfth and for the thirteenth century, even a systematic use of the printed evidence to be found in the *Documenti e studi per la storia del commercio*[5] allows us to know more than the few facts already mentioned by Schaube in his *Handelsgeschichte der Romanischen Völker der Mittelmeergebietes*. Besides, parallel evidence is now available for several Spanish regions; the archives of the cathedral of Barcelona from the first

[3] P. Peragallo, *Cenni intorno alla colonia italiana in Portogallo nei secoli xiv, xv, xvi* (Genoa, 1907); P. Canestrini, "Intorno alle relazioni commerciali dei Fiorentini coi Portoghesi avanti e dopo la scoperta del Capo di Buona Speranza," *Archivio Storico Italiano*, Appendix, III (1846), 95 ff.; R. Almagià, "Commercianti, banchieri ed armatori genovesi a Siviglia nei primi decenni del secolo xvi," *Rendiconti Academia dei Lincei*, 1935; P. Gribaudi, "Navigatori, banchieri e mercanti italiani nei documenti degli archivi notarili di Siviglia," *Bollettino della Società Geografica Italiana*, 1936.

[4] See, for instance, C. Verlinden, "La place de la Catalogne dans l'histoire commerciale du monde méditerranéen médiéval, I, avant 1300," *Revue des Cours et Conférences* (Paris, 1938), pp. 586 ff.

[5] First edited by F. Patetta and M. Chiaudiano. The first notary published is Giovanni Scriba (Genoa, middle of the twelfth century) (2 vols., Turin, 1935). Since then, a series of Genoese, Pisan, and Venetian documents has appeared. The Genoese notaries are being published by a group of United States scholars with Prof. R. L. Reynolds of the University of Wisconsin and Prof. H. C. Krueger, Cincinnati, as permanent links.

ITALIAN INFLUENCES IN IBERIAN COLONIZATION   201

half of the century and those of the cathedral of Seville from the second half, after the *reconquista*, provide a great many documents not yet sufficiently scrutinized.[6]

In Castile the importance of the Genoese continually increases from the middle of the century onwards. When Seville is taken by the Christians, in 1248, Genoa immediately is granted far-reaching privileges. In 1251, King Ferdinand III bestows on it a whole quarter with *fondaco*, chapel, oven, and bath. The taxation of the Genoese is fixed, and the relations of their consuls with the Castilian authorities are regulated. The oil trade, to which many of them give their time and money, leads to their permanent presence in Seville and makes them ask for citizenship in order to become *vecinos* of the town. The charter of 1251 that regulates their status is the starting-point for their subsequent legal condition during the whole of the later middle ages.

This Genoese *barrio* in Seville during the thirteenth and fourteenth centuries is the foremost center of activity in the Iberian peninsula for the subjects of the Ligurian Republic. A great many Genoese tradesmen are also settled there. The Genoese are even so numerous that they are able to play a part in the conflicts in which Castile is involved and above all in the wars on the sea. It is via the colony at Seville that the first Genoese to serve Castile as an admiral, Ugo Vento, became acquainted with King Alfonso X and was appointed by him.[7] He paved the way for a series of his countrymen such as Benedetto Zaccaria, Egidio and Ambrosio Boccanegra,[8] and later, Christopher Columbus. The Seville colony deserves to be better studied; one should begin with the file of privileges published in the *Liber jurium Reipublicae Genuensis* (H.P.M.) and then turn to the unpublished material in the Archivo di Stato in Genoa and, in the first place, to the acts of the notaries. For Seville, a few documents are to be found in the books of N. Tenorio, *El concejo de Sevilla* (1901), and A. Ballesteros, *Sevilla en el siglo xiii* (1913), but many others await the historian in the cathedral archives.

Already, during the thirteenth century, some Genoese are act-

---

[6] For Barcelona see A. E. Sayous, *Les méthodes commerciales de Barcelone au xiii*^e *siècle d'après les archives de sa cathédrale* (Estudis Universitaris Catalans, XVI) (Barcelona, 1932); For Seville: R. Carande, "Sevilla, fortaleza y mercado," *Anuario de Historia del Derecho Español*, Vol. II (1925).

[7] R. Lopez, "Alfonso el Sabio y el primer almirante genovés de Castilla," *Cuadernos de Historia de España* (Buenos Aires), Vol. XII (1950).

[8] R. Lopez, *Genova marinara nel duecento: Benedetto Zaccaria* (Messina-Milan, 1933); and L. Belgrano, "Un ammiraglio di Castiglia," *Archivio Storico Italiano*, 1884.

ing as money-lenders in favor of the Castilian king, but this happens more frequently from the fourteenth century onward, when some Placentines equally play a part in this financial business that had become a specialty to them.   In 1310, one Giovanni de Vivaldo, whose kinship with the celebrated traveler of the same name should be investigated, lends sums to the king of Castile.[9]   The same occurs with a member of the illustrious family of the Spinola.   Some of these businessmen collect municipal taxes.   Thus, in 1381, one Gaspar Cibon (Ital. Cibo) "genoes" is busy as "canbiador e recabdador del dinero de la carne." Already, in 1370, a prominent Genoese known as Micer Gaspar and no doubt identical with our Cibo, lends funds on several occasions to the town council.[10]   The fact that these Genoese of the fourteenth century are busy in Seville in public and private finance, prepares their successors for the task of money-lenders they fulfill in the time of the great discoveries, and enables them to act their parts in the Castilian civil service, a role they will be reluctant to give up for centuries.

In Portugal Italian influence during the thirteenth century is scarcely known.   But it is certain that Italians dealt with several aspects of economic life such as the whale and coral fishery in Algarve and especially in Lagos.[11]   They become principally numerous after that, at the end of the thirteenth and the beginning of the fourteenth century when Italian convoy navigation to northwestern Europe is growing important.   From this period onward the coasts of Spain and Portugal are navigated by Genoese, Venetian, and later on also by Florentine and sometimes Neapolitan convoys bound to England and Flanders.   In this way Lagos became, from about 1310, an important harbor on the route of the Italian convoys to northwestern Europe.[12]   If one remembers that Lagos, much more than Sagres, was the starting point of the first Portuguese discoveries,[13] the importance of the bonds,

[9] Tenorio, op. cit., p. 117.

[10] "Cuentas del dinero de la carne," Archivo Municipal, Sevilla, Carpeta I, siglo xiv; R. Carande, op. cit., p. 382.

[11] First appearance under Affonso III (1248-1279), also under King Diniz (1279-1325). On the development of economic life in Portugal during the later middle ages J. da Silva Marques, Descobrimentos portugueses (2 vols., Lisbon, 1944), contains a large amount of evidence that has scarcely been utilized.

[12] A. Schaube, "Die Anfänge der venezianischen Galeerenfahrt nach der Nordsee," Historische Zeitschrift, Vol. CI (1908); R. Doehaerd, "Les galères génoises dans la Manche et la Mer du Nord à la fin du xiiie et au début du xive siècle," Bulletin de l'Institut Historique Belge de Rome, Vol. XIX (1938).

[13] J. Mees, "Henri le Navigateur et l' académie portuguaise de Sagres," Bulletin de l'Académie Royale de Belgique, CI (1901), 33 ff.

established there with Italian seamen and businessmen, grows evident.

This Italian convoy navigation was, during the whole of the fourteenth and fifteenth centuries, of the foremost significance for Spain and Portugal.   To prove this, it will be sufficient to quote, for instance, the regulation of the Florentine Consuls of the Sea of 1447 that fixed the list of the ports where the galleys bound to Flanders had to anchor.   In Spain and Portugal these ports were San Feliú de Guixols in Catalonia, Palma in Mallorca, Valencia, and then still more to the South, Javea, Villajoyosa, Denia, Alicante, Almería, Málaga and, beyond the Strait of Gibraltar, Cádiz, Lisbon and La Coruña.[14] The other Italian convoys entered these or other Iberian ports.   All of them had an influence on the organization of Spanish and Portuguese convoys to the colonies in the Atlantic and the Indian Ocean that has been nearly completely neglected until now.   When it becomes possible to do so systematically, it will be worth while to compare carefully the late medieval Italian with the early modern Spanish and Portuguese practice of convoy navigation; the more since we know that in both Iberian countries Italians played a leading part in the organization of this kind of transportation.

Actually Italian influence in Iberian colonization starts with the period during which Italian convoy navigation was growing really important, i.e., the fourteenth century.   This may, at first sight, look somewhat paradoxical, since it is generally assumed that in Portugal the period of the great discoveries begins with Henry the Navigator, who took the lead after the conquest of Ceuta, in 1415.   As for Spain, it is even frequently stated that nothing of importance occurred before the first voyage of Columbus in 1492.   I believe that further study will make it necessary to give up such assumptions and that the history of Portuguese colonization will have to start with the reign of Affonso IV (1325-1357), while for Spain, above all for Castile, colonization hardly begins later.   This calls for a few words of explanation.

In 1317 King Diniz of Portugal had introduced into his country the Genoese merchant family of the Pessago[15] and since then a series of its members held, during nearly two centuries, the highest positions in the Portuguese navy. Such admirals were not only in command of the fleet; they also built ships and were concerned with trade and exploration.   Lanzarotto Malo-

[14] A. Grunzweig, "Le fonds du Consulat de la Mer aux archives de l'état a Florence," *Bulletin de l'Institut Belge de Rome*, 1930, p. 24.

[15] See the privilege of that year in J. da Silva Marques, *op. cit.*, I, 27.

cello, who discovered the Canary Islands between 1325 and 1339, was a Genoese acquainted with the Pessagno and had probably traded with them to England.[16]

From this time, Portugal, Castile, and Aragon were interested in the Canary archipelago. It was made a rule to promise feudal concessions to those who intended to discover and take possession of new territory. The same practice had long been a habit in Italian colonial procedure, especially among the Genoese. It would be worth while to undertake a careful analysis and comparison of the terms of such concessions both in Italy and in the Peninsula.

The expeditions to the Canary Islands went on during the whole fourteenth century, and gradually other archipelagos were explored and colonized with the same methods.[17] With all these events, whether for Portugal or for Castile, Italians were always concerned. Till now we knew this principally for a later time. Pedro Fernández Cabrón, for instance, with whom a contract is concluded by Ferdinand and Isabella in 1480 with a view to the occupation and cultivation of some of the Canary Islands,[18] is, in spite of his Spanish name, a true Genoese. Other Italians settled as captains-*donatários* on more than one of the Portuguese islands of the Atlantic. The most celebrated among them is Perestrello, the father-in-law of Columbus, who was born in Piacenza and settled in Porto Santo, one of the Madeira Islands. But there are Italians to be found as far as the Gulf of Guinea. It would be useful to have a list of these men with their exact chronology.

Notwithstanding general belief, Portuguese colonization was not from the very beginning a royal monopoly. For the time of Henry the Navigator, Mrs. H. Fitzler maintains that a large number of colonial undertakings were organized as companies. These companies were preceded by commercial and industrial concerns in the mother country in which Italians played a leading part. In 1456 the king founded a company for growing and

[16] Cf. contract of 1306 (L. T. Belgrano, *Atti della Società Ligure*, XV, 250) and of 1330 (M. Canale, *Nuova istoria della repubblica di Genova* [Florence, 1860], III, 343). F. Pérez Embid (*Los descubrimientos en el Atlántico y la rivalidad castellano-portuguesa hasta el tratado de Tordesillas* [Sevilla, 1948], pp. 18 ff.) is not quite satisfactory on this point.

[17] For the fifteenth and early sixteenth centuries there are thirty examples of grants in the Portuguese possessions in the Atlantic published in *Alguns documentos do archivo nacional da Torre do Tombo* (Lisbon, 1892). Cf. P. Merea, "A solução tradicional da colonização do Brasil," *Historia da coloniazção portuguesa do Brasil* (Lisbon, 1924), III, 167 ff.

[18] M. Fernández Navarrete, ed., *Colección de los viages y descubrimientos que hicieron por mar los Españoles desde fines del siglo xv* (5 vols., Madrid, 1825), II, 397 ff.

selling cork, of which the Genoese Domenico Scotto and Marco Lomelini were members, as well as the Florentine Giovanni Guidotti. Nearly at the same moment that these *societates* animated the internal economy of Portugal, colonial companies appear with a *mesa* or board of directors, a general assembly and a specialized management, i.e., with more than one aspect of the colonial companies established later on in northwestern Europe. There is a great deal of still unexplored evidence about these questions in Portuguese archives.[19] But it is already apparent that the Genoese *mahone* have, to some extent, been the pattern for the Portuguese achievements.

How can the role of the Italians at the beginning of Iberian colonization be explained?

First, and above all, by the place they were able to conquer in the key positions of the Iberian peninsula itself. In Portugal they were as numerous in Lisbon as in Algarve, whence the expeditions started. This has been already shown to some extent by P. Peragallo in his *Cenni intorno alla colonia italiana in Portogallo nei secolo xiv, xv, xvi.* But there is more! When, in 1415, the Portuguese began their new and final expansion under Henry the Navigator with the taking of Ceuta, Italians, and first of all Genoese, were everywhere concerned with it. In several instances, the latter were in Northern Africa even before the Portuguese. And how could it have been otherwise for they had visited the markets of Morocco since the end of the twelfth century.[20] Here, too, there exists continuity that has escaped us till now and which we should integrate into the history of Portuguese discovery and colonization.

It is not unimportant to emphasize Genoese connections with Morocco. When the Portuguese conquered Ceuta in 1415, they found there a Genoese *fondaco.* In Algiers, in 1437, in Fez in the following year, they met Genoese moneychangers. In Sale lived

[19] H. Fitzler, "Portugiesische Handelsgesellschaften des 15. und Beginnenden 16. Jahrhunderts," *Vierteljahrschrift für Sozial-und Wirtschaftsgeschichte,* Vol. XXV (1932). The evidence gathered here has to be reëxamined carefully. Dr. Bailey W. Diffie announces a study of the Portuguese material used by Fitzler, but this material should also be examined in connection with the Italian and Northern European developments. On the Genoese *mahone* cf. L. Goldschmidt, *Universalgeschichte des Handelsrechts* (Stüttgart, 1891), pp. 295 ff.

[20] H. C. Krueger, "Genoese Trade with North-west Africa in the Twelfth Century," *Speculum,* VIII (1933), 377-395. For the routine of commerce between Genoa and Northwest Africa during the twelfth century see *The Mariner's Mirror,* XIX (1933), 417-438. For wares of exchange in Genoese African trade in the twelfth century see *Speculum,* XII (1937), 57-71.

Genoese and Venetians, among whom several had business connections with northwestern Europe. Some were serving native kings, as did one Franco Doria, military engineer with the king of Fez. Italians were active, too, in the mountain villages of the Atlas. There they bought leather and wax and sent these wares generally to Portugal but sometimes directly to Genoa. The same occurs in Southern Morocco, although the country was a great deal more savage and colonial. Sometimes the Genoese sold weapons to the Moroccans of the time who were making the life of Portuguese garrisons difficult.[21]

This Italian trade with Morocco had its European bases in Lisbon or Lagos as well as in Cádiz and Jerez. Thence the Italians had their part in Iberian discovery and colonization along the African coast, on the continent as well as in the archipelagoes. This was the way the Venetian, Cà da Mosto, followed to become one of the most important collaborators of Henry the Navigator during the last years of his career. And in the same manner all Italian businessmen who went to the Canary Islands, the Azores, or Madeira established connections with the Portuguese or Castilian courts.

About the history of the Italian penetration in Southern Spain during the fifteenth century there is somewhat more evidence accumulated recently by H. Sancho de Sopranis.[22]

From the beginning of the fifteenth century representatives of the Genoese nobility settled in Jerez. They came there—just as they had to Seville at the end of the thirteenth century—with their ships, which they hired out to the king of Castile, but used also for trade, when no military duties engaged them. We know these men from the deeds of a Jerez notary called Hernando de Carmona, used by Sancho de Sopranis only for genealogical purposes. The register, however, should be published and thoroughly studied as to the trade methods of the Genoese.

The Spinola and the di Negro played a primary part here. As the latter were intimately acquainted with the Banco di S. Giorgio—which in Genoa was concerned with the Levant possessions and for a time directed them—one can be aware immediately of the influence they might have exerted on the first development of Spanish colonial administration and especially on the Casa de Contratación.

    [21] R. Ricard, "Contribution à l'étude du commerce génois au Maroc durant la période portugaise (1415-1550)," *Annales de l'Institut d'Etudes Orientales de l'Université d'Alger*, III (1937), pp. 53 ff.

    [22] *Los genoveses en Cádiz antes de 1600* (Larache, 1939); "Los genoveses en la región gaditano-xericiense de 1460 a 1500," *Hispania*, VIII (1948), 355 ff.

ITALIAN INFLUENCES IN IBERIAN COLONIZATION   207

The Genoese of Cádiz, Jerez, Puerto Santa María, and San Lúcar de Barrameda were very busy with trade with the Portuguese *presidios* in Africa, with the Azores, Madeira and the Canary archipelago. Numerous among them were the factors of the di Negro, Centurioni, Cibo, Franchi, and other great families They moved frequently, as did many businessmen and firms later on to play their part in the trade with America, to conquer their position in the Iberian colonial economy by first maintaining relations with the oldest colonial zone, which already during the fifteenth century was in full expansion on the shores and archipelagoes of northwestern Africa.

Many among the Genoese of Jerez and Cádiz went there when and because the Turks went forward in the Levant. As the Genoese colonies in the eastern part of the Mediterranean were waning, they became interested still more in the growing Iberian *imperium* in Africa. They hoped to have part in the earnings by settling in Portuguese and Spanish districts in which trade with the colonies developed. At the same time they had at their disposal good relay-stations along the convoy lines to northwestern Europe. From Seville and the southern Iberian ports they will, later on, easily trade with America. It looks as though Genoese colonization, after the loss of the Levant, was going on in the West, but now under foreign sovereignty.

As to the African archipelagoes, this activity persisted even when relations with America had already started. A young Italian scholar, Dr. Giofré, has shown this recently for Madeira at the very beginning of the sixteenth century, but without comparison between Portuguese and Italian evidence. The Genoese, Lorenzo Cattaneo, for instance, buys on one occasion in 1500, 50.000 *arrobas* of sugar in Madeira, while the Florentines Marchione and Sernigi also play an important part in this trade.[23]

Besides, sugar cane, according to Duarte Pacheco Pereira in his *Esmeraldo de Situ Orbis*,[24] was introduced into Madeira from Sicily.[25] Later on, in Brazil, sugar-growing came in via Madeira,

[23] D. Giofré, "Genova e Madera nel primo decennio del secolo xvi," to appear in the forthcoming publications of the Convegno Internazionale di Studi Colombiani held in Genoa in March, 1951.

[24] (Lisbon, 1892), pp. 17 ff.

[25] S. Crino, "Cenni sulla coltura della cana da zucchero in Sicilia," *Revista Geografica Italiana*, 1923, pp. 76 ff. The Italians had sugar-cane plantations in their Levant colonies. Cf. G. Padovan [G. Luzzatto], "Capitalismo coloniale nel trecento," *Populi*, I (Milan, 1941), 62 ff. Professor A. Petino projects a study of the expansion of Sicilian sugarcane plantation practice in the frame of an international inquiry on medieval influence on the colonization of America which I am organizing. See on the scope of this inquiry

thanks to both the Genoese Adorno and the Antwerp merchant Schetz.[26] If one keeps in mind that the Adorno were also interested in sugar-growing in Sicily and that some of them were settled in Jerez and in Portugal, whence Madeira, Brazil, and all the other sugar-growing districts of the Atlantic could easily be reached, the question arises whether this is not a kind of big concern about which we should like to know more.

The part of the Genoese in the colonization of Tenerife in the Canarian archipelago has been studied very recently in an excellent paper by Señorita Manuela Marrero.[27] Nevertheless, the evidence gathered there is only available for the years between 1496 and 1509, and more facts should be put at our disposal. This is really possible, thanks to the existence in Tenerife of well-preserved town and notarial archives.

In 1496 Alonso de Lugo, with royal Castilian consent and Italian financial participation, founded a company for the conquest and exploration of the island of La Palma. The Italian capitalists were awarded territorial concessions, among which some were operated by companies, a feature to be found also in the Levant possessions of the Italian republics.[28]

Manpower was partly supplied by trade in black and Guanche slaves in which Spaniards as well as Italians were very busy. Immediately, grain is raised and marshland is drained. One Italian gives land away by subinfeudation, just as it so often occurred in the Levant. Genoese play the leading part, but there are also Romans, Lombards, and Venetians. Without Italian capital and Italian experience the development of colonial economy in the archipelago would have been much slower. Still more important, the same may be said for Spanish, as well as for Portuguese, America.

As for Brazil, the company created in 1502 for trade in brazil-

C. Verlinden, "Les influences médiévales dans la colonisation de l'Amérique." *Revista de Historia de América*, 1950, pp. 440 ff. and *idem*, "Le problème de la continuité en histoire coloniale," *Revista de Indias*, 1951 (Madrid).

[26] A. Furtado, *Os Schetz da capitania de S. Vicente* (Publicações do Archivo Nacional, Rio de Janeiro, 1914), pp. 9 ff.; A. Marchant, *From Barter to Slavery, the Economic Relations of Portuguese and Indians in the Settlement of Brazil, 1500-1580* (Baltimore, 1942), p. 94.

[27] "Los genoveses en la colonización de Tenerife," *Revista de Historia, Universidad de La Laguna de Tenerife*, 1950. Srta. Marrero has agreed to collaborate under the direction of Prof. E. Serra Rafols in the inquiry mentioned in note 25 above.

[28] J. Wölfel, "Alonso de Lugo y compañía, sociedad comercial para la conquista de La Palma," *Investigación y Progreso* (Madrid, 1934), pp. 244 ff.; L. de la Rosa Olivera and E. Serra Rafols, *El adelantado D. Alonso de Lugo y su residencia por Lope de Sosa* (La Laguna 1949) (Fontes Rerum Canarium, Vol. III).

ITALIAN INFLUENCES IN IBERIAN COLONIZATION 209

wood, got its financial means from Portuguese and *maranos*, but also from Genoese and Florentines. Among the latter was the Marchione firm we have already met on Madeira. It is probably as a factor of Marchione that Americo Vespucci undertook his first voyage in 1503.[29]

But I should like to insist principally upon the part of the Seville Italian colony at the beginning of the trade with America.

We know something about this for the first years of the sixteenth century, thanks to the *Catálogo de los fondos americanos del archivo de protocolos de Sevilla*, published in 1930 by the Instituto de Historia de América in Seville. The evidence of this catalogue (not the actual documents) was used by two Italian scholars, R. Almagià and P. Gribaudi.[30] Both studied the question from the point of view of the history of geography and intended, principally, to supply a better knowledge of the sphere in which Columbus lived.

If the documents of the Seville notarial archives could be published systematically, it would be possible really to know the methods, and thus the exact influence, of the numerous Italians mentioned there. For some of them the evidence is particularly rich. For the years between 1508 and 1518, for the Genoese Gaspar Centurioni, *mercader* and *banquero*, the catalogue summarizes not less than 120 deeds. After 1513 he is nearly always associated with his compatriot, Giovanni Francesco Grimaldi. He is interested in so many ways in the trade with America that even an accurate study of only the contracts in which he was a partner would teach us much more than what A. E. Sayous has been able to infer from the catalogue.[31]

A large number of these Italians from Seville went to America and settled there. When ordinances are issued prohibiting them from remaining in the Spanish colonies they escape this difficulty by naturalization. In this way they were able to introduce into the New World their methods as well as their technique. This can be noticed especially in the exchange business, in which they

[29] Cf. Duarte Leite in *Historia da colonização portuguesa do Brasil* (Porto, 1923), II, 254 ff., and A. Baião, *ibid.*, pp. 330-332.

[30] See note 3 above.

[31] "Origen de las instituciones económicas en la América española," *Boletín del Instituto de Investigaciones Históricas*, Buenos Aires, 1928, pp. 1 ff.; "Le rôle des Génois lors des premiers mouvements réguliers d'affaires entre l'Espagne el le nouveau monde, 1505-1520," *Academie des Inscriptions et Belles Lettres* (Paris, 1932), pp. 287 ff.; "Les débuts du commerce de l'Espagne avec l'Amérique, 1503-1518," *Revue Historique* CLXXIV (1934) 185 ff.; "Partnerships in the Trade between Spain and America and Also in the Spanish Colonies in the Sixteenth Century," *Journal of Economic and Business History*, I, 282 ff.

had gathered vast experience.   They were interested, too, in mining to such an extent that in the second half of the sixteenth century Peru counted many naturalized Genoese among its inhabitants.

In the trade with America several Florentines also play an
important part.   On the other hand, Venetians are nearly completely absent.   The explanation is obvious.   In opposition to
what occurred for the other Italian colonies, those which Venice
owned in the Levant remained in her possession until far into
the seventeenth century.   Venice was not compelled to search
in America for the advantages that Genoa and Florence were no
longer able to find in the Levant.   Furthermore, the political
constellation of the time also had its part in these circumstances.

Whenever Italians entered into a company with Spaniards,
they invested more money than the latter.   Hence they succeeded in getting still more control over colonial trade.   And
since a great deal of the financial power of the Spanish monarchy
depended on this kind of commerce, they could gradually attract
state finance into their sphere of influence.   Here too the Genoese
were the leaders.

When studying the Genoese methods in the Spanish colonial
trade, A. Sayous emphasizes that it is impossible to understand
the working of Spanish companies for American commerce without knowledge of Italian medieval precedents, such as *commenda*
and *societas maris*.   For the explanation of the contracts he uses
the *Suma de tratos y contratos* by Tomaso de Mercado (Seville,
1571) but fails to remark that the sponsor of this Spanish econo-
mist, Angelo Bruengo, is also an Italian, about whom we should
like to be better informed.

Although he supplies many useful data, Sayous, in general,
has set in a wrong way the problem of Italian influence.   There
is more than one reason for this.   Sayous, as has already been
said, could use only the catalogue of the Seville notaries.   Futher-
more, he did not really insist upon concrete comparison with late
medieval Italian methods, above all with those concerning the
Levant colonies.   Besides, he did not try to investigate in what
kind of economic atmosphere Italian influence took root in Spanish soil and in the colonies.   This has been impossible for him, since
he neglected to examine the late medieval Spanish economy systematically.[32]

[32] See my article, "Modalités et méthodes du commerce colonial dans l'empire espagnol
au xve siêcle, I, La question des influences italiennes," to be published, shortly, in *Revista
de Indias* (Madrid).

ITALIAN INFLUENCES IN IBERIAN COLONIZATION 211

Sayous also believed that insurance had only reached a very slight development in Seville and that the old technique of the sea loan was generally used with Italians acting as moneylenders. Where this actually occurs, the reason is not the alleged backward state of Spanish commercial law, since legislation about sea-insurance was highly developed in Spain during the sixteenth century. Even on the basis of the very incomplete information used by the French scholar, one may notice that the contents of the company contracts concluded for American trade are much more extensive and complicated than the generally very short Italian *commenda* or *societas maris* agreements of the thirteenth century. This is an evident consequence of the fact that Italian commercial practice went on developing during the later middle ages, and that the Spanish economic atmosphere also exerted its influence.

This remark seems to me the necessary conclusion of this paper. I hope to have made evident that Italian influence was really very important in Iberian colonization during the later middle ages and early modern times. I hope to have emphasized, too, that this influence deserves an extensive systematic treatment, but, for such a investigation, it should always be kept in mind that external influence combines with internal development. There exists no Italian nor Spanish, nor Portuguese history of such evolution; there is only the general western one.

[33] C. Verlinden, "Code d'assurances maritimes selon la coutume d'Anvers promulgé par le consulat de Bruges en 1569," *Bulletin Commercial Royal des Anciennes Lois et Ordonnances de Belgique*, XVI (1949), pp. 38-140.

[34] This paper was read at the Conference on Latin-American History at the meeting of the American Historical Association, New York, December, 1951.

6
Prince Henry the Navigator

P.E. Russell

IN one respect, at least, my assignment today is an easy one. I suppose that no name from Portuguese history is so well-known in this country as that of Prince Henry the Navigator, unless it be that of Vasco da Gama. I do not, therefore, need to begin this lecture by seeking to persuade you of the importance of its subject. Indeed, some of the most important scholarly works about Prince Henry and the discovery of West Africa have been written by Englishmen. One thinks, in this connection, of names like R. H. Major, in the nineteenth century, and of C. R. Beazley and Edgar Prestage earlier in this century. It seems, indeed, to have been British historians and geographers who first applied the slightly misleading epithet of "the Navigator" to the prince. In our own time, too, at least one very important contribution to our understanding of Prince Henry has been made here. I have in mind E. W. Bovill's book *The Golden Trade of the Moors*, a work which not only describes in detail the working of the overland caravan trade between Guinea and North Africa in Prince Henry's time, but also brings out of the shadows the political history and organisation of the great Saharan and Senegambian kingdoms whose Atlantic perimeter was discovered by the Portuguese.[1]

As far as I have been able to ascertain, Prince Henry has always impressed the British. Early in the eighteenth century we already find the Scottish poet, James Thomson, lauding him, in the idiom of that age, as

1. See R. H. Major, *The Life of Prince Henry of Portugal, surnamed the Navigator* (London, 1868); *idem, The Discoveries of Prince Henry the Navigator and their results* (London, 1877); C. Raymond Beazley, *Prince Henry the Navigator, the hero of Portugal and of modern discovery* (*London*, 1901); C. R. Beazley and Edgar Prestage (ed. and translators), *The Chronicle of the Discovery and Conquest of Guinea, written by Gomes Eannes de Azurara* (Hakluyt Society: London, 1896–99); Edgar Prestage, *The Portuguese Pioneers* (London, 1933); E. W. Bovill, *The Golden Trade of the Moors* (London, 1958).

4   PRINCE HENRY THE NAVIGATOR

The Lusitanian prince, who, Heaven-inspired,
To love of useful glory raised mankind
And in unbounded commerce mixed the world.
            (*The Seasons*: Summer, ll., 1010–1012.)

Thompson, perhaps because of his racial origins, intuited
the importance of a motive for the prince's work—the
economic one—which was not to become fully respectable
for scholars until our own times.   Whether Prince Henry
had any inkling that he had shown mankind the way to
useful glory, or whether he was really concerned only with
older forms of renown is, however, a matter still much
debated.

The prince's high reputation in this country is unim-
paired today.   One has only to look at the observations
about him to be found in the many books about Portugal
which have recently been published in English to see that
this is so.   I note, however, nowadays, a tendency for
British writers to hint that the achievements of Prince
Henry had something to do with the fact that he was
Philippa of Lancaster's son, and grandson of John of Gaunt.
The point is, very likely, a valid one, but not, I think, in the
way those who make it intend.   Nothing we know about
the House of Plantagenet, or the House of Lancaster,
justifies our supposing that, from his English relatives, the
prince can have inherited any particular curiosity about
what lay beyond the bounds of the known world, or, still
less, any desire or talent for investigating it.   I ought to
add, here, that one will not find, in his immediate Portuguese ancestors, either, any trace of such interests or
capacities.   Neither in his heredity, nor in the rather
limited and highly conventional intellectual life of Portugal
when he was young, is there—at least at first sight—any
hint or explanation of the work which was to make him
famous.

If, for the reasons I gave at the beginning, my assignment
is, in one respect, easy, I must confess that, in many other

PRINCE HENRY THE NAVIGATOR 5

ways, I have found it difficult. This is because, once we start to ask ourselves what kind of a person Prince Henry really was and what sort of motives caused him, so surprisingly, to undertake to discover the west coast of Africa and the Atlantic Isles, we shall find that we scarcely have the material to provide completely satisfactory answers on a number of points. As a result, and particularly in Portugal itself, the figure of the prince has, in recent decades, been the subject of much polemical writing. A general impression that we have to do with a man of genius comes over clearly enough across the five centuries which separate us from him. But any final understanding of the man and his motives seems constantly to slip away just when we think we have secured it.

Earlier British students of his life like Major and Beazley felt much more certain of their man. Major depicts the prince as a student of mathematics, navigation and cartography, and tells us that, for an explanation of the discoveries, we need look no further than to "the patience, wisdom, intellectual labour and example of one man."[2] Beazley recognised that reliable information about him was, in fact, scanty, but concluded there was enough for us to discern "a hero, both of science and action."[3] The nineteenth-century Portuguese historian Oliveira Martins, though finding his character harsh and somewhat inhuman compared with that of his royal brothers, also claimed that he was a hero in the noblest sense of the word since, through him, European civilisation won one of its two or three fundamental conquests outside the European world.[4]

All these earlier assumptions about Prince Henry's achievements have been called in question by recent scholarship—much of it the work of Portuguese scholars.

2. *The Life of Prince Henry of Portugal*, p. viii.
3. *Prince Henry the Navigator*, p. xviii.
4. J. P. Oliveira Martins, *Os filhos de D. João I*, 7ª· edição (Lisboa, 1947), p. 60.

6   PRINCE HENRY THE NAVIGATOR

It has been argued, for example, that the credit for much of the work attributed to the prince should, in fact, go to his able elder brother, the Regent Dom Pedro. Others have stressed aspects of his career in which he played something less than a hero's role. It has been suggested by some, among them Mr. Bovill, that the religious motive put forward by Prince Henry for the exploration of the Guinea Coast was mere hypocrisy, and that his real aim was to lay hands on West African gold. On the other side, with great vigour, one contemporary Portuguese scholar has maintained not just that the religious motive was uppermost in the prince's mind, but that he was solely a Christian crusader with a well-thought-out plan to weaken the Islamic threat to eastern Europe by striking a blow against the Muslims in the west.[5] What strikes me as dubious about these opposing interpretations of the prince's character and motives is that they tend to assume that, at all stages, there must have been, in Prince Henry's mind, some single, clear-cut plan of discovery, and that the results he achieved were those he had planned to achieve.

The latter assumption is, I think, a rash one. If we approach the problem of motives with a ready-made assumption that there was such a plan and that our business is simply to identify it and state it we may well miss the real point altogether.

We must, I think, also beware of letting our admiration for the work associated with the prince's name cause us to attribute to him attitudes of mind which he cannot have had. Sixteenth-century writers like João de Barros tend to treat him as if he had been a humanist in their sense.

5.   For examples of these various opinions see Júlio Gonçalves, *O Infante D. Pedro, as "Sete Partidas" e a génese dos descobrimentos* (Lisboa, 1955); A. J. Saraiva, *História da cultura em Portugal*, I (Lisboa, 1950), especially pp. 404, 558, 578; *História da expansão portuguesa no mundo* I (Lisboa, 1937), especially pp. 327–8; Duarte Leite, "Talent de bien faire" in *Revista portuguesa de S. Paulo*, I (1930), pp. 89–99; Joaquim Bensaúde, *A cruzada do Infante D. Henrique* (Lisboa, 1943).

PRINCE HENRY THE NAVIGATOR   7

Nineteenth-century scholars—as I have shown—thought he was a scientist—again in their sense. I must declare frankly at this point that I have failed to discern any factual evidence which permits us to see in Prince Henry either a harbinger of humanism or a pioneer of modern science. He seems, in fact, to have been a great deal less literate than his brothers, King Duarte and Dom Pedro. No serious student today defends the old idea that he founded, at Sagres, a formal school of navigation. Much has been made of the fact that he assumed the title of Protector of Lisbon University, but it is noteworthy that the only university endowment left by him of which record remains was for the purpose of furthering theological studies. As for the supposed school of cartography also sometimes said to have been established at Sagres, it is surely significant that, in 1458, Afonso V had to send all available information about the discoveries to Venice in order to have a definitive map of them made.

It will probably he helpful, at this juncture, if we remind ourselves, very briefly, exactly what the work of discovery carried out under Prince Henry's aegis was. Portuguese sailors entered hitherto unknown waters in 1434 when a vessel under Gil Eannes succeeded in rounding Cape Bojador, just below latitude 27° north, in what now is the Spanish Saharan territory of Rio de Oro.[6]

During the next twenty-six years the caravels managed to round, one by one, the other great capes on the bulge of Africa—Cape Blanco, Cape Verde and Cape Roxo. Their advance was not, however, progressive. Thus it seems quite likely that the voyage of Alvaro Fernandes in 1446 marked the farthest distance beyond Cape Verde reached

6. Contemporary documents and chronicles fail to make it clear whether Prince Henry considered his captains had discovered the African coast from Cape Bojador southwards, or from Cape Nun (Port. Cabo Não), a good deal further north. It seems clear that Cape Nun was the normal limit of navigation before his day, but that Cape Bojador was the real beginning of the unknown Atlantic coast.

by any Portuguese discoverer in Prince Henry's life-time. The voyages were, moreover, suspended altogether for several years at a time when the prince was involved in military affairs in Morocco or political troubles at home. But, whatever the chronology, before he died Portuguese ships had certainly got beyond Cape Roxo, and possibly as far as Sierra Leone.[7]

For navigational reasons a very important accompaniment to this advance was the discovery and occupation of the Madeiran Archipelago (1418–20) and the occupation of the Azores (about 1439). The Canaries had been partly occupied and colonised in 1402 by a French knight, Jean de Béthencourt, with the support of the king of Castile. These islands, too, were more or less under Prince Henry's control from about 1451.

In terms of distance the Portuguese had thus discovered, at best, well under 2000 miles of unknown African coastline. A very important moment in the history of this exploration was when, at an early date, a permanently manned trading-post was set up on Arguin Island, just south of Cape Blanco, where there were abundant supplies of fresh water. A fort was built there in 1448. Another post was set up at Rio de S. João, somewhat further south. There may have been others much further south still before the prince's death. Some of the Portuguese and foreign captains in his service penetrated into the interior, notably up the Senegal, Gambia, and Geba rivers, but there was no serious attempt to colonise. At the beginning the early discoverers, for ideological reasons to which I shall allude presently, insisted on treating the Toureg and Senegambian inhabitants as enemies. Later, they entered into trading relations with the local rulers when the latter would permit it. The supply bases for the caravels, once they had left Portugal,

7. João de Barros, *Ásia: Primeira Década*, ed. António Baião (Coimbra, 1932), p. 61, says categorically that Pedro de Sintra, a knight of Prince Henry's household, reached Sierra Leone.

PRINCE HENRY THE NAVIGATOR   9

were in Madeira and the Canaries, and to some extent in the
Azores, for it was often necessary to tack across the north-
east trade winds from Cape Verde to the Azores on the
homeward journey and then pick up the westerlies to
Portugal.

To get Prince Henry's achievement into perspective,
it must be made clear that he was not the first prince in the
Iberian Peninsula to interest himself in geography and
navigation.   There is ample documentary evidence to show
that, in the closing decades of the fourteenth century,
John I of Aragon collected *mappamundi* and owned and used
navigational tables.   We also find him taking under his
special protection a family of Majorcan Jews which special-
ised in making *mappamundi* incorporating the latest
geographical information about the limits of the known
world. His successor, Martin I, had similar interests. So
did Charles V of France (1364–80), to say nothing of the
rulers of some of the Italian maritime states.[8]   An interest
in maps and in navigation was evidently not something
unique at the medieval courts of Europe, even before
Prince Henry's day.

Moreover, the interior of Africa, behind the coasts which
the prince's ships were first to discover, was not entirely a
terra incognita to Europeans at this time.   So much is clear
from the Italian and Majorcan maps of the fourteenth
century which have survived.   The Majorcan map made
by Abraham Cresques for Charles V of France about 1375
knows and depicts the general area of Guinea and more or
less correctly places the cities of Timbuktu, Gao and others.
It shows the pass through the Atlas Mountains followed,
as the lettering states, by the merchant caravans from
North Africa on their way "to the land of the negroes of
Guinea."   The veiled Touregs of the western Sahara are

8.   See particularly A. Rubió i Lluch, *Documents per l'història de la cultura
     catalana mig-eval*, I (Barcelona, 1908) nos. 302, 321, 386, 409, 463
     and II (Barcelona, 1921) nos. 213, 251, 258, 260, 262.

represented there pictorially.   The map-maker also knew of the Mandingo empire of Mali and its famous ruler, Mansa Musa (d. 1332), about whom he wrote on his map "this king is the richest and most noble lord of all this region on account of the abundance of gold which is gathered in his kingdom."[9]   Such a comment was not likely to go unmarked in a Europe chronically short of gold. It doubtless was the motive which had led to unsuccessful Genoese and Majorcan attempts to round Cape Bojador by sea long before Prince Henry's voyages began.   There is contemporary evidence that the lure of African gold, too, was one of the reasons why Jean de Béthencourt undertook the conquest of the Canaries in 1402.[10]

In a general way the information given about gold on the Majorcan map of 1375 was correct.   This gold, mined in the region of Bambuk, on the Upper Senegal River, and at Lobi on the Niger, came by bearer through Mali and the ancient kingdom of Ghana as far as Timbuktu, and thence by caravan up the Taghaza road across the Sahara to the Islamic rulers of North Africa.   The actual source of the gold, however, was a secret which even the latter did not know.

These early maps do not mention the other great export from Guinea to North Africa—negro slaves.

There is no problem in discovering how this knowledge

9.   "Aquest senyor negre es appellat Musse Melly, senyor dels negres de Gineva.   Aquest rey es lo pus rich e'l pus noble senyor de tota esta partida per l'abondança de l'or, lo qual se recull en la suua (*sic*) terra." The West African section of the Majorcan map of 1375 is conveniently reproduced as a frontispiece in Bovill, *op. cit.*   I have slightly altered the English translation of the passage as given by Mr. Bovill.   For a useful brief account of this and later Catalan maps see the memoir by G. H. T. Kimble which accompanies the reproduction of the fifteenth-century Catalan world map in the Biblioteca Estense, Modena, published by the Royal Geographical Society (London, 1934).

10.   See *The Canarian or Book of the Conquest and Conversion of the Canarians in the year* 1403.   Transl. and ed. by R. H. Major.   (Hakluyt Society: London, 1872), p. 95.

of the West African interior reached Europe in the fourteenth century.   Trading contacts with North Africa were
quite close.   Genoese ships, in particular, frequented the
North African ports.   The Aragonese, too, had close
political and maritime relations with some of the North
African kingdoms, as did the Granadine Moors.   The
Portuguese themselves carried on a profitable export of
fruit from the Algarve to Morocco; the gold they received
in exchange was an important source of bullion for Portugal.
Genoese merchants were established at Fez.   Genoese and
Castilian merchants were also resident at Arzila, in
Morocco, with their own church, in 1437.   However,
the main source from which the Jewish cartographers of
Majorca got their information about the African interior
was from their co-religionaries, who were allowed to travel
without much hindrance far inland.

It was, however, one thing for the prince to know at
second-hand what sort of country lay beyond Bojador.   It
was quite another to persuade his squires, pilots and sailors
to go there.   A distillation of legends taken from both
classical and Arab geographers made Cape Bojador a place
of neurotic terror to medieval seamen.   Beyond it, they
believed, stretched the Green Sea of Darkness, or, according
to other tales, the sea boiled, terrifying monsters lurked in
the ocean, men exposed to the tropical sun turned permanently black, or Satan himself lay in wait for the first
men foolish enough to venture beyond a point which
tradition had always declared to be the furthermost south
on the Atlantic to which men were permitted to sail.
Cape Bojador projects 25 miles westwards from the mainland.   The violence of the waves and currents on its
northern side, the shallows which exist near it, the difficulty
of returning northwards on account of the prevailing winds,
were all seen merely as proof of the truth of the legends by
sailors able only, at first, to navigate close in-shore.   Other
facts supported them, too.   It had been noted by the

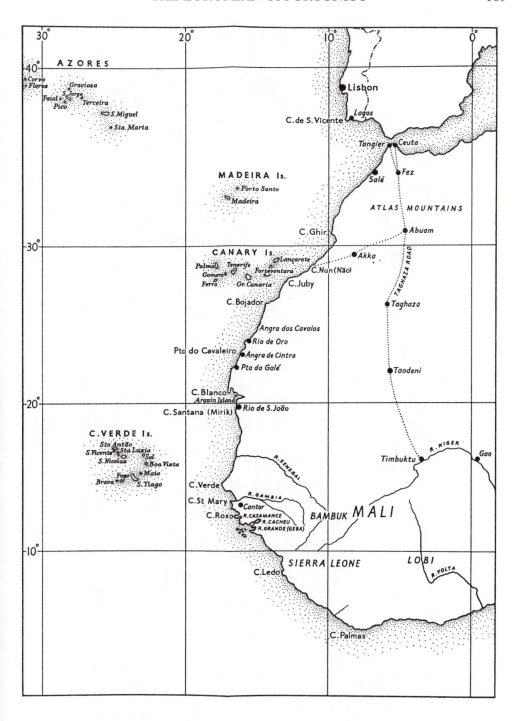

30°   20°   10°   0°

40°

A Z O R E S

Corvo
Flores
Graciosa
Faial S. Jorge
Pico Terceira
S. Miguel
Sta. Maria

● Lisbon

Lagos

C. de S. Vicente

Tangier ● Ceuta

MADEIRA Is.
● Porto Santo
● Madeira

● Fez
● Salé

ATLAS MOUNTAINS

C. Ghir ● Abuam

30°

CANARY Is.
Palma Tenerife Lançarote
Gomera Forteventura ● Akka
Ferro Gr. Canaria C. Nun (Não)
C. Juby

TAGHAZA ROAD

C. Bojador

● Taghaza

Angra dos Cavalos
● Rio de Oro
Pto do Cavaleiro ● Angra de Cintra
● Pta da Galé

● Taodeni

C. Blanco
Arguin Island
C. Santana (Mirik) ● Rio de S. João

20°

C. VERDE Is.
Sto Antão
S. Vicente Sta Luzia
S. Nicolau Sal
Boa Vista
Fogo Maio
Brava S. Tiago

● Timbuktu
R. NIGER
● Gao

C. Verde

C. St Mary
R. GAMBIA
C. Roxo ● Cantor
R. CASAMANCE
R. CACHEU
R. GRANDE (GEBA)

R. SENEGAL

BAMBUK MALI

SIERRA LEONE
LOBI

10°

C. Ledo
R. VOLTA

C. Palmas

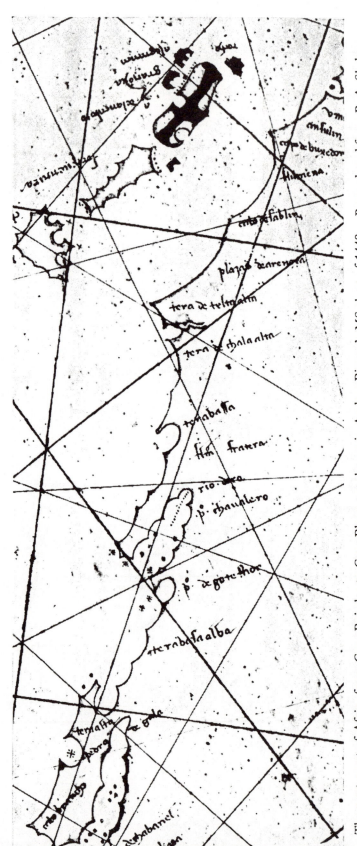

The west coast of Africa from Cape Bojador to Cape Blanco as shown in Andrea Bianco's MS chart of 1448. Reproduced from R. A. Skelton, *Explorers' Maps* (London, 1958), fig. 15.

medieval map-makers that, at the end of the thirteenth century, some Genoese galleys had sailed beyond the accepted limits and had never been seen again.   The same had happened in 1346 to a Majorcan captain, Jaume Ferrer, who had tried to reach the River of Gold, beyond the terrible cape.   Jean de Béthencourt, though established on the Canaries only a short distance to the north of it, had also failed to round it, or make good his hope of making a settlement on the African shore.

It took, perhaps, twelve years of battle between Prince Henry's will on the one hand and the inherited superstitions of those who manned his ships on the other before Cape Bojador was, at last, rounded.   As many as fifteen unsuccessful attempts may have been made before success came.   The deed was done, at last, in 1434, when, as I have said, a squire of the prince's household, Gil Eannes, after faltering in the neighbourhood of the cape the previous year, tried again and returned to Portugal bearing a handful of rosemary gathered on the Saharan coast beyond Bojador.

The rounding of Cape Bojador must, I think, be rated as the most important achievement of Prince Henry's connection with African exploration.   To do it he had had to show not only will-power, but also patience, and a readiness to expend very large sums of money on which no immediate return could be expected.   Until 1434 the traditional terrors of the unknown Atlantic had rendered impotent even his seafaring household squires, avid for glory as these were.   Once the psychological barrier represented by the famous cape had been dissolved, however, further progress down the African coast was restrained only by real problems of navigation, equipment, and supply. These were, of course, serious.

The few contemporary documents we have, either written in the prince's name or summarising his achievements, show that he himself was well aware of the significance of this particular moment in his career.   As late as

PRINCE HENRY THE NAVIGATOR   13

1457, in a document issued by his chancery, we find him writing about it in these terms:

> Knowing how, within the memory of men, there was no information among Christians about the seas, lands, and people beyond Cape Nun towards the south . . . I set about enquiring and discovering, from many years past to the present time, what lay from the said Cape Nun onwards, not without great efforts by me and endless expenses . . . sending during this time many ships and caravels with my dependants and servants who, by God's grace, passed beyond the said Cape. . . .[11]

I must, however, stress that—as in all similar documents referring to the rounding of Capes Nun and Bojador—the Prince at once goes on to speak of the crusading and missionary consequences of his achievement. There is no suggestion that the discoveries could be justified purely in scientific terms as an addition to human knowledge. Whether this represented the prince's own view of his work, or whether he felt bound to speak of it as he did because nearly all the documents are concerned either with obtaining papal and royal privileges or with justifying the expenditure of the revenues of the military order of Christ on the discoveries, is clearly a point we shall have to consider.

I do not think it unduly far-fetched to suggest that there is a certain parallel between the prince's part in the rounding of Cape Bojador and the preparations which are today being made for men to travel in still more alarming regions. As in the case of the politicians, physicists, engineers and psychologists involved in current space projects, there never seems to have been any question of Prince Henry himself actually going on any of the voyages made in his name. This should cause us no surprise; indeed, it is a point which arises only because, as I have mentioned, English-speaking writers have bestowed on the prince the

11. J. M. da Silva Marques, *Descobrimentos portugueses: documentos para a sua história*, I (Lisboa, 1944), no. 426, p. 544.

ambiguous title of "the Navigator." Medieval protocol and custom made it unthinkable for a royal prince to sail on voyages of discovery, especially in tiny vessels such as the Portuguese used.[12]   His task was to provide the ships, the finance, the information, and the psychological preparation needed to make it possible for his pilots, captains and seamen to carry out his plans.

What, however, were the motives behind these plans? This seems to me to be the really important question we have to ask ourselves about Prince Henry.   At first sight the most promising source of information on this point is the *Crónica dos feitos de Guiné* of Gomes Eannes de Zurara.[13]

The *Chronicle of Guinea* was finished about 1453, though evidently touched up after Henry's death in 1460.   Zurara was both keeper of the royal archives and chronicler royal of the prince's nephew, Afonso V (1438–81).   He was closely connected with the court.   He knew the prince himself well and was, as a *comendador* of the military order of Christ, the latter's dependant, since the prince had been appointed Administrator-General of the Order of Christ in 1420.   All this should add up to a very useful and reliable account of the discoveries and the motives for them. Unfortunately grave reservations have to be made about Zurara's work.   He was, in fact, too familiar with the court and the prince to be able to write objective history and his work is quite frankly intended to be a piece of panegyrical writing about his hero and patron.   I think some modern critics have blamed Zurara too much for this, for he could hardly have written objectively about the prince's career and motives when Henry was still living and

12.   The three-masted caravels which explored West Africa in the prince's time were, it has been established, not much more than 60–90 feet in length.

13.   For the purposes of this lecture I have used the edition edited by A. J. Dias Dinis—vol. II: *Texto* (Lisboa, 1949).   Also important for a study of textual and other problems relating to Zurara and his chronicle is vol. I: *Introdução* (Lisboa, 1950).

was, at least after the king, the most important man in Portugal. Less excusable is Zurara's vagueness about chronology and topography, his very subdued interest in the kind of things modern readers want to know about the newly discovered lands, and the extreme paucity of the information he gives us about the organisation and technical aspects of the voyages of discovery themselves.

Zurara is, in fact, a man deeply imbued with what Huizinga called the "illusion of society based on chivalry." In his pursuit of this illusion he constantly tries to turn the discovery of Guinea into a tale of chivalry. To this end, petty engagements between bewildered groups of Toureg and Senegambian tribesmen and the strongly-armed, if numerically inferior, Portuguese are written up as occasions of knightly prowess. Mere slave-raiding expeditions are, by the same process, transformed into occasions for a squire literally to win his spurs. Like Froissart, Zurara usually seems incapable of seeing the contradiction between his general concepts and the facts he has to narrate. Since his chronicle is the only original source which survives for the early voyages, all this is, doubtless, highly regrettable. Characteristic of Zurara's approach to the whole matter is the fact that he stops his chronicle in 1448 with a comment that, from this point, "things were not conducted with the same effort and fortitude as those which had happened before, since, from this year onwards, the affairs of those parts were always managed more through treaties and trading agreements than by endurance or force of arms."[14]

A. J. Saraiva and some other contemporary scholars have written of Zurara with severity, seeing in him a chronicler not up to the level of the events he was called upon to describe. I am not sure this will do. Zurara, as we have seen, was in close touch with Prince Henry and with the Portuguese court. He wrote to please these patrons and

14. Zurara, *Crónica dos feitos de Guiné*, II, cap. xcvi, pp. 425–6. For the later voyages we have accounts by Cà de Mosto and Diogo Gomes.

he succeeded in doing so.   This, surely, makes it necessary at least to consider the possibility that the *Chronicle of Guinea* accurately depicts the spirit in which the discoveries were carried out, or, at any rate, the spirit in which the prince, his explorers, and the court of Afonso V wished posterity to believe they had been carried out.

I have already mentioned that contemporary Portuguese documents describing the prince's discoveries nearly always associate these with crusading or missionary ends.   We saw, however, that—since these documents are concerned either with obtaining privileges for Prince Henry or with justifying his use of the revenues of the Order of Christ— it could be held that such an association was made with an ulterior motive.   There is, however, one piece of writing which can safely be attributed to the prince himself and which does, undoubtedly, contain a sincere statement of his views about religion, chivalry, and the doctrine of the crusade.   Unlike his brothers, King Duarte and the Regent Dom Pedro, or his nephew, King Alfonso, Henry did not leave any literary works behind him.   But he did, when at Estremoz in 1436, write a memorial giving his reasons for supporting the much-debated project for a Portuguese attack on Tangier.[15]   It is not a very well-argued or even well-written paper.

He begins by observing that the accepted aims of this life are to save one's soul and the honour of one's person, name, lineage, and country, to make the body joyful and, in last place, to achieve temporal gains.   He then goes on to stress the supreme importance of honour, and to state his own contempt for the physical pleasures such as eating, drinking, sleeping, singing and the company of women. From this he concludes—somewhat erratically—that the only permissible purpose of life is to serve God and achieve honour.   War against the Moors will satisfy both purposes and should, therefore, be undertaken.   Since God may be

15. Silva Marques, *op. cit.* I, no. 287, pp. 360–3.

expected to help the Portuguese the king should not fear its outcome. The memorial ends with an encouraging assessment of the supposed military weakness of the kingdom of Fez which, in the event, was to be revealed as wholly erroneous.

Now the Prince Henry who reveals the workings of his mind here is about as far away as possible from the nineteenth-century concept of him as humanist and scientist. He sounds like a character out of a medieval romance of chivalry, not like a field commander staking a claim to be charged with the task of invading a dangerous shore. One is reminded of another aspect of the prince's life which also belongs to the world of romance. I refer to his supposed life-long cult of perfect chastity which three writers who knew him—Zurara, Cà da Mosto and Diogo Gomes—all refer to with undisguised admiration. Whether they spoke the truth or merely sought to flatter him we cannot tell. Obviously there is a possible problem here which deserves greater attention than I can give it. But I think it signifi-cant of Prince Henry's exaltation of medieval chivalric ideals that he wished to be remembered for his exceptional chastity.

Despite the intelligent and far-sighted objections set out by his brothers to the plan for an attack on Tangier, and the whole notion of a Portuguese empire in Morocco which went with it, Prince Henry had his way—as he usually did. Before the expedition sailed King Duarte handed him detailed instructions for the military conduct of the cam-paign. These show that the king—an inveterate believer in rules for dealing with all situations—feared that the prince would manage the expedition imprudently. He reminded him, therefore—among other things—that his famous English relatives had won their successes in their wars by good discipline and tactics.[16] The king's fears were well-founded. As is common knowledge, the prince

16. Silva Marques, *op. cit.* I, no. 300, p. 384.

showed himself to be an impetuous and unskilled commander.   In the disaster at Tangier a Portuguese army
was lost and his young brother, Dom Fernando, left to die
as a prisoner of the king of Fez.

How did Prince Henry react to this disaster?   All we
know for certain is that he used—successfully—all his
influence to make the Portuguese king reject a Moorish
offer to release Dom Fernando in exchange for the sur-
render of Ceuta.   He then went back to the business of
discovering Guinea.   He remained, however, firmly
attached to the idea of a Portuguese conquest of Morocco.

The whole Tangier episode shows that, whatever else
he was, the prince was a genuine believer in the doctrine of
the crusade and, moreover, that his attitude to it was
distinctly bookish and Quixotic.   One can see why his
brothers thought him rather dangerous as an army commander.   One can also see why some modern critics have
concluded that such a man cannot have been capable of the
careful planning and—above all—the patience which went
into the discoveries.   Yet, unless we are arbitrarily to
discard all the evidence of all his contemporaries, he was
so capable.   Is this contradiction capable of explanation,
or should we simply accept it as a curious but inexplicable
fact about Prince Henry's temperament?

Zurara gives six reasons for his patron's interest in the
discovery of Guinea and the Atlantic Islands.   He recog-
nises, first, that the prince was moved by a desire to find out
what lay beyond Cape Bojador in order to open an unknown
sea passage to mariners and merchants.   But he immediately
follows this up with four more reasons, all of which are
concerned, in one way or another, with showing that the
prince's main concern was with the crusade against the
Moors in Africa and with the discovery of infidel souls
which might be converted.   Zurara ends by explaining
that there was one other explanation for the discoveries
more powerful than any of these.   This was Prince Henry's

horoscope. The chronicler describes it in detail and—as far as I can judge—correctly, and then notes that it showed the prince to be predestined to work to achieve great and noble conquests, especially by seeking out secret things hidden from other men.[17]

Zurara's suggestion that astrological prediction in- fluenced Prince Henry's career more than anything else usually gets scant attention from students of his life. This may well be a mistake. Credence in astrology and horoscopes was general in Europe at this time, and no- where more so than at the courts of kings and princes. Henry's father, John I, was interested in astrology. His brother, King Duarte, also concerned himself with it. Medieval science was, indeed, completely mixed up with astrology—few branches of it more so than navigation, about which the prince clearly knew something—even if the extent of his knowledge has possibly been somewhat exaggerated. I think it very likely, therefore, that what Zurara has to say on this matter, too, may faithfully reflect Prince Henry's own beliefs about his destiny. The predictions of his horoscope may explain, perhaps, not only why he was always ready to abandon West African exploration for chivalric and crusading adventures in Morocco, and *vice versa*, but also why, for a considerable period, he insisted—otherwise inexplicably—on treating the discovery of Guinea itself as if it were also a war of conquest against the Moors.

Mr. E. W. Bovill discounts the sincerity of the claims of Prince Henry and his seamen that the discovery of Guinea was carried on for missionary purposes. "Their real purpose," he writes, "was not, as they pretended, to spread the Gospel, but to discover the source of the gold which was being imported into Morocco overland by the

17. Zurara, *op. cit.* II, pp. 45–6.   It is, perhaps, relevant here to note that Prince Henry was born on Ash Wednesday (4 March), 1394.   He died on 13 November, 1460.

20   PRINCE HENRY THE NAVIGATOR

Taghaza road."[18]   The observation may well be true of
many of those who—especially after 1443—took part in the
African voyages.   But, as far as Henry himself is concerned,
the suggestion that he was hypocritical is, I think, impossible
to sustain.   It was clearly not hypocrisy which led him to
abandon temporarily the work of discovery and hurl himself
into the disaster at Tangier.   We may disregard Zurara's
evidence on the question of motive as possibly suspect.
The constant assertion of a crusading and missionary
purpose in contemporary documents may, too, be explained
away as belonging to the conventions of self-interest.   But
there remains what Cà da Mosto has to say.   This Venetian
captain knew the prince personally and made two voyages
to Guinea under his direction in 1455 and 1456.   He
himself had, as his account of his journeys shows, no
particular interest in crusading or in missionary work.
Cà da Mosto declares, however, that the prince's wish to
discover the African coast was connected with his desire to
attack the Moors and refers, also, to the prince's desire to
make converts.[19]

It would, all the same, be unrealistic to deny that the
desire to lay hands on the gold of Guinea must, nevertheless, have entered largely into Prince Henry's calculations.   The problem is to discover how—if at all—he
justified this desire in terms of the ideology by which he
lived.

The reign of John I, so successful in political and
military affairs, had been economically disastrous for those
who depended on the land.   The general European shortage of gold was particularly acute in Portugal, where, at the
same time, there had been a galloping inflation of the
currency.   There was, too, an acute shortage of labour in

18.   *Op. cit.* p. 28.
19.   See the text of Cà da Mosto's work published, with a Portuguese
      translation, in Silva Marques, *op. cit.* I (Suplemento), pp. 165 (2) and
      (3), 166 (6) and 183 (44).

the countryside.   As a result, the new nobility of Portugal, which was led by the ambitious sons of John and Philippa, could not look forward to finding, at home, the revenues which would allow them to live in the state kept up by their English and Burgundian relatives, or by their Castilian neighbours.   The nobles were, however, totally unwilling to accept the consequences of their economic situation. Their prospects became worse after the conclusion of a permanent peace with Castile in 1411, which ended all opportunities at home for gaining knightly reputation and wealth by war.   There is, thus, much to be said for the view that John I, when he inexplicably attacked and conquered Ceuta in 1415, did so partly in order to create a Portuguese equivalent of the border between Castile and Granada where his young nobles might satisfy their chivalric urges and desire to acquire booty in war.

Prince Henry himself was a great spender.   He always maintained a large household of young knights and squires. He was, therefore, in financial trouble from the beginning of his career as an independent magnate, and was to remain in it to the end of his life.   Neither the governorship of the Algarve—which he held from 1419—nor the revenues of the dukedom of Viseu and the lordship of Covilhã were sufficient to satisfy his domestic needs.   Nor, apparently, did the control he was given, in 1420, over the ample revenues of the Order of Christ save him from financial embarrassment; these proved quite insufficient to cover the great costs involved in financing the early voyages of discovery.

In these circumstances it would be difficult to maintain that Prince Henry did not see, in the gold of Guinea, a way by which his own fortunes and those of his country might be saved.   This is not merely a matter of deduction. Diogo Gomes, one of his captains, declared categorically of him that—when the prince began his explorations in West Africa—he wished to make contact with the lands from which West African gold reached the north "in order to trade with them and to sustain the nobles of his household."[20]

There was, in principle, no contradiction between the prince's crusading interests and this search for gold. It was proper to deny to the infidel, if possible, one of the sources of his military strength and use it to finance expeditions against him. No one had ever sought to maintain, either, that a crusader might not make as much profit as he could from his crusading—provided he did not forget that his main duty was to wage religious war. The late medieval code of chivalry—as set out, for example, in the *Siete Partidas* of Alfonso the Wise—had, however, added some new complexities to this position. Theoretically at least, any form of buying or selling except in connection with war or the holding of land was considered incompatible with the status of knight. This belief must have caused some difficulty to Prince Henry when it began to look as if he was becoming the leader of an enterprise in which trade, not crusading or conversion of the infidel, was the dominant objective.

It is possible, I think, to see the commercial history of the conquest of Guinea as the story of the way in which the hard realities of economic fact and ordinary human motivation gradually forced themselves into the sublimated world of chivalry and religious zealotry in which the prince sought to live. From the beginning, if Zurara is correct, he openly admitted an intention to trade in Africa, but only if

20. The journeys of Diogo Gomes took place between 1444 and 1463. About 1483 he gave an account of them, and of the discovery of Guinea, to Martin Behaim of Nürnberg, who wrote it down in Latin. The text is published by Dr. Schmeller in the *Abhandl. der Phil.-Philolog. Classe der k. bayerischen Akademie der Wissenschaften*, IV (München, 1847), under the title "Über Valentim Fernandez Alemão und seine Sammlung von Nachrichten über die Entdeckungen und Besitzungen der Portugiesen in Afrika und Asien bis zum Jahre 1508." For the quotation given in the text see p. 19.

he could find Christian peoples there to trade with.   This hope had very soon to be relinquished, because no such peoples were found and trade with the non-Christian inhabitants of Senegambia and the western Sahara became essential if the voyages were to continue.   The establishment, in 1443, of Arguin Island as a permanent trading-post for doing business with the Mauretanian Touregs confirms that the pretence of a predominantly crusading objective had already started to break down.   Nevertheless, the documents suggest very clearly that the prince was always unwilling fully to accept this situation.   He goes on talking—anachronistically—about wars of conquest and the conversion of the natives, even when peaceful trading and the importation of large numbers of slaves purchased by barter from local chiefs had become the order of the day and exploration had largely ceased.[21]   Meanwhile the Portuguese merchants and shipowners who, at the beginning, had viewed the prince's high-minded intentions in West Africa with total indifference, now clamoured to have his permission to join him.   They were impressed by the sight of the lucrative cargoes of seal-oil, fish, skins, ostrich eggs, sugar from Madeira, dragon's blood and all the other merchandise of Guinea, to say nothing of gold, both yellow and black, which arrived at Lagos and Lisbon in the prince's caravels.   After 1446, discovery, as such, takes second place.

We know very little about the exact quantities of gold which reached the homeland after 1441 or 1442, when the first precious dust was brought back.   The Portuguese never succeeded in finding the elusive source of West African gold; that secret was kept from Europeans until the time of Mungo Park, though the curiosity and intelligence of Cà da Mosto nearly discovered it when he sailed up the Gambia River in 1456.   Gold, however, probably did

21.   See Silva Marques, *op. cit.* I, no. 401, pp. 503–513; no. 407, pp. 518–9; no. 420, pp. 535–7; no. 426, pp. 544–5.

reach Portugal in sufficient quantities to make a useful contribution to the country's economy. But it was soon found that black gold—slaves—was the most attractive cargo Guinea had to offer. This, it is certain, did make an important contribution to Portuguese economic life by relieving the long-standing and acute shortage of man-power there.

A good deal has been written recently about the extent of the borrowings made by the peoples of the Iberian Penin-sula from Moorish civilisation. The organised slave-trade from Africa represents, I think, a new borrowing to be added to the list. Through many centuries of Islamic domination in North Africa the slave caravans had moved northwards across the Sahara to supply labour to the Moorish kingdoms there. Now the slaves were transported thence by sea to Portugal for the same ends. Cà da Mosto says that, in his day, 700–800 captives were shipped yearly from Arguin Island alone. At the beginning they had been obtained by armed raiding. This made it possible to reconcile the trade with Prince Henry's private ideologies. It could be said that the slaves were captives taken in war; they were, or were declared to be, Muslims. Such slaves were, of course, an accepted feature of medieval Iberian society. But this method had unexpected con-sequences. The native tribes concluded that the Portu-guese must eat the men, women and children they so inexplicably seized and carried away. Not unnaturally they, therefore, rather tended to regard the discoverers as enemies. It was soon found more convenient to obtain slaves by the accepted African method of bartering with Toureg, Mandingo, and Joloff merchants and chiefs.[22] The main instrument of barter seems to have been horses. Diogo Gomes, describing the situation in 1458, complains that a Genoese merchant on the Guinea coast lowered the

22. Not all the slaves imported into Portugal were, however, African. Some came from the Canary Islands.

PRINCE HENRY THE NAVIGATOR   25

customary rate on the Gambia of one horse for twelve slaves to one horse for six slaves.

This is a matter which, in the circumstances of 1960, it is necessary to approach objectively, but as honestly as we can.   It is certain that the Portuguese generally treated these fifteenth-century African slaves much more humanely than other European peoples were to treat them.   Leo of Rozmital, a Bohemian knight who, with his friends, wrote down his impressions of a visit to Portugal a few years after the death of Prince Henry, noted that a slave who had been baptised could not, in any circumstances, be sold by his master.   There is other evidence that, at this time, the Portuguese made little difference between African slaves and other servants of their households.   But, when everything has been said, I cannot accept the claim of a recent writer that "the captives found, in Portugal, under the aegis of the Infante [Prince Henry], a new way of life, more dignified, more human."[23]   I think few people with imagination enough to consider what had happened to these captives before they were put up for auction in the slave-markets of Lagos and elsewhere could venture to go that far.   Nor will the doctrine of *autres temps, autres moeurs* serve in this case.   The evidence against that comes from a very unexpected quarter.   In 1445 the chronicler Zurara was present at an auction of over 200 slaves at Lagos.   The spectacle, for once, forced Zurara to face realities.   The result was that he wrote a pained and honest account of the sheer human suffering he saw on that occasion, though, characteristically, he then goes on to try hard to justify it because most of the slaves subsequently accepted baptism.[24] This justification is hardly impressive if one considers both the psychological pressure put on the captives and the great advantages in treatment which came to them after

23. Padre António Brásio, *A acção missionária no período henriquino* (Lisboa, 1958), p. 86.
24. *Op. cit.* II, pp. 124–7.

baptism.   It seems to me beyond argument that the reasons for bringing the slaves to Portugal were exclusively economic ones and that, if these had not existed, they would have been left at home—perhaps to be converted by normal missionary methods.

Prince Henry's attitude towards this new trade, of which fate had made him the unexpected patron, seems to have been characteristic.   Zurara describes his presence on horseback at the 1445 slave-market and clearly finds it embarrassing.   The prince, he says, took the customary fifth—forty-six slaves—which belonged to him, but—he hastens to add—showed little interest in the profit to be made from them, preferring instead, "to mediate with great satisfaction on the salvation of those souls which had previously been lost."   Certainly, as the documents show, the prince never ceased to justify the development of the slave-trade in terms of conversions.   But, by the end of his life, he had evidently come to be rather less contemptuous of the commercial value of African slaves than Zurara would have us believe.   In 1457 he ceded to the Order of Christ 1/21 of the value of all merchandise reaching Portugal from the lands over which his commercial monopoly extended.   Among the main commodities listed as im-ported from Guinea he puts—first of all—slaves, male and female, placing them before even gold and fish.   They are described as 'cousas' (*things*) just like any other form of merchandise.[25]   Yet earlier in the same document, when summarising his achievements, he had explained how, first by war and then by trade, "a very great number of infidel

25. Silva Marques, *op. cit.* I, no. 426, p. 545: ". . . tenho, Estamdo em cabidoo per campaa tamgida, com acordo do Comendador mõõr, Craueiro, Comendadores, dom prioll, e o procurador da dicta hordem e freires: que, de todallas cousas que sse em a dita terra de gujnea des o dicto cabo de nam por diante resgatarem e ouuerem per quallquer guisa e modo que seja, asi descrauos, escrauas, ouro, pescarias, como quaẽẽs quer outras cousas e mercadorias, dem a dicta hordem e paguem, em loguo de dizema de cada hũũas das dictas cousas, de vijnte hũũa."

PRINCE HENRY THE NAVIGATOR   27

captives had come to the Christian world, the greater part
of whom, offering great praise to Our Lord, have turned
to his holy faith; and everything is well-prepared for many
more to come." Clearly he found the whole business of his
connection with the slave-trade equivocal.

Prince Henry, one may therefore be sure, was never able
to disembarrass himself sufficiently of his preconceptions
to understand, except dimly and reluctantly, what he had
really done. He possessed a variety of commercial
monopolies on a great scale, including not only that over all
trade with West Africa and the Atlantic Isles, but also over
such humdrum things as the fishing rights off the Algarve,
the import of dyes and sugar and the control of the soap
industry in Portugal. But he remained, it seems, always
a *commerçant malgré lui*. Perhaps this was one of the
reasons why, despite all the resources he controlled, the
prince seems to have lived and died heavily in debt. And
the old hankering after great and noble victories against
the Moors never ceased to seduce him. In 1458 he
succeeded in persuading his nephew and disciple, Afonso V,
to attempt, once again, the conquest of Morocco. Henry,
now an old man, did not hesitate, once more, to abandon his
West African enterprises in order to take part. Thanks
to the prince's obsession the Portuguese were committed to
an imperialist programme in North Africa which was, in the
end, as the Regent Dom Pedro had predicted, to come near
destroying Portuguese independence for good, though that
consequence was still far off. Still, it must be remembered
when we try to evaluate his achievements.

Our attempt to get at Prince Henry's motives, then,
seems to establish two important facts about him and them.
His mind was always dominated by a zealous devotion to
the twin doctrines of chivalry and crusade. He also
exhibited a notable reluctance, or inability, to modify his
preconceptions when he was confronted by unforeseen
situations—even those which he himself had created. It

is important, I think, to note that the doctrines of chivalry and crusade to which be adhered were not Hispanic. In Henry's time the Spaniards were engaged in the penultimate stages of their difficult love-hate relationship with the Moors of Granada. Long practical experience, sometimes painfully acquired, had taught them that their relationship with the Spanish Moors was a subtle and complicated affair. In it, religious zeal and chivalrous idealism had to be tempered by the remembrance of practical realities—especially economic ones. The Portuguese, on the other hand, had no tradition of practical crusading. This was, perhaps, why offers by Prince Henry to join in the war with Granada were politely but firmly turned down by the Castilians. The sort of approach set out in the prince's memorial of 1436 was too Quixotic for them.

It seems likely that the prince partly derived his ideas about chivalry from his English relatives—but at secondhand. One notices an unexpected interest in chivalry and crusading in the later career of the prince's father, the severely practical soldier of former years, John I. Zurara may be right when he hints that the influence of Philippa of Lancaster was at work here. Certainly one has only to read the writings of Henry's brother, King Duarte, to see how strong was the belief of those of Philippa's sons who had not been there, that England was the land *par excellence* of great feats of arms and noble living. The Regent Dom Pedro, who actually had visited England, learnt rather different things from the English, such as that talk of fame and honour could be overdone, that they thought the Portuguese occupation of Ceuta to be a great indiscretion: even how to run a university properly.[26] But one may be fairly sure Prince Henry did not care overmuch for his brother's down-to-earth attitude to Portugal's problems and capacities. Perhaps that was one of the reasons why he let him be killed on a civil war battlefield in 1449.

26. Oliveira Martins, *op. cit.* (appendix of documents), p. 349.

PRINCE HENRY THE NAVIGATOR 29

I have tried, in this lecture, to bring out the importance of medieval crusading and chivalric ideas in Prince Henry's life because, without them, it seems to me that we get nowhere near the man and his motives. For that reason I conclude that the prince belongs essentially to the later Middle Ages, rather than to the humanist and scientific Renaissance, where a long tradition has tended to place him. I think there is much to be said for the conclusion of Dr. Veiga Simões that he was one of the builders of the modern world without intending to be. But if he clung, with characteristic tenacity, to the illusion that his life was dedicated to the crusade and to chivalry we must not forget that it was from this same illusion that he very likely drew the moral strength and the single-mindedness which made it possible for him to carry through the great enterprises of discovery associated with his name. The anachronistic vision of Prince Henry led, past Africa, towards the Indian Ocean and a great commercial empire. Dom Pedro's prudence perhaps would have led to no more than acceptance by the Portuguese of a modest provincial status on the confines of western Europe.

I am reminded of the famous portrait of Henry in the painting (*c.* 1465) by Nuno Gonçalves. Perhaps it is not really a portrait from life. But Nuno Gonçalves seems, at any rate, to have visualised very exactly the personality of the prince as we may suppose it to have been towards the end of his life. Strength, even rigidity, is there. The expression of the eyes is firmly ultramundane still. But there is also a sense of melancholy and disillusion, not of achievement. One thinks, inevitably, of the parallel with Columbus, another man with a clutter of medieval notions in his mind and an unshakeable sense of mission, who also found a new world which was not the one he expected to find. Who, too, could never quite reconcile himself to accepting what he had found for what it was, rather than what he had wanted it to be. Neither is less great, and

30   PRINCE HENRY THE NAVIGATOR

certainly not less human, because of this inability to trim his dreams to fit actualities obvious to lesser men. Indeed, when one comes to think about it, it seems certain that both discoverers owed everything to this furrow of Quixotism in their natures.

Thanks are due to Mr. R. A. Skelton and to Messrs. Routledge & Kegan Paul for permission to use the block of the map facing p. 12.

7

Fernand Colomb et le traité d'astrologie d'Henri le navigateur

Guy Beaujouan

Le cinquième centenaire de la mort du grand Infant portugais vient de donner un certain regain d'actualité aux vieilles polémiques sur les rapports entre la culture scientifique et l'art nautique à l'époque des grandes découvertes maritimes : la question des origines de la navigation astronomique reste, plus que jamais, à l'ordre du jour [1].

Comment, pourtant, se défendre d'une certaine impression de tourner en rond lorsque, comme le disait naguère V. Magalhaes Godinho, on retrouve sans cesse « les mêmes sources mâchées et remâchées avec une enviable patience de bovin »[2].

Raison de plus pour ne négliger aucun texte inédit ! Ceci nous encourage à présenter ici, malgré le caractère assez conjectural de sa lecture et de son interprétation, un document jusqu'ici inconnu, sur le traité d'astrologie attribué à l'Infant Henri.

Cette attribution remonte à l'année 1866 : c'est alors, en effet, que fut, pour la première fois, signalée, parmi les si pré-

---

1. G. Beaujouan, *Science livresque et art nautique au XVe siècle* (tirage ronéotypé) ; cet assez long rapport sera prochainement imprimé dans *Le navire et l'économie maritime : travaux du cinquième colloque... tenu à Lisbonne les 14-16 septembre 1960, présentés par Michel Mollat*, Paris, S.E.V.P.E.N.

2. V. M. Godinho, *Les grandes découvertes* dans *Bulletin des études portugaises*, XVI, 1952, p. 3.

LE TRAITÉ D'ASTROLOGIE D'HENRI LE NAVIGATEUR 97

cieuses notices que Fernand Colomb nous a laissées de ses propres livres, l'importante description que voici.

« 4129. Libro en español de mano llamado secreto de los secretos de astrologia compuesto por el infante don Enrrique de Portugal. *Incipit* : « aqui se comiença un libro que se llama segredo... ». *Desinit* : « ...a Dios fazer como su merced fuere; a Dios gracias ». Es en 4°. Costo en Salamanca tres reales a 21 de abril de 1525 [1] ».

Dès le XVIIe siècle, le volume ainsi décrit avait disparu de la Bibliothèque colombine de Séville où il devrait normalement se trouver [2].

Un ancien catalogue de manuscrits ayant appartenu à l'érudit, également sévillan, Argote de Molina (1548-1598) fait justement état de « *Secretos de astrologia por el infante Don Enrique de Portugal* ».

Argote de Molina a-t-il fait copier l'exemplaire de la Colombine ou se l'est-il, plus simplement, approprié ? La question ne peut être tranchée avec certitude [3].

---

1. B. J. Gallardo, *Ensayo de una biblioteca española de libros raros y curiosos*, t. II, (Madrid, 1866) col. 553. Le *Registrum B* de Fernand Colomb a été, depuis, reproduit en fac-similé : A. M. Huntington, *Catalogue of the library of Ferdinand Columbus*, New-York, 1905. Il sera prochainement publié par D. Tomás Marin, professeur de paléographie à l'Université de Séville.

2. Ce n'est pas le lieu de présenter ici l'amoureux passionné des livres qu'a été le fils du découvreur de l'Amérique, Fernand Colomb (1488-1539). Les travaux classiques publiés sur lui par H. Harrisse, S. de la Rosa, J. Babelon, A. Esteban Romero, J. Hernandez Diaz, etc. sont recensés dans E. Jos, *Investigaciones sobre la vida y obras iniciales de Fernando Colón*, Sevilla, 1945. Y ajouter M. Ruffini, *Fernando Colombo e i libri italiani di Siviglia*, Torino, 1960 et A. Cioranescu, *Primera biografia de Cristobal Colón : Fernando Colón y Bartolomé de Las Casas*, Tenerife, 1960.

3. A. Millares Carlo, *La biblioteca de Gonzalo Argote de Molina* dans *Revista de filologia española*, X, 1923, p. 137-152. Il existe une troublante ressemblance entre les manuscrits 2, 14, 25, 27, 29, 41 d'Argote et ceux portant dans le *Registrum B* de F. Colomb les nos 3282, 3291, 4127, 4176, 4129 et 4174. Tous cependant n'ont pas été volés puisque le 41 = 4174 semble être l'actuel 5-2-21 de la Bibliothèque colombine. Autre exemple :

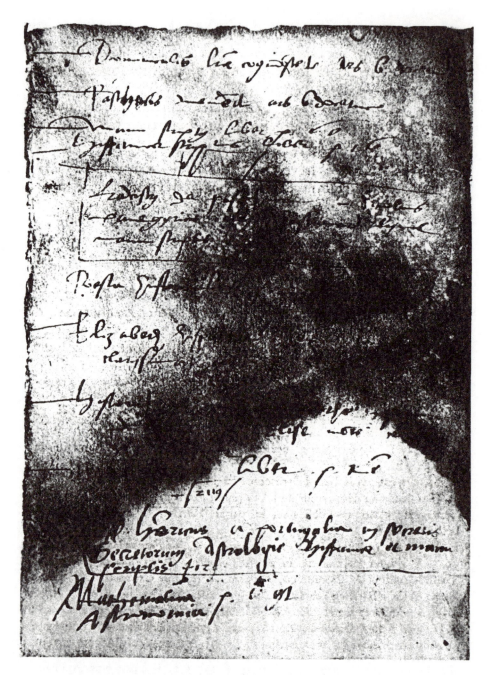

Résumé du traité d'astrologie de l'infant Henri de Portugal

LE TRAITÉ D'ASTROLOGIE D'HENRI LE NAVIGATEUR   99

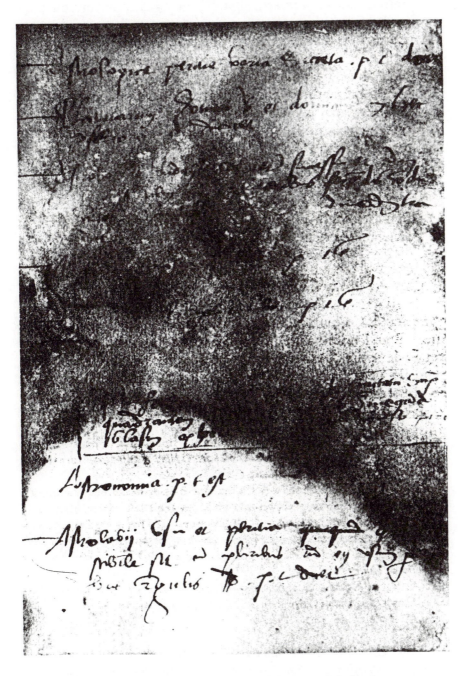

dans le *Compendium librorum* de Fernand Colomb.

100

Armando Sousa Gomes a signalé, en 1938, une version portugaise du *Secret des secrets* connu au moyen âge sous le nom d'Aristote : il a, du même coup, ébauché la thèse selon laquelle l'Infant Henri aurait, de quelque manière, participé à l'élaboration de cet important manuscrit [1].

Il serait prématuré (voire imprudent) d'épiloguer sur ce *Segredo dos segredos* jalousement gardé jusqu'ici dans une collection privée, mais dont M. A. Moreira de Sá annonce la prochaine publication [2].

On ne saurait pourtant oublier les objections soulevées par Joaquim de Carvalho [3] : il a catégoriquement nié que le secret des secrets portugais pût être identifié avec le secret des secrets d'astrologie composé, en espagnol, par l'Infant Henri de Portugal et acheté, à Salamanque, par Fernand Colomb.

*
* *

Fernand Colomb a rédigé ou fait dresser de sa bibliothèque un si grand nombre de répertoires que la tentation nous est venue de rechercher s'il n'était pas possible de trouver, à l'intérieur de l'un d'eux, quelques indications supplémentaires sur ce mystérieux traité d'astrologie.

---

le 42 « *Ludovicus Vegius de astrologia* » (resté inidentifiable pour Millares) est sans doute à rapprocher du « *Ludovici Rigii libri 2 de judiciis astronomicis de mano* » (F. C. nº 10768, actuel 5-6-22).

Si donc Argote a emprunté à la Colombine d'assez nombreux manuscrits, il en a du moins restitué quelques-uns après les avoir fait copier. Mais comment, dans ces conditions, pouvait-il écrire que les livres de Fernand Colomb étaient alors « emprisonnés » sans servir à personne ? « *...agora estan encarcelados... no siendo a nadie de provecho lo que se dejó para aprovechamiento y estudio de los ingenios* ».

1. A. Sousa Gomes, *O livro « Segredo dos Segredos » e o Infante D. Henrique* dans *O Instituto* (Coimbra) XCIII, 1938, p. 193-220.

2. A. Moreira de Sá, *O Infante D. Henrique e a Universidade*, Lisboa, 1960, p. 93.

3. J. de Carvalho, *A propósito da atribuição do « Secreto de los secretos de astrologia » ao Infante D. Henrique* dans ses *Estudos sobre a cultura portuguesa do século XV*, Coimbra, 1949, p. 283-361.

LE TRAITÉ D'ASTROLOGIE D'HENRI LE NAVIGATEUR   IOI

Joaquim de Carvalho s'était déjà, du reste, engagé sur cette voie : non content de collationner la notice de Fernand Colomb maintes fois reproduite d'après le *Registrum B*, il s'était reporté à l'*Abecedarium* B (qui en est, en quelque sorte, la table alphabétique)[1] et il y avait relevé, à la colonne 552, l'indication suivante :

« *Enricus a Portugalia in secretis secretorum astrologie hispanice et manuscriptis. 4129* ».

Le numéro 4129 (souligné) renvoie à la notice du *Registrum B*. Mais il est aussitôt suivi — et cela J. de Carvalho ne le dit pas — du nombre |2119| inscrit dans un rectangle dont il manque le côté supérieur.

Bien qu'il fût le meilleur spécialiste des autographes de Fernand Colomb, A. Esteban Romero a cru qu'il fallait renoncer a trouver la signification des chiffres ainsi encadrés[2]. La solution est pourtant fort simple : il suffit de se reporter au témoignage même du secrétaire de Colomb, la « *Memoria de la orden que llevaba Colon en su libreria* » par le bachelier Juan Perez[3]. « *...el que esta entre tres rayas de esta manera |321| es el numero que tiene la materia del tal libro en el libro de las materias de que arriba hicimos mencion* ».

Les quatre volumes de ce *libro de las materias* se retrouvent aujourd'hui encore à la Bibliothèque colombine, mais sous une autre dénomination, celle de *Compendium librorum*. Les trois premiers tomes, déreliés et en partie pourris par l'humidité, ont été retirés de la vitrine où sont exposés les autres anciens répertoires de Fernand Colomb. Leur mauvais état de conservation matérielle en rend malaisées la consultation et la lecture. On peut cependant y déchiffrer sous le n° 2119 le résumé suivant :

---

1. Dans l'original du *Registrum B*, le n° 4129 est suivi des nombres 134, 552 et 866 : ces nombres renvoient aux colonnes de l'*Abecedarium B*.

2. A. Esteban Romero, *Don Fernando Colón, su personalidad literaria, repertorios bibliográficos y manuscritos*, Sevilla, 1939.

3. H. Harrisse, *Excerpta colombiniana*, Paris, 1887, p. 277.

102

2119

Dominus Henricus a Portugalia in secretis ‖

secretorum astrologie hispanice et manu ‖

scriptis 4129.

Mathematica [*rayé*]

Astronomia p. t. est.

— Astrologice peritie varia secreta p. t. docet ‖

— Planetarum *vir*tutes b. et dominiu*m* in hec ‖

inferiora d. docet.

— Astrologicis judiciis de re*rum* successu et a*n*ni ‖

tempestatibus atque qualitatibus ferendis condu-‖

centes canones per totum admod*um* tra-‖

dit.

— Manu scriptus liber p. t. e*st*.

— Hispanice scriptus liber p. t. e*st*

Le papier est, par endroits, à tel point délavé et décomposé que, sans une méticuleuse comparaison avec des formules analogues employées aux feuillets épargnés par l'humidité, il serait impossible de déchiffrer certains mots comme *admodum,* ou *manu* et *hispanice* dans les deux dernières lignes. Les sigles *b.,* *d.* et *p. t.* auraient, d'autre part, gardé tout leur mystère si, dans le mémoire déjà cité, le propre secrétaire de Fernand Colomb n'avait jugé utile d'en donner la clef à la postérité [1] :

---

1. H. Harrisse, *Excerpta,* p. 272.

LE TRAITÉ D'ASTROLOGIE D'HENRI LE NAVIGATEUR   103

« *Tambien se ha de advertir que en estos libros hay algunas abre-
viaturas y adoquiera que hallaren una* b *quiere decir* breviter, *y
una* d *quiere decir* diffuse, *y adonde esta una* t *quiere decir* per totum, *porque fue necesario y muy provechoso que se dijese si el autor
o libro que trata aquella materia la trata breve o difusamente o en
el todo. . .* »

* *
*

Il est dès lors possible de récapituler. Le traité de l'Infant
pris dans son ensemble (*per totum*) enseigne divers secrets du
savoir astrologique. Il enseigne brièvement les vertus des planètes et, de façon diffuse, leur influence sur le monde d'ici-bas.

Il transmet comme il se doit (*admodum*) des règles commodes
conduisant à porter des jugements astrologiques sur la marche
des événements (ou le succès des choses) et les qualités... de
l'année. Il est entièrement (*per totum*) manuscrit et rédigé en
espagnol.

Ces indications sont sommaires : elles ruinent cependant
l'idée qu'il puisse s'agir d'un manuel d'astronomie nautique
tombant sous le coup de la fameuse « politique du secret » si
chère au regretté Jaime Cortesão.

Elles ne s'accordent pas, non plus, avec le contenu du traité
d'astrologie attribué à Enrique de Villena [1] : il n'y a donc pas
eu confusion entre les deux Henris [2].

Reste le *Secret des secrets* pseudo-aristotélicien. Si importantes
que soient les variantes entre ses différentes versions, ce texte
comprend, dans le meilleur cas, quatre parties [3].

---

1. Madrid, Bibl. nac. ms. reservado 2. Cf. F. Vera, *El tratado de astrologia
del marqués de Villena* dans *Erudición ibero-ultramarina*, I, 1930, p. 19-67
et J. M. Millás Vallicrosa, *El « Libro de astrología » de don Enrique de Villena*
dans ses *Estudios sobre historia de la ciencia española*, Madrid, 1949, p. 399-
420. L'attribution de ce traité à Enrique de Villena nous paraît beaucoup
moins certaine que ne le prétend le Prof. Millás.

2. J. de Carvalho, *Est. cult. port. do sec. XV*, p. 327-329.

3. R. Steele, *Secretum secretorum cum glossis et notulis* dans *Opera hactenus
inedita Rogeri Baconi*, fasc. V, Oxford, 1930. Cf. J. Monfrin, *Le secret des
secrets, recherches sur les traductions françaises* dans *École nat. des chartes.
Positions des thèses*, Paris, 1947, p. 93-99. — Sur les versions espagnoles
indications encore utiles de Knust, *Ein Beitrag zur Kenntnis der Eskurialbi-*

104

— Conseils moraux à l'usage des rois.
— Régime de santé.
— Mélanges de philosophie naturelle et de politique.
— Traité de physiognomonie.

Même s'il est bien spécifié que les rois doivent s'entourer des conseils d'un bon astrologue et qu'il ne leur convient pas de recourir aux médicaments ou à la saignée, de déclarer la guerre ou de partir en voyage sans tenir compte des positions respectives des planètes, à supposer même que ces sporadiques allusions à l'astrologie judiciaire aient paru justifier le titre « *Secreto de los secretos de astrologia* », on ne saurait dire du *Secretum secretorum* ou de l'un quelconque de ses commentaires que « *astrologice peritie varia secreta* per totum *docet* » [1]. Mais ne préjugeons pas de ce que sera exactement le contenu de l'ouvrage dont M. Moreira de Sá annonce la publication; gardons-nous, en un mot, de nous poser en partie ou en arbitre dans une polémique à laquelle 'nous n'avons voulu participer que pour apporter une pièce à conviction.

*
* *

Si mince que soit le présent article, il voudrait dépasser son objet propre en attirant l'attention du monde érudit sur les immenses possibilités qu'offrent encore les anciens inventaires de la Bibliothèque colombine de Séville.

Les deux tiers environ des volumes jadis possédés par le fils du découvreur de l'Amérique sont aujourd'hui perdus : certains

bliothek dans *Jahrbuch f. rom. u. engl. Litt.*, X, 1869. Cf. L. A. Kasten, *Seudo Aristoteles, Poridat de las poridades*, Madrid, 1957. — Sur le contenu de la version portugaise, A. Sousa Gomes, *loc. cit.*, p. 199-200.

1. On penserait plutôt aux trois derniers livres du « *Libro complido en los judizios de las estrellas* » d'Alin Aben Ragel dont il existe, du reste, une version judéo-portugaise de 1411. Cf. l'éd. de G. Hilty, Madrid, 1954; I. Gonzalez Llubera, *Two old portuguese astrological texts in hebrew characters* dans *Romance philology*, VI, 1952-1953, p. 267-272. — A. Moreira de Sá, *loc. cit.* Mais il a dû circuler dans l'entourage de l'Infant bien d'autres traités cf. G. Beaujouan, *Note additionnelle sur l'horoscope de l'Infant Dom Henrique* dans G. Eanes de Zurara, *Chronique de Guinée : (préf. et trad. de L. Bourdon)*, Dakar, 1960, p. 269 sq. (texte p. 68).

LE TRAITÉ D'ASTROLOGIE D'HENRI LE NAVIGATEUR   105

d'entre eux contenaient (les registres et les abécédaires en font foi) des textes, par ailleurs, complètement inconnus. Il serait urgent d'en dresser la liste et d'en relever les analyses dans le *Compendium librorum* avant que ce précieux répertoire, jamais consulté mais déjà très endommagé, finisse irrémédiablement de tomber en ruine. On souhaiterait que soient systématiquement entreprises la lecture, sous rayons ultraviolets, des parties les plus détériorées et leur prompte restauration au *laminator*.

Note additionnelle : Le présent article était déjà mis en pages lorsque parut un nouveau travail du professeur A. Moreira de Sá, *A próxima edição de tres traduções portuguesas inéditas do século XV* dans *Boletin internacional de bibliografia luso-brasileira*, vol. I, n° 4 (oct.-déc. 1960), p. 563-585. Les pages 579 et suivantes y sont consacrées à la version portugaise du *Secretum secretorum* déjà décrite par A. Sousa Gomes : elles ne modifient pas les données du problème, nous dispensant ainsi d'apporter le moindre correctif à notre démonstration. — G. B.

Note de 1991 concernant la republication de cet article dans le présent volume de "Variorum": Dans la transcription donnée à la page VIII 102, quelques mots illisibles ont pu, maintenant, être restitués grâce aux recherches de D. Tomas Marin, d'après les *Proposiciones* constituant la seconde partie du *Libro de las materias* de Fernand Colomb. Voir Tomas Marin Martinez, *Obras y libros de Hernando Colon* (Madrid, 1970), p. 375-380 et 846-847. Guy Beaujouan, *Hernando Colon, adquiridor de manuscritos cientificos*, dans *Hernando Colon y su época* (Sevilla, 1991), p. 47-59, spécialement p. 51-52, ou dans *Boletin de la Real Academia Sevillana de Buenas Letras*, XVIII (1990), même pagination.

8
Back to Gold – and Silver[1]

Andrew M. Watson

QUICK glance at the monetary history of Europe and the Muslim world from 1000 to 1500 shows that in monetary matters the two halves of the Mediterranean followed very different courses. Whereas Europe minted virtually no gold until the middle of the thirteenth century,[2] but greatly increased its supplies of silver coins, the Islamic countries through much of this same period were experiencing an acute silver famine during which they were able to mint *only* gold, billon, and base metals. Then a remarkable reversal occurred. Towards the end of the twelfth century, silver reappeared in abundance in the Arab world and soon displaced gold as the basis of many currencies. A little later, Europe began minting gold coins in large quantities and her silver currencies began to falter. The dissimilarity seems total. The one side of the Mediterranean mirrored in reverse what was happening on the other shore.

It would be wrong, however, to conclude from this divergence that the monetary histories of these two worlds were independent of one another. On the contrary, they were inextricably bound together. The disappearance of silver from the East in the eleventh and twelfth centuries seems traceable to the same causes which drove gold out of the West. And the return to silver in the East depended heavily on silver imported from Europe, while the return to gold in the West relied—perhaps to a slightly lesser extent—on gold released from the East. In monetary matters, therefore, the two regions should be treated as a whole. To study the monetary history of the one in isolation from the other is like watching a football match from a seat which overlooks only half of the field.

---

[1] In writing this article I have had generous help from Mr Philip Grierson, Prof. Karl Helleiner, Dr George C. Miles, and Prof. Michel Mollat.

[2] Some gold *was* minted in Europe between 1000 and 1250, mostly, however, in peripheral regions. There were, for instance, the imitation Muslim coins struck in Sicily and Barcelona in the eleventh century and in Castille during the twelfth century, as well as other gold coins struck by the Normans in Sicily and southern Italy. There also seems to have been an early issue of gold in Genoa at the end of the twelfth or the beginning of the thirteenth century. *Vide infra*, p. 7, n. 3. Finally, of course, there was Byzantine gold coinage in this period.

2   ANDREW M. WATSON

                              I

The "silver famine" which spread over the Muslim world during the eleventh, twelfth, and thirteenth centuries has been little studied and never explained.[1] Yet the fact of the famine seems clear—though its extent and severity may have been exaggerated by earlier writers. Whereas every part of the Muslim world had produced an abundant silver coinage throughout most of the tenth century, one region after another gave up striking silver as the eleventh century progressed, until almost no silver whatever was minted in the heartland of the Islamic world. In the Levant and Asia Minor, silver coins, previously struck at more than a dozen towns, became rare after 970 and had completely disappeared by 1027/8.[2] Baghdad and the other territories under Buwaihid rule had stopped

---

[1] It is surprising that so little has been written about this important phenomenon. *Vide* R. P. Blake, 'The Circulation of Silver in the Moslem East down to the Mongol Epoch', *Harvard Journal of Asiatic Studies*, II (1937), 291–328; E. A. Davidovich, 'Gorod, remeslo i denezhnoe obrashchenie v sredniei Azii perioda tak nazyvaemogo "serebrianogo krizisa" (XI–XIII v)', *Materialy vtorogo sovieshchania arkheologov i etnografov srednei Azii* (Moscow/Leningrad, 1959); W. Heyd, *Histoire du commerce du Levant au moyen-âge* (Amsterdam, 1959), I, 57 ff.; Kh. A. Mushegian, *Denezhnoe obrashchenie Dvina po nomizmaticheskim dannym* (Erevan, 1962); and E. A. Paxomov, 'The Monetary Circulation of Azerbaijan in the 12th and the Beginning of the 13th Century', *Trudy Gos. Isd. Muzeja, Numizmaticeskij Sbornik* (Moscow, 1957), pt 2, pp. 82–90. I cannot, however, agree with the various explanations of the onset of the famine offered by Davidovich (and I believe that his ratio of gold to silver has not been correctly calculated). The article by Blake requires extensive revision.

[2] It would be impossible to give complete references for each statement concerning the onset of the silver famine. I have arrived at my conclusions after studying all the published catalogues of the world's major collections of Islamic coins and much other literature as well. My research covered the activities of well over 100 minting towns between the years 950 and 1330. The following are the main sources: P. Balog, 'Dirhems ayoubites inédits du Yemen', *Bulletin de l'Institut d'Egypte*, XXXVI (1953–4); P. Balog, 'Etudes numismatiques de l'Egypte musulmane', *Bulletin de l'Institut d'Egypte*, XXXIII (1951), 1–41, XXXIV (1952), 17–55, XXXV (1953), 401–29; P. Balog, 'Monnaies islamiques rares', *Bulletin de l'Institut d'Egypte*, XXXVI (1953–4), 326–46; P. Balog, 'Table de référence des monnaies ikhidites', *Revue belge de numismatique*, CIII (1957), 107–34; P. Z. Bedoukian, *Coinage of Cilician Armenia* (New York, 1962); A. Bel, 'Contribution à l'étude du dirhem de l'époque almohade', *Hespéris*, XVI (1933), 1–68; O. Blau, *Die orientalischen Münzen des Museums der Kaiserlichen Historisch-Archäologischen Gesellschaft zu Odessa* (Odessa, 1876); J. D. Brethes, *Contribution à l'histoire du Maroc par les recherches numismatiques* (Casablanca, 1939); R. Brunschvig, 'Esquisse d'histoire monétaire almohado-hafside', *Mélanges William Marçais* (Paris, 1950); *Catalogue of the Coins in the Numismatic Cabinet belonging to J. Gerson da Cunha* (Bombay, 1888–9), 4 vols.; B. A. Dorn, *Inventaire des monnaies des khalifes orientaux et de plusieurs autres dynasties* (St Petersburg, 1882), II; J. Faruggia de Candia, 'Monnaies fatimites du Musée du Bardo', *Revue tunisienne*, n.s. XXVII–XXVIII (1936), 89–136; J. Faruggia de Candia, 'Monnaies hafsites du Musée du Bardo', *Revue tunisienne*, n.s. XXXV–XXXVI (1938), 231–88; J. Figanier, *Moedas Arabes* (Lisbon, 1949), pt I; I. Ghaleb Edhem, *Catalogue des monnaies turcomanes* (Constantinople, 1894); H. Goodacre, *A Handbook of the Coinage of the Byzantine Empire* (London, 1960); H. W. Hazard, *The Numismatic History of Late Medieval North Africa* (New York, 1952); Abdul Karim, *Corpus of the Muslim Coins of Bengal* (Dacca, 1960); J. Karst, *Précis de numismatique géorgienne* (Paris, 1938); B. Lagumina, *Catalogo delle monete arabe* (Palermo, 1892); S. Lane-Poole, *Catalogue of Oriental Coins in the British Museum* (London, 1875–90), 10 vols.; S. Lane-Poole, *Catalogue of the Collection of Arabic Coins Preserved in the Khedivial Library at Cairo* (London, 1897); S. Lane-Poole, *Catalogue of the Mohammadan Coins Preserved in the Bodleian Library at Oxford* (Oxford, 1888); D. Lang, *Studies in the Numismatic History of Georgia in Transcaucasia* (New York, 1955); H. Lavoix, *Catalogue des monnaies musulmanes de la Bibliothèque Nationale* (Paris, 1887–96), 3 vols.; H. Longuet, *Introduction à la numismatique byzantine* (London, 1961); A. K. Markov, *Inventarnyi katalog musulmanskikh monet Imperatorskogo Ermitazha* (St Petersburg, 1896–1904), 1 vol. and 3 supps.; W. Marsden, *Numismata orientalia illustrata* (London, 1823–5), 2 vols.; G. C. Miles, 'The Ayyubid Dynasty of the Yaman and their Coinage', *Numismatic Chronicle*, 5th ser. XIX (1939), 62–97; G. C. Miles, *Fatimid Coins* (New York, 1951); G. C. Miles, *The Numismatic History of Rayy* (New York, 1938); G. C. Miles, *Numismatics, Rayy: 1934, 1935, 1936* (unpublished typescript at the American Numismatic Society); H. Nützel, *Katalog der orientalischen Münzen* (Berlin, 1898–1902), 2 vols.; J. Østrup, *Catalogue des monnaies arabes et turques du Cabinet Royal des Médailles du Musée National de Copenhague* (Copenhagen, 1938); A. Prieto y Vives, *Los Reyes de Taifas* (Madrid, 1926); C. J. Rodgers, *Catalogue of the Coins of the Indian Museum* (Calcutta, 1893–6), 4 vols.; N. Siouffi,

GOLD AND SILVER   3

striking silver by 1009/10.[1] Farther to the north and east, silver continued to be minted somewhat longer: in the Central Asian reaches which they controlled, the Il Khans, successors to the Samanids, struck silver of decreasing fineness in apparently large quantities until the third quarter of the eleventh century, while the Ghaznavids during this same period issued silver coins in Ghazneh, Walwaliz, Balkh, Mahmudpur, and probably other unidentified towns. But in these areas, too, silver had almost completely disappeared by the end of the third quarter of the eleventh century.[2] With the exception of intermittent and probably unimportant issues from Seljuk territories,[3] the only part of Muslim Asia to strike silver after 1075 was Ghaznavid India.

By this time the famine had also begun to move slowly westwards. In Fatimid Egypt, the fineness of the dirhem, originally a coin of pure silver, fell gradually from 86 per cent at the close of the tenth century to 34 per cent by the end of the eleventh century. During the same period the weight of the coins was slightly reduced and full dirhems became increasingly rare.[4] By the end of the eleventh century silver had also virtually disappeared from Fatimid Tunisia.[5] In Spain and the western part of North Africa, a gradual disappearance of silver can also be traced. From a fineness of 99 per cent in early Omayyad times, the dirhem had become only 73 per cent fine by the early eleventh century and then fell to 37 per cent fineness towards the middle of the century.[6] During the period of the Kings of the Taifas, who succeeded the Omayyads, the quality of the dirhem continued to be very low. Although some good silver was again struck in Spain and North Africa by the Almoravids and the early Almohads, mostly after the

---

Catalogue des monnaies orientales. Collection Siouffi (Mosul, 1879–91), 1 vol. and supp.; D. Sourdel, *Inventaire des monnaies musulmanes anciennes du Musée de Caboul* (Damascus, 1953); Ahmed Tevhid, *Catalogue des monnaies des Khakans Turcs, Gaznewides, Seldjoukides . . .* (Constantinople, 1903); E. Thomas, 'Notes on Colonel Stacey's Ghazni Coins', *Journal of the Asiatic Society of Bengal*, XXI (1852), 115–27; E. Thomas, *On the Coins of the Kings of Ghazni* (London, 1848); W. Tiesenhausen, 'Mélanges de numismatique orientale', *Revue de numismatique belge*, XXXI (1875), 189–214, 329–79; W. Tiesenhausen, *Moneti vostochnavo khalifata* (St Petersburg, 1873); W. Tiesenhausen, 'Vostochniya moneti N. P. Linevitcha', *Zapiski Vostochnavo Otdeleniya Russkavo*, IV (1889), 289–320; W. Tiesenhausen, *Notice sur une collection de monnaies orientales de M. le Comte de Stroganoff* (St Petersburg, 1880); A. Vives y Escudero, *Monedas de las dinastías arábigo-españolas* (Madrid, 1893); Jeanette Wakin, *The Coinage of the Ayyubids* (unpublished typescript at the American Numismatic Society); J. Walker, *The Coinage of the Second Saffarid Dynasty in Sistan* (New York, 1936); H. N. Wright, *Catalogue of the Coins of the Indian Museum, Calcutta* (Oxford, 1907), vol. 2; W. Wroth, *Catalogue of the Coins of the Vandals, Ostrogoths and Lombards in the British Museum* (London, 1911); E. von Zambaur, 'Contribution à la numismatique orientale', *Numismatische Zeitschrift*, XXXVI (1904), 43–122.

[1] This date, obtained by examining the numismatic evidence, is confirmed by Al Makrizi. Text in *Chrestomathie arabe*, ed. Silvestre de Sacy (Paris, 1826–7), I, 250.

[2] These coins, overlooked by Blake, are mostly reported in Markov, op. cit. Davidovich, op. cit. reports that an analysis of the dirhems struck in the region of the Karakhans shows that the amount of copper rose from 12 or 13 per cent (early eleventh century) to 35 per cent (second decade of the century) and then 50 per cent (1030's and 1040's); later in the century the dirhem in this region contained 70 to 80 per cent copper, and by the end of the century it was a coin composed entirely of base metals.

[3] Seljuk silver, extremely rare, is reported in Miles, *Numismatics, Rayy . . .*, op. cit.; von Zambaur, op. cit.; and Tiesenhausen, 'Vostochniya . . . ,' op. cit.

[4] P. Balog, 'History of the Dirhem in Egypt', *Revue numismatique*, 6th ser. III (1961), 122.

[5] P. Balog, 'Etudes numismatiques . . .', op. cit. p. 6. The pieces described by Balog in this article are very debased. According to Ibn Adhari, who is clearly wrong on this point, silver disappeared from North Africa in 888/9. *Histoire de l'Afrique et de l'Espagne*, ed. R. P. A. Dozy, I (Leyden, 1848), 114–15.

[6] G. C. Miles, *The Coinage of the Umayyads of Spain* (New York, 1950), I, 92; and H. Sauvaire, *Matériaux pour servir à l'histoire de la numismatique et de la métrologie musulmanes* (Paris, 1882), pp. 263–4.

ANDREW M. WATSON

beginning of the twelfth century, no more silver seems to have been minted in these regions after the year 1164. Then the famine was at its height. From the Atlantic coast to the western borders of Ghaznavid India no Islamic ruler was striking silver coins. Nor, it is believed, did the older silver coins circulate. The area seems to have been almost completely drained of silver coins. Its bimetallic system of classical Islamic times had collapsed. Over this vast geographical expanse gold had come to be the basis of all currency systems, supplemented only by low-quality billon, copper, brass, lead, iron, and—in some regions perhaps —by glass.[1]

In the Byzantine Empire, too, the same phenomenon is found. After 1000 silver coinage, though it did not completely disappear, became rare, and there were no important issues until the second quarter of the thirteenth century.[2] In monetary matters, at least, Byzantium seems to have belonged to the East rather than to Europe.

Not enough is yet known about this famine for an explanation to be given with any assurance. Part of the answer may lie in the history of silver mines in the Muslim world, a few of which were lost in wars while others may have stopped being worked for technical or political reasons.[3] Owing to the paucity of source materials throwing light on the history of mining in this period, and the difficulty of interpreting these sources, however, these hypotheses are usually not easy to test. In any case, it remains to be explained how the vast quantities of silver which were in circulation before the onset of the famine disappeared. In all probability they were drained off towards neighbouring regions: perhaps partly towards India and China, and certainly towards Europe. One such outflow has been well charted. From the early years of the ninth century until the middle of the tenth century, Samanid coins moved across the Caspian Sea and by caravan through Khwarizm into Russia, Poland, Sweden, Finland, and Norway, and thence to Western Europe and even to Iceland. The hoards found along the route, revealing the direction of flow "as with the silver point of a compass", show that the loss of silver in this direction must have been enormous: at least 120,000 such coins have been discovered in Russia[4] and more than 85,000 in Scandinavia,[5] and those which have been found in hoards can be only a tiny fraction of the total. When, in the second half of the tenth century, the trade over these routes came to an end, silver coins continued for a time to flow into the

[1] Recently, two scholars have argued convincingly that the large numbers of glass objects made in Egypt, formerly thought to have been weights or alumets, were in reality—at least after 985/6—fiduciary money. P. Balog, 'Jetons fatimites en verre', *Revue belge de numismatique*, CVII (1961), 171–83, and M. Jungfleisch, 'Jetons (ou poids?) en verre de l'Imam el Montazer', *Bulletin de l'Institut d'Egypte*, XXXIII (1952), 359–74. Curiously, however, no documentary evidence has yet been found to support this thesis.

[2] See Philip Grierson, 'Coinage and Money in the Byzantine Empire', in *Moneta e scambi nell' alto medioevo*, Settimane di studio del Centro Italiano di Studi sull' alto Medioevo, VIII (Spoleto, 1961), 430, and Longuet, op. cit. pp. 11–13. A fair number of silver coins struck during this period *are* listed in Goodacre, op. cit. but most are extremely rare.

[3] Thus the mines of Sardinia, for example, mentioned by Al Idrisi (E. Fagnan, *Extraits inédits relatifs au Maghreb* [Alger, 1924], 109), were lost when the island fell to the Christians early in the eleventh century.

[4] J. Duplessy, 'La circulation des monnaies arabes en Europe occidentale de VIIIe au XIIIe siècle', *Revue numismatique*, 5th ser. XX (1956), 105. Some of the literature on this subject is cited in S. Bolin, 'Mohammed, Charlemagne and Ruric', *Scandinavian Economic History Review*, I (1953), 34, n. 37.

[5] U. S. Linder Welin, 'Arabiska mynt', *Kulturhistorisk leksikon for nordisk middelalder* (Copenhagen, 1956), I, 182–94.

GOLD AND SILVER   5

southern Slavic territories, and then the outflux stopped. Its stoppage corresponds with the onset of the silver famine in Muslim Asia.

At the same time as this leakage was occurring, another process may have been
at work which drew additional silver towards Europe and served to prolong the
famine in the East. In an important article Mr Philip Grierson has suggested
that differences in the silver–gold ratios of the West, Byzantium, and the Islamic
Empire in the late seventh century caused movements of precious metals which
resulted in a redistribution of the supplies of gold and silver in these regions.[1]
The West in this period, he maintains, had a ratio of 12, Byzantium 18, and the
Islamic Empire 14. Because of these differing values of the two precious metals,
gold was drawn away from the region where it was least valued in terms of silver
and moved towards the region where its value was highest; silver moved in the
opposite direction. As a result, Europe lost her gold and received more silver,
Byzantium lost much of her silver but received gold, and the Islamic Empire was
able during the ninth and tenth centuries to maintain a bimetallic currency. To
explain why such a disequilibrium in silver–gold ratios should have continued
in the face of changes in supply, Prof. Cipolla[2] has argued that the abandoning
of gold coinage in the West reduced demand for gold just at the time when
supplies were becoming scarce; thus the price of gold was kept low, with the
result that gold continued to move eastward and silver westward.

This line of argument can be extended to explain, in part at least, the silver
famine of the Muslim world. For the silver–gold ratio in the West was considerably below 12—and often below 10—up till the middle of the thirteenth century,[3]
and the West may therefore have attracted silver throughout this period from
regions which valued it less highly. In the East, however, the high price of gold
in terms of silver continued, rising in the Arab countries during the ninth century
(when the production of the great silver mines at Banjahir was at its peak) and
remaining high during the tenth and probably the eleventh centuries (perhaps
because of the high demand for gold following the abandonment of silver coinage).[4] Quite possibly, the ratios in Byzantium and the Arab countries drew together in this later period, and both were certainly high above that prevailing
in Europe. Such a convergence of ratios in the East, and the continuing disparity
between East and West, could account for the brief reappearance of a bimetallic
currency in Byzantium during the tenth century and for the later disappearance
of silver from *both* Byzantium and the Islamic world. If this argument is correct,
the same forces which drained gold from the West also drew silver out of the East
(though it took longer to exhaust the rich silver stocks of the East than the gold
stocks of the West). The European gold famine and the Muslim silver famine,
according to this interpretation, are thus two sides of the same coin.

The beginning of the end of the silver famine was signalled in the year 1174/5,
when the Ayyubids in Damascus resumed the coining of silver.[5] A few years later,

---

[1] Philip Grierson, 'The Monetary Reforms of 'Abd al-Malik', *Journal of the Economic and Social History
of the Orient*, III (1960), 241–64.
[2] C. Cipolla, 'Sans Mahomet, Charlemagne est inconcevable', *Annales. Economies, Sociétés, Civilisations*,
XVII (1962), 130–6.
[3] *Vide infra* Table 1.   [4] *Vide infra* Table 2.
[5] The sources which have been used to document the return of a silver coinage to the Muslim world
are the same as those cited above on p. 2, n. 2.

6 ANDREW M. WATSON

in 1183/4, they also began minting silver in Hama and Aleppo;[1] and by the 1240's silver had completely displaced gold as the basis of Ayyubid currency in Syria, accounting for roughly 85 per cent of all coins minted.[2] Shortly afterwards silver began to be minted in the territories of the Seljuks of Rum, being struck first in Konia (1185/6) and Kaiseri (1199/1200), and then moving along well-travelled trade routes to reach Siwas (1207/8) and Erzerum (1210/11). Some time between 1196 and 1220 the Christian kingdom of Lesser Armenia in the Gulf of Alexandretta also began minting her silver "trams". From these focal points the minting of silver spread slowly outwards, reaching the Nicaean Empire (between 1222 and 1254), Duneysir (1226/7), Hisn Qaifa (1227/8), Baghdad (1233/4), and the towns of Al Hilla, Wasit, and Basra (between 1298 and 1300). Along another route, farther to the north, silver reappeared in Byzantine Trabizond (between 1235 and 1238), Tiflis in Georgia (1240/1 or shortly thereafter), and Berdaa (1284/5). To the south of Trabizond, silver seems to have followed the main trade routes across Asia, reaching Arzanjan (1260/1), Tabriz (1271/2), Bukhara (1281/2), Samarkand (1283/4),[3] and Tashkent (1284/5). Indeed, in the 1280's and 1290's silver coins began to be struck by dozens of towns which had never struck silver before—towns in Asia Minor, Russia, Persia, and Turkestan —so that no clear direction of flow is by then apparent. Quite possibly, as one scholar has argued, monetary reforms introduced by the Mongols released great quantities of silver from China after 1260, and this silver moved westwards through Central Asia and perhaps into Arab countries.[4] However this may be, another direction of flow—from Christian West to Muslim East—is also apparent in this period, and the rate of flow was undoubtedly quickened by the ease of trade and travel in Mongol Asia.

In Egypt, North Africa, and Spain the end of the silver famine is more difficult to date precisely than in those eastern reaches of the Muslim world. Some dirhems of good quality must have been minted by towns in North Africa before the end of the twelfth century, but these have not yet been identified.[5] However, from 1229/30 onwards the Almohads in North Africa and Spain, as well as the Beni Hudid in Spain, struck recognizable silver coins at a number of towns; and although much of Muslim Spain was lost to the Christians shortly thereafter, the towns of the Maghreb probably continued to mint silver of varying fineness until the end of the Middle Ages.[6] In Egypt the return to silver came later than in the Maghreb. Although three Ayyubid rulers—Saladin, 'Adel I, and Saleh

---

[1] This date, like all other dates given for the return to silver in the East, has been obtained from the numismatic evidence. One documentary source, however, puts the return to silver in Aleppo a year earlier. *Vide* Abou Shamah, 'Le livre des deux jardins', *Recueil des historiens des croisades. Historiens orientaux*, IV (Paris, 1898), 238.

[2] Wakin, op. cit. In the very large sample of Ayyubid coins examined by Miss Wakin, only 32 per cent of those struck between 1174/5 and 1193/4 were silver. From the period after 1242/3, however, 85 per cent of all the coins were silver.

[3] Actually, Markov, op. cit., mentions four silver coins struck at Samarkand during the silver famine.

[4] Blake, op. cit. As already suggested, however, this article is not altogether reliable. In G. Tullock, 'Paper Money—A Cycle in Cathay', *Economic History Review*, 2nd ser. IX (1957), 393–407, further information is given which could be used in support of this hypothesis.

[5] *Vide infra* the discussion of the *millarès*. The Muslim coin which the Europeans were imitating must have been at least 10/12 fine.

[6] This at least is what is stated in Faruggia de Candia, 'Monnaies hafsites...', op. cit. p. 231, and seems to be implied in Brunschvig, op. cit. The later coins, however, do not seem to have been identified.

GOLD AND SILVER   7

Ayyub—attempted to reintroduce a good silver coin, their efforts all failed and throughout the Ayyubid period the silver coinage struck in Cairo remained very debased.[1] In consequence, the good silver coins struck in Syrian mints began to filter into Egypt and probably circulated widely. Only in 1256/7, with the coming of the Bahri Mamluks, did Egypt get her own strong silver coinage.[2]

The return to silver in the Muslim world thus began towards the end of the twelfth century, and one hundred years later the triumph of silver was complete. In Europe, at roughly the same time, a bimetallic currency was also being re-introduced. The first step was taken by Genoa, which apparently began to mint gold coins at the very end of the twelfth or early in the thirteenth century.[3] But the real turning-point was not until 1252: in that year Florence and Genoa, by striking their new gold coins, the florin and a new *genovino*, touched off "one of the greatest chain reactions in monetary history". This was to end with the victory of gold in almost every part of Europe by the middle of the fourteenth century.

Thus both Christian Europe and the Muslim world underwent a monetary revolution at about the same time. Can it be mere coincidence that the silver famine in the East ended only a little before gold reappeared in the West?

II

Much of the silver which allowed Islamic mints to strike silver coins again seems to have come from Europe. It proceeded over a number of different routes and for a variety of reasons. In the long run, however, the result was everywhere the same: the Muslim countries all received enough silver to bring the famine to an end.

The first such outflow of silver from Europe began with the Crusades, and as long as the Christian warriors held a stronghold in the Levant they continued to draw silver from West to East. It seems likely, of course, that the crusaders tried to take with them as much *gold* as they could secure, since gold was the basis of all currencies in the Arab East. Thus there was a considerable demand for the gold pieces which from the eleventh century onwards had been struck in Christian Spain in imitation of Arab coins,[4] as well as for the later *augustales* of thirteenth-century Sicily; gold was also sent to the East in the form of bars and ingots.[5] In this way, it seems, the crusaders succeeded in keeping Europe drained of gold and probably delayed the West's return to a gold currency. But such gold as

---

[1] Balog, 'History of the Dirhem . . .', op. cit. p. 130.

[2] Ibid. p. 141. Balog has found the silver of the Bahri Mamluks to be 62 to 78 per cent fine, while that of the Burji Mamluks was more than 90 per cent fine. According to the tests carried out by Balog, the monetary reform of 1225/6 involved a change only in the shape of the dirhem, not in its fineness. Al Makrizi thus appears to have been wrong about this reform.

[3] The case for a golden *genovino* issued around the year 1200 was accepted by many numismatists in the nineteenth century and seems, to this writer, to have been proved in C. Astengo. 'L'inizio della coniazione dell' oro ed una pubblicazione del prof. R. S. Lopez della Yale University', *Rivista italiana di numismatica*, LXIII (1961), 13–57. This position is also taken in *Corpus nummorum Italicorum*, III (Rome, 1912), 16.

[4] O. Gil Farrés. *Historia de la moneda española* (Madrid, 1959), pp. 135–6, 198–9, discusses these coins. That they were greatly demanded by crusaders is stated in H. de Marchéville, 'Le rapport entre l'argent et l'or au temps de St Louis', *Annuaire de la Société de Numismatique*, XIV (1890), 157.

[5] E.g. the shipment mentioned in H. Lavoix, *Monnaies à légendes arabes frappées en Syrie par les croisés* (Paris, 1877), pp. 26–7.

A N D R E W   M.   W A T S O N

could be procured in Europe was not nearly enough to take care of the needs of the crusaders: it had to be supplemented by large quantities of silver. Indeed, all the moneys mentioned by one of the chroniclers as being used on the First Crusade were silver,[1] and silver probably made up the greater part of the coins and specie carried to the East by early crusaders, pilgrims, and traders. In later shipments of moneys to the Latin East silver seems also to predominate. In the funds sent to Alfonse, Count of Poitiers, in 1250, for instance, there were only 71 marks of gold but 1,772 marks of silver.[2] "Crusader" coin hoards also suggest that large quantities of silver coins flowed out of Europe towards the East in the period of the Crusades. The ten such hoards found in the eastern Mediterranean dating from the eleventh and twelfth centuries contain more than 2,000 silver or billon coins—the great majority from France—but only one gold coin.[3] Although the evidence of these hoards is still too limited to justify any conclusion about the use that was made of these and similar coins brought eastwards by Europeans, it does suggest that in the twelfth century silver coinage from the West, especially from France, circulated widely in the Latin East and probably beyond. In short, the boundaries of the European monetary zone seem to have been extended eastwards.

Such a displacement of European silver was no doubt what permitted the Latins to begin striking their own silver coinage in the East—long before the neighbouring Muslim regions of the East resumed the minting of silver. Almost immediately after the First Crusade silver or billon coins were issued by Count Bertrand of Tripoli, and before 1131 by the kings of Jerusalem; in 1149, and probably earlier, the counts of Antioch were also striking silver. By the early thirteenth century, the number of crusader mints which were active had increased considerably: silver was being struck not only at the places already mentioned, but also in Jaffa, Sidon, Beirut, Cyprus, and, after Constantinople capitulated to the Venetians, through much of Greece. In the thirteenth century, too, heavier silver coins were struck, first under Jean de Brienne (d. 1250), and after the middle of the century under the last two counts of Tripoli, who issued a *gros* and a *demi-gros*.[4] And finally, after the Ayyubids resumed the minting of silver coins in Damascus, Aleppo, and Hama, Christian minters in Tripoli and Acre took advantage of the new opportunities presented and began to counterfeit these Muslim coins. Only in 1250, when a shocked Innocent IV learned that papal funds were subsidizing warriors who struck coins praising Mohammed and his god, was this manufacture stopped—or driven underground. But even after this date, at least until the year 1253, silver coins with Arabic legends (from which, however, the offending words had been removed) continued to be struck by the Christians at Acre.[5] Both the earlier counterfeit Muslim coins and these later

---

[1] Raymond d'Aguilers, as cited by Lavoix, 'Monnaies...', op. cit. p. 28.

[2] E. Cartier, 'Or et argent, monnoyés ou non monnoyés, envoyés en Palestine à Alfonse, Comte de Poitiers, frère de Saint-Louis dans l'année 1250', *Revue numismatique*, XII (1847), 121–50.

[3] This conclusion was arrived at from an analysis of the data in J. Duplessy and D. M. Metcalf, 'Le trésor de Samos et la circulation monétaire en Orient Latin aux XIIe et XIIIe siècles', *Revue belge de numismatique*, CVIII (1962), 202–4.

[4] G. Schlumberger, *Numismatique de l'Orient Latin* (Graz, 1954), *passim*.

[5] P. Balog and J. Yvon, 'Monnaies à légendes arabes de l'Orient Latin', *Revue numismatique*, 5th ser. XXII (1958), 160. These coins were first identified by Balog in op. cit. *Bulletin de l'Institut d'Egypte*, XXXIV (1952), 45 ff.

coins seem clear proof that silver was passing farther eastward, from Christian into Muslim hands.

The very large output of silver coins in the Latin kingdoms in the thirteenth century seems to have displaced somewhat the European coins which, it has been suggested, circulated widely in the East during the previous century. Thus in the "crusader" hoards of the *thirteenth* century silver coins from the Latin East are preponderant and European coins in the minority.[1] One should not, how-ever, conclude that silver ceased to flow eastwards from Europe to the Levant. Even in the thirteenth century, the "crusader" hoards *do* contain a considerable number of European coins, enough to lead two scholars to conclude that Euro-pean silver coinage was still used on a wide scale in the Aegean and the Levant at least until about 1250.[2] Undoubtedly, the influx of such coins and of silver in bars was what enabled the Latins to strike so much silver in the East.[3] And it was probably this European silver, filtering farther eastwards in trade, or cap-tured, which allowed the Ayyubids in Syria and the Seljuks of Rum to return to a silver standard.

While they were in this way reintroducing silver into the Levant, the Christians in the East also came to handle more and more gold. Part of this gold probably came from Europe as papal subsidies and other transfers to warriors and mer-chants in the Holy Land. Though the amount of gold which Europe could send may at first have been small, larger shipments may have been made after the opening of trade with the North African ports during the eleventh century; in-deed the movement of African gold from Italy to the Levant may explain the prolongation of the European gold famine until the middle of the thirteenth century. A greater part of the gold used by the crusaders, however, seems to have been of eastern origin. It came from subsidies paid by the Emperor of Constanti-nople to the Franks;[4] tribute exacted from Arab potentates who bought off the Christians or enlisted their help;[5] dowries, such as that brought by the widow of Roger I of Sicily, whom Baldwin I bigamously married;[6] booty, such as the 20 golden lamps weighing 20,000 mithqals, removed by Tancred from the temple of Jerusalem;[7] payments made by Arab merchants to their Christian counter-parts; and taxes raised in conquered areas where the basis of the currency had long been gold. The sums so obtained were truly enormous, though they were often quickly spent. They permitted the crusaders to make very large payments in gold: to buy twice, for instance, the island of Cyprus for 100,000 bezants,[8] to

---

[1] D. H. Cox, *The Tripolis Hoard of French Seignorial and Crusaders' Coins* (New York, 1933); H. Longuet, 'La trouvaille de Kessab en Orient Latin', *Revue numismatique*, 4th ser. xxxviii (1935), 163–83; and C. P. Seltman, 'A Hoard of Coins in Frankish Greece', *The Numismatic Circular*, lxxii (1964), 135.

[2] Cox, op. cit. and Longuet, 'La trouvaille...', op. cit. This view is also put forward by Schlumberger, op. cit. p. 5. Duplessy and Metcalf, in op. cit., are more cautious in interpreting the evidence.

[3] Balog, in *Bulletin de l'Institut d'Egypte* (1952), op. cit. believes that some of these coins may have been struck in Venice.

[4] E.g. the subsidies paid by Alexis Comnenus to those participating in the First Crusade, as reported by Albert of Aix. Other examples are given in Yvon and Balog, op. cit. p. 134, nn. 1–2.

[5] E.g. two payments of 1,000,000 dinars made by Chawar to the Christians, mentioned in E. Minost, 'Au sujet du Traité des Monnaies Musulmanes de Makrizi', *Bulletin de l'Institut d'Egypte*, xix (1936–7), 50. It is not clear, however, that these sums were actually paid in full.

[6] Mentioned in L. Blancard, *Le besant d'or sarrazinas* (Marseilles, 1880), p. 8.   [7] Ibid. p. 8.

[8] The island was purchased by the Templars in 1191 and sold by them to Guy de Lusignan in 1192. *Chronique d'Amadi*, ed. R. de Mas Latrie (Paris, 1841), pp. 83, 85.

free Raymond of Tripoli at a cost of 150,000 bezants of Tyre,[1] and to ransom the
army of Saint Louis for 800,000 dinars.[2]

Having thus fallen heirs to lands in which gold was the basis of the currency,
and having themselves acquired large quantities of gold, it is small wonder that
the rulers of the Latin Orient also began to strike gold coins. According to an
Arab source,[3] the Christians who captured Tyre (in 1124) continued to mint
gold there in the name of the Egyptian sovereign, Al-Amir, for a period of three
years, after which they stopped. Very probably, these coins were struck with dies
that had been captured, and are therefore indistinguishable from the coins they
counterfeited.[4] It seems, however, that by the third quarter of the twelfth century,
if not much earlier,[5] gold coins were again being produced in Tyre—coins which
can be identified because they were imperfect imitations of Faṭinḍ dinars,
deficient in weight and fineness, and often crude in lettering. Simḷla. besancii
sarracenati, as these coins were known, were being made in Acre, Tripoli, and
Antioch by the first decades of the thirteenth century and perhaps much earlier.
At Acre and Tripoli, at least, these counterfeit coins were still being struck in the
middle of the thirteenth century. Only in 1250, when an indignant Innocent IV
excommunicated those involved, did the official production of these coins stop.[6]
But from 1251 to 1257, at least, and perhaps over a longer period, a mint in Acre
continued to strike imitation dinars; these later coins, however, could give the
Pope no offence, since their legends, though in Arabic, did not mention Mohammed or the Islamic year.[7] That the coins to which the Pope objected also
continued to be made in clandestine workshops is not unlikely. By this time,
however, the need for such coins was less: Europe was already minting its own
gold coins which were quickly to become *the* international currency. (Indeed the
striking of gold in Europe may have been precipitated by the papal ban two years
earlier on the minting of the *besancii sarracenati* in the East. Initially, the one may
have been just a substitute for the other.)

The appearance of these imitation dinars in the Latin Orient is far more than
a numismatic anomaly. It is an occurrence which is crucially linked to the
monetary history of both East and West.[8] By the end of the eleventh century the
gold coins of most regions in the East had been considerably debased and were

---

[1] Ibn al Athir in *Recueil des historiens des croisades. Historiens orientaux*, I (Paris, 1872), 619.

[2] Joinville and Villehardouin, *Chronicles of the Crusades*, ed. M. R. B. Shaw (Harmondsworth, 1963),
pp. 249 ff. It is not certain, however, that the sum was all paid in gold, or that the second instalment
was paid at all.

[3] Ibn Khallikan, *Kitab wafayat al 'ayan* (Cairo, 1882), II, 189.

[4] This point is discussed in Yvon and Balog, op. cit. pp. 141–2.

[5] The dating of these coins is extremely difficult, if not impossible, until more evidence from hoards
is available. However, the texts, e.g. Ibn Al Athir and Ibn Jubair, seem to suggest that this coin was
being struck in the 1170's and 1180's.

[6] The letter is reproduced in Schlumberger, op. cit. pp. 139–40.

[7] Another type of crusader gold coin with a Latin legend, probably dating from after 1251, has been
identified by P. Grierson in 'A Rare Crusader Bezant with the *Christus Vincit* Legend', *American Numismatic Society. Museum Notes*, VI (1954), 169–78.

[8] A link between crusader gold coins and the return to gold in the West has already been suggested in
R. S. Lopez, *Settecento anni fa: Il ritorno all' oro nell' Occidente duecentesco* (Naples, 1955), and in A. Ehrenkreutz, 'Arabic Dinars struck by the Crusaders', *Journal of the Economic and Social History of the Orient*, VII
(1964), 167–82. An earlier study by G. I. Bratianu, 'L'hyperpère byzantin et la monnaie d'or des ré-
publiques italiennes au XIIIe siècle', *Mélanges Charles Diehl* (Paris, 1930), I, 37–48, suggested a con-
nexion between the decline of Byzantine gold coinage and the return to gold in Italy.

losing prestige: this was the case of the Byzantine *nomisma* and of the dinars of the Abassid caliphate. No gold whatever seems to have been struck in the areas controlled by the Seljuks. Only the Fatimid dinars minted in Egypt and (for a time) in Syria could boast the fineness and the uniformity of weight necessary for an international currency.[1] Perhaps because of their prestige, it was these Fatimid dinars which the crusaders chose to counterfeit. But the imitation dinars struck by the crusaders may have eventually undermined the Fatimid gold currency. For the influx of these coins, lighter in weight and less pure than the originals, appears to have set in operation Gresham's Law, causing hoarding and export of good gold coins.[2] This process was accelerated in Syria by the return to a sound silver coinage in 1174/5: the new silver coins, by providing an alternative to gold, made it unnecessary to strike more gold, and allowed the stocks of gold in circulation to be released to areas where they were more in demand.[3] In fact, gold seems to have disappeared from the Levant shortly after the reappearance of silver. In Egypt, the Ayyubids were not successful in introducing a strong silver coinage, but here, too, gold coinage faltered,[4] the metal probably moving to the Christian Levant and Europe. So acute did the shortage of gold become that, according to Makrizi, "to say the name of a pure gold coin was like mentioning the name of a wife to a jealous husband, while to get such a coin in one's hands was like crossing the gates of paradise."[5] The way was prepared for an influx of the fine silver coins being minted in Syria and for the eventual return to a silver-based currency.

The Latin kingdoms were therefore a point of leverage around which the monetary history of both East and West turned. Through them the East obtained the silver which brought the silver famine to an end. And in these kingdoms Europeans again began minting gold, drew considerable supplies of gold out of the neighbouring countries, and undermined what had been the strongest gold currency in the world. The need thus arose for a new gold coinage of high quality which could be used in international trade, and Europeans were getting into position to fill that need.

While the Near East was receiving from Europe enough silver to revive its silver coinage, enormous quantities of silver were escaping from Europe to North Africa in a commerce which, had it been more widely known, would have scandalized all Christendom.[6] It seems some mints in Western Europe had been

[1] Ehrenkreutz, op. cit. p. 174.

[2] Ibid. pp. 177 ff. This argument, however, assumes that the crusader dinars circulated at par, or nearly at par, with Fatimid dinars.

[3] An exchange of gold from the Arab countries for silver from the Latin Orient is suggested by C. Cahen in 'Notes sur l'histoire des croisades et de l'Orient Latin', *Bulletin de la Faculté des Lettres de Strasbourg.* XXIX (1950), 338.

[4] A. Ehrenkreutz, 'The Crisis of the *Dinar* in the Egypt of Saladin', *Journal of the American Oriental Society*, LXXVI (1956), 178–84.

[5] Al Makrizi, *Traité des monnoies musulmanes*, ed. Silvestre de Sacy (Paris, 1797), p. 43. Cited in Ehrenkreutz, 'The Crisis...', op. cit. p. 178. Al Makrizi also states that silver was in short supply at the same time, but we know that silver eventually returned to Egypt.

[6] The standard literature on this subject is L. Blancard, *Le millarès* (Marseilles, 1876); A. de Longpérier, 'Le millarès, étude sur une monnaie du XIIIe siècle...', *Journal des savants* (1876), pp. 428–41; A. Germain, *De la monnaie mahométane attribuée à un évêque de Maguelone* (Montpellier, 1854); and L. Blancard, *Essai sur les monnaies de Charles Ier* (Paris, 1868), pp. 480–93. More recent discussion of the coin in Spain and Italy may be found in P. F. Casaretto, *La moneta genovese in confronto con le altre valute mediterranee* (Genoa, 1928), pp. 203–19; F. Mateu y Llopis, 'La repoblación musulmana del Reino de Valencia

counterfeiting the half-dirhem of the Almohads for shipment to certain ports in North Africa—Bougie, Ceuta, Oran, and Tlemcen—and occasionally to Sicily and Spain from at least as early as 1202.[1] The manufacture of the *millarès*, or *milliarensis*, as this money was called, was sanctioned in concessions granted to minters by temporal and spiritual rulers, a number of which documents have survived.[2] The scandal lay not in the fact that the counterfeiting of coins was officially condoned by these concessions, for it was fair enough (perhaps even commendable) to cheat the infidel. It was rather that the *millarès* bore legends such as "There is no god but Allah; Mohammed is his apostle; the Mahdi is our Imam." Even worse, the highest officials in the Christian world were implicated in this sordid commerce. The Bishop of Melgueil, whose diocese fell under the direct jurisdiction of the Pope, granted one of these concessions, and doubtless profited greatly from it; another was given in the name of the Bishop of Agde; and a third was in the gift of the Count of Toulouse, the brother of Saint Louis. Similar coins, all destined for the North African coast, were struck in such widely scattered places as Arles, Montpellier, Marseilles, Tarascon, the Bishopric of Agde, the Bishopric of Maguelone, the Venaissin, the Island of Oléron, Majorca, Barcelona, Lérida, Valencia (after its reconquest), Genoa, Savignone, Pisa, and Montieri.[3]

The manufacture of the *millarès* went on unhindered for over sixty years, and may have continued in secrecy still longer. In the late 1260's and in the 1270's, however, the trade in these coins seems to have slowed down and then came to a halt. Saint Louis, who had already persuaded Innocent IV to ban the striking of coins with Muslim legends in the East, could hardly allow such sacrilege to continue in his own country, and in the second half of his reign he pursued a policy of forbidding all imitations of Muslim coins.[4] He also brought pressure to bear on the rulers of neighbouring regions lying beyond his control. Thus in 1266 he successfully persuaded Clement IV to command the Bishop of Maguelone to stop this manufacture in his diocese.[5] Similarly, in 1266 he prevailed upon his brother Alfonse II, the Count of Toulouse, to prohibit the manufacture of the *millarès* in the territories under his control,[6] and in the following year letters to this effect were sent by the Count to his officials in the Venaissin and on the Island of Oléron.[7] Saint Louis was not, however, able to suppress altogether the striking

---

en el siglo XIII y las monedas de tipo almohade', *Boletín de la Sociedad Castellonense de Cultura*, XXVIII (1952), 29–43; and J. Botet y Sisó, *Les monedes catalanes* (Barcelona, 1909), II, 52–61.

[1] This is the date given by Blancard, *Le Millarès*, op. cit. p. 27, based on a Statute of Arles which, it is believed, can be dated not later than 1202 and probably somewhat earlier. Genoese documents from the end of the twelfth century mention the coin, as does the *Liber Abaci* of Leonardo Pisano, written in 1202. Casaretto, op. cit. pp. 203, 206.

[2] See, for example, the concession reproduced in Alvaro Campaner y Fuertes, *Numismática Balear* (Palma de Mallorca, 1879), pp. 263–4, or that in R. S. Lopez, *La prima crisi della Banca di Genova* (Milan, 1956), pp. 155–6.

[3] Blancard, *Le Millarès*, op. cit. p. 7; Lopez, *La prima crisi...*, loc. cit.; Mateu y Llopis, op. cit.; Gil Farrés, op. cit. p. 138.

[4] T. N. Bisson, 'Coinage and Royal Monetary Policy in Languedoc during the Reign of Saint Louis', *Speculum*, XXXII (1957), 457.

[5] Arch. dép. de l'Hérault, Cartulaire de Maguelone, Reg. D. fo. 279v. Reproduced in Longpérier, op. cit. p. 431.

[6] Germain, op. cit. p. 6.

[7] *Correspondance administrative d'Alfonse de Poitiers*, ed. A. Molinier (Paris, 1894–1900), I, nos. 556, 695. Cited in Bisson, op. cit. p. 466.

of these coins.[1] Thus in areas lying beyond the jurisdiction of the Pope and the king of France permission to strike the *millarès* was still being granted in the 1270's: Charles I, the Count of Provence, issued such an authorization in 1272 to the lessees of the mint of Tarascon,[2] and Jaime I of Aragon granted the right to strike these coins in Majorca in 1273.[3] By the later 1270's, however, this commerce seems to have ended. Perhaps the purer silver coinage which appeared in Hafsid territories some time between 1262 and 1287[4] displaced the *millarès* (which was by the 1270's considerably debased) and made the striking of Muslim silver coins unprofitable for Europeans. Perhaps, too, the general decline in trade between North Africa and the ports of France and Italy, which a number of scholars believe occurred in the second half of the thirteenth century, may have brought about a decline in the trade in Muslim coins.[5] The opposite, however, is more likely true: the decline in the export of *millarès*, the most important commodity sent by Europe to the Maghreb, probably brought about the general decline of trade with North Africa.

We have no way of telling how much silver was lost to Europe in this commerce, but everything suggests that the leakage was of paramount importance. In the notarized trading documents from thirteenth-century Marseilles there are some 40 contracts (out of about 1,200 cited) which mention the purchase of *millarès* with European currencies; in almost every case, these coins were to be shipped to North Africa "ad laborandum".[6] Another glimpse of this traffic is afforded by some curious Genoese documents relating to an incident which occurred in 1234. In that year a number of Genoese ships lying at harbour in Ceuta had been attacked by the Moors, and in order to press claims against the Sultan the Italians drew up a list of losses. In almost all of the 34 cases for which documents have survived, the coins which were carried by the ships were *millarès*; the total losses reported amount to almost 55,000 of these coins.[7] The revival of silver mining in Sardinia, under the control of Genoese lessees, seems to have been closely connected with the great demand of the merchants of Genoa and nearby cities for this coin. One document shows that a partner in the mining venture also dealt in the *millarès*.[8] Another glimpse of the great output of these coins is afforded by a receipt sent by Jaime I of Aragon to the master of the mint in Montpellier which struck these coins stating that in the years 1267 and 1268 a total of 54,509 marcs of silver were converted into *millarès*.[9] On the basis of this figure, one scholar has

---

[1] Indeed it may be that as the number of mints empowered to strike the *millarès* was reduced the production of those which remained in business increased. The high output of the mint in Montpellier in the years 1267 and 1268 may perhaps be accounted for in this way. *Vide infra* in text.

[2] Blancard, *Essai....* op. cit. pp. 459–61 reproduces the document.

[3] Campaner y Fuertes, loc. cit.   [4] Brunschvig, op. cit. pp. 71–2.

[5] E.g. R.-H. Bautier, 'Les relations commerciales entre l'Europe et l'Afrique du Nord', *Bulletin philologique et historique* (1953–4), pp. 399–416; E. Baratier, 'Influence de la politique angevine sur le déclin commercial de Marseille aux XIIIe et XIVe siècles', in *VI Congreso de Historia de la Corona de Aragón* (Madrid, 1959), p. 683.

[6] L. Blancard, *Documents inédits sur le commerce de Marseille au Moyen Age* (Marseilles, 1884), 2 vols. *passim*.

[7] Calculated from the documents in Raffaele di Tucci, 'Documenti inediti sulla spedizione e sulla mahone dei Genovesi a Ceuta (1234–37)', *Atti della Società Ligure di Storia Patria*, LXIV (1935), 271–340.

[8] R. S. Lopez, 'Contributo alla storia delle miniere argentifere di Sardegna', *Studi economico-giuridici*, XXIV (Cagliari, 1936), 13.

[9] Document reproduced in Germain, op. cit. pp. 12–13.

hazarded the guess that more than three billion (3,000,000,000) such coins were struck in the Christian world and exported during the thirteenth century.[1] These would have contained about 4,000 metric tons of silver.[2] (According to A. Soetbeer, the *total European output of silver* during the twenty-eight years from 1493 to 1520—a time when the silver mines in Eastern Europe were flourishing—was only 47 metric tons.[3])

How the North African cities were able to pay for such enormous quantities of silver our sources do not explain. Clearly, the agricultural and industrial goods exported from the Maghreb, counterbalanced as they were by imports of cloths and oriental wares from Europe, could have paid for only a small part of this bullion. *The rest was almost certainly paid for in gold.* For centuries the "gold of Ghana" had been moving northwards across the Sahara to the ports of the Maghreb, to Egypt, and to Spain; and thence, from the twelfth century onwards, some of this gold went to Christian Europe.[4] Significantly, *all* the Arab coins which have been found in European hoards buried during the twelfth and thirteenth centuries are *gold* coins; significantly, too, all these coins were struck in African or Spanish mints.[5] It was most probably this African gold reaching the shores of Italy which allowed Genoa to issue her precocious gold coins at the end of the twelfth century or the beginning of the thirteenth.[6] But during the first half of the thirteenth century some of this gold entering Europe seems to have been drained off towards the Latin kingdoms of the Orient to supply part of the raw material for the *besancii sarracenati* which the Christians were striking in the East. (Quite possibly, some of these counterfeit dinars were even struck in the West for export to the East: thus the notarial documents of Marseilles show that the very merchants who were sending *millarès* to the Maghreb, and presumably receiving payment partly in gold, were also shipping *sarracenati* to the Levant.[7]) When Europe went "back to gold" in the 1250's, however, and the Latin East ceased striking gold coins, this pattern of trade changed. From that time onwards, the gold which flowed into Europe from the ports of North Africa and Spain largely remained in Europe.[8] It provided an important part of the raw material from which Europe's new gold coinage was struck.

The decline of the *millarès* did not spell the end of the drain of European silver toward the Muslim world or of the inflow of gold which was received in exchange. For the movement of precious metals between the two monetary zones was to

---

[1] Longpérier, op. cit. p. 436. The figure is perhaps excessive, as it was based on the performance of what may have been one of the most active mints during its busiest period. On the other hand, we now know of more mints which produced the *millarès* than Longpérier was aware of.

[2] The calculation is based on the assumption that each *millarès* weighed 1·36 gr. and was 10/12 fine.

[3] A. Soetbeer, *Edelmetall-Produktion und Wertverhältnis zwischen Gold und Silber...* Petermann's Mittheilungen, Ergänzungsheft LVII (Gotha, 1879), 107.

[4] The main literature on this subject is C. de la Roncière, *La découverte de l'Afrique au Moyen Age* (Cairo, 1924), I, 77 ff.; E. W. Bovill, *The Golden Trade of the Moors* (London, 1958); E.-F. Gautier, 'L'or du Soudan dans l'histoire', *Annales d'histoire économique et sociale*, VII (1935), 113-23; and V. Magalhães Godinho, 'O "Mediterraneo" saariano e as caravanas de ouro', *Revista de história*, VI (São Paulo, 1955), 74-134.

[5] Duplessy, op. cit. pp. 130-1.   [6] *Vide supra*, p. 7, n. 3.

[7] Blancard, *Documents...*, op. cit. shows that the Manduel family engaged in both kinds of business. Cf. docs. 3 and 4.

[8] Blancard, *Essai...*, op. cit. p. 297, believes that there was a considerable circulation of Islamic gold in Provence in the time of Charles I.

continue for at least another two centuries and was to displace still greater amounts of bullion. A new peak of activity seems to have been reached in the last decade of the thirteenth century and the first two decades of the fourteenth century—at precisely the time when large quantities of gold coins were being struck at Venice and in France. Another burst of activity occurred in the 1330's and 1340's, when much of northern Europe, as well as parts of Spain, returned to a gold coinage. And after this crisis had been weathered, the exchange of precious metals continued—indeed it was to last until the very end of the Middle Ages. What can be noticed, however, are certain changes in the character of the trade. Fewer counterfeit coins were sent, though they were by no means unknown; more of the metal exchanged was in the form of genuine coins, plate, and bars of gold and silver. By the end of the thirteenth century, too, the export of precious metals had become illicit in those European countries which were striking gold, as governments struggled vainly to achieve some stability in their bimetallic currencies. In consequence, the traffic became clandestine. Hidden from view in secret account-books, concealed in ledgers and notarial documents by moneys-of-account, escaping the detection of customs officials of the time (and of scholars today), this fugitive commerce seldom came to light except when flagrant violation of the rules provoked an inquiry and perhaps a lawsuit.

But continue it did. From the southern coast of France, and particularly from Montpellier, silver still escaped from the European monetary zone. In a document which dates from about the end of the thirteenth century, the master minter of France pleaded that laws be passed similar to those of England against the export of silver ("*l'argent métal*"); he estimated that "l'on a bien trait en la terre des sarrasins 400,000 marcs [or about 100 tons] et plus."[1] Barely had the silver been taken out of the mines, according to one writer, when it was secretly shipped out. For a slightly later period, Prof. Bautier has collected documents which compromise the patricians of Montpellier in about a dozen cases of illegal export of silver over a period of about twenty-five years. In *one* of these cases witnesses evaluated the silver melted down in two (of several) mills at between 100,000 and 120,000 marcs; but the amount of copper extracted from the silver and sold apparently suggests that the silver obtained actually weighed between 200,000 and 400,000 marcs (or 50 to 100 tons).[2] Another episode in this commerce concerns the smuggling out of the kingdom of 100,000 marcs of *monnaie noire*.[3] Small wonder it is, then, that in this period France was afflicted with an acute silver crisis, such that for years on end (e.g. from 1308 to 1314) no good silver coins were struck; although gold coins were becoming increasingly plentiful, there was an acute shortage of silver in circulation.[4] Later in the fourteenth century Montpellier was still apparently a centre for the bullion trade, in spite of ever stricter laws against the export of precious metals and in spite of the city's gradual loss

[1] Quoted in A. Grunzweig, 'Les incidences internationales des mutations monétaires de Philippe le Bel', *Le Moyen Age*, LIX (1953), 118.

[2] R.-H. Bautier, 'L'or et l'argent en occident de la fin du XIIIe siècle au début du XIVe siècle', *Académie des Inscriptions et Belles-Lettres. Comptes rendus* (1951), pp. 169–70. This is a preliminary article without footnotes or other references to sources. The main article has still not appeared, and I have been unable to learn what sources Professor Bautier used.

[3] Ibid. p. 170.

[4] See Grunzweig, op. cit. and L. Borelli de Serres, 'Les variations monétaires sous Philippe le Bel', *Gazette numismatique française*, V (1901), 245–367, VI (1902), 9–67.

16   ANDREW M. WATSON

of independence. A letter of 1368 from "Loys, filz du roy de France . . . au recteur de Montpeslier et a touz commissaires . . ." ordered legal proceedings against merchants and money-changers of the town who "feissent aler les billons hors du royaume, ou feissent autre si grant trespassement [against the King's monetary regulations] que nous ne le peussons bonnement souffrir a passer soubz dissimulacion".[1] These proceedings, if they were initiated, could not have been very effective: as will be shown below, the city in the fifteenth century was still one of the most important centres for this commerce.

Although the evidence from the Italian cities is more fragmentary, it suggests that they also played an important role in the exchange of precious metals during the late thirteenth century and throughout the fourteenth century. Genoese merchants, drawing on the silver resources of the Alpine areas and of Provence,[2] shipped silver to Pera,[3] Caffa, Tabriz,[4] and Tunis[5] in the 1290's and 1300's; the port books of Genoa from the years 1366–7 show shipments of silver to Sicily, Tunis, Cyprus, and Beirut. At the same time, these port books show that the city was receiving enormous quantities of gold, almost all of which came from "Yspania" and was doubtless of African origin.[6] Florence was another centre for the export of silver: in 1345, Villani reported that there was "grande difetto e nulla moneta d'argento", and that "tutte le monete d'argento si fondeano e portavansi oltramare."[7] Apparently the striking of new silver coins of good quality did not end the shortage, for he informs us that in 1347 "i mercatanti per guadagnare ricoglievano [l'argento] e portavanlo oltremare ov' era molto richiesto."[8] Naples, too, became a centre for the export of European silver towards the East. From the early years of the fourteenth century this city began striking large quantities of a new silver coin, the *gigliato*, for export to many parts of the eastern Mediterranean, where it quickly became the leading international silver currency, imitated by the Turkish emirs and the Knights of St John in Rhodes and counterfeited by others.[9] So high had the output of these coins risen by 1326 that the

---

[1] Document quoted in Germain, *Histoire du commerce de Montpellier* (Montpellier, 1851), II, 274–5.

[2] J. Day, *Les douanes de Gênes, 1376–77* (Paris, 1963), gives a number of customs documents testifying to an outflow of silver from Provence to Genoa. *Vide*, e.g., pp. 289, 386, 802, 830.

[3] F. Balducci Pegolotti, *La pratica della mercatura*, ed. A. Evans (Cambridge, Mass., 1936), p. 219. For a revision of the traditional dating of this work, see P. Grierson, 'The Coin List of Pegolotti', in *Studi in onore di Armando Sapori* (Milan, 1957), I, 483–92.

[4] See, e.g., the document reproduced in G. I. Bratianu, *Recherches sur le commerce gènois dans la Mer Noire au XIIIe siècle* (Paris, 1929), pp. 319–20.

[5] Balducci Pegolotti, op. cit. p. 133.

[6] Day, op. cit. gives a very large number of entries of gold from Spain, the total value of which, according to my calculations, was L.Gen. 134,080. Much smaller quantities of gold, the total value of which was only about one-sixth of the above amount, were received from Sicily, Naples, Provence, Flanders, Gaeta, and Calabria. Exports of gold amounted to L.Gen. 25,569, and were sent to Alexandria (mainly), Sicily, Famagusta, Beirut, Ibiza, and Malaga. "Yspania" probably means Muslim Spain and Morocco, but some of this Spanish gold came through Barcelona and Valencia. According to Prof. Earl Hamilton, a large part of the gold coined in Valencia came from Moorish *doblas* which were melted down. "On September 6, 1405, the city council wrote Francesco Ferrer, master of the mint, that his absence was depriving foreign and native merchants of an outlet for their doblas, and that 'thereby the city is losing a great deal ... because gold is leaving the country'." *Money, Prices and Wages in Valencia, Aragon, and Navarre, 1351–1500* (Cambridge, Mass. 1936), p. 17, n. 4.

[7] *Croniche di Giovanni, Matteo e Filippo Villani*, ed. A. Racheli (Trieste, 1857), I, 476 (XII, 53).

[8] Ibid. I, 476 (XII, 97).

[9] P. Grierson, 'La moneta veneziana nell'economia mediterranea del Trecento e Quattrocento', *La civiltà veneziana del Quattrocento* (Venice, 1962), pp. 83–6; and Schlumberger, op. cit. pp. 478–90. Silver for the mint of Naples seems to have been brought from Sardinia. R. Davidsohn, *Geschichte von Florenz* (Berlin, 1896–1925), IV, 25, and Balducci Pegolotti, op. cit. p. 120.

GOLD AND SILVER 17

number of minters had to be increased "ex argenti copia quae in dicta sicla auxit et auget assidua monetae argenti".[1]

Venice also became an important minter of silver coins for the eastern Mediterranean, and hence a middleman in the trade in precious metals between East and West. Receiving silver from the mines of Germany and Bohemia,[2] and after 1340 from the rich new mines of Bosnia and Serbia,[3] she struck a series of silver coins which were widely used in her eastern territories and other parts of the East. The first of these, the *grosso*, was originally minted in preparation for the Fourth Crusade, but by the middle of the thirteenth century it had become the principal money of the Aegean area.[4] The export of *grossi* to the East was greatly increased after the minting of the ducat in 1284, since the gold coin, it seems, was almost consistently overvalued and silver was therefore shipped abroad in greater quantities.[5] Severe shortages of silver were experienced in the first two decades of the fourteenth century and again in the 1340's. (During precisely these periods gold abounded: in 1315 a committee was appointed to consider the problem of "monetarum bizanciorum . . . quae omnia reperiuntur",[6] while in the 1340's the activities of the mint had to be expanded to take care of "aurum quod ducatur per mare per mercatores in maxima quantitate".[7]) All the measures taken by the government to stop the outflow of silver—the forbidding of the export of precious metals, the exclusion of foreigners from the oriental trade, the striking of new coins exclusively for the local market, and the adoption of differential rates of exchange for silver coins depending on the market in which the coins were used —seem to have failed. By 1353 the *grosso* had to be abandoned. Even this tactic, if it was one, did not succeed. The export of *soldini*, coins originally struck for the local market, increased greatly,[8] and silver bars were exported in greater quantities.[9] What is more, the government, probably bending to pressure from the merchants, began minting new silver coins intended exclusively for the Orient; these *tourneselli*, struck in imitation of the *denier tournois*, were minted from about the middle of the fourteenth to the middle of the fifteenth century, and were followed by another coin also designed for the Eastern market, the *grosetto per navigare*. The total loss of silver caused by the export of these coins seems to have been very considerable.[10]

The silver coins and bars which Venice and the other Italian cities sent to the East often passed through the hands of a number of intermediaries as they gravitated farther and farther eastward. It is sometimes possible to trace these successive stages in the transfer of European silver to the East. The island of Cyprus,

---

[1] Grierson, 'La moneta . . .', op. cit. pp. 83–4.

[2] The great merchants of Regensburg, such as the Runtinger family, usually brought back silver on their return trip from Prague; only the smaller merchants brought "Bohemian wares". This silver, as well as coins which were no longer current, was often taken to Venice. F. Bastian, *Das Runtingerbuch, 1383–1407* (Regensburg, 1935–44), I, 86, 548–9.

[3] D. Kovačević, 'Les mines d'or et d'argent en Serbie et Bosnie', *Annales. Economies, Sociétés, Civilisations*, xv (1960), 248–58.

[4] Grierson, 'La moneta . . .', op. cit. p. 81.

[5] R. Cessi, 'Problemi monetari e bancari veneziani del secolo XIV', *Archivio Veneto-Tridentino*, ix (1926), 217–301, *passim*.

[6] Ibid. pp. 219–20.   [7] Ibid. p. 241.   [8] Grierson, 'La moneta . . .', op. cit. p. 81.

[9] Cessi, op. cit. p. 259.

[10] Schlumberger, op. cit. p. 473, gives a document of 1385 stating "quod in cecha nostra Venetiae cuduntur marchae XII. milia tornesellorum annuatim . . .".

for instance, received silver from Sardinia, Bohemia, and the Tirol via Genoa and Venice;[1] much of this silver may have travelled farther eastward in the same form, either as bullion or as European coins, but some was sold to the mint in Famagusta for coining before reshipment. Moving in the other direction—from the East toward Cyprus and thence presumably to Europe—was a flow of gold coming from Damascus, Beirut, Latakia, Tripoli in Syria, and Trabizond.[2] Another entrepôt in this trade was the city of Constantinople, which shipped gold coins intermittently to Venice[3] and silver farther east. Here the merchant traversing the Mongol route could buy bars of silver which "si portano in Gazera [the Crimea] e insino al Gattaio [Cathay]".[4] Another current of silver flowed from Constantinople towards Trabizond[5] and thence farther East: hoards of Byzantine coins concealed in the Caucasus region of the U.S.S.R. from the thirteenth to the fifteenth century contain almost exclusively silver coins (whereas the earlier hoards, laid down during the silver famine, contained only gold).[6] Doubtless these hoards lay along the path of merchants carrying silver into Persia and perhaps into Central Asia.

By the fifteenth century the flow of precious metals between the two monetary zones seems to have lost momentum, and at times the direction of flow may have been reversed. Indeed, toward the end of the fourteenth century the Venetian gold ducat began to circulate in Egypt, where it became the main currency for international transactions, and not long afterwards it was in ascendancy in other parts of the Muslim East.[7] Other European gold coins, such as the florin, also began to be used more widely in the East.[8] This influx of gold from Europe (much of which may originally have come from the East) may reflect a growing shortage of silver in Christendom: just as in the time of the Crusades Europeans could not find enough gold to send to the Levant, and had to send silver as well, so by the end of the fourteenth century gold may have been used to supplement the silver which was being sent eastwards. No doubt the collapse of all gold currencies in the East created conditions which were favourable to the use of good foreign gold coins. It is even possible that much eastern gold was minted in Venice in this period and then re-exported to the East.

Basically, however, the directions of flow seem to have remained unchanged. It was still silver that was shipped in largest quantities to the Muslim world, and it was still gold that moved in the other direction. All across Europe there seems to have been a steady flow of silver southwards towards Italy and France, and thence across the Mediterranean; this silver came in part directly from the mines

[1] Day, op. cit. p. 343; Balducci Pegolotti, op. cit. pp. 81, 120; Davidsohn, op. cit. IV, 396.

[2] Balducci Pegolotti, op. cit. pp. 90–1; R. Thiriet, *Régestes des délibérations du Sénat de Venise concernant la Romanie* (Paris. 1958), I, 57.

[3] T. Bertelè, 'L'iperpero bizantino dal 1261 al 1453', *Rivista italiana di numismatica*, LIX (1957), 73.

[4] Balducci Pegolotti, op. cit. pp. 40–1.   [5] Bertelè, op. cit. p. 73.

[6] V. V. Kropotkin, *Klady vizantiskikh monet na territorii SSSR* (Moscow, 1962), Maps 8 and 10.

[7] A. R. van Gennep. 'Le ducat vénitien en Egypte', *Revue numismatique*, 4th ser. 1 (1897), 373–81, 494–508; H. E. Ives, *The Venetian Gold Ducat and its Imitations* (New York, 1954); and F. Babinger, 'Contraffazioni ottomane dello zecchino veneziano nel XV secolo', *Annali del Istituto Italiano di Numismatica*, III (1956), 83–99. Al Makrizi mentions the first appearance of the ducat as being in 1414 (op. cit. p. 47), but it was clearly earlier.

[8] In the late fifteenth century Florence made several attempts to have the florin circulate at par with the ducat in Egypt. See the documents in M. Amari, *I diplomi arabi del R. Archivio Fiorentino* (Florence, 1863), pp. 208, 385.

GOLD AND SILVER   19

and in part via northern trading centres such as Bruges and London.[1] By the last half of the fourteenth century a new and very important source of silver had been developed in the rich mines of Bosnia and Serbia, the output of which was immediately harnessed to the needs of the Orient.[2] Some of this Bosnian and Serbian silver was sent by inland routes southwards into Ottoman domains and towards Byzantium;[3] some passed through Ragusa and was sent thence to the East;[4] and very large quantities of it were shipped by firms like that of the Caboga family to Venice, whence it was exported to the East.[5] Fed by silver from these new mines, as well as from Bohemia and other parts of Europe, the mint of Venice throughout the fifteenth century was able to continue striking coins for the East, and these were carried by merchants such as Andrea Barbarigo to Levantine and other eastern ports.[6] More interesting, however, is a new *westward* expansion of the Venetian trade in precious metals: from at least the 1440's Venetian merchants were trading with the Barbary coast, shipping out silver coins and "Venetian wares" and bringing back mainly gold.[7]

But during the whole of the fifteenth century the "gold of Ghana" still reached Italy *mainly* through the port of Genoa, and from Genoa it was pulled farther north by silver coming southward. A monetary crisis was provoked in the city toward the middle of the century by an influx of foreign silver coins coming to buy up gold, and in an effort to control the trade the city prohibited foreign moneys and set a higher official value for gold.[8] Toward the end of the century, however, the same directions of flow may be observed: the mint in Genoa, in 1493, bought silver of German origin in the Milan market and paid for it with Spanish *scudi* (struck, no doubt, from African gold).[9] Although much African gold was still probably arriving via Spain, there are signs that Genoese and other Italian merchants, wishing to avoid intermediaries, were penetrating farther and farther into the Sahara in search of its source. Thus, for instance, towards the middle of the fifteenth century the house of Centurione sent a Genoese, Malfante, to Touat, and it is possible that he reached the city of Timbuctu.[10] About two

[1] R. de Roover, 'La balance commerciale entre les Pays-Bas et l'Italie au quinzième siècle', *Revue belge de philologie et d'histoire*, XXXVII (1959), 374–86, shows that the deficit in the balance of trade of the Lowlands with Italy had become considerable by the fifteenth century. It was covered by the shipment of moneys and bullion, as well as by multilateral arrangements. See also R. de Roover, *The Rise and Decline of the Medici Bank* (Cambridge, Mass. 1963), p. 317.

[2] D. Kovačević, op. cit. and *Trgovina u Srednjovjekovnoj Bosni* (Sarajevo, 1961), pp. 139–41.

[3] B. Krekić, *Dubrovnik (Raguse) au Moyen Age* (Paris, 1961), pp. 68–9. That Serbian mines were an important source of silver for the Byzantine Empire is shown by a document in Karl Dietrich, *Byzantinische Quellen zur Länder- und Völkerkunde* (Leipzig, 1912), II, 79. See also C. Jiriček, *Die Handelsstrassen und Bergwerke von Serbien und Bosnien während des Mittelalters* (Prague, 1879), *passim*.

[4] Krekić, op. cit. p. 122.   [5] Kovačević, *Trgovina ...*, op. cit. p. 52.

[6] F. C. Lane, *Andrea Barbarigo, Merchant of Venice* (Baltimore, 1944), pp. 61, 132, 105.

[7] Ibid. pp. 31, 37, 170.

[8] H. Sieveking, 'Studio sulle finanze genovesi nel medioevo', *Atti della Società Ligure di Storia Patria*, XXXV (1906), 105, quotes a document of 1444 which states that "civitatem plenam esse monetis extraneis argenteis auro nequaquam respondentibus que ob id ipsam causam afferunt, ut aureus et precio augeatur et propter ea hinc exportetur."

[9] C. Cipolla, 'Argento tedesco e monete genovesi alla fine del Quattrocento', *Rivista italiana di numismatica*, 5th ser. IV (1956), 2. The position of Milan as an entrepôt in the trade in precious metals slightly earlier in the century is shown in Emilio Motta, 'Documenti Visconteo-Sforzeschi per la storia della zecca di Milano', *Rivista italiana di numismatica*, VIII (1895), 379.

[10] C. de la Roncière, 'La crise des changes au Moyen Age et la découverte du nouveau monde', *Académie des Sciences Coloniales. Comptes rendus* (1926–7), p. 256. See also R. S. Lopez, 'I genovesi nell' Africa occidentale', in *Studi sull' economia genovese nel Medioevo* (Turin, 1936).

decades later, a Florentine traveller writes as if the trip to Timbuctu were a commonplace.[1] In at least partial payment for the gold which reached Genoa from the North African cities, silver still moved southward across the Mediterranean. It seems, moreover, that some of the tricks of days gone by which made the trade more profitable had not been forgotten. A treaty of 1433 between the Republic of Genoa and the King of Tunis, Bône, and Bougie repeats the stipulation of 1272 that counterfeit moneys brought in by Genoese merchants should be broken or cut.[2] Not to be deterred by this clause, however, Genoese merchants stole a die from a Hafsid mint, and began striking in Genoa counterfeit coins which they marketed in Sfax and Tripoli.[3]

From fifteenth-century France, too, there is evidence of continuing activity in the trade in precious metals. By analysing documents showing the output of all French mints from 1401 to 1403, and by comparing these documents with those from other periods, Mr Maurice Rey has been able to detect an important decline in the minting of silver coinage in France lasting from about 1392 to 1410.[4] No silver whatever appears to have been minted in Paris during the years studied, and little silver was struck in the south and west of France. What minting took place was mainly at Tournai and to a lesser extent in certain towns lying along the eastern and south-eastern borders of France. In the light of the present study, the interpretation of these facts seems clear. Silver was being drawn into France from the great silver market at Bruges and from Alpine areas, and it was minted or reminted near the point of entry before being taken farther southward.[5] Gold, on the other hand, shows an entirely different pattern. Although large quantities of gold were also minted at Tournai in the years studied, the output of the Paris mint was considerable and mints in Normandy and the Midi (including Montpellier) were relatively active. The gold that was being struck by these latter mints, it seems, was gold brought into France from Spain, North Africa, and the Middle East. It is significant that the eastern and south-eastern towns, which were active in the minting of silver, struck almost no gold.

That the south of France, a little later in the fifteenth century, was still a centre of the trade in precious metals is shown from the activities of Jacques Coeur. As chief *argentier* to the king of France, and operator of his own silver mines, the famous French merchant was admirably placed to take part in this illicit commerce and he seems to have taken full advantage of his position. In the *arrêt de condamnation* of 1453, he was accused of having "transporté ou fait transporter ausdiz Sarrazins . . . grande quantité d'argent blanc, et telement qu'il en avoit ainsi que l'en disoit avoir du tout exillé et desnué nostre dit païs du Languedoc".[6] If the report of Coeur's own testimony at his last interrogation is to be believed, these charges were not trumped up. He is alleged to have admitted that each of

---

[1] de la Roncière, 'La crise . . .', op. cit. p. 526.

[2] M. L. de Mas Latrie, *Traités de paix et de commerce* . . ., op. cit. (Paris, 1866), pp. 134-5.

[3] Brunschvig, op. cit. p. 84.

[4] M. Rey, 'Les ZiB 305 (deuxième partie). Etude d'histoire monétaire en France au début du XVe siècle', *Annales littéraires de l'Université de Besançon*, 2nd ser. 1 (1954), 27-52.

[5] This is not, however, the explanation offered by Rey, who links this minting pattern with the needs of the army during the Hundred Years' War.

[6] Michel Mollat, *Les affaires de Jacques Coeur. Journal du Procureur Dauvet* (Paris, 1952), 1, 5. See also ibid. 1, 7, where it is stated that Coeur had "fait fondre et mectre en lingotz . . . grant quantité d'argent blanc alayé . . . jusques à 20.000 marcs et plus, mené ou fait mener . . . ou païs d'Alexandrie".

his galleys sailing to Syria carried between 1,800 and 2,000 marcs of silver, and that one of his ships once took between 9,000 and 10,000 marcs of silver.[1] To increase the profits of the trade, the silver was melted down (often, it seems, in royal mints), alloyed with copper, poured into bars, and stamped with the royal fleur-de-lys, which was supposed to guarantee that the bars were of the same degree of fineness as that which was sold by the French mints.[2] In vain did Coeur plead that "ce n'estoit pas grant mal de la faire hors du Royaume," and that "pour chacun marc d'argent a fait venir ung marc d'or au Royaume."[3]

III

Il a prouffit a porter argent blanc en Suyrie, car quand il vault 6 escus par deca il en vault 7 par dela.[4]

JACQUES COEUR

Gold and silver tend to shift away from areas where they are undervalued (either in terms of goods or in terms of the other metal) and to go where they are more highly valued. When such flows affect regions of the world which have large stocks of bullion, and when they continue over long stretches of time, an important redistribution of the world's supply of precious metals may take place.

In the movement of precious metals between the medieval Islamic world and Christendom, a crucial role was played by the silver–gold ratio, the figure which expresses the number of units of silver required to buy a unit of gold. Whenever this ratio was not the same in the two regions—and it almost never was—the difference in ratios signified that gold was valued more highly, and silver less highly, in one region than in the other. Gold thus tended to travel to the region which placed a higher value on it, while silver moved the other way. This shifting of metals occurred for a number of different reasons. In the first place, at least enough metal had to move to cover one region's deficit in the balance of trade with the other; the metal which would be chosen for this purpose, if both were available, would be the one which was valued less highly at home than abroad. As long as the imbalance in trade continued, one precious metal would therefore tend to flow in one direction. Should the balance of trade be reversed, the other precious metal would flow in the opposite direction.[5] In fact, however, *much more specie moved between these two regions than was needed merely to cover the balance of trade.* Since "clearing-house" arrangements between Arabs and Christians were poorly organized, each merchant trading with the other bloc usually had to use cash to cover his own *personal* deficit, i.e. to pay for the part of his travelling expenses and purchases not covered by the return from his sales.[6] If he made a surplus abroad, he usually received it in cash. In consequence, the amount of precious metals flowing between the two blocs was much greater than the trade deficit of one towards the other, *and the flow was in both directions.* Again, gold moved out

---

[1] Arch. Dépt. de la Loire. Fonds du Duché de Roannais, E 4, fo. 3*v*. I am indebted to M. Robert Guillot for furnishing me with this and other information from the same source which will be published in a forthcoming study of his.

[2] Ibid. fo. 4. See also Mollat, op. cit. p. 7. [3] Ibid. fo. 4*v*. [4] Ibid. fo. 4.

[5] I do not intend to join others in speculating about the nature of the balance of trade between the Arab countries and Europe. As will be seen, this balance is only one of several factors causing the movement of precious metals, and not the most important one.

[6] This was the case for Andrea Barbarigo. See Lane, *Andrea Barbarigo* . . ., op. cit. p. 58.

of the country where its value in silver was lower. At the same time silver went the other way.

What is more, this exchange of precious metals was accelerated when the difference in the silver–gold ratios was great enough, and the obstacles were sufficiently few, to make profitable the trading of one metal against the other. In the example given above from a cross-examination of Jacques Coeur, the merchant is alleged to have said that silver would buy more gold in "Syria" than in France, and a relatively small differential in the silver–gold ratios (amounting in this case to about 16 per cent) apparently allowed traders to make a profit by shipping silver to Syria and bringing back gold. Though the risks in such trade might be high, the cost of transporting precious metals seems to have been negligible. In 1345 the Venetian Senate fixed the cost of moving gold in galleys from Trabizond to Venice at one hyperperion per centenario.[1] To ship silver from Genoa to Pera in an armed galley cost five pennies per monetary *lira*, or 2 per cent of its value.[2] Nor was the overland transport of gold and silver dear: it cost only 0·015 per cent of the purchase price to send silver from Milan to Genoa.[3] Other obstacles there certainly were, in the form mainly of prohibitions against the export of precious metals and taxes on their import and export; but they hampered the enterprising merchant but little, the prohibitions being almost universally disregarded and the taxes, where they were collected, being low.

Naturally, the profits of this trade could be enhanced by judicious fraud. If the merchant could pass off as pure silver a metal that was actually alloyed with copper—as Jacques Coeur was accused of doing—he stood to gain more. Again, by sending counterfeit *coins* instead of bullion the merchant could take advantage of the higher value invariably placed on metal that had been minted. Hence springs the desire of merchants of the first half of the thirteenth century to send coins, even if they bore Muslim legends, to the Latin East and to the Maghreb. And if the counterfeit coins were of a lower alloy and a lighter weight than the originals, and this difference was not detected, profits rose still higher. The merchant shipping the *millarès* to Bougie, for instance, made a profit (a) by taking advantage of the differential in the silver–gold ratio, (b) by avoiding minting charges, and (c) by hoodwinking his clients into accepting inferior, counterfeit coins as the real thing. Essentially, however, it was the difference in the silver–gold ratios which gave direction to this commerce by creating a preference for shipping silver out of Europe and bringing back gold. The other gains were just the frosting on the cake—sometimes, it is true, spread very thick.

The scholar who wishes to make use of silver–gold ratios will find his path strewn with thorns. In the first place, the calculation of such ratios is tricky: it has tripped up distinguished numismatists and given rise to some of the nastiest quarrels in numismatic history. The ratios, moreover, are of different kinds which should not be mixed (though they usually are, and sometimes will be here). To name only some of the varieties that may be met, there are market ratios for unminted metals; market ratios for coins (which depended not only on the intrinsic value of the coins but also on their prestige and their official rate of exchange);[4] the

[1] Thiriet, op. cit. p. 57.   [2] Balducci Pegolotti, op. cit. p. 220.
[3] Cipolla, 'Argento tedesco ...', op. cit. p. 5.
[4] Variations in ratios depending on the prestige of the coins concerned are shown in L. Blancard,

GOLD AND SILVER   23

ratio at which mints purchased metals or sold coins; ratios used in books of account; ratios stated in commercial documents; ratios used by tax collectors; and ratios given in treaties between states. Some of these ratios—those given in treaties, in books for the collection of papal taxes, and in international trading documents—cannot be given any precise geographical locus. They may reflect the ratio in one of two places, or be a compromise between the two. Finally, silver–gold ratios, like other prices, are subject to fluctuations; and one cannot be sure that the ratio of one day was the same on the morrow. Seemingly trivial occurrences, it appears, could upset the ratio. The payment of an army in silver coin, by creating a considerable demand for silver in one area and releasing large supplies of it in another, could play havoc with the ratio of both regions. According to one legend, a king of Mali, on a pilgrimage to Mecca around the year 1324, brought to Cairo so much gold that the value of gold in that city fell dramatically and stayed low for many years after.[1] A Hungarian scholar has claimed—probably wrongly—that a similar drop in the value of gold in Italy during the 1340's was caused by the visit from the Queen of Hungary, who brought with her 10,000 marks of pure gold and almost half a bushel of florins and sent for another 4,000 marks of gold during her stay.[2]

Fortunately, however, the calculations which are available from Italy, France, England, Germany, and Hungary for the period under discussion are so numerous, and the trend which they show is so clear, that we may speak of *general movements* in the ratio—though not of specific ratios—with some confidence. The results of these calculations are given in Table 1. They show that before Europe returned to gold the ratio in most parts of Europe was generally between 9 and 10, though it was sometimes a little more or less. Whether the minting of gold

Table 1. *Silver–Gold Ratios in Europe, 1100–1400*

Date	England	France	Germany	Hungary	Piedmont	Venice	Genoa	Florence	Rome
1104	9·0								
c. 1106–11			8·0						
1113		12·5							
1156?	9·0								
1159							9·6–10·1		
1199	10·0								
end 12th c.		7·5							
1207		9·6							
1208	9·0								
1213	9·0								
1227?	9·0								
1230		10·0							
1250		8·9–9·5							
1253		8·4					c. 8·5	10·7	
1257	9·3–10·0								
1258							8·5–9·7		

'Le rapport de l'or à l'argent sous Saint Louis et ses successeurs', *Annuaire de la Société de Numismatique* (1890), p. 15. The effect of minting charges on ratios is demonstrated in A. Luschin von Ebengreuth, 'Das Wertverhältnis zwischen den Edelmetallen in Deutschland', *Congrès international de numismatique organisé à Bruxelles* (Brussels, 1891), pp. 436–7. See also Soetbeer, op. cit. p. 117.

[1] Al 'Omari, *Masalik al absar*, ed. Gaudefroy-Demombynes (Paris, 1927), p. 78.

[2] Bálint Hóman, 'La circolazione delle monete d'oro in Ungheria dal X al XIV secolo e la crisi europea dell'oro nel secolo XIV', *Rivista italiana di numismatica* (1922), pp. 151–2.

24

Date	England	France	Germany	Hungary	Piedmont	Venice	Genoa	Florence	Rome
1260			8·0						
1262	9·6						9·3		
1267	11·1	9·2–9·8							
1271		11·2							
1273		11·2							
1275							10·7		9·7
1278	10·0	9·9–12·5							
1280			10·1						11·6
1283					10·0				
1284			7·15			10·6–11·3			
1285		12·0				10·9–11·1			
1287							12·7		
1291									11·4
1292	12·5								
1295		11·5–12·0			10·0				8·6
1296		11·6	9·2		11·4	12·9	10·0–11·1	10·9–11·1	12·0
1297						13·1			
1298		10·0							
1299		13·8							
1300					13·1				
1301						13·4		11·0	
1302					13·7		13·7		12·8
1303		10·3				13·0			
1304		12·9–15·2							
1305		15·9	10·0		13·6	13·0		10·8–10·9	13·6
1306		15·2							13·7
1307		15·2							
1308		14·5	9·23			14·2			
1309		16·0					13·4		
1310		15·6							
1311		19·6		14·4					
1312		15·3							
1313		14·4	13·4–14·7						
1315		15·0							
1317			14·1–14·5						
1318		12·0	16·9			14·2			
1319			14·1–15·2	16·2–17·3					
1322		15·0–16·0							
1324						13·9		13·6	
1327					12·8		13·6		
1328		14·1				14·1			
1329		13·7							
1332				19·7–21·0					
1334			15·4	23·6–25·2	12·3				
1336			16·8–17·3						
1337		11·5–12·0		19·7–21·0				12·9	
1338		12·6	18·9						
1339	12·6		21·6				11·4		12·2
1340		12·0		14·0–15·2					
1341		11·7							
1342		11·9	10·0	13·0		15·2			
1344	11·0–12·6							10·0	11·4
1345		11·8		13·7				11·0	
1346	11·6	11·1	11·3						
1347								9·4–10·9	
1348			12·5						
1349	11·6								
1350		12·0		10·0		9·4–14·4			
1351	12·0	6·6	12·3						
1352	11·2								
1354		10·0							

GOLD AND SILVER 25

Date	England	France	Germany	Hungary	Piedmont	Venice	Genoa	Florence	Rome
1355		10·5							
1356	11·2								
1357			10·6						
1358		9·9							
1359		6·8							
1360		10·5							
1361		12·0							
1364		12·0							10·0
1365		10·5	11·4				10·3		
1368									11·0
1370							10·2		10·3
1375		10·1	12·4					10·8	
1379						10·2–13·2			
1380						11·4			
1382									10·5
1385		10·8	9·3						
1387			10·6						
1389		10·2							
1390							10·0		
1391		10·7	11·8						
1393									10·0
1399			11·3		11·3–11·7				
1400			10·4						10·0–11·6

Sources: A. Blanchet and A. Dieudonné, *Manuel de numismatique française* (Paris, 1912–36), II; E. Born, *Das Zeitalter des Denars* (Leipzig/Erlangen, 1924), pp. 396–7, 440–1; C. Cipolla, 'Studi di storia della moneta. I movimenti dei cambi in Italia dal secolo XIII al XV', *Università di Pavia. Studi nelle scienze giuridiche e sociali*, XXIX (1948), 153; J. Craig, *The Mint* (Cambridge, 1953); Desimoni, op. cit.; Hóman, 'La circolazione ...', op. cit.; F. C. Lane, 'Le vecchie monete di conto veneziane ed il ritorno all'oro', *Atti del'Instituto Veneto di Scienze, Lettere ed Arti. Classe di Scienze Morali e Lettere.* CXVII (1958–9), 49–78; Luschin von Ebengreuth, *Das Wertverhältnis ...*, op. cit.; A. Nagl, three articles in *Numismatische Zeitschrift*, XXII (1890), 47–84, XXIII (1891), 177–80, and XXVI (1894), 41–258; N. Papadopoli, *Le monete di Venezia*, I (Venice, 1893), App. I, Table 3; W. A. Shaw, *The History of Currency, 1252–1894* (London, n.d.), p. 40; Soetbeer, op. cit.

coins in the 1250's and 1260's in Florence, Genoa, Rome, Milan, and France caused an immediate rise in the value of gold is a question that was much debated in the later part of the nineteenth century (when the controversy over bimetallism stirred up some interest in the history of the silver–gold ratio) and the issue has perhaps not been settled.[1] But by the last two decades of the century gold prices clearly *had* risen in those states which were minting gold and in some neighbouring states: the ratio in Italy and France in the early 1290's seems to have been between 11 and 12. Such an increase in the value of gold was no doubt what attracted much of the gold that in this period flowed into Europe from the southern and eastern shores of the Mediterranean. It also drew gold out of northern Europe, in particular from Germany, where the ratio remained very low throughout the thirteenth century; this well-documented export of gold from the North probably kept the North drained of gold and postponed its return to a gold currency.[2]

By the early fourteenth century signs appeared of what was to become a spec-

[1] This controversy is summarized in C. Desimoni, 'La moneta ei l rapporto dell' oro all' argento nei secoli XII al XIV', *Atti della R. Accademia dei Lincei*, 5th ser. Classe di Scienze Morali ..., III, pt I (1895), pp. 47 ff.

[2] A. Luschin von Ebengreuth, 'Goldgeschäfte Meinhards II, Grafen von Tirol und seiner Söhne', *Veröffentlichungen des Museums Ferdinandeum*, VIII (1928), 441–58; and Aldo Stella, *Politica ed economia nel territorio Trentino-Tirolese dal XIII al XVII secolo* (Padua, 1958).

ANDREW M. WATSON

tacular boom in the price of gold. The South of Europe was hit first: in Venice
the success of the ducat seems to have caused such a demand for gold that the
ratio rose to over 13 by 1297 and over 14 by 1308, while in France the coining
of large quantities of gold under Philip the Fair brought the ratio up to nearly
14 in 1299, 16 in 1309, and apparently over 19 in 1311. By then, however, the
crisis seems to have spread northward, affecting gold prices in Hungary and
Germany, where the ratio rose to over 14. The ratio seems to have remained high
(between 12 and 15) over most of Europe during the 1320's, without, however,
any decisive tendency to rise or fall. Then the crisis entered a new and final phase.
Whereas in southern Europe the price of gold seems to have eased gently downwards during the 1330's, in the North the price skyrocketed upward in a dizzying
fashion—and then plummeted downwards. Reflecting, perhaps, the increase in
the demand for gold after 1325, the year in which both King John of Bohemia
and King Carlo Roberto of Hungary began to strike gold, the ratio in Germany
reached 15·5 in 1334, rose to between 16·8 and 17·3 in 1336, and hit a peak of
21·6 in 1339. (Seven electoral princes in Germany were granted the right to
strike gold in 1339, though few or none used it till some years later.) In Hungary,
despite the output of local gold mines, the inflation in the price of gold reached
still greater heights: by 1334 the ratio stood between 23·6 and 25·2. *In the course
of less than a century the price of gold (expressed in silver) had almost doubled in the South
and almost trebled in the North.* Or, to put it another way, *the price of silver (expressed
in gold) had fallen to somewhere between a half and a third of what it had been in the age
of the penny and the grosso.* It was precisely in this period of rapid appreciation of
gold that Europe attracted from the Islamic world (and no doubt from the Hungarian mines) much of the stock of gold which was to make the return to gold
successful. And at the same time she lost much of her undervalued silver.[1]

The bubble seems to have burst towards the end of the 1330's. In Germany
the ratio fell sharply to a level of 10 in 1342, while in Hungary the ratio reached
the same level by 1350. The rest of Europe also felt this collapse in gold prices;
and during the 1350's the market was extremely unsteady, with the French ratio,
for instance, fluctuating between 6·6 and 12. By the 1360's, however, a new
stability had been achieved in the ratio of silver to gold, a stability which was to
last until the end of the Middle Ages. Almost everywhere in Europe the ratio
remained at a level between 10·5 and 12 until the year 1500.[2] In spite of the
increase in demand for gold occasioned by the striking of new gold coins in much
of northern Europe, the value of gold remained low—low, at least, in comparison
to what it had been. The next shock to the ratio was not to occur till American
gold and silver arrived on the scene.

[1] The speculative nature of this rapid rise in gold prices seems to be indicated by some documents in
Cessi, op. cit. p. 280. The effects of this boom and the ultimate collapse in the gold market have not
been sufficiently studied. Obviously, those who had acquired gold in the expectation that its price would
remain high were hurt. It is possible that some of the Italian banks which had to close their doors in the
1340's held large stocks of gold, or that those who owed them money did. The various explanations
given for the fall in the price of gold by Bálint Hóman in *Geschichte des ungarischen Mittelalters,* II (Berlin,
1943), 359, and in 'La circolazione . . .', art. cit. do not seem acceptable.

[2] Some fifteenth-century silver–gold ratios may be found in J. Heers, *Gênes au XVe siècle* (Paris, 1961),
p. 680; E. Hamilton, op. cit. pp. 37, 136; C. Trasselli, *Note per la storia dei banchi in Sicilia nel XV secolo,*
pt I (Palermo, 1959), 109; W. A. Shaw, *The History of Currency, 1252 to 1894* (London, n.d.), p. 40; C.
Cipolla, 'Studi di storia della moneta', *Studi di scienze giuridiche e sociali,* XXIX (Pavia, 1948), 154.

GOLD AND SILVER 27

The European ratio, however, tells only part of the story. The ratio on the other side of the Mediterranean—in Byzantium and in the Arab countries—is equally important.

Table 2. *Silver–Gold Ratios in Arab Countries*

Date	Ratio	Place
1. early 7th c.	9·0–11·0	various
2. c. 695	14·0	Caliphate
3. c. 800	15·0	Eastern Caliphate
4. c. 847–61	17·3	Eastern Caliphate
5. c. 907–32	15·4	Eastern Caliphate
6. after 928	11·6	Eastern Caliphate
7. 941	12·0	Eastern Caliphate
8. 986	15·4	Egypt
9. 1003	15·2	Egypt
10. c. 1175–1200	6·4	Tunisia (or Sicily?)
11. 1234/5	7·0	Eastern Caliphate
12. 1239	4·8	Syria
13. c. 1250	5·0	Egypt
14. 1278	9·3 or 11·6	Tunisia
15. 1339/40	12·4	Egypt
16. 1340/1–1359/60	8·3	Egypt
17. 1368/9	12·4	Egypt
18. before 1400	9·6	Egypt and Syria
19. 1404–5	14·1	Egypt and Syria
20. 1422	8·0	Egypt and Syria

Sources: Nos. 1, 3, 4, 5, and 7 from Bolin, op. cit. pp. 16–17; No. 2 from P. Grierson, 'The Monetary Reforms . . .', op. cit. p. 260; Nos. 8 and 9 calculated from exchange rates given in S. D. Goitein, 'The Exchange Rate of Gold and Silver Money in Fatimid and Ayyubid Times', *Journ. Ec. Soc. Hist. of the Orient*, VIII (1965), 3–4, and numismatic information given in P. Balog, 'History of the Dirhem in Egypt', *Revue numismatique*, 6th ser. III (1961), 109–46; No. 10 from L. Blancard, 'Besants d'or et d'argent de Tunis au XIIIe siècle', *Annuaire de la Société Française de Numismatique*, XIX (1895), 5–14; No. 11 from P. F. Casaretto, op. cit. p. 208; No. 12 calculated by the author from information given in C. Cahen, *La Syrie du nord à l'époque des croisades* (Paris, 1940), p. 470, n. 16, assuming after Balog that the dirhem concerned weighed 2·85 gr. and was 80 per cent fine and that the dinar referred to was the dinar-of-account of 4·25 gr. of pure gold, No. 13 from L. Blancard, 'Le rapport de l'or à l'argent sous Saint Louis et ses successeurs', *Annuaire de la Société de Numismatique* (1890), p. 18; No. 14 calculated by the author from information given in Brunschvig, 'Esquisse . . .', op. cit., the difference depending on whether the documents refer to old or new dirhems; Nos. 15, 16, and 17 calculated by the author from information given in P. Balog, op. cit.; Nos. 18, 19, and 20 from William Popper, *Egypt and Syria under the Circassian Sultans*, University of California Publications in Semitic Philology, XVI (Berkeley and Los Angeles, 1957), 43–4, 58.

Unfortunately, much less is known about the silver–gold ratio in those regions. Although for over eighty years a wealth of documentary evidence has been available, giving equivalences of dinars and dirhems at different times and places,[1] scholars have been able to use these sources but little. For one thing, the documents do not make clear whether the coins mentioned are actual coins or moneys-of-account. If moneys-of-account are referred to, are these the "canonical" dinar and dirhem, or have they moved away from the standards of classical times? And if they are real coins, the scholar may have to choose from a proliferation of different dirhems in circulation at one time, or from dinars whose weight fluctuated widely even though they were issued by the same mint in the same year. About the fineness of these coins, almost nothing was known until recently.[2] Our un-

[1] *Vide* Sauvaire, op. cit. *passim*.
[2] The work of Balog, Grierson, and Ehrenkreutz has considerably advanced our understanding of these important points, but much remains to be done.

derstanding of this all-important question has thus advanced slowly. What calculations have already been made are open to question and new calculations are hazardous. The discussion which follows must therefore be regarded as very tentative.

Nevertheless, everything suggests that the silver–gold ratio in Arab countries followed a very different path from that of Europe. During the ninth and tenth centuries, the Arab ratio appears to have been extremely high, reaching a peak of 17·3 some time between 847 and 861. Prof. Bolin has argued that this high-point was caused by the very great output of silver mines in Transoxania, as well as by the relative scarcity of gold;[1] no doubt it was during this period of high gold prices that much of the silver of the Muslim countries escaped to other parts of the world, while their gold stocks were increased. During the silver famine (a crucial period for which no ratios are yet available) the price of gold may have remained high; for while silver was in short supply, the demand for it fell off when the minting of silver coins was abandoned. Thus the outflow of silver from Muslim countries to other parts of the world (and the inflow of gold) may have continued until perhaps the middle of the twelfth century, prolonging the silver famine in these regions and the gold famine in Europe.

But by the later part of the twelfth century the picture had completely changed, and the direction of flow of precious metals was on the point of being reversed. What caused this turnabout seems to have been an extraordinary conjuncture of events which brought about a fall in the silver–gold ratio in the Arab countries so steep that the ratio was thereafter considerably *below* that prevailing in Europe. Changes in both demand and supply probably played a part in this sharp rise in the value of silver in terms of gold. The demand for silver in the Arab countries rose, and that for gold fell, as one country after another shifted from gold to silver as the basis of its currency system. Equally important, however, was the great increase in the supply of trans-Saharan gold that occurred, as chance would have it, just when the demand for gold was falling off. This gold, brought in great caravans across the desert, appears to have been in such plentiful supply that in the regions where the gold-dust was washed the silver–gold ratio was 1 to 1: a pound of silver could buy a pound of gold.[2] Salt was also said to be exchanged at parity with gold.[3] Only 1·5 pounds of copper were needed to buy a pound of gold. (It is hardly surprising, therefore, that the North African merchants sent salt and copper, rather than silver, to the gold-producing regions.) As the volume of the caravan trade grew and more and more cheap gold poured into North Africa, Egypt, and the Levant, the ratio of silver to gold in these regions fell greatly, reaching 6·4 in Tunisia towards the end of the twelfth century and remaining very low till the middle of the thirteenth century. Thus when the price of gold in Europe was high and rising, the price in the Arab countries was at its lowest point. Small wonder then that during the period from about 1200 to 1350 the traffic in precious metals was most active.

As Table 3 shows, even those parts of Europe which bordered on the Muslim world—Spain, Portugal, Byzantium, and perhaps Serbia—seem to have been affected by the spillover of trans-Saharan gold. When elsewhere in Europe the ratio was high, in these countries it remained low (though perhaps above that of

---

[1] Bolin, op. cit. pp. 20–1.   [2] Lopez, *Studi sull' economia genovese* ..., op. cit. p. 39.
[3] Al 'Omari, op. cit. p. 83.

GOLD AND SILVER   29

the Arab countries). Very probably it was this intermediate ratio which allowed merchants in these peripheral areas of Europe to act as middlemen in the exchange of precious metals between the two great monetary blocs.

Table 3. *Silver–Gold Ratios in Christian Countries near the Arab World*

Date	Portugal	Spain (usually Valencia)	Navarre	Ragusa and Serbia	Byzantium
1146	7·0				
1162–76	6·7				
1253	7·3				
1268		8·0 (Catalonia)			
1296	7·7				
end 13th c.				9·3	
1328					12·3–13·5
1336				9·4	
1340					6·6
1355	7·8				
1355 and after					7·5
1357–67	7·7				
1365				10·7	
1367				10·4	
1367–73	8·1				
1376				11·3	
c. 1376–9					9·4
1377–80			12·8		
1380			8·4		
1380–3			8·1		
1382–3	7·1				
1385–6			3·7		
1386			7·4		
1393–1406		9·1			
1407		8·9			
1408–25		8·6			
1426–48		9·9			
1427					10·7
1428–9			5·8		
1431			6·4		
1449–72		10·0			
mid-15th c.				10·0	

Sources: T. Bertelè, 'L'iperpero bizantino dal 1261 al 1453', *Rivista italiana di numismatica*, LIX (1957), 70–89; L. Blancard, *Essai* ..., op. cit. p. 198; V. Vinaver, 'Prizoli istoriji plemenitih metala, cena i nadnica (srednjovekovni Dubrovnik)', *Istoriski glasnik*, XIII (1960), 79; Earl Hamilton, *Money, Prices* ..., op. cit. pp. 37, 136; J. Ferraro Vaz, *Numaria medieval portuguesa*, I (Lisbon, 1960), 157. I am grateful to my colleague, Mr M. Surducki, for translating the relevant passages of the article by Vinaver.

After 1350 the differential in the ratios of the two zones gradually narrowed. As we have seen, the European ratio, once the crisis of the first half of the fourteenth century had passed, settled down to between 10·5 and 12 and remained remarkably stable at this level until the end of the fifteenth century. The few data which we have for the Arab countries in this later period suggest that the ratio there was much more subject to fluctuations, being sometimes higher and sometimes lower than in Europe. This instability may reflect the monetary chaos of the region in the later Middle Ages. As the evidence already given above shows, however, silver continued in this period to leave Europe for Byzantium and the

ANDREW M. WATSON

Muslim countries, and gold sometimes returned; this prevailing direction of flow suggests that the ratio in the East was still usually lower than that in the West. But it is true that in this later period there may also have been cross-currents in these flows, probably reflecting short-lived rises in the ratio in the East which made it profitable to reverse the usual direction of trade. In any case, the profit margin in this trade, as in other kinds of late medieval commerce, was falling, in spite of a lowering of transportation costs. The merchant who wished to do well in trading precious metals, therefore, had to keep a sharp eye on both markets and respond more sensitively than had been necessary in an earlier age. He could no longer take advantage of the great disequilibrium in prices of precious metals that prevailed when both Europe and the Muslim countries were in the throes of their monetary revolutions. On the contrary, he had to face the fact that, with ever closer contacts being established, the two lakes were once more slowly merging into one.

In summary, the mechanism which governed the distribution of precious metals between Europe and the Muslim world during the later Middle Ages was sensitive to many influences which combined to produce a changeover in the monetary systems of both regions. During the eastern silver famine and the western gold famine a *modus vivendi* had been achieved which allowed, indeed encouraged, the two zones to go their separate ways. But the balance was disturbed by the arrival of large quantities of European silver in the Levant and North Africa and seriously shaken when these regions, and later others in the East, reverted to silver as their principal coinage. The overthrow of the old order was completed in the late thirteenth and early fourteenth centuries when Europe, once again able to procure gold, but feeling a drain on her silver supplies, returned to gold as the basis of her currency systems. In both regions, therefore, changes in *supply* of precious metals seem to have initiated the monetary revolutions; but the switches in minting policy were in turn to bring about great changes in the *demand* for gold and silver—changes which made the revolutions enduring. The new minting policies, once in operation, were not to be reversed, though circumstances might change: even when gold became dear, it was still gold which European rulers wished to make their prestige currency, while in the Muslim world the availability of cheap gold, shortly after the return of silver, seems to have had little effect on minting policies. Indeed, so considerable were the changes in demand for both metals in both zones that the disequilibrium in prices between the two regions persisted, though the gap gradually narrowed, till the end of the Middle Ages, *in spite of the great movements of metals over this long period.*

Vagaries in the history of mining, by affecting supplies of metals, doubtless also played their part in these monetary changes. The opening or closing of a mine in one region, for instance, or the capture of a mine which had previously belonged to the other bloc, could be of some importance to the distribution of the world's supply of precious metals. Thus the gold mines in Hungary added to Europe's supply of that metal and contributed some of the raw material needed for the return to gold.[1] Similarly, the capture of Sardinian silver mines by the

---

[1] A Hungarian scholar has estimated that in the later Middle Ages eleven-twelfths of Europe's gold production came from Bohemia and Hungary, and by far the greater part of this came from Hungary. Hóman, *Geschichte* . . ., op. cit. II, 349. The same writer goes on to say that in this period almost two-

GOLD AND SILVER   31

Christians, or of Crimean silver mines by the Mongols, probably had some effect. *But it is easy to exaggerate the importance of mines as a cause of monetary disturbances.* The relative increase in the total stock of precious metals which could be achieved over a short period of time through opening of new mines or increasing the output of old mines must, in all but the most exceptional cases, have been insignificant. What is more important is the way in which the available stocks were distributed. In any case, mines are not altogether "independent variables" in economic history. Their profitability depends in part on the price for their output; when the price of gold (in terms of goods *or* silver) is high, new gold mines can be expected to open and others to increase their production, while output will fall as the price goes down. And when two monetary zones trade with one another, the fact that a mine is located in one zone, or brought into it by conquest, is of little importance. Time and again, we have seen that mines in one zone could produce largely for markets lying in the other: perhaps the greater part of the output of the silver mines of the south of France, of Bosnia, and of Serbia went to the Arab countries, while much of the gold washed in the Guinea region was drawn towards Europe. What mattered most, therefore, was not which region had what mines, but rather what was the demand for each metal in each region.

IV

It is commonly held that the last two centuries of the Middle Ages were a time of bullion famine in Europe. What constitutes such a famine, however, is not clear, and it is difficult to know how one would recognize this kind of crisis. Certainly, on *a priori* grounds, any shortage of precious metals seems improbable. If the output of some silver mines in this period fell off, other important mines continued to produce at high levels[1] and new mines, some extremely rich, were opened in Bohemia, Serbia, and Bosnia.[2] What is more, the fall in population caused by the Black Death and its aftermath, and the perhaps even greater shrinkage of trade, must have reduced the need for precious metals. Supplemented as it was by credit instruments, the money supply already in circulation in 1340 should therefore have been adequate for Europe's needs until 1500. Indeed, one could argue that the ratio of money to transactions was higher in the century following the outbreak of the plague than it had been for some time before.[3]

Without doubt, much of the evidence which has been used to support the thesis of a bullion famine has been misread. When governments resorted to debasement to finance their activities, it was more likely because of overspending or fiscal inadequacy than because of a general shortage of precious metals. Or again, the disappearance of certain coins from one city or area was most often the result of the operation of Gresham's Law; it does not prove that precious metals were in short supply.[4] When, for instance, new and more debased pennies were given the

thirds of the world's production of gold came from Africa (and most of the remainder came from Hungary). Ibid. p. 353.

[1] F. Graus, 'La crise monétaire du 14e siècle', *Revue belge de philologie et d'histoire*, XXIX (1951), 452.

[2] Ibid. and Kovačević, op. cit.

[3] It can, however, be argued that larger marketable surpluses from rural areas resulted in an extension of the scope of the money economy, thereby raising "T".

[4] See, for example, H. Laurent, *La loi de Gresham au Moyen Age* (Brussels, 1933), and H. Van Werveke,

ANDREW M. WATSON

same value as older coins with a higher intrinsic value, the older coins were driven out—and perhaps replaced by an inrush of inferior coins. But the total supply of bullion in the region affected was not much changed. The same result could be achieved when a government gave two silver coins different values (relative to their content of silver) in terms of the money-of-account: the undervalued coins would be the first to be exported. But provided the coins remained in Europe, the continent's supply of precious metals remained the same. The trade in precious metals that arose from regional differences in the ratio of silver to gold might also give the illusion of a bullion famine where none existed. In such trade one city might be relieved of most of its silver, but received gold in return; a neighbouring city might lose its gold and receive silver. Both cities suffered a shortage of *one* of the precious metals, but there was no overall shortage. That such exchanges did exist in Europe is certain, and some examples have been well documented.[1] However disrupting this kind of trade might be for the regions affected, it did not reduce the total supply of bullion. It merely redistributed it.

Finally, one cannot plausibly argue that there was a shortage of *gold* in Europe during the last two and a half centuries of the Middle Ages. For it is in this very period that gold coinage was adopted by one city, one country, one region after another, until finally there was almost no part of Europe that did not strike gold. The output of gold coins, moreover, was high,[2] and almost every region maintained at least one kind of gold currency of excellent quality until the very end of the Middle Ages.[3] It was thus a time of vastly increasing, and not decreasing, supplies of gold.

Only when we turn to *silver* do we find signs of a real shortage. Almost as soon as gold was minted in a region, difficulties were experienced in maintaining a silver coinage, and shortages often became acute. To guard against the loss of silver, laws were passed in most parts of Europe forbidding the export of coins and unminted metals. That these laws (which usually appeared as soon as a bimetallic currency was introduced, if they were not already in force) were not successful is evident. Almost everywhere the coming of gold enfeebled silver. In Genoa, for instance, the debasement of silver occurred in 1252, the same year as the return to gold.[4] In Venice, the silver coinage underwent a series of crises which culminated in 1353 with the abandonment of the *grosso*;[5] from that date onwards the ducat was the standard money-of-account. In France, the striking of large quantities of gold under Philip the Fair was accompanied by a hectic debasement of both the penny and the *gros tournois*, the latter of which had maintained its full weight and fineness until the end of the thirteenth century.[6] In

'Currency manipulation in the Middle Ages: the case of Louis de Mâle, Count of Flanders', *Transactions of the Royal Historical Society*, 4th ser. XXXI (1949).

[1] *Vide* p. 25, n. 2, and A. Girard. 'La guerre monétaire (XIVe–XVe siècles)', *Annales d'histoire sociale*, II (1940), 207–18. However, I do not believe that the money market was quite so sensitive to small fluctuations in the silver–gold ratio as Girard suggests.

[2] J. Craig, *The Mint* (Cambridge, 1953), pp. 410–13, shows that for almost every year after 1344 the value of gold minted exceeded that of silver. During the years 1357–1438, the disproportion was striking, the *weight* of gold struck often exceeding that of silver.

[3] A. Dieudonné, 'Des espèces de circulation internationale en Europe depuis Saint Louis', *Revue suisse de numismatique*, XXII (1920), *passim*. The only area without high-quality gold coinage seems to have been the Rhenish currency union.

[4] Desimoni, op. cit. p. 34.   [5] Cessi, op. cit. *passim*.   [6] *Vide* p. 15, n. 4.

England, the first appreciable debasement of the silver coinage occurred between 1344 and 1351, immediately after the striking of the noble by Edward III.[1] The pattern was everywhere the same. Rulers in all parts of Europe were ready to procure the metal needed to maintain a strong gold currency by sacrificing silver. They were prepared to let the common people, who received their incomes in silver, bear the burden of keeping intact a prestige coinage for the use of princes and merchants.[2]

The shortage of silver, however, was not everywhere equally acute. Generally speaking, the northern regions of Europe were much less affected than the South. In England, Germany, and Hungary, for instance, only silver coins were minted until the middle of the fourteenth century (if the brief English experiment with gold in the 1250's be excepted). Throughout the whole period when the price of gold was rising and the price of silver was falling, therefore, this part of Europe based its currency system on the metal which was becoming cheaper and was able to keep its silver supplies more or less intact. Only when the price of gold fell, and that of silver rose, did this region go over to gold; because of the change in relative prices of the two metals, the North could make the shift with less sacrifice of silver than the South. Thus in England, for instance, the penny of 1500 contained more than half of the silver of the penny of 800. Debasement was relatively restrained.[3] On the other hand, the southern regions of Europe—France and Italy—were caught both ways. These areas, which went over to gold early, had to acquire their gold supplies during a period when the price of gold was rising rapidly, and they did so only by shipping out very great amounts of silver. If, after 1340, they tried to strengthen their silver coinage, they found the price of silver had risen and the cost of doing so was too high. In consequence, the downward drift of French and Italian silver coins continued. By 1500 the penny of Milan contained only 1/43 of the silver it had had in 800, and the penny of Venice had depreciated still further.[4] The larger silver coins which had been issued from time to time in these areas also went the same way. Much of southern Europe thus entered the modern era with its currency system in a state of chaos and its economy as a result weakened.

But France and Italy suffered from more than bad timing: they were also in a poor geographical position. Separated from the other monetary zone by only a body of water, they were the regions most vulnerable to the pull on Europe's silver exercised by the Arab world. By contrast, the northern regions were to some degree insulated. As silver continued to be drawn out of Europe for three centuries, it is not surprising that the damage wreaked on the countries with a Mediterranean exposure was great. Of course, the gold which was received in return for some of the silver mitigated the evils of the drain. But this gold which reached southern Europe from across the Mediterranean was in turn subject to the attractive power of northern Europe, and often stayed in the South only long enough to change hands. In short, these southern regions, which were the first

[1] A. Feaveryear, *The Pound Sterling* (Oxford, 1963), p. 439.
[2] This view seems to be shared by Villani, op. cit. xii, 53 and 97, who thinks that Florentine monetary policy was designed to suit the interests of the cloth manufacturers.
[3] C. Cipolla, 'Currency Depreciation in Mediaeval Europe', *Economic History Review*, 2nd ser. xv (1963), 422.
[4] Ibid. p. 422.

ANDREW M. WATSON

to try to cope with a bimetallic currency system, were exposed to pulls on their money supplies from two sides, and they suffered continual upsets in their currency systems. This was the price they had to pay for being intermediaries between East and West. Though from a commercial viewpoint this position may have had many advantages, from a monetary standpoint there was little to commend it.

Nor did Europe and the Muslim world together constitute a closed system. Especially was this fact apparent in the trade in precious metals, for gold and silver could pass swiftly over long distances to reach in a few years places which had no direct contact with the source of the metals. Thus the Muslim countries, too, like southern Europe, were caught between two worlds: between Europe on the one hand and the Far East on the other. And like southern Europe, the Muslim countries felt the gravitational attraction exercised on their money supplies by these two powerful economies which surrounded them. They, too, were unable to maintain any stability in a bimetallic currency system. In particular, the *Arab* countries, whose economies were already in decline, were little able to resist the pressures coming from two sides; and by the end of the Middle Ages they had suffered prolonged monetary disorders and severe shortages of *both* precious metals. (In fifteenth-century Egypt, copper became the basis of the currency system.) These monetary upheavals can only have hastened the downward slide of the economies of the Arab world and prepared the region for the final Ottoman conquests.

En fin de compte, therefore, in this period as perhaps in an earlier one, a decisive factor in Europe's economic history may have been the strange power of India and China to attract precious metals from other parts of the world. How Europe and the Muslim countries were affected by monetary events in the Far East, however, is not yet known, the history of monetary conditions in Asia being still largely *terra incognita*. The answer, which may be of greatest importance, will emerge only as the horizons of monetary history widen.

9

The Quest for Prester John

C.F. Beckingham

FEW[1] scholars can have taken greater delight in discovering historical facts than did John Boyle. He endeavoured above all to ascertain exactly what had happened, and to identify as precisely as possible the place and date of events and the persons involved in any incident. It was this quality which made him such a superb commentator on the Persian histories, to the study and interpretation of which he devoted so much of his energies with such impressive results. There have been other scholars with whom he shared this characteristic, his teacher Minorsky, for instance. But Boyle joined to this, unusually, an affection

[1] The text of a lecture delivered by Professor Beckingham at Manchester University on 31 October 1979 in memory of Professor John Andrew Boyle.

292 THE JOHN RYLANDS UNIVERSITY LIBRARY

for legends, and an appreciation of the way in which they develop under the influence of changing conditions as they pass from one century or one people to another, and of how they in their turn may influence events. Very few men have derived more enjoyment at once from factual and from legendary history. Today I propose to speak about a legend which he did something to elucidate, which has had an immense influence on history, especially on the history of geographical discovery, and which affords a remarkable example of the courage and persistence of men in seeking evidence for something in which they would like to believe.

Among the historical episodes which Boyle has helped us to understand better is the struggle for power which took place among the tribes of Mongolia at the end of the twelfth and beginning of the thirteenth century, which eventuated in the supremacy of Chingiz Khan over the whole people. His principal rival in this conflict, who was eventually defeated and killed, was a man whom the European travellers of the thirteenth century, William of Rubruck and Marco Polo, call Unc or Unc Can. In a characteristically concise and informative note to his translation of Juvaini Boyle remarks that Unc is intended to represent the Mongol pronunciation of Wang, a title conferred upon him by the Chinese emperor, that his personal name was To'oril, and that he was the Khan of the Kereit, a tribe which was then Christian though of the Nestorian persuasion. It was this last fact that persuaded Marco Polo to identify him with Prester John, the mysterious priest and emperor, of prodigious wealth, power and sanctity, who was believed to rule over 72 subordinate kings and an enormous but vaguely located territory somewhere on the other side of the Saracens. Polo's identification enjoyed great success. As late as the middle of the sixteenth century, when Prester John had long been the name by which the Emperor of Ethiopia was usually known in Europe, we find the sober Portuguese historian Castanheda saying that the real Prester John was the one of whom Marco Polo spoke, who had reigned in the hinterland of India, and whose territory had adjoined that of the Great Khan of Cathay, by whom he had been defeated and killed, since when his empire had

THE QUEST FOR PRESTER JOHN   293

ceased to exist. Polo was nevertheless demonstrably wrong. The earliest literary reference to Prester John that has been traced is in the chronicle of Otto of Freising under the year 1145. This in turn relates to a battle which can be dated to September 1141. At this time Chingiz Khan had not been born and it is improbable that Wang Khan had been either ; if so he can only have been a child. Moreover, there are slight hints that the legend may be yet older. I incline to think that its origin should be sought not so much in a historical event as in a very under-standable aspiration.

The immense popularity of the story was attributable to the famous letter, supposedly addressed by Prester John to the Byzantine Emperor Manuel II Comnenus. This preposterous document must have been composed between 1143 and 1180. Originally written in Latin it spawned a multitude of versions, with different addressees, in the languages of western Europe. There are even some in Hebrew which Professor Edward Ullendorff and I are hoping to publish with a commentary.

The process by which Prester John, from being Khan of the Kereit and a Nestorian, became the Emperor of Ethiopia and a Monophysite, was protracted.   The decisive stages in the process were two embassies, not, as one might have expected, European embassies looking for him, but African embassies to Europe. The first was sent by the Emperor of Ethiopia and was in Genoa in 1306 ; the second was sent by the King of Benin in West Africa to Portugal in 1486. The first is known to us only from a chronicle by Jacopo Filippo Foresti of Bergamo entitled *Supplementum chronicarum*, first published at Venice in 1483. Foresti relates that in 1306 thirty members of an embassy from Prester John to the king of the Spains, *ad Hispaniarum regem*, who were returning home after seeing the Pope at Avignon and visiting Rome, were detained at Genoa by contrary winds. The rector, *praepositus*, of St. Mark took the opportunity to question them about Ethiopia and compiled a treatise, which he called a map. The Rector was the cartographer Giovanni da Carignano. His treatise has not survived and we do not know whether all that is meant may not be the legends on a map. A planisphere by Giovanni was preserved at Florence but was destroyed by fire

294 THE JOHN RYLANDS UNIVERSITY LIBRARY

during the Second World War, though not before several reproductions had been made. Unfortunately the lower edge had
been badly mutilated and we cannot be certain that Prester John
was shown on the upper Nile. Certainly a map drawn in
Mallorca by the Genoese Angelino da Dalorto in 1339 did put him
there and this is the earliest surviving map to do so. It is now
generally believed that Giovanni da Carignano was first responsible for locating Prester John in Africa.

It is rather surprising that this new habitat, for which there
was good evidence, did not at once gain general acceptance.
There must have been many Europeans who had some awareness
of the existence of a Christian kingdom in Ethiopia. From an
uncertain but early date Ethiopian pilgrims had been coming to
Jerusalem and some of them remained there to form a small
resident community. The first Christian pilgrim after the Arab
conquest to have left a record of his travels, the Englishman St.
Willibald, who became bishop of Eichstatt in Bavaria, relates that
he accompanied an Ethiopian across the plain of Esdraelon.
This was probably in the third decade of the eighth century.
Pilgrims from Europe came to be numerous and were highly
organized, eventually as much so as modern package tourists.
Many accounts of their journeys are to be found in medieval and
Renaissance libraries, often mercifully unpublished, for they are
frequently no more interesting than a narrative of a fortnight in
Torremolinos. There were, however, some pilgrims, especially
priests, who stayed longer in the country and learnt something of
the other Christian communities established there. Their
narratives contain many references to the Ethiopians ; it was
primarily from these that Cerulli was able to compile his authoritative book *Etiopi in Palestina*. There must have been many
returning European pilgrims who had met Christians from
Ethiopia.

It is a common mistake to assume that no accurate knowledge
of Asia or sub-Saharan Africa was available in late medieval or
Renaissance Europe. In fact there was a great deal known about
not only the Near East, but Central Asia, China, India and
Ethiopia, though less about Japan and South-East Asia. The
difficulty which confronted scholars or statesmen who needed such

THE QUEST FOR PRESTER JOHN 295

information was not that there was none, but that it was so difficult to distinguish which information was trustworthy. There was a vast quantity which was wholly fictitious though equally well attested. Various descriptions of Prester John's domain incorporate in inextricable confusion genuine information about the Christian Turks of Central Asia, the Christians of St. Thomas in South India, and the Christians of Nubia and Ethiopia, but mingled with much that has never been true of Christians or anyone else anywhere on earth.

How correct and how pertinent information about Asia and Africa could be is exemplified by a short work about which I propose to say something, partly because it seems to me less well-known than it deserves to be. This is largely to be blamed upon the odd way in which it was published. William Adam's tractate *De modo Sarracenos extirpandi* was printed in the great French collection of sources for the history of the Crusades, *Recueil des historiens des Croisades*, but it was perversely included in the second volume of Armenian documents. William Adam's nationality is not known but he was certainly not an Armenian. Nor did he write in Armenian ; had he done so Boyle might have, indeed almost certainly would have, read his book, but it would have been unintelligible to me.

We do not know much about him. He was a Dominican who was made a suffragan to the archbishop of Sultanieh, the newly built capital of the Mongol rulers of Persia, the so-called Ilkhans. He then became bishop of Smyrna and, in 1322, archbishop of Sultanieh, whence he was translated to Antivari, the modern Bar in Yugoslavia, only two years later. He died between 1337 and 1341, having spent most of his later years in France, though without vacating his see.

His book seems to have been written in 1316 or 1317. It is a solution of the Palestine problem as it presented itself to contemporary statesmen. Then, as more recently, there were those who believed that the most effective course of action would be to concentrate attention on Egypt. You will recall that in the late twelfth century the Kings of Jerusalem had contended with the rulers of Damascus for mastery of Egypt, that Renaud de Châtillon had attempted to destroy Egyptian power by attacking

296 THE JOHN RYLANDS UNIVERSITY LIBRARY

the Red Sea shipping, on which the country's wealth largely depended, and that Louis IX had led a Crusade against Egypt. William Adam advocated the restoration of the Latin Empire of Constantinople and a sustained effort to prevent the supply of war materials to Egypt by European merchants, too many of whom were ready to risk excommunication for the profits obtainable. He even wished the Pope to forbid pilgrimages to Palestine on pain of excommunication in order to deprive the Sultan of an important source of revenue. The most interesting section of his book is the fifth and last in which he explains how Egyptian commerce could easily be ruined by a small fleet operating in the Indian Ocean. Here he displays some knowledge of the political alignment of the principal powers of Asia. He knew that the Mongol conquests had resulted in the formation of four states, China of the Yüan dynasty, of whose pre-eminent position he was aware, the Khanate of the Golden Horde, which he calls Gazaria, i.e. the country of the Khazars, Persia of the Ilkhans, and the Chaghatai Khanate, which he calls Doa or Caydo, both in fact names of Mongol princes prominent in the recent or contemporary politics of Central Asia. Moreover, he appreciated the important fact that the Persian Ilkhans and the Golden Horde were enemies, and that there was a consequent rapprochement between the latter and the Mamluk Sultans of Egypt. Indeed he advised that a Papal squadron should be formed and placed under the command of the Genoese lords of Chios, the Zaccaria brothers, to sail in the waters of the Levant and prevent communication between the Horde and Egypt. He also realized that the Ilkhans would welcome the friendship of Europeans hostile to the Muslims.

Like Renaud de Châtillon over a hundred years before, William Adam understood the importance of the trade of the Indian Ocean to the prosperity of Egypt. "Everything that is sold in Egypt," he says, "like pepper, ginger and other spices, gold and precious stones, silks and those rich textiles dyed with Indian colours, and all the other valuables, to buy which the merchants from these countries go to Alexandria and expose themselves to the snare of excommunication, all these are brought to Egypt from India. As food is transferred from the head to the

THE QUEST FOR PRESTER JOHN   297

throat, and from the throat to the stomach, and from the stomach to the other parts of the body, just so the aforesaid precious goods have an outlet from the Indian Sea as if from the head, and are dispersed through the said Gulf of Eden as if through the throat, and thence to Egypt through the Red Sea, as if through the stomach, to the other countries of the world, as if to the other parts of the body.   If then the head were to be cut off, the whole stomach would wither away from lack of nourishment, and the other limbs would perish."

William Adam's notions of the geography of at least the western part of the Indian Ocean were correct.   He seems to have believed that Africa was circumnavigable, since he speaks of the Indian Sea, *mare Indicum*, as a branch of the Ocean, *brachium maris Oceani*, by which we should presumably understand the circumambient ocean surrounding the habitable world.   He knew that the Red Sea was a gulf of the Indian Ocean and that it extended between Arabia and a range of mountains beyond which was the real Ethiopia, *ultra quos montes veram Ethiopiam habet*.   The adjective is significant.   It means that, unlike many others of his own and later times, he understood that Ethiopia was in Africa and was quite different from, and some distance from, India, with which it was frequently confused, a geographical misunderstanding to which I shall revert.   He was aware of the position of Aden, which he calls Eden, in relation to the Red Sea, and of its commercial importance, and he knew about Socotra and its adjacent islands, their strategic position in the Gulf of Aden and the fact that their population was Christian, for he had spent nine months there when attempting to reach Ethiopia where he and others of his order intended to preach, *fui in dictis insulis novem mensibus commoratus, quando volebam, causa predicandi fidei, cum quibusdam aliis ordinis mei, meis sociis, in Ethiopiam proficisci*.   He may well have reached Ethiopia but I do not think it should be assumed that he did, as it usually is. He goes on to say that he could tell many astonishing things about Ethiopia if it were not that he intended to write only a short book, but many other travellers have written amazing accounts of places to which they have not been.   One thinks of Marco Polo and Odoric of Pordenone, to mention only two.

298 THE JOHN RYLANDS UNIVERSITY LIBRARY

His recommendation was that four galleys should be built in the Indian Ocean and based on Socotra. With the enthusiastic help of the population of several countries and islands of the region the trade of Egypt could then be harried. He had, he claims, spent twenty months in that part of the world, and he knew that these people would welcome the opportunity to attack Aden if aided by the superior military technique of the Europeans. There were three places where the galleys could be built, which were beyond the reach of the Aden merchants, who would naturally try to wreck the undertaking.

The first place was Ormuz, which was in the territory of the emperor of Persia, that is, the Ilkhan. He probably had in mind Öljeitü, who died in December 1316. Like so many of the Mongols he was a man of unstable religious affiliations. In the authoritative chapter on the political and dynastic history of the Ilkhans which he contributed to the *Cambridge History of Iran*, Boyle noted that he was christened Nicholas, was for a while a Buddhist, then became a Sunni Muslim, and finally an Imami Shi'i. Like several of his predecessors he was interested in co-operating with Christian Europe against the Mamluks and had addressed a letter to Philip IV of France in April 1305 ; there is no trace of a reply, but a similar letter to Edward I of England was acknowledged by his successor in the autumn of 1307. In the winter of 1312-13 Öljeitü had made an unsuccessful incursion into Syria, which was then part of the Mamluk empire. William Adam's assumption that he would have been sympathetic to his project was almost certainly justified.

The second possible site for constructing the galleys was what he calls *Dive insule*, said to be some 3,000 miles away. It has been argued whether this phrase refers to the Maldives or the Laccadives. It seems to me likely that William, in common with many other writers, did not distinguish between them. It is certain that the Maldives, and possible that the Laccadives, had been converted to Islam from Buddhism and Hinduism respectively, but in both instances the occurrence must have been recent and it is probable that the new religion still sat lightly on its adherents, if we can judge by the scandalized description of Maldivian morals written by the pious Ibn Battuta a few decades later.

THE QUEST FOR PRESTER JOHN   299

The third possibility was Further India, *ultima India*, in which he names three cities, Thana, Cambay and Quilon. India could provide ample timber for shipbuilding. Nowhere else had he seen such tall trees with sound wood so free from knots. There were 20,000 islands in the Indian Ocean, of which 6,000 were inhabited. There were so many pirates in these that it would be easy to man forty or fifty ships with 600 or 800 men in each to join in an attack on Aden and other coastal cities. They had already once taken Aden, even without European help, and had looted and burnt the entire city which they were not able to hold. I should add that I have not so far found any reference to this incident in the Arabic sources, some of which are fairly detailed.

William wished to entrust the execution of his scheme to the Genoese, for several reasons. They had greater maritime experience than other peoples, were readier to go to remote regions, and were more eager to make money. Already in the time of the Ilkhan Arghun (1284-91) they had built two galleys at Baghdad with the intention of using them to blockade the Gulf of Aden. They had done this at the instigation of Arghun himself. The scheme had failed only because of their internecine quarrels. They had begun calling one another Guelfs and Ghibellines and killing each other. William tactfully omits to mention what must have been a very important reason for resorting to the Genoese, their hostility to the Venetians and consequent eagerness to see the latter's trade with Egypt collapse.

William Adam's plan was not acted upon and his knowledge of the geography and foreign policy of the principal Asian empires was not emulated in the next century. Prester John was constantly sought and, apparently under the influence of Giovanni da Carignano and the Genoese and Mallorcan cartographers, was often shown on maps as residing on the upper Nile. However, an extraordinary confusion between India and Ethiopia persisted throughout the fourteenth and fifteenth centuries. This confusion, almost incredible though it may seem to us, was of long standing. Already in the sixth century Isidore of Seville had described the Ethiopians with the words that Julius Solinus had applied to the Indians some centuries before. Anywhere vaguely south of the

300 THE JOHN RYLANDS UNIVERSITY LIBRARY

Muslim countries was liable to be called India. A factor which must I think have contributed to the confusion, or at least have impeded its resolution, is the influence of a book which enjoyed unchallenged authority and which was until very recently read by almost every literate European, the *Book of Genesis*. You will remember that in Chapter II it is stated that a river flowed from Paradise and formed four branches which are named Pison, Gihon, Hiddekel and Euphrates. The Euphrates is the Euphrates. The Hiddekel is certainly the Tigris ; the names are cognate. The identification of the Pison and the Gihon is more difficult but in medieval times one or the other, usually the Gihon, was thought to be the Nile. For our purpose it does not matter which river the original writer had in mind. It is obvious, however, that if the Tigris, the Euphrates, and the Nile, let alone an unidentified fourth river, are to be regarded as branches of one river, even allowing, as some commentators did, for rivers running underground for a considerable distance, our conception of the geography of the Near East and Africa requires substantial modification. If we are to rearrange the topography of the area so that these three rivers become branches of one stream which have flowed in opposite directions it will be uncertain whether that stream is in Ethiopia or in India. It can be located comfortably in either without creating any more difficulty.

This confusion between India and Ethiopia, the belief that Prester John was to be found in either and that the two might in some sense be the same, gave encouragement to the Portuguese when in the fifteenth century they commenced those voyages of discovery along the west coast of Africa usually associated with the name of Prince Henry the Navigator. There is ample evidence that they hoped to find India as well as Prester John and believed that Africa would lead them to both. The argument about whether Henry was concerned to find India or only Prester John, which has preoccupied some scholars, is somewhat ridiculous. The two were part of the same problem. As early as 1441 Antão Gonçalves proposed to the Prince that an African of rank who had been captured on the coast of that contentious territory which later became the Spanish Sahara should be taken back and ransomed in the hope of obtaining information about the interior.

THE QUEST FOR PRESTER JOHN   301

Henry replied that he wanted to know also about the Indies and the country of Prester John. This quest recurs constantly throughout the fifteenth century explorations. Indeed Ruy de Pina, the chronicler of João II, says that the famous padrões, the inscribed pillars surmounted by crosses which the Portuguese erected at various points along the African coast, were intended to prove that they were Portuguese and Christians " all with the object of gaining knowledge of the Prester John, who was said to be Christian ". The Portuguese frequently captured Africans, took them to Portugal, made them Christians, taught them Portuguese and then returned them to some part of the African coast in the hope that through them Prester John might become aware of their search for him. The fate of these ladies and gentlemen is easier to imagine than to ascertain. Like many of their successors in Africa, though with more excuse, the Portuguese had no conception of the immense complexity of the political and linguistic map of sub-Saharan Africa. They do not seem to have realized that if an African was kidnapped at the mouth of the Senegal, his command of his native Wolof would avail him nothing in trying to penetrate Bantu speaking areas of central and southern Africa. They entertained similar misapprehensions about the political map. They were liable to apply the name Ethiopia to the whole of Africa south of the Sahara. The historian Barros speaks of the fort of São Jorge de Mina as being in the midst of the great region of Ethiopia. He also tells us that information about the interior was gained not only from people indigenous to the places occupied or visited by the Portuguese, but also from strangers, including some Arabs and Abyssinians, *abexis*, who came to the castle of Arguim. Who the latter were it is difficult to say, but it is very unlikely that they came from the country we know as Ethiopia. As late as 1564 we find Gastaldi's map showing Damot and Gojam in the latitude of Mombasa, the Gurage country adjoining Kilwa, and the country of the Falasha still further south. Begamedr, which he calls Bagametro, is in the latitude of Mozambique. Indeed Africa, or at least the interior as far as the Cape of Good Hope, was considered to be part of Ethiopia. I do not think we should assume that the Portuguese supposed that every Hottentot at the Cape

302 THE JOHN RYLANDS UNIVERSITY LIBRARY

paid taxes to the Emperor of Ethiopia or obeyed his injunctions, but they did evidently think that many of them would have heard of him and would be able to give their envoys helpful information about the direction in which he should be sought, and would perhaps be able to transmit to him information about the Portuguese. The assumption was not unreasonable. After all, had an Ethiopian landed in Brittany or Jutland in the fifteenth century and said he was looking for the Pope—we must remember that Prester John was an amalgam of a Pope and a Holy Roman Emperor—there would have been many people who would have known enough to tell him he should make for Rome, and that Rome was somewhere in Italy.

The form taken by this quest was partly determined by a geographical misapprehension which proved remarkably persistent. It was that there were one or two large lakes in the centre of Africa from which the principal rivers of the continent all flowed. This notion may have owed something to the four branches of the river of Paradise which I mentioned earlier. As the rivers reaching the Atlantic were discovered it was thought that the Senegal and then the Congo belonged to this remarkable river system. Ruy de Pina tells us that Prince Henry in his maps and memoranda called the Senegal the Nile, " not the one that comes into the Levant Sea at Alexandria but another branch of it which the cosmographers say reaches this Ocean ", but he adds " the certain truth of this is now in the time of the King Dom Manoel I still to be ascertained ". Gastaldi shows the Congo, the Zaire as he calls it, and the Nile both flowing from a great lake, the northern part of which he names Lago de Zaire and the southern Lago de Zembere, this being no doubt a corruption of the Ethiopian Dambya. So long as this conception of the hydrography of Africa prevailed it seemed that the easiest way to reach Prester John would probably be to mount one of the rivers entering the Atlantic, follow it to the lake in which it originated and near which he was likely to be, and then if necessary return to Europe by following the Nile to Egypt and the Mediterranean.

This concept continued to influence the activities of the Portuguese long after the sea route to India had been established and even after their fleets had entered the Red Sea. This is

THE QUEST FOR PRESTER JOHN 303

exemplified by the adventures of someone who has received little notice. Gregorio da Quadra was in command of a brigantine in a Portuguese fleet which was sent to blockade the Gulf of Aden. They called at Malindi which was a friendly port, and in August 1509 made their way northwards along the Somali coast. One night when they were anchored off Mogadishu the cable of Quadra's ship broke ; everyone was asleep and the vessel was driven by winds and currents past Cape Gardafui and into the Gulf of Aden. There, off Zeila, it was captured and the crew made prisoners. Da Quadra was sent to Zabid in the lowland plain of the Yemen where he was imprisoned for the next seven years, earning a livelihood by knitting woollen caps. In 1516, however, an Egyptian army overthrew the ruler of the Yemen, and da Quadra and five other survivors were released. He pretended to be a pious Muslim, accompanied the new ruler to Mecca and Medina and then claimed that he wished to visit Kerbela. He tried to overtake a caravan, nearly lost his life in the desert, was saved by what he regarded as a miracle, not unreasonably, and eventually reached Iraq. He made his way to Basra and so to Ormuz where he was welcomed by the Portuguese Captain and enabled to return to Portugal, where he arrived in 1520. He doubtless anticipated a tranquil retirement. However, King Manoel was so fascinated by what he told him about Ethiopia and the great lake from which the Nile and the Congo both flowed that he despatched da Quadra on a mission to the King of the Congo who was requested to send him on to Ethiopia.

The ruler of this Congo kingdom was one Mobemba Amosinga who had been converted to Christianity. His principal territory was not so much in the present Republic of Zaire but rather in northern Angola, in the area bounded by the Atlantic, the Congo, the Kwango and the Kwanza rivers. He received da Quadra warmly and took the advice of his Portuguese counsellors whom he trusted more than those of his own race. These advised against sending on da Quadra. They urged that the Portuguese were so eager to establish close relations with Prester John that if they were enabled to do so by the Congo route they would gradually annex the kingdom and all the intervening

304 THE JOHN RYLANDS UNIVERSITY LIBRARY

territory until they had a common frontier with Ethiopia. However improbable this was, their advice was fortunate for da Quadra. It is very hard to believe that he could ever have made his way successfully across Africa from northern Angola to Ethiopia. Instead he was sent back to Portugal where he found that King Manoel had died and he spent the rest of his life in tranquillity as a discalced Capuchin friar, expiating his temporary profession of Islam while in Arabia. He did however tell his story to the chronicler Damião de Goes.

In 1486, and therefore after the discovery of the mouth of the Congo, they received great encouragement from an embassy sent to Portugal by the King of Benin. Its object was to ask for priests to be sent to his kingdom to instruct his subjects in Christian beliefs and practices. This ambassador told King D. João that 20 moons' travel to the east of Benin, which was reckoned to mean about 250 leagues, there was a powerful king called Ogané, revered by the pagan princes of Benin as the Pope was among the Portuguese. There was an ancient custom by which the Kings of Benin, on their accession, used to send a present to Ogané and ask him to confirm them in office. In response he would send a staff, headgear and a cross to be worn round the neck; without these insignia the new King was not considered a legitimate ruler by his subjects. The ambassador sent to Portugal claimed that he had himself been an ambassador to Ogané and during the whole time he had been there he had never seen Ogané himself; he had always been concealed behind curtains, except that at the final audience one foot had been revealed. The ambassador had also been given a little cross, apparently a miniature version of the one sent to the King of Benin, and this, he told King João, made him a privileged man, free from all service, like the Commendadores in Portugal. When Barros was writing his account of all this in 1540 there were ambassadors from Benin in the country, one of whom, a man of about 70, was wearing one of these crosses. Barros interrogated him and he confirmed the whole story.

Scholars have not reached agreement on the identity of Ogané. A former colleague of mine in London proposed the Oni of Ife. Certainly, as the Portuguese came to know, the

THE QUEST FOR PRESTER JOHN   305

Emperor of Ethiopia sat behind a curtain at his audiences and revered the cross, but it is unthinkable that at this or any other time he should have exercised even a shadowy suzerainty over any part of West Africa. Whoever Ogané may have been in reality, he was a powerful inducement to the Portuguese to press forward their exploration of the African coast. King João had gathered from friars who had been to Jerusalem, and who had no doubt talked to Ethiopian pilgrims there, and also from Ethiopian monks who had come to Portugal, that the country of Prester John lay above Egypt and extended to the South Sea. His cosmographers compared Ptolemy's description of Africa with what the Benin ambassadors said and concluded that Ogané must be Prester John. The King inferred that if his ships persisted they would reach Cape Prason, the most southerly place in Africa known to the ancients, in fact, probably to be identified with Cape Delgado.

It was at this juncture that King João decided on a double attempt to settle the problem by sending two missions, one by land and the other by sea. The latter is much better known. It was commanded by Bartolomeu Dias and it succeeded in discovering the Cape of Good Hope. The overland expedition was an almost farcical failure. Two men, Frei Antonio de Lisboa and one Pero de Montarroio, went as far as Jerusalem but because they did not know Arabic, did not dare to accompany the monks they met there, by whom is no doubt meant the Ethiopian pilgrims, whom they had hoped to join on their journey home. The excuse, as it is given in Barros, seems lame indeed. It is not impossible to acquire the rudiments of Arabic and one would have expected them to do so. It seems to me more likely that the Ethiopians may have travelled as Muslims and were perhaps afraid that the two Portuguese would not be willing or able to pass as Muslims, or that they themselves thought so. In any event they returned to Portugal and the king then despatched Pero da Covilhã and Afonso de Paiva. We know something, though nothing like as much as we could wish, about the former because, over thirty years after his departure from Portugal, the first properly accredited Portuguese embassy to Ethiopia found him living there, married with a family of children, and endowed

306 THE JOHN RYLANDS UNIVERSITY LIBRARY

with an estate and in favour at court. His knowledge and in particular his command of Amharic were very useful to the embassy and they left him in Ethiopia when they sailed from the country in 1526.

Covilhã's story is well-known and he is the subject of an excellent monograph in Portuguese by the Conde de Ficalho, published in 1898. I do not intend to repeat the details now. I would however remark upon one circumstance which has, I think, escaped attention hitherto. The Conde de Ficalho concluded that, as he was known by the name of a town and not a patronymic or surname, he must have been of fairly humble origin. This may be so but it has not been noticed in this connection that the town of Covilhã, which is in the province of Beira Alta, was a seignory of Prince Henry the Navigator. It was conferred upon him with the dukedom of Viseu as a reward for his services in Africa. Henry died in 1460. Though Pero was old enough to have been entrusted with several delicate missions before he was sent to look for Prester John in 1487, he was still alive in 1526. If therefore he was born before Henry died it is very improbable that he was more than a child. All the same, there may well have been a family tradition of service to the lord of the town, service that perhaps entailed some connection with voyages of discovery.

Covilhã and Paiva made their way to Valencia, Barcelona, Naples, Rhodes, Alexandria, Cairo, Tor in Sinai and Aden. There they parted, Paiva making for Ethiopia, presumably by way of Zeila in Somalia, and Covilhã going to the Malabar coast, then to the east coast of Africa as far as Sofala, the usual southern limit of Arab trade, and perhaps to Madagascar. He may then have visited Ormuz before returning to Cairo to keep his rendezvous with Paiva. When he reached Cairo he found that Paiva had died. According to some authorities he died in Cairo and we do not know whether he had been to Ethiopia or not. It has been argued that if he had he would not have been allowed to leave. It is true that Covilhã was not allowed to leave but the emperor who was reigning when he arrived seems to have been willing for him to do so. I do not think there is any reason to suppose that Paiva would have been detained in Ethiopia and the probability, though not more than a probability, seems to me to be that Paiva

THE QUEST FOR PRESTER JOHN   307

reached Ethiopia from Zeila and returned to Cairo before he died.

Covilhã now prepared to return to the wife he had left in Portugal, when he encountered two Jews, one Joseph, a shoe-maker of Lamego, and Rabbi Abraham of Beja, whom the King had sent to look for him. Their instructions to him were that if he had done all that the King had asked him to do he was welcome to return ; if not he should send an account of what he had dis-covered to the King with Joseph and then take the Rabbi to Ormuz ; it was especially important that he should not return before having found Prester John. It appears from the account given by Barros that Joseph had recently been in Baghdad and had learnt about the importance of Ormuz. Barros tells us that it was not long since he, Joseph, had been in that region. If, then, he had returned to Portugal from the East only recently he had probably not left again before Bartolomeu Dias had come back with news of the discovery of the Cape of Good Hope. The date of Dias's return is uncertain. Barros says that he arrived back in Portugal in December 1487, having been away for 16 months and 17 days. This implies that he must have left in August 1486, very soon after the visit of the Benin ambassador with his news of Ogané. There is, however, good reason to think that the date given by Barros is one year too early and that Dias did not return till nearly the end of 1488, having discovered the Cape in the spring of the year. It is thus highly probable that Joseph of Lamego and the Rabbi were sent by the King after he knew that the African coast did not continue indefinitely southwards but reached a point where it turned east and then north. It was probably this that prompted him to send messen-gers to seek Covilhã and to insist upon his finding Prester John. Covilhã wrote a letter to the King, despatched it with Joseph, took Rabbi Abraham to Ormuz as he had been instructed to do, and then parted from him, made his way to Mecca and Medina, to Tor and so to Zeila, whence he reached Ethiopia. Abraham returned by the Aleppo caravan from Iraq. Covilhã, as is well known, was welcomed by the Emperor of Ethiopia, Eskender, who, however, died soon afterwards. His successor Na'od refused to allow him to leave and, as I have mentioned, he settled

308 THE JOHN RYLANDS UNIVERSITY LIBRARY

in Ethiopia, and was found there by the Portuguese when at last
a fully accredited embassy reached the country in 1520 by way of
the Portuguese possessions in India.

The importance of Covilhã's travels is debatable and has been
debated at great length. If his letter reached Portugal then the
information it contained must have been of the greatest value in
determining what instructions were to be given to Vasco da
Gama, indeed in deciding whether the attempt should be made
to send a fleet to India. It was argued by Ficalho that the fact
that da Gama was sent to Calicut strongly suggests that
Covilhã's letter had arrived and that the King was therefore aware
of the great importance of this port. On the other hand Covilhã's
letter has not yet been traced in the Portuguese archives, but their
contents are very imperfectly known, as I have found from my
own experience. Certainly there seems no reason why a letter
should not have arrived. It has not usually been remarked that
it had two chances of reaching its destination. Joseph set out
from Cairo and the Rabbi from Ormuz ; both must have carried
detailed reports. It was not difficult, especially for Jews, to make
the journeys in question.

There is one important item of evidence about this which I
should like to discuss in some detail. In his book *The Portuguese
Pioneers* the late Edgar Prestage made what has often been assumed to be an authoritative statement : " Some authors have
doubted whether John II received Covilhan's letter. In the
first edition of his history of the Portuguese in the East, Castanheda says that he did ; in the second he denies it." Castanheda
was perhaps the most cautious of the early Portuguese historians
of the Indian enterprise, and his testimony is of great importance.
It does not seem to me that Prestage's words accurately represent
what he said.

The first edition of the first book of Castanheda's *History of
the Discovery and Conquest of India by the Portuguese* was published in 1551. Books II and III followed in 1552. In 1554
another edition of Book I appeared. The first fact to be noted is
that, contrary to what is sometimes suggested, we are not dealing
with the excision or alteration of a single statement ; the whole
book has been not so much revised as rewritten. Thus we do not

THE QUEST FOR PRESTER JOHN   309

have to consider the omission or alteration of a particular statement, perhaps at the instigation of a censor, official or unofficial.
There are a number of significant differences in what is said
about Covilhã.   For example, in the first edition he is said to have
gathered information about Madagascar, the Island of St.
Laurence as it was called, in Sofala ; in the second he is alleged
to have visited it.   An important error is corrected.   In the first
edition it is stated that Frei Antonio and his companion were
despatched after the return of Bartolomeu Dias when the King
learnt that, although Dias had found that the coast of Africa
trended eastwards and then to the north, he had found no news
of India and had met only with people who were half savages.
Now Covilhã and Paiva were not sent until after the failure and
return of Frei Antonio and Pero de Montarroio.   We know from
several sources that Covilhã and Paiva were received by João II
and the heir apparent at Santarem for their final audience on 7
May 1487.   Even if Barros's dates for Dias's voyage are correct,
and there is strong evidence to suggest that they are not, he did
not return till seven months after they had left.   Concerning the
letters carried by Joseph of Lamego and Rabbi Abraham, in the
first edition Castanheda says that after Covilhã had gone to
Ethiopia the King heard no more of him and supposed him to be
dead ; he was left with the information contained in the letters
the Jews had brought him.   There is another interesting detail.
When Covilhã was first despatched he was given what is called
a *carta de marear*, a chart, copied from a map that had been
prepared by the Licentiate Calçadilha, Dom Diego Ortiz de
Villegas, a Spaniard not a Portuguese by birth, who was bishop of
Viseu and a celebrated cosmographer.   Castanheda's narrative
makes clear what the other authorities do not, that this map was
not intended to help Covilhã and Paiva find their way, as one
might suppose, but was for them to enter the names of places in
Prester John's empire and through which they went.   In the
first edition of his history Castanheda tells us that Covilhã added
to the map the names of all the places he visited in India, " even
though badly written ", *ainda que mal escriptos*.   I do not think
that this is to be understood as a criticism of his penmanship but
rather of his spelling of names which must have been familiar to

310 THE JOHN RYLANDS UNIVERSITY LIBRARY

Castanheda who had spent some years in India. It is likely enough that an attempt to represent Swahili, Arabic, Persian, Canarese and Malayalam names in accordance with the ortho-graphical conventions of fifteenth century Portuguese should have presented difficulties. But whatever the phrase means, how could Castanheda, who was a cautious historian, have made such a comment if he had not either seen the chart or at least talked to someone who had seen it? If so it must have reached Portugal. This seems to me important evidence. I do not think the fact that this particular sentence is omitted in the second edition is necessarily significant ; other items are omitted, some of which we have no reason to doubt as they are confirmed by the best source we have for his adventures, Francisco Alvares, who knew him later in Ethiopia from 1520 to 1526. Nor is Prestage correct in claiming that in the second edition of his book Castanheda denies that King João received the letters which Covilhã sent him with the Jews. What he does say is that he did not know whether João received them. Even if he did not, they may still have arrived after his death, though, as this occurred in October 1495, they must have taken very much longer than we should have expected.

It is, of course, possible that the *carta de marear* and the letters will one day be found in the archives in Portugal. Until further evidence is discovered we cannot be sure whether the influence of Covilhã's journeys was of immense importance, or quite negli-gible. Like so much else in the story of Prester John it serves to remind us of something which no historian should ever forget, something which John Boyle never forgot, that what we know of the past is not always what it would most interest us to know, not what we should most expect to know, and not even what the past did most to ensure that we should know, and that, in the words of Sir Thomas Browne, " the iniquity of oblivion blindly scattereth her poppy, and deals with the memory of men without distinction to merit of perpetuity ".

10
Prophecy and Discovery: On the Spiritual Origins of Christopher Columbus's 'Enterprise of the Indies'

Pauline Moffitt Watts

> And I saw a new heaven and a new earth: for the first heaven and the first earth were passed away; and there was no more sea.
> —Revelations 21:1

> God made me the messenger of the new heaven and the new earth of which he spoke in the Apocalypse of St. John after having spoken of it through the mouth of Isaiah; and he showed me the spot where to find it.
> —Christopher Columbus, 1500[1]

CHRISTOPHER COLUMBUS WANTED TO BE REMEMBERED as the Admiral of the Ocean Sea. It was a formal title that he had struggled to win from his king and queen, Ferdinand and Isabella of Spain, in recognition of his discovery and exploration of the Indies. And for the last one hundred fifty years scholars have almost without exception elaborated the image of Columbus as the bold and innovative explorer who, armed with a "rational" or "scientific" geography, battled the ignorance and superstition of influential ecclesiastics at the Aragonese court until he finally won royal support for his "Enterprise of the Indies." Samuel Eliot Morison's well-known biography, *The Admiral of the Ocean Sea* (1942), is a prime example of this traditional line of scholarly interpretation.[2]

Morison's image of Columbus coincides with but one of two images that

An early version of this paper was presented in May 1981 at Villa I Tatti, while I was a fellow at the Harvard University Center for Italian Renaissance Studies. I would like to thank the staffs of the Biblioteca Berenson, Villa I Tatti, and of the William L. Clements Library, Ann Arbor, Michigan, for the generous help they have given me during the past several years. W. G. L. Randles initially stimulated my interest in this subject; I am especially indebted to him for the information and encouragement that he unfailingly provided. Both he and Nicholas Steneck read this essay in the course of its preparation, and I am grateful for their comments and suggestions. I would also like to express my appreciation to Delno C. West, Burdette C. Poland, and the anonymous readers for the *American Historical Review* for their insights and advice.

[1] This passage occurs in a letter written by Columbus to a member of the royal court in 1500, after his third voyage when he was returned from the New World Indies to Spain in chains; G. B. Spotorno, *Memorials of Columbus* (London, 1823), 224.

[2] After almost seven years of petitioning at the Spanish royal court, Columbus won acceptance for his Enterprise of the Indies—his plan to reach the oriental archipelago by sailing west—from Queen Isabella in

Columbus had of himself. The second image tended, particularly in his later years, to take precedence over the first and seemed to consume him. He came to believe that he was predestined to fulfill a number of prophecies in preparation for the coming of the Antichrist and the end of the world. According to his calculations, these events were not far off. This second self-image is epitomized in the signature that Columbus adopted: Christoferens. It is an awkward latinization of his given name and means "Christ-bearer." Until recently, little attention has been paid to Christoferens—that is, to the spiritual dimension of Columbus's personality, to the religious and cultural environment out of which it developed, and to its possible influence on the genesis of his voyages of discovery.[3] Yet Columbus's apocalyptic vision of the world and of the special role that he was destined to play in the unfolding of events that would presage the end of time was a major stimulus for his voyages. Moreover, his apocalypticism must be recognized as inseparable from his geography and cosmology if a balanced picture of the historical significance of his Enterprise of the Indies is to be achieved.

The origins and development of the two-fold conception that Columbus had of himself, and of the sense of mission that grew out of it, are not easy to trace. Details regarding his background and education are sparse. According to his son Ferdinand's biography and to Bartolomé de Las Casas's *Historia de las Indias,* the two principal early sources for the mariner's life, Columbus studied for a while at the University of Pavia. There, Ferdinand wrote, he "studied enough . . . to understand the geographers, of whose teaching he was very fond; for this reason he also gave himself to the study of astronomy and geometry, since these sciences are so closely related that one depends upon the other. And because Ptolemy, in the beginning of his *Geography,* says that one cannot be a good geographer unless one knows how to draw too, he learned drawing, in order to be able to show the position of countries and form geographic bodies, plane and round."[4] Scholars have long doubted that Columbus studied at the University of Pavia. Many follow instead the argument advanced by Cornelio Desimoni in 1894 that Pavia refers not to the famous Italian

---

1492. For at least a year prior to that acceptance he insisted that he be granted the title Admiral of the Ocean Sea and a generous portion of all future profits from any lands that he might discover as conditions for undertaking his voyage. These demands almost cost him the royal support he so persistently sought. See Ferdinand Columbus, *The Life of the Admiral Christopher Columbus by His Son Ferdinand,* trans. Benjamin Keen (New Brunswick, 1959), chap. 14. It should be noted that this translation was made from the first Italian edition of Ferdinand's biography, published in Venice in 1571; the Spanish original is lost. See Samuel Eliot Morison, *Admiral of The Ocean Sea,* 1 (Boston, 1942), chap. 8. For the texts of the seven documents signed by Columbus and the Spanish monarchs regarding the Enterprise of the Indies, see Samuel Eliot Morison, *Journals and Other Documents on the Life and Voyages of Christopher Columbus* (New York, 1963).

[3] Columbus first signed himself Christoferens in a 1493 memorandum addressed to Ferdinand and Isabella. On virtually everything he signed from 1493 until his death in 1506 he used the following sigil, which has never been definitively deciphered:

.S.
.S. A .S.
X M Y
Xp̄o FERENS.

On this curious sigil and the various attempts to decode it, see Paolo Emilio Taviani, *Christophe Colomb: Genèse de la grande découverte,* 2 (Paris, 1980), 38–40. Taviani provided an excellent bibliography of the relevant scholarship; *ibid.,* 45. Also see Alain Milhou, *Colón y su mentalidad mesiánica en el ambiente franciscanista español,* Cuadernos Colombinos, vol. 11 (Valladolid, 1983), 59–90.

[4] Ferdinand Columbus, *Life of the Admiral Christopher Columbus,* chap. 3, p. 9. On Columbus's education, compare Bartolomé de Las Casas, *Historia de las Indias,* ed. José Sancho Rayón, 1 (Madrid, 1875), 46.

university but rather to the Vicolo Pavia—an alleyway in Genoa where, in the mid-fifteenth century, the guild of the wool workers ran a well-known school for the children of their members. Columbus's father was a wool maker in Genoa.[5] While the question of where and when Columbus received his education remains unresolved, evidence regarding some of the more important sources of his thought survives.

Columbus apparently acquired much of his knowledge of geography, cosmology, history, astronomy, and other related subjects from a number of popular and quite widely diffused compilations that he read and annotated. Prominent among them were Pliny the Elder's *Naturalis historia*, Plutarch's *Lives*, Marco Polo's *Il milione*, the *Historia rerum ubique gestarum* of Pius II, and Pierre d'Ailly's *Imago mundi*. In these works Columbus would have encountered the following names: Aristotle, Averroes, Avicenna, Eratosthenes, Marinus of Tyre, Strabo, Ptolemy, Solinus, Seneca, Julius Capitolinus, Flavius Josephus, Augustine, Ambrose, Isidore of Seville, the Venerable Bede, Alfraganus, Roger Bacon, John Mandeville, Joachim of Fiore, Thomas Aquinas, Peter Comestor, Nicholas of Lyra, Francis Mayronnes, and Paolo Toscanelli. The depth of Columbus's knowledge of these figures would have varied greatly had it been limited to these compilations; some are barely mentioned, while the views of others are described in considerable detail. Finally, it is important to bear in mind that Columbus, like most Christians of his age, was deeply and thoroughly acquainted with the Old and New Testaments and with the Apocrypha (which would have been included in the Vulgate version of the Old Testament that he used).[6]

Without doubt, Columbus did not have the advanced, specialized education of a professional academic. But he did read and annotate works composed in Latin (for example, d'Ailly's *Imago mundi* and Pius II's *Historia*), Castilian (Alfonso de Palencia's translation of Plutarch's *Lives*), and Italian (Cristoforo Landino's translation of Pliny's *Naturalis historia*). His script was clear and not unsophisticated. As Ferdinand noted and Las Casas repeated, "So fine was his hand that he might have earned his living by that skill alone." His interest in history, geography, astronomy, and cosmology and his readings in these subjects were likely shared by many of the better-educated merchants, navigators, bankers, and business entrepreneurs of his day. And this is precisely what Columbus was—an experienced sailor and sometime merchant who married into a family belonging to the minor nobility of Portugal, a man whose fortunes had prospered on a modest scale.[7]

[5] Desimoni, *Questioni colombiane*, in Cesare de Lollis, ed., *Raccolta di documenti e studi pubblicati della R. Commissione Colombiana*, pt. 2, vol. 3 (Rome, 1894), 29. For a summary of the debate over whether Columbus studied at the University of Pavia, see Taviani, *Christophe Colomb*, 60–62. Las Casas's history seems to support Desimoni's theory, for Las Casas wrote that Columbus had an elementary rather than an advanced level of instruction. Columbus "estudió en Pavía *los primeros rudimentos* de letras"; *Historia de las Indias*, 46.

[6] Columbus's copies of the following works survive: d'Ailly's *Imago mundi* (1480 or 1483), Pius II's *Historia rerum ubique gestarum* (1477), Marco Polo's *De consuetudinibus et conditionibus orientalium regionum* and a resume of it in Italian (*Il milione*) by Pipino of Bologna (1485), Pliny's *Naturalis historia* (the Italian translation by Cristoforo Landino, Venice, 1489), Plutarch's *Lives* (in a 1491 Castilian translation by Alfonso de Palencia), and a fifteenth-century palimpsest of Seneca's *Tragedies*. On the sources to which Columbus had access, see Ferdinand Columbus, *Life of the Admiral Christopher Columbus*, chaps. 6–9; Las Casas, *Historia de las Indias*, chaps. 6–11; Taviani, *Christophe Colomb*, 231–38; and S. de La Rosa, *Libros y autógrafos de Cristobal Colón* (Seville, 1891).

[7] Ferdinand Columbus, *Life of the Admiral Christopher Columbus*, chap. 3, p. 9; and Las Casas, *Historia de las*

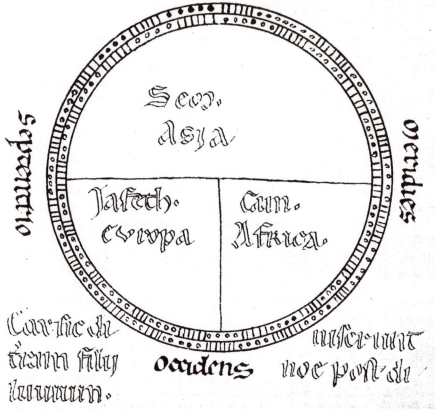

Figure 1: T-O Map of the Thirteenth Century. Diagram reproduced from Vicomte de Santarem, *Atlas composé de mappemondes, de Portulans, et de cartes hydrographiques et historiques depuis le VIᵉ jusqu'au XVIIᵉ siècle* (Paris, 1849), plate 5, no. 11.

The vision of the cosmos that Columbus shared with many of his contemporaries was derived from a variety of well-known ancient and medieval sources, including many by the authors mentioned above. It seems likely that Columbus's vision came principally from d'Ailly's *Imago mundi* and opuscula and from Pius II's *Historia*. From these works he arrived at a composite picture of a cosmos that was finite and geocentric. The world was located at the center of the seven concentric planetary spheres, themselves enclosed by the outermost shell of the fixed stars. The composition of the heavens and the movements of the planets and stars were permanent and unchanging and could and did influence actions and events on the earth, which was always subject to change—to generation and corruption.

The world itself was commonly depicted as a disk divided into three parts: Europe, Asia, and Africa. This disk was circumscribed by a band of ocean, the impassable sea whose unknown expanses had been feared since antiquity. The tripartite division of the world corresponded to the known land masses and was corroborated by a passage from the Old Testament. "The sons of Noah who went forth from the ark were Shem, Ham, and Japheth. . . . These three were the sons of Noah; *and from these the whole earth was peopled*" (Gen. 9:19). Accordingly, the most common form of the medieval *mappaemundi*, the so-called T-O map, was a circle, with the tripartite division resulting from the placing of the "T" within the circle "O." Since Shem was considered to be the eldest of Noah's sons, his domain was the largest of the three land masses, Asia. Ham's portion was Africa, and Japheth's was Europe (see Figure 1).

East was at the top of most medieval *mappaemundi*. There the terrestrial paradise was located, again in accordance with Scripture. "And the Lord God planted a garden *eastward in Eden* and there he set the man he had formed" (Gen. 2:8). Frequently the terrestrial paradise was depicted as an island, separated from the world by the waters of the flood. On the northern shores of Africa were the "monstrous races," first catalogued by Pliny and subsequently incorporated into various popular medieval Christian legends. Somewhere in the northern stretches of Asia, according to these legends, were the tribes of Gog and Magog, imprisoned within walls constructed by Alexander the Great. These tribes would be loosed upon mankind when the end of the world was imminent, as prophesied in the *Revelation* of John of Patmos and other influential apocalyptic visions, such as that of the pseudo-Methodius. Until these events occurred, the cosmos was the place where men and women were fated to live after Adam and Eve had been cast out of the Garden of Eden. This was the setting of fallen humanity's struggle to redeem itself in the eyes of its Maker and to recover the lost paradise so prominently and so nostalgically depicted on so many *mappaemundi* (see Figure 2).[8]

Indias, 46. On Columbus's knowledge of Spanish, Italian, and Latin, see Taviani, *Christophe Colomb*, 42–43, 45; and V. I. Milani, "The Written Language of Christopher Columbus," in *Forum Italicum* (Buffalo, 1973). On the connections among literary, scientific, and mercantile cultures during the age of discoveries, see J. H. Parry, *The Age of Reconnaissance: Discovery, Exploration, Settlement, 1450–1650* (Berkeley and Los Angeles, 1981), pt. 1; Boies Penrose, *Travel and Discovery in the Renaissance, 1420–1620* (New York, 1962), chaps. 16–17; Leonardo Olschki, *Storia letteraria delle scoperte geografiche* (Florence, 1937); and Irving Leonard, *Books of the Brave* (New York, 1964).

[8] On medieval conceptions of geography—"spiritual" and otherwise—and their representations in *mappaemundi*, see Milhou, *Colón y su mentalidad mesiánica*, 403–11; W. G. L. Randles. *De la terre plate au globe*

Figure 2: Ebstorf World Map of the Thirteenth Century.
Facsimile reproduced from Konrad Miller, *Die Ältesten Weltkarten* (Stuttgart, 1895–98), vol. 5

Men saw themselves essentially as *viators*, "strangers and pilgrims" St. Francis called them, journeying through the time and space of a tainted cosmos in search of a redemption that would occur only with the termination of that cosmos. These journeys were individual and collective. Sometimes they were voluntary, sometimes not. The peregrinations of the body were often inextricable from those of the soul. The *ecclesia peregrina* of Augustine's *The City of God*, the *imrams* of the Irish saints who set themselves adrift at sea, the Crusades, the lengthy pilgrimages undertaken by many thousands of nameless men and women to the grid of sacred sites that

terrestre: *Une mutation épistémologique rapide, 1480–1520* (Paris, 1980); George H. T. Kimble, *Geography in the Middle Ages* (New York, 1938), chap. 8; John K. Wright, *Geographical Lore of the Time of the Crusades* (New York, 1925), pt. 1, chap. 4; and John Block Friedman, *The Monstrous Races in Medieval Art and Thought* (Cambridge, Mass., 1981), chap. 3. For two fundamental catalogues of medieval *mappaemundi*, see Konrad Miller, *Mappaemundi: Die Ältesten Weltkarten*, 6 vols. (Stuttgart, 1895–98); and Marcel Destombes, *Mappemondes, A.D. 1200–1500: Monuments cartographiques anciens* (Amsterdam, 1964).

stretched across Europe to the Holy Land, the deliberate dependence of mendicant orders on the randomly encountered charity of others—all are manifestations of the symbiotic relationship between the internal and external journeys necessarily undertaken by post-lapsarian man.

Guided more often than not by prophecies regarding the appearance of an emperor-messiah, the conversion of all the peoples of the world to Christianity, the final recovery of the Holy Land from the infidel, and the advent of the Antichrist, Columbus and his contemporaries sought to discover and play out their historical roles in a cosmic drama they perceived as inexorably unfolding from the moment that Adam and Eve had been expelled from the Garden of Eden. Their searches and their enactments produced proto-nationalistic "duels of prophecies" and could also result in a civic apocalypticism, such as that of Savonarola of Florence, the quintessential urban prophet. But the drama took place on a larger stage as well, encompassing less particularized experiences of time, space, and place.[9] The striving to fulfill prophecy on a cosmic or global scale was a major stimulus to travel and discovery, from the early Franciscan missions into Asia to Columbus's Enterprise of the Indies, which led to his discovery of "a new heaven and a new earth" in the Americas.

MODERN STUDY OF THE ORIGINS of Columbus's Enterprise of the Indies can be traced back to the first half of the nineteenth century. In the years 1836–39, Alexander von Humboldt published his *Examen critique de l'histoire de la géographie du Nouveau Continent*, an important five-volume study of European discovery and exploration of the Americas during the fifteenth and sixteenth centuries. In the first volume of that work Humboldt wrote what remains the classic analysis of how and why Columbus made his famous voyages. Humboldt recognized the "persuasive force" of a "mystical theology," which increasingly gripped the "great soul" of Columbus, but he was basically puzzled by this "strange combination of ideas and sentiments in a superior man, gifted with a high intelligence and with an invincible courage in adversity, nourished on scholastic theology, very apt, however, in the management of business, of an ardent and sometimes disorderly imagination, unexpectedly ascending from the simple and naive language of a sailor to felicitous poetic inspirations, reflecting in himself at the same time, so to speak, everything sublime and bizarre that the middle ages produced."[10] In spite of his uncertainties regarding the religious dimension of Columbus's personality, Humboldt took greater pains to accommodate it than did any of his successors. He argued that the

---

[9] On the medieval image of the *viator*, see Gerhart Ladner, "*Homo viator*: Medieval Ideas on Alienation and Order," *Speculum*, 42 (1967): 233–59; and Jonathan Sumption, *Pilgrimage: An Image of Medieval Religions* (Totowa, N.J., 1975). On medieval apocalypticism, see Norman Cohn, *The Pursuit of the Millennium* (New York, 1961); Marjorie Reeves, *The Influence of Prophecy in the Later Middle Ages: A Study in Joachimism* (Oxford, 1969); and Bernard McGinn, *Visions of the End: Apocalyptic Traditions in the Middle Ages* (New York, 1979). On "civic" apocalypticism, see Donald Weinstein, *Savonarola and Florence: Prophecy and Patriotism in the Renaissance* (Princeton, 1970).

[10] Humboldt, *Examen critique de l'histoire de la géographie du Nouveau Continent et du progrès de l'astronomie nautique aux quinzième et seizième siècles*, 1 (Paris, 1836), 110.

mariner was heir to a long medieval tradition of a "géographie mystique," which he traced in considerable detail.[11] In Humboldt's judgment, Christoferens represented a discomfiting but probably inevitable medieval residue in the great explorer's mind that rose to the surface as his rational powers declined in his unhappy waning years. Humboldt clearly felt most comfortable with the conclusion that Columbus's voyages were actually based on a "scientific" geography gleaned from a variety of ancient and medieval sources.

In writing his account from these sources, Humboldt closely followed chapters 6–9 of Ferdinand's biography in which Ferdinand discussed his father's reasons for believing that he could reach the Indies by sailing west. According to Ferdinand, Columbus believed that the world was a sphere, that it could be circumnavigated, and that the only unexplored region was the area extending from the eastern shores of Asia to the Azores. Following ancient authorities, such as Aristotle, Pliny, Seneca, Solinus, and Julius Capitolinus, Columbus argued that the extent of this unknown region was not as great as commonly supposed. But Ferdinand suggested and Humboldt strove to demonstrate that the most important sources of Columbus's cosmographical knowledge and the principal stimuli for his voyages were *Imago mundi* by d'Ailly, the French cardinal and conciliarist, and two letters purportedly written to him by Paolo Toscanelli, the famous Florentine physician and astronomer.[12]

Two serious problems impede any assessment of the historical significance of the Toscanelli-Columbus correspondence. The first problem concerns the authenticity of the two letters received by Columbus and the dating of the correspondence. The earlier, and by far the more significant, of the two letters is in large part a copy of a letter, dated June 25, 1474, that Toscanelli sent to Alfonso V of Portugal via his friend Ferdinand Martins. It apparently included a map, which remains lost in spite of numerous attempts to locate it. The second letter seems to have been written soon after the first, in response to one that Toscanelli received from Columbus. Considerable controversy surrounds the dating of the letters. Some scholars (for example, Humboldt) have placed them within two years of the Toscanelli letter to Alfonso V. Others, such as Henri Harrisse and Henry Vignaud, have placed them later, in 1480 or 1481.[13]

---

[11] *Ibid.*, 110–206.

[12] For Humboldt's discussion of Toscanelli and Columbus, see *ibid.*, 210–56, esp. 255. Humboldt concluded that Toscanelli "was, as Ferdinand Columbus said, the most powerful cause of the spirit [*anima*] with which the admiral launched himself upon the immensity of an unknown sea; strangely, posterity has almost forgotten the influence of this Florentine mathematician." On Columbus and d'Ailly, see *ibid.*, 60–70. Humboldt began his discussion by stating, "Among the authors that Columbus consulted . . . no one is cited with greater predilection than the Cardinal, Pierre d'Ailly." The statistics bear out Humboldt's assertion; there are 898 annotations on d'Ailly's *Imago mundi* in Columbus's hand, more than he devoted to any other single work; Taviani, *Christophe Colomb*, 233. Humboldt did not know Las Casas's biography, which was not edited until 1875. On Columbus's sources, see Ferdinand Columbus, *Life of the Admiral Christopher Columbus*, chaps. 6, 7; and Edmond Buron, *Imago mundi de Pierre d'Ailly*, 3 vols. (Paris, 1930), 1: 206–15. Ferdinand Columbus cited "the conclusion of the second book" of Aristotle's *De caelo et mundo*, the second book of Pliny's *Naturalis historia*, the first book of Seneca's *Quaestiones naturalis*, chapter 68 of Solinus's *Collectanea rerum memorabilium*, and chapter 19 of Julius Capitolinus's *Geographia* as sources for Columbus's belief that the extent of the western ocean was not so great as commonly supposed; *Life of the Admiral Christopher Columbus*, 17–18.

[13] For Vignaud's description of the various versions of the two letters and the different dates assigned to them, see his *Toscanelli and Columbus: The Letter and Chart of Toscanelli* (New York, 1902), 9–20. He gave the texts

No originals of the Toscanelli-Columbus correspondence survive. There is a Spanish translation of the letters (which were written in Latin) in Las Casas's *Historia* and a sixteenth-century Italian translation of them based on Ferdinand's lost Spanish text. In 1871 Harrisse discovered a Latin version of the first letter written in Columbus's own hand on a blank page of his copy of a 1477 edition of Pius II's *Historia*. That Columbus copied out Toscanelli's letter, however, is not proof that Toscanelli actually sent it to him. Because the originals do not survive and there is no other evidence of an exchange of letters between Toscanelli and Columbus, the authenticity of the correspondence has on occasion been hotly contested. The most famous challenge is that of Vignaud, put forth in a torrent of articles and several books published around the turn of this century. On the basis of what is currently known, it seems extremely unlikely that Toscanelli and Columbus corresponded directly, although Toscanelli wrote most of the first letter and Columbus no doubt read it.[14]

The second problem that arises out of the Toscanelli-Columbus correspondence concerns the content. The letters are general in nature: they evoke the marvels of the East, argue that the Orient can be reached more quickly by sailing westward rather than by traveling overland eastward, and provide various calculations in support of the opinion that the stretches of unknown sea to the west are relatively short. Humboldt's analysis of the correspondence has withstood the test of time. Although he stressed the importance of the Toscanelli letters, Humboldt was careful to point out that Columbus could have gotten virtually all of the information contained in them from other sources available to him, particularly the works of Marco Polo, Nicolò de Conti, and d'Ailly.[15] It is difficult to escape the conclusion that the drama inherent in a direct exchange between two such famous figures on the eve of the discovery of the Americas has hitherto diverted scholars from a sober evaluation of the letters themselves in relation to other sources at Columbus's disposal. Toscanelli's influence on Columbus was probably inspirational or corroborative, perhaps both.

D'Ailly's *Imago mundi*, the other traditional source for Columbus's Enterprise of the Indies, is far from being original or forward-looking. Written in 1410, this work is a compendium of ancient and medieval cosmology and geography, intended for the instruction of the ordinary lay reader, which apparently circulated quite extensively in Western Europe during the fifteenth century. Borrowings from

of each version along with an English translation; *ibid.*, appendixes A–E, pp. 275–327. Taviani provided a clear, balanced presentation of the complicated controversy regarding the Toscanelli-Columbus correspondence and included an extensive bibliography; *Christophe Colomb*, 190–211.

[14] For the Spanish version, see Las Casas, *Historia de las Indias*, 92 *passim*. For the Italian version, see *Historie del S. D. Fernando Colombo* (Venice, 1571), f. 16r. For a facsimile of the Latin version in Columbus's hand, see Harrisse, *Biblioteca Vetustissima, Additions* (Paris, 1872), 16–18; and Cesare de Lollis, *Raccolta di documenti e studi pubblicati della R. Commissione Colombiana*, part 1, volume 3: *Autografi di Cristoforo Colombo* [hereafter, *Autografi*] (Rome, 1892), plate 63. Vignaud's attempt to disprove the authenticity of the Toscanelli-Columbus correspondence is a major theme of his *Toscanelli and Columbus* and his *Histoire critique de la grande enterprise de Christophe Colomb* (Paris, 1911).

[15] Humboldt, *Examen critique*, 213–16. Humboldt thought that Nicolò de Conti might well have been a major source for Toscanelli's account of the "Marvels of the East," either through conversation or through book 4 of Poggio Bracciolini's *Historiae de varietate fortunae*, which contained Nicolò's account of his travels. According to Humboldt, Nicolò is one of the anonymous travelers to the East mentioned in Toscanelli's second letter.

other sources, particularly Roger Bacon's *Opus maius*, are evident throughout *Imago mundi*, and *Opus maius* was itself a compendium of thirteenth-century knowledge. What we have here is not esoterica but a lineage of texts containing well-known and widespread sorts of information.[16]

Columbus carefully read and annotated d'Ailly's *Imago mundi*. The incunabulum that he used survives in the Biblioteca Colombina in Seville, Spain. Examination of Columbus's copy of *Imago mundi* reveals that chapter 8, "De quantitate terrae habitabilis," is heavily annotated. For this reason, Columbus scholars have consistently pointed to it as central to an understanding of the intellectual origins of Columbus's project. Humboldt demonstrated that chapter 8 is cribbed from Bacon's *Opus maius*; whether Columbus knew that is unclear. Scholars have long assumed that Columbus did not know of Bacon's existence since he nowhere mentioned him by name. But this assumption is incorrect, for Columbus did mention Bacon in his marginalia to another work by d'Ailly contained in the same incunabulum as *Imago mundi*. Whether he knew that in reading d'Ailly he was frequently reading Bacon is another matter that is difficult, if not impossible, to resolve.[17]

The Bacon-d'Ailly argument of chapter 8 that so interested Columbus again concerned the relatively short width of the western ocean. Authorities such as Aristotle, Seneca, and Pliny are cited in support of the conclusion that the ocean does not cover three-fourths of the earth's surface, as some had supposed. Conclusive proof is supplied by a passage from the Apocrypha, where it is written that six-sevenths of the world is dry (therefore inhabitable) and only one-seventh is covered by water (2 Esd. 6:42).[18]

Columbus's theoretical basis for the assumption that the western ocean was not vast was borne out by his practical experience as a sailor. According to a note in his own hand in his copy of *Imago mundi*, Columbus navigated by the erroneous calculations of the tenth-century Arabian astronomer Alfraganus. Alfraganus, whose figures were recorded by Bacon in *Opus maius* and incorporated into *Imago mundi* by d'Ailly, underestimated the length of a degree at the equator. Using Alfraganus's figure of 56 2/3 land miles per equatorial degree (the correct figure is 60 land miles per equatorial degree), Columbus estimated that he had only to sail approximately twenty-five hundred miles westward from the Canary Islands in order to reach the Orient. In two letters written to Ferdinand and Isabella, one

[16] The text of d'Ailly's *Imago mundi* and Columbus's annotations on it have been edited and translated into French by Buron; *Imago mundi de Pierre d'Ailly*. A facsimile of the incunabulum of d'Ailly's works that Columbus used has been published. See Massachusetts Historical Society, *Imago mundi by Petrus de Aiaco (Pierre d'Ailly) with annotations by Christopher Columbus* [hereafter, d'Ailly, Incunabulum] (Boston, 1927). For a listing of the manuscripts and the incunabulum of the *Imago mundi*, see Ludovico Salembier, *Petrus de Alliaco* (Lille, 1886), xxiii.

[17] Humboldt, *Examen critique*, 60–70; Buron, *Imago mundi de Pierre d'Ailly*, 1: chaps. 2, 3. Columbus mentioned Bacon in an annotation on d'Ailly's *Elucidarium astronomice concordie cum theologia et hystorica veritate*; f. 129v; d'Ailly, Incunabulum. In the course of a discussion of the month in which the world was created, d'Ailly remarked that Bacon stated in a letter to Pope Clement that the world was created in October. Columbus noted this, writing in the margin: "Bachon [sic] wrote to Pope Clement that without doubt the world was created in October." For a facsimile of the note, see de Lollis, *Autografi*, series C, plate 91, no. 821.

[18] For the Latin text of chapter 8 of *Imago mundi* and Columbus's annotations on it, see Buron, *Imago mundi de Pierre d'Ailly*, 1: 206–15.

from Hispaniola in 1498 and the other from Dominica in 1503, Columbus asserted that his voyages had confirmed the cosmography of *Imago mundi* and the calculations of Alfraganus. In the latter of these two letters describing his fourth voyage, Columbus proclaimed:

The world is but small; out of seven divisions of it the dry part occupies six, and the seventh is entirely covered with water. Experience has shown it, and I have written it, with quotations from the Holy Scripture, in other letters, where I have treated of the location of the terrestrial paradise, as approved by the Holy Church; and I say that the world is not so large as vulgar opinion makes it, and that one degree from the equinoctial line measures fifty-six miles and two-thirds. This is a fact that one can touch with one's own fingers.[19]

Columbus's readings and his own testimony indicate that his image of the world was traditional rather than innovative. He did not believe that his Enterprise of the Indies would essentially alter a geography and cosmology that had existed since antiquity; he thought that his expedition would simply fill out that picture.

THE PREVAILING MODERN IMAGE OF COLUMBUS as intrepid sailor and enlightened geographer—the Admiral of the Ocean Sea—does not substantially differ from that established by Humboldt in the 1830s. This image continues to be based on the same slender repertoire of texts: the two letters from Toscanelli, the annotations on *Imago mundi*, and selections from Columbus's letters describing the four voyages of discovery. The works of well-known Columbus scholars, such as Harrisse, Cesare de Lollis, and J. N. Fiske in the nineteenth century and Vignaud and Morison in the twentieth, have not significantly revised the account of the genesis of Columbus's ideas given by Humboldt in the *Examen critique*. None of these scholars took seriously the possibility that Columbus's personal spirituality or the spirituality of his age might also have inspired him to undertake his voyages of discovery.[20]

John Leddy Phelan—in his pioneering study, *The Millennial Kingdom of The Franciscans in the New World*, first published in 1956—was the first modern scholar to attempt to restore Christoferens to Columbus. In the second chapter of that book, "The Apocalypse in the Age of Discovery," Phelan emphasized the importance of contemporary apocalypticism, specifically Joachimism, to understanding the mentality of Columbus and his motivations for travel and discovery. More

[19] R. H. Major, trans. and ed., *Christopher Columbus: Four Voyages to the New World* (New York, 1961), 177–78. Humboldt considered this citation to be important evidence of "l'impression profonde" that Columbus's reading of chapter 8 of *Imago mundi* had on his voyages of discovery; *Examen critique*, 61. On Columbus as a practical, as distinguished from a theoretical, navigator and geographer, see George E. Nunn, *The Geographical Conceptions of Columbus* (New York, 1977), 1–30. Nunn argued that Columbus used a degree that measured 56 2/3 Italian nautical miles, which was not equivalent to Alfraganus's figure, calculated on the basis of Arabian nautical miles. Columbus himself thought that he was navigating according to Alfraganus's figures. In a lengthy note to d'Ailly's *Epilogus mappae mundi*, he wrote: "Observe that in sailing often from Lisbon southward to Guinea, I carefully measured the course . . . and in agreement with Alfragan I found that each degree answered to 56 2/3 miles. So that we may rely upon this measure." J. N. Fiske, trans., *The Discovery of America*, 1 (Boston, 1983), 377–78. For the Latin original, see Buron, *Imago mundi de Pierre d'Ailly*, 2: 530–31; d'Ailly, Incunabulum, 42; and de Lollis, *Autografi*, series C, plate 82, no. 490.

[20] Vignaud's conclusion is representative of this prevailing point of view: "It is also necessary to mention that Las Casas and [Ferdinand] Columbus assigned a fourth source to the grand design of Columbus: divine inspiration. But that is an order of ideas that permits no critical discussion and one into which we need not enter here; it suffices to have mentioned it." *Histoire critique*, 8.

recently, well-known students of apocalypticism such as Morton Bloomfield and Bernard McGinn have pointed out the apparent importance of Joachimism and other apocalyptic movements in the age of discovery and have called for further study in this area.[21] Only in the past several years have scholars begun to respond to these calls and to the argument that Phelan first sketched almost thirty years ago. In his *Colón y su mentalidad mesiánica en el ambiente franciscanista español*, published in 1983, Alain Milhou presented a much more detailed picture of Franciscanism in fifteenth-century Spain than has heretofore been available and followed Phelan in arguing that it is a principal source for Columbus's "messianic mentality." Although the historical background of Columbus's apocalypticism has become clearer with this study, the apparent paucity of sources that link Columbus's Enterprise of the Indies to contemporary apocalypticism or to the medieval prophetic tradition has remained a serious obstacle. But sources there are.

The incunabulum of d'Ailly's works that came into Columbus's hands was published sometime between 1480 and 1483 by John of Westphalia.[22] In addition to *Imago mundi*, it contained a number of other opuscula by the Cardinal of Cambrai and by his contemporary Jean Gerson, the important nominalist and mystic. D'Ailly's opuscula, written in 1414, focused on the problem of the interrelationships between history, theology, astronomy, and prophecy. They included *Tractatus de legibus et sectis contra supersticiosos astronomos*, *Tractatus de concordia astronomice veritatis cum theologia* (known as the *Vigintiloquium*), *Tractatus de concordia astronomice veritatis et narrationis hystorice*, *Elucidarium astronomice concordie cum theologia et hystorica veritate*, *Apologetica defensio astronomice veritatis*, *Secunda apologetica defensio astronomice veritatis*, and *Tractatus de concordia discordantium astronomorum*. These opuscula involved a debate with Gerson over the legitimacy of astrology for forecasting the fulfillment of various biblical prophecies and the end of the world. Columbus read and annotated these short works by d'Ailly and Gerson as well as *Imago mundi*. He seems to have been considerably more interested, however, in d'Ailly's opuscula than in those of Gerson, with which this essay will not deal. Surprisingly, scholars have paid little attention to the content of d'Ailly's opuscula and to Columbus's annotations on them. What follows here is intended to fill in this lacuna, if only in a preliminary way.

Columbus intended to set forth his vision of history and the role that he was

---

[21] Phelan, *The Millennial Kingdom of the Franciscans in the New World* (Berkeley and Los Angeles, 1970), 17–28; Bloomfield, "Recent Scholarship on Joachim of Fiore and His Influence," in Ann Williams, ed., *Prophecy and Millenarianism: Essays in Honour of Marjorie Reeves* (Essex, 1980), 37: "The need of investigations of Joachim in the New World is so obvious that it hardly needs saying"; and McGinn, *Visions of the End*, 284: "To those accustomed to seeing the discovery of America as the work of a hard-headed practical seaman flouting the traditions of the past, the picture of Columbus as a religious visionary strongly influenced by centuries of apocalyptic hopes may seem strange but the existence of this element in the great explorer's personality is undeniable."

[22] Buron believed that the incunabulum of d'Ailly's works was published in 1483 and pointed out that Humboldt and others merely repeated the date of 1490 that Jean de Launoy assigned to it. Salembier and de Lollis, refuting Humboldt, gave 1480 or 1483 as the date of publication. Lynn Thorndike used another copy of the same incunabulum that Columbus annotated and dated it "about 1480." Thorndike's discussion of d'Ailly's opuscula and the controversy with Gerson is the most extensive published to date. See Buron, *Imago mundi de Pierre d'Ailly*, 1: 29; Humboldt, *Examen critique*, 62; de Launoy, *Regii navarrae gymnasii parisiensis historia* (Paris, 1677), 477–78; Salembier, *Petrus de Alliaco*, xxiii; de Lollis, *Autografi*, vii; and Thorndike, *A History of Magic and Experimental Science*, 4 (New York, 1934), 101–31.

destined to play in it in a volume called the *Book of Prophecies*, which he worked on for a number of years, including the period of the last of his four voyages to the New World, but never completed. What survives is a collection of materials assembled by himself and a friend, the Carthusian monk Gaspar Gorricio, that Columbus apparently planned to incorporate into the *Book of Prophecies*. It consists of excerpts from the Bible and from a number of well-known ancient and medieval authors, some fragments of verse in Spanish (most likely not by Columbus), and an incomplete letter (written by Columbus sometime between September 13, 1501, and March 23, 1502, and addressed to Ferdinand and Isabella of Spain) that became the preface to the work.[23]

De Lollis, who edited the *Book of Prophecies* in 1894, and more recently Phelan, among others, have stressed its importance for understanding Columbus. Because of its incomplete and composite nature, however, the *Book of Prophecies* has defied extensive analysis. This essay contends that it is Columbus's reading of d'Ailly's opuscula that provides the key to his plan for the *Book of Prophecies*. A plan, though latent, can be discerned in the pattern of sources selected by Columbus and Gorricio. Columbus discussed this latent plan more explicitly in the prefatory letter to the *Book of Prophecies* and in other letters describing his voyages to the New World. If the testimony in Columbus's marginalia and his letters is taken into account, these opuscula of d'Ailly played at least as important a role in motivating him to make his voyages of discovery as did his reading of *Imago mundi* and his alleged correspondence with Toscanelli.

When did Columbus read d'Ailly's opuscula? The question is vexing yet crucial for any argument regarding the genesis of the Enterprise of the Indies. It is well known that in a note at the beginning of chapter 8 of *Imago mundi* Columbus referred to a voyage made by Bartolomeu Dias in 1488, which makes that year a *terminus post quem*. But what has not been previously pointed out is a note in Columbus's hand to one of the other pieces in the incunabulum of d'Ailly's works,

---

[23] For a discussion of the text of the *Book of Prophecies*, see de Lollis, *Raccolta di documenti e studi pubblicati della R. Commissione Colombiana*, part 1, volume 2: *Scritti di Colombo* [hereafter, *Scritti*] (Rome, 1894), lvii–lx. De Lollis found the earliest mention of the *Book of Prophecies* in an inventory of items belonging to Columbus's son, "Admiral Don Diego." The *Book of Prophecies* is listed in a catalogue, compiled by Ferdinand, of Columbus's books, and Ferdinand mentioned it in the biography of his father, including a passage from the beginning of Columbus's letter to Ferdinand and Isabella contained in the *Book of Prophecies*. De Lollis said that this excerpt occurs in chapter 8 of Ferdinand's *Life of the Admiral Christopher Columbus*; it is in fact at the beginning of chapter 4. Also see Las Casas, *Historia de las Indias*, 47–48. In a note at the beginning of the script of the *Book of Prophecies*, Columbus wrote that, while resting from his third voyage to the New World (completed in October 1500), he decided to compile a series of excerpts illustrating "tragic events," which he hoped someday to put into verse, and asked Gorricio to gather other relevant passages. The letter is dated September 13, 1501; de Lollis, *Scritti*, 75. On March 23, 1502, when Columbus was preparing to depart for the fourth voyage, Gorricio sent some additional "jottings" that he had compiled. Columbus's letter to Ferdinand and Isabella intended as the preface to the *Book of Prophecies* can be dated between September 1501 and March 1502, that is, between the third and fourth voyages. Although the date of the prefatory letter has caused controversy, de Lollis believed that the letter is an autograph of Columbus; *Autografi*, xx–xxi. Four hands can be distinguished in the manuscript of the *Book of Prophecies*: Columbus's, Gorricio's, Ferdinand's, and that of Columbus's brother Bartolomeo; de Lollis, *Autografi*, xviii–xxii. De Lollis concluded that the work should be regarded essentially as Columbus's: "Let us repeat: considered in its purpose and its entirety, the *Book of Prophecies* serves marvelously to make sense out of the complex spirit of Christopher Columbus"; *Scritti*, lx. The manuscript of the *Book of Prophecies* is in the Biblioteca Colombina, Seville, Spain. For de Lollis's edited version, see *Scritti*, 75–160. He also published a facsimile of those parts of it that he considered to be in the hand of Columbus; *Autografi*, series F, plates 102–159.

De correctione kalendarii. In chapter 3 of that work, "De errore ex mutatione equinoxiorum et solstitiorum," d'Ailly discussed the problem of accurately determining the date and time of the annual solstices and equinoxes. Using the Alphonsine tables (which Columbus also knew), d'Ailly made calculations for "this year 1411." Columbus followed d'Ailly's notations carefully, paraphrasing them in the margin. At the bottom of the page Columbus, using d'Ailly's figures in *De correctione kalendarii* and others in *De legibus et sectis*, made his own calculation of when the vernal equinox would occur in "*this year 1491.*" On the basis of this note it can be argued that Columbus read *Imago mundi* and the other opuscula prior to his initial voyage of discovery in 1492.[24]

As ALREADY SHOWN, d'Ailly's significance as a source for Columbus lies not in his originality as a thinker but in his diligence as a reader and digester of authoritative or influential works by other writers. In composing his opuscula on the interrelationships between history, astronomy, and theology, d'Ailly relied on a number of earlier medieval treatises that discussed the events to occur on the eve of the end of the world and that predicted when they would happen on the basis of planetary movements and conjunctions. Paramount among d'Ailly's sources was book 4 of Roger Bacon's *Opus maius*, especially sections on the application of mathematics to sacred subjects and on astrology. Not coincidentally, this was the same book containing Bacon's discussion of geography, large sections of which d'Ailly incorporated into *Imago mundi*.[25]

According to Bacon, the patriarchs and prophets discovered mathematics. Citing Josephus, Jerome, and Cassiodorus as his sources, he said that "the sons of Adam discovered geometry, astronomy, arithmetic, and music; and Noah and his sons taught the Chaldeans; then Abraham taught the Egyptians." These ancients applied their knowledge of mathematics to a number of different sacred subjects, including the following: cosmography, which "stirs us to reverence the creator"; geography, "for the whole series of scripture deals with the regions, states, deserts, mountains, seas, and other places of the world"; and chronology, "for the whole course of history is traced through times and generations and ages from the beginning of the world to Christ the Lord, and all things have been set in order on his account, that no other legislator might be expected, but that he alone may be the saviour of the world by his own law."[26]

---

[24] For the text of Columbus's note to chapter 8 of *Imago mundi*, see Buron, *Imago mundi de Pierre d'Ailly*, 1: 207; d'Ailly, Incunabulum, 13; and de Lollis, *Autografi*, series C, plate 70. For Columbus's notes paraphrasing d'Ailly's calculations for the solstices and equinoxes of 1411, see d'Ailly, Incunabulum, 60; and de Lollis, *Autografi*, series C, plate 90, nos. 619, 620. Columbus's note to d'Ailly's *De correctione kalendarii* mentioning "this year 1491" reads: "Note that in the calendar, the ascending of the solar year is ten minutes and forty-four seconds in any year, as is demonstrated at the end of the treatise on laws and sects [*De legibus et sectis*]. And it is confirmed that we can designate the vernal equinox of this year 1491 as the eleventh day of March at one hour, thirty-seven seconds, and forty-seven tierces past noon, accepting as a base that in the year 1411 the Sun entered the first point of Aries on the eleventh of March at fifteen hours, fifty-six minutes, seven seconds and forty-seven tierces after noon." D'Ailly, Incunabulum, 60; and de Lollis, *Autografi*, series C, plate 90, no. 621.

[25] D'Ailly's sources also included Albert the Great, Henry Bate, William of Auvergne, Vincent of Beauvais, Nicholas Oresme, and Henry of Hesse (Henry Langenstein). See Thorndike, *History of Magic*, 103–09.

[26] Robert Belle Burke, trans., *The* Opus maius *of Roger Bacon*, 1 (Philadelphia, 1928), 195–96. On the

The mathematical knowledge of the astronomers was essential to determining the configuration of the planets and hence the time of the year when the world began. From these determinations the dates of other important past events, such as the flood and the birth of Christ, and the time of future events prophesied in Scripture could be calculated. What Bacon particularly wanted to forecast was the coming of the Antichrist, which portends the imminent end of the world.[27]

In his calculations Bacon relied on the theory of planetary conjunctions set forth by Albumasar, the ninth-century Arabian astronomer. Albumasar argued that the universe is a *sympatheia* in which the terrestrial and celestial worlds are bonded together in a reciprocally harmonious whole, governed by the movements of the planets and stars. Whoever comes to comprehend any part of the universe through the techniques of theurgy and astrology comprehends the whole and can predict the future, for all events are imprinted on the present. Important religious and historical events can be predicted as well as events in an individual's life. Following Albumasar's theory of planetary conjunctions, Bacon (and others) calculated the "horoscopes" of the great religions and empires in much the same way that one would cast a personal horoscope.[28]

In *De legibus et sectis*, d'Ailly closely followed the theory of conjunctions set forth by Bacon in *Opus maius*. As he had done in *Imago mundi*, d'Ailly incorporated substantial sections of *Opus maius* directly into his own text. And, just as he had done with *Imago mundi*, Columbus carefully annotated *De legibus et sectis*, acquainting himself with Bacon's and d'Ailly's eschatology and theory of conjunctions. According to the ancient tradition expounded by Bacon and d'Ailly, Jupiter, one of two "benevolent and fortunate" planets, occupies the ninth house in the heavens, the "house of peregrinations and journeys of faith and deity and religion." Jupiter can enter into conjunction with six planets (including the sun and moon), each of which reigns over one of the great religions of the world. When one of these planets enters into conjunction with Jupiter, its religion becomes historically ascendant. The conjunction of Jupiter with Saturn signifies the ascendancy of the Jews, with Mars the Chaldeans, with the Sun the Egyptians, with Venus the Saracens, with Mercury the Christians, and with the moon the final sect of the Antichrist. Columbus followed this argument, presented by d'Ailly in chapters 1 and 2 of *De legibus et sectis*, noting that "there are six principal sects from the beginning of the

---

discovery of mathematics and the sacred subject of cosmology, see *ibid.*, 200–03. On geography, see *ibid.*, 203–08. On chronology, see *ibid.*, 208–32.

[27] Burke, *The* Opus maius *of Roger Bacon*, 276: "By the means offered by mathematics not only are we [theologians] made certain respecting our profession, but we are fortified in advance against the sect of the Antichrist, about which at the same time with the Church of Christ mathematics is concerned. A very excellent examination of this kind is made by considering all the principal sects from the beginning of the world... namely Jews, Chaldeans, Egyptians, Agarenians or Saracens, who descended from Agar and Ishmael, the Church of Christ, and the sect of the Antichrist. Nor is it strange if philosophers have spoken regarding these, since they were after the patriarchs and prophets and were instructed by their sons and books, as we have previously shown."

[28] Albumasar's major works, *Introductorium maius in astronomiam* and *De magnis coniunctionibus*, were translated into Latin in the twelfth century by John of Seville. Through these translations the so-called "theory of conjunctions" entered the Western tradition of cosmological speculation. See Richard J. Lemay, *Abu Ma'shar and Latin Aristotelianism in the Twelfth Century: The Recovery of Aristotle's Natural Philosophy through Arabic Astrology* (Beirut, 1962); Pierre Duhem, *Le système du monde: Histoire des doctrines cosmologiques de Platon à Copernic* (Paris, 1958), vol. 8, chap. 13; and Eugenio Garin, *Astrology in the Renaissance: The Zodiac of Life* (London, 1983), chap. 1.

world: the sects of the Hebrews, the Chaldeans, the Egyptians, the Saracens, Christ, and the Antichrist." "The conjunction of Jupiter with Saturn signifies the law of the Hebrews; if Jupiter is conjoined with Mars, it signifies the Chaldean law, which teaches the worship of fire; if Jupiter is conjoined with the Sun, it signifies the Egyptian law; if it is conjoined with Venus, it signifies the law of the Saracens; if it is conjoined with Mercury, the law of the Christians; if conjoined with the moon, the law of the Antichrist."[29]

The point of ascendancy of each of these religions and the length of its stay in power is determined by the conjunctions of Jupiter and Saturn, which are of three kinds. As discussed by d'Ailly in chapter 4 of *De legibus et sectis*, they are as follows: a "great conjunction," which takes place every twenty years and refers to "the elevation of kings and potentates and to dearness in the cost of provisions, and to the rise of prophets"; a "greater conjunction," which takes place every 240 years and refers to "a sect and to its change in certain regions"; and a "greatest conjunction," which takes place every 960 years and refers to "changes in empires and kingdoms, to impressions of fire in the air, to flood, earthquakes, and dearness in the price of food." The fortunes of a particular sect may shift more quickly or slowly within this framework of great conjunctions depending on "the properties of the planets bearing sway over different regions": Saturn controls India; Jupiter, Babylonia; Mars, Thrace; the Sun, the Romans and their empire; Mercury, Egypt; the moon, Asia. Columbus absorbed this material as well, noting that "there are three kinds of conjunctions of Jupiter and Saturn, namely, a great conjunction, a greater conjunction and a greatest conjunction. . . . The greater conjunction takes place every 240 years . . . the greatest conjunction every 900 years," and "Saturn rules over India, Jupiter over Babylonia, Mars over Thrace, the Sun over Rome, Mercury over Egypt, the moon over Assyria."[30]

Columbus's reading of the first four chapters of *De legibus et sectis* led him to a passage by d'Ailly copied directly from Bacon's *Opus maius*, which was apparently of such significance to him that he included it in the *Book of Prophecies*. Located in chapter 4 of *De legibus et sectis*, the passage concerns the length of time that the law of Muhammad (the law of the Saracens) will last and under what circumstances its demise might be predicted. D'Ailly (following Bacon) noted that "according to what Albumazar said, that law [of Muhammad] cannot last more than 693 years." Columbus marked this passage and copied it out verbatim in the margin. Albumasar, Bacon, and d'Ailly predicted that the followers of Muhammad, the Saracens, would be destroyed by either the Tatars or the Christians. Columbus also marked this passage, saying "the Saracens have already in large part been conquered by the Tatars and their capital, Baldac, and their caliph, 'who was like a Pope to them,' have been destroyed."[31]

---

[29] Burke, *The Opus maius of Roger Bacon*, 276–80. On Jupiter and its conjunctions with each of the other planets signifying the ascendancy of one of the major world religions, compare d'Ailly, Incunabulum, ff. 44v–45; and de Lollis, *Autografi*, series C, plate 83, nos. 513–18, 524.

[30] Burke, *The Opus maius of Roger Bacon*, 284–87; d'Ailly, Incunabulum, ff. 46v–47; and de Lollis, *Autografi*, series C, plate 83, nos. 535–37, 543.

[31] For Bacon's text, see Burke, *The Opus maius of Roger Bacon*, 287. For a Latin edition, see John Henry Bridges, *The Opus maius of Roger Bacon*, 1 (London, 1900), 266. For the passage from d'Ailly's *De legibus et sectis*

In *Opus maius*, Bacon noted that these events had taken place only twelve years earlier. In *De legibus et sectis*, d'Ailly lamented the "big lapse since that time," during which the sect of the Tatars had not been finally destroyed. It would be useful for the church, he suggested, to determine when the final destruction of "that sect of perdition" was to come, since, according to "this doctor" [Bacon] and the "astronomers," "no sect comes after the law of Mohammed, only the Antichrist." Using a passage from *Opus maius*, d'Ailly predicted that the advent of this last sect was not far off:

Ethicus, the philosopher, says in his *Cosmography* that a race that has been shut up within the Caspian gates shall burst forth upon the world and meet the Antichrist and call him God of gods. This has already come true, just as he said: Have not the Tartars who were within those gates gone forth from them? For those gates have been broken as some Christians who travelled through the middle of them have returned. Therefore, he introduces this as a sign of the imminent advent of the Antichrist. In conclusion he says, "I know that, if the Church would be willing to unroll the sacred text and the holy prophecies of the Sybilline oracle and of Merlin, of Aquile and Joachim and many others, and besides the histories and the books of the philosophers, and if the Church were to order that the methods of astronomy be considered, it would discover what it needs to know, that is, some idea of greater certainty regarding the time of the Antichrist."[32]

This passage was one of five excerpts from d'Ailly's opuscula that Columbus included in the *Book of Prophecies*.

It is significant that in their seminal article, "The Penetration of Joachimism into Northern Europe," Morton Bloomfield and Marjorie Reeves quoted the latter part of this passage (from Bacon's *Opus maius*) as indicative of the thirteenth-century sense "of crisis, of impending doom in history, that turned men's thought towards the Calabrian abbot." This "sense of crisis, of impending doom" still prevailed in the early fifteenth century when d'Ailly picked out the passage from Bacon for inclusion in *De legibus et sectis* and in the late fifteenth century when Columbus chose it for the *Book of Prophecies*. The *fortuna* of this passage from *Opus maius* is evidence of the perennial power of the apocalyptic vision of history derived from the prophetic tradition, regardless of shifting historical circumstances.[33] The extent to which it can be specifically or exclusively associated with Joachimism is problematic. Of this more below.

A second important passage that Columbus marked for the *Book of Prophecies* is located in another of the opuscula, *Tractatus de concordia astronomice veritatis et narrationis hystorice*, which consists of eight preambles, future events that will presage the appearance of the Antichrist. In the left-hand margin at the beginning of the

included in the *Book of Prophecies*, see d'Ailly, Incunabulum, f. 47v. For the text edited by de Lollis, see *Scritti*, 105–06. For facsimiles of the two marginal annotations by Columbus, see de Lollis, *Autografi*, series C, plate 83, nos. 544, 545.

[32] D'Ailly, *De legibus et sectis*, chap. 4, in d'Ailly, Incunabulum, f. 47v; and de Lollis, *Scritti*, 106: "But not withstanding these matters, and though much time has passed since then, yet experience teaches that the ruinous sect has not yet been destroyed, for, alas, it has often strongly prevailed against the Christians." For the passage that d'Ailly copied from Bacon, which has been slightly edited here, see Burke, *The* Opus maius *of Roger Bacon*, 289–90. For the Latin text, see Bridges, *The* Opus maius *of Roger Bacon*, 268–69. For the transcription in the *Book of Prophecies*, see de Lollis, *Scritti*, 106–07.

[33] Bloomfield and Reeves, "The Penetration of Joachimism into Northern Europe," *Speculum*, 29 (1954): 772–93. The passage quoted is on page 786.

passage, Columbus drew a hand whose index finger pointed to the text. He used this common medieval device throughout the incunabulum of d'Ailly's works to mark passages that apparently were of particular significance to him. Accompanying this indicator is a notation in Columbus's hand, "Jerome mentions that Methodius the martyr writes many things concerning the completion of the ages," a reference to Jerome's brief entry on Methodius in chapter 83 of his *Liber de viris illustribus.* The entire passage is marked by a line drawn parallel to it.[34]

D'Ailly's eight preambles for the advent of the Antichrist are taken directly from chapters 10–13 of the pseudo-Methodius's *Sermo de regno cantium et in novissimis temporibus certa demonstratio,* one of the most influential apocalyptic texts among the many that circulated throughout the Middle Ages and Renaissance. The section that d'Ailly lifted and Columbus took for the *Book of Prophecies* is one of the best-known parts of that well-known work.[35]

The first preamble describes the coming of the "son of perdition" as predicted by Paul in the second letter to the Thessalonians: "The day of Christ is at hand. Let no man deceive you by any means: for that day shall not come except there come a falling away first, and that man of sin be revealed, the son of perdition; who opposes and exalts himself above all that is called God."[36] Paul's "son of perdition" was widely believed in the Middle Ages to be the Antichrist. The second preamble predicts the uprising of the sons of Ishmael, of whom Daniel spoke, against the Roman empire. This will take place in the seventh millennium, on the eve of the end of time. During this millennium, according to d'Ailly's third preamble, the sons of Ishmael, whom he identified with the Saracens, will overrun the promised land of the Christians, which Paul predicted in 2 Thessalonians. On account of their sins, the inhabitants of the promised land will fall victim to other, more horrible perversions—for example, sodomy. The fourth preamble further discusses this period of dissension and torment, saying that the spirit of the faithful will be much diminished and that many will abandon their faith altogether. Preambles 3 and 4 paraphrase chapters 11 and 12 of the pseudo-Methodius's sermon on the end of the world.[37]

According to d'Ailly's fifth preamble, the sons of Ishmael will celebrate the desolation that they have wrought throughout the world, saying that the Christians will never escape their domination. But suddenly an emperor-messiah, "the king of the Romans," will appear from the "Ethiopian Sea in a great fire" and will conquer the sons of Ishmael, imposing "his yoke upon them seven times as much as their

[34] D'Ailly, *Tractatus de concordia astronomice veritatis et narrationis hystorice,* chapter 61, in d'Ailly, Incunabulum, ff. 120–120v; and de Lollis, *Scritti,* 108–09. For a facsimile of Columbus's annotation, see de Lollis, *Autografi,* series C, plate 91, no. 795.

[35] I used the edition of the pseudo-Methodius's sermon contained in Ernst Sackur's *Sybillinische Texte und Forschungen: Pseudo-Methodius, Adso und die Triburtinische Sibylle* (Halle, 1898). On the place of the pseudo-Methodius in the prophetic tradition, see Paul J. Alexander, "Byzantium and the Migration of Literary Works and Motifs: The Legend of the Last Roman Emperor," *Medievalia et Humanistica,* new ser., 2 (1971): 47–82; Reeves, *Influence of Prophecy,* pt. 3; and McGinn, *Visions of the End,* pt. 1, chap. 7.

[36] 2 Thess. 2:2; and Sackur, *Sibyllinische Texte und Forschungen,* 78.

[37] For the second preamble, see d'Ailly, Incunabulum, f. 120; and de Lollis, *Scritti,* 108–09. For chapter 10 of the pseudo-Methodius, see Sackur, *Sibyllinische Texte und Forschungen,* 80. For the third and fourth preambles, see d'Ailly, Incunabulum, f. 120; and de Lollis, *Scritti,* 109. For chapters 11 and 12 of the pseudo-Methodius, see Sackur, *Sibyllinische Texte und Forschungen,* 80–88.

yoke weighed upon the earth." The sixth preamble states that, after the fiery revenge of the "king of the Romans," "there will be a time of great peace and tranquillity upon the earth such as there has never been, for there is nothing like that final peace that is at the end of time." This is the peace of which Paul spoke in the second letter to the Thessalonians. Both of these preambles closely follow the contents of chapter 13 of the pseudo-Methodius and the sequence of his presentation.[38]

D'Ailly's seventh preamble follows the latter part of the pseudo-Methodius's chapter 13. It predicts, after this period of profound tranquillity, another period of great turmoil during which the forces of Gog and Magog will be unleashed. "The gates of the north will be opened and the strength of those nations which Alexander enclosed within them will go forth." The "enclosed nations" will corrupt the earth for "a week of years," whereupon a divinely sent warrior prince will conquer them in an instant. The eighth preamble, directly quoting the conclusion of the pseudo-Methodius's chapter 13, completes the sequence of events that will precede the coming of the Antichrist. Following the defeat of the "enclosed nations," the "king of the Romans" will live in Jerusalem for ten and one-half years, at which time the "son of perdition" will appear.[39]

D'Ailly's opuscula also provided Columbus with a larger chronological framework within which to place the rise and decline of the great religions of the world, the defeat of the Saracens by the Christians, and the events leading to the appearance of the Antichrist. In *Vigintiloquium*, d'Ailly discussed the duration of the world. In verbum 11 of that work, he took Augustine as his authority, specifically citing book 22, chapter 30, of *The City of God* and Augustine's sermon on the Sixth Psalm. D'Ailly may himself have selected these texts. The passage from *The City of God*, a succinct summary of the Augustinian periodization of history, was again well known and influential throughout the medieval and Renaissance periods. In it Augustine listed seven ages corresponding to the number of days in the week of creation:

The first age, corresponding to the first day, is from Adam to the flood, the second from then on til Abraham. These are equal, not in years, but in the number of generations, for each age is found to have ten. From this point, as the evangelist Matthew marks off the periods, three ages follow, reaching to the coming of Christ, each of which is completed in fourteen generations: one from Abraham to David, the second from then until the deportation to Babylon, the third from then until the birth of Christ in the flesh. Thus there are five ages in all. The sixth is now in progress and is not to be measured by any fixed number of generations, for the scripture says: "It is not for you to know the times which the Father has fixed by his own power" (Acts 1:17). After this age God will rest, as on the seventh day, when he will cause the seventh day, that is, us, to rest in God himself. . . . This will be our sabbath and its end will not be an evening, but the Lord's day, an eighth eternal day, sanctified by the resurrection of Christ, which prefigures the eternal rest of both spirit and body.[40]

---

[38] For the fifth and sixth preambles, see d'Ailly, Incunabulum, f. 120v; and de Lollis, *Scritti*, 109. Also see Sackur, *Sibyllinische Texte und Forschungen*, 89–91.

[39] For the seventh and eighth preambles, see d'Ailly, Incunabulum, f. 120v; and de Lollis, *Scritti*, 109. Also see Sackur, *Sibyllinische Texte und Forschungen*, 91–93.

[40] William M. Green, trans., *Saint Augustine: The City of God against the Pagans*, 7 (Cambridge, Mass., 1972),

D'Ailly also noted that Augustine in his sermon on the Sixth Psalm said that the world would last for seven thousand years, a millennium for each of the seven days in the week of creation. Columbus followed this presentation, noting in the margin next to d'Ailly's text Augustine's reference in the sermon on the Sixth Psalm to "those who believed that there were seven thousand years from Adam to the coming of the Lord to judge." He included the passage from *The City of God* cited above in the *Book of Prophecies*.[41]

THESE EXAMPLES SUGGEST THAT D'AILLY (and through him Bacon, the pseudo-Methodius, Augustine, and others) must now be considered a principal source of Columbus's apocalypticism and of his "scientific" geographical knowledge. Put another way, d'Ailly in *Imago mundi* and in the opuscula provided Columbus with summaries of contemporary knowledge about the physical cosmos and about that cosmos's eschatology. It was a cosmos with a mathematically determinable beginning and end, unfolding in time and space according to divine plan. Certain events forecast by the prophets would have to take place in order for that plan to be completed. Through proper application of the mathematical arts, discovered by the patriarchs and prophets, to the sacred subjects of cosmology, geography, and chronology, men could understand the past, present, and future of this divine plan. In the *Book of Prophecies* Columbus intended to set forth that eschatology and to explain his role in it.

Set against the background provided by d'Ailly, the selections from the Psalms and the Old Testament prophets that form a large part of the texts assembled for inclusion in the *Book of Prophecies* begin to manifest certain themes. Two themes emerge consistently in the selections from the Psalms. The first is a virtual obsession with the recovery of Mount Zion, symbol of the Holy Land. A typical example is the following citation from Psalm 2:6–8:

> I indeed have anointed my king
> On Zion, my holy hill.
> Let me tell of the decree of the Lord:
> He said to me, "you are my son;
> Today I have begotten you.
> Ask of me and I will make the
> nations your inheritance,
> and the ends of the earth your possession.

The second theme that runs through the selections from the Psalms is the conquering and conversion of the heathen, as, for example, in Psalm 18:43–44:

> Thou dost establish me as the head of the
> nations;
> People that I have not known
> serve me;
> As soon as they hear of me they submit to me.

383–85. The passage from Augustine's sermons on the Psalms to which d'Ailly referred may be found in *Sancti Aurelii Augustini Enarrationes in Psalmos*, in Jacques Paul Migne, ed., *Patrologia Latina*. vol. 36, col. 90.

[41] For the text of the passage from d'Ailly's *Vigintiloquium* included in the *Book of Prophecies*, see de Lollis, *Scritti*, 107. For a facsimile of Columbus's annotation, see de Lollis, *Autografi*, series C, plate 88, no. 716.

Prophecy and Discovery 93

Another example is Psalm 22:27–28:

> All the ends of the earth will remember
> and turn unto the Lord;
> And the clans of the nations will worship
> before him.
> For the kingdom belongs to the Lord;
> And he rules over the nations.

Many other similar excerpts from the Psalms compiled in the *Book of Prophecies* could be cited.[42]

The selections from the prophets collected in the *Book of Prophecies* also center on predictions concerning the recovery of Mount Zion by the faithful and the demise of the enemies of God. But there are others foretelling the triumph of Jerusalem following a period of world-wide conflict and the unleashing of Gog and Magog. These events are described in considerable detail in chapters 11 and 12 of the Book of Daniel and chapters 38 and 39 of Ezekiel, all cited in the *Book of Prophecies*. But a briefer and more general prediction from Isaiah, to whom Columbus accorded special status as a prophet in the prefatory letter to the *Book of Prophecies*, is the best example:

For the Lord will have mercy on Jacob, and will yet choose Israel, and set them in their own land: and the strangers shall be joined with them, and they shall cleave to the house of Jacob. And the people shall take them, and bring them to their place: and the house of Israel shall possess them in the land of the Lord for servants and handmaidens: and they shall take them captives, whose captives they were; and they shall rule over their oppressors (Isa. 14:1–2).

As in the case of the Psalms, many similar examples drawn from other prophets were collected in the *Book of Prophecies*.[43]

Columbus's preoccupation with the final conversion of all races on the eve of the end of the world is also reflected in the particular attention that he paid to John 10:16: "And other sheep I have, which are not of this fold: them also I must bring, and they shall hear my voice; and there shall be one fold, and one shepherd." This famous verse, which lay at the heart of so many medieval and Renaissance apocalyptic texts, was quoted in its entirety in the *Book of Prophecies* along with glosses from Augustine, John Chrysostom, Gregory the Great, and Nicholas of Lyra.[44]

The *Book of Prophecies* concludes with what at first seems to be a baffling collection of biblical passages in which the islands of Tarshish, Cathyr, and Ophyr are mentioned. Columbus's fascination with islands might be part of what Leonardo Olschki, the great Italian scholar, has called the medieval "romanticismo insulare" stemming from Marco Polo's *Il milione* and other popular travel literature. It seems

---

[42] On the recovery of Mount Zion by the faithful, see, for example, Pss. 2:6–8, 48:1–2, 79:1, 50:1–2, 102:13, 122:1–2. On the final conquest and conversion of the heathen, see Pss. 18:43–44, 22:27–28, 46:10, 57:9–11, 67:3–4, 72:10–11, 86:8–10, 96:1, 106:47, 115:1–6.

[43] For other examples, see Isa. 14:1, 25, 35:10, 24:23, 41; Jer. 4:31, Bar. 5, Dan. 11–12, Ezek. 38–39, Joel 2, Amos 9, Micah 4, 5, 6. A greater part of the book of Isaiah is included in the *Book of Prophecies*, which is probably not coincidental. Phelan mentioned that Isaiah was one of the most popular Old Testament prophets among the Joachimites; *Millennial Kingdom*, 135 n.25. Reeves noted that Joachim in *Liber concordiae* made Isaiah the symbol of the second status—the *ordo clericorum*; *Influence of Prophecy*, 18.

[44] De Lollis, *Scritti*, 105.

more plausible, however, that this fascination is an aspect of his more general interest in the *unum ovile et unus pastor* theme. A passage from Augustine's *De divinatione daemonum* included in the *Book of Prophecies* supports this theory:

God will prevail, it is said, against them and he will wipe out all the gods of the peoples of the earth, and they will adore him, each one from its own place, all the peoples of the islands. And indeed not only the peoples of the islands, but all peoples, so that elsewhere he does not name all the peoples of the islands, but the universal orb of the earth, saying: the universal ends of the earth will remember God and be converted to him and the people of the earth will adore his fatherly aspect since God is king and rules over the people.[45]

Even the most remote, undiscovered islands will be converted to Christianity before the world ends. In the prefatory letter to the *Book of Prophecies* Columbus affirmed his certainty that his own discoveries—islands he thought to be part of the oriental archipelago described by Marco Polo—had greatly accelerated this final process of world-wide conversion.

Against this backdrop of material relating to the universal eschatology that Columbus intended to unfold in the *Book of Prophecies* may be placed a number of selections that appear to be part of the personal role he meant to establish for himself in this drama. A prophetic passage taken from *Soliloquiorum animae ad Deum*, a popular devotional work attributed to St. Augustine, evokes the inevitability of personal destiny in a general sense. "Before you formed me in the belly, you knew me, and before I left the womb, whatever pleased you was preordained for me. And those things that concerned me were written in your book, in the secret of your counsel."[46] Two others make more specific predictions. Not coincidentally one evokes the achievement of the Admiral of the Ocean Sea and the other, that of Christoferens. The first passage, one of a number of entries under the general heading "de presenti et futuro," is taken from Seneca's tragedy *Medea* (376): "The years will come, in the succession of the ages, when the Ocean will loose the bonds by which we have been confined, when an immense land shall lie revealed, and Tethys shall disclose new worlds, and Thule will no longer be the most remote of countries." This passage is followed by its paraphrase in Spanish. Written next to it in the hand of Ferdinand is the sentence, "My father, the Admiral Christopher Columbus, fulfilled this prophecy in the year 1492."[47]

The second prophecy that can be applied to Columbus is attributed by him to Joachim of Fiore. It predicts that "he who will restore the ark of Zion will come from Spain." Neither Phelan nor Reeves could identify this prophecy, though

---

[45] *Ibid.* Also see *De divinatione daemonum*, in Migne, *Patrologia Latina*, vol. 36, col. 584. For Olschki's discussion, see his *Storia letteraria*, chap. 2, sect. 3, 38–55.

[46] This passage is not from Augustine's *Soliloquies* but from *Soliloquiorum animae ad Deum*, one of a triumvirate of popular devotional works widely attributed to him (the other two were known as the *Liber meditationum* and *Manuale*). Marcel Bataillon concluded that these works (translated into Spanish) were extremely widespread and influential in early sixteenth-century Spain, that is, during the period in which Columbus and Gorricio were compiling the *Book of Prophecies*; Bataillon, *Erasmo y España: Estudios sobre la historia espiritual del siglo XVI* (2d edn., Mexico, 1966), 47. For the Latin text of the passage quoted from the *Book of Prophecies*, see de Lollis, *Scritti*, 97. Also see Migne, *Patrologia Latina*, vol. 40, col. 884; and Jer. 1:5.

[47] De Lollis, *Scritti*, 141. Ferdinand also cited this passage from the *Medea* in chapter 8 of his biography and added, "Now it is considered certain that this prophecy is fulfilled in the person of the Admiral"; *Life of the Admiral Christopher Columbus*, 18.

Phelan believed that it stemmed from Arnold of Villanova (ca. 1250–1312), a Joachite and diplomat for the brothers James II of Aragon and Frederick III of Sicily. Phelan's guess was correct. In fact, José Pou y Martí had already published (in 1940), in his *Visionarios, beguinos y fraticelos catalanes (siglos XIII–XV)*, the section of Arnold's *De cymbalis ecclesiae* containing the prophecy attributed to Joachim. Pou y Martí's materials and themes were such that he had no reason to make the connection with Columbus, and he did not. But Milhou made the connection in his *Colón y su mentalidad mesiánica*. He has now unveiled the origins of the *Ve mundo* prophecy and its complicated medieval *fortuna*. The *Ve mundo* prophecy circulated in Aragon from Arnold's lifetime onward, being interpreted in various ways according to changing political circumstances. The version of the *Ve mundo* prophecy that Columbus knew was contained in a letter apparently addressed to Ferdinand and Isabella by Genoese legates in 1492 on the occasion of the Spanish capture of Granada from the Muslims. This event was interpreted by Columbus and others as evidence of the key role to be played by the house of Aragon in restoring the "ark of Zion" to the faithful—that is, the recapture of Jerusalem from the infidel. The letter from the Genoese delegates containing the *Ve mundo* prophecy attributed to Joachim was thus probably an example of the curious medieval mixture of political propaganda and eschatology discussed by Milhou.[48]

THE THEMES THAT HAVE EMERGED in this examination of the materials that Columbus and Gorricio gathered for the *Book of Prophecies*—the recovery of the Holy Land and the final conversion of all peoples of the world set against the universal eschatology provided by d'Ailly's opuscula—were pulled together by Columbus in the prefatory letter addressed to Ferdinand and Isabella of Spain. Somewhat rambling and incomplete, this letter is nonetheless essential for understanding Columbus's self-image as the Christ-bearer.

Columbus began this letter by recalling his lifelong experience as a navigator and mapmaker and his many encounters with learned men:

When I was very young I went to sea to sail and I continue to do it today. This art predisposes one who follows it towards the desire to know the secrets of the world. More than forty years have already passed in which I have engaged in this activity; I have gone to every place that has heretofore been navigated. I have dealt with and held conversations with learned men, ecclesiastics and secular, Latins and Greeks, Jews and Moors, and with many others of other sects. I have found Our Lord very well disposed towards my desire, and I have from him the spirit of intelligence for carrying it out. He has bestowed the marine arts upon me in abundance and that which is necessary to me from astrology, geometry, and arithmetic. He has given me adequate inventiveness in my soul and hands capable of drawing spheres and situating upon them the towns, the rivers, mountains, islands, and ports, each in its proper place.[49]

[48] For the text of the prophecy as it appeared in the *Book of Prophecies*, see de Lollis, *Scritti*, 148. For Phelan's discussion of it, see *Millennial Kingdom*, 135–36, and n. 27. Also see Reeves, *Influence of Prophecy*, 316–17. For the text of the *Ve mundo* prophecy contained in Arnold of Villanova's *De cymbalis ecclesiae*, see José Pou y Martí, *Visionarios, beguinos, y fraticelos catalanes (siglos XIII–XV)* (Vich, 1930), 54–55. For Milhou's discussion of the *Ve mundo* prophecy, see *Colón y su mentalidad mesiánica*, 375–483. For the role that Spain and its rulers were destined to play, see Phelan, *Millennial Kingdom*, chap. 1.

[49] De Lollis, *Scritti*, 79.

But he explicitly denied that these activities and encounters were what ultimately caused him to succeed in the Enterprise of the Indies. Nor, in fact, did he believe that this enterprise was his final goal:

I spent six years here at your royal court, disputing the case with so many people of great authority, learned in all the arts. And finally they concluded that it all was in vain, and they lost interest. In spite of that it [the voyage to the Indies] later came to pass as Jesus Christ our Saviour had predicted and as he had previously announced through the mouths of His holy prophets. Therefore, it is to be believed that the same will hold true for this other matter [the voyage to the Holy Sepulchre]. If what I myself say does not seem to be sufficient evidence of this, I offer that of the Holy Gospel, which says that everything shall pass save for His marvelous Word. And in saying that, it says that everything must come to pass as it has been written by Him and by the prophets. . . . *I have already said that reason, mathematics, and mappaemundi were of no use to me in the execution of the enterprise of the Indies.* What Isaiah said was completely fulfilled and that is what I wish to write here in order to remind Your Highnesses of it so that you may rejoice when I tell you by virtue of the same authorities that you are assured of certain victory in the enterprise of Jerusalem if you have faith.[50]

It was divine inspiration that Columbus believed had come to him—and to Ferdinand and Isabella—and that urged him on to the final goal—the reconquest of the Holy Land:

Who would doubt that this light, which comforted me with its rays of marvelous clarity . . . and urged me onward with great haste continuously without a moment's pause, came to you in a most deep manner, as it did to me?

In this voyage to the Indies Our Lord wished to perform a very evident miracle in order to console me and the others in the matter of this other voyage to the Holy Sepulchre.[51]

And it was the opuscula of d'Ailly, not the "Joachimism" that Phelan suggested but was unable to substantiate, that provided Columbus with the eschatological framework within which to place his Enterprise of the Indies and what he conceived as his final mission.

In the prefatory letter he made this clear, drawing on the references to Augustine and d'Ailly that he had gathered for the *Book of Prophecies* and calculating that the end of the world was but 155 years away:

St. Augustine says that the end of this world will come in the seventh millennium from its creation; the holy theologians follow him, especially the Cardinal Pierre D'Ailly in Chapter XI of his *Vigintiloquium* and in other places, as I will mention below.

From the creation of the world, or from Adam, until the coming of Our Lord Jesus Christ are five thousand three hundred and forty-three years and three hundred and eighteen days according to the reckoning of King Alfonso, a reckoning that is held to be the most certain. Pierre D'Ailly, in Chapter X of his *Elucidario astronomice concordie cum theologica et hystorica veritate*, adds to it a little under one thousand five hundred and one years to make altogether a little under six thousand eight hundred and forty-five years.

According to this calculation, there are lacking about one hundred and fifty-five years for the completion of the seven thousand at which time the world will come to an end, as is said in the authorities mentioned above.[52]

---

[50] *Ibid.*, 80, and 82 [my emphasis].

[51] *Ibid.*, 79–80.

[52] *Ibid.*, 81. A single sentence taken from d'Ailly's *Elucidarium astronomice concordie cum theologia et hystorica*

Columbus went on to refer his monarchs to the last nine chapters of d'Ailly's *Tractatus de concordia astronomice veritatis et narrationis hystorice* for details regarding the coming of the Antichrist. These nine chapters include chapter 63, discussed above, in which d'Ailly presented the eight preambles for the coming of the Antichrist. All of the preambles blended Bacon's theory of planetary conjunctions with the eschatology of the pseudo-Methodius. D'Ailly considered Joachim to have been an important prophet and mentioned him frequently throughout the opuscula, more often than not in a distinguished list that included Hildegard, Merlin, and the Sybilline prophet. But he nowhere discussed Joachim's eschatology in any detail as he did the eschatologies of Bacon and the pseudo-Methodius. So, if Columbus was indeed a "Joachimite," we do not know where he derived his knowledge of Joachim's theory of history and how it figured in his plan for the *Book of Prophecies*. On the other hand, he did read d'Ailly's opuscula, and the evidence suggests that he intended to incorporate the eschatology set forth in them into his own work.[53]

This eschatological framework was probably already in place when Columbus made his initial voyage of discovery in 1492. In the letter to Ferdinand and Isabella that prefaces the journals of the first voyage and describes events leading up to that voyage, Columbus evoked the intermingled destinies of himself and his monarchs:

Most Christian and most exalted and most excellent and most mighty princes, King and Queen of the Spains and of the islands of the sea, our Sovereigns: . . . in this present year of 1492, after Your Highnesses made an end of the war with the Moors who reigned in Europe, and had brought that war to a conclusion in the very great city of Granada . . . in that same month, on the ground of information which I had given Your Highnesses concerning the lands of India, and concerning a prince who is called "Grand Khan," [and concerning] how many times he and his ancestors had sent to Rome to beg for men learned in our holy faith, in order that they might instruct him therein, and how the Holy Father had never made provision in this matter, and how so many nations had been lost, falling into idolatries and taking to themselves doctrines of perdition, Your Highnesses, as Catholic Christians and as princes devoted to the holy Christian faith and propagators thereof, and enemies of the sect of Mahomet and of all idolatries and heresies, took thought to send me, Christopher Columbus, to the said parts of India, to see those princes and peoples and lands and the character of them and of all else, and the manner which should be used to bring about their

narratione for the *Book of Prophecies* reads: "From the creation of Adam to the time of Christ, according to Alfonso, there are five thousand, three hundred and forty three years and three hundred and eight days"; de Lollis, *Scritti*, 107. Columbus closely followed verbum 9 of d'Ailly's *Elucidarium*, where d'Ailly discussed the duration of the six ages of the world; Incunabulum, ff. 125–26. Columbus annotated it copiously. See de Lollis, *Autografi*, series C, plate 91, nos. 800–07. At the conclusion of d'Ailly's discussion (d'Ailly, Incunabulum, f. 126) Columbus noted, "From the creation of the world up to Christ, according to Alfonso, there are 5,326 years, 3 days, 16 hours, and thirty minutes of the hour, according to one calculation; and according to another, otherwise"; de Lollis, *Autografi*, series C, plate 91, no. 807.

[53] The last nine chapters of *Tractatus de concordia astronomice veritatis et narrationis hystorice* are as follows: "De aliis decem revolutionibus saturnalibus et postea gestis"; "De his que ante complementum decem aliarum revolutionum gesta sunt"; "De scismatibus ecclesia"; "De magnis ecclesiae scismate"; "De octava coniunctione maxima"; "De adventu antichristi et eius secta"; "De sex sectis principalibus secundum astronomos"; "De octo preambulis adventus antichristi secundum methodium"; "De antichristi ortu et fine et de consummatione seculi secundum eundem." On Columbus's "Joachimism," see Phelan, *Millennial Kingdom*, 22, and nn. 25, 26. There is evidence that in his later years Columbus was associated with the Franciscan Tertiaries—the branch of the order open to laymen. According to Las Casas, Columbus appeared in public in Seville dressed in the robes of a Franciscan; *Historia de las Indias*, 89. Columbus's son Diego related that his father was buried in the robes of a Franciscan Tertiary; Phelan, *Millennial Kingdom*, 19, and nn. 6, 7.

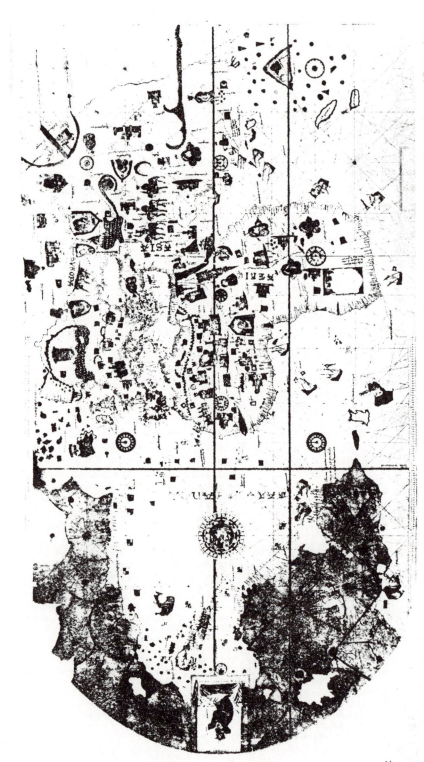

Figure 3: The 1500-05 map of Juan de la Cosa. Reproduction made from a nineteenth-century photolithograph in the collection of the William L. Clements Library, Ann Arbor, Mich. Photograph reproduced courtesy of John Dann, director of the Clements Library.

conversion to our holy faith, and ordained that I should not go by land to the eastward, by which way it was the custom to go, but by way of the west, by which down to this day we do not know certainly that anyone has passed.[54]

Columbus's sentiments echoed those of many of his contemporaries who were convinced that, with the victory over the Moors at Granada, the time when the Spanish monarchy would play a special role in history had arrived. Phelan demonstrated how the ancient emperor-messiah myth, which was an essential part of medieval apocalypticism, was applied to the Spanish monarchy by early Franciscan missionaries such as Gerónimo de Mendieta.[55] And Marcel Bataillon and Milhou have written about the more general revival of Joachimism and other forms of apocalypticism, particularly among the Franciscans and their Tertiaries, in fifteenth- and sixteenth-century Spain. Events such as the conquest of Granada and the discovery of the Americas fired contemporary expectations that the recovery of Jerusalem from the infidel and the final conversion of all races prophesied in the Apocalypse would soon come to pass.[56]

Columbus clearly shared these expectations. In his letter to Ferdinand and Isabella describing the fourth voyage of discovery, Columbus offered his services for one last journey:

Jerusalem and Mount Zion are to be rebuilt by the hands of the Christians as God has declared by the mouth of his prophet in the fourteenth Psalm (vv. 7–8). The Abbé Joaquim said that he who should do this was to come from Spain; Saint Jerome showed the holy woman the way to accomplish it; and the Emperor of China has, some time since, sent for wise men to instruct him in the faith of Christ. Who will offer himself for this work? Should anyone do so, I pledge myself, in the name of God, to convey him safely thither, provided the Lord permits me to return to Spain.[57]

This was Columbus's ultimate goal, the purpose of all his travels and discoveries— the liberation of the Holy Land.

IN THE FINAL YEARS OF HIS LIFE, with his discovery of the unknown islands of the Indies, Columbus came increasingly to see himself as a divinely inspired fulfiller of prophecy, the one who inaugurated the age of the *unum ovile et unus pastor* forecast by John the Evangelist and John of Patmos. Columbus's vision of himself as the Christ-bearer was depicted by one Juan de la Cosa, who made what is generally considered to be the earliest map of the New World (see Figure 3).[58] Historians of

---

[54] Cecil Jane, trans., *The Journal of Christopher Columbus* (London, 1960), 3–4.

[55] Phelan, *Millennial Kingdom*, 11. On the emperor-messiah myth, see Reeves, *Influence of Prophecy*, pt. 3, "Joachimist Influences on the Idea of a Last World Emperor," *Traditio*, 17 (1961): 323–70; Franz Kampers, *Die deutsche Kaiser-idee in Prophetie und Sage* (Munich, 1896); and R. Folz, *Le souvenir et la legende de Charlemagne*, (Paris, 1950).

[56] Bataillon, *Erasmo y España*, 51–61, "Évangélisme et millenarisme au Nouveau Monde," *Courants religieux et humanisme à la fin du XVᵉ et au début du XVIᵉ siècle* (Paris, 1959), 25–36; Robert Ricard, *The Spiritual Conquest of Mexico: An Essay on the Apostolate and the Evangelizing Methods of the Mendicant Orders in New Spain, 1523–1572*, trans. Lesley Byrd Simpson (Berkeley and Los Angeles, 1966); Adriano Prosperi, "America e apocalisse," *Critica Storica*, 13 (1976): 1–61; and Milhou, *Colón y su mentalidad mesiánica*, pt. 2.

[57] Major, *Christopher Columbus*, 197–98.

[58] The map is in the Museo Naval, Madrid, Spain. Whether there is more than one Juan de la Cosa has

Figure 4: Detail of Columbus as Christoferens from the map of Juan de la Cosa. Frontispiece reproduced from R. H. Major, ed., *Select Letters of Christopher Columbus* (London, 1870).

Prophecy and Discovery 101

cartography have paid much attention to the configurations of the islands and the coastlines, and other technical details, while ignoring the larger religious and cosmological content of the map.

The map represents, in fact, the dissolution of the world picture presented in the medieval *mappaemundi*. The geometrically proportioned disk composed of Europe, Asia, and Africa surrounded by the ocean is gone. In its place is a much more uncertain picture. To the east is a highly articulated drawing of the coast of Western Europe, yet its overall location remains ambiguous. To the west is the emerging coastline of the New World, which the mapmaker can trace with accuracy in only a few places. The interior is unknown and depicted as a vague, swampy, brown-green land mass on which stands a figure—Columbus—carrying the Christ child on his shoulders. The figure is an adaptation of the ancient image of the converted pagan giant, St. Christopher, who carried the Christ child across a swift river on his shoulders—only now it is Christoferens, the bearer of Christ across the ocean to the unknown shores of the New World (see Figure 4).

Ferdinand put this image into words in the biography of his father. Writing about the "mystery" of his father's name, symbolic of the role he was destined to play in history, Ferdinand explained that "Columbus" meant dove:

> If we consider the common surname of his forebears, we may say that he was truly Columbus or Dove, because he carried the grace of the Holy Ghost to that New World which he discovered, showing those people who knew Him not·Who was God's beloved son, as the Holy Ghost did in the figure of a dove when St. John baptized Christ; and because over the waters of the ocean, like the dove of Noah's ark, he bore the olive branch and oil of baptism, to signify that those people who had been shut up in the ark of darkness and confusion were to enjoy peace and union with the Church.[59]

And Columbus's given name linked him with St. Christopher:

> We may say that just as St. Christopher is reported to have gotten that name because he carried Christ over deep waters with great danger to himself, and just as he conveyed over people whom no other could have carried, so the Admiral Christophorus Colonus, asking Christ's aid and protection in that perilous pass, crossed over with his company that the Indian nations might become dwellers in the triumphant Church of Heaven.[60]

In a letter dating from his later years, Columbus himself wrote that he had

---

caused controversy. A Juan de la Cosa was the owner of the Santa Maria and second in command on Columbus's first voyage. A Juan de la Cosa, a well-known mapmaker, accompanied Columbus on his second voyage and subsequently sailed with Amerigo Vespucci. On the controversy, see Taviani, *Christophe Colomb*, 294–96, 302. On the map itself, see G. E. Nunn, *The Mappemonde of Juan de la Cosa* (Jenkintown, Penn., 1934).

[59] Ferdinand Columbus, *Life of the Admiral Christopher Columbus*, 4. Also see Las Casas, *Historia de las Indias*, 43.
[60] *Ibid.*

Pauline Moffitt Watts

discovered the "new heaven and the new earth" prophesied in the Apocalypse: "God made me the messenger of the new heaven and the new earth of which he spoke in the Apocalypse of St. John after having spoken of it through the mouth of Isaiah; and he showed me the spot where to find it."[61] In his mind then, the New World was identified with the end of the world—the first heaven and earth were passed away, there was no more sea—and the journey of the *viator*, which had begun in the deserts of the Old Testament prophets, was surely almost over.

[61] Columbus, as quoted in Spotorno, *Memorials of Columbus*, 224. Later in the same letter Columbus again spoke of the "New World": "My confidence in God and her Highness, Isabella, enabled me to persevere.... I undertook another voyage to the new heaven and earth, which land, until then, remained concealed"; *ibid.* 225.

11
The Transfer of Colonial Techniques from the Mediterranean to the Atlantic*

Charles Verlinden

The colonization of the Atlantic world is generally considered to be an unprecedented and completely original phenomenon. This view is erroneous, however, since colonies existed in the eastern Mediterranean or Levant at the end of the Middle Ages. It was there that the technique of colonization which spread across the Atlantic world originated. The study of medieval influences on colonization in the Atlantic zone, i.e. America and Africa, opens up a new field of historical research and modifies the traditional perspectives from which we are accustomed to examine relations between the Old and New Worlds. Such a study, moreover, implies a conception of colonial history different from the old "external" conception. This point requires some explanation.

During the colonial era historians were interested almost exclusively in the colonies as a function of the metropolises. They studied the colonies founded by a particular nation from a nationalist perspective. The study of the medieval precedents of Atlantic colonization requires, on the contrary, knowledge of reciprocal influences in a very large area and cannot be accomplished unless one deals with the American continent, the Atlantic archipelagoes, and a large part of Africa on the one hand, and western and southern Europe on the other, as well as Italian, Catalan, and French medieval colonies in the

* Translated, with revisions, from "Le transfert des techniques coloniales: De la Méditerranée à l'Atlantique," ch. 9 of *Les origines de la civilisation atlantique*, by C. Verlinden (Neuchâtel: Editions de la Baconnière, 1966), pp. 157–178.

4   Europe and America

Mediterranean. Reciprocal contacts and influences, in both administrative and economic terms, are so important that we must consider the various colonies and metropolises as forming part of one large historical area. Instead of merely examining the external diplomatic and commercial history of the colonies, we must study and compare their internal economic, social, and institutional development. By doing this, we find that certain phenomena are continuous, and we are thus able to understand the transfer of colonial techniques.

I am not suggesting that Spain, Portugal, France, England, the Netherlands, and the Scandinavian countries introduced identical economic and social institutions and structures into their Atlantic colonies. The obvious differences in the development of the metropolises, in the eras in which the colonies were founded, and in the geographical and anthropological environment prevented such similarities. Their common atmosphere, characterized by phenomena of filiation or continuity, is undeniable, however. If we adhere constantly to the influence exercised over the various Atlantic colonies by the economic, social, and administrative institutions of the colonies in the later Middle Ages, and of the metropolises, if we combine this study with an analysis of the influence and transformations of the indigenous populations, it becomes possible to follow the development of colonial history in a way that will be useful not only to those interested in the past, but equally to those who are studying the contribution of the West to the countries now in the process of developing.

We have too often lost sight of the fact that from the early twelfth century the eastern Mediterranean countries provided an outlet for the European desire to colonize, and this situation continued not only after Columbus but, for the Venetians at least, long after the beginning of English colonization in America.

Colonization in the Mediterranean began immediately

Transfer of Colonial Techniques   5

after the First Crusade in the Holy Land with the Crusade principalities and the Italian establishments—Genoese, Pisan, and Venetian—which were founded there. These establishments were even more truly colonial than the Crusade seigneuries, since politically they were more closely connected with their various Italian metropolises than the French barons of Palestine and the Peloponnesus were with the king of France, whose feudal ascendancy rapidly became purely theoretic. Besides, the Italians far more than the barons pursued specific economic objectives. The Venetians, for example, became immediately involved in the sugar-cane plantations with the object of exporting. We shall see later in this chapter that it is possible to establish continuity from their activity as planters in the Holy Land in the twelfth century to the introduction of sugar cane to the French and English Antilles in the seventeenth century.

Colonial activity in the eastern Mediterranean spread from the Holy Land to the islands, archipelagoes, and mainland of southeastern Europe. At the end of the twelfth century, Cyprus became a Franco-Italian possession and remained so until the beginning of modern times. A large part of Palestine was conquered by the Turks in the thirteenth century, but the colonies in existence there were replaced by more valuable colonies, in Crete by the Venetians after the Fourth Crusade, and by the French and Italians on the islands of the Aegean and Ionian seas as well as along the coast of the Balkan Peninsula.

After the fall of the Latin Empire of Constantinople, held under the protection of the Venetians, in 1261, the Genoese, allies of the Byzantine emperors who had just reconquered their throne, were able to penetrate as far as the Black Sea, where they began to colonize the Crimea. With this as their starting point, they proceeded to occupy various well-situated spots further east. This whole region later became known as the Khazarian empire, from the name of the Khazars or Chazars, who had once dominated the South of Russia. It is

6   *Europe and America*

evident that even the idea of a maritime and colonial empire, whatever its dimension, was familiar to the later Middle Ages.

While the colonies in the eastern Mediterranean were still in their early stages of development, Europeans, and especially Italians, were beginning to explore, map, and populate the Atlantic archipelagoes. As early as a generation before 1300, the Genoese had begun regularly sending their galleys beyond the straits of Gibraltar. Together with other Italians and sailors from the coastal regions of western Europe they pushed further and further to the southwest of the Atlantic, and even to the northwest, though to a lesser extent. It is interesting to discover, in the course of this expansion, scientists, captains, sailors, and merchants who had already been involved in the colonies in the eastern Mediterranean. Methods and techniques passed from one colonial zone to another. Inhabitants of the Iberian Peninsula, with the strong support of Italians, began to colonize the Canary Islands in the second half of the fourteenth century; some years later, it was the turn of the Madeiras and the Azores, where lands were distributed by methods very similar to those followed by the Italians in their colonies in the Levant. The settlement of the Atlantic archipelagoes, where a plantation economy was already in operation before the middle of the fifteenth century, attracted colonists from the Iberian Peninsula, and also from Italy, Normandy, and later from Flanders. On the other hand, the Iberian colonies in the Balkans, especially those developed by concerns like the Catalan and Navarrese companies in the duchies of Athens and Nauplia, assumed, beginning in the first half of the fourteenth century, a form very similar to that introduced two centuries later into Mexico and Peru by Cortez and Pizarro. With no break in continuity, Iberian colonization, assisted by Italian admirals, pilots, sailors, merchants, and scientists who were charged with the important technical tasks, extended along the African shores and reached the

Transfer of Colonial Techniques   7

Far East as well as the Caribbean and the rest of America. Almost immediately, English, Breton, Norman, and even Danish sea expeditions followed in the wake of the Italo-Iberian explorers and colonizers. Until the end of the sixteenth century, however, the French, Dutch, and English could not be considered serious rivals by those who until that time had had the monopoly of colonial activity. These nations, too, had made an early bid for the collaboration of technicians from Venice, Genoa, Seville, and Lisbon. English colonial ambitions were aimed simultaneously at three objectives: the colonial absorption of Ireland, penetration of the zones previously monopolized by the Iberians, and the gaining of a foothold in regions of the Western Hemisphere that the latter had not yet penetrated. To achieve these ends they could not in the beginning do without the aid of Italian and Iberian specialists. Only later were the English, French, and Dutch colonists able to manage without those who had learned the secrets of colonization in the Italo-Iberian world.

During the centuries following the Crusades the attractiveness of overseas expansion and the profits to be made from overseas colonies contributed greatly to the development of European commercial methods. There is a direct line of development between the *compere* or companies that administered the municipal finances of Genoa, the *mahonas* or colonial Genoese companies of the fourteenth century, the Bank of St. George (also Genoese) which played a role of prime importance in the administration of the colonies in the Crimea and the Levant, and the Spanish and Portuguese organizations for the control of commerce and colonial settlement on the one hand, and the Dutch, French, and English companies which directed the colonial expansion of those nations on the other. Even in medieval Genoa close ties existed between the colonial *mahonas* and the national debt; regarded from this angle, the famous Mississippi and South Sea companies are only a link in a long tradition.

8   Europe and America

Individual connections can be similarly traced. A good example of this is provided by Sebastian Cabot, a Genoese who belonged to a merchant family originally from Venice and held a very high position in Spanish colonial administration; he became the chief promoter of the English Muscovy Company for whose organization he was responsible. The fact that the Muscovy Company was a joint-stock company was certainly attributable to the experience acquired by Cabot in Italy and Spain, since this type of organization was new in England, even though it had existed for some time in southern Europe.

Another individual example of the continuity between medieval colonization and colonial activity in the Atlantic— in this case up to the beginning of the seventeenth century— is a man named Pallavicino, one of the most important shareholders of the Virginia Company. He belonged to a family mentioned since the thirteenth century in hundreds of documents concerning overseas trade in the archives of Genoa. His ancestors had possessed and governed a colonial marquisate in Greece since the fourteenth century.

If we turn to institutional aspects we can establish, during the whole period that concerns us in this volume, a real continuity in the organization of colonial societies and in the methods of internal administration of the colonies. Frequently earlier institutional forms served as models for new. Here is an example originating in medieval England. Shortly after 1066 the Normans founded what was to become the Palatinate of Durham; though its organization and function were modified in the course of succeeding generations, the institutional framework could still be used for the proprietor's colonies in Ireland and for those in Maryland and other American possessions in the seventeenth century.

But generally the connections are neither so direct nor so simple. Colonial organization in the Mediterranean in the Middle Ages and in the Atlantic area at the beginning of the modern era can be divided into three main types. First,

Transfer of Colonial Techniques   9

there is the feudal type of colonial landowning that existed in the Crusade colonies in Palestine, Cyprus, and medieval Greece, and on an even vaster scale in the Spanish, Portuguese, Dutch, and English colonies in the Atlantic. A second type of colony involved the formation, in the metropolis, of a company which received a charter from the government and thus enjoyed almost complete administrative autonomy. These company-controlled colonies were as much in existence in the Middle Ages as during the early modern period. Genoa, for example, administered the Aegean island of Chios by means of a *mahona* similar to the English companies in Virginia or Massachusetts and the French or Dutch companies in the East and West Indies. A third type of colony was based on an agreement between free citizens. In the Middle Ages the most striking examples of such agreements concerned communal or military groups. The constitutions of some of these communes served as models in certain colonial areas. Genoa, for example, used its own communal constitution in the colonies of Pera on the Bosporus and Caffa in the Crimea. So-called free companies fought in nearly all the European wars in the later Middle Ages, and their members were bound together by an agreement. In some cases these companies were transplanted overseas, and a new agreement was established with the object of regulating not only their internal government but also the control of the conquered country. This was done by the Catalan and Navarrese companies in their colonies in Greece in the fourteenth century. When the English colonists in the New World reached lands that had not previously been controlled by the government or by a company, they drew up agreements or covenants. In this way the English separatists put into effect the Mayflower Agreement when they arrived in New England instead of disembarking in Virginia, where they had received permission to land. Roger Williams' followers established the Providence Agreement, which covered civil government, when they were banished from Massachusetts; the Connecticut colonists did the same in their Fundamental Orders. One of the origins of these agreements was the idea of covenant so dear to the English Calvinists and Nonconformists, but there was a precedent for them which goes back to the Mediterranean colonies at the end of the Middle Ages, long before the appearance of Protestantism.

The connections are simpler as far as maintaining colonial politics under the control of the metropolitan government is concerned. The Casa de Contratación, which administered Spanish colonial commerce, was derived largely from Genoese colonial administration, as can be seen from the statutes drawn up by the Genoese Pinelli in 1503. The Spanish and Portuguese administrative bodies in charge of the colonies exercised an influence on the institutions created for the same purposes by England, France, and Holland. Men like Usselinx, the founder of the Dutch West Indies Company, or Linschoten, who did the groundwork for Dutch expansion in the East Indies, to mention only two, had learned the principles of colonial administration while working in the Portuguese colonial service. Even the main provisions of the Navigation Acts, which were so important, had been applied in the Mediterranean several centuries before Cromwell.

All this does not mean that the institutions established in the Atlantic colonies were merely copies of those in western Europe and the Levant at the end of the Middle Ages. In the Atlantic colonies there was a gradual and active adaptation to the new milieu. But from the Atlantic point of view, the common origin is much more important than the adaptation which is an inevitable law of life. This common origin is European and goes back to the Middle Ages. That is why, from the beginning of the colonial era, the direction followed by history has been identical on both sides of the great interior ocean of the Western world.

Transfer of Colonial Techniques II

Land Concessions in the Mediterranean Colonies and in the Atlantic Zone

The study of land concessions made in the Atlantic colonies reveals both a direct descent from medieval colonization and an adaptation of medieval metropolitan institutions to the new colonial milieu.

Forms of landowning that originated in the western and southern European feudal systems were transplanted, particularly in their French and Italian versions, to the Levant during the later Middle Ages. The colonial lords, like those in the metropolis, would possess domains inhabited by a half-free class who owed them fairly heavy work dues. Moreover the manpower they employed—and this is an essentially colonial characteristic—also included slaves captured during the continual frontier wars against the infidels of Palestine or bought in the slave markets of other colonies in the Levant. The seigneury was held from the King of Jerusalem, the Latin Emperor of Constantinople or the King of Cyprus, all of whom came from western Europe like their barons; and even in the colonial regions, where there was no king or emperor, the landowners were always vassals of a suzerain of western origin. To be invested with a fief one had to provide the suzerain with a knight's service and as large a following as possible.

Crete was the most important Italian colony in the Levant. From the beginning of the thirteenth century Venetians possessed *casalia* or rural domains in that island and cultivated them by means of the work imposed on the *parici* (Greek serfs). They often employed slaves as well. These landowners owed military service to the Venetian government, just as did the Greek nobles who had joined the colonial regime.

The Genoese colonies in Palestine were much less extensive than the huge Venetian colony of Crete but they had been acquired more than a hundred years earlier. The first

12   Europe and America

land concession received by the Genoese in the Holy Land was granted on July 14, 1098, by Bohemond of Antioch, a Christian lord and Crusader. Bohemond thus created, within the framework of his own colonial principality, a condominium administered by himself and the Genoese state. It was not a question in this case of an agricultural domain given to a nobleman in exchange for a knight's service but of the concession of an urban district to an allied state. Later other Crusaders in Palestine granted similar possessions to the Genoese, for, like Bohemond, they wished to show their gratitude for the help they had received in their struggle against the Moslems. Such concessions always included a warehouse, or fonduk, and exemption from taxes. The Venetians and Pisans obtained similar benefits for the same reasons, but the former sometimes managed to have important rural zones included. In the seigneury of Tyre they received 21 entire villages and a third part of 51 others, out of a total of 114.

After obtaining a series of concessions along the Palestinian shore the state of Genoa began to enfeoff a portion to members of its nobility. This explains how the powerful Embriaci family held from Genoa, for a theoretically limited time, a series of urban areas in Palestine. For the state of Genoa it was a means of paying the debts it had contracted with the Embriaci for maritime expeditions that they had undertaken. This is the first example of the connection between national debt and colonial concession: the state wished to discharge what it owed or at least to postpone its liquidation.

Similarly, Genoa granted concessions to companies; here is proof that colonial companies were not the creation of northern European countries in modern times, as is often believed, but that their origin goes back to the Middle Ages and that they existed first among the Mediterranean nations. This is true of almost all the commercial techniques in general and colonial techniques in particular.

Transfer of Colonial Techniques 13

Within the Genoese colonial system these companies were called *mahonas*, which signifies reimbursement, indemnification, thereby emphasizing their connection with the national debt. The first example was the *mahona* of Chios. Twenty-nine galleys had been equipped for the state at private expense, and since the government was not in a position to reimburse these citizens, their leader was authorized, in 1346, to conquer the Greek island of Chios, which possessed at that time nearly all available vegetable mastic. The creditors would hold the island from the doge of Genoa with the right to administer and exploit it economically and fiscally for twenty years, after which the state would pay the 203,000 pounds that it owed. In fact, the Republic was never in a position to keep to its agreement, and the colony remained in the hands of the company formed by the mahonists, i.e. by those who should have been indemnified and their descendants or successors. This company later acquired other islands and continued to increase its constituted capital by stocks, a procedure repeated later by colonial companies in the Atlantic zone and in the Indies.

The various types of colonial concessions that existed in the Genoese possessions in the Levant were handed on to the Iberian nations and merged with the feudal forms inherited from the medieval past of those countries. This is particularly evident in the colonization of the Canary Islands, begun by the Portuguese in the middle of the fourteenth century. Lanzarotto Malocello, one of the Genoese captains serving the king of Portugal, discovered a part of the Canary Islands, took possession of it in the name of the king, and held by his authority two of these islands for several years. In this way Mediterranean colonial practices were transplanted to the Atlantic zone. About the same time, Catalans and Castilians also became interested in the Canary Islands. The discoverers and colonists sent there by those nations had to pay their own expenses and were reimbursed by means of feudal concessions. This system was applied throughout the Atlantic archipelagoes that were colonized as much by the Portuguese as by the Castilians. Since these concessions were granted by the kings of Portugal and Castile, their institutional characteristics derived from feudal law as elaborated in those two countries during the Middle Ages. The process, however, was the same as in the Levant; moreover, the beneficiaries were sometimes Italians.

Land concessions in the Madeiras and the Azores were granted first by Henry the Navigator, and then by the king of Portugal to hereditary captains who held public authority. At Porto Santo, in the Madeira Islands, the captaincy was given, in 1446, to Bartolomeo Perestrello, a knight of Italian origin, whose daughter later married Christopher Columbus. He had the right to will the captaincy to his male heirs and their descendants. He administered justice in the name of Henry the Navigator, who himself held the island from the king. He could levy special taxes on the mills and machines used in the sugar plantations and he was allowed to subenfeoff lands.

There were also examples of gifts to groups. In 1496 the Castilian Alonso de Lugo set up a company for the conquest and settlement of the island of Palma, in the Canaries. Several Italian capitalists were members and received territorial concessions in reimbursement of their expenses. This is how the Genoese Cristóbal de Ponte came to hold from the Crown of Castile a castle surrounded by lands, a part of which he subenfeoffed to a third party.

It would be wrong, however, to believe that the feudal type of colonial concessions was the only system employed by the Iberian governments. They also created colonies by settlement and, as soon as the colonists were numerous enough, created municipalities which had a development parallel to that of the seigneuries of the first colonists. In the course of the sixteenth century, when the central power

Transfer of Colonial Techniques 15

succeeded in exercising a more effective control over the colonies, it tried to suppress the feudal privileges of the first discoverers and colonists. In behaving this way the kings were only following the normal tendencies of absolute states at the beginning of modern times. Functionaries then began to replace the feudal lords, and they strove to make the common law of the monarchy prevail over the privileges of the first colonists; but, everywhere, the state had left the first risks to private initiative, since its fiscal system was still too primitive to provide the necessary funds.

In America this system was maintained as long as the central authority was not strong enough to take over the complete control of the colonies. The Spanish conquerors went to America with the intention of acquiring lands and free manpower. They were prepared to risk their lives to become lords, with all the powers and possessions that would involve; but, when the king wished to diminish their privileges, bloody revolts broke out, especially in Peru, when the Crown suppressed the privileges of Pizarro's and Almagro's companions.

The Portuguese in Brazil had recourse first to the system of hereditary captaincies, as in their Atlantic archipelagoes. But in the middle of the seventeenth century the government succeeded in strengthening its control, thus putting an end to the golden age of Brazilian feudalism while at the same time maintaining the system of demesnes. This was also true of the Spanish possessions. The Spanish *hacendados* and the Portuguese *fazendeiros* were from then on powerful lords who, even if they had lost a great part of their political power, remained masters of the land and people from an economic and social point of view, like European nobles of the same period.

The situations were analogous in the majority of American possessions belonging to the colonial powers of northern Europe, even though those states had not founded colonies before the seventeenth century. Though it is true that the

16   Europe and America

colonists of Massachusetts and Connecticut concluded agreements among small landowners, it must also be noted that the feudal type of land concession was by far the most numerous and extensive among the English colonies of North America. Moreover the companies held their territories equally from the king and played the role of a sort of collective lord. In French Canada the seigneurial system formed the basis of colonization, and what is even more surprising at first sight, in the American possessions of the Republic of the United Provinces, where no prince could be considered the keystone of a feudal hierarchy, the colonial concessions still maintained the traditional form.

The Dutch example is so striking that it is worth closer examination. The Dutch state was born of the revolt against the despotism of Philip II; it was a product of the Reformation and of the emancipation of the middle class resulting from the development of commerce and industry. The politics of the West India Company, was no less feudal so far as land concessions were concerned. It was a chartered company exercising public authority, which it held from the Dutch Estates General in the same way as a vassal held land and powers from his lord. The company's very position was feudal, so it is not surprising that its method of land distribution should be so. The people to whom the company gave seigneuries in fief were "patrons," and the land tenure involved military obligations as well as agricultural prestations. Default in one of these obligations could mean seizure, as a European fief could be seized.

Here is a concrete example of a colonial Dutch fief. As late as 1669 the company directors signed an agreement with a German nobleman, the Count of Hanau, establishing a fief on the coast of Cayenne, in South America. It was understood that the Count owed homage for the land granted him and that the fief would owe the company a special tax on the death of the vassal. The fief in question was quite large; it covered thirty miles of coast and might stretch as much as a hundred miles into the interior if the Count could find enough people to occupy it. The coastal region had to be cultivated within twelve years or the noncultivated lands would revert back to the company. The Count of Hanau also received every sort of public power including jurisdiction over lesser crimes (whenever bloodshed was not involved), which he wielded in the name of the Estates General. He owed a knight's service for his fief, and he was guaranteed the right of inheritance and the right to subenfeoff. The company would act as the feudal court if the Count should encounter difficulties with his own vassals, who owed him homage just as he owed it to the company.

The Dutch granted fiefs not only on the South American continent but also in the Antilles. In the whole of this zone the "patron" would receive land together with seigneurial rights. In New Holland, the valley of the Hudson, on the other hand, the soil became the property of the grantee and only the seigneurial rights that went with it were held in fief. Certain seigneuries carried with them the right of jurisdiction over more serious crimes involving the death sentence, others involved only jurisdiction over lesser crimes. Certain patrons could levy tithes and rents, others could tax only the fishing and hunting preserves. When the Dutch extended their dominion to northeastern Brazil, it was decided, by a decree of 1634, that the colonial municipalities would receive lands in hereditary fief, as well as the right to elect a governor to be assisted by regents or magistrates. This was indeed a strange mixture of European municipal and feudal law, handed down directly from the Middle Ages but transplanted into this new Atlantic milieu.

The Transfer of Sugar Production from the Mediterranean to the Atlantic

Historians of colonization often believe that the medieval colonies in the Levant were solely commercial centers which served as ports of call on the routes leading to the interior of Africa or Asia. From a commercial standpoint this view would be exact, but it overlooks certain aspects of medieval Mediterranean colonization which foreshadowed Atlantic colonization in modern times, especially the agricultural and industrial activities.

A combination of agriculture and industry characterized the sugar-cane production in which the Italian republics became interested when they acquired possessions in Palestine after the First Crusade. Sugar cane had been introduced into the Holy Land by the Arabs, who thus became the liaison for sugar between the Asiatic East and the Mediterranean world as they were for paper, the compass, and Arab numerals. In the course of the wearisome marches in Palestine during the First Crusade the warriors of the West came to know the sweetness of what one chronicler called "this unsuspected and inestimable present from Heaven." We have seen that Palestine after its conquest was divided into seigneuries according to the rules of Western feudalism. Tyre, conquered in 1123, was the first of these to manufacture sugar. A series of villages was conceded to the Venetians, who immediately drew profit from the fields of sugar cane and the sugar presses that they found there. The dues on the lands were often paid in sugar, and certain Crusaders received the right to send their sugar duty-free to the port of Acre, where it was bought by exporters, some of whom were equally exempt from paying duty. The knights of the Teutonic order and the Hospitalers possessed sugar-cane fields near the Palestinian towns of Tripoli and Tiberias. Thus it was not surprising that the Assize of Jerusalem should contain a large number of provisions concerning sugar.

During the thirteenth century sugar production increased in Syria and in Palestine, especially around Sidon, Tripoli, Galgala, and Jericho. A castle near Mamistra, in the interior of Palestine, was even called "Canamella," which means sugar cane, obvious proof that this crop was harvested in its fields. Even in 1300, when there was hardly anything left

Transfer of Colonial Techniques 19

of the colonial economy in Palestine, the domain of Krak, near the Dead Sea, and Jericho and Beirut were producing sugar to be exported to western Europe.

After the fall of the last Christian bastions and their conquest by the Turks at the end of the thirteenth century, Syria, which had provided Europe with sugar during the Crusades, relinquished its role to Cyprus. This did not mean that the sugar industry disappeared from Palestine but that henceforth the sale of sugar was oriented toward the Moslem world. The French dynasty of the Lusignan had established a prosperous colonial kingdom in Cyprus. Here, too, the cultivation of sugar cane had been introduced by the Arabs who had conquered the island in the seventh century, but it was not until the fourteenth century, after the collapse of Christian Palestine, that Cyprus became a truly important center of production.

The richest plantations were found on the southern coast of the island, where the sugar-producing royal domains of Lemva, Paphos, Aschelia, and Kuklia were situated, as well as the lands of the Venetian Cornaro family, near Piscopi, the Bishop of Limassol, the Catalan Ferrer family, and the Hospitalers' monastery near Kolossi.

The Cornaros managed their plantations according to capitalist methods. The agricultural work was done by slaves of Arab or Syrian origin, by local serfs, and by emigrants from the Holy Land. Arguments over the use of water often involved the landowners in conflict with their neighbors, and more than once they were faced with problems of canalization or handling. Hydraulic mills were used to press the sugar cane, but the Cornaros' industrial activity was not limited to this first step in the transformation of the product. In the seventeenth and eighteenth centuries sugar cane grown in America was not refined on the spot but was processed in specialized European factories, whereas Cyprus in the fifteenth century supplied the finished product in the shape of sugar loaves or powdered sugar. For this purpose the Cornaros used huge copper boilers manufactured in Italy; every year they invested large sums of money in the enterprise and assigned a special budget to its maintenance and administration.

The kings of Cyprus themselves produced great quantities of sugar which were sent to the warehouses in Nicosia where they were taken over by exporters. Often this sugar was used to pay royal debts, and in the fifteenth century the king gave his plantations as securities to private capitalists, to the state of Venice and to the famous Bank of St. George in Genoa.

The Venetian colony of Crete, like Cyprus, played a part in sugar production, but much more sugar was produced by Sicily in the central Mediterranean. The Arabs had first introduced it there too at some time during their possession of the island up to the middle of the eleventh century. When the Normans conquered Sicily, the sugar industry continued to prosper in the Palermo area, and in the twelfth century the king and the great monastery of Monreale owned sugar presses. About 1200 a crisis arose which Frederick II later tried to remedy by sending for master sugar-makers from the oldest production centers in Palestine. He had very little success, and in the fourteenth century the cultivation of sugar cane decreased. But in 1449 a new press was invented which restored prosperity. Production increased immediately in the coastal regions, and the Sicilian refineries became more numerous than before.

In the western Mediterranean, Moslem Spain was also familiar with sugar-cane cultivation. About 1300, the sugar of Málaga was sold as far away as Bruges, and a large commercial company in Ravensburg, in southern Germany, which had previously been engaged in the sugar trade in Valencia, began to produce the product there about 1460. This company used the new Sicilian press, another proof of the transfer of techniques from one end of the Mediterranean to the other. In Portugal sugar cultivation began in 1404, when the Genoese Giovanni della Palma was the first to

Transfer of Colonial Techniques 21

produce it in Algarve, the southernmost province of the country.

By the early fifteenth century, then, the production of sugar had spread from the eastern basin of the Mediterranean to the shores of the Atlantic. Three colonial regions —Palestine, Cyprus, and Crete—had played a part in this development; three noncolonial zones—Sicily, Spain, and Portugal—had participated in it. Spain and Portugal produced less than Sicily, but all three contributed to the expansion of sugar-cane production across the Atlantic zone.

Again it was the Genoese who served as the liaison between the Mediterranean and the Atlantic, and it was their capital that stimulated production in the Madeiras, a Portuguese colony, as well as in the Canary Islands, a Spanish possession. The Genoese had already been involved in the cultivation of sugar cane in Sicily, and from there the plant and the indispensable agricultural techniques were carried to Madeira. Production had begun there in 1455, but it was only after 1472, when sugar from Madeira was exported directly to Antwerp without first going through Lisbon, and when, as a result, northern Europe absorbed the product in ever increasing quantities, that the island experienced a real boom in industry. Already in 1480 some seventy vessels sailed to and from Madeira with full loads of sugar, and the output, which consisted of six thousand arrobas in 1455, rose to eighty thousand in 1493. At that time there were eighty master sugar-manufacturers on the island, which meant that there were eighty different establishments. Soon exportation had to be controlled to avoid a fall in price, and in 1498 quotas were fixed for the different ports of destination. But this system was soon suspended; demand grew to such an extent that Madeira supplied Italian markets and even Constantinople and the Aegean island of Chios, both areas close to the former centers of production in the Levant which had at one time provided sugar for the whole of Christian Europe.

22   *Europe and America*

The boom in the sugar industry in the new Atlantic colonies was due, in the first place, to the fact that as Turkish dominion extended over the eastern Mediterranean, it caused a general setback in trade and industry and, in particular, the complete suppression of sugar exportation. This was the cause of the development of sugar-cane production in the Portuguese empire, from the Madeiras first to the Azores, later reaching São Tomé, in the Gulf of Guinea on the coast of West Africa, and finally Brazil, while in the Spanish empire it spread from the Canary Islands to Santo Domingo, Puerto Rico, Mexico, Peru, and finally Cuba. European demand increased more rapidly than the production in the colonies; this is what enabled Barbados, Jamaica, and the other English Antilles, and Guadeloupe and Martinique in the French Antilles to enjoy a late prosperity.

In the Spanish Canary Islands as in the Portuguese Madeiras the Genoese again played a large part in initiating sugar production. In 1526 there were no less than twelve Italian and Spanish plantations on Grand Canary Island, eleven on Tenerife and one on Gomera; the majority were always held by the Spanish. Other foreigners were equally interested and the powerful German firm of the Welsers, from Augsburg, even tried at one time to produce sugar on the island of Palma.

Columbus had come from the Canary Islands on his second voyage in 1493 when he introduced sugar cane into Haiti, which was called at that time Española. In addition to the small establishments which employed only Indian slave manpower, larger establishments soon appeared which used horses or hydraulic power for the mills. The increase in production augmented the need for slaves on the big plantations, and since the supply of Indians was rapidly exhausted, Negroes were brought from Africa in ever increasing quantities. The first technicians came from the Canary Islands, but the boilers were at first imported from the metropolis. Soon they were manufactured on the island itself thanks to the

Transfer of Colonial Techniques 23

credit granted by the Crown. The Welsers of Augsburg, who engaged in much colonial speculation, invested capital both in the sugar plantations and in the slave trade.

The first hydraulic press was built in Puerto Rico in 1527. The beginnings were not easy, but in 1547 production began to increase. Here, too, the influence of the Canary Islands can be seen, and in 1569 the Canary authorities were still sending to Puerto Rico master sugar-manufacturers and other technicians.

The first *ingenio de azúcar* (plantation) appeared in Jamaica in 1527. Production was aided by Portuguese immigration from the Atlantic archipelagoes, but it never assumed great importance during the period the island was held by the Spaniards. In Cuba, where the sugar industry enjoyed a spectacular rise during a relatively recent epoch, the beginnings were slow and not very promising. Although sugar cane was introduced as early as 1511, production only became important after 1600, and even then the returns were poor.

Cortez brought sugar cane from the Antilles into Mexico during the years immediately following his conquest, and he himself owned plantations in the valley of Oaxaca. Pizarro introduced it into Peru in 1533, a year after his arrival.

Such were the beginnings of sugar production in the Spanish possessions in America. In the Portuguese empire we have seen it spread from the Madeiras to the Azores, and to São Tomé in the Gulf of Guinea, where in 1554 there were some sixty sugar-making establishments. Sugar cane had been introduced there in 1529, at the same time as it had been brought to the archipelago of Cape Verde, from where it spread to Brazil.

During the years following 1530, the Portuguese began to grant portions of the Brazilian coast to hereditary captains, and they alone had the right to possess mills or hydraulic machines for sugar pressing. Nevertheless in 1570 there were sixty *engenhos* or plantations between Itamaracá and São

24   Europe and America

Vicente, but none as yet in the region of Rio de Janeiro, although there were twenty-three in the North of the country around Recife and eighteen in the region around Bahia. Genoese in association with merchants from Antwerp again played a part in this expansion by creating plantations and supplying capital. In 1628 there were as many as 235 plantations in Brazil, and at that time Portugal was supplying the refineries of England, Flanders, and Germany. The old centers of production in the Mediterranean had completely given up competing, and the Atlantic zone had achieved complete supremacy. Despite the ever increasing Brazilian sugar production, Madeira sugar was still the most valuable during the sixteenth century. It was only in the seventeenth century, as a result of the constant shift in production toward the west, that Brazilian sugar took first place. The Azores and São Tomé stopped planting sugar cane at that time, and even Madeira lost much of her importance. The slave trade thrived as the sugar production increased, so it is possible to say that sugar was the principal cause of the development of slavery in the colonies. The big establishments where mills and melting-pots were used employed between 150 and 200 Negroes, and we know how greatly the numbers of Negroes increased in the population of Brazil beginning with the seventeenth century.

Although Brazil continued until the early eighteenth century to play the main role in production, the French and English Antilles began in the seventeenth century to send increasing quantities of sugar to the European market. In 1625 parts of the island of Saint Christopher had been occupied at almost the same time by the English and the French, and twenty years later both nations began to sell the sugar of this island in the metropolitan markets. By the Treaty of Utrecht in 1713 the English became sole masters of the island, and the sugar industry began to be quite important.

In 1627 the English settled on Barbados. Like Madeira

at the beginning of the Portuguese colonization, this island was too thickly wooded for the settlers to establish significant plantations right away, but exportation began in 1646. However, only after 1655 and the immigration of the Dutch, who had been chased out of Brazil by the Portuguese reconquest, did sugar production become wholly satisfactory, especially after the adoption of the *tayche*, a boiler of Portuguese origin. Manpower was supplied by white prisoners—mainly Scottish and Irish—during the Protectorate of Cromwell, and later by imported Negroes. Under Charles II, thirteen planters were raised to the rank of baron, obvious proof of the wealth they had acquired. The Negroes on Barbados at this time numbered about twenty-five to thirty thousand.

In 1656 the Spaniards lost Jamaica to the English, who in 1664 introduced, or to be precise reintroduced, sugar cane from Barbados. In 1675 there were seventy-five mills, and around 1700 sugar became the principal export. Production continued to grow throughout the eighteenth century, as it did in the other English islands of the Lesser Antilles: Nevis, Antigua, Saint Vincent, Dominica, and Granada.

The French set out from their base on Saint Christopher in 1635 and occupied Guadeloupe and Martinique. The sugar technique in these islands followed the Brazilian methods used by the Dutch and the Jews in Recife before the Portuguese reconquest. On these islands too there was a large increase in production during the eighteenth century. Even before this time the French had added an important portion of Santo Domingo to their possessions in the Caribbean and had restored prosperity to its sugar industry, which had been badly neglected by the Spaniards after 1600. Under the French regime production greatly increased and remained very substantial until the great slave revolt of 1791, which ended in the independence of Haiti.

This revolt was a catastrophe for the planters of the island, but Jamaica, Brazil, and particularly Cuba benefited from it.

26   Europe and America

The latter island, a Spanish possession, did not assume any importance in sugar production until the middle of the eighteenth century: the circumstances were then favorable and Cuba was ready to profit from them. This was not the case for the other Spanish possessions, but the Danish possessions of Saint Thomas and Saint Croix had for some time been enjoying a truly advantageous situation.

At about this time, as a result of Napoleon's continental blockade, sugar cane began to suffer from competition with the sugar beet. The details of sugar production, its localization, and its international market changed completely. There is no need here to go into these new characteristics or their repercussions on prices and consumption. We simply want to show that the history of sugar-cane production presents a particularly striking example of the passage from the medieval economy of the Mediterranean to the colonial economy of modern times in the Atlantic area. The methods invented in the Middle Ages in the Mediterranean zone made possible the expansion of sugar production across the Atlantic world, where, in the beginning, both capital and technical personnel came from the Mediterranean region. In this particular area of economy the continuity is evident. There has been a gradual shift to the West, from the Palestinian sugar plantations in the twelfth century to those in Cuba in the eighteenth century. This is certainly very convincing evidence of the filiation which bound medieval colonial economy with that of modern times.

From Roman to Colonial Slavery

Everyone knows that in the modern era slavery reached an impressive stage of development in the colonies, particularly in the American colonies. On a superficial level the relationships between colonial slavery and medieval European social history are not obvious since slavery is generally believed to have disappeared from most European countries at the end of Antiquity. In actual fact, although serfdom was

Transfer of Colonial Techniques   27

a structure much more characteristic of medieval society than was slavery, nevertheless the latter did exist in many European countries during the period between the fall of the Western Roman Empire and the time of the great discoveries. It even continued to exist up to the beginning of the nineteenth century, for there were still some slaves in Sicily in 1812, in Spain in 1820, and in Portugal in 1836.

Christianity had an extremely important influence upon slavery but, being centered on spiritual values, the Gospel did not aim at suppressing this social condition. Christ, according to one text, did not come to change the condition of men but their minds. The changes brought about by Christianity had more influence on the progressive transformation of slavery than did the often contradictory teachings of the Church Fathers, but they did not bring about its disappearance. In fact the Church allowed believers and even its dignitaries to possess slaves but recommended that they should be treated humanely. Emancipation was a pious work; it was neither obligatory nor even expressly recommended.

It is not surprising, then, that slavery existed in the German states at the beginning of the Middle Ages. The source of slaves, just as under the Roman Empire, was, above all, war, and even war among Christians. The slave trade was equally important. The biography of a seventh-century saint relates that whenever the hero heard that slaves were going to be sold he hastened to redeem them. Sometimes, according to this account, one ship alone would transport more than a hundred of these unfortunate creatures, among them Welshmen, Bretons, North Africans, and especially Saxons, great numbers of whom were thrown onto the market at that time. The slave boats which our seventh-century saint met were thus no less laden than the Portuguese sailing ships of the middle of the fifteenth century which plied the seas between the western coasts of Africa and Lisbon with their holds full of Negroes.

28   Europe and America

In the eighth or ninth century, slavery was replaced by serfdom in almost all of western Europe, but slave trade across the sea continued. Pagan Slavs were captured along the banks of the Elbe and sold in Moslem Spain. They were brought through Germany and France and shipped from the ports of Provence to the Caliphate of Córdoba. In Great Britain prisoners taken in the wars between Anglo-Saxons, Welsh, Irish, and Scots were often enslaved. As late as 1102, a council held in London forbade everyone "henceforward to follow the guilty practices which until that time in England had permitted the sale of men like wild animals." Actually by that time slavery had become rare in Great Britain; it was only the condition of a small fraction of British society in the border regions. When political unity was achieved slavery disappeared as it did in other states populated by diverse races but controlled by one central authority.

The slave trade between the Slavic regions and Moslem Spain decreased in the tenth century and disappeared completely after the fall of the Caliphate of Córdoba. The Christians of southern Europe, instead of selling slaves to the Moslems, strove to deprive the latter of their liberty, and in this way slavery continued in Mediterranean Europe.

As a result of the war against the infidels slavery was a matter of course in the Iberian Peninsula as long as Christian kingdoms were at war with Moslem states. In central Spain the struggle continued until the conquest of Granada in 1492, the same year as the discovery of America. But even later, Moslems captured at sea were regularly sent to the slave markets in Spain, just as Spaniards and other Christians were sent to slave markets in Moslem North Africa.

In Catalonia, in the Roussillon—French today but belonging to Aragon in the Middle Ages—in the kingdom of Valencia, more slaves came from the slave trade than from war. Generally the deeds of sale guaranteed that they were not Christian, not stolen, and not protected by the King's Peace. The first of these clauses disappeared in the fourteenth cen-

Transfer of Colonial Techniques 29

tury, and many Greeks and Christian Slavs were sold at that time in Spain, Italy, and the South of France.

In Spain female slaves were generally cheaper than males, although the opposite was true in most of Italy. This was because much of the slave manpower in Spain was used in agriculture and in industry, whereas in Italy the domestic slave predominated in the cities and therefore more female workers were required.

During the fourteenth and fifteenth centuries a great number of slaves were imported into eastern Spain and other Mediterranean regions. Most of the trade was carried on by Italians, and the slaves came from the Italian colonies on the Black Sea and the Balkan Peninsula. These Tartars, Russians, and Caucasians, both men and women, were sold all over the Mediterranean world by Genoese and Venetians who bought them from the men who hunted them.

In Portugal and in Castile slaves were still captured in frontier raids until the middle of the thirteenth century. About this time the Portuguese *Reconquista* came to an end, and no independent Moslems were left in the country. From then on slaves could be acquired only outside the kingdom. During the fourteenth and fifteenth centuries, when a series of African islands were discovered, the slave hunt began immediately. Castilians and Portuguese hunted the Guanches of the Canaries—a race that is now extinct—but they bought even more slaves from the interior of the African continent.

These black slaves had for a long time been imported into southern Europe through the Moslem countries of Africa. The demand during the fourteenth century had increased to such proportions that a special caravan route had been created from the Sudan across the Sahara to the peninsula of Barca in Cyrenaica. The Portuguese under Henry the Navigator created a direct sea route for the black slaves like the one they would establish for the spice trade at the time of Vasco da Gama. There was no longer any need for intermediaries along the caravan routes and in the Moslem ports of North Africa. The Portuguese themselves loaded their holds full of slaves directly in the Senegal or in Guinea. After the death of Henry the Navigator, Diogo Cão went as far as the Congo, and from there, as well as from Angola, increasing quantities of slaves were sent first to Portugal and later to America when the sugar plantations began to grow in number and size.

Since the fifteenth century *asientos* or concessions for the slave trade were granted by the Portuguese government. Thus the Florentine firm of Bartolomeo Marchionni bought the monopoly of slave trade on the Slave Coast, just as later monopolies were sold for buying in Africa and selling in America. The control of this ignominious traffic was in the hands of a special administration, the Casa dos Escravos, or Slave Bureau, a subdivision of the Casa da India, the Portuguese colonial ministry. This traffic along the African coast at the end of the Middle Ages was a transition toward colonial slavery in America. Since the American aborigines, enslaved at the beginning of Spanish colonization in the Antilles, became extinct with frightening rapidity, they were replaced by Negroes imported according to the rules of the *asientos* at the end of the Middle Ages. The passage of medieval slavery in the Mediterranean and southern Europe to colonial slavery in America was thus scarcely noticeable; it was a phenomenon of simple continuity.

When we turn, however, to the study of medieval precedents in the use of slaves in the colonial economy it becomes a question of derivation. Slavery as a sad aspect of colonial technique in its early stages first appeared in the Italian colonies of the eastern Mediterranean. The Italians, accustomed to slavery at home, found the institution flourishing in the regions of the Byzantine Empire or Moslem states where they settled. Slaves were already present in their first possessions in Palestine, either on the plantations or as domestics.

Transfer of Colonial Techniques   *31*

Some of them were to be found on ships as merchandise or as servants. Later, in the smaller Italian colonies that served mainly as markets or ports, slaves were used primarily as servants, whereas in the larger colonies they were used both in agriculture and in industry. There could often be found for sale in the Italian colonial markets women taken in raids in the Caucasus, Tartar children sold by their own parents, and Greeks and other orthodox Christians. Some of them assisted the merchants in their trades, others worked in the fields, still others were domestic servants. When Salveto Pessagno, a member of the Genoese family that supplied Portugal with six admirals, died at Famagusta, Cyprus, early in the fourteenth century, he left two Greek slaves of mixed blood and two other captives, all four of them his personal servants.

The Venetians had for some time played a part in the slave trade in these regions, and Tana, at the mouth of the Don, was their most important market. Crete was also a prosperous slave market, and many Catalans did business there in the fourteenth century. They sold entire herds of slaves taken in raids in Greece or in the numerous islands in the Aegean. Such quantities were not absorbed by the island alone, for Crete was also an important transit market on the sea routes of the slave trade; but some of the slaves were employed in the *casalia* or agricultural settlements in the interior of the island, and the Venetian government was careful to import them for this purpose. The Genoese did the same for their sugar plantations in Cyprus and mastic plantations on Chios. Sometimes slaves were also used in mines, as in the alum mines in Phocaea, a Genoese colony on the coast of Asia Minor. This variety of uses to which slaves were put illustrates clearly the degree to which medieval colonial slavery served as a model for Atlantic colonial slavery. Slave manpower had been employed in the Italian colonies in the Mediterranean for all the kinds of work it would be burdened with in the Atlantic colonies. The only important change was that the white victims of slavery were replaced by a much greater number of African Negroes, captured in raids or bought by traders.

This chapter has shown that the majority of the techniques of colonization that developed in the Atlantic area in modern times had their origin in the later Middle Ages in the colonies of the eastern Mediterranean. It is clear that there was a general movement from east to west, from the time of the Crusades until the seventeenth and eighteenth centuries. This movement was a complicated process of reciprocal influences among European colonies in the Levant and the European metropolises on the one hand, and the colonies of the Atlantic archipelagoes, the African continent, and the American continents on the other. In the course of this evolution all the geographical and cultural elements of the Western world appeared to be parts of one great historical area. What was true of early colonial techniques also became true in the course of time for the whole of Western civilization, since it spread across the immensity of the Atlantic zone precisely by the techniques whose transplantation from east to west has been described in the preceding pages. Continuity provides a living identity, that is to say of the same essence on both sides of the ocean, despite the indispensable adaptation to different environments. The basis of the various civilizations in the Atlantic zone, is found to be of common origin, however diverse the nuances may be. From the very beginning, history follows the same direction on the two shores of the Atlantic. Nowhere is there a simple copying of precedents, but all parts of this immense zone appear to have a single, fundamental identity when compared with the situations which characterize non-Atlantic civilizations.

12

The Castilian as Plainsman:
The Medieval Ranching Frontier in
La Mancha and Extremadura

Charles Julian Bishko

FEW GENERALIZATIONS in Spanish historical thought command readier assent than that which affirms the profound influence of the Reconquest on the making of Castile. Yet it is only in recent decades that scholars like Claudio Sánchez-Albornoz, J. M. Lacarra, Julio González, and others have established the thesis that those eight centuries of now slow, now rapid southward advance against the Moors were not merely an Iliad of military and political combat, but above everything else a medieval *repoblación,* or recolonization, of the Iberian Peninsula.[1] From this standpoint, the Reconquest appears as a frontier movement in the authentic American sense—the occupation and development of relatively empty territories on the margin of an expanding society.

Like all new historical interpretations, this frontier approach to medieval Iberian history raises many questions for investigation. Furthermore, it imposes the necessity of advancing beyond traditional lines of political, constitutional, and juridical research into the as yet little explored fields of medieval peninsular demography, ecology, anthropogeography, and agrarian history. At the same time it suggests the great utility of exploiting, on a comparative basis, the rich body of methods and interpretations evolved by frontier historiography in the study of other frontiers, medieval and modern, and not least that of the United States, where the subject of the frontier has been pursued more intensely, more heatedly, and surely more fruitfully, than anywhere else.[2]

It is in the light of such reflections as these that the frontier historian might reappraise what has always been one of the obscurest,

48

least understood, and most hastily treated of all the major geographic and chronological subdivisions of the Castilian Reconquest. This is the great region of the southern tableland or *meseta* of inner Iberia, the rolling plains and flat steppelands between the valley of the Tajo and the Sierra Morena that constitute the historic provinces of La Mancha and Extremadura. Historians concerned with more typical elements of medieval European life—agriculture and land tenures, peasants and nobles, secular churchmen and monks, towns, middle classes, and urban economy—have tended to dismiss this curious part of Spain where all these things were either lacking or of secondary importance. But it is precisely here, under such conditions, that a fresh approach in terms of the frontier holds much promise.

From this point of view, the Guadiana River Basin can be seen as one of the most interesting stages in the long advance. Its problems and their solutions are significant not only for Spanish history but also for the pastoral-plains society which the Castilian eventually transplanted to Northern Mexico and Texas, the Orinocan Llanos, the Chilean Central Valley, and the limitless pampas of the Río de la Plata.

North American historians are familiar with the classic work of Walter Prescott Webb, *The Great Plains*, which so brilliantly traces the institutional and psychological adaptations made by American frontiersmen moving from the humid, forested, agricultural East into the level, timberless, semiarid spaces of the plains.[3] Medieval Castilian frontiersmen, on both the northern and southern halves of the *meseta*, as again in Andalusia, confronted parallel difficulties in establishing a new society in a dry plains environment of climatic extremes, insufficient water, limited cultivable soil, treelessness, and xerophytic brush vegetation; but in La Mancha and Extremadura these conditions were more widespread, more intense, more hostile to human occupation than anywhere else between the Cantabrians and the Sierra Nevadas. In addition, the land was virtually unpeopled—the desert of the Guadiana is a southern frontier counterpart to Sánchez-Albornoz' desert of the Duero—and under the shadow of Almorávid and Almohade military power, which halted or slowed the Reconquest here for a significant century and a half.

The Guadiana Basin, still today the least populated major region of Spain, is a land of long, parching summers and cold, snowless winters; of an inadequate and irregular rainfall (ranging from under

The Castilian as Plainsman   49

sixteen inches in eastern La Mancha to thirty-two inches in favored
parts of Extremadura), the effects of which are aggravated by a
high evaporation rate and an extreme permeability of the soil; and
of a drainage system of lakes and rivers which, like long stretches
of the broad, shallow Guadiana itself, become in summer dry ar-
royos or mere trickles.[4] To a limited degree, the high watertable
offsets the surface shortage, permitting the sinking of wells and the
raising of ground water through the *noria*, the vertical waterwheel
with pots fastened to its rim which is turned by animal power; such
wells determined in large part the distribution of frontier settlements, but they never became the basis for more than a very limited
regadío or irrigated farming system. Throughout the year the wind
blows, raising in the dry season from the grey, bleak Manchegan
steppes the dust-haze of the *calina;* but not until the end of the
Middle Ages, with the expansion of cereal production, was it apparently deemed profitable to introduce the medieval invention, the
windmill, into this area naturally suited to its use.

Climatic conditions and the lateritic Mediterranean red earth soils
of clayey, sandy or saline structure account for the advanced treelessness of most of the basin, not, as so often alleged, medieval
deforestation. The predominant vegetation is the *matorral*, which
includes various woody, aromatic, deep-rooted, leathery-leaved,
evergreen, drought-resistant bushes and shrubs—broom, gorse,
heather, sage, rosemary, cistus, and others. Ignacio Olagüe, who
attempts to explain Spain's decline in the later sixteenth century as
due to an alleged radical change in *meseta* climate, attributes forests,
extensive grasslands, and flourishing crop farming to medieval La
Mancha and Extremadura, but his thesis rests more on personal
conviction than factual proof.[5] It seems highly probable, however,
that in medieval times the region's grasslands were much more extensive than today, after centuries of overgrazing and spring burn-
ings, for it is upon grass, not *matorral*, that the medieval documents
on grazing rights lay stress. In La Mancha this grass was to be found
at its richest in the Murcian plains around Chinchilla and Albacete,
on the *campos* of Montiel and Calatrava, in the sheltered Sierra
Morena valleys near Alcaraz and the Vale of Alcudia; and in Extremadura, in the renowned pastures of La Serena, the Tierra de
Barros, the *campos* of Badajoz, Cáceres, Alcántara, and Coria, and
the Vale and Vera of Plasencia. One characteristic of Guadiana Valley grass is especially to be noted: it grows not only in the spring,

50

when grass is available in most of the Peninsula, but abundantly in the fall rainy season. This fact accounts for the great drives of transhumant sheep and cattle from the north, stock movements that play a central role in the history of the Manchegan and Extremaduran frontier period.

The other major factor in shaping the course of Castilian occupation of the Guadiana plains was military: the fact that between 1085 and 1235 La Mancha and Extremadura were the invasion corridor and battleground of Berber armies based in Andalusia and of Castilian-Leonese forces raised on both sides of the Central Sierras.[6] For a century and a half frontier warfare swept the plains, in four principal phases: (1) the Almorávid period, 1085–1150, which commenced disastrously, but under Alfonso VII in the early 1140's saw the first permanent establishments in the plains country at Coria in Extremadura and Calatrava in La Mancha; (2) the two extremely critical decades, 1155–1175, when ferocious Almohade offensives wiped out Ferdinand II's gains in León and recovered virtually all of La Mancha except the key fortress of Calatrava; (3) the period 1175–1212, of long-delayed Leonese arrival in the Tajo Valley and steady Castilian advance in La Mancha, culminating in the victory of Las Navas; and, finally, (4) the period 1212–1235, when the Almohades were driven from the remaining portions of La Mancha and Extremadura.

Carrying on this prolonged struggle imposed important changes upon Castilian military organization, changes that were to have lasting effects upon the methods of colonizing the plains.[7] For both Moors and Castilians, the endless warfare itself was a typically plains affair, where occasional major campaigns aimed at conquest of the settled territory on the other side of the *despoblado*; but it was normally characterized by incessant raids and hit-and-run attacks (*algaras, correduras*) which sought to surprise the enemy, devastate and pillage his towns and farms, and then swiftly withdraw across the intervening plains with captured humans, livestock, and other booty. In consequence the Guadiana zone forced Castilian and Leonese rulers into a costly defense in depth by means of castles and towns, and into desperate efforts to maintain control of strategic routes and mountain passes, such as Muradal, also called Despeñaperros.

In the first half of the twelfth century the kings depended increasingly upon the powerful municipal militias, such as those of Sala-

The Castilian as Plainsman 51

manca, Avila, Segovia, Madrid, Toledo, and Cuenca, which came
to be characteristic of the new *concejos* or towns of the region
between the Duero and the Tajo. From the Fuero de Cuenca (1189–
1190) and similar sources, it can be gathered that these urban
armies, adapting themselves to the exigencies of plains warfare, included a cavalry of *caballeros villanos* or petty nobles resident in
the town; an infantry of *peones*, the free but non-noble citizen-
soldiers; and archers, both mounted and foot. Elaborate procedures
were developed for defense of the town during the army's absence;
the siting and layout of encampments; the use of scouts and spies;
compensation for wounds and losses of equipment; and division of
spoils. Thus, in a very literal sense, urban frontier warfare was economic warfare. On campaigns, to judge by Cuencan practice, it was
customary for the host to divide itself into equal halves; one, called
the *azaga*, constructed a defensible base-camp, from which the other
half, the *algara* proper, departed to launch its lightning thrust into
enemy country, and to which it returned to await the inevitable
counterattack.[8]

But by the second half of the century, the advent of the Almohades
and continuous bitter fighting in the Guadiana Basin proved con-
clusively that the frontier military needs of the crown could not be
adequately met by municipal armies and nobles, resident at often
considerable distances from the scene of combat, slow to muster,
privileged in respect to length and frequency of service, and dis-
inclined to take up homesteads or promote settlements in the plains.
What was required in addition to these regular forces, as the Almohade crisis of 1155–1175 revealed, was fighters stationed in close
proximity to frontier defense points in or below the Tajo Valley,
capable of garrisoning exposed castles and fortresses, constantly
alert for instant action against raiders, and willing to undertake the
permanent conquest and colonization of La Mancha and Extremadura. This is the background for the sudden rise to prominence in
Castilian-Leonese history of the six great military orders of the
Templars, Hospitalers, Calatrava, Alcántara and the two branches
of Santiago, San Marcos in León and Uclés in Castile. Before the
mid-twelfth century, significantly enough, the older Temple and
San Juan had not fought the infidel in the two western kingdoms
of Spain; and it was the two decades of dire Almohade peril that
brought into existence all the native orders, whose founding members were nearly all well-blooded in Guadiana Valley fighting. These

52

paramonastic warriors, the *freires caballeros* of the orders, whom the *Rule* of Calatrava pictures as sleeping dressed and armed, ready at a moment's notice to mount their chargers and ride against the Moor, along with the vassal *caballeros* and *peones* of their patrimonies, henceforth become the standing protectors of the frontier settlements and a persistent scourge of the Almohades.[9]

The Castilian conquest of the Guadiana Basin, except in the lowest reaches of the river, was terminated by 1235; but the era of colonization extends to at least the end of the thirteenth century.[10] Throughout this period, royal efforts to promote settlement and economic development of the area depended almost exclusively upon two agencies, the town and the military order. Compared with its striking predominance in the twelfth-century colonization of the Duero-Tajo belt, where it served as the principal basis of political, ecclesiastical, social, and economic life, the royal *concejo* plays a distinctly secondary role in La Mancha and Extremadura. To be sure, towns founded by the king on his crownland (*concejos de realengo*), and largely self-governing under a royal *fuero* defining municipal laws and liberties, sprang up both in Extremadura, where we find notable examples in Coria, Cáceres, and Badajoz, and also in La Mancha, for example, Alarcón, Alcaraz, Chinchilla, and Villarreal (modern Ciudad Real). Yet such towns were comparatively few in number, partly because urban agglomerations remained scattered in the plains country, partly because so much of the territory was entrusted to the military orders. It is noteworthy that of these royal towns, only two, Coria and Badajoz, attained the level of episcopal sees.

Far more important than the *concejos de realengo* as colonizers were the military orders, which throughout La Mancha and Extremadura directed the settlement and Castilianization of the frontier. The military was but one of four vital functions these great corporations performed. From the governmental standpoint their broad patrimonies constituted palatine lordships, outside the law and jurisdiction of the king and his officials, lands where the orders ruled and administered justice through their capable directorate of grand masters or priors, and subordinate district *comendadores*. Over much of the Guadiana Basin, until the days of the Catholic kings, government was thus the monopoly of the orders, as the royal laws and charters recognize when the king speaks of "mi tierra e la de las ordenes." But the orders largely replaced not only the king's

government, but also that of the secular church. The new Extremaduran bishoprics carried on the ecclesiastical policy followed in
the Duero-Tajo settlement; but all La Mancha remained part of a
huge diocese of Toledo, where the orders, secure in their papal,
Cistercian, or Compostellan exemptions from episcopal control, administered their domanial churches, providing clergy and collecting
tithes. No less startling, the orders entirely prevented monasticism
from establishing itself in the Tierra de las Ordenes, and because
Cáceres, Badajoz, and other towns in *realengo* prohibited the gift,
sale, or exchange of land to religious orders, the plains country was
a strangely monkless land, the one large subdivision of the medieval
West where monasticism—Benedictine, Cluniac, Cistercian, Carthusian, Franciscan, Dominican—plays no part whatsoever in religious life.

Lastly, the orders were active colonizers of the Guadiana frontier,
making grants to nobles who undertook settlement projects, and
establishing towns and villages to which they conceded, in order to
attract colonists, liberal *fueros*, often those of Cuenca or Cáceres.
Alcázar de San Juan, Consuegra, Madridejos, Calatrava, Almadén,
Quintanar de la Orden, Mérida, Usagre, Alcocer, Medellín, Montán-
chez, Trujillo: such are some of the many pueblos sponsored by the
orders. Yet most of these towns remained small and overwhelmingly
rural in social and economic composition, partly again because of
environmental handicaps to urban growth, but also because the
often more limited rights of self-government allowed by the orders,
the retention of various seigneurial rights and monopolies, the exclusion of royal law, and prohibition of appeals in judicial cases to
the crown repelled settlers.[11] The well-known case of Cáceres, where
the colonists compelled Alfonso IX to swear that the town would
never be transferred to an order, is indicative of the hostility frontiersmen felt.[12]

Population in all the plains towns, whether of the orders or of the
crown, belonged mostly to the two social classes characteristic of
the Castilian meseta frontier: the *caballeros villanos* and the *peones*.[13]
Each charter member of the town, of either class, received a town
lot, and often a piece of arable land just outside it, at the time of
its foundation; a land distribution or *repartimiento* was effected,
either by the order's *comendador* (as at Madridejos in 1238), or, in
the royal towns like Cáceres, through a two-stage partition by
cuadrelleros to soldiers of the conquest and subsequently by *sex-*

54

meros to later arrivals.[14] These land cessions, in line with Castilian frontier practice, were full allodial grants. After at most a three-year period, the settlers could sell, exchange, or give them away, although both the crown and the royal *concejos* forbade land transfers to religious orders, and the military orders required prospective owners to promise vassalage to them.[15]

That farming, particularly the raising of grain, was carried on in the land close to the town is evident from references in the sources to units of arable land and to wheat, barley, and the like; to plow-teams of oxen and mules, the latter probably a Moorish carryover; and to various tithes and taxes levied on crops. Olive culture is rarely mentioned, but viticulture on the other hand was obviously widespread and the subject of promotion by at least one order, Calatrava. This order, in establishing Miguelturra near Ciudad Real in 1230, compelled *caballeros* to plant two *arranzadas*, and *peones* one, of vineyard under threat of losing their allotments.[16]

Far more economically significant, however, than cereal agriculture or viticulture was stock raising in that advanced form, more fruitfully developed in the Iberian Peninsula than anywhere else in the medieval world, which is properly called ranching.[17] The systematic ranging of large numbers of sheep, cattle, horses, and other livestock on the open *meseta* plains had first developed above the Duero River; all the way from the Rioja and Burgos westwards to León, Zamora, and the trans-Miño country there occurred in the late ninth and the tenth centuries, as part of the Asturoleonese—Castilian colonization of the desert of the Duero, a shift towards the pastoral side of the balance in the old Cantabrian-Pyrenean mixed farming system of crops and livestock. After 1085 both the limited arable and water resources of the northern *meseta*, and the military conditions of the Reconquest that favored mobile property over easily destroyed crops and orchards, promoted the rapid expansion of ranching into the new frontier settlements of the Duero-Tajo region such as Segovia, Sepúlveda, Avila, Valladolid, Salamanca, and Ciudad Rodrigo above the Central Sierras, and Soria, Guadalajara, Madrid, Cuenca, Toledo, and Talavera beyond them.

From the middle twelfth century this flourishing Castilian pastoralism, made aware of the rich pasturage resources of the trans-Tajo plains, must have acted as a powerful if now little-mentioned factor in Castilian southward expansion. Certainly by the second half of the century towns like Cuenca, Toledo, and Plasencia, and

The Castilian as Plainsman   55

the military orders of Calatrava, the Hospital, and Uclés, were sending their herds and flocks into the Guadiana Basin in spite of the
ever-present danger of Almohade attack. With the final expulsion
of the Moors under Alfonso IX, Ferdinand III, and Alfonso X in the
succeeding century, and the opening up of the richest Manchegan
and Extremaduran grasslands, there occurred, simultaneously with
a parallel development in Lower Andalusia, an explosive expansion
of the ranching industry of the plains. This movement is strongly
reflected in the extraordinarily numerous chapters which such *fueros*
as those of Coria and Cáceres devoted to pasturage rights, stock
taxes, and tithes, disputes among stockmen, compensations for crop
damage, and similar topics; and it appears also in the many pastoral
references of the charters of the military orders and the Guadiana
towns.[18]

These sources also throw considerable light upon three central
questions in the rise of frontier ranching in La Mancha and Extremadura: the social status of the stockmen themselves; the grazing
system upon which the industry was based; and the evolution of
new regulatory institutions. Aside from a small number of seigneurial
ranchers, of whom we know next to nothing, the frontier stockmen
of the Guadiana Basin were either the orders with their great flocks
and herds, or the many small and middle-sized ranchers living in
the towns. Early in their history, as their records prove, the orders
became heavily engaged in stock raising; as usual, figures are hard
come by, but the Templar-Alcántara quarrel in 1243 over 42,000
sheep in the vicinity of the Tajo Valley town of Ronda, is suggestive.[19] Thirteenth-century Calatrava diplomas show that great
Manchegan order protecting its brand against use by others, and
driving its animals eastward into the pastures of Uclés and northwards into the Sierras of Guadarrama and Malagón, where they
aroused the opposition of Segovia and Avila.[20] Ferdinand III's
generous grants to the Templars of wide pasturelands around Almorchón, Alcocer, and Capilla, in the heart of the most prized
grazing ranges; Sancho IV's extension to Uclés of free pasturage
rights throughout the realm; and the appointment of special pastoral
administrators, *frayles veedores* and *comendadores de las vacas,* by
Calatrava, Uclés, and San Marcos, all bear witness to the basic importance of pastoral enterprise in the economic activity of these
corporations.[21]

On the other hand, there were numerous small and middle-sized

56

ranchers, the townsmen, both *caballeros villanos* and ordinary free-men. In the Guadiana region even more than above the Tajo, it is patent that the majority of such townsmen were in no significant sense landed proprietors; although they possessed small holdings in or near the town, their real wealth was not in land but in livestock, and in the cherished right of access to the grazing grounds not only of the town, but very commonly also of either the military orders or of the crown. Such stipulations as those of the Fuero de Cáceres requiring stockmen to combine their separate herds of animals into *cabañas* of 400 cattle, 200 mares, or 2,000 sheep, and the royal pro-visions on exemption of herdsmen from military service, which con-template ranchers owning fewer than 40 cows or 100 sheep, or between 40 and 100 cows and 100 and 1,000 sheep, prove that the small-ranching class, which is also typical of northern *meseta* ranching, was strongly established throughout La Mancha and Extremadura.[22]

In the more northern centers of Castilian ranching, on both sides of the Duero, the grazing of livestock was normally carried on through seasonal rotation of pastures within the confines of the mu-nicipal bounds; lowland pastures near the town served in the winter, while the summer months saw the stock driven into the upland grazing grounds of the nearest sierra. Such a pasturage system, which is really more sedentary than truly transhumant, required a minimum of special institutions. *Pastores* and *vaqueros* at the duly specified times drove the stock to or from the pastures and kept it under constant herding; *montaneros* might be named to patrol the municipal *montes* or pastures against entry of outsiders; and the regular alcaldes or other town officials, on the basis of provisions in the *fuero* or unwritten custom, handled all questions of stray ani-mals, pasturage rights, and stock damage to vineyard or arable, the wages and misdeeds of herdsmen, the settlement of disputes, and the imposition of penalties.

When the frontier moved southward, from the reign of Alfonso VI on, municipal grazing and pastoral regulation under the control of the alcaldes remained the general rule in the new *concejos* of the Duero-Tajo region. But certain important changes soon appear. These were due chiefly to the fact that many of these towns, par-ticularly those near the Central Sierras, like Avila, Segovia, Madrid, and Escalona, came to possess much larger municipal territories than were common hitherto. These often stretched far up into the

Guadarramas and Sierra de Gredos, where were the highly desirable *agostaderos,* or summer pastures. At the same time, other towns on the edge of the plains, among them Cuenca, Toledo, and Talavera, began to winter their livestock southwards in the Guadiana Valley. Thus, for the first time, absence from the town during several months on the part of herdsmen driving sheep and cattle in far parts of a town's own territory or, on the southern plains, completely outside it, became a frequent occurrence; and this in turn naturally raised new problems of protecting the livestock and the herders, and of municipal control over the latter.

One consequence of this, in the towns of the Central Sierras, and on the margins of the Guadiana plains, was the introduction of an organized escort of armed riders and men on foot, who accompanied the animals during their sojourn in distant feeding grounds, with the function of guarding both them and their herders. The oldest and fullest description of such a pastoral military escort survives in the Fuero de Cuenca, a frontier town only a dozen years old in 1189–1190, which, although located up in the Serranía de Cuenca, stood on the very edge of La Mancha Alta. According to the Fuero, each year at the beginning of December the sheep and cattle of the Cuencan ranchers were placed under the formal guard of what is called the *esculca,* which was clearly a company of armed, mounted men who were provided by the stockowners on the basis of one *caballero* for each herd of cattle or for every three flocks of sheep they owned. Accompanied by these *esculqueros,* who elected *alcaldes de la esculca* as their officers, and by the *pastores* and *vaqueros,* the sheep and cattle were driven southward onto the plains of La Mancha, very likely as far down as Villora, Tabarrosas, and Iniesta, points mentioned elsewhere in the Fuero as limits within which Cuencan livestock might be found. Here four and a half months were spent in winter grazing. By mid-March the whole outfit returned to the environs of Cuenca, where the *esculca* disbanded and the *concejo,* between that time and St. John's Day (June 24), supervised what must have been the spring branding of calves and lambs, and the cutting out of animals for sale or slaughter. On St. John's Day the herds were driven north into the summer pastures high in the Serranía; this time, however, they were escorted only by sixty herdsmen on foot, supplied by seven of Cuenca's villages, who were commanded by the *alcaide* of Cuenca. By the first of November, when the *alcaide's* term of office expired, the herds

58

were once again trailed back to Cuenca, presumably for some sort of fall roundup and in readiness to be entrusted at the start of December to the protection of the *esculca*.[23]

This Cuencan innovation of an armed guard for herds and *pastores* on the plains was certainly in use among plains towns that adopted the Fuero de Cuenca; these would include not only *concejos de realengo*, such as Alarcón, Alcaraz, and Plasencia, but also many settlements of the military orders which used it either in its original form or in the adaptations of the Fueros of Consuegra and Montiel. Furthermore, the existence of an armed pastoral escort, this time under the name of *rafala*, can be discovered in a number of ranching towns well to the west of Cuenca. The *rafala* first turns up, so far as we now know, in the pasturage agreements made ca. 1200 among the *concejos* of Plasencia, Escalona, and Avila; and in the Fueros of Coria and Cáceres a few years later.[24] The latter codes give us some data regarding the terms of service of the mounted *rafaleros*, and certain regulations governing them during the months when the *rafala* was away from the town on duty. So, too, the Fuero de Salamanca refers to a *rafala* guarding the municipal herds of swine when they were driven across the sierra, doubtless the Sierra de Peña de Francia.[25]

The *rafala-esculca*, however, was not the only new institution developed by Castilian municipal pastoralism to meet the frontier conditions of long-range grazing. Historically more important is the concomitant evolution of a system by which the herdsmen and their armed guards could be governed during their now prolonged seasonal absence from their homes. In his able book on the Mesta, Julius Klein assumes that from a very early date medieval Iberian towns possessed a kind of local stockmen's association called the *otero* or *mesta*, which met two or three times a year to restore stray animals to their owners, regulate the hiring of shepherds and cowboys, and punish violations of pastoral law. These meetings, which he sees continuing throughout the Middle Ages, Klein distinguishes carefully from what he regards as their institutional offshoot, the celebrated Real Mesta, or national association of Castilian stockmen which Alfonso X founded in the thirteenth century.[26] But the existence before the middle of the twelfth century of such local pastoral organizations is highly dubious, and indeed contradicts the many *fuero* references we have to the regulation of all aspects of stock raising, including specifically the restoration of strays to their owners, by the regular town officials, normally the alcaldes. Why are not such assemblies ever mentioned in the Leonese-Castilian *fueros* of the tenth to thirteenth centuries, such as those of Soria, Molina de Aragón, Guadalajara, Alcalá de Henares, Zamora, Salamanca, Alba de Tormes, Ledesma, and other pastoral centers? To assume that *otero* and *mixta* or *mesta*, place names common in northern Spain, designate the customary meeting places of these hypothetical assemblies would be unwarranted.[27] The truth is rather that so long as municipal stock raising operated within the more or less narrow territories of northern Castilian and Leonese towns, the ability of local officials to handle pastoral matters was adequate; but, as with the *rafala-esculca*, it was the growing practice of transhumant grazing and its southward extension that produced changes from the traditional pattern.

The earliest sure instance of this innovation appears in the Fuero de Cuenca, which shows that before starting south in early December the *caballeros* forming the *esculca* chose special alcaldes, and that these *alcaldes de la esculca* exercised not merely military but judicial and general governmental authority over herdsmen and *esculqueros*, serving in fact as substitutes for the ordinary alcaldes to enforce the pastoral and other provisions of the Fuero. This authority, furthermore, was final, decisions of these special alcaldes not being open to appeal or rehearing when, on returning home in mid-March, they surrendered their authority to the *concejo*. The arrangement was quite different from the one Cuenca followed for the summer interval, when in the upland grazing grounds the sixty village herders were subject to the authority of the *alcaide*. The principle, in the case of the *esculca* and the winter herdsmen (who were men of Cuenca, not villagers) is the same as that which other sections of the Fuero show governed the organization of the town army, and even of the town hunt club (*recloba*). That is to say: a collective group of townsmen, absent from municipal territory on official business, remained subject to the rights and obligations of the Fuero, and continued to be governed by it under what were in effect itinerant alcaldes.[28]

Whether, or how often, the whole company of guards and herdsmen assembled for special meetings at which the *alcaldes de esculca* gave judicial decisions and distributed strays, we are not told; but in the Fuero de Cáceres, which unlike that of Coria mentions both *rafala* and *otero*, some additional light is thrown on what must have

60

been a growing practice where long-distance grazing was involved. The Cáceres *fuero* in several chapters speaks of the compulsory assembly of *rafala* guards and herdsmen, apparently three times a year, for the holding of an *otero,* at which judicial matters were settled.[29] So too the Fuero de Salamanca's chapter on the *rafala* that guarded the driving of pigs across the sierra mentions the *otero,* only in this case the *otero* meets daily, doubtless out of the need for frequent re-deployment of lithe but distinguishable porkers.[30] Presumably, Mérida, Usagre, and other towns using the Cáceres *fuero* followed the same pattern, so that at least here in Extremadura, if not in La Mancha, the existence of municipal pastoral assemblies in the thirteenth century seems certain.

In none of these texts, it may be noted, is the term *mesta* applied to meetings of herdsmen and guards; indeed, the use of the word in the Fuero de Cáceres to mean a stray animal shows that at least in northern Extremadura the terms were by no means synonymous.[31] What would appear to be the oldest documentary occurrence of *mesta* in the sense of an *otero*-like pastoral assembly is to be found in two diplomas of Alfonso X, issued at Seville on the same day in 1266; in these the king authorizes the holding of *mestas* at Seville and at Alcaraz in deep southern La Mancha.[32] The Seville charter, which thus sets up the later famous municipal *mesta* of Seville, has not yet been published, but was probably of the same tenor as the Alcaraz text, which has been. In the latter document the king orders that compulsory *mestas* of the sheepmen and cowmen of Alcaraz be held (literally 'made') three times a year at the forks of the Guadalmena River; and lays down a number of brief rules regarding the handling of strays, brawling among the herdsmen, and similar topics. Pretty clearly, this is what in Extremadura would have been called an *otero;* on the other hand, no less clearly, it hardly reflects the necessity of having regulations for stockmen who are encamped on ranges some distance away from their regular municipal government, since the Guadalmena forks are not far from Alcaraz. Whether the background for this was Andalusian is uncertain; Alcaraz possessed the Fuero de Cuenca, and the king advises the Alcaraz stockmen to consult Cuenca or Alarcón if problems arise, which suggests that before 1266 such *mestas* were to be found at those two places. The prime mystery here is why the king intervened to establish a *mesta*—which, unlike *otero,* seems to be the royal term for a pastoral organization—at Alcaraz; whereas, so far as we know, he did not do so in the case of the *oteros* already cited. The matter is not without wider implications. First, because from this type of royal-founded municipal *mesta* is descended a series of others in later medieval and early modern Spain, which are the prototypes of those eventually founded in a very few towns of the Indies, principally Santo Domingo and Mexico City.[33] Elsewhere in the New World pastoral matters were handled, according to the older tradition, by the town governments, or *cabildos*. Secondly, the Alcaraz and Seville *mestas* are somehow linked with the earliest evolution of the great Real Mesta of Alfonso X. If we hypothesize that these *privilegios* represent royal assent to local *mestas* and, in effect, exempt these from inclusion in the Real Mesta, then we may assume that the latter was already in existence before 1273, the usually assigned date of foundation, as is also indicated from other quarters.

The solution to this question, if it can be found, is involved in an even larger problem of the Castilian ranching frontier in La Mancha and Extremadura, that of the origins of the Real Concejo de la Mesta itself. In its main lines, the history of the Real Mesta has been admirably surveyed in Julius Klein's standard work on the subject, which, although published in 1920, stands up remarkably well after many years. Yet Klein's treatment of the Mesta's beginnings leaves something to be desired, especially when one attempts to determine to what extent the Mesta was really the product of the Guadiana Basin frontier.

The origins of the Mesta are more obscure than commonly supposed. What is often called Alfonso X's foundation charter is in fact four separate documents, dated in 1273 but claiming to replace older ones worn out by hard usage.[34] These texts do not set up an organization; they assume its existence and grant it royal protection and certain grazing and other privileges. Thus the Mesta must have existed before 1273, and its beginnings can be postulated not so much in the wide period 1212–1273, as Klein suggests, but more narrowly in the interval between the conquest of the Extremaduran pasturelands and a date as much before 1273 as it might have taken to wear out the original parchments. If we set 1230–1263 as approximate limits, we shall not be far wrong.

Now within this period the most important development leading towards the creation of the Mesta was certainly the initiation by northern stockmen in Galicia, Asturias, León, and Old Castile, of

62

the great autumnal transhumant drives of sheep and cattle into Extremadura and La Mancha. Klein's assumption that these drives had been going on for centuries before the conquest of the plains on the basis of agreement with the Moors seems completely without foundation; his chief proof-text, a Cuencan charter of 1200, actually deals with the driving of stock south for sale in Moorish markets, a very different thing.[35] The *Chronicle of Alfonso VII* and other sources, which depict the incessant warfare of the plains and the no less incessant cattle and sheep lifting by both sides, emphatically contradict this view.[36]

To ignore the novelty of the northern entry into the Guadiana ranges is to misunderstand what happened. That this entry began immediately on the morrow of the Reconquest is manifest. Ferdinand III's charter of 1237, authorizing the Templar towns to collect grazing fees (*montazgos*) on the transhumants, follows by only one year his grant to the Templars of Almorchón, their earliest big southern Extremaduran acquisition. This document, along with Alfonso X's establishment in 1253 of Alcántaran and Templar toll-collecting stations at Capilla, Alcocer, Benquerencia, and an unidentifiable "Burgo" in the same region, and his 1255 *privilegio* to Logroño exempting that town's livestock from tolls except at Toledo, Murcia, and Seville, show a rapid development of transhumant drives along fairly fixed routes, the historic *cañadas*.[37] It must be remembered that these drives southward involved large numbers of animals; the *montazgo* payments were calculated on the basis of flocks of sheep numbering between 500 and 5,000, and cattle herds of 50 to 500. In accordance with the century-old custom, small urban ranchers would bunch their individual holdings into a municipal herd, so that the *cañadas* must have presented the colorful spectacle twice a year of one municipal herd after another, trailing along, under the command of its alcaldes and surrounded by its herdsmen and guards. Under these circumstances, mix-ups of strays between different town outfits and disputes among townsmen appealing to different *fueros* must have multiplied, and stressed the need for new regulatory machinery on a supra-municipal level.

But the handling of interurban strays and disputes was not the only or most serious problem confronting transhumant stockmen in their southern drives. Even more pressing was assurance of grazing rights, and defense against attack by Guadiana Basin stockmen who could hardly be expected to welcome these annual encroachments

The Castilian as Plainsman   63

on their grass and water. Current views, largely shared by Klein, that it was farmers in general, or townsmen everywhere defending their liberties, who opposed transhumant pastoralism, and that Alfonso's Real Mesta was a nationwide association of stock raisers set up in reaction, are particularly distorting.[38] The plain fact is that the violent antagonism to the transhumants was largely Extremaduran and Manchegan. It was the military orders, and the towns of the Guadiana Basin—not those of trans-Tajo Castile, which were mostly members of the Mesta—which became the bitterest enemies of the northern stockmen and, after its formation, of the Real Mesta. This hostility, as the earliest Mesta charters make plain, found outlet in various forms, violent and nonviolent: in excessive impositions on the transhumants of *montazgos, portazgos,* and restrictions designed to impede passage or pasturage of the livestock; in seizures of animals, including breeding rams and the indispensable bell-wethers, and the killing or dispersal of whole flocks and herds; in armed attacks upon the herdsmen, resulting in injuries and deaths; and in the deliberate closing of *cañadas* by converting sections of them into enclosed pastures across which transit was forbidden. The struggle was basically one between two competing groups of cowmen and sheepmen, northern and southern, each fighting for possession of the winter grass in the choice pasturelands of the southern plains. It was a conflict in which the northerners, far from home and faced with determined opposition, welcomed royal intervention.

By just what steps, and in what chronological order, events led to royal recognition of the Mesta, it is at present impossible to determine. The more eastern towns, trailing through Cuenca into the grasslands of La Mancha, Murcia, and Andalusia, became united at some time in the second half of the thirteenth century in what was called the *concejo de la mesta de la cañada de Cuenca,* which held meetings attended by representatives from the towns using this *cañada.*[39] But did the towns or the king take the initiative in establishing it? We cannot now say, anymore than we can in the parallel case of Extremadura, the region primarily the subject of Alfonso X's pre-1273 charters. Several trunk *cañadas* terminated in Extremadura; whether, as in La Mancha, single *mestas* first developed for each route, is uncertain. The king was to name royal itinerant justices (*entregadores*) for each *cañada,* but whether this action preceded or followed a union of northern stockmen wintering in Extremadura is at present unanswerable. All we can be sure of is that out of the

64

autumnal influx into Extremadura there emerged, probably between 1260 and 1265, the Real Concejo de la Mesta. And in this sense, the Mesta can be recognized as the product of the ranching frontier of the Guadiana Basin.

It lies beyond the bounds of this paper to estimate the full significance of the Guadiana Basin frontier, but certain broad consequences may be briefly suggested. For Iberian frontier history the Guadiana chapter presents unique features of considerable interest: the successful Castilian adaptation to semi-arid plains conditions unsuited to normal medieval agrarian and urban institutions; the development more than anywhere else in the Peninsula of an intensely pastoral society of small towns and small stockmen ranching great numbers of sheep and cattle on the open ranges; the supremacy—military, governmental, and religious—of the military orders at the expense of town, crown, and church; the transhumant invasions that produced the fateful establishment of the Mesta. In some measure the predominance of pastoralism, and of the Mesta, in sixteenth- and seventeenth-century Spanish economic life may be traced to the very success of the Guadiana Valley frontier; when, in the eighteenth century Jovellanos attacked pastoralism and the Mesta as responsible for most of the ills of Spanish society, he represented the reaction to the undue degree to which for so long the world of the plains, and notably that of La Mancha and Extremadura, had dominated the economic life of the nation.[40] For America also the Guadiana frontier has its implications, and not only in the conquistadores, Pizarro, Valdivia, and thousands of others, whom the region early sent to the Indies and who there created New Extremaduras in Mexico and Chile.[41] We are often told how in the New World the Spaniard succeeded only where he could conquer and exploit Indian agrarian societies, and critics lament his supposed failure to fill American plains regions from Texas to Argentina with farms and bustling urban communities. But it should be remembered that the development of a plains country through ranching was a Castilian frontier experience, as rule over great subject masses was not; that pastoralism has its own legitimate claims to respect in the early civilization of many regions and the permanent economy of some; and that where, from the sixteenth century on, the New World frontier of the Americas has fostered the rise of pastoral societies, they have been—with all their own many original con-

The Castilian as Plainsman   65

tributions—deeply indebted to the way of life and institutional patterns of an Iberian plains background in which the Guadiana Basin was a central and integral element.

NOTES

Research grants from the Institute for Research in the Social Sciences and from the Research Committee, both of the University of Virginia, materially aided the preparation of this paper and are gratefully acknowledged.

1. C. Sánchez-Albornoz, *España, un enigma histórico* (2 vols. Buenos Aires, 1956), II, Chap. xii; José María Lacarra, ed., *La reconquista española y la repoblación del país*, Escuela de Estudios Medievales, Estudios XV (Zaragoza, 1951); J. González, "Repoblación de la 'Extremadura' leonesa," *Hispania*, III (1943), 195–273; J. González, *Repartimiento de Sevilla*, Escuela de Estudios Medievales, Textos XV–XVI (Madrid, 1951); and cf., despite its errors, Jean Gautier, "Le repeuplement de l'Espagne au moyen âge (régions du nord, du centre et du sud)," *Revue de Géographie Humaine et d'Ethnologie*, I (1948–1949), No. 2, pp. 91–94.

2. For the evolution, bibliography, and foreign applications of American frontier methodology, see, most recently, Gene M. Gressley, "The Turner Thesis—a Problem in Historiography," *Agricultural History*, XXXII (1958), 227–249.

3. W. P. Webb, *The Great Plains* (Boston, 1931).

4. For the geography of the Guadiana Valley see especially Juan Dantín Cereceda, *Regiones naturales de España* (2nd ed., Madrid, 1942), I, 11–84; G[onzalo] de R[eparaz] R[odríguez], Vol. I of José Gavira, ed., *España, la tierra, el hombre, el arte* (Barcelona, 1943), pp. 300-304, 340–342, 344 ff., 451–452, 469 ff.; Hermann Lautensach, "Spanien und Portugal," in Fritz Klute, ed., *Handbuch der geographischen Wissenschaft*, IX (Potsdam, 1936), 426–557; and the virtually inaccessible E. W. Gilbert, R. P. Beckinsale, and S. da Sá, *Spain and Portugal*, British Admiralty, Naval Intelligence Division, Geographical Handbook Series (4 vols. Oxford, 1941–1944), Vols. I and III. On La Mancha there is the excellent study by Otto Jessen, "La Mancha: Ein Beitrag zur Landeskunde Neukastiliens," *Mitteilungen der geographischen Gesellschaft in Hamburg*, XLI (1930), 123–227; also published as "La Mancha: Contribución al estudio geográfico de Castilla la Nueva," *Estudios Geográficos*, VII (1946), 269–312, 479–524. Unfortunately, there is no comparable geographic survey of Extremadura.

5. See his *La decadencia española* (4 vols. Madrid, 1950–1951), IV, Chaps. 24–25; and "El paisaje manchego en tiempos de Cervantes," *Anales Cervantinos*, III (1953), 215–279.

6. On the military history of the Guadiana Basin in the twelfth and thirteenth centuries, see Luis G. de Valdeavellano, *Historia de España*, (2nd ed., Madrid, 1955), I, Part 2, Chaps. xvi–xxi; A. de Ballesteros, *Historia de España* (2nd ed., Barcelona, 1943–1956), II, 307–407; III, Part I, pp. 1–13; Julio González,

66

Regesta de Fernando II (Madrid, 1943); González, *Alfonso IX* (2 vols., Madrid, 1944).

7. No good study of the organization and tactics of the medieval Castilian army has yet appeared, but certain aspects are well treated, largely from the juridical standpoint, in A. Palomeque, "Contribución al estudio del ejército en los estados de la reconquista," *Anuario de Historia del Derecho Español*, XV (1944), 205–251; cf. also Jaime Oliver Asín, *Origen árabe de rebato, arrobda y sus homónimos* (Madrid, 1928) and Ferdinand Lot, *L'art militaire et les armées au moyen âge* (2 vols., Paris, 1946), II, 260–297.

8. Rafael de Ureña y Smenjaud, ed., *Fuero de Cuenca* (Madrid, 1935), Chaps. XXX–XXXI.

9. Of the early history of the military orders in Castile only that of the Hospitalers has yet been carefully scrutinized: Santos A. Garcia Larragueta, *El Gran Priorado de Navarra de la Orden de San Juan de Jerusalén* (2 vols., Pamplona, 1957) I, 35–61; García Larragueta, "La Orden de San Juan en la crisis del imperio hispánico del siglo XII," *Hispania*, XII (1952), 483–524. For the native Castilian orders I have depended chiefly upon I. J. Ortega y Cotes, *et al.*, *Bullarium ordinis militiae de Calatrava* (Madrid, 1761); Francisco Uhagón y Guardamino, "Indice de los documentos de la Orden Militar de Calatrava existentes en el Archivo Histórico Nacional," *Boletín de la R. Academia de la Historia*, XXXV (1899), 5–167; A. F. Aguado de Córdova, *et al.*, *Bullarium equestris ordinis s. Iacobi de Spatha* (Madrid, 1719); Consuelo Gutiérrez del Arroyo de Vázquez de Parga, *Privilegios reales de la Orden de Santiago en la edad media* (Madrid, 1946); I. J. Ortega y Cotes, *et al.*, *Bullarium ordinis militiae de Alcántara* (Madrid, 1759).

10. For colonization by both crown and military orders in southern New Castile and Extremadura, the basic guides are the *Colección de fueros y cartas-pueblas de España, Catálogo*, edited by Tomás Muñoz y Romero for the R. Academia de la Historia (Madrid, 1852), and the *Bullaria* of the orders cited in n. 9 above.

11. Illustrations in FMonreal [Fuero de Monreal], granted in 1207 by Uclés (Luis Salazar y Castro, *Historia genealógica de la Casa de Lara* [4 vols., Madrid, 1636], IV, 678 [bis]); FMiguelturra, 1230, Calatrava (Eduardo de Hinojosa, *Documentos para la historia de las instituciones de León y de Castilla* [Madrid, 1919], pp. 148–150); FMérida, 1235, San Marcos de León and Archbishop Bernard of Compostela (*Bullarium s. Iacobi*, p. 106); FMadridejos, 1238, San Juan (Hinojosa, pp. 151–152); FSalvaleón, 1253, Alcántara (Hinojosa, pp. 158–160; *Bullarium de Alcántara*, p. 68); FVillasbuenas, 1256, Alcántara (*Bullarium de Alcántara*, p. 91).

12. Latin Fuero of Cáceres, 1229: Gónzalez, *Alfonso IX*, II, 691–692.

13. Claudio Sánchez-Albornoz, "Las behetrías," *Anuario de Historia del Derecho Español*, I (1924), 196–205; Sánchez-Albornoz, "El precio de la vida en el reino astur-leonés hace mil años," *Logos: Revista de la Facultad de Filosofía y Letras*, Universidad de Buenos Aires, III (1944), 244–249; Sánchez-Albornoz, *España, un enigma histórico*, II, 7–55; Sánchez-Albornoz, "La frontera y las libertades de los castellanos," in these *Proceedings*.

14. Hinojosa, pp. 151–152; Antonio C. Floriano, "Cáceres ante la historia:

The Castilian as Plainsman 67

El problema medieval de la propiedad de tierra," *Revista de Estudios Extremeños.* V (1949), 3–29, especially pp. 7–10; Esteban Rodríguez Amaya, "La tierra en Badajoz desde 1230 a 1500," *op. cit.,* VII (1951), 395–497.

15. Cf., for example, FCuenca, II, 2; the *reales privilegios* of Alfonso X to the Concejo of Badajoz (A. Tomás González, *Colección de cédulas, cartas-patentes, provisiones, reales órdenes y otros documentos* [6 vols. Madrid, 1829–1833], VI, 112, 116); and the *fueros* of Mérida, Madridejos, Salvaleón and Villasbuenas, cited above, n. 11.

16. FMiguelturra, c. 6 (Hinojosa, p. 150).

17. For what follows, and for bibliography on medieval Castilian ranching of sheep and cattle, see Julius Klein, *The Mesta* (Cambridge, Massachusetts, 1920; Spanish translation, Madrid, 1936); C. J. Bishko, "The Peninsular Background of Latin American Cattle Ranching," *Hispanic American Historical Review,* XXXII (1952), 491–515.

18. *El Fuero de Coria,* ed. José Maldonado y Fernández del Torco (n.p., 1949), *passim; Fueros y privilegios de Cáceres,* ed. Pedro Ulloa y Golfín (n. p., ca. 1657 ?); Antonio C. Floriano, *Documentación histórica del Archivo Municipal de Cáceres* (Cáceres, 1934); Esteban Rodríguez Amaya, "Inventario general de los Archivos de la S. I. Catedral y Ciudad de Badajoz, formado por D. Ascensio Morales en 1753–1754," *Rev. Estud. Extrem.,* VIII (1952), 389–492; *Fuero de Usagre,* ed. Rafael de Ureña y Smenjaud and Adolfo Bonilla y San Martín (Madrid, 1907), títulos 432 ff.; Miguel A. Ortí y Belmonte, "Las conquistas de Cáceres por Fernando II y Alfonso IX de León y su fuero latino anotado," *Rev. Estud. Extrem.,* III (1947).

19. *Bull. de Alcántara,* pp. 51–53.

20. Uhagón, *Indice de documentos de Calatrava,* p. 22, No. 104 (1255); *Bull. de Calatrava,* pp. 683–686 (1221); Antonio Benavides, *Memorias de D. Fernando IV de Castilla* (2 vols., Madrid, 1860), II, 813–815, Nos. dlii–dliii (*reales* of 1311 but referring to reigns of Alfonso X and Sancho IV).

21. *Bull. de Alcántara,* pp. 73–75 (1236, in *inspeximus* of Alfonso X, 1255); A. López Ferreiro, *Fueros municipales de Santiago y de su tierra* (2 vols., Santiago, 1895), I, 365; Gutiérrez del Arroyo, *Privilegios de Santiago,* No. 495 (1282); *Bull. de Calatrava,* p. 685 (1221), pp. 150–151 (1293); Benavides, *Fernando IV,* II, 728, Col. 2 (1310).

22. FUsagre (= FCáceres), títulos 456, 464; *Memorial Histórico Español,* I (1851), 178, 225; Hinojosa, *Documentos,* p. 169; Benavides, II, 292, Col. 1.

23. FCuenca, cc. XXXIX, 1–3; XXXI, 16.

24. Texts published by Luis Suárez Fernández, "Evolución histórica de las hermandades castellanas," *Cuadernos de Historia de España,* XVI (1951), 47, 49; FCoria, título 163; FUsagre (= FCáceres) títs. 167, 443–466, 479, 482, 498–505.

25. FSalamanca, tít. 196, in Américo Castro and Federico de Onís, *Fueros Leoneses* (Madrid, 1916), p. 148.

26. Klein, *The Mesta,* pp. 9–13.

27. Pending a careful philological examination of Iberian pastoral nomenclature in its historical as well as etymological aspects, it seems unwise to attempt as yet any inferences based upon philological evidence alone. Juan

68

Corominas, *Diccionario crítico etimológico de la lengua castellana* (4 vols., Berne, 1954) regards *esculca* as of Germanic origin (II, 369); *rafala* as probably Arabic (III, 1069–1071, s.v. "rehala"); and *otero* (I, 173 s.v. "alto") and *mesta* (III, 358–359) as from the Latin. But his retention of Klein's mistake (*The Mesta*, p. 12, n. 3; p. 74) about the *rafala* at Cáceres as being concerned primarily with horse trading, his almost certainly erroneous derivation of *mesta* in its pastoral sense from Latin, *mixta*, and his surprising failure to discuss the well-known equation of *mesta* with Berber *mechta*, a winter encampment of nomadic shepherds (Klein, p. 10), all sufficiently underline the need for a study of Spanish pastoral vocabulary on the scientific level of, e.g., Y. Malkiel, "Estudios de léxico pastoril: 'piara' y 'manada'," *Bulletin Hispanique*, LIII (1951), 41–80.

28. FCuenca, XXXIX, 1–3; XXX, 1, ff.; XXXIX, 4.

29. FUsagre (= FCáceres), títs. 448, 451, 467; note the reference in tít. 448 to the "dia de la descamia" on which the "caualleros de rafala" are required to attend the *otero*.

30. FSalamanca, tít. 196.

31. FUsagre (= FCáceres), tít. 463.

32. González, *Repartimiento de Sevilla*, II, 347; González, *Colección de cédulas*, VI, 142–145.

33. Klein, *The Mesta*, pp. 8–9; José Miranda, "Notas sobre la introducción de la Mesta en la Nueva España," *Revista de Historia de América*, No. 17 (June 1944), pp. 1–26.

34. The texts have been published by Klein, "Los privilegios de la Mesta de 1273 y 1276," *Bol. R. Acad. Hist.*, LXIV (1914), 202–219.

35. *The Mesta*, pp. 166–170.

36. See, for example, *Chronica Adefonsi imperatoris*, ed. Luis Sánchez Belda (Madrid, 1950), cc. 36, 39, 88, 122, 131, 187; E. Lévi-Provençal, "Un recueil de lettres officielles almohades," *Hespéris*, XXVIII (1941), 52–53.

37. Klein's description and map of the *cañadas* (*The Mesta*, pp. 18–20) have been corrected in various respects by the much more detailed studies of the geographer Juan Dantín Cereceda, "Las cañadas ganaderas del Reino de León," *Boletín de la R. Sociedad Geográfica*, LXXVI (1936), 464–499; "Cañadas ganaderas españolas," *Congresso do mundo português, Publicações* (Lisbon, 1940), XVIII, 682–696; "La cañada ganadera de La Vizana," *Bol. R. Soc. Geog.*, LXXVIII (1942), 322–335. See Robert Aitken, "Routes of Transhumance on the Spanish Meseta," *The Geographical Journal*, CVI (1945), 59–69. It should however be noted that both Klein and Dantín Cereceda draw chiefly upon nineteenth-century accounts of the cañada system as then still surviving rather than upon the medieval documentation for the original network of the thirteenth and fourteenth centuries.

38. Klein, pp. 75 ff., 301 ff., 351–352; in certain passages, e.g., p. 98, where he seems to recognize that the conflict centered in the Guadiana Valley, Klein fails to reckon with the predominantly pastoral character of the Mesta's southern opposition.

39. Benavides, *Fernando IV*, II, 222–224.

40. Gaspar Melchor de Jovellanos, *Informe de la Sociedad Económica de*

The Castilian as Plainsman   69

Madrid . . . en el Expediente de Ley Agraria [1795] in *Biblioteca de autores españoles,* Vol. L (Madrid, 1898), 80–98.

41. See the suggestive comments on continuities between the medieval Iberian and the Ibero-American frontier by Silvio Zavala, "The Frontiers of Hispanic America," in Walker D. Wyman and Clifton B. Kroeber, eds., *The Frontier in Perspective* (Madison, Wisconsin, 1957), pp. 35–58; and "Las fronteras de hispanoamérica," *Cuadernos Americanos,* XVII (July–Oct., 1958), 374–384.

13

Atlantic Exploration before Columbus: The Evidence of Maps

Felipe Fernández-Armesto

Anyone who has ever seen a late medieval mappamundi or portolan chart will be able to appreciate the sentiments of a Sicilian songster, captured in a mass-setting of the third quarter of the fifteenth century: enchanted by the beauty of the maps, he searched them for a lovelier isle than his own, albeit without success.[1] The finest surviving example of the cartography of the period, the 'Catalan Atlas' of the Bibliothèque Nationale, Paris, generally attributed to Cresques Abraham of Majorca, is as rich and intricate as a spilled jewel casket, resplendent with powerful images of exotic beings and untold wealth.[2] Maps of even greater magnificence, larger and more densely illuminated, are recorded but lost.[3] These were royal gifts, intended for ostentation as well as use, but the more modest and practical portolan charts would be drawn with grace and adorned with illustrations or, at least, with fine calligraphy and a delicate web of rhumb-lines. It was a period in which maps could inspire more than music. It was almost certainly a map – perhaps even the Catalan Atlas itself – that in 1402 induced the Poitevin adventurer, Gadifer de la Salle, to embark on a quest for the mythical 'river of gold' which led to his ruin. In the late fourteenth century, the anonymous author of the *Libro del conoscimiento de todos los reynos* constructed from the legends of maps a fantastic journey of the imagination which reached beyond the limits of the known, even of the accessible world.[4]

In the present century, some historians have been enthralled by these maps, over-estimating their value as evidence; others, more prudent, have been reluctant to succumb to their siren-like allure. The maps give a true picture of their makers' mental images of the world: that is not in question. But whether they can be

[1] *Johannes Cornago, Complete Works: Recent Researches in the Music of the Middle Ages, and Early Renaissance*, ed. R. L. Gerber, XV (Madison, 1984), viii-ix.

[2] The best reproduction is *Mapamundi: the Catalan Atlas of the Year 1375*, ed. G. Grosjean, (Zurich, 1978); where the map is cited hereafter, a reference to sheet III of this edition may be understood. On the problems of authorship, the correct form of the name of Cresques Abraham and general questions concerning the atlas, see *El Atlas Catalán*, (Barcelona, 1975).

[3] R. A. Skelton, 'A Contract of World Maps at Barcelona, 1399-1400', *Imago Mundi*, XXII (1968), 108-09.

[4] P. E. Russell, *El Infante Dom Henrique e as Ilhas Canárias* (Lisbon, 1979), p. 19; *Fontes Rerum Canariarum*, XI, 106; *Libro del conoscimiento de todos los reynos, tierras y señoríos que hay en el mundo*, ed. M. Jiménez de la Espada, (Madrid, 1877).

Atlantic Exploration before Columbus   13

accepted as proof of a growth in real knowledge is a matter on which opinions are sharply divided. In 1969, Professor Charles Verlinden's contribution to the Colloque International d'Histoire Maritime was greeted with something very close to derision because of his ready acceptance of cartographical evidence of a fourteenth-century discovery of the Azores; towards the end of his life, the distinguished Portuguese historian, Armando Cortesão, jeopardised his considerable reputation by his dogged insistence on basing his theory of a pre-Columbian discovery of America on the evidence of maps; and the late Eva Taylor incurred accusations of excessive susceptibility as a result of her championship of the reliability of maps in this connection.[5] Credulous assessments of the value of map evidence, in default and even in defiance of other documents, have had redoubtable defenders; but some of their most zealous partisans have carried their interpretations to such extremes of excessive protestation that the maps have lost all credibility.[6] Today their spokesmen seem to work in isolation from other scholars, advancing theories, ignored elsewhere, in circles of their own.

In partial consequence, for instance, fourteenth-century exploration of the Azores (the particular point of dubious orthodoxy for which I wish to argue in these pages) is dismissed or ignored by textbooks in current use, because of, rather than despite, the cartographic evidence in its favour.[7] Respect for fifteenth-century traditions that the Azores, together with Madeira (to which many of the same arguments apply), were discovered by followers of the Infante Dom Henrique of Portugal has played a part in this. Henrique may have been the first to colonise and exploit these islands, but that does not preclude earlier discovery and exploration; it is possible, without contradiction, to admit both a fourteenth-century exploration, which imparted awareness of the archipelago's existence and a fifteenth-century exploration which determined its exact whereabouts and configuration. The example of Madeira is, in a sense, decisive: as we shall see, all

---

[5] *IXe Colloque International d'Histoire Maritime* (Seville, 1969), pp. 276-9. Verlinden has replied in 'La découverte des archipels de la "Méditerranée Atlantique" (Canaries, Madères, Açores) et la navigation astronomique primitive', *Revista portuguesa de história*, XVI (1978), 105-31; A. Cortesão, 'A Carta Náutica de 1424', *Esparsos* (3 vols, Coimbra, 1975), III, ix-211 [hereafter Cortesão, 'Carta']. I cite this edition because it includes the author's last revisions, but the maps and diagrams can be consulted in a larger and clearer format in *The Nautical Chart of 1424* (Coimbra, 1954); E. G. R. Taylor, 'Imaginary Islands: a Problem Solved', *Geographical Journal*, CXXX (1964), 105-07.
[6] The credulous tradition has its origin in H. Yule Oldham, 'The Importance of Mediaeval Manuscript Maps in the Study of the History of Geographical Discovery', *Report of the VIth International Geographical Congress* (London, 1895), pp. 703-06, and its *reductio ad absurdum* in W. H. Babcock, *Legendary Islands of the Atlantic* (New York, 1922). For recent statements, see, for example, V. H. Cassidy, 'New Worlds and Everyman: Some Thoughts on the Logic and Logistics of pre-Columbian Discovery', *Terrae Incognitae*, X (1978), 7-13, esp. p. 8, and Taylor, loc. cit., p. 105.
[7] G. Winius and B. W. Diffie, *Foundations of the Portuguese Empire* (Minneapolis, 1977), pp. 25, 61; G. V. Scammell, *The World Encompassed* (London, 1981), p. 245; S. E. Morison, *The European Discovery of America; the Northern Voyages* (New York, 1971), p. 95. Cf., however, the use of portolan charts by Mediterranean historians in M. Quaini,'Catalogna e Liguria nella cartografie nautica e nei portolani medievali', *Atti del I Congresso Storico Liguria-Catalogna* (Bordighera, 1974), p. 551.

surviving Atlantic maps datable, without question, to the last quarter of the fourteenth century, show Madeira, Porto Santo and the Desert and Savage Islands with a verisimilitude that defies disbelief. Thus we cannot exclude the possibility of prior knowledge of the Azores, either, merely out of deference to traditions associated with Dom Henrique. In part, too, scruples concerning the evidence of fourteenth-century knowledge of the Azores may have derived from the widespread conviction that navigators were incapable – from timidity or technical insufficiency – of sailing so far out to sea: the Azores are over 700 miles from the nearest land. Yet this may be to underestimate the mariners' proficiency and daring. Equally prejudicial to the cool consideration of the evidence is the repugnance we may feel at unwarrantable inferences made from map evidence in favour of pre-Columbian theories of the discovery of America. The reputation of the maps should not be allowed to suffer, as it were, by contagion, but evaluated on its merits.

The purpose of these pages is to offer a tentative word in vindication of the maps. I hope to suggest that it is possible to reach different conclusions on the problems respectively of a fourteenth-century discovery of the Azores and a pre-Columbian discovery of America and to show the limits of the usefulness of cartographic evidence in determining the extent of Atlantic penetration by Columbus's day. My guiding principles will be that maps must be read with caution; that, without corroboration from other documents it would be rash to accept cartographers' evident growing interest in the Atlantic as proof of growing knowledge; and that the appearance of new lands on maps does not necessarily signify new discoveries. We should remember the warning, uttered by the Infante Dom Pedro of Portugal in 1443, that in the maps of his day unknown regions 'were not drawn except according to the whim of the men who made them'[8]. Though a considerable body of secondary literature is available, offering a variety of readings, I take it for granted that only the maps themselves or the best available facsimiles can yield reliable readings of place-names and legends and the versions I give are my own. Finally, I shall advocate a stricter discipline in the dating of surviving maps than has characterised previous discussion; this, I believe, tends to make the case for fourteenth-century knowledge of the Azores more cogent.

Atlantic exploration before Columbus can usefully be divided into three overlapping phases: first, the breaking out of Mediterranean vessels into Atlantic waters in the late thirteenth and early fourteenth centuries; second, from the early fourteenth to the early fifteenth centuries, the creation of a zone of navigation in previously unexplored waters, bounded by the Azores in the north, the Canaries in the south and the Iberian and African coasts in the east, and linked by the Atlantic wind-system; finally, a period of increased interest in and speculation about the remoter Atlantic, which stimulated further exploration and yielded new discoveries, but which cannot be shown to have led navigators to the New World before 1492. My concern is with the second of these phases, because its effect was

---

[8] 'nem direitamente nas cartas de marear nem mapamundo non estavam debuxadas senão a prazer dos homens que as faziam'. J. Martins da Silva Marques, *Descobrimentos portugueses*, 3 vols, (Lisbon, 1944-71), I. 435; *Monumenta henricina*, 15 vols, (Lisbon, 1960-74) VIII, 107.

broadly to fix the configurations of pre-Columbian knowledge of the Atlantic; but to be understood it must be set briefly in the context of the other two.

In the first phase, some seafarers turned northwards when they reached the Atlantic, like the Zaccaria family of Genoa, who tried to monopolise the English alum market, or the Frescobaldi of Florence, who acquired a sizeable stake in English wool. They made something of an economic breakthrough, but added nothing to geographical knowledge or to the reach of exploration. Others, however, turned south into waters unsailed – as far as we know – for centuries, off the west coast of Africa. Record of only one such voyage has survived: that of the brothers Vivaldi, who from Genoa in 1291 departed *ad partes Indiae per Oceanum*, thus apparently anticipating the task Columbus was to set himself almost exactly two hundred years later. The Vivaldi presumably envisaged a circumnavigation of Africa rather than a transnavigation of the Atlantic, but the galleys they deployed were hardly suited to either purpose, too low and shallow for rough Atlantic waters, too dependent on inshore sailing for the inhospitable African coast. The Vivaldi were never heard of again, but it is likely that there were other journeys in the same direction, albeit with less ambitious aims. It was probably in the course of such expeditions that the Canary Islands were discovered: according to Petrarch, writing in the 1340s, Genoese armed ships had sailed to the Canaries *memoria patrum*. In 1337, he had professed himself almost as well informed about the 'Fortunate Isles' as about Italy or France.[9]

The third phase, beginning in the 1420s, was distinguished by what one might call the discovery of Atlantic 'space': of navigable – and potentially exploitable – stretches of ocean beyond the zone of established navigation. The number of Atlantic charts or of charts which included the Atlantic multiplied. Mapmakers invested costly blank parchment in the depiction of the ocean, which was strewn – to a far greater extent than in the fourteenth century – with imagined or reputed islands. Known archipelagoes were charted with a new precision, and in the second half of the century the islands of Cape Verde and of the Gulf of Guinea were added to them.

It was in the second phase, however, that the other archipelagoes of the eastern Atlantic, including the Azores, were first explored and mapped. This phase can be said to have begun in the 1330s. To summarise: in 1339, some of the Canary Islands, albeit misplaced slightly to north, with three islands, in a position suggestive of those of the Madeira archipelago, appeared for the first time on a surviving map.[10] Thereafter, within the span of a couple of generations, there were so many voyages, accumulating so much knowledge, that an almost complete picture of the islands of the east-central Atlantic became available in Latin Christendom. The transformation of that picture by the time of maps reliably dated to the 1380s, in which, as we shall see, the Canaries are shown almost

[9] *De Vita Solitaria*, ed. A. Altamura (Naples, 1943), II, vi, 3, p. 125; *Le familiari*, ed. V. Rossi, 4 vols. (Florence, 1933), I, 106; R. Caddeo, *Le navigazioni atlantiche di Alvise da Cà da Mosto, Antoniotto Usodimare e Niccoloso da Recco* (Milan, 1928), p. 51.

[10] Y. Kamal, *Monumenta Cartographica Africae et AEgypti*, 5 vols in 16, (Cairo, 1926-51) [hereafter Kamal], IV, fasc. 2, no. 1222; K. Kretschmer, *Die Italianische Portolane* (Berlin, 1909), p. 118.

16   F.F.R. Fernández-Armesto

complete, with the Savage Islands, the Madeira archipelago and most of what I take to be the Azores, was a remarkable achievement: hazardous to the vessels, novel to the technology and unparallelled in the experience of sailors of the time. To understand why and how knowledge of the Atlantic was so thoroughly revolutionised in such a relatively short span, it is necessary to reconstruct the stages of the change in some detail. Because the winds of the Atlantic naturally constitute a system of ducts, which tend to take ships south-west from the pillars of Hercules and at most seasons force a wide northward sweep out to sea upon returning sail traffic, the exploration of the Canaries was necessarily the first stage.

Like patches of twilight in the Sea of Darkness, the Canary Islands in the middle ages lay, never utterly unknown, but long unvisited, except by susceptible imaginations. By the time of their rediscovery at the end of the thirteenth century or early in the fourteenth, knowledge of them transmitted from antiquity was encrusted with fables of St Brendan and St Ursula, Merlin and the Earthly Paradise. Indeed, the exact notions of the archipelago which early explorers took with them on their first forays into the Atlantic are hard to identify among the myths. Of the supposed references to the Canaries in ancient literature, only those of Pliny are convincing. Pliny's circumstantial details – concerning, for instance, the number of islands and their climatic heterogeneity – seem to correspond to the geographical realities of the Canaries. His 'Nivaria' evokes Tenerife, with its snow-capped peak, and his 'Pluvialia' may well refer to one of the relatively rainy westerly isles. His description, repeated by Solinus and Isidore (those great mediators of classical learning in late antiquity) was identified with the Canaries in the era of rediscovery: his collective name, 'The Fortunate Islands', was appropriated by mapmakers. The rest of his nomenclature was borrowed in humanist circles. The terms 'Canary Isles' or 'Isles of Canary', current from the 1340s, also seem indebted to Pliny's name, 'Canaria', for one island.[11]

Although some historians have 'detected' real places and events in the undergrowth of any myth or legend, no other demonstrable references to the Canaries were inherited from ancient writers. Mentions of remote islands by Plutarch and Horace are too vague to inspire reliance and might refer to any or all of the great mass of islands known or thought, in antiquity and the middle ages, to lie in the western ocean. The same applies to the western isles, Hesperides and Elysian Fields, which have sometimes been taken as allusions to the Canaries or even the Azores, but which might equally be wholly fabulous, without any basis in actual islands. Yet all this material helped, in the period of rediscovery, to shroud Pliny's relatively precise information in mystery, which was deepened by confusion with other island myths of late antique (Brendan and Ursula) or (in the case of the Merlin legend) even earlier origins.[12] It is hard to say whether the enchantment

---

[11] *Naturalis Historia*, VI, 37; J. Alvarez Delgado, 'Las Islas Canarias en Plinio', *Revista de historia* (La Laguna), XI (1945), 26-51.
[12] Plutarch, *Vita Sertorii*, VII, IX; Horace, *Epod.*, XVI, 42; A. O. Lovejoy and G. Boas, *Primitivism and Related Ideas in Antiquity* (Baltimore, 1935), pp. 280-303; G. Boas, *Essays on Primitivism and Related Ideas in the Middle Ages* (Baltimore, 1948), pp. 168-69; E. Faral, *La légende arthurienne*, 3 vols, (Paris, 1929-34), III, 334; E. Benito Ruano, 'Nuevas singladuras por las Canarias fabulosas', *Homenaje a E. Serra Ràfols* (3 vols, La Laguna, 1970), I, 203-21.

spun into this tissue of fable increased or diminished the lure of the Atlantic for late medieval explorers. If Arab navigators were deterred by the Sea of Darkness, the mariners of Latin Christendom seem to have evinced a more adventurous spirit. While Arab geographers recorded no advances in the field, in western Europe the corrupt traditions gradually changed, in the fourteenth century, in the light of observation and experience.[13]

The chronology of late medieval exploration of the Canaries cannot be reconstructed with any certainty. The first authenticated visit, at an unknown date probably prior to 1339, was attributed in most sources to the Genoese, Lanzarotto (or Lancelotto or Lanzarote) Malocello, who found the island which still bears a version of his name. The dating and authenticity of many of the earliest documents are so debated that the exact circumstances of Malocello's voyage – whether under Genoese or Portuguese auspices, whether of reconnaissance, conquest or trade – are matters for speculation. But his vagabond career (in Ceuta, Portugal and, perhaps, France as well as his native city) and attainment of fame are features of the tradition of explorers and early conquistadores as it was to be established over the next century or so.

It was perhaps diffusion of knowledge of Malocello's achievement by Genoese and Majorcan mapmakers that excited efforts to trade, evangelise, enslave and conquer in the islands, with great intensity in the 1340s and a modest regularity thereafter. Whoever commissioned Malocello's voyage, it is certain that the first expedition of which a detailed account survives (copied, apparently, by Boccaccio and dated 1341) was in part, at least, a Portuguese enterprise.[14] The point is worth emphasising, as it contributes towards a growing picture of Lusitanian maritime activity in the fourteenth century.[15] This expedition, moreover, demonstrates co-operation between Portugal and Italian – specifically, in this case, Genoese and Florentine – experts, which characterises the early history of Portuguese overseas expansion and establishes a *prima facie* case for continuity between the 'medieval' colonial experience of western Mediterranean peoples in their home waters and the 'modern' history of empire-building in the Atlantic. Moreover, although it sailed from a Portuguese port under Italian command, the '1341' expedition included, at a lower level, Castilian personnel and mariners 'from other parts of Spain'. Thus almost at the very outset of the story, a modest Castilian presence can be detected which would eventually grow to preponderance. And it was via Italian merchants in Seville that the surviving account was transmitted to Florence and to Boccaccio's hand. Seville, therefore, appears already in its future role as the data bank – so to speak – the overseer and information exchange, of Atlantic navigation.

---

[13] *La géographie d'Aboulféda*, ed. J. T. Reinaud, 2 vols, (Paris, 1848), II, 263-64; [Al-Idrisi], *Description de l'Afrique et de l'Espagne par Edrisi*, ed. R. Dozy and M. J. de Goeje (Paris, 1866), p. 197; R. Mauny, *Les navigations médiévales sur les côtes sahariennes* (Lisbon, 1960), pp. 81-88.

[14] *Monumenta henricina*, I, 201-06 replaces earlier editions.

[15] C. Verlinden, 'Les génois dans la marine portugaise avant 1385', *Actas do Congresso de Portugal Medievo*, 3 vols (Braga, 1966), III, 388-407.

Because of changes in toponymy, the route of the voyage cannot be re-traced accurately. But it is not hard to recognise the Canaries in the account. Depending on how one reads the text, the expedition can be seen to have visited at least thirteen islands (and perhaps as many as nineteen): if all the islets and great rocks are counted, the Canary archipelago can be said to contain thirteen islands (Lanzarote, Fuerteventura, Gran Canaria, Tenerife, La Palma, Gomera, Hierro, Graciosa, Lobos, Alegranza, Santa Clara or Montaña Clara, Roque del Este, Roquete). The possible references to more islands may be explained as the product of duplication or ambiguity. Six of the isles visited were inhabited: this fits the real situation in the Canaries closely enough, for, at the time, there were seven inhabited islands, and visitors may not have had an opportunity to observe signs of life on all of them. The description of Tenerife – with its numinous combination of high mountains and low clouds, snow and fierce defenders – is unmistakable. While less obviously unequivocal, the descriptions of the other islands fit the real topography of the Canaries. To the author of this account, the Canaries were *insulas nuncupatas Repertas* – or perhaps the punctuation should be made to read, *insulas nuncupatas 'repertas'*. The excitement of new discovery rapidly communicated itself to merchants, like the Florentines of Seville who reported it home; mapmakers like Angelino Dulcert, who (if a later interpolation is not responsible) recorded the discovery of Lanzarote on his map of 1339; and humanists, like Boccaccio, who had a particular interest in the anthropological implications of the news. Over the next few years, would-be missionaries and would-be conquerors formed an equally receptive public.

It was in Majorca that the news from the Canaries had the greatest impact. This is not surprising, although the Majorcans' role as early leaders in the late medieval 'space-race' in the Atlantic is too often forgotten or ignored. Majorca was itself something of a 'colonial society' and 'frontier zone': reconquered from the Moors only a century previously in 1229, it was briefly, from 1276 to 1343, the centre of an independent kingdom which lived by trade and, therefore, from the sea. It was a centre, too, for the technical developments in shipping and cartography which helped to make Atlantic navigation practicable on a large scale. Majorca's mapmakers, the most renowned in Europe, were assiduous gatherers of geographical information, aided by the large Jewish community, from whom many of them were drawn. Exploration of the Canaries was, in a sense, a natural extension of existing Majorcan interests in Africa and the Atlantic: Majorcan shipping carried Catalan trade to northern Europe in the late thirteenth and early fourteenth centuries; and the dispensations Majorcans enjoyed to trade with infidels peculiarly fitted them to take part in navigation along the African coast. The island, moreover, had long been a Genoese staging-post for westward navigation; indeed, the Vivaldi themselves had called there. Finally, it was the home of a school of missionaries, chiefly Franciscans, inspired by Ramon Llull's methods of evangelisation: peaceful persuasion, enhanced by charity and apostolic example, expressed in native tongues. Llullian missionaries were to be among the most frequent early travellers to the Canaries.

At least four voyages from Majorca to the Canaries were licensed in April 1342. Françesc Desvalers, Pere Margre and Bartolomeu Giges – we know nothing of them save their names, though the first has been linked with a certain

Atlantic Exploration before Columbus   19

En Valers, said to be lately returned from Tartary in a document of 1379 – were authorised to make two expeditions in the cogs, *Santa Creu, Santa Magdalena,* and *Santa Joan* to islands *vocatas perdudes vel de Canaria,* also referred to as *repertas.*[16] This nomenclature seems to establish a link in contemporary minds between these islands, the *insulae repertae* of the '1341' account, the Plinian 'Canaria' and the islands of the Brendan myth, one of which was traditionally called 'Perdita'. That at least one of this pair of licences bore fruit in an actual voyage is shown by the chance survival of a mariner's claim for wages. Other licences were issued in the same month for voyages by Bernat Desvalls and Gillem Safont, *simile mandatum,* and to Guillem Pere, citizen of Majorca, 'to equip and make a voyage to the isles newly found in the parts of the west', again expressly in a cog. A detailed account of what may be a fifth expedition of about this time survives in a corrupt version in a printed book of the next century, which describes a fortuitous landfall in the islands by pirates (probably, though not expressly, Majorcan) pursuing a galley or fleet of the King of Aragon: though dated 1370, the account can be shown from internal evidence more plausibly to relate to the early 1340s. These pirates seem to have regarded themselves as the first discoverers of the islands: this raises the possibility of a casual Majorcan discovery independently of the voyages of Malocello and of the Portuguese, but may be explained alternatively as the result of a corruption in our text:[17] or a claim advanced, like those of the Portuguese to the discovery of Madeira, in despite of earlier explorations.

A gap in the Majorcan archives conceals the next few years' activity, though it seems unlikely that the hectic pace of the early 1340s can have been long sustained. The wage claim of Guillem Joffre indicates the commercial failure of the voyage on which he shipped and the death of one of its leaders, Pere Margre. This may have been a disincentive to other potential explorers but continued activity during the sparsely documented years is indicated by the record in the Catalan Atlas of the voyage down the coast of Africa to the 'river of gold' (perhaps the Wad Draa, alchemically transmuted, or arguably the Senegal) of Jaume Ferrer in 1346.[18] It was formerly thought that Atlantic exploration suffered a 'check' in the mid-fourteenth century because of the effects of the Black Death and the technical insufficiency of ships and nautical aids.[19] When archival records become available again from 1351, there is little evidence to support this. It may be, however, that some of the commercial impetus of the earliest voyages was lost, as most of the expeditions of the next generation appear, from surviving records, to have been the work of missionaries.

---

[16] F. Sevillano Colom, 'Los viajes medievales desde Mallorca a Canarias', *Anuario de estudios atlánticos,* XXIII (1978), 27-57; A. Rumeu de Armas, 'Mallorquines en el Atlántico', *Homenaje a E. Serra Ràfols,* III, 265-76.

[17] A. Lütolf,'Zur Entdeckung und Christianisung der Westafrikanischen Inseln', *Theologische Quartalschrift,* XLVII (1877), 319-32; A. Rumeu de Armas, *El obispado de Telde* (Madrid, 1960), p. 31. I offer a new study of this text in chapter IX of *From the Mediterranean to the Atlantic* (in press).

[18] *Mapamundi,* ed. Grosjean, sheet III; Mauny, op. cit., pp. 96-97.

[19] P. Chaunu, *L'Expansion européenne du XIIIe au XVe siècle* (Paris, 1969), pp. 95-98.

The voyage of Joan Doria and Jaume Segarra of 1351 is exceptionally well documented. In May, they obtained a Bull from Clement VI for a mission to the Canaries: they were to be accompanied by twelve Catalan-speaking natives of the islands (evidence here of the influence of Llullian methods of evangelisation) who had been captured by previous expeditions. The following month they obtained a royal licence to sail from Majorca. The completion of their journey is strongly suggested by the fact that in November of the same year Clement VI founded the diocese of 'Fortuna' or of the Fortunate Islands, which was established at Telde in Gran Canaria and lasted until 1393.[20] Records survive of five further missionary expeditions between 1352 and 1386, and it is not unreasonable to suppose that there were others of which no notice has come down to us. It may be that the apparent shift of emphasis in the Majorcan voyages from commerce and conquest to conversion and pastoral care is connected with the re-absorption of Majorca into the Crown of Aragon in 1343.[21] Thereafter, Majorca had no specific interest in making sovereign conquests. On the other hand, it is apparent that the Crown of Aragon inherited, at least for a time, Majorcan pretensions in the region, for a precious document of 1366 preserves royal instructions to the sea-captain, Joan Mora, to patrol the archipelago and exclude interlopers from other states. This shows that shipping from outside the Crown of Aragon was active in these latitudes at the time, though, unfortunately, its provenance is not given.[22]

Slavers and perhaps fishermen might be presumed to have been frequenting the islands at the time, but no notice has survived of a renewed attempt at conquest from outside the Crown of Aragon until 1370, when the first partial or temporary success seems to have been achieved, though the disappearance of the original documents, which might constitute the evidence, has cast doubt on the whole episode. According to presumed copies of much debated authenticity, on 29 June 1370, the King of Portugal granted two islands, which he called 'Nossa Señora a Franqua' and 'Gumeyra', to Lansarote da Framqua, who is described as 'admiral' and 'our vassal' and who is said to have found and conquered the islands in question for the Portuguese king ('trobou e nos gannou'). An interpretation consistent with other known facts of the islands' history is that this conquest saw the erection of the tower on Lanzarote, attributed by later conquistadores to Lanzarote Malocello, who may have been the same 'Lansarote da Framqua' to whom the grant of 1370 was addressed. The cognomen 'da Framqua' could refer to the island seigneury, part of which the admiral may have wished to dedicate to Our Lady under that avocation for reasons of personal devotion or even possibly as a result of having been in French service, though there is no firm evidence to link Malocello, or any other 'Lancelot' who may be in question here, with France. By this interpretation, the island of 'Nossa Señora' would be Lanzarote, as a marginal note to the lost document is said to have claimed. As the toponymy of the Canaries was not yet definitively established, it is not necessary to suppose that

---

[20] Rumeu, 'Mallorquines', pp. 264-73.
[21] M. Mitjà, 'Abandó des Illes Canaries per Joan d'Aragó', *Anuario de estudios atlánticos*, VIII (1962), 329.
[22] A. Rumeu de Armas, 'La expedición mallorquina de 1366 a las Islas Canarias', ibid., XXVII (1981), 15-23.

'Gumeyra' was the island we now call 'Gomera', but the balance of probabilities seems to incline that way, as the cartography of the time assigned more or less accurate positions and standard names to all major islands of the archipelago (see p.11 below). Other copies of documents relating to this lordship, of 1376 and 1385, of the same provenance as that of 1370, purport to show that Lansarote da Framqua continued to hold or attempt to hold at least part of his island possessions and died in their defence on Lanzarote in or shortly before 1385. This recalls the tradition that Lanzarote Malocello spent about twenty years on his homonymous island.[23]

By the time of his death, he had been disputing possession with Castilian interlopers, as well as native Canarians, for at least ten years, in what the 1376 document called '*ficada guerra que ouve com os ditos gaanchos e castellaos*'. It was natural that Castilian interest in the islands should have grown. The expedition ascribed to 1341 included Castilian mariners and it was through Seville that news of it was brought to Italy. In 1344, a prince of Castilian antecedents had been enfeoffed with the islands by the Pope. Reacting to that event the following year, the Castilian king had staked a claim of his own to the conquest of the archipelago on the spurious grounds that the islands, with much of the African mainland, had belonged to his remote Visigothic predecessors and that 'the kingdoms of Africa are of our conquest'.[24] Frequently in the third quarter of the century, Majorcan and Catalan missionaries must have sailed through Castilian waters to reach the islands. And Aragonese defence in the 1360s or – more doubtfully – Portuguese conquest in the 1370s may have made the Canaries a theatre of war involving Castilian interlopers in a period when, according to tradition, expeditions were being sent from Seville (though such traditions are not confirmed by contemporary evidence until the 1390s). It is not necessary, however, to admit such traditions, or make any assumptions about presumed Castilian navigation to the Canaries, for purposes of the present argument. Frequent communications with the islands, from the 1330s onwards, are sufficiently attested by an impressive variety of sources.

This period of fairly intensive activity by navigators was accompanied by a gradual increase in geographical precision concerning the Canaries, reflected in contemporary maps. In cartographic sources, the discoveries seem, as it were, to take shape. Whereas, in the early fourteenth century, the Hereford Mappamundi characteristically showed only a speculative mass of Atlantic islands, as though torn from the ragged western hem of Africa, by the time of the Dulcert map of 1339, at least three of the islands of the archipelago were clearly distinguished. These two maps served different purposes: the first was devotional, designed to

---

[23] C. Verlinden, 'Lanzarotto Malocello et la découverte portugaise des Canaries', *Revue belge de philologie et d'histoire*, XXVI (1958), 1173-1209; see his debate with E. Serra Ràfols in *Actas do Congresso de Portugal Medievo*, III, 388-407; *Revista de historia canaria*, XXVII (1961); and C. Verlinden, 'La découverte' (cited n.5 above), pp. 109-119. Verlinden has answered adequately the charge that the documents in question contain anachronisms; it remains true, however, that their provenance is tainted.

[24] *Clément VI: Lettres se rapportant à la France*, ed. J. Glénisson, E. Déprez and G. Mollat (Paris, 1958), no. 1317.

adorn an altar as an image of the perfection of God's creation (though the visitor to Hereford Cathedral today will find it dismissed to an aisle), while the second was practical, intended as an aid to navigation; but the differences between them also reflect the achievements of Lanzarotto Malocello. Dulcert has 'insula capraria' and 'Canaria' − both names associated with the Canaries − in what are probably speculative positions, though suggestive of Madeira, about the latitude of northern Morocco, with the legend, *Insulle s[an]c[t]i brandani sive puellarum*, nicely blending the myths of Brendan and Ursula. What could be 'Pluvialia' (one of Pliny's names for the Canaries) lies close by. But off what is perhaps the Wad Draa the map shows *Insula de lanzarotus malocelus, vegimarin* (corresponding to the present Isla de Lobos, a small islet between Lanzarote and Fuerteventura) and *la forte ventura*. All are recognisably marked and the first is emblazoned with a St George's Cross, perhaps in honour of Malocello's provenance. The somewhat later but evidently closely dependent British Library map, Add. MS. 25691, shows *[Ca]praria* just below the latitude of the westernmost extension of Africa, with a large *Insula de columbis* to the south (possibly alluding to the Brendan myth), then just to the south-east *Canaria*, below which comes the legend, *Insulle de sanbrandini*. But to the south-east again, in roughly correct position, come the identifiable Lanzarote, Fuerteventura and Lobos.[25]

The next relevant map of reliable date is the Pizigani portolan chart of 1367 in Parma (Kamal, IV, fasc.1, no. 1289). Here place-names associated with the Canaries begin to coalesce into a recognisably single archipelago. Gomera and Hierro seem to be consciously depicted: certainly, there are eight distinct islands shown. The Catalan Atlas allows no room for doubt concerning the identities of the islands depicted in the position of the Canaries. Of the eleven largest islands, only La Palma is omitted. *Graciosa, laregranza, rocho, Insula de lanzaroto maloxelo, Insula de li vegi marin, forteventura, Insula de Canaria, Insula del infernio, Insula de gomera, Insula de lo fero* appear as we read in order. The corresponding modern names are: Graciosa, Alegranza, Roque, Lanzarote, Lobos, Fuerteventura, Canaria, Tenerife, Gomera, Hierro. Mount Teide, the great peak of Tenerife, is graphically depicted. The *Libro del conoscimiento*, compiled perhaps at about this time, names eleven islands of the Canaries and includes the name *tenerefiz*, as well as *Infierno* for the first time.[26] The roughly contemporary work of Guillem Soler (one version of which bears the date 1385) improves on the Catalan Atlas and excels some later maps in placing the archipelago in its true position relative to the trend of the African coast. The depiction of the Canaries is also remarkably complete: Santa Clara is added, so that eleven of the twelve largest islands are shown; Hierro has been thought to have been omitted but is in fact faintly visible in the Florentine version of the map, whereas in the other version (in Paris) the relevant section is torn.[27]

---

[25] See n. 10 above; on whether Madeira is represented, I concur with the reservations of J. Mees, 'Les Açores d'après des portolans', *Boletim da Sociedade de Geographia de Lisboa* (1900), 457, *Acta Cartographica*, III, 382.

[26] ed. Jiménez, p.50.

[27] Kamal, IV, fasc.3, nos. 1320-1322; A. Cortesão, *História da cartografia portuguesa*, 2 vols, (Coimbra, 1969-70) [hereafter Cortesão, *História*], II, 49-50, 59.

In view of the ample evidence of frequent sailings to the islands in the period concerned, there is no reason to question the substantial reliability of these maps. It is worth stressing that, even were corroborative documents not available, the evolution of the cartographic image of the islands, from the speculations of the Hereford Mappamundi to the information recorded in late fourteenth-century portolan charts, would raise a strong presumption in favour of a thorough exploration of the islands. This evolution can, as we have seen, be demonstrated from maps of unimpeachable authenticity, without calling any of questionable date into consideration. If it is admitted that the maps we have cited are evidence of knowledge of the Canaries in the period, it must be admitted that they show knowledge of Madeira, too. In the Catalan Atlas and the work of Soler, Madeira, Porto Santo, the Desert Islands and the Savage Islands are all shown in creditably authentic positions, under recognisable versions of their modern names. Although unconfirmed by explicit references in any other contemporary documents, the proposition that they were genuinely known must benefit from the same presumption in its favour as we have claimed for the case of the Canaries. Finally, as we turn to consider the more problematical case of the Azores, the slow evolution of the cartographic tradition of the Canaries should also be kept in mind – an evolution occupying at least two generations' span in time. It would not be unreasonable to expect the accurate mapping of the Azores to take at least as long.

To understand the early cartography of the Azores it is essential to set all prejudice aside and, in particular, to distinguish the case of the Azores from that of America. The presumed cartographic evidence for pre-Columbian navigation to the New World rests on three sources: the maps that depict an island under the name 'Antilia' with other commonly associated islands[28]; the world maps of German provenance that show an antipodean land (insular or, in one case, apparently continental in character), usually called 'Hesperides', in or beyond a narrow Atlantic[29]; and the Atlantic Chart of Andrea Bianco of 1448, which depicts an 'authentic island' *(ixola otinticha)* at its extreme southern margin (but well short of the left-hand or 'western' edge), south of the western part of the Gulf of Guinea: in a superimposed legend the island is said to be 1,500 miles *longa a ponente*.[30] These lands are not shown on any of the maps whose reliability we have so far established (although it must be said that the Bianco map is generally well informed). Nor, of course, have they the support of any non-cartographic evidence of the sort available for the Canaries. The Antilia group is anyway unlikely to be intended for America (even setting aside the perhaps deceptive argument that it is in quite the wrong place) because of its early first appearance (1424), its traditional character, its indebtedness to a well attested legend[31] and its

[28] Cortesão, 'Carta', pp. 146-202.
[29] D. Bennett Durand, *The Vienna-Klosterneuburg Map Corpus of the Fifteenth Century* (Leiden, 1952), plates XIII, XV, XVI reproduce some examples. See also, J. Parker, 'A Fragment of a Fifteenth-century Planisphere in the James Ford Bell Collection', *Imago Mundi*, XIX (1965), 106-107 for the most remarkable example.
[30] Kamal, V, no. 1492; the reproductions in H. Yule Oldham, 'A pre-Columbian Discovery of America', *The Geographical Journal*, V (1895), 221-239, are more serviceable than the arguments.
[31] Cortesão, 'Carta', pp. 146-202.

confusion – as we shall see – in some mapmakers' minds with the Azores. None of these considerations is sufficient to refute the identification of Antilia with America, but, in default of other evidence, they justify our wariness. The maps which show the Hesperides are all *mappaemundi*, not portolan charts; they are classifiable as literary compilations to which practical navigation contributed little or nothing. Bianco's *ixola otinticha* is a unique case, inexplicable as it stands and unillumined by any other source; any interpretation of it is necessarily speculative; whatever the meaning of the phrase *1,500 mi[li]a longa a ponente*, the actual location of the island on the map, within the Gulf of Guinea and perhaps about a hundred miles from the African coast, suggests no part of the New World.

Nor should we allow the case of the Azores to be obscured by the insubstantial arguments which have characterised some discussion of the early cartography of the Cape Verde Islands. Though, from 1413 onwards, islands of apparently mythical origin appear in portolan charts south of the Canaries – a large island known as Ymadoro or Himadoro and two sausage-shaped ones under the names of 'Illes de Gades' and 'Dos ermanes' – the presumption that these are pre-figurations of the Cape Verde Islands can only be justified on the hypothesis that every rumoured or fabled island must be a reflection of perceived reality. There is no evidence outside these apparent cartographical speculations of any reported discovery of the Cape Verde Islands in the first half of the fifteenth century.[32]

The presumed early cartography of the Azores, however, is of a much more impressive and substantial character. The archipelago does not appear fully and accurately mapped, on surviving charts, from before the 1480s. Yet, even at the most conservative estimate, most of the islands had by that time been thoroughly explored and much frequented for some fifty years. Their colonisation is documented from 1439 onwards. We should not, therefore, expect too much of the earliest attempts at depiction. We should also make allowance for the technical problems faced by high-seas navigators of the late middle ages in recording their course in little-known waters.

Previous attempts to identify the Azores on portolan charts and to reconstruct the process of their mappings have foundered on the unreliable chronology of the maps. In the attempt which follows, I avoid arguments which rely on assigning dates to undated maps or on assuming a date equivalent, where an almanac is included, to the start of the almanac. The Medici Atlas of the Laurentian Library (Kamal, IV, fasc.2, nos 1246-1248), for instance, opens with an almanac beginning in 1351[33]; but the Atlas has every appearance of being a collection of folios by more than one hand, drawn at different times. The fifth folio, which shows the Atlantic, most closely resembles the versions of Guillem Soler, one of which is dated 1385, and other maps of similar date or in the same

[32] A. Cortesão, 'Descubrimento e representação das Ilhas de Cabo Verde na cartografia antiga', *Memorias da Academia das Ciências de Lisboa: Classe de Ciências*, XXI (1976-7), 229-50.

[33] On problems of dating see G. H. T. Kimble, 'The Laurentian World Map with special reference to its Portrayal of Africa', *Imago Mundi*, I (1935), 29-33; Cortesão, *História*, II, 45.

tradition. The Catalan Atlas is conventionally attributed to 1375, because that year is used as the starting-point for the computation of the Golden Number, but 1376 and 1377 are also mentioned in its accompanying texts; it conforms closely to the description of such an atlas in the French royal library catalogue, dated 1380, but possibly interpolated or revised later; and its date should also be considered in the light of the record of the imminent despatch of a mappamundi by Cresques Abraham to the King of France by the Infante of Aragon in November, 1381.[34] In view of the fact that Guillem Soler's map of 1385 is almost identical in its representation of the Atlantic, save that it is slightly more complete, the Catalan Atlas can be assigned with some confidence to the late 1370s or early 1380s. For most undated maps, however, it is impossible to suggest anything like so narrow a range of possibilities.

Two Venetian maps, the 'Pinelli-Walckenaer' of the British Library (sometimes said to be Genoese) and the dependent 'Combitis' Atlas of the Biblioteca Marciana, are traditionally dated 1384 and c.1400 respectively, the former because of the starting-point of its almanac.[35] But both have features which suggest a much later origin: the perfunctory treatment of a group of islands in the eastern Atlantic, probably derived from early attempts to represent the Azores, is a common feature of maps of the mid- and late fifteenth century and is not found on any known late fourteenth- or early fifteenth-century example. The Mediterranean toponymy of both maps includes features not found before the fifteenth century[36]. Unless and until reliable dates can be assigned, it is best to leave these maps out of account when trying to establish the chronology of the mapping of the Azores.

By using the handful of reliably dated maps as points of reference, three stages can be discerned in the depiction of islands which might be intended for the Azores. First, in maps of or about the 1380s, clusters of islands reminiscent of groupings of the Azores, or some of them, appear in the latitudes of the Azores but displaced well to the east of the archipelago's true position; these are the only possible attempts to represent the Azores until the 1420s[37]; secondly, from the 1420s onwards, in positions overlapping with the true position of the Azores, a tradition is established of placing a large, rectangular island or islands, usually bearing names associated with the myth of Antilia and the Isle of Seven Cities.[38] Only one map in this tradition attempts to give these islands, with other, smaller ones nearby, anything resembling the true relationship of the Azores to each other.[39] Mapmakers who knew the true position of the Azores, from 1439 onwards, either excluded this group altogether or retained it in a new, speculative position. Thirdly, a group of three maps of 1439-48 shows a string of islands which even the most sceptical scrutineer would willingly identify as the Azores, in

[34] Kamal, IV, fasc.3, nos. 1301-1307; see no. 1307 for the documents concerning the date; Cortesão, História, II, 48; see also n.2 above.
[35] Kamal, IV, fasc.3, nos. 1316-1319, 1333; Cortesão, História, II, 49-50.
[36] Information of Mr. Tony Campbell of the British Library Map Collection.
[37] Soler maps (Kamal, IV, fasc. 3, nos. 1320-1322); Catalan Atlas (n. 2 above).
[38] Cortesão, 'Carta', pp. 146-63.
[39] Cristofalo Soligo: Kamal, V, no. 1510.

roughly their correct position: the first two of these replace the old Azores-like clusters of fourteenth-century origin with these new depictions, suggesting that, in the minds of the cartographers, the traditional clusters were identified with what we think of as the Azores[40]; in the third map, by Andrea Bianco, the traditional clusters are reinstated, but the Azores are included in place of the Antilia group, suggesting that in Bianco's mind the Antilia group represented a prior attempt at depiction of the Azores.[41] Finally, it is common for fifteenth-century maps to retain schematic versions of the fourteenth-century clusters, or of the Antilia group, or both, long after the true position of the Azores had become known, presumably in deference to their cartographic sources; this shows what an important influence tradition had become in the mapping of the Atlantic. It should not be taken to mean that these islands must have been imaginary or fabulous at the time of their first inclusion.

What I have called the first phase can be discerned in the Guillem Soler maps and their contemporaries and derivatives: the fifth folio of the Medici Atlas, the Catalan Atlas, the Catalan portolan charts of Paris (Kamal, IV, fasc. 4, no. 1390) and Naples (Kamal, IV, fasc. 3, no. 1331) and the dated maps of Niccolò de Pasqualini (1408) and Mecia de Viladestes (1413). These all have features in common in their depiction of an Azorean group of islands. All, except the Catalan Atlas, show eight islands, which share a more or less common sequence of names; the Medici Atlas omits or conflates certain names: a central cluster of three islands, for instance, is called 'Insule de ventura sive de columbis' while most of the maps show 'Ventura' and 'columbis' or 'li columbi' as the names of two islands of the group. The Catalan Atlas omits the two most southerly islands – otherwise called 'Capraria' and 'Lovo' – altogether, perhaps by inadvertence. The *Libro del conoscimiento*, of the late fourteenth century, lists eight islands, with recognisably the same names (in a Castilian or Aragonese form) as are shown in the maps. All the maps show the Azorean group on more or less the same meridian as the westerly isles of the Canaries (well displaced to the east, of course, from the Azores' true position) and on a rhumb north by north-west from a centre near Lanzarote or Fuerteventura, through the Madeira group: although one would actually have to steer a course to the north-west to reach the Azores from the Canaries, magnetic variation, variable winds, unfamiliar currents and cartographical error (assuming that all these maps belong to a single tradition) might account for the difference. The entire archipelago, in all these maps, is 'stretched' over a far greater area of ocean than in reality and the size of the islands is much exaggerated: this is also a feature of the early cartography of the Canaries.

For the identification of the islands depicted, or rather for the solution of the problem of whether they are identifiable, the way they are clustered in definable groups is the most important common feature of maps of the first phase. To understand the significance of this, it is important to consider how the Azores

---

[40] Kamal, IV, fasc. 4, no. 1463; Cortesão, *História*, II, 150-52; *The Nautical Chart of 1424* (Coimbra, 1954), plate V.

[41] Kamal, V, no. 1492; cf. Bianco's 1436 version of the Atlantic in A. E. Nordensköld, *Periplus* (Stockholm, 1897), p. 19; R. A. Skelton, T. E. Marston and G. D. Painter, *The Vinland Map and the Tartar Relation* (New Haven, 1965), plate VI.

appear as one approaches them under sail from the south-east. Santa María is encountered first, lying well to the south of the main archipelago. São Miguel appears as a relatively large island, 'broadside on' to the north. To the north-west again, the central group of the archipelago is formed by two small clusters: Pico, Faial and São Jorge make up the more southerly cluster, Graciosa and Terceira lie slightly to the north-east in relation to it. Beyond the central group again, to the north-west, lie Flores and Corvo.

How does the reality of the Azores, thus described, correspond to the clusterings on the early maps? Superficially, the resemblance seems clear: the substitution of an archipelago of eight islands for one of nine might be explained by the fusing of two outlines on the horizon, or the omission of a small island like Graciosa. The maps all show a central cluster of islands, with two isles well out to the north and others well removed to the east and south: to that extent, reality and cartographic image seem well matched. It is against the background of these general similarities that Armando Cortesão has tried to link particular islands found on the map with real ones.[42] His effort, however, has been unconvincing. In particular, the relationship between Santa María and São Miguel does not fit that of the two small southerly islands called Capraria and Lovo in the maps; nor can one feel satisfied with the displacement of Terceira from a position on the north-east flank of the central group to one south of it: how could a navigator approaching the islands from the south-east have made such an error of observation, or a cartographer, following his account, such an error of interpretation? The omission of Graciosa rather than, say, Faial, appears arbitrary, and is made largely in order to permit the identification of the two most northerly isles of the maps as Flores and Corvo. Yet that identification also seems unsatisfactory, since in every case the maps show these two islands slightly to the east of the meridian of the central group, whereas in fact they are well to the west.

We may do better by abandoning Cortesão's identifications and starting again from scratch. The central cluster of three islands shown in all the maps could represent more than three 'real' islands, particularly observed when standing well out to windward. But it seems unlikely that vessels should normally have chosen to make such an approach and, as a matter of common sense, it is appropriate to try first the tentative hypothesis that the cluster of three represents São Jorge, Faial and Pico: indeed the relationship one to another of these islands on the map does closely resemble the real relationship of these islands, arranged like the apices of a triangle. From this central group, two islands stand out to the north and east on the maps, as in reality: Terceira and Graciosa; to be sure, the 'Corvi Marini' and 'Conigi' of the maps lie far to the north of the cluster of three, whereas Terceira and Graciosa are within sight of their neighbours; but this sort of elongation is not atypical of the early cartography of Atlantic archipelagoes generally. To the south-east of the central cluster, we find in the maps, as in reality, a relatively long island, looming broadside on as one approaches from the south-east. The 'Brazil' of the maps thus corresponds to São Miguel. This leaves the problem of identifying the two small islands of Capraria and Lovo well to the

---

[42] Cortesão, História, II, 58-59, largely following Kretschmer, Italianische Portolane, pp. 686-87.

south. When one recalls, however, that Santa María lies well to the south of the
rest of the archipelago; that a little way off Santa María to the north we find the
rocky Formigas, and that early cartography habitually exaggerated the size of islets
and rocky outcrops, particularly, to take a pertinent example, in the case of the
Canaries, the problem seems to dissolve. It does not appear to me that Flores and
Corvo are represented on any map of the fourteenth or early fifteenth centuries, or
that there is any reason to suppose that they must have been discovered along with
most of the rest of the archipelago. They lie much further to the west than the
other islands; there is no record from before 1452 that they were known to the
Portuguese settlers who had begun to colonise Santa María and São Miguel from
1439; and though a freak wind or a deliberate attempt at exploration might have
led seamen to them, there is neither point nor merit in such a speculation, whereas
it is satisfactory and consistent with the evidence to suppose that fourteenth-
century knowledge of the Azores was limited to the southern and central islands of
the archipelago.

Maps of what I call the second stage – those which introduce islands whose
nomenclature is connected with the legends of Antilia and the Seven Cities –
belong to the history of the mapping of the Azores only in a modified sense. It is,
on balance, marginally more likely that the appearance of Antilia, from 1424,
reflects, if anything, a sighting of the Azores than of the New World: the position
of Antilia, at its first appearance, on the Nautical Chart of 1424 in the James Ford
Bell Collection, Minneapolis, does at least coincide with that of the Azores. But
neither identification is satisfactory. The main islands of the Antilia group, in all
cases of their inclusion in fifteenth-century maps, have conventional, rectangular
shapes; and although, at the start of the tradition, Antilia is placed in a position
suggestive of the Azores, other islands are dotted around at random. Only two
mapmakers seem to have identified the Antilia group with the Azores: the
Cristofal Soligo map, of uncertain date, groups eleven islands, including some
bearing the traditional shapes (and in one case a traditional name) of islands in the
Antilia group, in a fan-shaped archipelago covering much of the central north
Atlantic; Soligo gives to this archipelago and its islands names associated with the
Azores in the fifteenth century.[43] This looks like a late attempt at synthesis of two
cartographic traditions. In the other case, that of Andrea Bianco, the identity of
the Azores and the Antilia group does appear to be presumed (p.15 above); and it
may be worth adding that in a chart of Battista Beccario of 1435, the Antilia group
is labelled, *de novo reperte*, which could be interpreted as a reference to
Portuguese voyage to the Azores of the early 1430s.[44] But these indications in
favour of identifying the Antilia group with the Azores – while more impressive
than those which link Antilia with America – amount to very little. Even if a real
sighting of the Azores (or *a fortiori* of any other land) did lie behind the Antilia
tradition or contribute to it, it would still be necessary to assert a literary or

---

[43] Kamal, V, no. 1510. cf. Cortesão, 'Carta', pp. 125, 152-53. For the contemporary use of
Soligo's nomenclature see documents of 1460 in *Monumenta henricina*, XIII, 345-46, XIV,
20.

[44] Cortesão, 'Carta', p. 147. The relevant section is reproduced in R. Hennig, *Terrae Incognitae*, 4 vols (Leipzig, 1944-56), IV, plate III.

legendary origin for the tradition as well. As the necessary explanation is also sufficient, it is supererogatory to adduce others. Like Cipangu, whose traditional shape it resembles, Antilia was, as far as we know, an island reputed, not reported.

Within a few years of the first appearance of Antilia, however, the cartography of the Azores was genuinely transformed by what I have called the three maps of the third phase: the Gabriel Vallseca map, dated 1439, now in Barcelona[45]; an undated Catalan map in Florence (Kamal, IV, fasc. 4, no. 1463); and the Atlantic portolan of Andrea Bianco, dated in London in 1448, now in Milan.[46] All these maps show the Azores as a group of islands strung out serially or, in the case of Vallseca, almost serially, on a north-west to south-east axis, in a position corresponding very closely to that really occupied by the archipelago, except that it extends rather too far north. Both Catalan maps show nine islands, Bianco's seven. On the maps in Florence and Venice, each island bears a name of its own. One name which occurs in both, Isle of Hawks (*faucols* in the Catalan, *falconi* in the Venetian map) anticipates the toponymy of the Azores as it would come to be fixed: this was the Portuguese collective name for the archipelago from 1439. The remaining names are descriptive or traditional. The size and mutual relationships of the several islands are random; but their position and orientation make them clearly intended for the Azores. The makers of all three maps seem to identify the newly depicted archipelago with traditionally depicted islands: with it the two Catalan maps replace the traditional Azorean clusters – Vallseca omitting the latter altogether while the map now in Florence retains only *liconigi* and *Illa de corps marins*, which had always been shown as a pair remote from other islands, in their traditional position. This suggests that Vallseca identified the Azores with the traditional Azorean clusters as a whole, while the second author made broadly the same identification, excluding only the two most marginal of the traditional islands. Bianco evidently took a different view. His 1448 map retains the traditional clusters, while omitting the Antilia group, to which he had given some prominence in his maps of 1436.[47] Hence Bianco appears to have regarded the Antilia group as an attempted representation of the Azores: as we have seen, this was an unusual identification at the time, duplicated, as far as we know, only by Cristofal Soligo. Most mapmakers, on becoming aware of the real position of the Azores, continued to represent the traditional islands as well, shifting the Antilia group westward.[48]

How can this new precision, at least in the position and orientation of the Azores, arising relatively suddenly in maps of the 1430s and 1440s, be explained? Vallseca offers some elucidation in a famous gloss, still legible beneath an equally famous ink-blot, made when George Sand was looking at the map. 'These islands were found by Diego de Silves pilot of the King of Portugal in the year 1427'.[49]

---

[45] Cortesão, *História*, II, 150-52.

[46] see n. 30 above.

[47] see n. 41 above.

[48] Cortesão, 'Carta', p. 58, notes this westward shift but regards it as evidence that the Antilia group was meant to depict part of the New World.

[49] 'Aquestes illes foram trobades per Diego de Silves pelot del rey de portogall'. See Cortesão, *História*, II, 150-52. In the quotation, the reading 'Silves' is conjectural, except

This is broadly compatible with other traditions about the beginnings of Portuguese exploration of the Azores, which date it to the early 1430s, and with the almost continuous documentation of the Portuguese colonies in the islands from 1439.[50] It is thoroughly consistent with the character of late medieval mapmakers' techniques that Vallseca should have departed from cartographical tradition to include a reported new discovery in this way. A note on the 'Yale Map of 1403' by Francesco Beccario expressly states that the author modified the map to take account of mariners' information.[51] Andrea Bianco's 1448 map is by universal assent an attempt to incorporate recent news about the African coast culled by Portuguese explorers. The world map of the Laurentian Medici Atlas was modified at least twice in the fifteenth century to accommodate new contributions.[52] It is therefore reasonable to accept Vallseca's adjustment of the position of the Azores as based on an authentic report.

This begs the question of how his informants fixed their position with an accuracy so superior to that of their fourteenth-century predecessors. Unless this question is satisfactorily answered, confidence in the validity of the evidence of fourteenth-century Azorean voyages is bound to be undermined. It is hard to discern any haven-finding technique that may have been new to the generation of 'Diego de Silves'. We know of no direct computations of longitude made by professional seamen until the 1480s at the earliest, and even then with indifferent accuracy. Navigational tables, trigonometrically based, which enabled pilots to correct their course when deflected by wind or current, were evidently in practical use in the 1430s, when Andrea Bianco, himself a ship's captain, included a set in his atlas of 1436. But they had been known since the late thirteenth century, at least, when they were described by Ramon Llull, and the history of their diffusion among practical navigators is obscure.[53] The problems of dating the emergence of the use of the astrolabe and quadrant for determining latitude are not relevant here. For purposes of navigation in the area of the Azores, latitude can be adequately determined by an experienced sailor with the naked eye, and even the earliest presumed cartographic records of the Azores were roughly right as far as latitude was concerned. In all probability, 'Diego de Silves' and his contemporaries navigated by means of the same aids as their predecessors: compass, hourglass and a good eye for the speed of the ship, the drift off course and the height of the sun or the Pole Star. If they were able to judge their course on the high seas more accurately than their forbears, it can only have been because of the progressive effects of experience of the Atlantic, gradually but decisively accumulated over a long period. For the same reasons, similar 'breakthroughs' appear in the cartographical evolution of the image of the Canary Islands: it is not surprising to find them also in the case of the Azores.

It is, of course, one thing to say that the islands depicted on the maps genuinely resemble the Azores and another to claim that these resemblances

---

for the initial 'S'.

[50] *Monumenta henricina*, II, 361; VI, 335; VIII, 43; IX, 235.

[51] For a description of this map, see H. Kraus, *Catalogue no. 55* (New York, 1955), pp. 62-6.

[52] Kimble, 'The Laurentian World Map' (cited n. 33), 33.

[53] E. G. R. Taylor, *The Haven-Finding Art* (London, 1956), pp. 117-21.

derived from real knowledge; one thing to aver that sailors of the time were capable of finding the islands, another to demonstrate that they actually did so. We may, however, advance the argument some way further, first by meeting the remaining objections to the cartographic evidence, then by adducing such corroborative material as we have.

The strongest reasons for doubting the maps lie in the difficulty of verifying their data. Many bear no reliable date; they are vulnerable to emendation by later hands; their treatment of the Azores, in particular, is open to charges of vagueness and, as we have seen, islands are often almost unrecognisably displaced from their true positions. Moreover, the toponymy of fourteenth-century cartographers is classical and mythological and they include many unquestionably speculative islands. None of these caveats, however, definitely invalidates the maps, nor is anything in the cartographers' depictions of the Azores demonstrably unauthentic. That the Azores appear only as a result of interpolation is possible but improbable: the Catalan Atlas and the Soler maps, which constitute the essential evidence, betray no hint of the intervention of later hands, and fourteenth-century mapmakers are unlikely to have wasted parchment in order to leave space for interpolators to work in; it gradually became normal to allow increased space to the Atlantic – and that in itself is a strong indication of the vibrancy of late medieval interest in exploration of the ocean – but, among surviving maps, it is only with the Nautical Chart of 1424 that space seems to be included speculatively, to be filled in later. The surviving maps represent only a small sample of those which must have been available in widely dispersed centres: interpolation would have had to be widespread and systematic to yield consistent results. Imprecision in the location of islands is only to be expected: if they were completely accurate, it would be a sure sign that they were forgeries, as no means of fixing one's position at sea with exactitude were available in the period. Navigators could take rough readings of latitude and, in our maps, latitudes are always roughly right or, at least, within the margin of error to be expected from cartographers who relied on readings obtained without instruments by direct observation of celestial bodies with the naked eye.[54] Longitudinal accuracy was unknown until the fifteenth century. As far as the classical and mythical toponymy of the maps is concerned, this is again just what one ought to expect of the period. The modern nomenclature was not fixed until well into the fifteenth century: a fourteenth-century map which appeared to anticipate it would be highly suspect. Learned cartographers who received mariners' reports of newly discovered islands naturally assigned them names which, if not purely descriptive (as, in some cases, they were) would be drawn from existing tradition. As for the inclusion of speculative islands, it was not only in the fourteenth century that such speculations were recorded as if they were facts. Notional islands continued to appear on nineteenth-century Admiralty charts. Genuine discoveries tend to breed speculation in their turn and Atlantic conditions are, as experienced sailors know, conducive to false sightings.[55] Inclusion of speculative islands might as well be read

---

[54] P. Adam, 'Navigation primitive et navigation astronomique', *VIe Colloque International d'Histoire Maritime* (Paris, 1966), pp. 91-110 (with discussion); C. Verlinden, 'La découverte des archipels' (cited n. 5 above), 129-30.

[55] S. E. Morison, *The European Discovery of America: the Northern Voyages* (New York,

as evidence of the sailors' knowledge of the Atlantic, as of their ignorance. Finally, we must confront the most influential of all objections to the cartographical evidence: S. E. Morison's insistence (unquestioned even by advocates of the maps) that whereas the Azores are aligned from east to west the early alleged cartographic depictions show them running from north to south.[56] This is simply false on both counts. The Azores are grouped around a roughly north-west to south-east axis. They are encountered, as one approaches from the south, in the clusters defined above (p.16): Santa María and Formigas well to the south; to the north, São Miguel on its own; then the cluster of Pico, São Jorge and Faial, well to the north-west, with Terceira and Graciosa separated from them a little to the north-east. Flores and Corvo, lying well to the west, do not enter into the picture. It is in clusters of this sort, arranged in the same way, that the islands are depicted in late fourteenth-century maps: the admitted exaggerations of size and distances are characteristic, visible to a lesser extent in the early cartographic tradition of the Canaries. There are maps which show eastern Atlantic islands bearing names traditionally associated with the Azores, strung out from north to south, but those maps are not of the fourteenth century. The 'Pinelli-Walckenaer' and the 'Combitis' are, as we have seen, wrongly attributed to the fourteenth century. Others – such as the Benincasa and Bertran charts of the 1460s to 1480s – date indisputably from a period after the position of the Azores was accurately determined.[57] Their sketchy onion-strings of eastern Atlantic islands may ultimately have derived from early attempts to depict the Azores, but in the second half of the fifteenth century had become traditional.

One vital objection to the cartographic evidence remains: why, if the Azores were indeed explored in the fourteenth century, are there no documents of the time, apart from the maps, which explicitly refer to them? Clearly, spurious traditions of later invention, which would throng the North Atlantic in the middle ages with imaginary precursors of Columbus, must be discounted. But it is hardly surprising that uninhabited islands should be ignored by our surviving sources: they were understandably of little interest to slavers, conquistadores and missionaries, who, for instance, were responsible for the Canarian voyages documented above. It may be worth pointing out that the Majorcan sailing licences which speak of 'islands of the west' do not specifically exclude the Azores, but it is only common sense to take them as referring to the Canaries.

It is, however, possible to claim the discovery of the Azores as a by-product of the Canary run and to assign a corroborative value, for alleged voyages to the Azores, to the evidence of navigation to the Canaries; in other words, the documents which refer to the Canaries may be treated by implication as evidence of knowledge of the Azores. Two circumstances may be cited in favour of this

---

1971), p. 82.
[56] S. E. Morison, *Portuguese Voyages to America in the Fifteenth Century* (Harvard, 1940), p. 12.
[57] For a good reproduction of the relevant section of the Grazioso Benincasa map of 1467, see M. Mollat du Jourdin, C. M. de La Roncière et al., *Sea Charts of the Early Explorers* (London, 1984), plates 18-19, and of that of Bertran of 1482, Kamal, V, no. 1503. Cortesão, *História*, II, 184-96, provides a useful critical list of the Benincasa maps.

proposition. First, there is the sheer scale of navigation to and from the Canaries in the fourteenth century; secondly, the influence of the Atlantic wind system. Since the discoveries, made by Rumeu de Armas, of a formidable body of documents on the activities of the missionary see of Telde, from the 1350s to the 1380s, and of the document on Joan de Mora's expedition of 1366, (above, p.9), the Canary voyage can no longer be seen as an occasional or sporadic indulgence of the period. Whether or not one accepts Verlinden's contentious reconstruction of the career of Lanzarotto Malocello (above, pp.9-10), the Canaries continue to appear as much frequented islands. Once that is admitted, a context in which to understand the discovery of the Azores begins to emerge. It will be remembered (above, p.8) that most of the early sailing licences for the Canaries refer to cogs, which were generally unsuitable for tacking against the wind. Though the name 'cog' was relatively new, it does not seem to have denoted a different type of ship from a traditional Mediterranean *navis* (Catalan *nau*). There is no reason to suppose that it was other than square-sailed. Rigged to catch a following wind, such vessels could only return from the Canaries by either of two expedients: they could limit homeward navigation to the most favoured season of the winter, when south-westerlies are frequent enough to grant a safe passage. Indeed, from what we know of the timing of early voyages, that was understandably the most favoured method and route. But given the frequency of sailings, the duration of the period over which they took place, and the unreliable nature of the winds, it is unreasonable to suppose that the alternative route, making use of the pattern of prevailing winds, was not also employed. This meant striking north in search of the westerlies that would take one home. Such a course would touch or skirt Madeira and it would be generally expedient, and sometimes necessary, to reach the latitude of the Azores before turning east. The same return route is well attested for some Guinea voyages of the fifteenth century.[58] Against the background of current knowledge of frequent sailings to the Canaries, the roughly contemporary discovery of the Azores seems natural, even inevitable. The process can be compared with the Portuguese discovery of Brazil in 1500 in the course of a wide sweep out into the south Atlantic in search of the westerlies that would carry the fleet round the Cape of Good Hope. This, on a larger scale and in reverse, was a reflection of the journey the Majorcan cogs might have made on their return from the Canaries in the north Atlantic in the fourteenth century, like an image in a shaving mirror.

Thus fourteenth-century maps of the Azores should be considered vindicated, while fifteenth-century maps of America should not. Yet it is possible to wrest evidence of another, hitherto largely unremarked discovery, from fifteenth-century Atlantic maps. In what I have labelled the third stage of Atlantic exploration, Columbus's was not the only practical attempt to exploit the alluring uncertainties of the Atlantic. Flores, Corvo, the Cape Verde Islands and the isles of the Gulf of Guinea were explored in the 1450s and 1460s. Cartography, lagging as usual behind discovery, did not incorporate them – or, indeed, delineate

---

[58] Verlinden, 'La découverte', 129; the evidence, though not the argument, of G. Coutinho, *A náutica dos descobrimentos*, 2 vols (Lisbon, 1951), I, 165-95, suggests this, too. See the wind maps in Cortesão, 'Carta', pp. 166-69.

34   F.F.R. Fernández-Armesto

previously known islands with perfect accuracy – until the 1480s. Yet, while slow
to reflect discovery, maps were quick to encourage it: Bristol voyages of the last
years of the century in search of the Isle of Brasil, or those of the Portuguese of the
Azores to find Antilia, or of Columbus himself, suggest this. Even in world maps
– which gave their compilers a welcome chance to speculate about the Orient –
the greatest concentration of novelties of the fifteenth century, after those drawn
from the reception of Ptolemy, lay in the Atlantic. The extent of speculation
about the Atlantic, in both world maps and sea charts, is the most remarkable
feature of the cartography of the time. It shows what a stimulus to the imagination
Atlantic exploration was, and how consciousness of an exploitable Atlantic grew in
the century before Columbus's voyages. Maps helped to induce potential
explorers to see the ocean in a new light. In that respect, whatever one thinks of
the cartographic record of discoveries of new lands, they are evidence of at least
one authentic discovery of transcendant importance: the discovery of Atlantic
space.

14

European Merchants in the Medieval Indies: The Evidence of Commercial Documents

Robert S. Lopez

I

S TRANGELY enough, up to the present day, commercial documents have contributed almost nothing to our knowledge of trade between Europe and India or China in the Middle Ages. The actual management of a voyage to "the Indies," as India and China were designated in the thirteenth or fourteenth century, has remained obscure because our evidence about commerce has come from sources mainly concerned with other matters.

Marco Polo deserves our gratitude more than anybody else, because his account is by far the most detailed and accurate; moreover, our admiration grows deeper when we compare the amount of accurate knowledge so charmingly presented in the nonchalant pages of the *Milione* with the hurried, unreliable, and swashbuckling relation of Ibn Batūta on China, where he pretended to have been some fifty years later. Polo was the only professional merchant who left a written account of his own experience; and no other European merchant had as brilliant a political career in the Indies. It should also be remembered that the Polo family was one of the first to go as far as Peking. Marco's father and uncle had gone there for the first time between 1260 and 1269; Marco himself was introduced to Kubilai in 1275.[1] By the time he was back in Venice the rush to the Farther East had already begun: Indeed in 1291, the Vivaldi brothers had tried to reach the Indies from the West. This drive to go further into the East laid open to western peoples for the first time an immense part of the world of which very little had been known by Europeans—a world where the largest cities, the highest mountains, the widest rivers, the most immense plains and plateaus could be found, dwarfing the familiar, restricted horizons of Europe—a world where gunpowder, coal, paper money, printing, and so many other curious and useful goods, unavailable or rare elsewhere, were everyday objects. The westerners called all this region of wealth and wonder the Indies,

---

[1] The *Milione* cannot have been written before 1297. Its influence grew deeper as time went on—not so much when there still were travelers who could actually relate what they had seen in Cathay, but later, long after the first witness was dead. The best edition of Marco Polo is that of L. Foscolo Benedetto (Firenze, 1928). The older editions by Pauthier (Paris, 1865) and by Yule, revised by Cordier (New York and London, 1926), are still useful for their footnotes and bibliographies.

Merchants in the Medieval Indies   165

partes Indiae, often lumping together in their thought China, Indo-China, India, and Malaya.

The commercial infiltration eastward into the regions beyond Persia, Egypt, and Arabia is indicated by incidental mention of merchants in letters, reports, and martyrologies of missionaries. Commercial expansion and religious propaganda advanced jointly. A European merchant, Peter of Lucalongo, was the fellow traveler of Friar John of Montecorvino; later, he offered some land to the missions of Khanbalik (Peking), where he had been a trader for some ten years. The Franciscans, in turn, built a *fondaco* and a bath in Zaitun, opposite Formosa —probably the earliest European "concession" in China. Zaitun was at that time the greatest harbor of China, and one of the four greatest in the world according to Ibn Batūta, who saw the other three also (Soldaia in Crimea, Alexandria in Egypt, and Calicut in India). Genoese merchants were not an uncommon sight in this harbor in 1326.[2] About 1320 the Genoese "Jacobus mercator" was the only person—aside from Friar Jordan—who escaped the martyrdom inflicted on the Franciscan mission of Tana, near modern Bombay. But twenty years later another Italian merchant, apparently a Genoese, shared martyrdom with the whole mission of Almalīgh, in Central Asia.[3] Friar Jordan mentions some "Latin" merchants who were trading along the whole western coast of India, from Tana to Quilon, and who reached Ethiopia from there. The names of two more merchants are revealed by the accounts and the legends connected with Jordan's mission: Lanfranchino di Gatuccio, a Genoese, and John, son of Ugolino, a Pisan.[4]

The diplomatic records of European sovereigns and popes[5] have preserved for us the names of several other merchants, who conveyed ap-

---

[2] Nearly all the documents and the accounts of missionaries have been collected and reprinted by G. Golubovich, *Biblioteca bio-bibliografica della Terra Santa e dell' Oriente Francescano* (5 vols., Firenze, 1906-1927) and by A. van den Wyngaert, *Sinica Franciscana* (Vol. I, Firenze, 1929); further bibliographic information is found in these works. As for Pietro di Lucalongo, cf. *Sinica Franciscana,* I, 332, 352, 353; as for the *fondaco* of Zaitun, *ibid.,* I, 536; *Biblioteca,* IV, 279 (with a text slightly different); as for the Genoese in Zaitun, *Sinica Francescana,* I, 375-376.

[3] *Biblioteca,* II, 69-71; *Sinica Franciscana,* I, 528; *Analecta Franciscana* (Firenze, 1886), III, 559. The name of the merchant killed in Almalīgh is given as "Gillottus mercator" by Friar Giovanni Marignolli, as "Gulielmus de Mutina mercator Januensis" by the *Chronica XXIV Generalium.*

[4] *Analecta Franciscana,* III, 607-612. W. Heyd, *Histoire du commerce du Levant au moyen-âge* (Leipzig, 1885), II, 149, regards as an evidence of Genoese merchants in India the fact that Marignolli met in this country a native who had been once ransomed from the pirates and baptized by a Genoese merchant. Still, the account of Marignolli does not say whether the ransom and the baptism themselves occurred in India.

[5] I take the opportunity to publish here an interesting item concerning an ambassador from the Mongolian court of Persia (although this ambassador was not a merchant):

166 *Robert Sabatino Lopez*

peals for new crusades to the Mongolian khans. Especially important among these were three Genoese. Neither Buscarello de Guizulfis nor the banker Tommaso de Anfussis, however, seems to have reached the Far East; but the third, Andalò di Savignone, resided in China and, in 1338, was put in charge of a diplomatic mission by the Great Khan. Unfortunately, he left no written record of his travels.[6]

Thus it is in the work of a Florentine professional merchant, Francesco Balducci Pegolotti, that we find the most detailed account after that of Marco Polo. It is true that Pegolotti, the famous agent of the Bardi company, seems to have known only one of the three main routes to China; moreover, he never went to China himself. But he drew valuable information from the narratives of a great number of eyewitnesses. For, when he wrote his book (1310-1340?), there were many European travelers on the route from the Crimea to China, the route that he describes as being "entirely without danger," only fifty years after Marco Polo left Venice![7] It is not unlikely that some of his informants were his fellow citizens; as a matter of fact, a contemporary account of the English customs shows that already in 1340 the agents of the Frescobaldi company (the great Florentine rival of the Bardi) imported into London China silk, "serico nominato Catewy." It is quite possible that the Frescobaldi obtained this silk from its original source.[8]

What we have hitherto known about medieval trade between Europe and the Far East has been derived almost exclusively from these

Public Record Office, London, *Various Accounts E/101*, 375/8 (Account of Antonio Pessagno, Genoese merchant, to the Royal Wardrobe): "Episcopus de partibus Persarum. Fratri Guillielmo de Villanova Episcopo in partibus Persarum, venientis ad Regem in nuncium Imperatoris Tartarorum et redeunti, de dono ipsius Regis, in recessu suo de eodem per manus Oliverii de Burdigala, ibidem [apud Pissiacum] IIII^{to} die Julij, sicut patet per dictas particulas [Johannis de Okhami], X Lb. II s. I d. ob." (Year 1313; cf. also C. P. R., same year, index of names, *Villanova*).

[6] Cf. P. Pelliot, *Mongols et Papes aux XIIIe et XIVe siècles* (Paris, 1922) and G. Soranzo, *Il Papato, l'Europa cristiana e i Tartari* (Milano, 1930), with bibliography. On Andalò di Savignone, in particular, cf. C. Desimoni, *Archivio Storico Italiano*, Ser. IV, Vol. I (1878), 307.

[7] "The larger part of the book [of Pegolotti] . . . derives from the decades 1310 to 1340" (A. Evans, introduction to F. Balducci Pegolotti, *La Pratica della mercatura* (Cambridge, Mass.: The Mediaeval Academy of America, 1936), xv. The description of the China Road is found in Pegolotti, pp. 21-23.

[8] Public Record Office, London, *Customs Accounts E/122*, 68/11. It is also possible that the Frescobaldi company had bought its silk from Genoese merchants, who, in turn, would have purchased it in China. A few years later another Tuscan merchant, "Ravaldus de Pisis draperius," bought in Genoa from a Genoese a quantity of "seta Chattuya"; the record shows that he was going to Southampton (Archivio di Stato, Genova, *Notaio Bartolomeo de Fornari*, IV, F. 125 r.). Mentions of Chinese silk are very frequent in Genoese records of the late thirteenth century and of the early fourteenth, but there is no telling whether this silk was directly imported from China.

sources. To the foregoing list we could add only some narratives half-way between history and fantasy (such as the *Libro del Conoscimiento* and the pretended travels of Sir John Maundeville) and the medieval maps, both European and Oriental.[9] No commercial documents had been discovered that added to our knowledge. In the case of Venice and Florence, the lack of such evidence may perhaps be explained by the loss of a large part of the documents of this kind for the thirteenth and early fourteenth centuries. But for Genoa we have notarial instruments connected with trade by the tens of thousands; we might expect that at least some of these instruments refer to the Indies, inasmuch as Genoese formed the majority of European merchants in the Far East. Even in Florence, Giovanni Boccaccio quoted the Genoese as the best authority to vouch for a story allegedly taking place in China: "It is absolutely certain—if we may put faith in the narrative of some Genoese and other persons who have been there—that in the regions of Cathay there once lived a man . . . ." Elsewhere, he tells of a false missionary who displayed pretended relics and a mockingly distorted geography of the

---

[9] Italian and Jewish-Catalan maps have formed the subject for several excellent essays; see bibliography in I. Hallberg, *L'Extréme Orient dans la littérature et la cartographie de l'Occident des XIIIe, XIVe et XVe siècles*, Göteborgs Kungliga Vetenskaps och Vittershets Samhället, Ser. IV, Vol. VII-VIII (Göteborg, 1906); H. Yule, *Cathay and the Way Thither*, 4 vols. (2d ed. revised by H. Cordier; London, 1913-1916); C. R. Beazley, *The Dawn of Modern Geography* (London, 1901), Vols. I and II. Cf. also Berthelot, *L'Asie ancienne centrale et sud-orientale d'après Ptolémée* (Paris, 1930); P. Revelli, *Cristoforo Colombo e la scuola cartografica genovese* (Roma, 1938). But the Chinese map of the King-shi-ta-tien, compiled about 1331, did not receive all the attention it deserves. This map and the Si-pei-ti (a contemporary document, cf. E. Bretschneider, *Mediaeval Researches from Eastern Asiatic Sources* [London, 1888], II, 3) point out the main stations of the three routes from China to Europe so clearly that one is led to wonder whether the compilers drew some information from Italian merchants. It is true that such a great scholar as P. Pelliot, "Le nom du Khwārizm dans les textes chinois," *T'oung Pao*, XXXIV (1938), 146, maintains that the Chinese map was copied from an Arabic original. But the former has mistakes that can hardly come from an Arabic map; for instance, Damietta is placed north of Constantinople, and the Tūs is placed east of the Badakhshān. Besides, those earlier Chinese geographers, Chou K'u-fei and Chan Ju-kua, who certainly are indebted to Arabic sources, have some information about Sicily and the Almoravid Empire (neither of which is found on the map of the King-shi-ta-tien) and next to nothing on the western portion of the land routes used by the European merchants in the thirteenth and fourteenth centuries (which are clearly shown in that map). On the other hand, the leading Arab geographers of the thirteenth century, Yākūt and Abu'l fidā, have no information on China except for accounts which they copy from travelers of the ninth and tenth centuries. Indeed, Yākūt points out that he never met anybody who had been in China. A little later, it is true, Ibn Sa'īd is better informed; but it can be suggested that he may have drawn his information from Italian merchants in Genoa or in Tana, for he is particularly well informed about these cities. Sources in Chan Ju-kua, *Chu-fan-chi*, ed. F. Hirth and W. Rockhill (St. Petersburg, 1911), and in G. Ferrand, *Rélations de voyages et textes géographiques arabes, persans et turks relatifs à l'Extrême-Orient* (Paris, 1913-1914), with bibliographies.

Robert Sabatino Lopez

Middle and Far East.[10] Missionaries and Genoese—these were the principal experts on the Orient, who peddled their stories to the half-fascinated, half-incredulous ears of the medieval Florentine man in the street.

Unfortunately the Genoese were far less talkative than the missionaries. They left us not even one general account like that of the Venetian Marco Polo or the Florentine Pegolotti. The reason, I believe, lies in the difference between the open and talkative Venetians and Florentines, fond of any social gatherings, and the individualistic, taciturn, and reserved Genoese. Jealous of their business secrets, the Genoese not only refrained from leaving accounts of their travels, but often refused to mention the final destination of their trips in the contracts they drew up before notaries. The reasons for this secrecy can only be guessed at. Could not the notaries, for example, disclose to the outsiders the routes which the parties preferred to exploit either alone or within a small circle of relatives and friends? Were there not already too many Genoese on the trails to the Indies? Very obviously, owing to the great costs involved, a trip could be profitable only if there was but little competition.[11] I have already pointed that out with regard to equatorial Africa;[12] the best descriptions of these regions were written by the Venetian Alvise Ca'da Mosto and the Florentine Boccaccio. In contrast, the Genoese, although their expeditions into Africa were more numerous and more daring, have left us only two confidential letters, intended to inform and to appease discontented creditors. Thanks to these letters not destined for publicity, we know about Antoniotto Usodimare and Antonio Malfante; other information comes from maps, religious texts, and historical or pseudohistorical accounts; only a very small minority is revealed by notarial instruments. It is possible that such a formula as "promitto ire quo Deus mihi administraverit" was intended to conceal from intruders information historians would very much like to have. Other formulae, such as "[promittit ire] apud Septam *et quo maluerit,*" "[portabit] Sale *et quo iverit,*" announce only the first and not unusual destination, but give no hint about the final goal.[13]

---

[10] G. Boccaccio, *Decameron,* VI, 10; X, 3.

[11] *See,* for instance, *Libro che tracta di mercatantie et usanze de paesi,* ed. F. Borlandi (Torino, 1936), 165; and cf. our Venetian document for the profits of a journey to Delhi (*see* below, 174-180).

[12] R. Lopez, *Studi sull'economia genovese nel Medio Evo* (Torino, 1936), 5 ff.; 54-55; 57 ff.

[13] Cf. A. Lattes, *Il diritto marittimo privato nelle carte liguri dei secoli XII e XIII* (Città del Vaticano, 1939), 71; R. Ciasca, "Un centro marocchino del traffico genovese nel Medioevo," *Rivista internazionale di scienze sociali* (1935), 445 ff.; Lopez, 46 ff.

Merchants in the Medieval Indies

II

A characteristic example is provided by the notarial instruments drawn up for the brothers Ugolino and Vadino Vivaldi in 1291. They were preparing to find a western route to the Indies exactly two hundred years before Columbus; they drew up partnership and loan agreements "for the different parts of the world" (*per diversas mundi partes*), for Majorca, even for the Byzantine Empire—that is, for the direction opposite to their true one.[14] Perhaps we would know nothing of their deeds, if a chronicler, a relative of the capitalist who advanced the funds for the voyage, had not devoted to the heroes a short account and a prayer, after their galleys were lost.[15] Even so, the chronicler has raised only one side of the veil. His ambiguous words do not allow us to reconstruct the route projected by the daring men; they tell us only that the brothers were seen for the last time off the coast of Gozora, at the edge of Darkest Africa. Some years later, it seems, a son of Ugolino, who could not resign himself to believe that his father was dead, left by the normal route for the Indies, where he felt sure he would find him. He did not. Legends flourished almost at once: Dante idealized the Vivaldi in his Ulysses, who was swallowed by the waves when he first saw on the horizon the mysterious earth of the new hemisphere, promising the sciences and the virtues for which he thirsted. A hundred and fifty years later, Usodimare believed that he had met in Senegal a descendant of a survivor from the expedition. Other chroniclers maintained that only one of the galleys perished, while the other one reached Ethiopia. Who was right? The sea has the bodies and the secret; it will not yield them.[16]

The reasons that prompted the voyage of the Vivaldi, like those that later were to impel Columbus toward the unlooked-for Americas, were many, but a thirst for discovery of the ways of the unknown certainly was present. Moreover, the Vivaldi, like Columbus, wanted to carry the word of Christ to the savages.[17] The main aim, however, was to open a

---

[14] Sources in L. Belgrano, "Nota sulla spedizione dei fratelli Vivaldi," *Atti della Società Ligure di Storia Patria*, XV (1891), 317 ff., and in R. Caddeo, *Le Navigazioni atlantiche* (Milano, 1929), 111-114.

[15] Jacopo D'Oria, *Annales Januenses*, ed. Belgrano and Imperiale, V, 124; cf. Lopez, 8 ff.

[16] For the bibliography of this debated question, *see* the brilliant monograph of A. Magnaghi, *Precursori di Colombo? Il tentativo di viaggio transoceanico dei fratelli Vivaldi* (Roma, 1936).

[17] *See* p. 170.

170   *Robert Sabatino Lopez*

route entirely by sea for trade with the Indies. The advantages would have been twofold: A maritime trip would have been less expensive, and it would have replaced completely the southernmost of the three usual routes to the Levant (that through Egypt). Trade with. Egypt had been prohibited more strictly than ever by the Pope in 1291, as an answer to the Sultan's offensive against the last remnants of the kingdom of Jerusalem (1289-1291). In the face of the final collapse of the Christian holdings, and in view of the impossibility of gathering sufficient forces for an immediate reconquest, the effective enforcement of an embargo seemed to be the only reprisal possible. But in Genoa even those who would have been the most favorable to military action against Egypt could not see without deep concern the "very harsh" sentence of the Pope.[18] There was a flourishing Genoese colony in Alexandria, and its consul was Guizulfo de Guizulfis, a relative of that Buscarello who had done so much to bring about a Mongolian-European coalition against Egypt.[19] Neither the colony nor the consul was called back. But if the voyage of the Vivaldi brothers had been successful it would have supplied the Genoese with an alternative sea route to the Indies, and, as a result, the decay of Egypt in international trade would have followed as a matter of course.[20]

The embargo was never fully enforced, but it certainly contributed to channeling most of the China and India traffic away from the southernmost route. The central and northern routes were more expensive, for

[17] Jacopo D'Oria, V, 124; and cf. G. Pessagno, *Il commercio dei Genovesi,* in *La Consulta dei Mercanti Genovesi* (Genova, 1928).

[18] For the background of these measures, cf. W. Heyd, II, 23 ff.; R. Lopez, *Storia delle colonie genovesi nel Mediterraneo* (Bologna, 1938), 234-245; 271-275. There were two currents of opinion in Genoa. Many, including the heads of the Commune and the historian D'Oria (the words *sententia durissima* are his own), wanted business as usual. Others wanted all-out war against Egypt, and alliance with the Mongolians; the admiral Benedetto Zaccaria was perhaps their outstanding leader. But almost no one approved of the half-hearted hostility, based on an ineffectual embargo, which the Popes advocated. The Vivaldi expedition, organized by two cousins of Zaccaria and financed by a cousin of D'Oria, would have made the embargo a practicable measure. Another attempt along the same line was the maintenance of Genoese galleys (paid for by the Ilkhāns of Persia) on the strait of Bab-el Mandeb. These galleys tried to intercept all the oversea trade from Egypt to India and China, making the overland routes the only ones feasible. But this attempt was frustrated by the outbreak of hostilities between Guelfs and Ghibellines in Genoa.

[19] G. M. Thomas, *Diplomatarium Veneto-Levantinum* (Venezia, 1880), 31. A certain "J. de Ghisulphis" is found among a group of women who tried to organize a crusade against Egypt in 1301, under the leadership of Benedict Zaccaria and with the backing of the Ilkhāns. Cf. R. Lopez, *Benedetto Zaccaria ammiraglio e mercante* (Milano, 1933), 217 ff.

[20] *See* Symon Simeonis, *Itineraria,* ed. Nasmith (Cambridge, 1778), 19 ff.; William

Merchants in the Medieval Indies   171

they ran entirely overland; but they were shorter, safer, and protected by the friendly Mongolians. Besides, the Italian colonies at the western end of these itineraries (respectively in Southern Russia and the Crimea, and in Asia Minor and Persia) were expanding rapidly. Finally the Sultan of Egypt himself, wanting to reserve for his own subjects direct trade with India and China, did not allow foreign merchants bound for the Far East to cross his states; if they wanted to reach the Indian Ocean, they had to take long detours overland, through Asia Minor or Syria. Thus the direct trade with India and China by routes which avoided Egypt made steady progress in the first half of the fourteenth century. Some light is thrown on this progress by a Genoese notarial instrument, which, so far, has been known only through an incomplete summary of a modern scholar.[21]

In 1315 Benedetto Vivaldi (doubtless a relative of Ugolino and Vadino) left Genoa on the galley of Angelino de Mari, carrying with him in *accomendatio* £ 303. 17. 6 of Genoese denarii, which had been entrusted to him by Filippo, Simone, and Ginevra Vivaldi.[22] His announced destination was the Byzantine Empire; but, in fact, he was bound for the Indies, where he engaged in business with another Genoese, Percivalle Stancone. Benedetto died in the Indies some time later.[23] In 1322 his death was known in Genoa, so that a guardian was appointed for his minor sons. Stancone, without leaving India, informed the creditors and heirs of his associate that he was ready to send back Vivaldi's goods at their own risk. But the creditors preferred to transfer the *accomendatio* to Stancone himself. He was to invest the money in his own business and to bring the proceeds back to Genoa.

Adam, *De modo Sarracenos extirpandi,* ed. Köhler, *Recueil des historiens des Croisades,* 524 ff.; Marin Sanudo, *Secreta Fidelium Crucis,* ed. Bongars, *Gesta Dei per Francos,* II, 22 ff.; cf. W. Brandt, "Pierre Dubois, Mediaeval or Modern?" *The American Historical Review,* 1930, 507 ff.

[21] L. Belgrano, *Della vita privata dei Genovesi* (2d ed.; Genova, 1875), 191 ff. Besides omitting all the details of the document, Belgrano incorrectly speaks of a permanent society (*ratio Vivaldorum*). The term *ratio* in this document refers only to shares in a temporary *accomendatio* or partnership, such as were currently formed by the Genoese merchants for single voyages.

[22] Archivio di Stato, Genova, *Notaio Giovanni Gallo,* I, f. 136 v. and 137 r. Philip had given £150 (instrument of the notary Giorgio Boccaccio); Simon had given £79, 1s. 6d., and Ginevra, a niece of Philip, had given £74, 15s. (instruments of Filippo Avondo).

[23] "[Benedictus de Vivaldis] dictur navigasse de Janua in galea Angelini de Mari ano curente MCCCXV versus Romaniam, et . . . decessit in partibus Indie. Racio cuius Benedicti pervenit ex causa accomendacionis vel alio titulo ad Percivalem Stanconum, civem Januensem, qui est in dictis partibus Indie . . . ." (*Notaio Giovanni Gallo,* I, f. 136 v.)

172   *Robert Sabatino Lopez*

The names of some of the foremost Genoese traders in the Middle and Far East—de Anfussis, de Guizulfis, de Camilla—are brought in, directly or indirectly, by this document.[24] As for the Stancone family, it appears from other sources that it was especially prominent in trade with Tuscany and Rome; but there are no other records of its activity outside Europe.[25] On the other hand, it should be pointed out that we owe the mention of India in a notarial document to a special circumstance, the death of Vivaldi in that country; the original contracts of *accomendatio,* it will be recalled, mentioned only the Byzantine Empire.

The trip of Stancone and Vivaldi took place at a very favorable moment for overland trade with the Far East. The embargo against Egypt had never been so near to complete enforcement; even Venice, usually the best customer of that country, sent no convoys there from 1323 to 1345.[26] In contrast, the routes through the four great Mongolian empires were wide open. Pegolotti's statement about the northern route ("entirely without danger") refers to this period.[27] As for the other

---

[24] The guardian of the heirs of Benedict Vivaldi, Leone di Ricaldone, was also guardian of the heirs of Anfreone and Ugolino de Guizulfis (Archivio di Stato, Genova, *Notaio Giovanni Gallo,* I, fol. 124 r.). One of the witnesses of our document was Benedetto de Anfussis, of the same family as Thomas, the banker, whose diplomatic missions to the Mongolic courts were mentioned before. (The Anfussis family was also engaged in oversea trade with Flanders as early as 1310; cf. R. Doehaerd, "Les Galères génoises dans la Manche et la Mer du Nord," *Bulletin de l'Institut Historique Belge de Rome,* XIX [1938], 56 ff. and 62 ff.) The other witnesses are a notary (Ventura di Manarola) and Giovanni de Camilla, belonging to another family prominent in the Byzantine Empire, in Persia, and in the Crimea.

[25] At the end of the twelfth century the Roman merchants residing in Genoa used to meet in a *lobia* rented from the Stancone family, and, in the thirteenth century, the merchants of Lucca, Florence, Pisa, Pistoia, and Arezzo held frequent meetings in the house or in the square of the Stancone. In 1307, on the other hand, Simone Stancone was the consul of the Genoese merchants in Pisa (Archivio di Stato, Genova, *Notaio Lanfranco,* II A, fol. 113 r.; *Notaio Ignoti,* Busta I; *Notaio Andreolo de Laneriis,* I B, fol. 40 r.; cf. also A. Ferretto, "Codice diplomatico . . . ," *Atti della Società Ligure di Storia Patria,* XXXI [1903], index of names, *Stancone*). In 1278 and in 1281 Tommaso Stancone made business trips to Majorca; the second time he was a partner of Percivalle de Mari (Archivio di Stato, Genova, *Notaio Giovanni de Corsio,* I, 174 v. and 183; *Notaio Leonardo Negrini,* I, fol. 78 v.).

[26] Cf. Heyd, II, 43 ff., with sources. As a matter of course, this does not imply that single ships did not go to Egypt from time to time, with or without a special license from the Pope.

[27] Likewise, Friar John of Montecorvino wrote in 1305: "per terram Cothay Imperatoris aquilonarium Tartarorum est via brevior et securior, ita quod cum nunciis infra V vel VI menses poterunt pervenire" (*Sinica Franciscana,* I, 349). (According to Pegolotti, the journey from Tana to Peking took from 259 to 284 days.) On the other hand, Montecorvino states that the sea route is dangerous, and has been particularly dangerous for the last twelve years "propter guerras"; it takes at least two years to go from Europe to "Peking by sea." The *nuncii* mentioned by Friar John are the messengers of the state mail. It is worth remarking that the second successor of Kubilai, Kaishan Kuluk (1307-1311), prohibited western merchants from using the horses of the official mail (cf. H. Cordier, *Histoire générale de la Chine et de ses*

route, through Asia Minor and Persia, it is true that Pegolotti speaks of numberless customs, and of brigands who defied repeated efforts of the Ilkhāns to wipe them out.[28] Nevertheless, so long as the descendants of Hulāgū-khān held Irak, Iran, and Eastern Anatolia as a solid bloc,

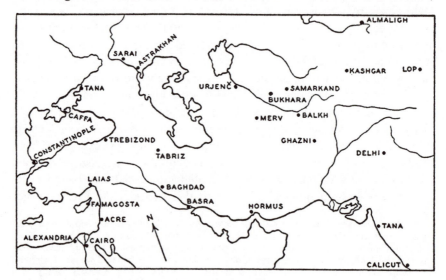

ROUTES TO THE INDIES

the dangers for the merchants could not be too great. But in 1338, after the death of Abū-saʿīd, the empire of the Ilkhāns split into several small states. Tabrīz, the former capital and one of the most important road junctions, fell under the jobanide Hasan, and then under his brother Ashraf, a bloody tyrant.[29] On the other hand, in 1339 a usurper got temporary control of the capital of the central empire, Almalīgh. He

---

relations avec les pays étrangers [Paris, 1920-1921], II, 345). This probably was a consequence of the increase of unauthorized use of these horses by the merchants, among whom there may have been some Europeans.

[28] Cf. Heyd, II, 117 ff.; G. I. Bratianu, *Recherches sur le commerce génois dans la Mer Noire au XIIIᵉ siècle* (Paris, 1929), 179 ff., with sources. There were along the way numerous state guards (*tataul*), to whom the merchants were expected to pay a special tax. But, despite the severe regulation enforced by Ghāzān-khān (who is enthusiastically praised for that by his historian Rashīd al-Dīn) and again by Abū-saʿīd, the merchants were still subjected to illegal contributions both by the brigands and by the guards. We cannot agree with Heyd, who accepts uncritically the statements of Rashīd al-Dīn; Pegolotti, a few years after the death of Ghāzān, set apart in the budget of a trip from Lajazzo to Tabrīz 50 aspers "per forza che fanno i moccoli, cioè tartari scherani." For robbers along other stretches of the route *see,* for instance, Marco Polo, ch. 5, 18, 19.

[29] Cf. Hammer-Purgstall, *Geschichte der Ilkhane* (Darmstadt, 1842-1844), II, 337; H. H. Howorth, *History of the Mongols* (London, 1876-1888), III, 650; B. Spulber, *Die Mongolen in Iran* (Leipzig, 1939), 135 ff., with sources.

Robert Sabatino Lopez

stirred up the people of this important station on the northern route to a pogrom against European missionaries and merchants.[30] Both the over-land routes to China were therefore blocked; but it was still possible to go to India by taking the northern route from Tana to Urjench (in the Mongolian empire of Kipchak) and then cutting south through Ghaznī. The latter city, once a splendid capital, had been ruined by the Mongolian conquest, although the travelers still used the trail thither.[31]

III

The only extant (and hitherto unprinted) information about a journey of European traders to India via Ghaznī[32] is, once more, explained by the fact that some of the merchants died on the way. In 1338, six merchants left Venice, bound for Delhi. At least four of them belonged to the upper bracket of the Venetian aristocracy: Giovanni (nicknamed Vacca) and Paolo Loredano, Marco Soranzo, and Marino Contarini.[33] At that time the Sultan of Delhi, Muhammad ibn-Tughluk, was vig-orously engaged in the conquest and the Islamization of the whole Dekkan.[34] Although he was monstrously cruel toward his enemies, as he often was toward his own subjects, he had frequent impulses of lavish generosity, especially toward foreigners. Rumors spread from the Khurāsān to Arabia that he liked strangers better than natives, and that he called them "a'izza" ("illustrious ones") lest the name "foreigners" might "tear their heart and trouble their spirit."[35]

These rumors certainly were reported in Europe by the numerous Venetian merchants settled in Persia; probably that is why neither love for his wife and his three sons, nor the prayers of his mother, his brother, and the family priest could make Giovanni Loredano desist from his planned trip.[36] The efforts of his brother to prevent loans

[30] Cf. P. Pelliot, "Chrétiens d'Asie Centrale et d'Extrême-Orient," *T'oung Pao*, III (1914), 630 ff.; W. Barthold, *Vorlesungen über die Geschichte der Türken Mittelasiens* (Berlin, 1935), 206 ff.; R. Grousset, *L'Empire des steppes* (Paris, 1939), 414 ff., with sources.

[31] Heyd, II, 140, maintains that no Europeans used the route from Persia to India via Ghaznī (cf. also M. Longworth Dames, "Ghazna," *Encyclopedia of the Islam*). But our documents prove that they did.

[32] I am indebted to Professor Gino Luzzatto for this document and for his transcription of it.

[33] On the Soranzo, for instance, cf. G. Luzzatto, "Les Activités économiques du patriciat vénitien," *Annales d'histoire économique et sociale*, IX (1937), 42, 51 ff. Each one of these families gave more than one doge to the Republic.

[34] Cf. T. W. Haig, *Cambridge History of India*, III, 136 ff., with sources.

[35] Ibn Batūta, ed. Défréméry and Sanguinetti, III, 243-244.

[36] Archivio di Stato, Venezia, *Procuratori di San Marco, Misti*, Busta 122 (Testimony of Leonardo de Cagnolis, parson of S. Gemignano, February 22, 1344?) : "Quando ser Zaninus Lauretano dictus Vacha intimus meus disposuit se ire ad viagium a Delli,

being made to Giovanni had no greater success, especially since
Giovanni's father-in-law, Alberto de Calli, more business-minded than
family-conscious, loaned him £80 veneziane di grossi, *in muodo de
colleganza*.[37] Another nobleman Francesco Marcello loaned £3, also as
a *colleganza,* while Antonio of Cremona loaned some 20 lire, probably
as a sea loan.[38] Perhaps a loan was made also by Caterina, the mother
of Giovanni.[39]

The merchants doubtless landed in the Crimea, and proceeded with no
recorded incidents as far as Astrakhan, one of the main stations of the
route to Cathay as described by Pegolotti.[40] Here they were obliged to
stop for fifty days before crossing the river, "because of the ice."[41] This
seems to confirm a contemporary account (of Ibn Batūta) that all
communications between the two shores of the Volga were interrupted

---

de quo non redivit, mater sua domina Chaterina et ser Bertonus Lauretano non semel
sed pluries et pluries in mea presentia ipsum rogabant quod ab isto viagio desisteret
omnino, et ego pluries ipsum rogavi tam ex parte mea quam ex parte predictorum
quod sibi placeret desistere. Qui mihi respondebat quod bene faciebat illud quod faciebat,
et cum Dei adiutorio ipse rediret consolatus. Item conquestus fuit michi de ser Bertono
qui nolebat quod mater sua dare [sic] sibi denarios ad istum viagium . . . ."

[37] Archivio di Stato, Venezia, *Procuratori di San Marco, Misti,* Busta 122. The
attorney of Alberto de Calli produced the following document, written by Giovanni
Loredano: "1338 de luio, Io Zanin Loredan son contento d'aver rezevudo da mio
suocero ser Alberto da Calle Libre 80 de grossi per portar al viazo ch'io anderò
a vostro pro e danno in muodo de colleganza, dagando vui a mia mare lirre [sic]
3 soldi 10 de grossi . . . ." *See also* the defense of the sons of the deceased, September
23, 1346.

[38] From the request of the attorney of Alberto de Calli, September 23, 1346: "Con-
tentabatur tamen dictus Albertus quod in dicto viagio fuerunt de ratione ser Francisci
Marcello libre 3 grossorum pro quibus non credebat ei fuisse satisfactum; item quod de
ratione Antonii de Cremona circa libre 20 grosse que non fuerunt reportate de Delli
ad civitatem Venetiarum, sed in Delli dicto Antonio fuit de ipsis et de prode et lucro
integre satisfactum de monte partis dicti Johannis." The last sentence might lead one
to think that Antonio da Cremona went with the others to India. But Antonio was not
one of the six partners, and there is nothing in the documents which allows us to conclude that he went with them. More probably the sum was withdrawn from further
speculation in Delhi because it was a sea loan, due on safe arrival there.

[39] The attorneys of the heirs of Loredano tried to prove "quod ultra rationes predictas
dictus Johannes extraxerat de Veneciis denarios a multis personis et maxime a matre
sua." But their evidence was not regarded as sufficient by the Judges of the Procuratori di
San Marco. In general the documents and testimony produced by the defense made no
explicit mention of a loan for the trip to the Far East, except for a few lines entered
in a book of the priest Marco de Viviano, as follows: "1339 del mese decembre
rezevé Nicolina da soa mare [Caterina Lauretano] per nome de lo dicto Vacha da Cha
Loredan £ 13 e soldi 15 de grossi de pro e de cavedal che 'l pié in lo viazo del Cataio."
The book was in the possession of Caterina; but the priest declared that he had not
actually seen her giving the money to John.

[40] Pegolotti, 21.

[41] Archivio di Stato, Venezia, quoted above, testimony of Andrea Giustiniani (who,
at that time, was the podestà of Mestre), September 20, 13. . ?: "dum iret ad viagium
de Organzi, ipse applicuit in Citracham, ubi invenit quamplures, inter quos erat nobilis
vir Johannes Lauretano dictus Vacha cum societate que ire debebat ad viagium del
Delli, et propter glaciem ipsi morati fuerunt ibidem per dies 50, et inde non potuerunt
discedere."

Robert Sabatino Lopez

at the beginning of winter; whereas, when the ice was thick, the river could easily be crossed by sleds. In summer, as Pegolotti tells us, it was possible to cross by boat, a cheaper means of transportation.[42]

Pegolotti had advised merchants leaving from Genoa or Venice for Cathay to bring cloth to Urjench, where it could be sold at a profit. But Giovanni Loredano was obliged to cut a part of the cloths he had carried from home, and to send them back to be sold at Tana. He was selling them at a loss, as he told Andrea Giustiniani, another Venetian nobleman who met our merchants in Astrakhan, where he, too, had to stop on his way to Urjench.[43] A little later, the goods of Loredano were appraised at about 105 lire by his associates; that is, at a sum just about equal to the loans he had contracted in Venice. So far, there was no profit.[44]

The next part of the journey, especially the stretch from Bukhara to the Pamir plateau, was very trying. Half a century earlier Marco Polo fell sick before reaching this plateau; but he recovered his health, thanks to a long stay on the Badakhshān, whose miraculous salubrity he exalted.[45] Loredano was not so fortunate; he died in or near Ghaznī, not far from this region. Now, in the Mongolian states, according to a custom mentioned by Pegolotti, the goods of a merchant who died en route were seized unless a brother could take them over.[46] This is certainly why a new partition of the *monte* (the capital) was made at once. Each of the surviving merchants contributed a minimum of 205 to 210 lire; Paolo Loredano took over also the share of his brother, and added enough money of his own to bring that share to 210 lire.[47]

---

[42] Ibn Batūta, II, 410 ff.; Pegolotti, 21.

[43] Testimony of Andrea Giustiniani, quoted above: "et infra dictum tempus pluries se invenit in stopa [*sic*] dicti ser Johannis, ubi ipse ser Johannes morabatur. Et vidit quod de certis pannis quos ipse habebat, ipse incidebat et faciebat cavicios et mittebat in Tanum ad vendendum." Giustiniani did not know definitely whether this cloth belonged to Loredano, or its worth, or the amount of loss sustained by Loredano in the sale; but he believed that the cloth had been brought from Venice. *See also* the defense: "dictus Johannes multum amisserat de ratīone pannorum quos dicebant habuisse a dicto Alberto pro dictis libris 80 grossorum."

[44] *See* below, note 47.

[45] Marco Polo, ch. 29; *see also* Yule's notes, I, 163.

[46] Pegolotti, 22: "se il mercatante che va o che viene morisse in cammino ogni cosa sarebbe del signore del paese . . . e tutto prenderebbono gli ufficiali del signore . . . . Veramente s'egli avesse suo fratello o stretto compagno che dicesse che fusse suo fratello, sì gli sarebbe dato l'avere del morto, e camperebbesi in questo modo l'avere." This shows that Chingis Khan's Yasa ("In case the dead man has no heir . . . . In no case his estate is confiscated") did not apply to foreign merchants. Cf. G. Vernadsky, "Juwaini's version of Chingis Khan's Yasa," *Seminarium Kondakovianum*, XI, 1340.

[47] Archivio di Stato, Venezia, first testimony of Marco Soranzo, August 30, 1343; "Eo Marco Soranzo de S. Apostolo . . . dentro quello ch'io missi in queste terre e

Merchants in the Medieval Indies 177

When the merchants finally arrived at Delhi, their hopes of gain were realized. The Sultan gave them as a gift 200 thousand bezants, the equivalent of about 7,500 Venetian lire,[48] a deed not unworthy of him. Ibn Batūta (who probably was at Delhi when our merchants arrived there, but who does not speak of them) quotes a more lavish gift; the Sultan gave to the Persian merchant Shihāb al-Dīn a thousand thamgas of gold, with the right of pre-emption of wares of any kind worth that much, and three ships complete with sails, food, and sailors to carry the wares home. But Ibn Batūta adds that later on Shihāb al-Dīn lost all his substance in a civil war, and philosophically concludes: "Such is the usual end of treasures acquired in India. Seldom does a man leave that country with the goods he has accumulated; if he does God sends him a misfortune which swallows up all his goods."[49] This reflection was doubtless suggested by Ibn Batūta's own ill luck after he left Delhi. And, in fact, two more of the Venetian merchants died on the way home, which makes us think that there might be something to the Arab traveler's omen![50]

One tenth of the Sultan's gift was kept back by the customs, and the merchants had to give one per cent to the chief customs officer, perhaps as a bribe. Besides, the Venetians deemed it prudent to buy the

---

tutte spese ch'io fici in Casni fo da libre 105 infin 110 de grossi, et infin questo luogo aviso che 'l dicto ser Zan Loredan metesse tanto. Pasando puochi zorni el dicto ser Zane si mori." First testimony of Marino Contarini: "Marin Contarini fiol de messer Dardi Contarini de la contrada de S. Salvador. . . . Dentro quello ch'io missi in questa terra e quello ch'io spisi de fin che nui fosemo in Casni fo da libre 105 de grossi. E infin a questo luogo aviso che ser Zan Loredan mettesse tanto anche ello. Passando certi zorni ello manchò, de che so frar ser Polo in tute le spese che bisogna implir in questo sesto, nui consentissemo che lo implisse. E fo dentro quello che fo messo in la compagnia per homo o che fo speso dapuò da libre 210 de grossi. E s'el no avesse implido questo sesto, sì l'avessemo implido nuy e trato l'utel de quelo che 'n de fosse meso." Similar testimonies were given by these and other witnesses in later hearings. Marco Soranzo and Marino Contarini, in another hearing, declared that the new repartition of the *monte* occurred at about fifteen days' distance from Delhi.

[48] Second testimony of Marco Soranzo, January 9, 1943 (*more veneto*, that is, 1344): "nui avessemo de dono dal signor del Delli . . . bizanti 200,000, de li qual el de romase in la casena bizanti 20,000, e bizanti 2000 avè el scrivan de la dita casena." Testimony of Soranzo and Contarini, on request of Alberto de Calli: "domandado . . . quanto rezevé tuta la compagnia del signor del Delli, responderunt 200,000 bizanti, de li qual de romase a la casena del signor 20,000."

[49] Ibn Batūta, III, 244 ff.

[50] The merchants who left Venice were six (see the expressions "in questo sesto" in the testimony quoted above, note 47, and that quoted below, note 55). Three came safely home, and were heard in court: Soranzo, Contarini, and Paolo Loredano. As for the others, their death must be inferred from these words of the testimony of Soranzo and Contarini on request of Alberto de Calli: "domandado . . . se ordenamento di compagni fo che le parti di morti vegna del Delli in Famagosta et infin a Marina senza spesa alguna, responderunt sic in parte ser Balduini et in aliis partibus non." Thus

Robert Sabatino Lopez

friendship of the courtiers by distributing nine hundred to a thousand bezants.[51] Next they set aside a sum for paying back special loans not included in the *monte,* such as that of Antonio of Cremona.[52] Then they bought pearls worth 102 thousand bezants, after which they allotted 10 thousand bezants to each one of the six partners (Paolo Loredano receiving both his own share and that of his deceased brother), and finally they invested what was left in thamgas, the local currency.[53] They began their return trip without dividing the pearls among themselves.

When they reached Urjench, however, they distributed the pearls in equal shares, 17 thousand bezants worth to each partner.[54] As for the thamgas, the division could hardly have been in equal parts, inasmuch as some of the partners had contributed more than the minimum share of 210 lire.[55] About the rest of the journey we have no direct information, but the division of goods points to a separation of the merchants. We only know that the share of one of those who died on the way home, Baldovino, was sent to Venice via Famagosta; that is, by a different way from that used on the outward journey.[56] Why the division and why the change of route? Possibly each merchant wanted to try his own chances at selling his wares on the way home in view of the fact that pearls

---

one of the deceased was Baldovino (his family name is not revealed by our documents). The others ("in aliis partibus," a plural) must have been two—John Loredano, and another merchant whose name is not given.

[51] *See* above, note 42. "Ancor de fo donadi via a quelli che 'n de avea fato molto honor, zoè da li baroni del signor, da bizanti 9000 in 10,000" (second testimony of Marco Soranzo).

[52] Ancor domandado . . . se Polo pagò in Delli alguni debiti per so frar, digo de si, ad un Antonio da Cremona, ma non so quanti" (second testimony of Marco Soranzo). "[Polo Loredano] satisfecerat in Delli rationem Antonii" (request of the attorneys of Albert). *See also* above, note 38.

[53] "Ancor trazessemo in Delli del monte bizanti 10,000 per zascadun, che vien bizanti 60,000 . . . . Alguni altri dener fo investidi in tangade. E quello che resta, che fo da bizanti 102,000 sì fo investidi in perle" (second testimony of Marco Soranzo).

[54] First testimony of Soranzo: "Et avè ser Pollo in Organzi quando nui partissemo tante perle che costa bizanti 17,000." (Six times 17 thousand makes exactly 102 thousand.) Likewise Marino Contarini, and the attorneys of Alberto de Calli.

[55] First testimony of Soranzo: "Eo . . . aviso aver trato da questo viazo da fiorin 3500, ben ch'io avì in Delli bizanti 2000 plui ch'el dito ser Polo Loredan per questo sesto. E ben posso dir con vero ch'io ò vendudo assé meio le mie cosse che non à fato algun de loro, perch'io le mandie in Franza." First testimony of Contarini: "Eo . . . . aviso de aver trato da questo viazo libre 300 grossorum, ben ch'io avesse in Delli da bizanti 4000 plui che no avè ser Pollo per questo sesto." Testimony of Soranzo and Contarini on request of Albert: "Item quanto rezevè in Delli zascun de li compagnoni e Pollo per la parte del Vacha de la dita gracia oltra li 17,000 bizanti e centenara rezevudi in Organzi per zascun de compagni e per ser Polo per la parte del Vacha, responderunt nescire."

[56] *See* above, note 50.

were exempt from customs charges in Persia as well as in Tana.[57] At any rate Marco Soranzo sent his gems to be sold in France.[58]

The change of route might have been connected with the disorders started at Tana in the first months of 1343. A Tartar was killed by a Venetian merchant; the angry populace therefore slaughtered all those Occidentals who had no time to take shelter on the galleys; they also plundered the houses of the westerners. This popular reprisal was followed by an official opening of hostilities against westerners by the khan of Kipchak, who besieged Caffa, the main Genoese colony on the South Russian shores.[59] News of these disorders might have reached our merchants in Urjench, giving them sufficient reason to avoid the northern route, and to try separately to reach the Mediterranean by either the central or the southern route. It would seem unlikely, however, that the merchants could have been informed in time, for Soranzo was back in Venice as early as the end of August 1343. Perhaps there had been unrest in the Crimea even before the massacre at Tana.

The profits of a journey so long, so adventurous, and altogether so fortunate, thanks to the generosity of the Sultan, were not as exceedingly high as one might expect. When Alberto de Calli—quite a stingy person, as appears from this and other documents—sued the heirs of Loredano for his part of the profit, it was found that the total proceeds of Giovanni Loredano's journey had been liquidated to the guardian of his heirs as 230 lire.[60] This was less than twice the amount of the loans received by the merchant when he left Venice. The proceeds were higher for Marino Contarini, about 300 lires; but he had invested 4,000 bezants more than Loredano. Marco Soranzo, who gained 330 florins, had invested 2,000 bezants more than Loredano and he had sent his pearls

---

[57] Pegolotti, 24 and 28.

[58] *See* above, note 55.

[59] Cf. E. Skrzinska, "Inscriptions des colonies génoises en Crimée," *Atti della Società Ligure di Storia Patria*, LVI (1928), introduction; Lopez, *Storia delle colonie . . .* 330 ff.; Grousset, 481 ff., with sources.

[60] First decision of the Judges of the Procuratori di San Marco, September 22, 13..?: "quod Paulus Lauretanus olim frater Johannis Lauretani dicti Vacha de bonis habitis et receptis in manibus dicti Pauli que fuerunt dicti Johannis ad viagium del Delli, deductis omnibus imprestitis, uxuris et presis et provisionibus et prode, tam de denariis acceptis per suprascriptum quondam dominum Johannem Lauretano quam per suprascriptum Paullum Lauretano occasione dicti colomelli et maxime denariorum quos dictus Johannes habuit ab Antonio de Cremona, dare et restituere deberet suprascriptis dominis procuratoribus tutoribus dictorum pupillorum libras 230 grossorum, nectas a suprascriptis omnibus . . . . " The guardians were Marco Loredano and Francesco Querini, Procurators of San Marco.

Robert Sabatino Lopez

to France, an additional trip which involved further risks, expenses, and time.[61]

It should be said, however, that no regular accounting was produced in court. Was this a strange negligence, or a shrewd maneuver in order to make Loredano's profits appear smaller, and thereby give a smaller sum to his creditors? The practice of the *accomendatio* and of the *collegantia* in the fourteenth century no longer required the traveling partner to supply the passive investor with any specific proof, or even to support his statement with an oath.[62] We cannot help wondering whether this case was not similar to that of a Genoese merchant, Daniel Fontanella, who declared to the guardian of the heirs of a fellow citizen that he had lost 20 per cent out of an *accomendatio* received from the latter, while it was known that he had gained fifty per cent or more; nevertheless, the guardian could not recover the money and had only the meager comfort of having a notary public write down his protest.[63] Be that as it may, Alberto de Calli was able to obtain from the heirs of Loredano all the acknowledged proceeds of the Indian trip, except the sums due to the other investors, and the share reserved to the traveling partner by the customs of *collegantia*.[64] Soon after the lawsuit was concluded, the widow of Giovanni Loredano provided for her own future—both in this and in the next world—by going into a convent.[65]

---

[61] *See* above, note 55.

[62] Cf. especially G. Luzzatto, "La commenda nella vita economica dei secoli XIII e XIV . . . ," *Atti della manifestazione pro Tabula d'Amalphi, I, convegno di studi di Diritto Marittimo* (Napoli, 1934), with sources. In the fourteenth century some statutes fixed a minimum percentage of profit that the traveling partner was obliged to give the passive investor, if he was unable to produce an account. Cf. Lattes, 77, 154.

[63] Cf. R. Lopez, "Aux origines du capitalisme génois," *Annales d'histoire économique et sociale*, IX (1937), 447 ff.; also R. L. Reynolds, "A business affair in Genoa in the year 1200," *Studi di storia e diritto in onore di Enrico Besta* (Milano, 1937-1939), II, 165 ff.

[64] The customary share of the traveling partner was one fourth, and, therefore, should have been £36. 15 out of a declared profit of £147. But the Procuratori di San Marco, in agreement with the demands of the attorneys of Alberto de Calli, left to the heirs of Loredano £44. 8. The difference was due "tam pro repromissa uxoris dicti Johannis Lauretani quam pro aliis expensis dictorum pupilorum et eorum occasione" (final decision of the Judges of the Procuratori di San Marco, September 23, 1346: it was a widespread, although not a universal use that the share of the capitalist was to be accounted for *sine expensis*). Of the remaining part of the profit £3. 14, £2. were assigned to Francesco Marcello, and £98. 17. 10 to Alberto de Calli.

[65] *See* four other parchments of the same Busta 122, dated May 19 and 26, 1339; August 10, 1344; January 19, 1341 (*more veneto*).

IV

The political disasters that have been mentioned were only the first of a series: the *pax Mongolica* was rapidly approaching its end, and as a result the overland routes of Asia were being closed to trade one after the other. Moreover, in China, where all foreigners had for centuries enjoyed hospitality, good order, and religious tolerance, a critical situation developed. The missionary archbishop of Peking, Giovanni Marignolli, was received in a solemn audience by the Great Khan as late as 1342; but this was the last known overland journey to China by an Occidental for centuries. A few years later a Moslem was entrusted with the presidency of the Ch'ung-fu-ssu, the office concerned with the centuries-old relations of the Chinese government with the Christian clergy.[66] Meantime, internal disorders, which began in 1337 with the rebellions of Chu-kuang-k'ing and of Pang-hu, undermined the Mongolian dynasty. In 1368 the Ming drove off the Mongolians forever and confronted the Europeans with much less tolerance than had the Yuan. At the same time, the Mongolian empire of Central Asia (Chaghatāi) was split into two states. The western part (Mā warā'al-Nahr) was ruled by powerless and do-nothing kings; the eastern underwent a period of anarchy, and fell prey to frequent explosions of xenophobe fanaticism. As for the empire of Kipchak, Khan Djānī-beg was obliged by the stern defenders of Caffa to withdraw and to conclude an agreement in 1350. His death was followed by years of anarchy. Finally, the relations of Genoa with the tyrant of Tabrīz grew so bad that the city had to enforce *devetum* (a commercial embargo) against his states.

The effect of so many disasters was promptly felt. In 1340, Chinese silk had been considered in Genoa one fifth less valuable than the silk of Merv, so much nearer to Europe.[67] But three years later, a chronicler states that the events in the Crimea had caused both the silk and the spices to rise from fifty to a hundred per cent in price.[68]

Italian merchants, however, did not give up at once. Evidence of another trip to the Far East is found in a notarial document; once again, we have a record because one of the travelers got into trouble.[69]

---

[66] A. C. Moule, *Christians in China* (London, 1930), 228 ff.

[67] Cf. H. Sieveking, *Aus Genueser Rechnungs- und Steuerbücher* (Wien, 1909), 15.

[68] Giovanni Villani, *Cronaca*, XII, ch. 27. This statement, while doubtless containing some truth, is likely to be exaggerated; but we have no direct way to check on it.

[69] Archivio di Stato, Genova, *Notai Domenico Durante e Oberto Osbergerio*, I, fol. 223 v. This document was brought to my attention by Mlle Renée Doehaerd.

Robert Sabatino Lopez

In 1343 Tommaso Gentile, a Genoese, arrived at Hormuz on the Persian Gulf, bound for Cathay. The document does not tell by what route he reached this city, but a guess is not difficult. He could not use the approach from the Crimea, because of the war against Djānī-beg. The shortest route, via Tabrīz, was barred by the newly enforced embargo, as we learn from the document itself.[70] Egypt, or the Egyptian-dominated harbors of Syria, were no thoroughfares for a European. The only available access was Lajazzo (Laias or Ayās), the main harbor of the Christian kingdom of Armenia; from there, Gentile could reach Hormuz, passing between the Egyptian possessions and the state of al-Ashraf. This was apparently the route selected by Marco Polo and his uncles some seventy years earlier; but the Venetian merchants, instead of sailing from Hormuz around India and Indo-China, had gone back to the Pamir plateau, where they had reached the main overland trail from Tabrīz. Probably they had intended at first to sail, but were discouraged by the fragility of the local ships, of which many travelers (including Polo) speak profusely.[71] In 1342, one year before Gentile arrived at Hormuz, Ibn Batūta was shipwrecked while going from India to China and had to take shelter at the Maldive islands.[72] In contrast, Friar Oderic of Pordenone sailed from Hormuz and arrived happily in China. But he stated that all the foreigners who went through this torrid place fell sick unless they took a curious precaution.[73]

Perhaps our merchant neglected to take the precaution; at any rate, he did fall sick. This was all the more unpleasant because, if he died, local custom prescribed that his goods be seized.[74] So Tommaso Gentile entrusted his merchandise to his companions, who went ahead toward Cathay, and he went home by the shortest way. Unfortunately the

---

[70] There were two decrees to this effect, one dated June 7, 1340, and the other April 12, 1341.

[71] Marco Polo, ch. 19; Giovanni di Montecorvino, *Sinica Franciscana*, I, 344-345; Oderico di Pordenone, *ibid.*, I, 422. Marco Polo arrived again at Hormuz from China on his way home via Tabrīz.

[72] Ibn Batūta, IV, 94 ff.; *see,* however, the objections of Ferrand, 426-433. Giovanni Marignolli, too, was in imminent danger of shipwreck between Columbus and Madras (*Sinica Franciscana*, I, 537).

[73] Oderico di Pord., *Sin Franc.*, I, 422: "In ea tantus et ita immensus est calor, quod virilia, id est testiculi hominum, exeunt ex corpore et descendunt usque ad dimidiam tibiarum. Ideoque gens illius contrate si vivere volunt, sibi faciunt unam unctionem qua illa ungunt. Nam aliter omnes penitus morerentur, et sicut sunt uncta, in quibusdam saculis illa portant circumcirca se cingentes." *See also* Marco Polo, ch. 19; for similar remarks in Arabic sources, cf. P. Schwarz, *Iran im Mittelalter nach den arabischen Geographen* (Leipzig, 1896-1929), III, 242 ff.; for additional material from European sources, cf. Hallberg, 242 ff.

[74] Marco Polo, ch. 19.

shortest way was via Tabrīz.[75] When news of his journey reached Genoa, his father had to justify his transgression of the *devetum* with the "Eight Wisemen of Navigation and the Major [Black] Sea," the superior colonial board of the Commune. These officers accepted the thesis of an act of God, and acquitted Gentile from every penalty, inasmuch as he had gone through Tabrīz with no merchandise.[76]

A few months later, in 1344, ambassadors of al-Ashraf arrived in Genoa. The tyrant promised an indemnity for everything which had been stolen from the Genoese, and favorable treatment in the future. But it was only a trap. As soon as Genoese merchants were allowed to go back to Persia they were robbed, and many were slaughtered. The material damage reached the exceedingly high sum of 200 thousand lire di grossi.[77] Persia had to be erased from the map of Genoese traders, and from that of the Venetians. Furthermore, in 1347 the Sultan of Egypt conquered Lajazzo (Laias). This bottled up all Far Eastern trade, for the only route which avoided both Tabrīz and the Egyptian possessions went through Almalīgh, and no one would dare crossing the Mā warā al-Nahr after Marignolli. It is true that after the middle of the fourteenth century the new sovereign of Tabrīz, Uwais I, tried to reestablish trade relations with both the Venetians and the Genoese. But he could not give them the guarantees they required, and the Italian merchants, eager as they were to recover their prosperous trade in Persia

---

[75] Archivio di Stato, Genova, quoted above: "ut oppressum gravi et valida egretudine remanserit in Ormes derelictum a sociis iter eorum arripientibus versus Cathayum, propter quam oportuit ipsum [Thomaynum Gentilem] transire Taurixium in reditu, ut avidum ad propria remeare . . . ."

[76] Archivio di Stato, Genova, quoted above: "Officium octo sapientium constitutorum super factis navigandi et Maris Maioris in quo interfuit sufficiens et legitimus numerus ipsorum officialium, et ipsi officiales concorditer, visa requisitione Chonfredi Gentilis requirentis Thomaynum filium suum absolvi non obstante ipsum pergisse Taurixium seu transisse per dictas partes Taurixii, cum casu necessario pergerit, et non habentem mercimoniam [sic] . . . considerando quod ad partes Cathay non poterat profici [sic], quo primo proposuerat ambulare; ad eciam ex Commissione ducali facta diligenti inquisitione de hiis ad hoc ut reperiri possit et valeat veritas, scrutatis diligenter omnibus possibilibus erga hoc, et reperto per patentes litteras fidedignorum ostensas dicto officio ac eciam presentatas, necnon fama publica quorundam civium expertorum ad hoc, dictum Thomaynum non ivisse seu transisse ad dictas partes Taurixii voluntatis actu, set necessario ut permittitur . . . tractavit, statuit et ordinavit necnon declarando voluit dictum Thomaynum non incidisse in aliquam penam occasionibus predictis, non obstantibus decretis, statuitis seu prohibicionibus." The document bears no date.

[77] Giorgio Stella, ed. Muratori, XVII, 1081; Giustiniani, *Annali*, fol. 131 (cf. on the latter Heyd, II, 131-132). These historians do not explain why the ruler of Tabrīz felt the need of sending ambassadors; our document makes it evident that he wanted the lifting of embargo.

Robert Sabatino Lopez

and to reopen the routes to India and China, felt it unsafe to trust a mere promise.[78]

General conditions became a little less unfavorable for inter-Asiatic trade in the first half of the fifteenth century. After the bloody exploits of Tamerlane, his son Shāhrukh successfully held together Irak, Persia, and Turkestan, and sent embassies to India and China. The Ming emperor, Yung-lo, sent Chinese warships as far west as Hormuz, and ambassadors as far as Aden and East Africa. But the commercial benefits were exploited by the Chinese and the Arabians. Only one European merchant seems to have profited by this Indian summer of peace, Athanasius Nikitin of Tver (between 1468 and 1474). He certainly reached India through the Kipchak and Hormuz.[79]

As for the Italians, they made concentrated efforts to get around the prohibition of the Egyptian Sultan against crossing his states toward the Red Sea. In the last years of the fifteenth century some Italian merchants succeeded in doing this, the most important among them being Nicolò de Conti, a Venetian, and Gerolamo di Santo Stefano, a Genoese. The Venetian dictated a long and interesting account of his voyage to the Florentine Poggio Bracciolini. The Genoese—you could have guessed it —only hinted at his experience in a very short letter addressed to a business partner.[80] This letter tells of voyages effected some years earlier, but is dated September 1, 1499. One year before, the caravels of Vasco da Gama had anchored at Calicut. A new era was dawning.

---

[78] Cf. Heyd, II, 129 ff., with sources, and the additional evidence recently published by G. I. Bratianu, *Les Vénitiens dans la Mer Noire au XIVᵉ sièle* (Bucarest, 1939), and "Les Vénitiens dans la Mer Noire . . . après la deuxième guerre des Détroits," *Echos d'Orient*, XXXIII (1934), 148 ff.

[79] This situation is reflected by the list of the merchants who went to Hormuz from the seven climates, according to "Abd al-Razzāk of Samarkand, who lived in India from 1422 to 1444 as an ambassador of Shāhrukh. This list includes, among others, merchants from Egypt, Syria, Rūm (Turkish Asia Minor), Mesopotamia, Adharbaidjān, Khurāsān, Transoxiana, Turkestan, Kipchak, Kalmak (Oirats), Peking, Java, Bengal, Tenasserim, Socotra, Abyssinia, Zanguebar, Aden, etc. (cf. Ferrand, *Relations*, 473-474, *see* above, note 9, p. 473-474). The renaissance of Arab trade and geographical science has its highest expression in the Instructions of Ibn Mādjid; China, too, produced a number of important geographical works, on which cf. P. Pelliot, "Les grands voyages maritimes chinois au début du XVᵉ siècle," *T'oung Pao*, XXX (1933), 237-452 (*addenda in T'oung Pao*, XXXI [1935, 274 ff.], with sources. Cf. also Bretschneider, II, 329 ff. and J. J. L. Duyvendak, "The true Dates of the Chinese Maritime Expeditions in the early fifteenth century," *T'oung Pao*, XXXIV (1938), 340 ff. As for Nikitin, *see* the translation published by the Hakluyt Society, XX (London, 1857). On the successors of Tamerlane, cf. L. Bouvat, *Les Timourides* (Paris, 1927), with bibliography.

[80] Nicolò de' Conti, Girolamo Adorno, Girolamo da Santo Stefano, *Viaggi in Persia, India e Giava*, ed. Longhena (Milano, 1929).

15
Frontier Arrangements in Fragmented Societies: Ireland and Wales

Rees Davies

From the late eleventh century onwards—in other words from the period of 'the awakening of Europe' and 'the making of the Middle Ages'—Ireland and Wales may appropriately be regarded as two of the western frontier zones of medieval Europe. They stood at one of the peripheries of the area of feudal imperialism associated with Norman conquest and colonization and indeed seemed to slow down and even to frustrate its apparently remorseless advance. They were also frontierlands in cultural terms, where a new, confident, aggressive, north-western European, Latin- and French-dominated aristocratic and ecclesiastical culture came into contact, and often confrontation, with native cultures profoundly different from it in their economic configuration, political assumptions, ecclesiastical norms, social customs, and literary and artistic traditions.[1]

It is appropriate, therefore, to consider Ireland and Wales, for all their differences, alongside each other as frontier societies. They certainly shared many common features. In both countries the process of domination, conquest, and settlement by the Anglo-Normans was slow, spasmodic, and long drawn out. In Wales it began virtually on the morrow of the battle of Hastings, but for much of the twelfth and thirteenth centuries its progress was uncertain and it was only with the two major royal campaigns of 1276–7 and 1282–3 that it was eventually and suddenly brought to a triumphant conclusion. The saga of the Anglo-Norman penetration of Ireland began in 1169, almost exactly a century later than that of Wales. After making rapid and impressive initial progress, it was already clearly faltering by the second half of the thirteenth

---

[1] This theme is explored, through the writings of Gerald of Wales, in Robert Bartlett, *Gerald of Wales 1146–1223* (Oxford, 1982). See also Huw Pryce, 'In Search of a Medieval Society: Deheubarth in the Writings of Gerald of Wales', *Welsh History Review*, 13 (1986–7), 265–81.

century. Thereafter the English government and English settlers in Ireland had gradually to come to terms with the painful truth that the conquest of Ireland was, and was to remain, piecemeal, uncertain, and incomplete. Consequently Ireland in the fourteenth century—like Wales in the twelfth and for much of the thirteenth century—was a country of halves, half under native and the other half under Anglo-Norman rule.[2] The boundary between these two halves—or whatever other more sophisticated fractions we may care to employ—was one of the obvious frontier zones of medieval Wales and Ireland.

The two countries shared a further common experience: English settlement within them was very uneven in its geographical distribution and density. Parts of the eastern borderlands, river valleys, and southern coastal lowlands of Wales and much of southern and eastern Ireland were intensively settled and became proudly and defiantly English in customs, language, place-names, law, agriculture, social structure, and so forth. But rarely did these alien settlements form extensive consolidated blocs which can be neatly and confidently represented on a map. More often were they fairly small and more or less isolated enclaves, separated from each other by mountains, estuaries, forests, or bogs and interspersed with large native districts where English settlers had scarcely penetrated and where English governance was frequently skeletal, nominal, or non-existent.[3] Thus to travel the few miles from the thoroughly Anglicized lowlands of Radnor into the uplands of Maelienydd, from the security of Pembroke to a frontier fortress such as Cilgerran, from Dublin into the treacherous fastnesses of the Wicklow mountains, or from Thurles and Tipperary into the Irishry of Ely O'Carroll was to enter a different world and to cross a frontier, or rather frontiers, all the more profound for not being neatly delineated on a map. Civil and ecclesiastical administrators might attempt to acknowledge the fact by defining the respective

---

[2] The concept of Ireland as 'a country of halves' has been explored in Robin Frame, *English Lordship in Ireland, 1318–1361* (Oxford, 1982), 25, 53–4, 80. See also Map 7, below.

[3] Rees Davies, *Lordship and Society in the March of Wales 1282–1400* (Oxford, 1978), 303–6; C. A. Empey, 'Conquest and Settlement: Patterns of Anglo-Norman Settlement in North Munster and South Leinster', *Irish Social and Economic History Journal*, 13 (1986), 5–31; id., 'The Norman Period, 1185–1500', in William Nolan (ed.), *Tipperary: History and Society: Interdisciplinary Essays on the History of an Irish County* (Dublin, 1985), 71–92; Art Cosgrove (ed.), *New History of Ireland*, ii: *Medieval Ireland, 1169–1534* (Oxford, 1987), 221–5.

Fragmented Societies: Ireland and Wales   79

districts as Englishries and Welshries or as *inter Anglicos* and *inter Hibernicos*; but their categories could hardly begin to do justice to the complexity of the situation. This uneven pattern of conquest, control, and settlement meant that both Wales and Ireland in the medieval period were societies of multiple and highly localized frontiers (in the loose sense of that term) where two peoples met, overlapped, and confronted each other. This highly fragmented and fluid situation was the very reverse of the definitiveness and clarity which characterized the frontier between the realms of England and Scotland (disputed lands and march districts notwithstanding).[4]

The contrast between Scotland on the one hand and Wales and Ireland on the other likewise stands out in another direction. In Scotland the Anglo-Norman settlers were introduced into the country by invitation and were, on the whole, readily and smoothly assimilated into Scotland's society, while subtly transforming it. In Ireland and Wales, however, alien settlement came largely, though not exclusively, in the wake of conquest and the English settlers entrenched their position in the host society by institutionalizing the separation between themselves and the native peoples. So it was that the governmental terminology of Wales and Ireland from at least the thirteenth century predicated a duality in the peoples and institutions of both countries: English and Welsh, *Gaedhil* and *Gaill*, *pura Wallia* and *marchia Wallie*, 'land of war' and 'land of peace', native law and customs and English common law and mores, and so forth. Such a duality— 'distinction and diversity' as the Act of Union of England and Wales in 1536 called it—sanctioned and promoted a mentality of separation and discrimination which in its turn begat a profound psychological frontier within both countries. A deep and officially sanctioned fissure of race and culture ran through the societies of medieval Wales and Ireland; the attempts, conscious or unconscious, either to deepen or to bridge that fissure were one leading motif in the histories of both countries in the later Middle Ages.[5] Both societies were, in that respect, truly frontier societies.

---

[4] Geoffrey Barrow, *The Kingdom of the Scots* (London, 1973), ch. 4, 'The Anglo-Scottish Border'; Denys Hay, 'England, Scotland and Europe: The Problem of the Frontier', *TRHS*, 5th ser., 25 (1975), 77–93.
[5] For Ireland see James F. Lydon, 'The Problem of the Frontier in Medieval Ireland', *Topic: A Journal of the Liberal Arts*, 13 (1967), 5–22 and P. J. Duffy, 'The Nature of the Medieval Frontier in Ireland', *Studia Hibernica*, 22–3 (1982–3),

80   *Rees Davies*

Wales and Ireland shared yet another common experience
which profoundly shaped their histories: they were, governmentally
and politically, deeply fragmented countries. Deep as was the
conviction of ultimate cultural, linguistic, and legal unity in both
countries,[6] it is the intensely regional character of loyalties,
politics, religion, and power which is the dominant feature of the
native, pre-Norman histories of both countries. As the Anglo-
Normans pushed forward their conquest of Wales and Ireland,
they became the heirs of this particularism and indeed seemed to
exult in it, adjusting the forms, formal and especially informal, of
their authority to the pre-existing patterns and geography of
power.[7] Countries in which the units of political power and
governance are multiple and which lack a central, stable,
unchallenged supervisory source of jurisdiction and power have
their own internal complex frontiers and have to devise their own
working solutions for dealing with the problems raised by such
frontiers. Such were both medieval Ireland and Wales, both in the
pre-Norman and Anglo-Norman periods.

Wales and Ireland may, therefore, be considered as countries of
plural frontiers, none of which exactly coincided with one another,
notably the frontiers of conquest, settlement, peoples, culture,
and units of power. One reflection of the community of experience
and problems shared by the two countries was the prominence of
the word 'march' (or 'marches') in the vocabulary of authority and
in the geography of power in both countries. 'Marches' are not, of
course, peculiar in any way to these two countries. They were a
common feature of border districts within and at the boundaries of
medieval Europe. Some of the problems they posed—especially in
terms of feudal loyalties and fiscal and jurisdictional status—have
been closely studied by historians.[8] Nevertheless marches and

---

21–38; for Wales, Rees Davies, 'Race Relations in Post-Conquest Wales',
Transactions of the Honourable Society of Cymmrodorion (1974–5), 32–56.

  [6] Donnchá Ó Corráin, 'Nationality and Kingship in Pre-Norman Ireland', in
T. W. Moody (ed.), *Nationality and the Pursuit of National Independence* (Histor-
ical Studies 11, Belfast, 1978), 1–35; Rees Davies, *Conquest, Coexistence and
Change: Wales 1063–1415* (Oxford, 1987), 15–20.

  [7] See esp. for Wales, David Walker, 'The Norman Settlement in Wales', in
R. Allen Brown (ed.), *Proceedings of the Battle Conference on Anglo-Norman
Studies*, i (Woodbridge, 1978), 131–43 and, for Ireland, Robin Frame, 'Power and
Society in the Lordship of Ireland, 1272–1377', *Past and Present*, 76 (1977), 3–33;
Cosgrove, *New History of Ireland*, ii. 37, 311–12.

  [8] Jean-François Lemarignier, *Recherches sur l'hommage en marche et les*

Fragmented Societies: Ireland and Wales 81

their associated institutions figure particularly prominently in the histories of medieval Ireland and Wales. That this was so was largely a consequence of the hesitant and faltering character of Anglo-Norman conquest in both countries and the need, accordingly, to develop and institutionalize a vocabulary which reflected that uncomfortable fact. That seems to have happened in Wales from the later twelfth century, as the prospect of the total subjugation of the country receded ever further beyond the immediate political and military horizon. Hitherto the term 'march' or 'marches' seems to have been used in a loose geographical sense to describe the borderlands of Wales.[9] It is, apparently, only from c.1200 that the phrases 'March of Wales', 'law of the March', and 'barons of the March' enter regularly as official and fairly precise categories into English governmental vocabulary.[10] The adoption of such a vocabulary reflected the acceptance of the fact that there was an extensive area between native-controlled Wales on the one hand and the kingdom of England on the other which was intermediate in its status, laws, and governance and had its own recognizable and recognized habits and institutions. The March of Wales, therefore, was an extensive frontier zone shaped by the character and chronology of the Anglo-Norman penetration and conquest of Wales. Likewise in Ireland in the thirteenth century the term 'marches' came to be used regularly to describe the areas which lay between Gaelic-controlled and English-dominated areas, and soon terms such as 'marchers' and 'law of the march' became part of the common vocabulary of Irish life.[11]

Significant and illuminating as are such similarities between Ireland and Wales, the differences between the two countries are equally striking. A cursory examination of the terminology soon alerts us to some of those differences. In Wales the term 'March'

frontières féodales (Lille, 1945); J. Balon, 'L'Organisation judiciaire des marches féodales', *Annales de la société archéologique de Namur*, 46 (1951), 5–72.

[9] e.g. *Domesday Book*, ed. Abraham Farley (2 vols., London, 1783), i, fo. 186ᵛ ('in Marcha de Walis'); *Welsh Assize Roll 1277–84*, ed. James Conway Davies (Cardiff, 1940), 237 ('quinque villas de Marchia', 1167–75).
[10] *Littere Wallie*, ed. John Goronwy Edwards (Cardiff, 1940), p. xlvii; Davies, *Conquest, Coexistence and Change*, 213, 272, 287–8.
[11] Cosgrove, *New History of Ireland*, ii. 240, 270, 272–3; Robin Frame, 'War and Peace in the Medieval Lordship of Ireland', in James F. Lydon (ed.), *The English in Medieval Ireland* (Dublin, 1984), 118–41, esp. 133–5.

(or 'Marches') was regularly and consistently used from the thirteenth to the sixteenth centuries to describe a large collection of lordships which had gradually been brought under Anglo-Norman rule—ultimately some forty or so in number and extending over more than half of the surface area of Wales. Before the Edwardian conquest of 1282–3 this March was contrasted with native Wales, *pura Wallia* or simply *Wallia*; after the conquest with the royal or principality lands in north and west Wales.[12] In other words in Wales the March by the end of the thirteenth century was an area well defined in geographical terms and institutional status. In Ireland, on the other hand, there was no single march; rather 'marches' were those districts of uncertain control which lay between 'the land of peace' (under English rule) and 'the land of war' (under Irish control); as such they were often associated with violence and danger.[13] In Wales the law of the March, *lex Marchie*, was accorded from at least *c.*1200 an official status alongside native Welsh law and English common law; its official acceptance as an identifiable body of law was sanctioned by no less august a document than Magna Charta (clause 56).[14] In Ireland, on the other hand, the law of the march was regarded as a perversion, an unofficial and regrettable concession to the customs of the Irish by those who lived cheek by jowl with them. It was officially classed with brehon law as 'not law but bad custom' and was even more dramatically condemned by others as being synonymous with 'the law of the devil'.[15] In Wales the process of Anglo-Norman conquest which had initially brought the March into being was complete by 1283; thereby the military *raison d'être* of the March was extinguished. In Ireland, on the contrary, the process of English conquest was stalled by the late thirteenth century and thereafter went into retreat. War continued to be a normal and recurrent feature of life in Ireland; the institutions and conventions of

[12] See Map 8.
[13] See e.g. *Cal. Justic. Rolls (1295–1303)*, 199 ('the marches outside the land of peace'); Goddard H. Orpen, *Ireland under the Normans, 1169–1333* (4 vols., Oxford, 1911–20), iv. 42 ('in the land of war or in the marches'); John A. Watt, *The Church and the Two Nations in Medieval Ireland* (Cambridge, 1970), 93 n. 4 ('in pessima namque marchia et periculosa inter Anglicos et Hibernicos').
[14] Rees Davies, 'The Law of the March', *Welsh History Review*, 5 (1970–1), 1–30.
[15] *Statutes . . . of the Parliament of Ireland: King John to Henry V*, ed. Henry F. Berry (Dublin, 1907), 388–9, 436–7; Cosgrove, *New History of Ireland*, ii. 343.

Fragmented Societies: Ireland and Wales 83

a military frontier were thereby perpetuated long after they had become historical memories in Wales.

The contrasts between Wales and Ireland are, therefore, as suggestive as the similarities. By studying the two countries together it may be possible to see how frontier institutions and conventions shaped to deal with the experience of war in a fragmented and partially conquered society could be adapted to cope with the assumptions of peace in a similarly fragmented but fully conquered society. It is to the former type of society—and therefore more particularly to the Irish evidence—that we turn first.

Medieval Ireland was a society habituated to war. It had been so in pre-Norman times; it remained so throughout the later Middle Ages.[16] The parties to warfare might change with confusing complexity; the methods and technologies employed altered over time; but the essential assumptions, practices, and purpose of war remained largely unchanged. They have been brilliantly characterized by Dr Katharine Simms and Dr Robin Frame.[17] Raids and counter-raids were almost seasonal in their occurrence; the taking and distribution of preys and plunder were central to the economy and power of native chieftains; military prowess of the most bloodthirsty variety was still at a priority, as might be demonstrated, for example, by the compliments paid to, and charges levelled against, Piers Bermingham (d. 1308);[18] military obligations remained meaningful, particularly from 'those who are nearest to the marches there'.[19] 'The Irish', as one observer remarked wearily, 'are more often at war than at peace.'[20] The same in truth could likewise have been said of the Anglo-Norman settlers, who quickly adopted the native idiom of warfare and who were more often than not at odds among themselves as well as at war with the

---

[16] Phrases such as 'when through general war the land is untilled' are common in the legal documents of the period, e.g. *Dowdall Deeds*, ed. Charles McNeill and A. J. Otway-Ruthven (IMC, Dublin, 1960), no. 43, pp. 20–1.

[17] See esp. Katharine Simms, 'Warfare in the Medieval Gaelic Lordships', *Irish Sword*, 12 (1975–6), 98–108; Robin Frame, 'The Justiciarship of Ralph Ufford: Warfare and Politics in Fourteenth-century Ireland', *Studia Hibernica*, 13 (1973), 7–47; id., 'English Officials and Irish Chiefs in the Fourteenth Century', *EHR* 90 (1975), 748–77; id., 'War and Peace'.

[18] Cosgrove, *New History of Ireland*, ii. 267–8.

[19] Quoted in Frame, 'War and Peace', 135.

[20] *Calendar of Documents Relating to Ireland (1171–1307)*, ed. H. S. Sweetman (5 vols., London, 1875–86), v, no. 335, p. 117.

native Irish. Ireland was indeed *terra guerre*, a land of war—or rather wars.

The situation had not been very dissimilar in Wales for much of the twelfth and thirteenth centuries. During that period it also was a country where the eventuality of war or wars seemed more certain than the prospect of peace.[21] Native princes and Anglo-Norman *conquistadores* alike resorted to war between and among each other as a regular and accepted way of promoting their ambitions and rearranging their relationships. Local raids and 'private' wars were common in their occurrence—such as the 'war' between William Vescy and Morgan ap Hywel in Caerleon or the dispute, conducted with banners displayed, between Fitzwarin of Whittington and Fitzalan of Oswestry.[22] Such a militarized society generated its own etiquette on issues such as the proper display of banners, the exchange of prisoners, and the division of booty.

Societies where power is essentially decentralized and wars frequent and local soon devise mechanisms to contain such wars, to provide a breathing space in the calendar of hostility, and to introduce a measure of peace in the feud. So it was that the institutions and conventions of a military frontierland were created in Wales and Ireland. The evidence is richer (and later) for Ireland, but there are clear hints that the situation had once been not dissimilar in Wales.

The most immediate need was for procedures to bring hostilities to an end, however temporarily. Ecclesiastics no doubt played a crucial role as intermediaries: two leading churchmen in twelfth-century Wales were appropriately commemorated as 'a mediator between Gwynedd and Powys' and as 'a peaceful arbitrator between various peoples'.[23] But others might also play the role of go-between: an Irish source provides a fascinating glimpse of an O'Toole woman who went on regular missions to the mountains, where she stayed with other women, in order to recover stolen goods and cattle carried off by her kinsfolk.[24] Sooner or later,

[21] Rees Davies, 'Kings, Lords and Liberties in the March of Wales, 1066–1272', *TRHS*, 5th ser., 29 (1979), 41–61 at 45.
[22] *Close Rolls of the Reign of Henry III (1247–51)* (London, 1922), 136; *Calendar of the Close Rolls (1296–1302)* (London, 1906), 495; Robert W. Eyton, *Antiquities of Shropshire* (12 vols., London, 1853–60), xi. 40.
[23] *Brut y Tywysogyon: or, The Chronicle of the Princes, Red Book of Hergest Version*, ed. Thomas Jones (Cardiff, 1955), 111, 121.
[24] *Cal. Justic. Rolls (1305–7)*, 480–1. For the fate of this female go-between, see Cosgrove, *New History of Ireland*, ii. 261 n. 5.

Fragmented Societies: Ireland and Wales 85

however, the parties at war or hostility would have to enter into direct negotiations or parleys. Many such parleys were, doubtless, informal and unofficial, arranged simply to mend fences and to end recriminations so that life could continue more or less normally. Anglo-Norman lords conducted such parleys with native Irish or Welsh leaders in order to bring them, or to bring them back, into a framework of acknowledged dependence, however loose and fragile. So it was that Maurice fitz Thomas, the future earl of Desmond (d. 1356), defended his right to negotiate (*ad parliamentandum*) with certain Irish on the grounds that other lords in Ireland did the same.[25] The government in Dublin might fulminate against such unlicensed parleys in a desperate attempt to keep alive its pious hope of 'one peace and one war',[26] but behind the theoretical aspiration and legislative bluster, it had to come to terms with a world which lay largely beyond its control. English families were given permission to treat with the attackers 'in the manner of marchers',[27] while the justiciar himself resorted to raids and parleys alternatively and complementarily to try to deal with the intractable problem of the native Irish.[28] Parleys could be used to defuse feuds between local parties, as was the case in the parley between the O'Carbraghs and the Barrys in 1307.[29] But equally they might be arranged to try to terminate frontier disputes of much graver political import, as in the parley between the Welsh princeling Maredudd ab Owain and the vassals of the earl of Pembroke in 1244 or that between Llywelyn ap Gruffudd, prince of Wales, and the earl of Gloucester called to settle an explosive dispute over control of upland Glamorgan in 1268.[30] Such a useful device naturally developed its own conventions: fixed places were appointed where parleys might be held;[31] covenants might be entered into to ensure that the parties attended;[32] and so regular

[25] Quoted in Frame, *English Lordship*, 39.
[26] *Statutes . . . of Ireland*, 204–5, 278–81.
[27] Quoted in Geoffrey J. Hand, *English Law in Ireland 1290–1324* (Cambridge, 1967), 35–6.
[28] For a good example see the roll of expenses of the justicar John Sandford, 1288–90: *Cal. of Docs. Relating to Ireland*, iii, no. 559, esp. 265–6, 271–2.
[29] *Cal. Justic. Rolls (1305–7)*, 385.
[30] *Calendar of Ancient Correspondence Concerning Wales*, ed. John Goronwy Edwards (Cardiff, 1935), 48; *Littere Wallie*, 101–3; J. B. Smith, *Llywelyn ap Gruffudd: Tywysog Cymru* (Cardiff, 1986), 241–2.
[31] Mills and bridges seem to have been particularly favoured venues for parleys.
[32] *Cal. Justic. Rolls (1305–7)*, 385.

Rees Davies

were such parleys that, like attendance at the host, they were regarded as a common obligation of marcher life.[33]

The success of parleys was, of course, not guaranteed. They might be abused: under the cover of a parley at the bridge of Carmarthen the Welsh, 'throwing off their tunics and sounding a horn', attacked the army of the earl of Pembroke in 1233, just as the author of *Caithréim Thoirdhealbhaigh* (*The Triumphs of Turlogh*) noted indignantly that it was 'a fundamental principle of that specious rascal, Thomas de Clare, to make peace when he had just been preyed, but to prey others at once upon ratification of peace'.[34] In such circumstances a parley might end in a bloodbath, such as that in 1335 when thirteen of the family of Archdeacon were slaughtered.[35] But a parley could also terminate hostilities and pave the way to a truce or even a peace. Submissions might be made; hostages surrendered or exchanged; herds of cows given as compensation for past depredations; and promises made for the future.[36] But parleys were more likely to be about mutual concessions than unilateral submission. Accordingly a settlement often involved the appointment of mutually acceptable arbitrators: when the English of Louth struck an agreement with the MacMahons the compensation was to be determined 'by the consideration and ordinance of the natives of their marches, as well English as Irish, to be chosen for the purpose', just as the treaty between the earl of Ormond and Rory O'Kennedy involved the establishment of a panel of arbitrators, four from each side.[37] As such examples indicate, a parley could on occasion lead to the drawing up of a formal public instrument by a public notary.[38] Arrangement might also be made for future breaches of such truces to be amended by mixed juries, drawn equally from

[33] *Cartae et alia munimenta . . . de Glamorgan*, ed. George T. Clark (6 vols., Cardiff, 1910), ii. 360 ('non permittatis venientes ad parliamentum vel exercitum hospitari vel comedere'), 550.

[34] *Calendar of Ancient Correspondence*, 34; *Caithréim Thoirdhealbaigh*, ed. and trans. Standish H. O'Grady (2 vols., ITS 26–7, London, 1929), ii. 17–18.

[35] John Clyn, *Annals of Ireland by Friar John Clyn and Thady Dowling*, ed. Richard Butler (Dublin, 1849), 26.

[36] *Cal. Justic. Rolls (1295–1303)*, 61.

[37] *Cal. Justic. Rolls (1304–14)*, 161; *Calendar of Ormond Deeds*, ed. Edmund Curtis (6 vols., IMC, Dublin, 1932–3), ii, no. 34, pp. 21–2.

[38] Such as that concluded between Donal O'Hanlon and the community of Louth in 1337: James F. Lydon, *Ireland in the Later Middle Ages* (Dublin, 1973), 50. Cf. the agreement between Llywelyn ap Gruffudd and the earl of Gloucester, *Littere Wallie*, 101–3.

Fragmented Societies: Ireland and Wales   87

both parties, at a day of parley (*dies parliamenti*). Such at least is the implication of one notable example from Glamorgan.[39]

Mediation, parley, arbitration, and truce were among the mechanisms whereby two warring and militarized societies attempted to contain and curtail their own aggression in partly conquered countries. They are the frontier institutions of a society at war. Two other observations may be briefly made about these institutions. First, they were essentially local in character. Conquest in Wales and Ireland had been and remained largely 'private' and unco-ordinated; so, therefore, by definition was peace-making. Marcher lords in Wales could and did conclude their own peace treaties with native Welsh lords and princes.[40] They could ask to be, and were, exempted from any general peace into which the king of England might enter with native Welsh princes.[41] In Ireland the king in theory claimed that he alone had the right to make general peace and war and to license parleys; but in truth the situation on the ground was very different. It is little wonder that the lord of Trim claimed that he could conclude 'private' truces with the Irish who were against the king's peace, so long as the justiciar was not actually out on campaign against them.[42] Peace-making, like war, in a fragmented society was largely devolved into the hands of local *potentes*.

Secondly, it is as well to place the institutions of the frontier in the context not only of a warring society but also of two peoples who, in spite of and indeed through war, were having to come to terms with each other. The habits of the frontier—especially of frontiers which were so fluid, local, and slow in the making—make for give and take. However much central directives might preach the necessity of uniformity with metropolitan norms and the desirability of the separation of peoples, a fusion of the practices and outlook of two contiguous and overlapping societies was bound to take place. In Wales part of that fusion was formally

[39] *Cartae . . . de Glamorgan*, ii. 550.
[40] e.g. Ranulf earl of Chester concluded a peace with Llywelyn ab Iorwerth in 1218 and Roger Mortimer of Wigmore with Llywelyn ap Gruffudd in 1281: *Annales Cestrienses*, ed. Richard C. Christie (Lancashire and Cheshire Record Society 14, 1887), 50–1, *s.a.* 1218; *Littere Wallie*, 99–100.
[41] *Close Rolls of the Reign of Henry III (1231–4)* (London, 1905), 568–9; *Littere Wallie*, 54–8; John Goronwy Edwards, 'The Normans and the Welsh March', *Proceedings of the British Academy*, 42 (1956), 155–77, at 171–2.
[42] *Calendar of the Gormanston Register*, ed. James Mills and M. J. McEnery (Dublin, 1916), 181–2.

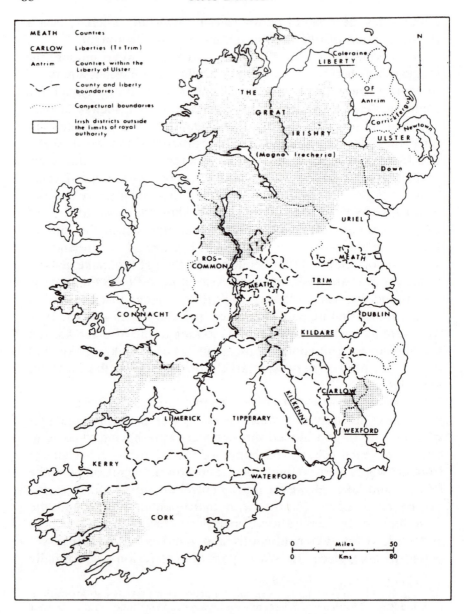

Map 7. Ireland in the Late Thirteenth Century
(*Source*: K. W. Nicholls's map in *New History of Ireland: Medieval Ireland 1169–1534*, ed. Art Cosgrove (Oxford, 1987), p. 174.)

Fragmented Societies: Ireland and Wales 89

acknowledged in that capacious phrase 'the laws and customs of the March'; the rest can be documented in the hybrid institutions and practices so characteristic of Marcher life.[43] In Ireland the theoreticians legislated and fulminated, but recent research increasingly emphasizes that 'the differences in any region between the lordships of Anglo-Norman and of Gaelic sur- name . . . appeared imperceptible' and that 'the position of the Gaelic Irish chiefs' approximated ever 'closer to that of their neighbours, the Anglo-Irish barons'.[44] The habits of war and the mechanisms of peace in a fragmented frontier society are but part of a larger process of confrontation and accommodation between two societies and two cultures.

In Wales, unlike Ireland, the process of conquest was eventually completed by the end of the thirteenth century. To that extent Wales ceased to be a military frontierland. With the exception of the native revolts of 1287, 1294–5, and 1316 and of localized 'private' wars between Marcher lords (of which the Gloucester– Hereford dispute of the 1290s and the Despenser war of 1321 are the best known examples), Wales henceforth enjoyed a remarkable period of peace. Nevertheless Wales still retained for the remainder of the Middle Ages many of the features of a frontier zone. It was a conquered country where two cultures and peoples met, confronted, and adjusted to each other; it was also a country where the distinction between native and settler, Welsh and English—however artificial it often was on the ground—still remained basic in the governance of the country. Wales also still retained the vestiges of its former frontier status in the way it was ruled. After the final Edwardian conquest of 1282–3, Wales was not integrated within itself institutionally nor was it assimilated into the body politic of England. The recently conquered lands in north and west Wales were, it is true, shired after the English fashion; but no attempt was made to dismantle the virtually

---

[43] Davies, *Lordship and Society*, 443–56.
[44] Kenneth Nicholls in Cosgrove, *New History of Ireland*, ii. 422 (cf. the comments of James F. Lydon, ibid. 269); Katharine Simms, *From Kings to Warlords: The Changing Political Structure of Gaelic Ireland in the Later Middle Ages* (Woodbridge, 1987), 30. For two studies of particular topics see Gearóid MacNiocaill, 'The Interaction of Laws', in James F. Lydon (ed.), *The English in Medieval Ireland* (Dublin, 1984), 105–17, and C. A. Empey and Katharine Simms, 'The Ordinances of the White Earl and the Problem of Coign in the Later Middle Ages', *PRIA* 75 C (1975), 161–87.

Rees Davies

independent collection of lordships in southern and eastern Wales which had been forged out of the slow process of Anglo-Norman conquest. These lordships were now known collectively as the March of Wales. They stood as the fossilized mementoes of an earlier age, monuments to the previous particularism of power in Wales and to the uncoordinated and piecemeal way in which the country had been gradually conquered by the Anglo-Normans. Their continued survival as units of lordship and power until the sixteenth century perpetuated the fragmentation of Wales; it also allows us to glimpse how virtually sovereign lordships regulated their frontier relations with each other in an age of peace as they had once done in an age of war.[45]

In the later Middle Ages the March of Wales consisted of forty or so lordships arranged in a solid bloc from north-east Wales, down the eastern border, and along the whole extent of the southern coastline. Some of these lordships were very old and had been in the making for centuries; others, especially in the north-east, were recent creations called into being by the territorial grants made by Edward I in 1282–3. Yet regardless of age and size, they all shared—and came to be regarded in the period itself as sharing—certain distinctive and, by English standards, extraordinary features which may be briefly itemized. They were territorially concentrated lordships; all land within them, other than church land, was held immediately or mediately of their respective lords.[46] Administratively, they were self-contained units of governance, at least in their relation with the king's administration. Powers of governance within them lay in the hands of officials appointed by the lord and answerable exclusively to him. There were no coexistent, alternative, or superior sources of authority; no royal sheriff, judge, escheator, or tax-collector exercised his office within them. It is little wonder that a later commentator referred to Marcher lords as 'soveraigne governors of their tenantes and people'.[47] So indeed they were. Fiscally, likewise,

---

[45] Davies, *Conquest, Coexistence and Change*, 285–8, 391–4. The evidence on which the remainder of this essay is based is reviewed more fully in Davies, *Lordship and Society*, esp. ch. 11; but I have revised some of the opinions expressed there and added some new evidence.

[46] As the earl of Gloucester put it in 1290, 'all lands and tenements within the land of Glamorgan are of his demesne': *Rotuli Parliamentorum* (6 vols., London, 1767–77), i. 43.

[47] George Owen, *The Description of Pembrokeshire*, ed. Henry Owen (4 vols., Cymmrodorion Record Series 1, 1892–1936), iii. 140.

Fragmented Societies: Ireland and Wales   91

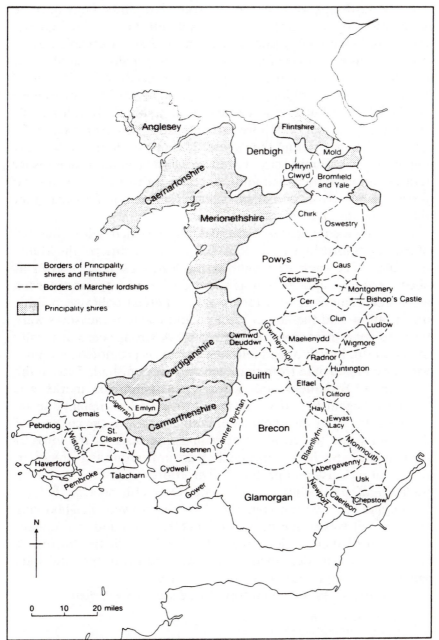

Legend:
——— Borders of Principality shires and Flintshire
--- Borders of Marcher lordships
▨ Principality shires

Map 8. Wales in the Fourteenth Century: Principality and March
(*Source*: Rees Davies, *Conquest, Coexistence, and Change: Wales*
1063–1415 (Oxford, 1987), 393

Marcher lordships were in effect independent units. Only once, in 1292, was a royal tax raised in the March; for the rest, the Marcher lords taxed their own tenants frequently and under a whole host of pretexts, but exclusively for their own ends. Finally, each Marcher lordship was a self-sufficient legal and judicial unit. The law of each individual lordship was its own peculiar amalgam of English and Welsh law, feudal practice, and local custom.[48] Jurisdictionally the immunity of the March from royal justice was expressed in the lawyer's dictum that the king's writ did not run there; but equally important is it to emphasize that there was no common supervisory judicial authority between and above the individual lordships, no jurisdiction in error, and no possibility (normally) of appeal other than to the lord's own council.

Utter fragmentation and the jealously guarded self-sufficiency of each of its lordships were, therefore, the hallmarks of the March of Wales. The men of neighbouring lordships were known as aliens, *extranei*, and treated as such. Each lordship was regarded as an autonomous unit in terms of commercial policy, economic organization, and the labour market, and vigorous measures were taken to try to preserve this autarchy.[49] A strong sense of loyalty to one's lord, lordship, and fellow tenants was promoted and those who dared to deviate from that loyalty were punished. Thus in the lordship of Bromfield and Yale a penalty of 100 marks was threatened against anyone who prosecuted a fellow tenant outside the lordship, since such behaviour was 'contrary to the customs of the country and the royal liberties and franchises of the lords of Bromfield'.[50] Such an approach was not grounded solely in seignorial jealousy and protectionism. It drew also on a very long tradition of particularism within native Welsh society and on intense and often vicious communal rivalries between neighbouring districts.[51] It was in the pursuit of such rivalries and as a defiant expression of their regality that Marcher lords in the thirteenth century vigorously defended their right to resort to 'private' wars against their neighbours to settle their disputes.

The March of Wales, therefore, is the area *par excellence* within

[48] Davies, 'Law of the March', esp. 10–12.

[49] Davies, *Lordship and Society*, 233–7.

[50] NLW Peniarth MS 404 D. fo. 103. For other comparable proclamations and for actual fines imposed in pursuit of such a policy, see Davies, *Lordship and Society*, 238–9.

[51] Davies, *Lordship and Society*, 241–2.

Fragmented Societies: Ireland and Wales 93

the British Isles where the uninhibited character of seignorial power and the fragmentation of authority can be most clearly studied. The problems posed by such a situation and the abuses to which it could give rise were manifold. Wanted men fled from one lordship to another to avoid prosecution; tenants in arrears with their rent or anticipating a heavy seignorial fine drove their herds and flocks to neighbouring lordships to avoid distraint; men were abducted from one lordship to another and only released on payment of a ransom; a man charged with murder might defend his refusal to reply in court simply by asserting that he was a stranger and had not been caught red-handed; while a chaplain's exemption from the jurisdiction of a Marcher court could be bluntly explained in these terms: 'he is not to reply between the two lands (viz. the lordships of Maelienydd and Clun) for any felony . . . because he is not in our jurisdiction.'[52] The March seemed to be a criminal's paradise, a land of multiple bolt-holes and loopholes. The basic procedures of medieval law-keeping—distraint, outlawry, and pledging—were subverted by the frag-mentation of judicial authority, while communal raids could be, and were, undertaken under the cloak of Marcher immunity. Indeed one might almost say that the abuses of judicial frag-mentation and immunity were institutionalized in the March by two practices. The first, disclaimer, was the practice whereby a man charged with an offence in court could disclaim the lordship of the lord of the court and thereby terminate proceedings on the grounds that the court and its lord had no jurisdiction over him.[53] The second practice, avowry, was a complementary one, whereby a lord avowed a man—in other words accepted him into his judicial protection—for a nominal sum, often no more than fourpence a year, even though he was not one of his tenants.[54]

These practices were on occasion loudly condemned by English parliaments,[55] and were eventually to be cited as a pretext for the

---

[52] *Calendar of the Patent Rolls (1327–30)* (London, 1891), 80, 82; Shropshire Record Office 552 (Clun Court Rolls) 1/10, m. 12; 1/3, m. 3.

[53] Thus a man hauled before the earl of Stafford's court in the lordship of Caus was challenged to declare whether he disclaimed the earl's lordship in full court in the presence of the steward. He did so and was promptly handed over to the bailiff of the earl of March: NLW Peniarth MS 280 D, fo. 71.

[54] For the practice of avowry in Ireland, Cosgrove, *New History of Ireland*, ii. 298.

[55] See esp. *Rotuli Parliamentorum*, iii. 508, 615–16.

Rees Davies

abolition of Marcher franchise. Such condemnations need, however, to be placed in perspective. The abuses diagnosed in the March of Wales are those which confront any society where power and governance is dispersed and where there is no single supervisory or appellate authority. They are not a pathological condition peculiar to the March of Wales. Indeed given the essentially decentralized character of power and governance in the Middle Ages and the proliferation and vigorous defence of immunities and franchises, it is surely the evolution of a unitary 'national' jurisdiction and of a single common law which is the phenomenon which demands an explanation. In other words on a broad perspective, geographical and historical, it may well be that it is the kingdom of England rather than the March of Wales which should be classified as the exception.

Furthermore the morcellement of the March was no more than a continuation of the fragmentation of authority already prevalent in native Wales. Native Welshmen, princes and communities alike, had already addressed themselves to the problems posed by such fragmentation. So much is suggested by the use of the vernacular term *cydfod* (literally 'coexistence') to describe agreements between communities and lordships in the later Middle Ages and by the survival of texts of such agreements (*cydfodau*) in Welsh antiquarian manuscripts.[56] So much is suggested also by references in pre-Edwardian conquest documents to 'accustomed places on the borders of those parts' where disputes might be settled between neighbouring jurisdictions and to the practice whereby Welsh magnates hold pleas in the borders of their lands 'in the manner of parliaments'.[57] But it is in the fourteenth and fifteenth centuries, under the rule of English lords, that we can study in detail the procedures adopted to cope with the fragmentation of authority and jurisdiction in Wales. The evidence testifies to the existence of what is virtually an international law of the March.

There was, first, a great deal of correspondence and meetings between stewards of neighbouring lordships to defuse quarrels, exchange information, and co-ordinate action; if problems proved intractable the councils of the two lords might meet to try to sort

[56] J. B. Smith, 'Cydfodau o'r Bymthegfed Ganrif', *Bulletin of the Board of Celtic Studies*, 21 (1965–6), 309–24; 25 (1972–4), 128–34.
[57] *Calendar of Ancient Correspondence*, 95; *Calendar of Various Chancery Rolls 1277–1326* (London, 1912), 206.

Fragmented Societies: Ireland and Wales   95

them out. Through such mechanisms fines might be respited or cancelled, cases deferred, and sealed copies of a judgement given in the court of a neighbouring lordship produced as evidence.[58] A letter of 1359 from the steward of Denbigh to his colleague in the neighbouring lordship of Dyffryn Clwyd illustrates what a close working relationship could be achieved through such arrangements: lists of wanted men were exchanged and such of them as could be arrested in a neighbouring lordship were bound over to appear at the next court of the march to face the prospect of extradition.[59]

Such mutual policing and exchange of information clearly helped to counter some of the fragmentation of authority in the March, but even more important were some of the formal mechanisms commonly employed to deal with the problem. One of the most prominent of these was the letter of the march, *littera marchie* or *littera de kedevot*.[60] Its operation is best illustrated by an example: when John Bowyer appeared before the justices of the duke of Lancaster at Monmouth in 1413 he produced letters of the march from Sir John Skidmore, steward of the neighbouring lordship of Goodrich Castle, asking that he be handed over as a tenant of Lord Talbot of Goodrich Castle. Accordingly he was released into the custody of Lord Talbot's bailiff and the case against him was deferred to the next day of the march, *dies marchie*.[61] The procedures followed on this occasion were common form throughout the March. So well established was the letter of the march as a legal instrument that an exemplar of it was copied into a contemporary formulary, and parchment was bought on the assumption that several such letters would be written annually.[62] Even case-law had developed to define the occasions when a letter of the march was not admissible, notably when an offender was caught red-handed or a claimant could be proved to be a serf or holding customary land.[63] Side by side with letters of the march—

[58] All these measures can be fully documented from the Dyffryn Clwyd court rolls in the PRO.

[59] PRO Court Rolls (SC 2) 281/7, m. 22 schedule.

[60] For this alternative name PRO SC 2/219/2, m. 24, m. 29; 219/4, m. 10; 219/5, m. 9.

[61] PRO Justices Itinerant (JI) 1/1152, m 18. Cf. T. B. Pugh (ed.), *The Marcher Lordships of South Wales 1415–1536: Select Documents* (Cardiff, 1963), 59, 65.

[62] BL Royal MS A xi, fo. 11; PRO Duchy of Lancaster, Ministers' Accounts (DL 29), 633/10317 Hay.

[63] BL Royal MS A xi, fo. 11; PRO SC 2/222/5, m. 16ᵛ; Pugh, *Marcher Lordships of South Wales*, 65.

which were normally delivered in court by an accredited seignorial official rather than by the defendant—should be placed letters of safe conduct granted to Marcher tenants about to embark on a journey outside their lordship in search of stolen cattle or goods.[64] Both safe conducts and letters of the march were genuine and well-established devices to deal with some of the problems posed by the fragmentation of authority and to discriminate between those who abused such fragmentation for their own ends and bona fide tenants, travellers, and litigants.

The successful production of a letter of the march normally required a defendant to appear at the next day of the march (or love day, *dies amoris*, or day of composition, *dies composicionis*, as it was alternatively called). Such days of the march can be documented for virtually every part of the March of Wales. Indeed in the case of three lordships—Dyffryn Clwyd, Caus, and Brecon—the evidence makes it clear that march days were held with *all* their respective contiguous lordships. The only lordships which were theoretically not included in such arrangements were those of the king, for it was held that, just as the king could not perform homage to any of his subjects, so 'he could not have a march with anyone'.[65] Even that prohibition was overlooked in practice for documentary evidence makes it clear that arrangements closely akin in form and substance to days of the march were entered into by some of the communities of the royal lands in Wales.[66] Days of the march were in fact a common and regular way in which relations between the fragmented units of late medieval Wales were organized. They were held at established venues or landmarks on the borders between lordships;[67] attendance at them was obviously considered to be so regular that it could be included among the list of obligations of local burgesses; while a letter on how to claim goods at a court of the march was of such

[64] For an example of such a safe conduct see Northumberland Record Office, Swinburne (Capheaton) Collection 1/99. I owe this reference to Mr D. A. L. Morgan.

[65] *Calendar of Ancient Correspondence*, 93; *Calendar of Various Chancery Rolls*, 336; *Rotuli Parliamentorum*, i. 397; *Calendar of Ancient Petitions Relating to Wales*, ed. William Rees (Cardiff, 1975), nos. 12708, 12780, pp. 425–6, 430–1.

[66] J. B. Smith, 'The Regulation of the Frontier of Meirionnydd in the Fifteenth Century', *Journal of the Merioneth Historical Society*, 5 (1965–6), 105–11.

[67] Fords (Welsh, *rhyd*) and passes (Welsh, *bwlch*) seem to have been favourite venues.

Fragmented Societies: Ireland and Wales   97

common form that it was included in a contemporary formulary.[68] Another negative indication of how central and regular a mechanism they were in frontier relations in Wales was the fact that their suspension was regarded as tantamount to a declaration of hostilities.[69]

Days of the march were not. of course, an exclusively Welsh or even frontier phenomenon. They were one of the devices employed in medieval society generally to reduce tension and settle quarrels by arranging 'extra-curial' arbitrations and mediations.[70] In Wales the most immediate antecedents of days of the march may be found on the one hand in a well-established native tradition (referred to above) of meeting at fixed places to sort out inter-regional disputes, on the other in the practice of encouraging feudal lords (*pares*) to hold pleas on the boundaries of their fiefs instead of resorting to arms. Such indeed is the context of some of the earliest references to a day of the march in Wales: for the earl of Gloucester in 1290, as for the earl of Arundel in 1293, it was an acknowledged way of terminating discord between two lordships through the judgement of 'neighbours and mutual friends who are, as it were, justices' in the matter. It was as such an expedient for settling frontier disputes in Wales that days of the march were fully sanctioned even by Edward I.[71]

By the fourteenth century, however, days of the march were not reserved merely for such inter-lordship disputes; instead they had become a regular feature of the dispensing of justice for ordinary litigants whose homes lay in different lordships. Nevertheless they were still regarded as one of the regalities of Marcher lords and as such the right to hold them was not to be usurped by lesser men.[72]

[68] Cardiff Free Library, Brecon Documents, 2 (rental of May, 1340); BL Royal MS A xi, fo. 12ᵛ.

[69] See the younger Despenser's letter of Mar. 1321 in *Calendar of Ancient Correspondence*, 260.

[70] See, most recently, Michael T. Clanchy, 'Law and Love in the Middle Ages', in John Bossy (ed.), *Disputes and Settlements: Law and Human Relations in the West* (Cambridge, 1983), 47–69.

[71] T. B. Pugh (ed.), *Glamorgan County History*, iii: *The Middle Ages* (Cardiff, 1971), 592 n. 140; *Placitorum abbreviatio* (Record Commission, London, 1811), 231; *Welsh Assize Roll*, 309.

[72] Pugh, *Glamorgan County History*, iii. 307; J. B. Smith, 'Marcher Regality: *Quo Warranto* Proceedings Relating to Cantrefselyf in the Lordship of Brecon', *Bulletin of the Board of Celtic Studies*, 28 (1978–80), 267–88, esp. 251, 285; *Cartae de Glamorgan*, iii. 992 ('salvis similiter querelis que die marchie inter terrras vicinas de consuetudine terminari debent').

Their official status, as part of the machinery of Marcher governance, was further indicated by the fact that the delegation to the day of the march was normally led by one or more of the lordship's major officials—the steward or his deputy, the constable, the receiver, or a local bailiff. But the occasion was one for assuaging communal tensions as well as for sorting out official problems. So it was that the officials were accompanied by some leading tenants, *probi*, from whose ranks were chosen the mixed juries—normally six jurors from each lordship—who decided cases at the day of the march.[73] For the day of the march was to all intents and purposes a court. It is regularly referred to as such, *curia marchie*, and the judicial records make it clear that it dealt with a whole range of matters judicial (both civil and criminal) and administrative.

So firmly established were mechanisms such as letters and days of the march that it comes as no surprise to learn that written codes of agreement were drawn up to determine what general issues could be dealt with in inter-lordship meetings and how they should be treated. No contemporary record of such an agreement— known as *convencio* in Latin, *cydfod* in Welsh—survives; but the range of issues covered by such an agreement can be guessed at from entries in contemporary court rolls and from later copies of such agreements preserved in antiquarian collections. They include matters such as the treatment of fugitives, extradition of wanted men, action on distrained goods, the status of safe conducts and letters of the march, arrangements for safeguarding the status of *bona fide* migrants, and so forth. It is clear that in north Wales at least such agreements were concluded between most lordships, often at the initiative of the steward and for fixed but renewable periods.[74]

The frontier arrangements and institutions of the March of Wales in the later Middle Ages were more sophisticated, complex, and regular than those of any other part of the British Isles. This should not occasion surprise. Governmentally and judicially, Wales was much more fragmented even than English Ireland, for though there were major liberties in Ireland they were, at least in theory, subsumed under the ultimate jurisdictional authority of Dublin, bound by obedience to the English common law, subject

---

[73] For references, which could be readily extended, see Davies, *Lordship and Society*, 245–6.

[74] Smith, 'Cydfodau'; Davies, *Lordship and Society*, 247, esp. n. 70.

Fragmented Societies: Ireland and Wales 99

to common taxation, and politically answerable to a single parliament. In the March of Wales, however, there was not even the veneer of unity; rather was it a collection of virtually autonomous lordships. Each lord, as one aggrieved litigant put it, was 'virtually king and justiciar' within his lordship.[75] Only through a mutual acknowledgement of the problems and dangers that such utter fragmentation posed could solutions to them be found and accepted. How far mutual necessity was the mother of frontier institutions in the March is sometimes revealed in the records with disarming frankness: a wanted man will be handed over to the steward of Denbigh provided that in similar cases in the future the lord of Dyffryn Clwyd is guaranteed like treatment for his men; a defendant agrees to appear in his lordship's court once the plaintiff has put in an appearance in his own court; a case from Clun involving men from Knighton is deferred until it is learnt how the men of Clun were treated in the courts of Knighton.[76] Such a tit-for-tat approach may appear petty (if familiar enough from our own international relations today); but from it were eventually woven the more permanent and institutionalized mechanisms of inter-lordship relations in the March of Wales.

Those mechanisms served to establish a workable, if fragile, relationship not only between neighbouring lords and their officials but also between neighbouring communities. Much of the cross-border tension in the March, as in so many frontier societies, was born out of communal rivalries generated by issues such as cattle-rustling, disputes over grazing rights, disagreements over boundaries, or vendettas prompted by a murder and fed by a tradition of enmity. If such rivalries were to be curbed the leaders of the communities would have to be involved in the negotiations. So indeed they were. Some of the inter-lordship agreements were in fact concluded by leading representatives of the communities, not by the lords.[77] At other times lords, officials, and tenants would co-operate (as indeed they did at days of the march). Thus it was by the counsel of the earl of Arundel and the lord of Stapleton

---

[75] *Cartae . . . de Glamorgan*, ii. 554.

[76] PRO SC 2/216/4, m. 34; 219/3, m. 10; 220/1, m. 15; Shropshire Record Office 552/1/19, m. 1.

[77] See the *cydfodau* published in Smith, 'Cydfodau', or the agreement of 1451 between 'the gentlemen, tenants, commoners and residents' of Elfael and Aberedw on the one hand and Hay, Blaenllyfni, and associated lordships on the other, NLW, Kentchurch Court, no. 1027.

and with the consent of the tenants that an inter-lordship feud, triggered by a vicious murder, was terminated in Clun by a *concordia* in 1401.[78]

It is this fumbling search for a *modus vivendi*, between units of power as well as between natives and settlers, which is one of the major motifs in the histories of medieval Wales and Ireland. The histories of both countries sit uneasily with some of the basic presuppositions of English historiography, notably its centralist point of departure in documentation and approach and its bias (all the stronger for being unspoken and unexamined) in favour of strong government, legal uniformity, and direct and clear lines of command and authority. Such a historiography finds it difficult to come to terms with societies which are institutionally fragmented, fluid in their frontiers, multiple in their loyalties, cultures, and laws, and normally well beyond the reach of the practical authority of metropolitan government. Such, however, are most medieval frontier societies. What we witness in Ireland are the frontier conventions devised within such a society to cope, however imperfectly, with the almost intolerable tensions of a bloody, piecemeal, and uncompleted conquest. In Wales similar institutions were eventually regularized and refined to cope with the problems of a fragmented society in an age of peace. It may, therefore, be not altogether inappropriate to hope that the evidence from both countries may have more than a local interest and that it might contribute to an understanding of medieval frontier societies in general.

[78] Shropshire Record Office 552/1/34, m. 4. In 1451 the steward of Brecon was ordered to compel the tenants of Hay to make restitution to their neighbours of Whitney and Eardisley 'with ye advise and help of other gentlemen of both countreis that rest and peace may be had between our lordships', NLW Peniarth MS 280 D, fo. 50.

Index